11th Global Wordnet Conference (GWC 2021)

Publications of the Astronomical Society "Rudjer Boskovic"
Number 20

Potchefstroom, South Africa
18-21 January 2021

Editors:

Sonja Bosch
Christiane Fellbaum
Marissa Griesel
Alexandre Rademaker
Piek Vossen

ISBN: 978-1-7138-2910-2

Printed from e-media with permission by:

Curran Associates, Inc.
57 Morehouse Lane
Red Hook, NY 12571

Some format issues inherent in the e-media version may also appear in this print version.

Association for Computational Linguistics
209 N. Eighth Street
Stroudsburg, Pennsylvania 18360

Phone: 1-570-476-8006
Fax: 1-570-476-0860

acl@aclweb.org

Additional copies of this publication are available from:

Curran Associates, Inc.
57 Morehouse Lane
Red Hook, NY 12571 USA
Phone: 845-758-0400
Fax: 845-758-2633
Email: curran@proceedings.com
Web: www.proceedings.com

GWC 2021

Proceedings of the 11th Global Wordnet Conference

**Sonja Bosch, Christiane Fellbaum, Marissa Griesel,
Alexandre Rademaker and Piek Vossen (Eds.)**

18–21 Jan, 2021
South African Centre for Digital Language Resources (SADiLaR)
Potchefstroom, South Africa

Foreword

We are excited to hold the 11th Global Wordnet conference on the continent where our human ancestors first created language tens of millions of years ago. South Africa today is home to eleven official and at least twenty-five other languages, and some joined the community of wordnet builders more than a decade ago when African Wordnet was launched. While the global pandemic has prevented us from meeting in person and forcing us to forego coffee and sightseeing breaks, the virtual format allows everyone to participate without incurring travel costs, and jetlag when attending talks outside of one's time zone is merely optional.

We received fifty submissions, and forty-one papers will be presented by colleagues from all continents except Antarctica. We will hear about wordnets covering languages that are new to our community (Uzbek, ancient Indo-European languages, taboo language), new approaches to the automatic construction of wordnets, enhancements of the "classic" WordNet model with additional relations and semantic information, crosslingual wordnet alignment, tools and applications for NLP tasks. Our invited speaker from Palestine, a short transcontinental hop across the Sinai, highlights the important distinctions between a Wordnet and an ontology, showing how ontology engineering can inform wordnet construction.

We are grateful to the South African Centre for Digital Language Resources (SADiLaR), without whose sponsorship and hosting this conference could not have taken place. Thanks go to the local organizers, who volunteered their time and effort, and to the members of the Program Committee, who read and reviewed submissions.

Christiane Fellbaum

Piek Vossen

Sonja Bosch

Marissa Griesel

Mampaka Lydia Mojapelo

Juan Steyn

Elsabé Taljard

Liané van den Bergh

January 2021

Conference Chairs

- Christiane Fellbaum (Princeton University)
- Piek Vossen (Vrije Universiteit Amsterdam)

Local Organising Committee

- Sonja Bosch – University of South Africa (UNISA)
- Mampaka Lydia Mojapelo – University of South Africa (UNISA)
- Marissa Griesel – University of South Africa (UNISA)
- Elsabé Taljard – University of Pretoria (UP)
- Juan Steyn – SADiLaR
- Liané van den Bergh – SADiLaR

Program Committee:

- Eneko Agirre (University of the Basque Country)
- Sina Ahmadi (Insight Centre for Data Analytics)
- Timothy Baldwin (The University of Melbourne)
- Francis Bond (Nanyang Technological University)
- Sonja Bosch (Department of African Languages, University of South Africa)
- Paul Buitelaar (Insight Centre for Data Analytics, National University of Ireland Galway)
- Bharathi Raja Chakravarthi (Insight Centre for Data Analytics, National University of Ireland, Galway)
- Janos Csirik (University of Szeged)
- Gerard de Melo (Rutgers University)
- Valeria de Paiva (Samsung Research America and University of Birmingham)
- Thierry Declerck (DFKI GmbH)
- Bento C. Dias-Da-Silva (UNESP)
- Umamaheswari E (Research Fellow NTU Singapore)

- Christiane Fellbaum (Princeton University)
- Leonel Figueiredo de Alencar (UNIVERSIDADE FEDERAL DO CEARÁ)
- Hugo Gonçalo Oliveira (University of Coimbra)
- Ales Horak (Masaryk University, Faculty of Informatics)
- Shu-Kai Hsieh (National Taiwan Normal University)
- Filip Ilievski (Information Sciences Institute, University of Southern California)
- Diptesh Kanojia (IIT Bombay)
- Kyoko Kanzaki Toyohashi (University of Technology)
- Shikhar Kr. Sarma (Gauhati University)
- David Lindemann (UPV-EHU University of the Basque Country)
- Ahti Lohk (Tallinn University of Technology)
- John P. McCrae (National University of Ireland, Galway)
- Verginica Mititelu (Romanian Academy Research Institute for Artificial Intelligence)
- Luis Morgado Da Costa (Nanyang Technological University)
- Sanni Nimb (Det Danske Sprog-og Litteraturselskab, DSL)
- Sussi Olsen (University of Copenhagen, Centre for Language Technology)
- Heili Orav (University of Tartu)
- Bolette Pedersen (University of Copenhagen)
- Maciej Piasecki (Department of Computational Intelligence, Wroclaw University of Science and Technology)
- Marten Postma (Vrije Universiteit Amsterdam)
- Alexandre Rademaker (IBM Research Brazil and EMAp/FGV)
- German Rigau (IXA Group, UPV/EHU)
- Ewa Rudnicka (Wrocław University of Technology)
- Kevin Scannell (Saint Louis University)
- Pia Sommerauer (Vrije Universiteit Amsterdam)
- Kadri Vider (University of Tartu)
- Piek Vossen (Vrije Universiteit Amsterdam)
- Shan Wang (University of Macau)

Invited Speaker

Mustafa Jarrar, Birzeit University, Palestine

Invited talk

Mustafa Jarrar: Linguistic Ontologies and Wordnets

Wordnets play an important role in understanding and retrieving unstructured information, especially in NLP and IR tasks. Their importance is also increasing to support managing and retrieving of structured data in new areas, such as Knowledge Graphs, multilingual Big Data, and medical informatics. Such new needs are demanding wordnets to be formal and play the role of ontologies.

The difference between wordnets and ontologies might not be obvious, especially because both have similar structures, e.g. considering synsets as concepts and hyponyms as subsumptions. However, synsets in wordnets are linguistically motivated concepts (i.e. units of thoughts), while concepts in ontologies are classes of instances. Additionally, subsumption is a subset relation, in the extensional or intensional sense, rather than a linguistic general-specific relationship. Furthermore, ontologies are typically application-specific rich axiomatizations, while wordnets are general-purpose mental lexicons, thus axiomatizing them would be a rigidification.

This talk will discuss the notion of linguistic ontology, which can play the role of being a wordnet and an ontology at the same time. The talk will also discuss what can be learned from the ontology engineering literature to build wordnets with ontologically and formally cleaner content.

The second part of the talk will present the Arabic Ontology, which is an Arabic wordnet built with formal and ontological analysis in mind. The ontology is represented in a similar structure as wordnets, and is fully mapped to the Princeton Wordnet, as well as with the WikiData knowledge graph and with many Arabic-multilingual lexicons. The ontology is being built at Birzeit University, in Palestine, and it is available at `https://ontology.birzeit.edu/concept/293198`.

Table of Contents

On Universal Colexifications

Hongchang Bao **Bradley Hauer** **Grzegorz Kondrak**
Alberta Machine Intelligence Institute, Department of Computing Science
University of Alberta, Edmonton, Canada
{hongchan,bmhauer,gkondrak}@ualberta.ca

Abstract

Colexification occurs when two distinct concepts are lexified by the same word. The term covers both polysemy and homonymy. We posit and investigate the hypothesis that no pair of concepts are colexified in every language. We test our hypothesis by analyzing colexification data from BabelNet, Open Multilingual WordNet, and CLICS. The results show that our hypothesis is supported by over 99.9% of colexified concept pairs in these three lexical resources.

1 Introduction

Colexification refers to the phenomenon of multiple concepts in the same language being lexified by a single word (François, 2008). For example, the English word *right* colexifies the concepts of RIGHT (side) and CORRECT (Figure 1). The term covers both polysemy and homonymy (Pericliev, 2015). In this paper, we posit and investigate the hypothesis that there are no universal colexifications, or more precisely, that *no two distinct concepts are colexified in every language*.

The universal colexification hypothesis is relevant for the task of word sense disambiguation because it would imply that any sense distinction in any language could be disambiguated by translation into some language. It is also related to a famous proposal of Resnik and Yarowsky (1997) "to restrict a word sense inventory to those distinctions that are typically lexicalized cross-linguistically". If there are no universal colexifications, then a sense inventory based on cross-lingual translation pairs would also include all core concepts in existing lexical resources, which would cast doubt on the commonly expressed opinion that WordNet is too fine-grained (Pasini and Navigli, 2018).

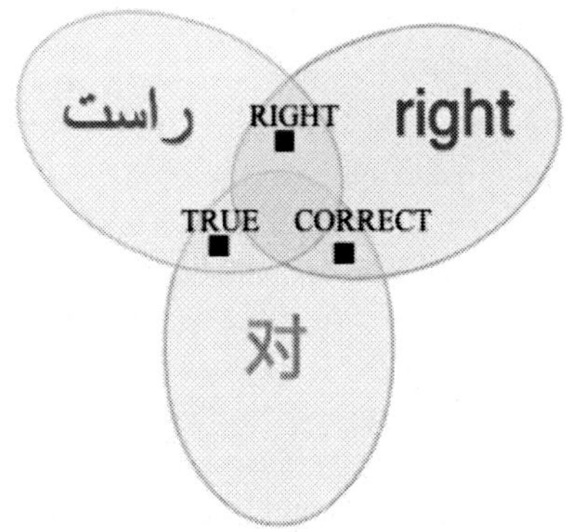

Figure 1: Three concepts (RIGHT, TRUE, CORRECT) that are colexified in Persian, English, and Chinese.

We test our hypothesis by analyzing the colexification data from three different lexical resources: BabelNet (BN), Open Multilingual WordNet (OMWN), and the Database of Cross-Linguistic Colexifications (CLICS). Taken together, these resources contain over a million lexifications in three thousand languages. The results show that our hypothesis is supported by over 99.9% of colexified concept pairs in these three lexical resources.

The structure of the paper is as follows: In Section 2, we introduce terminology and background knowledge, formalize the concepts of lexification and colexification, and state our hypothesis. In Section 3, we summarize previous research related to colexification. In Section 4, we discuss the sources of colexification information which we use to test the hypothesis. Section 5 describes how we construct a colexification database from each of these resources. In Section 6 we present the empirical verification of the colexification hypothesis and analyze these results further. Section 7 concludes the paper.

2 Colexification

We begin by describing the terminology and background knowledge which contextualizes our work. In particular, we discuss the phenomenon of colexification and how it relates to synonymy, translation, and WordNet. We then provide a formal treatment of these concepts, inspired by the formalization of homonymy and polysemy of Hauer and Kondrak (2020a). Finally, we formally state and discuss our hypothesis.

2.1 Background

Princeton WordNet (Fellbaum, 1998), and similarly structured resources, consist of *synsets*. Each synset contains one or more words that can be used to express a specific *lexicalized concept*, or simply *concept* (Miller, 1995). A word *lexifies* a concept if it can be used to express that concept; that is, if the corresponding synset contains that word. Each content word lexifies at least one concept. Each concept that a word can express corresponds to a *sense* of that word. *Word sense disambiguation*, the task of determining the sense of a word in context, is one of the central tasks in computational lexical semantics and natural language understanding (Navigli, 2018).

If two words in the same language lexify a single concept, such as *heart* and *core*, the words are *synonyms*. If two words in different languages lexify a single concept, such as *apple* and *pomme*, the words are *translational equivalents*. Synonymy and translational equivalence are the intra-lingual and inter-lingual components of the relation of *semantic equivalence*, or sameness of meaning (Hauer and Kondrak, 2020b). Indeed, multilingual wordnets (multi-wordnets) such as BabelNet (Navigli and Ponzetto, 2012) consist of multilingual synsets (multi-synsets), which contain words in many languages, each lexicalizing the concept that corresponds to that multi-synset. Multi-wordnets may be constructed by adding translations to the monolingual synsets of a pre-existing wordnet, typically WordNet itself (the *expand model*), or by linking the synsets of multiple independently constructed wordnets in different languages via an inter-lingual index (the *merge model*) (Vossen, 1996).

If two concepts are referred to by a single word, the concepts are *colexified* by that word. In WordNet terms, if two synsets have a non-empty intersection, each word in that intersection colexifies the concepts to which those synsets correspond. Some colexifications, such as the *bank* example above, are coincidental, arising only due to *homonymy*, the use of a single word to represent distinct, semantically unrelated entries in the lexicon (Hauer and Kondrak, 2020a). Other colexifications arise between concepts that are semantically related (Youn et al., 2016).

Lexification and colexification are language dependent. For any given concept, each language may have zero, one, or more synonymous words that lexify it, cases that correspond to the notions of a lexical gap, monolexical synset, and synonymy, respectively. For example, there is no Chinese word which colexifies the two concepts colexified by the English *right* in the example mentioned in Section 1. A language colexifies two concepts if it contains a word which colexifies them. For example, English colexifies the concepts RIGHT and CORRECT; Chinese does not.

2.2 Formalization

Let $\mathcal{C}$ be the set of all concepts. Let $\mathcal{L}$ be the set of all languages. For each language $E \in \mathcal{L}$, let $\mathcal{V}_E$ be the lexicon of E, the set of all words in E. Further, for each concept $c \in \mathcal{C}$, $w_E(c)$ is the set of words in E which lexify c; that is, w_E is a function from $\mathcal{C}$ to $\mathcal{P}(\mathcal{V}_E)$, where $\mathcal{P}$ denotes the *power set* of a set, the set of all the subsets of a set. If $w_E(c) = \emptyset$, c is a lexical gap in E; that is, no word in E lexifies c. Otherwise, if $w_E(c) \neq \emptyset$, c is lexified in E.

Two concepts $c_1, c_2 \in \mathcal{C}$ are colexified by language E if and only if $w_E(c_1) \cap w_E(c_2) \neq \emptyset$. We define $COL(c_1, c_2)$ as the set of languages that colexify c_1 and c_2, and $LEX(c_1, c_2)$ as the set of languages that lexify both c_1 and c_2:

$$COL(c_1, c_2) = \{E \in \mathcal{L} \mid w_E(c_1) \cap w_E(c_2) \neq \emptyset\}$$

$$LEX(c_1, c_2) = \{E \in \mathcal{L} \mid w_E(c_1) \neq \emptyset \neq w_E(c_2)\}$$

Obviously, $COL(c_1, c_2) \subseteq LEX(c_1, c_2)$.

For the purposes of analyzing colexification, we introduce the *colexification ratio*: for any pair of concepts, their colexification ratio is equal to the number of languages which colexify the concepts divided by the number of languages which lexify both concepts. Formally, we define the colexification ratio between two concepts as:

$$r(c_1, c_2) := \frac{|COL(c_1, c_2)|}{|LEX(c_1, c_2)|}$$

$r(c_1, c_2)$ is undefined if $LEX(c_1, c_2) = \emptyset$.

2.3 Hypothesis

We propose the following hypothesis: no pair of concepts is colexified in every language. More precisely, for any pair of concepts that are colexified in some language, there exists another language that lexifies both concepts but does not colexify them. Formally:

$$\forall c_1, c_2 \in \mathcal{C},\ \exists E \in \mathcal{L}\, s.t.\, w_E(c_1) \cap w_E(c_2) \neq \emptyset$$

$$\Rightarrow \exists F \in \mathcal{L}\, s.t.\, w_F(c_1) \neq \emptyset \neq w_E(c_2)$$

$$\wedge\ w_F(c_1) \cap w_F(c_2) = \emptyset$$

Equivalently, our hypothesis predicts that for every pair of concepts, the colexification ratio is either undefined or less than one:

$$\forall c_1, c_2 \in \mathcal{C}\ |LEX(c_1, c_2)| > 0$$

$$\Rightarrow r(c_1, c_2) < 1$$

This equivalence can be seen by simply substituting r, LEX and COL with the definitions given in Section 2.2, and applying some basic principles of set theory.

3 Related Work

Approaches to colexification can be divided into three types, which are based on semantic maps, graphs, and databases, respectively.

The semantic-map approach to colexification is introduced by Haspelmath (2000), who focuses on distinguishing senses in the grammatical domain. Semantic maps are constructed by cross-linguistic comparison, and contain concepts that have distinct colexifications in at least two different languages. Their experiments show that 12 diverse languages are sufficient to build a stable semantic map. Our hypothesis relates this statement to entire lexicons of core concepts. François (2008) also uses colexification data to build a semantic map for studying the world's lexicons across languages. He observes that the more languages are considered, the more distinctions between senses need to be made. This finding is consistent with our hypothesis, and also raises another open question: is a given pair of colexified concepts colexified universally?

The graph-based approach is introduced by List and Terhalle (2013), who analyze cross-linguistic polysemy. They build a weighted colexification graph using data from 195 languages representing 44 language families, and find that clusters of closely-related or similar concepts are often densely connected. Youn et al. (2016) construct colexification graphs in the domain of natural objects to verify if human conceptual structure is universal. Analysis reveals universality of similar patterns in semantic structure, even across different language families.

The database approach is used by Pericliev (2015), who studies colexifications of 100 basic concepts, and introduces heuristics for distinguishing between homonymy and polysemy. Georgakopoulos et al. (2020) use a colexification database to study commonalities between languages in the domain of perception-cognition. They analyze the colexification of four concepts related to perception (SEE, LOOK, HEAR, and LISTEN) to reveal connections between verbs of vision and hearing.

4 Resources

In this section, we describe our three resources: BabelNet (BN), Open Multilingual WordNet (OMWN), and CLICS. Table 2 contains the number of concepts and languages that we consider in each of these resources. For instance, CLICS contains approximately one million words in 3050 languages, which express 2919 concepts. The other two resources have fewer languages, but a higher average number of words per language.

BabelNet (Navigli and Ponzetto, 2012) is a multi-wordnet automatically constructed using the expand model based on the Princeton WordNet. It combines data from Wikipedia, Wikidata, OmegaWiki, and various other resources, supplemented by machine translation, to cover nearly 300 distinct languages. Each of the multisynsets in BN corresponds to a unique concept, with a unique eight-digit identifier, and an associated part of speech (noun, verb, adjective, or adverb), and contains one or more words which can express that concept in various languages. For instance, the nominal concept TREE is represented by synset `bn:00078131n` which includes the English words *tree* and *arbor*, as well as French *arbre* and Italian *albero*. We use BabelNet version 4.0.

Open Multilingual WordNet (Bond and Foster, 2013) is another multilingual wordnet, constructed by linking wordnets in 29 languages to WordNet version 3.0. Like BN, OMWN consists of multisynsets, each containing one or more words from

Resource	Colexified Concept Pair	COL	LEX	Ratio
CLICS	LEG - FOOT	336	1038	0.324
	WOOD - TREE	335	1036	0.323
	MOON - MONTH	313	538	0.582
BN	town.n.01 - city.n.01	100	121	0.826
	painting.n.01 - image.n.01	89	93	0.957
	house.n.01 - dwelling.n.01	88	117	0.752
OMWN	book.n.02 (work) - book.n.01 (object)	23	25	0.920
	wing.n.02 (airplane) - wing.n.01 (animal)	22	22	1.000
	shout.v.02 (cry) - shout.v.01 (with loud voice)	22	24	0.917

Table 1: The concept pairs colexified by the most languages in each of the three databases.

one or more languages which lexify a particular concept. For example, *sign* and *mark* (English), and *signe*, *témoignage*, *preuve*, and *point* (French) all share a multi-synset.

OMWN is based on a set of 5000 *core concepts*, constructed by Boyd-Graber et al. (2006)[1]. This list was updated to WordNet 3.0 by the creators of OMWN[2]. Every WordNet 3.0 synset in this list corresponds to exactly one multi-synset in OMWN, and exactly one multi-synset in BN. Indeed, both resources are created by applying the expand model to WordNet 3.0. For the purposes of our work, we limit OMWN and BN to their respective 5000 synsets corresponding to these core concepts.

The Database of Cross-Linguistic Colexifications (CLICS) (Rzymski and Tresoldi, 2019) is an online lexical database containing information on cross-linguistic colexification patterns across thousands of languages from hundreds of language families. CLICS does not follow any wordnet model, but instead integrates word lists representing thousands of languages, which vary greatly in terms of lexicon coverage. Colexification patterns are represented in the form of a network, where the weights express the number of languages that colexify the concept pair. We obtained the data following the procedure of List (2018), which directly facilitates access to colexification data for any concept pair. CLICS also contains information on the family each language belongs to.

5 Method

For each of the resources described above, we use the following procedure to create a database of concept pairs and colexification information.

The first step is to extract from each resource the set of concepts it contains, and the set of words lexifying each concept. For CLICS, this is relatively straightforward, as the resource is already structured as a database of concepts and lexifications for each language. We access OMWN through NLTK[3], and BN via its Java API[4]. Each concept in these resources is represented by a multi-synset, which can be extracted using the aforementioned APIs.

The second step is to map each of the three sets of concepts to each other, so that identical concepts in distinct resources can be associated with one another for our analysis. This is done by using WordNet 3.0 as a pivot. As described in Section 4, each of the 5000 core concepts in BN and OMWN is already linked to a WordNet 3.0 synset. However, mapping CLICS to WordNet is not trivial because, unlike BN and OMWN multi-synsets, CLICS concepts have no intrinsic connection to WordNet synsets. Therefore, we use a Concepticon mapping created by List et al. (2016) which links a subset of CLICS concepts to WordNet. Unfortunately, the mapping is incomplete, covering only 1368 (46.9%) of CLICS concepts.

The third step is to enumerate all pairs of distinct concepts. There are approximately 4.3 million possible concept pairs in CLICS, and 12.5 million possible concept pairs in BN and OMWN. Although there are millions of concept pairs in each resource, only a subset are lexified by some language (i.e. there exists a language with at least

[1] https://wordnetcode.princeton.edu/standoff-files/core-wordnet.txt

[2] http://compling.hss.ntu.edu.sg/omw/wn30-core-synsets.tab

[3] https://www.nltk.org/

[4] https://babelnet.org/guide

Resource	Languages	Concepts	Lexifications	Colexifications	Exceptions	Support
CLICS	3050	2919	1,377,282	75,089	64	99.9%
BN	284	5000	1,441,990	88,907	3	99.9%
OMWN	29	5000	267,503	54,615	4	99.9%

Table 2: The statistics on the lexical resources, and the empirical validation of our hypothesis.

one word for each concept), and only a subset of those are colexified by some language (i.e. there exists a language with a single word for both concepts). So, we are working with a subset of a subset of all concept pairs.

The fourth step is to determine which concept pairs are colexified, that is, have words in common. This consists of testing whether the intersection of the corresponding synsets (for BN and OMWN) or the corresponding database entries (for CLICS) are non-empty. We report the number of concept pairs which are colexified in at least one language in Table 2. For each pair of concepts, we record the number of languages that colexify the pair. For example, the CLICS database lists 980 languages that lexify both RIGHT (side) and CORRECT. Taking the intersection of the words lexifying each concept, we find that 41 languages have a word which lexifies both concepts, that is, 41 languages colexify these concepts in the CLICS database. Therefore, the colexification ratio for this concept pair, in CLICS, is $41/980 \approx 0.042$.

Our hypothesis states that the colexification ratio for any concept pair, for any of our databases, is always less than 1, given that it is defined. That is, there is always some language that lexifies both concepts, but does not colexify them.

6 Results

In this section, we describe the empirical validation of our hypothesis on the colexification data from CLICS, BN, and OMWN. Our results are summarized in Table 2, which shows that all three resources provide very strong evidence for our hypothesis. Namely, 99.9% of all colexified concept pairs have a colexification ratio less than 1 in all three resources. We find only 71 apparent exceptions in the individual resources.

The three most frequently colexified concept pairs in each resource are shown in Table 1. For example, the concepts LEG and FOOT are both lexified in 1038 languages (i.e. CLICS contains words for them in those languages) but only 336 languages colexify both concepts (i.e. have a single word that can express both of them). So, the colexification of LEG and FOOT is far from universal. In fact, approximately 76% of the 75,089 colexified concept pairs in CLICS are colexified in only a single language.

6.1 Analysis

The 71 apparent exceptions to our hypothesis must be qualified by the fact that none of the three resources makes any claim of completeness. For each seemingly universal colexification, it may be the case that there exists a language that lexifies both concepts, and does not colexify them, but this fact is not recorded in the corresponding database. In this section, we perform a cross-database analysis, to investigate how many, if any, of these apparent exceptions are actual counterexamples to our hypothesis, and how many are simply the result of resource incompleteness.

For example, there are only six languages[5] which lexify both of the concepts DULL and BLUNT in CLICS. This is surprising, as English words lexifying these concepts are, in fact, used to name them. However, the concept DULL does not have the English word "dull" listed in CLICS. All six of the languages which do lexify both of these concepts have a single word which lexifies both; based on our criteria, this would represent a universal colexification, if CLICS was fully complete and correct. However, by cross-checking this example against the information in the other two resources, we find several languages that do not colexify the two concepts.

The 64 apparent exceptions in CLICS involve 113 distinct concepts. Unfortunately, in all 64 cases, at least one of the concepts is not mapped any of the WordNet core synsets. To remedy this, we manually map a subset of the 64 exceptions to OMWN and BabelNet. We choose all four instances that are colexified in more than two languages, plus ten more instances that are selected at random. We find that none of the these 14 pairs are

[5]Indonesian, Klon, Lavukaleve, Mbaniata, Mbilua, Savosavo

Colexified Concept Pair	CLICS Ratio	BN Ratio	OMWN Ratio
RUN_AWAY - FLEE	**10/10**	24/36	13/17
DULL - BLUNT	**6/6**	34/37	6/8
RIVER - FLOWING_BODY_OF_WATER	**4/4**	2/69	0/20
FISHING - CASSOWARY	**3/3**	0/45	0/12
SKIN (human) - SKIN (animal)	**3/3**	10/13	7/10
SAME_SEX_OLDER_SIBLING - BROTHER	**2/2**	44/96	9/16
PIMPLE - BOIL (of skin)	**2/2**	37/63	5/15
MALE - BRASS_INSTRUMENT	**1/1**	0/41	0/13
GAZELLE - DEER	**1/1**	4/79	0/17
WRAPPER - DRESS	**1/1**	1/51	0/12
HYENA - CART	**1/1**	0/55	0/16
ECHIDNA - ANTEATER	**1/1**	6/58	4/10
STRIKE - CAST	**1/1**	0/20	0/14
WRAPPER - CLOTH	**1/1**	0/53	0/12
intention.n.03 - purpose.n.01	n/a	**19/19**	14/15
reserve.v.03-reserve.v.04 (hold)	n/a	**20/20**	14/16
increase.n.04 - increase.n.03 (increment)	n/a	**26/26**	20/22
wing.n.02 (airplane) - wing.n.01 (animal)	n/a	31/47	**22/22**
short.a.01 (time) - short.a.02 (length)	n/a	36/37	**20/20**
probability.n.01 - probability.n.02 (event)	n/a	32/33	**18/18**
new.a.01 (time) - new.s.11 (unfamiliar)	n/a	18/19	**16/16**

Table 3: The concept pairs with the ratio of 1 represent possible exceptions to our hypothesis. The fact that the corresponding ratio is less than 1 in another resource provides evidence against the exception.

exceptions in OMWN or BN (Table 3). In other words, there is at least one language in each of OMWN and BN that lexifies the pairs but does not colexify them. Based on this analysis, we conclude that the 14 exceptions are caused by data sparsity.

In BabelNet, there are only three apparent exceptions to our hypothesis (Table 3). Considering BabelNet alone, they appear to be counterexamples to our hypothesis. Unfortunately, the corresponding WordNet concepts are not mapped to CLICS concepts. However, we find that none of these three pairs are exceptions in OMWN; for all three, the OMWN colexification ratio is less than 1. For example, Chinese lexifies `reserve.v.03` as *liu* and `reserve.v.04` as *ding*. Based on this analysis, we conclude that the three apparent exceptions in BabelNet are artifacts of data sparsity.

The situation in OMWN is similar: we find only four apparent exceptions, and none of them are exceptions in BabelNet. For example, according to BabelNet, Icelandic lexifies "new.a.01 (time)" as *nýr*, and "new.s.11 (unfamiliar)" as *óþekktur*, but no Icelandic word lexified both concepts.

7 Conclusion

We have proposed a novel hypothesis which states that there are no universal colexifications. We provided evidence that the few apparent exceptions to the hypothesis that we found in three multilingual resources are attributable to omission errors in the resources. In the future, we plan to leverage our hypothesis to improve the accuracy of multilingual word sense disambiguation.

The validation of our hypothesis provides novel insights into several open issues in lexical semantics. It implies that every sense distinction in every language can be disambiguated by translation into some language. It also provides support for the informal conjecture of Palmer et al. (2007) that every possible sense distinction can be identified by translation into multiple languages. Finally, it furnishes evidence that the fine-granularity of wordnets and multi-wordnets is necessary for distinguishing between lexical translations of concepts.

Acknowledgments

This research has been supported by the Natural Sciences and Engineering Research Council of

Canada (NSERC), and the Alberta Machine Intelligence Institute (Amii).

References

Francis Bond and Ryan Foster. 2013. Linking and extending an open multilingual Wordnet. In *Proceedings of the 51st Annual Meeting of the Association for Computational Linguistics (Volume 1: Long Papers)*, pages 1352–1362, Sofia, Bulgaria, August.

J. Boyd-Graber, C. Fellbaum, D. Osherson, and R. Schapire. 2006. Adding dense, weighted connections to wordnet. In *In: Proceedings of the Third Global WordNet Meeting, Jeju Island, Korea*.

Christiane Fellbaum. 1998. WordNet: An on-line lexical database and some of its applications. *MIT Press*.

Alexandre François. 2008. Semantic maps and the typology of colexification: Intertwining polysemous networks across languages. *From Polysemy to Semantic change: Towards a Typology of Lexical Semantic Associations*, 163-215.

A. Georgakopoulos, E. Grossman, D. Nikolaev, and S. Polis. 2020. Universal and macro-areal patterns in the lexicon. *Linguistic Typology*.

Martin Haspelmath. 2000. The geometry of grammatical meaning: Semantic maps and cross-linguistic comparison. *The new psychology of language*.

Bradley Hauer and Grzegorz Kondrak. 2020a. One homonym per translation. In *Proceedings of the AAAI Conference on Artificial Intelligence*, volume 34, pages 7895–7902.

Bradley Hauer and Grzegorz Kondrak. 2020b. Synonymy = translational equivalence. *arXiv preprint arXiv:2004.13886*.

Johann-Mattis List and Anselm Terhalle. 2013. Using network approaches to enhance the analysis of cross-linguistic polysemies. *Proceedings of the 10th International Conference on Computational Semantics*.

Johann-Mattis List, Michael Cysouw, and Robert Forkel. 2016. Concepticon: A resource for the linking of concept lists. In *Proceedings of the Tenth International Conference on Language Resources and Evaluation (LREC'16)*, pages 2393–2400, Portorož, Slovenia, May. European Language Resources Association (ELRA).

Johann-Mattis List. 2018. Cooking with clics. *Computer-assisted language comparison in practice*, 14-18.

George A Miller. 1995. WordNet: A lexical database for English. *Communications of the ACM*, 38(11):39–41.

Roberto Navigli and Simone Paolo Ponzetto. 2012. BabelNet: The automatic construction, evaluation and application of a wide-coverage multilingual semantic network. *Artificial Intelligence*, 193:217–250.

Roberto Navigli. 2018. Natural language understanding: Instructions for (present and future) use. In *IJCAI*, pages 5697–5702.

Martha Palmer, Hoa Trang Dang, and Christiane Fellbaum. 2007. Making fine-grained and coarse-grained sense distinctions, both manually and automatically. *Natural Language Engineering*, 13(2):137–163.

Tommaso Pasini and Roberto Navigli. 2018. Two knowledge-based methods for high-performance sense distribution learning. In *Proc. of the 32th AAAI Conference on Artificial Intelligence*.

Vladimir Pericliev. 2015. On colexification among basic vocabulary. *Journal of Universal Language*, 63-93.

Philip Resnik and David Yarowsky. 1997. A perspective on word sense disambiguation methods and their evaluation. In *Tagging Text with Lexical Semantics: Why, What, and How?*, pages 79–86.

Christoph Rzymski and Tiago et al. Tresoldi. 2019. The database of cross-linguistic colexifications, reproducible analysis of cross- linguistic polysemies. *Scientific Data*.

PJTM Vossen. 1996. Right or wrong: combing lexical resources in the eurowordnet project. In *M. Gellerstam, J. Jarborg, S. Malmgren, K. Noren, L. Rogstrom, CR Papmehl, Proceedings of Euralex-96, Goetheborg, 1996*, pages 715–728. Vrije Universiteit.

Hyejin Youn, Logan Sutton, Eric Smith, Cristopher Moore, Jon F Wilkins, Ian Maddieson, William Croft, and Tanmoy Bhattacharya. 2016. On the universal structure of human lexical semantics. *Proceedings of the National Academy of Sciences*, 113(7):1766–1771.

UzWordNet: A Lexical-Semantic Database for the Uzbek Language

Alessandro Agostini[1,2], **Timur Usmanov**[1],
Ulugbek Khamdamov[1], **Nilufar Abdurakhmonova**[3], **Mukhammadsaid Mamasaidov**[1]
[1]LDKR Group*, Inha University in Tashkent, Uzbekistan
[2]ISGS, Inha University, Incheon, South Korea
[3]Tashkent State University of Uzbek Language and Literature, Tashkent, Uzbekistan
a.agostini@inha.uz
{t.usmanov,u.khamdamov,m.mamasaidov}@student.inha.uz
abdurahmonova.1987@mail.ru

Abstract

The results reported in this paper aim to increase the presence of the Uzbek language in the Internet and its usability within IT applications. We describe the initial development of a "word-net" for the Uzbek language compatible to Princeton WordNet. We called it UzWordNet. In the current version, UzWordNet contains 28140 synsets, 64389 sense and 20683 words; its estimated accuracy is 75.98%. To the best of our knowledge, it is the largest wordnet for Uzbek existing to date, and the second wordnet developed overall.

1 Introduction

By living in the world, we—human 'agents'—and machines as well do not just make meanings up from language independently of the world. This is the *language problem* (Wittgenstein, 1953; Steels, 1997; Steels et al., 2002), and it is crucial for IT applications worldwide (Knight, 2016).

Unfortunately, computer scientists and engineers are still learning how to efficiently solve the language problem in their theories or applications, and understand how language-based technologies called "universal language models" work. They are often surprised by the mistakes that new AI tools are making.[1] In short, new technologies proliferate, and language-based biases appear increasingly almost anywhere in applications.

A problem of current technologies is that if a language is endangered, it is possible it will never have a life within them—and in the Internet online. Far from infinite, usable technology seems only as big as the language(s) we speak as users.

Language is just as important for building human connections online as it is offline: it forms the basis of how users identify with each other, the lines on which exclusion and inclusion are often drawn, and the boundaries within which communities grow around common interests.

As a consequence, the relationship between language diversity and the Internet is a growing area of policy interest and academic study.[2] The story emerging is one where language profoundly affects our experience of the Internet. It is a matter of fact, for instance, that Google searching for "restaurants" in English may bring us back 10+ times the results of doing so in another language.

For "another language", we focus on the Northern Uzbek language, a Turkic language officially recognized as the state language of the Republic of Uzbekistan. In particular, in this paper we advance and discuss initial results on the ongoing development of UzWordNet (UzW in short), a prototypical version of a wordnet for the Uzbek language compatible to Princeton WordNet (Miller, 1995; Fellbaum, 1998).[3] Our long-term objective is to motivate, support and increase the study of computational aspects of Uzbek and, more generally, the usability of Uzbek within IT applications and the Internet. As a consequence, UzWordNet is added to the Wordnets in the world[4] and provided open source under a license and format compatible with the Open Multilingual Wordnet (Bond and Paik, 2012; Bond and Foster, 2013).[5]

This paper is structured as follows. Below are some elements of the Uzbek language, followed by a brief excursus on word-nets (Section 3). In

* The acronym "LDKR" means Language, Data, Knowledge, and Reasoning. The LDKR Group aims to discovering (learning), modeling, reducing and computing the "semantic gap" between users and the Universe of Language(s), Data, Information and Knowledge their ICT systems are based on.

[1]For instance, see https://medium.com/@robert.munro/bias-in-ai-3ea569f79d6a (accessed 30 Nov 2019).

[2]For instance, see http://labs.theguardian.com/digital-language-divide/ (accessed 17 Oct 2019).

[3]https://wordnet.princeton.edu/.

[4]globalwordnet.org/resources/wordnets-in-the-world/.

[5]http://compling.hss.ntu.edu.sg/omw/.

Section 4, we focus on the few previous attempts towards the construction of a wordnet for Uzbek. In Section 5 we advance and discuss the work that produced UZWORDNET. We validate and analyse the results in Section 7 and 8. We conclude with a summary and future work (Section 9).

2 Elements of Uzbek Language

Unless otherwise stated, in this paper by "Uzbek language" (native: *O'zbek tili*) we refer to the Northern Uzbek language. In fact, there is another Uzbek language—the Southern Uzbek—statutory language of provincial identity in Afganistan, spoken by about 6.5 million people wordwide (Eberhard et al., 2020).

Figure 1: Spread of Uzbek languages.

The (Northern) Uzbek language is a statutory national language in Uzbekistan.[6] It is a Turkic language and spoken by approximately 26.8 million people around the world (Ethnologue, 2020a), remarkably by a large group of ethnic Uzbeks residing abroad in Afghanistan, Kyrgyzstan, Kazakhstan, Turkmenistan, Tajikistan, Russia, Turkey, and Xinjiang (China), making it the second-most widely spoken Turkic language after Turkish (Ethnologue, 2020b). Figure 1 provides the rough geographical distribution of the Northern (majority) and Southern (minority) Uzbek languages.

[6]In spite of its status (1995, Official Language Law, amended, 3561-XI, Art.1), the Uzbek languange has been experimenting a number of issues for the disclosure of its full potentialities; see for instance cabar.asia/en/uzbekistan-why-uzbek-language-has-not-become-a-language-of-politics-and-science (accessed 12 Oct 2020).

The Uzbek languages are a descendant of Chagatai language, also known as the old-version of Uzbek. As a primary language of the Timurid dynasty, Chagatai represented the eclectic mixture of Turkic, Persian (or Farsi), and Arabic. After its extinction by the 19th century, its successor language lost its vowel-harmonization due to influence of Soviet standardization process (Hirsch, 2005) and became the standard (Northern) Uzbek we consider in this paper. Both languages belong to the Eastern subgroup of Turkic family, also known as the Karluk branch, along with the Uyghur language. In Figure 2, five most-spoken Turkic languages and their branches are depicted.

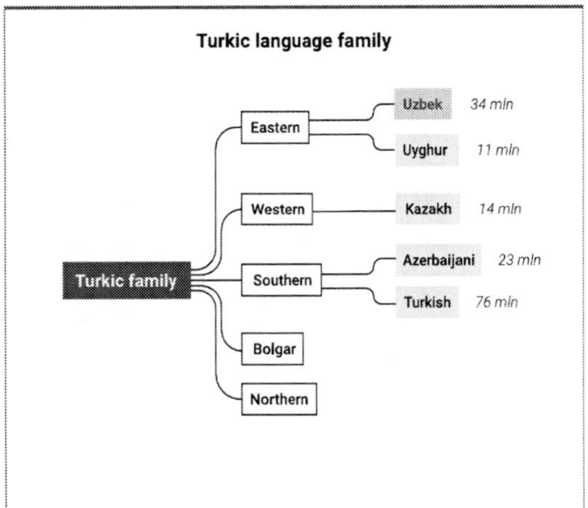

Figure 2: Widely spoken Turkic languages.

2.1 Dialects

The (Northern) Uzbek has three dialects: Karluk (or Karluk-Chigil-Uyghur), Kipchak, and Oghuz (Abdurokhmonov and Darvishev, 2011) (Figure 3). *Karluk* is a group of subdialects with a total number of 22-23 million speakers. It is divided into three main groups: Ferghana (covering almost the whole Ferghana Valley), Tashkent (the city and its region) and Qarshi, Samarkand and Bukhara groups. Karluk dialect became the standard form of Uzbek. *Kipchak* is a quite dispersed dialect. The total number of speakers is not yet calculated; that is to say, it accounts for the minority of speakers. Since the Karluk dialect is the standard on all levels of government and universities, the popularity of Kipchak is slowly declining. *Oguz* is spoken by approximately 2 million speakers, and it is widely spread in the Khorezm region, the Republic of Karakalpakstan, and the western part of the Bukhara region (To'ychiboev and Khasanov,

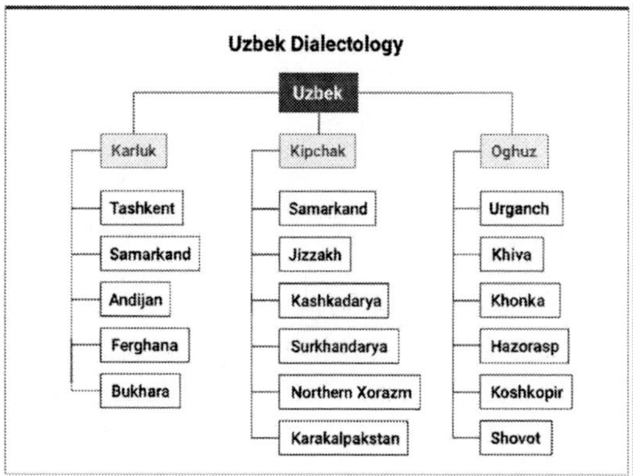

Figure 3: Uzbek dialects and their classification.

2004). Figure 4 is a roughly estimated visualization of Uzbek dialects spoken in Uzbekistan. Owing to the fact that Karluk and Kipchak dialects are dispersed throughout the country, each province is given the color of dialect of majority.

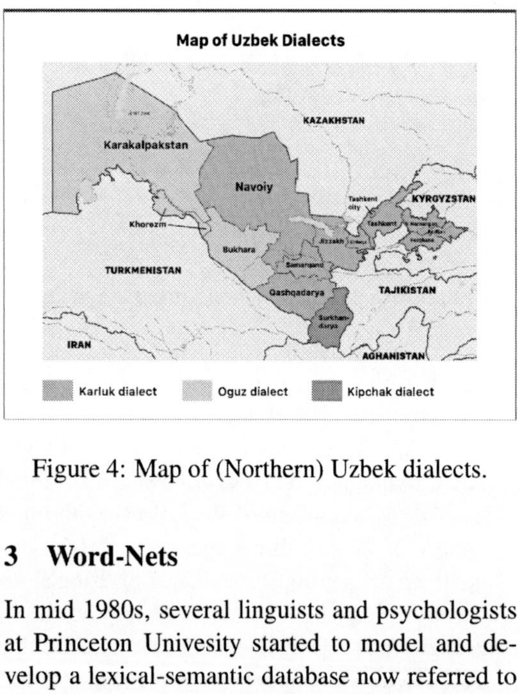

Figure 4: Map of (Northern) Uzbek dialects.

3 Word-Nets

In mid 1980s, several linguists and psychologists at Princeton Univesity started to model and develop a lexical-semantic database now referred to as Princeton WordNet (Miller, 1995; Fellbaum, 1998, PWN in short). The basic idea behind PWN has been to provide an aid in searching dictionaries conceptually, rather than merely alphabetically.

PWN divides the lexicon into four categories: nouns, verbs, adjectives, and adverbs. They are organized into synonym sets, each representing one underlying lexical concept (Miller et al., 1990).

PWN is based on synonyms and hyponyms of nouns and verbs, as well as antonyms of adjectives. In addition, it includes troponyms for verbs and hyponyms for nouns.

Princeton WordNet and a vast majority of wordnets (see for instance (Bond and Paik, 2012; Neale, 2018) for surveys and (Bond and Foster, 2013; Vossen, 1998) for extensions to open multilingual wordnet) were formed by expanding the semantic structure of PWN according to the *extend model*[7] (Vossen, 1998; Bond and Paik, 2012, p.67), which assumes that lemmas of the new language are created by translating English synsets of PWN. There is also possibility for creating semantic network by directly adding words and their definitions for the language under consideration. However, few wordnets have been created by using this method (*merge model*), due to the high cost of human expertise.

4 A Wordnet for Uzbek Language

Computational linguistics appeared as a field of research in Uzbekistan since the late 2000s; see for instance (Pulatov, 2011; Rakhimov, 2011; Abdurakhmonova, 2020, pp. 17-19). Since then, there have been few attempts to resolve lexical ambiguity in Uzbek by creating a sematic network, and none of them produced a word-net as we generally mean the term today after the pioneristic work at Princeton, see Section 3.

The very first wordnet for Uzbek—and, to the best of our knowledge, the only existing up to the present work on UzWordNet—is due to (Bond and Foster, 2013) as part of the Extended Open Multilingual WordNet project. The resulting wordnet (code **uzb**, accessible online[8]) is minimal in terms of available synsets and coverage of "core concepts" (Boyd-Graber et al., 2006):

Synsets	Words	Senses	Core concepts
889	1,115	1,157	8%

It also seems not clear what of two Uzbek languages the wordnet was built for. Moreover, we could not find a *specific* report on it (apart from the aforementioned numbers) and the estimated *specific* accuracy.[9]

In (Matlatipov et al., 2018), the authors focused on modeling a wordnet-like thesaurus for Uzbek, and tried to come up with a way to create rules for converting paper-based dictionary thesauruses

[7] Sometimes informally referred to as *expansion method*.

[8] http://compling.hss.ntu.edu.sg/omw/summx.html.

[9] The estimated accuracy is claimed to be 94% *over the 150+ languages* considered in the project.

into e-version using PROLOG. To develop a formal model of thesaurus, they built a dictionary's meta-language and defined its systematic properties. As a result, they obtained a *model*, not a wordnet as a computer system. (Abdurakhmonova and Khaydarov, 2019) surveys the main features of PWN towards its translation to Uzbek.

The list of works that explicitely target Uzbek (Northern or Southern) for the purpose of building a wordnet ends here. However, there have been numerous projects for other Turkic languages, for instance the development of a Turkish wordnet (Bilgin et al., 2004; Çetinoğlu et al., 2018). The project, started at Sabanci University of Istanbul as part of the BalkaNet project, uses a combination of the expansion and merge approaches. Another wordnet for Turkish is KENET (Ehsani et al., 2018). KENET is not based on PWN and is the most comprehensive wordnet for Turkish built from scratch using a bottom-up method. The wordnet was created by using the Contemporary Dictionary of Turkish (CDT) as lexical resource.

5 Our Approach

In this section we describe our approach to the construction of UZWORDNET. We divide it into three parts. First, the choice and pre-processing of the lexical resource. Second, the automatic construction of the PWN-like structure for (Northern) Uzbek, i.e., of UZWORDNET. Third, the expert human validation of the automatic construction.

5.1 Lexical resource

The lexical resource we used is the English-Uzbek Dictionary (*Inglizcha-O'zbekcha Lug'at*) by Shavkat Butayev and Abbos Irisqulov (Butayev and Irisqulov, 2008), a collaborative result by the authors and experts at the Uzbek World Languages University and the Uzbek Academy of Sciences. The dictionary is one of the largest existing bilingual dictionaries available electronically and with one of the richest collection of entries.

The 2008 edition contains 40,000 lemmas in the English-Uzbek part, and about 30,000 is the Uzbek-English part. For each English word, it provides Uzbek senses in the following format.

Example 1 For the English word "sense", the dictionary stores the following information:

sense [sens] n **1)** *his, tuyg'u, sezgi;* **2)** *aql, fahm, idrok, zehn,*

where numbers represent each sense of "sense". ⊣

Remark 1 Each lemma's entry of (English-Uzbek part of) the dictionary contains the major parts of speech (PoSs) associated with the lemma. However, we shall see that our "connectivity restoration algorithm" (Section 6) uses only nouns, adjectives, verbs, and adverb, because it generates UZWORDNET from processing PWN and its semantic network. ⊣

5.2 Processing the dictionary

Now we provide some details on the preparatory tasks performed before running the main algorithm and presenting the human validators with resulting synsets. Here we focus on the first issue that we faced in processing the dictionary: the bad quality of the scan of the dictionary. It is worth mentioning that the electronic copy we used is an optical scan converted to text, which caused errors in parsing the dictionary for further use.

Example 2 Consider the entry in the dictionary:

abbey ['æbı] n **1)** *abbatlik...*

Automatic reading produced:

abbey ['reblj n **1)** *abbatlik...*

(closing bracket of the entry is misidentified as character "j"). ⊣

Character misinterpretations increased difficulty of applying parsing rules on the dictionary when converting it into more structured computable form for further use.

Specifically, to make the dictionary readable for the machine, individual pages were first enhanced visually and processed by a free OCR (Optical Character Recognition) service.[10] Successively, a series of complex regular expressions were written to parse individual translations from the dictionary and get rid of misinterpreted characters. Those were developed on the basis of observed erroneous patterns similar to the one described in Example 2.

5.2.1 Tabular format

The dictionary was converted into a convenient machine-readable form. In particular, we converted it into a table format where each row consisted of three columns: source lemma(s) (English); part of speech of source lemma(s); target lemma(s) (Uzbek translation by dictionary).

Example 3 The entry for *abbey* in the dictionary (source lemma) is converted into the following table format: <abbey; n; abbatlik, monastir>. ⊣

[10]Available at https://www.onlineocr.net.

Because of PWN'structure contains distinct database files for nouns, verbs, adverbs, and adjectives, the dictionary in tabular format was split into four separate files, one for each respective part of speech. The resulting four tabular dictionaries were sorted alphabetically by source lemma(s), in order to increase the speed of search for a particular lemma from PWN when it is used in the automatic construction of the wordnet.

6 Automatic Construction

The main procedure for building up UZWORDNET is an automatic translation—called "connectivity restoration algorithm" in reason of the most significant part of it (CRA; Algorithm 1)—of PWN (version 3.0) into Uzbek provided by the lexical resource (subsection 5.1) preprocessed into tabular format and files for each part of speech (subsection 5.2). The algorithm exploits the expansion method, as we accept the temporary assumption (see Future Work; Section 9) that the semantic structure of PWN is similar to the semantic structure of target language, the Northern Uzbek for us.

Algorithm 1: Connectivity Restoration.

```
Input  : S, a data.pos file from Princeton
         WordNet (PWN, v3.0)
Input  : D, English-Uzbek dictionary in
         tabular form for a specific PoS
Output: W, the UZWORDNET (UZW, v1.0)
1  W ← ∅
2  for each synset ∈ S do
3      for each lemma ∈ synset do
4          if lemma ∈ D then
5              W ← W ∪ translate(synset,
               D[lemma])
6  for each w_synset ∈ W do
7      if parent(w_synset) ∉ W then
8          s_synset ← parent(w_synset)
9          while s_synset ∉ W and s_synset ≠
           top_level_synset(S) do
10             s_synset ←
               S[parent(s_synset)]
11             parent(w_synset) ← synset
12 return W
```

6.1 Connectivity Restoration Algorithm

UZWORDNET's development process is designed by the algorithm according to few related steps.

1. (lines 1-5): initial construction. The algorithm starts by initializing an empty set W for the resulting wordnet. English lemmas for each synset in S (file data.pos of PWN) are searched in D (dictionary in tabular format, cf. subsection 5.2.1). If a match is found, a new entry (Uzbek synset) in W is added. As the result, the algorithm produces the set W of synsets in Uzbek.

   However, not all synsets from PWN are translated into Uzbek. The reason is a lack of English entries in the lexical resource compared to the available lemmas from PWN. As a consequence, in W there may be disjoint synsets. This is the case of formation of *lexical gaps* for the target language, cf. (Giunchiglia et al., 2018; Giunchiglia et al., 2017), which means that the target language does not have, according to the lexical resource used, an equivalent synset.

2. (lines 6-12): connectivity restoration. For each synset from W (w_synset), the algorithm checks if the parent of w_synset exists in W. If it does not, then the algorithm extracts the parent of that synset from PWN (actually, from S in Algorithm 1) and checks if it exists in W. If not, it checks if the parent synset, say s, of that parent of w_synset exists in S. And so on until s is eventually found such that (a) s is translated into an Uzbek synset, say s', that is a (indirect) parent of w_synset, and (b) s' is in W. In the case that such a synset s satisfying conditions (a) and (b) above is not found, and the algorithm checked the synset from S, say s_r, that represents PWN's structural top level (root), then s_r becomes the parent of w_synset.

   As the result, all synsets in W are interconnected into the semantic hierarchy required.

Example 4 Consider Figure 5. Nodes denote synsets at a particular level in the structure; arrows denote the parental relationship between synsets.

The algorithm checks if an English synset, that is, a node from the structure of PWN, refers to a non-existent synset of Uzbek (target language) according to the lexical resource. In this case, we have a *lexical gap* for Uzbek language.

In the figure, S_D (synset S at level D in PWN) is referencing S_{C_2} (synset S at level C, child node 2 of parent node S_B in PWN). Assume that S_{C_2}

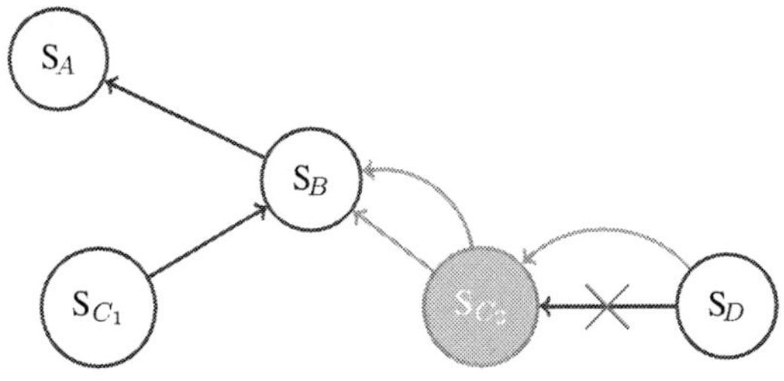

Figure 5: Visualization of the algorithm.

has no correspondent (equivalent) Uzbek synset, because the dictionary does not translate it. Then, S_{C_2} is not going to form a node of the emerging semantic network that eventually produced UZWORDNET. As a consequence, S_D references a synset (S_{C_2}) that is not represented in the resulting Uzbek wordnet. To avoid this problem, the algorithm searches out the parent node of S_{C_2} in the semantic structure of PWN and checks if it—node S_B in the figure—exists in the semantic structure that eventually builds the Uzbek wordnet.

For every synset s from PWN, the algorithm halts when run on s if either it finds a synset s' from PWN that is an *indirect* parent of s and s' has an equivalent Uzbek synset according to the dictionary, namely, s' exists in the Uzbek wordnet—like S_D and S_B, respectively, in Figure 5—or traversed the whole semantic network of PWN until it reached the synset at the root without finding a parental synset of s whose semantically equivalent Uzbek synset is provided by the dictionary—it would be the case of root node S_A that connects directly to S_D in Figure 5. ⊣

7 Expert Validation

Two native Uzbek speakers and one expert linguist—three co-authors of this paper—were asked to independently validate a sample of Uzbek synsets ("target lemmas") produced automatically.

For each part of speech (nouns, verbs, adverbs, and adjectives), an Excel file with 70 synsets ("lemmas") from PWN randomly selected was provided to the three "validators". For each file, the guidelines were the following:

1. Read each of the 70 English lemmas, its definition and example(s) if any.

2. For each lemma l, write 1 (meaning: "Yes, correct") in column "EVAL" you are provided for l, if you think that the target lemma, namely, Uzbek synset for l shares the same meaning of, or it is semantically equivalent to, l consistently with l's definition and, possibly, example(s). Write 0 ("No, wrong"), otherwise.

Some explanatory notes were also provided. In particular, this important one:

2.1 if English lemma l is translated into more than one word and *only some* of those words are the correct translation of l according to l's definition, *but some other words are not*, write 0 (i.e., "Translation incorrect").

8 Results

We run the CRA on PWN and the entries from the lexical resource as preprocessed (cf. subsections 5.2 and 5.2.1; also Input in Algorithm 1). The resulting semantic network, that is, UZWORDNET, contains 28140 synsets, 64389 sense and 20683 words, positioning UZWORDNET at the 18th place in the list of wordnets ranked by number of synsets, see Table 1 below (also cf. (Batsuren et al., 2019, Table 2).[11]

After the human evaluation over sample entries as described in the previous section, with a total number of instances processed be 17425 nouns, 5792 adjectives, 673 adverbs, and 4250 verbs, the estimated accuracy of the automatic translation by CRA resulted in 71.79% (Table 2).

8.1 Analysis

The estimated quality of UZWORDNET is rooted into a number of issues we encountered in processing the lexical resource. One important issue we mention here is strictly related to Uzbek rich semantics. Consider the following example.

Example 5 Suppose that our aim is to automatically extract from the dictionary the translation (synsets and senses, in particular) of the English word *body* stored in PWN and therein defined as follows: "The physical structure, including the bones, flesh, and organs, of a person or an animal".

Observe that, in the dictionary, *body*, as a noun, has the following Uzbek translations (senses):

1) *odam tanasi*; **2)** *so'zl. odam*; **3)** *murda*; **4)** *(nimaningdir) asosiy qismi*; **5)** *odamlar guruhi*.

Here is one example of sentence for each sense and its English translation (in parentheses):

[11]The list considers wordnets open source linked to PWN.

#	Language	Synsets	Senses	Words	Examples	Glosses	References
1	English	115424*	203145*	152059*	48459	109942	(Miller, 1995)
2	Finnish	107989	172755	115259	0	0	(Lindén et al., 2010)
3	Chinese	98324	123397	91898	17	541	(Wang and Bond, 2013)
4	Thailand	65664	83818	71760	0	0	(Thoongsup et al., 2009)
5	French	53588	90520	44485	0	0	(Sagot and Fišer, 2008)
6	Romanian	52716	80001	45656	0	0	(Tufiş et al., 2008)
7	Japanese	51366	151262	86574	28978	51363	(Bond et al., 2009)
8	Catalan	42256	66357	42444	2477	6576	(Gonzalez-Agirre et al., 2012)
9	Slovene	40233	67866	37522	0	0	(Fišer et al., 2012)
10	Portuguese	38609	60530	40619	0	0	(de Paiva et al., 2012)
11	Spanish	35232	53140	32129	651	17256	(Gonzalez-Agirre et al., 2012)
12	Polish	35083	87065	59882	0	0	(Piasecki et al., 2009)
13	Italian	33560	42381	29964	1934	2403	(Pianta et al., 2002)
14	Indonesian	31541	92390	24081	9	3380	(Noor et al., 2011)
15	Malay	31093	93293	23645	0	0	(Noor et al., 2011)
16	Basque	28848	48264	25676	0	0	(Pociello et al., 2011)
17	Dutch	28253	57706	40726	0	0	(Postma et al., 2016)
18	**Uzbek**	28140	64389	20683	0	0	this paper
19	Mongolian	23665	40944	26857	213	2976	(Batsuren et al., 2019)
20	Croatian	21302	45929	27161	0	0	(Oliver et al., 2016)

Table 1: Wordnets for number of synsets, cf. (Batsuren et al., 2019), *modified* (* our counting).

	Accuracy				
Validators	nouns	verbs	adverbs	adjectives	**Average**
MM	62.86 %	60.00 %	82.86 %	58.57 %	66.07%
NA*	78.57 %	71.43 %	84.29 %	72.86 %	*76.79 %*
UK	67.14 %	65.71 %	81.43 %	75.71 %	72.50 %
Average	69.52%	65.71 %	82.86%	69.05 %	**71.79 %**

Table 2: Human evaluation and accuracies (* expert linguist).

1) "*Faqatgina D va K vitaminlarini* ***odam tanasi*** *mustaqil ishlab chiqara oladi*". (The human body can only produce vitamins D and K.)

2) "***Odam*** *bu yerda yo'qolishi va hech qachon topilmasligi mumkin*". (A body could get lost out here and never be found.)

3) "***Murdalar*** *ertak aytmaydi*". (Dead men tell no tales.)

4) "*O'zbekistonda maoshlarning* ***asosiy qismi*** *oziq-ovqatga sarflanadi*". (In Uzbekistan a large part of salaries is spent on food.)

5) "*Bu* ***odamlar guruhi*** *o'zlarini xavf ostiga qo'yishmoqda*". (This group of people put themselves in danger.)

Further note that only the first translation, *odam tanasi*, matches PWN's definition of *body*.

However, our algorithm (CRA) extracts all five translations, even if we only need the senses of the source lemma that match the definition. ⊣

The example rises interesting questions about the semantic structure of UZWORDNET and polysemy. Although a deeper study into sense granularity in UZWORDNET and its effect on sense clustering is kept for future work, below we provide first answers and some further questions.[12]

8.2 Structure of UZWORDNET

Similarly to all word-nets created from PWN by expansion, nouns, verbs, adjectives and adverbs in UZWORDNET are grouped and classified into synonym sets (synsets), the major (lexical) relationship in the word-net. The semantic tree-like structure of synsets for nouns and verbs is based on the hypernym-hyponym relationship.

The structure for nouns, in particular, results the most representative among processed parts of speech, with 17425 nodes over the 28140 synsets total of the word-net produced. Its topologi-

[12]Thanks to the reviewer who asked some of the questions.

cal data, for instance the mean of distances of a node (synset) to the structure's root or, more precisely, the number of edges that connect consecutive nodes leading to the root—4.15, with standard deviation: 1.40—reveal a major downside of the structure, namely: its shallowness. In fact, UZWORDNET' structure contains many synsets with same sense high in the hyponym tree.

8.2.1 Polysemy

A main general issue in word-nets, which impacts on usability, is polysemy.

We quantified polysemy in the semantic structure of UZWORDNET for nouns (Figure 6) and verbs (Figure 7) by counting lemmas in synsets.

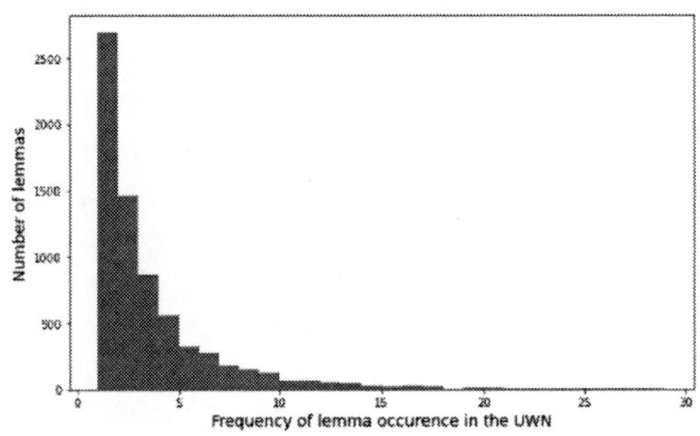

Figure 6: Degree of polysemy in nouns.

The mean of number of lemmas in synsets resulted in 2.05 (standard deviation: 3.56) for nouns and 2.99 (standard deviation: 4.78) for verbs.

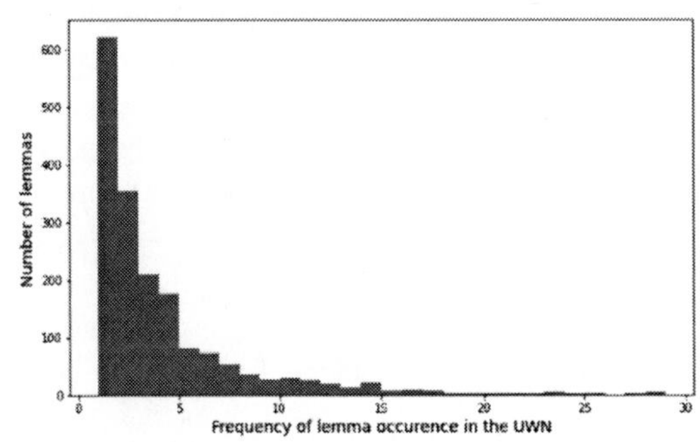

Figure 7: Degree of polysemy in verbs.

It turns out that polysemy is not present to a great degree on average in the structure. Moreover, most of the lemmas do not repeated more than mere several times in UZWORDNET.

A question is how polysemy and topological data we mentioned on average distance of nodes to UZWORDNET's root correlate. Precisely, the question here is: Where are synsets (for nouns, specifically) which contain more senses located on average within the semantic structure?

To assesses the degree of polysemy per level, namely, distance from root of the hypernym-hyponym tree, we run some scripts. The results are descriptive. Overall, the polysemy is higher closer to the root. An expected outcome, since senses closer to the root are more general, and therefore participating lemmas may express more concepts.

Remark 2 Another interesting question is: How much do sense granularity differ between the bilingual dictionary we used and UZWORDNET? Or, what senses for a given lemma in lexical resource we used are translated into senses for same lemma in UZWORDNET? An answer to the question, together with thoughtful analysis of sense granularity and sense coverage of UZWORDNET, would lead to interesting problems in the precision and recall of UZWORDNET and the issue of how to further improve it.[13] ⊣

Under a somewhat fortunate coincidence that most English lemmas in the dictionary we use do not have several senses in Uzbek, the issue of polysemy highlighted first by Example 5 and discussed further in this subsection could be solved by asking human experts to eliminate the translations automatically extracted that do not match the definition of the source lemma.

Although the extension of UZWORDNET by adding human expertise is out of the scope of this paper—and it is certainly part of future work, we like to foresee what would be the results.

8.3 Expert validation revised

We asked the validators to revise their validation over the identical set of sample files. The guidelines we gave to solve the task were identical to the previous, with the only exception over the explanatory note 2.1 (cf. Section 7).

The new explanatory note is:

2.1′ if English lemma l is translated into more than one word and *at least one* of those words is the correct translation of l according to l's definition, write 1 ("Translation correct").

The estimated accuracy of UZWORDNET after re-validation resulted in 75.98%. Table 3 reports in details the results of individual validations.

[13] For corpora to test our work on UZWORDNET upon coverage in words and senses, see for instance (Abdurakhmonova and Sobirov, 2019).

Validators	Accuracy (*revised*)				Average
	nouns	verbs	adverbs	adjectives	
MM	74.29 %	67.14 %	87.14 %	77.14 %	76.43 %
NA*	75.71 %	71.43 %	84.29 %	67.14 %	*74.64 %*
UK	71.73 %	70.00 %	85.71 %	80.00 %	76.86 %
Average	73.91 %	69.52 %	85.71 %	74.76 %	**75.98 %**

Table 3: Human evaluation *revised* and accuracies (* expert linguist).

9 Conclusion and Future Work

In this paper, we have advanced and discussed the results on the initial development of UZWORDNET, a lexical-semantic database, or a "word-net", for the Northern Uzbek language compatible by expansion (extend/expansion method) to Princeton WordNet. UZWORDNET contains 28140 synsets, 64389 senses and 20683 words and is the output of an automatic process whose central procedure is an algorithm of connectivity run on Princeton WordNet' semantic network and an external lexical resource. Evaluation by three validators of UZWORDNET's accuracy in the translation, run over 280 sample entries, 70 for each PoS (nouns, verbs, adjectives, adverbs), resulted in an estimated accuracy of 71.79% minimum and 75.98% maximum according to the methodology of validation; 74.64% to 76.79% if considering only the evaluation by an expert linguist.

9.1 Future work

In the short term, we aim to make UZWORDNET available[14] among the Wordnets in the world, and to provide it open source under a license and format compatible with the Open Multilingual Wordnet (Bond and Paik, 2012; Bond and Foster, 2013) and other lexicgraphic data sets like Wikionary or other open source resources.[15] Moreover, to make UZWORDNET more accessible, we plan to build a simple SQL server and interface for using it. At the same time, we will refocus attention on our algorithms, improve the overall quality of automatic translation, and further investigate questions only addressed in this paper.

UZWORDNET has been developed by accepting the assumption that its semantic network is similar to the semantic structure of PWN. Obviously, it is *not* the case that Uzbek and English share exactly the same concepts, due to quite diverse underlying cultures of each language. Thus, we plan to keep the cultural diversity of Uzbek into more account. Before doing it, however, we plan to extend and improve UZWORDNET by expert human *translation* (for English lemmas not included in the lexical resource) or expert, selective *validation* (for English lemmas translated into more Uzbek synsets that need to be chosen according to definition; cf. Example 5), possibly using crowdsourcing (Ganbold et al., 2018; Fišer et al., 2014; Giunchiglia et al., 2015; Huertas-Miguelážez et al., 2018). We partially addressed to work to carry along this research direction and foresaw the results in subsections 8.1 and 8.3.

Successively, we aim to expand the core semantic structure of UZWORDNET to capture those features of the language that are typically Uzbek, that is, strictly and uniquely depending on Uzbek culture and not be available, as a consequence, in English-based PWN and other wordnets. In this way, both unicity and diversity of Uzbek language and, as a consequence, culture, will be modeled for the future use in IT applications. This extended version produced shall be *not* compatible to PWN (over concepts that are uniquely depending on Uzbek culture) and will be provided by working in partnership within the *DataScientia* initiative[16] using the Universal Knowledge Core (Giunchiglia et al., 2017; Giunchiglia et al., 2018), a multilingual, high quality, large scale, and diversity aware machine readable lexical resource.

Acknowledgments

The first author would like to thank Fausto Giunchiglia for proposing us to join *DataScientia*. Enver Menadjiev has supported our work in perspective to make UZWORDNET available online. Thanks to the anonymous reviewers, Alexandre Rademaker, Piek Vossen, Thierry Declerck, and all other participants to the conference for the interesting questions, comments and remarks.

[14]http://uzwordnet.ldkr.org/.

[15]About the format, we are evaluating to use XML or RDF formats, cf. https://globalwordnet.github.io/schemas/.

[16]http://datascientia.disi.unitn.it/.

References

[Abdurakhmonova and Khaydarov2019] Nilufar Abdurakhmonova and Muhammad Khaydarov. 2019. On the tasks of creating a Wordnet in the Uzbek language (uzbek). *O'zbekiston Xorijiy Tillar (Foreign Languages in Uzbekistan)*, 4:19–27. In Uzbek.

[Abdurakhmonova and Sobirov2019] Nilufar Abdurakhmonova and Abdulhay Sobirov. 2019. Korpus yordamida tezaurus yaratishning konseptual ahamiyati (Conceptual peculiarities on creation thesaurus by corpus). In *Proceedings of the International Conference on Translation, Information, Communication: Political and Social bridge*, pages 36–39. In Uzbek.

[Abdurakhmonova2020] Nilufar Abdurakhmonova. 2020. *Computational Linguistics*. Lambert Academic Publishing, Germany. In Uzbek.

[Abdurokhmonov and Darvishev2011] Sh. Abdurokhmonov and I. Darvishev. 2011. Workbook on the Uzbek Dialectology Course. `http://library.ziyonet.uz/ru/book/39716`, Namangan. In Uzbek.

[Batsuren et al.2019] Khuyagbaatar Batsuren, Amarsanaa Ganbold, Altangerel Chagnaa, and Fausto Giunchiglia. 2019. Building the mongolian wordnet. In Christiane Fellbaum, Piek Vossen, Ewa Rudnicka, Marek Maziarz, and Maciej Piasecki, editors, *Proceedings of the Tenth Global WordNet Conference (GWC-2019)*, pages 238–244, Wrocaw, Poland. Oficyna Wydawnicza Politechniki Wrocawskiej.

[Bilgin et al.2004] Orhan Bilgin, Özlem Çetinoğlu, and Kemal Oflazer. 2004. Building a Wordnet for Turkish. *Romanian Journal of Information Science and Technology*, 7(1-2):163–172.

[Bond and Foster2013] Francis Bond and Ryan Foster. 2013. Linking and extending an open multilingual wordnet. In Hinrich Schuetze, Pascale Fung, and Massimo Poesio, editors, *Proceedings of the 51st Annual Meeting of the Association for Computational Linguistics (ACL-2013, Volume 1: Long Papers)*, pages 1352–1362, Sofia, Bulgaria. Association for Computational Linguistics.

[Bond and Paik2012] Francis Bond and Kyonghee Paik. 2012. A survey of WordNets and their licenses. In *Proceedings of the Sixth Global WordNet Conference (GWC-2012)*, pages 64–71, Matsue, Japan. Global WordNet Association.

[Bond et al.2009] Francis Bond, Hitoshi Isahara, Sanae Fujita, Kiyotaka Uchimoto, Takayuki Kuribayashi, and Kyoko Kanzaki. 2009. Enhancing the japanese wordnet. In *Proceedings of the 7th Workshop on Asian Language Resources (ALR7)*, pages 1–8.

[Boyd-Graber et al.2006] Jordan Boyd-Graber, Christiane Fellbaum, Daniel Osherson, and Robert Schapire. 2006. Adding dense, weighted connections to WordNet. In Petr Sojka, Key-Sun Choi, Christine Fellbaum, and Piek Vossen, editors, *Proceedings of the Third Global WordNet Conference (GWC-2006)*, pages 29–35, Brno, Czech Republic. Masaryk University.

[Butayev and Irisqulov2008] Shavkat Butayev and Abbos Irisqulov. 2008. *English-Uzbek, Uzbek-English Dictionary/Inglizcha-O'zbekcha, O'zbekcha-Inglizcha Lug'at*. O'zbekiston Respublikasi Fanlar Akad - Fan Nashriyoti, Tashkent, Uzbekistan.

[Çetinoğlu et al.2018] Özlem Çetinoğlu, Orhan Bilgin, and Kemal Oflazer. 2018. Turkish Wordnet. In Kemal Oflazer and Murat Saraçlar, editors, *Turkish Natural Language Processing. Theory and Applications of Natural Language Processing*, pages 317–336. Springer, Cham, Switzerland.

[de Paiva et al.2012] Valeria de Paiva, Rearden Commerce, and Alexandre Rademaker. 2012. Revisiting a brazilian wordnet. In *GWC 2012 6th International Global Wordnet Conference*, page 100.

[Eberhard et al.2020] David M. Eberhard, Gary F. Simons, and Charles D. Fennig. 2020. *Ethnologue: Languages of the World. Twenty-third edition.* SIL International, Dallas, Texas. Online version: http://www.ethnologue.com.

[Ehsani et al.2018] Elin Ehsani, Ercan Solak, and Olcay Yildiz. 2018. Constructing a wordnet for turkish using manual and automatic annotation. *ACM Transactions on Asian and Low-Resource Language Information Processing (TALLIP)*, 17(3):1–15, April.

[Ethnologue2020a] Ethnologue. 2020a. A Macrolanguage of Uzbekistan. `https://www.ethnologue.com/language/uzb`. Accessed: 2020-02-15.

[Ethnologue2020b] Ethnologue. 2020b. What are the Top 200 Most Spoken Languages? `https://www.ethnologue.com/guides/ethnologue200`. Accessed: 2020-02-15.

[Fellbaum1998] Christiane Fellbaum, editor. 1998. *WordNet—An Electronic Lexical Database*, Cambridge, MA. The MIT Press.

[Fišer et al.2012] Darja Fišer, Jernej Novak, and Tomaž Erjavec. 2012. slownet 3.0: development, extension and cleaning. In *Proceedings of Sixth International Global Wordnet Conference (GWC 2012)*, pages 113–117.

[Fišer et al.2014] Darja Fišer, Aleš Tavčar, and Tomaž Erjavec. 2014. sloWCrowd: A crowdsourcing tool for lexicographic tasks. In *Proceedings of the Ninth International Conference on Language Resources and Evaluation (LREC-14)*, pages 3471–3475, Reykjavik, Iceland. European Language Resources Association (ELRA).

[Ganbold et al.2018] Amarsanaa Ganbold, Altangerel Chagnaa, and Gábor Bella. 2018. Using crowd agreement for Wordnet localization. In N. Calzolari, K. Choukri, C. Cieri, T. Declerck, S. Goggi, K. Hasida, H. Isahara, B. Maegaard, J. Mariani, H. Mazo, A. Moreno, J. Odijk, S. Piperidis, and T. Tokunaga, editors, *Proceedings of the Eleventh International Conference on Language Resources and Evaluation (LREC-18)*, pages 474–478, Miyazaki, Japan. European Language Resources Association (ELRA).

[Giunchiglia et al.2015] Fausto Giunchiglia, Mladjan Jovanovic, Mercedes Huertas-Migueláñez, and Khuyagbaatar Batsuren. 2015. Crowdsourcing a large scale multilingual lexico-semantic resource. In Elizabeth Gerber and Panos Ipeirotis, editors, *Proceedings of the Third AAAI Conference on Human Computation and Crowdsourcing (HCOMP-15)*, Palo Alto, CA. AAAI Press.

[Giunchiglia et al.2017] Fausto Giunchiglia, Khuyagbaatar Batsuren, and Gabor Bella. 2017. Understanding and exploiting language diversity. In *Proceedings of the 26th International Joint Conference on Artificial Intelligence (IJCAI-17)*, pages 4009–4017, Menlo Park, CA. AAAI Press.

[Giunchiglia et al.2018] Fausto Giunchiglia, Khuyagbaatar Batsuren, and Abed A. Freihat. 2018. One world - seven thousand languages. In *Proceedings of the 19th International Conference on Computational Linguistics and Intelligent Text Processing (CiCling-18)*, Hanoi, Vietnam.

[Gonzalez-Agirre et al.2012] Aitor Gonzalez-Agirre, Egoitz Laparra, and German Rigau. 2012. Multilingual central repository version 3.0. In *LREC*, volume 2525, page 2529.

[Hirsch2005] Francine Hirsch. 2005. *Empire of nations: Ethnographic Knowledge & the Making of the Soviet Union*. Cornell University Press, Ithaca, N.Y.

[Huertas-Migueláñez et al.2018] Mercedes Huertas-Migueláñez, Natascia Leonardi, and Fausto Giunchiglia. 2018. Building a lexico-semantic resource collaboratively. In Jaka Čibej, Vojko Gorjanc, Iztok Kosem, and Simon Krek, editors, *Proceedings of the XVIII EURALEX International Congress: Lexicography in Global Contexts (ELX-18)*, pages 827–834, Ljubljana, Slovenia. Ljubljana University Press, Faculty of Arts.

[Knight2016] Will Knight. 2016. AI's language problem. *MIT Technology Review*, (Sep/Oct).

[Lindén et al.2010] Krister Lindén, Lauri Carlson, et al. 2010. Finnwordnet-wordnet på finska via översättning. *LexicoNordica*.

[Matlatipov et al.2018] San'atbek Matlatipov, Mirsaid Aripov, and Nilufar Abdurakhmonova. 2018. Modeling WordNet type thesaurus for Uzbek language semantic dictionary. *International Journal of Systems Engineering*, 2(1):26–28.

[Miller et al.1990] G. A. Miller, R. Beckwith, C. Fellbaum, D. Gross, and K. J. Miller. 1990. Introduction to WordNet: An on-line lexical database. *International Journal of Lexicography*, 3(4):235–244.

[Miller1995] G. A. Miller. 1995. Wordnet: A lexical database for English. *Communications of the ACM*, 38(11):39–41.

[Neale2018] Steven Neale. 2018. A survey on automatically-constructed wordnets and their evaluation: Lexical and word embedding-based approaches. In N. Calzolari, K. Choukri, C. Cieri, T. Declerck, S. Goggi, K. Hasida, H. Isahara, B. Maegaard, J. Mariani, H. Mazo, A. Moreno, J. Odijk, S. Piperidis, and T. Tokunaga, editors, *Proceedings of the Eleventh International Conference on Language Resources and Evaluation (LREC-18)*, pages 1705–1710, Miyazaki, Japan. European Language Resources Association (ELRA).

[Noor et al.2011] Nurril Hirfana Bte Mohamed Noor, Suerya Sapuan, and Francis Bond. 2011. Creating the open wordnet bahasa. In *Proceedings of the 25th Pacific Asia Conference on Language, Information and Computation*, pages 255–264.

[Oliver et al.2016] Antoni Oliver, Krešimir Šojat, and Matea Srebačić. 2016. Automatic expansion of croatian wordnet. *Metodologija i primjena lingvističkih istraživanja*, page 171.

[Pianta et al.2002] Emanuele Pianta, Luids Bentivogli, and Christian Girardi. 2002. MultiWordNet: Developing an aligned multilingual database. In *Proceedings of the First Global WordNet Conference (GWC-2002)*, pages 293–302.

[Piasecki et al.2009] Maciej Piasecki, Bernd Broda, and Stanislaw Szpakowicz. 2009. *A wordnet from the ground up*. Oficyna Wydawnicza Politechniki Wrocławskiej Wrocław.

[Pociello et al.2011] Elisabete Pociello, Eneko Agirre, and Izaskun Aldezabal. 2011. Methodology and construction of the basque wordnet. *Language resources and evaluation*, 45(2):121–142.

[Postma et al.2016] Marten Postma, Emiel van Miltenburg, Roxane Segers, Anneleen Schoen, and Piek Vossen. 2016. Open dutch wordnet. In *Proceedings of the Eight Global Wordnet Conference, Bucharest, Romania*.

[Pulatov2011] Abdumajid Qayumovich Pulatov. 2011. *Computational Linguistics*. Akademnashr, Tashkent, Uzbekistan. In Uzbek.

[Rakhimov2011] Azamatjon Rakhimov. 2011. *The Foundations of Computational Linguistics*. Akademnashr, Tashkent, Uzbekistan. In Uzbek.

[Sagot and Fišer2008] Benoît Sagot and Darja Fišer. 2008. Building a free french wordnet from multilingual resources. In A. Oltramari, L. Prévot, C-R. Huang, P. Buitelaar, and P. Vossen, editors, *Proceedings of OntoLex (OntoLex-2008)*, pages 14–19.

[Steels et al.2002] L. Steels, F. Kaplan, A. McIntyre, and J. Van Looveren. 2002. Crucial factors in the origins of word-meanings. In A. Wray, editor, *The Transition to Language*, pages 214–217. Oxford University Press, Oxford, UK.

[Steels1997] L. Steels. 1997. The synthetic modeling of language origins. *Evolution of Communication*, 1(1):1–34.

[Thoongsup et al.2009] Sareewan Thoongsup, Thatsanee Charoenporn, Kergrit Robkop, Tan Sinthurahat, Chumpol Mokarat, Virach Sornlertlamvanich, and Hitoshi Isahara. 2009. Thai wordnet construction. In *Proceedings of the 7th Workshop on Asian Language Resources (ALR7)*, pages 139–144.

[To'ychiboev and Khasanov2004] B. To'ychiboev and B. Khasanov. 2004. *Uzbek Dialectology*. Abdulla Qodiriy National Heritage.

[Tufiş et al.2008] Dan Tufiş, Radu Ion, Luigi Bozianu, Alexandru Ceauşu, and Dan Ştefănescu. 2008. Romanian Wordnet: Current state, new applications and prospects. In Attila Tanács, Dora Csendes, Veronika Vincze, Christiane Fellbaum, and Piek Vossen, editors, *Proceedings of the Fourth Global WordNet Conference (GWC-2008)*, pages 441–452, Szeged, Hungary. University of Szeged.

[Vossen1998] Piek Vossen. 1998. *EuroWordNet: A multilingual database with lexical semantic networks*. Kluwer/Springer, Dordrecht, Netherlands.

[Wang and Bond2013] Shan Wang and Francis Bond. 2013. Building the chinese open wordnet (cow): Starting from core synsets. In *Proceedings of the 11th Workshop on Asian Language Resources*, pages 10–18.

[Wittgenstein1953] L. Wittgenstein. 1953. *Philosophical Investigations*. Blackwell, Oxford, UK.

Practical Approach on Implementation of WordNets for South African Languages

Tshephisho Joseph Sefara
Council for Scientific and Industrial Research
Pretoria, South Africa
tsefara@csir.co.za

Tumisho Billson Mokgonyane
Department of Computer Science
University of Limpopo, South Africa
tumisho.mokgonyane@ul.ac.za

Vukosi Marivate
Department of Computer Science
University of Pretoria, South Africa
vukosi.marivate@cs.up.ac.za

Abstract

This paper proposes the implementation of WordNets for five South African languages, namely, Sepedi, Setswana, Tshivenda, isiZulu and isiXhosa to be added to open multilingual WordNets (OMW) on natural language toolkit (NLTK). The African WordNets are converted from Princeton WordNet (PWN) 2.0 to 3.0 to match the synsets in PWN 3.0. After conversion, there were 7157, 11972, 1288, 6380, and 9460 lemmas for Sepedi, Setswana, Tshivenda, isiZulu and isiXhosa respectively. Setswana, isiXhosa, Sepedi contains more lemmas compared to 8 languages in OMW and isiZulu contains more lemmas compared to 7 languages in OMW. A library has been published for continuous development of African WordNets in OMW using NLTK.

1 Introduction

WordNet consists of information about adverbs, adjectives, verbs and nouns in English and it organizes the words according to the notion of a synset. A synset can be defined as a set of words that are interchangeable in certain context. For example, the set {house, home, building} form a synset since the words can be used interchangeably referring to the same concept. Synsets can be linked to each other by means of semantic relations such as meronymy (leaf-tree), hypernymy versus hyponymy relation (flower-rose). The interlinked synsets create a strong semantic network that allows researchers (a) to automatically expand their search queries in information retrieval tasks (Azad and Deepak, 2019; Abbache et al., 2016), (b) to artificially expand their dataset by making use of data augmentation in natural language processing (NLP) tasks (Marivate and Sefara, 2020), (c) to improve cybercrime investigation in social network mining tasks (Iqbal et al., 2019).

WordNets have been applied in many domains such as machine learning classification to improve the performance of classification algorithms. An example is the role of WordNets is to increase the amount of NLP task data via data augmentation (Marivate and Sefara, 2020). This has been done for many well-resourced (European) languages. For low-resource languages such as South African languages, few studies have been done to build WordNets under low resources. African WordNets (Bosch and Griesel, 2017; Griesel et al., 2019) is a project that develop aligned WordNets for African languages spoken in South Africa. Initially, the project included five languages Sepedi, Setswana, Tshivenda, isiXhosa and isiZulu. During the development, DEBVisDic (WordNet editor) was used to build semantic networks. Due to limited resources, the expand model was followed during the development of the African WordNets. The expand model in WordNets creation is when the structure of Princeton WordNet is used to create other WordNets in other languages.

The goal of this paper is to build a multilingual lexical database with WordNets for South African languages based on the Princeton WordNet 3 to be utilized using the Python NLTK[1] library via open multilingual WordNets (OMW)[2]. We utilize the WordNets previously built by Bosch and Griesel (2017) for Sepedi, Setswana, Tshivenda, isiXhosa and isiZulu, to be compatible with OMW standard.

The main contributions of this paper are as fol-

[1]http://www.nltk.org/
[2]http://compling.hss.ntu.edu.sg/omw/

lows:

- A Python library has been released to allow inspection and improvement of the resource. The library can be found on Github[3] and Python repository[4].
- We released and published the data set (Sefara et al., 2020).

The outline of this paper is as follows: In Section 2 we discuss literature review of WordNets and their applications. Section 3 describes the methodology taken to create the resource. Section 4 concludes the paper with future work.

2 Literature Review

This section discusses the current WordNets and their applications in various domains.

2.1 WordNets

Bond and Foster (2013) created OMW that support more than 150 languages. OMW is made by combining WordNets published with open source licenses, Wiktionary data, and Unicode Common Locale Data Repository. The aim of OMW is to provide access to WordNets in multiple languages. All the WordNets in OMW are linked to PWN (Miller, 1995). The OMW and PWN can be accessed through NLTK.

EuroWordNet is a project created by Vossen (1998) to build multilingual WordNets for European languages based on PWN. The goal of EuroWordNet is to create multilingual database, build WordNets independently, obtain compatibility across languages, and to maintain language-specific relations.

Postma et al. (2016) created an open WordNet for Dutch that contains a total of 117,914 synsets using data from Cornetto database, open source resources, and the PWN. Authors also created a Python module[5] that can be applied to NLP applications.

ElKateb et al. (2006) proposed the development of WordNet for Arabic language using PWN for English as basis. Authors constructed the Arabic WordNet by using methods used to develop the EuroWordNet (Vossen, 1998). Regragui et al. (2016) added new content to Arabic WordNet that improved the performance of NLP applications such as question answering.

Bosch and Griesel (2017) discussed methods to build WordNets for low-resourced languages when the development of WordNets for South African languages was initiated using expand model based on PWN version 2. Authors created a total of 53982 synsets, 9279 definitions and 28853 usage examples. Due to low-resource environment, identification and translation of appropriate synsets was done by a human expert. One of the method is that authors used bilingual dictionaries to transfer information from dictionary to WordNet then a linguists make final approval for inclusion in the WordNets.

The Finnish WordNet is a lexical database for Finnish based on PWN structure (Lindén and Carlson, 2010). All word senses in PWN were translated into Finnish to make FinnWordNet. The PWN word senses were translated by a human translator to validate the quality of the content. The translation process is explained by (Lindén and Carlson, 2010). FinnWordNet has 117659 synsets and freely available under Creative Commons 3.0 license.

2.2 Applications of WordNets

Baccianella et al. (2010) annotated all the synsets of WordNet (Miller, 1995) with respect to the notions of positivity, negativity, and neutrality to create new dataset called SentiWordNet, an improved lexical resource that is designed to support opinion mining applications and sentiment classification. Authors published the dataset on Github[6].

Siddharthan et al. (2018) uses WordNet to create WordNet-feelings which is a new dataset that categorises word senses as feelings. Authors created ten categories and manually annotated the dataset by adding new categories and definitions.

WordNets are used as data sources in search and information retrieval tasks when building a query (Azad and Deepak, 2019). Abbache et al. (2016) improved the performance of information retrieval system for Arabic language by using WordNet and association rules to expand the search query. In their methodology, authors removed stop words (functional words) from the query before extracting and selecting synonyms using Arabic WordNet as the main source for word selection.

Marivate and Sefara (2020) used WordNet to

[3]https://github.com/JosephSefara/AfricanWordNet

[4]https://pypi.org/project/africanwordnet

[5]https://github.com/cltl/OpenDutchWordnet

[6]https://github.com/aesuli/SentiWordNet

create data augmentation technique for NLP classification applications. Authors compared the technique with semantic similarity augmentation and round-trip augmentation. The WordNet-based augmentation improved the performance of the classification models when using Wikipedia dataset. The same WordNet-based augmentation was used by Zhang et al. (2015) to train a temporal convolutional network that learns text understanding from character level input up to an abstract text concepts. Hasan et al. (2020) applied semantic similarity of WordNet to manage the ambiguity in social media text by selecting informative features to enhance semantic representation.

3 Methodology

This section discusses the design and implementation of the WordNets for South African languages. It first discusses sense map preparation, then WordNets conversion, and finally implementation.

3.1 Sense map preparation

In this section, we explain the sense map preparation process.

We used the sensemap(5WN) published on PWN website [7] for versions 2.0, 2.1, and 3.0. Sense map simply list each 2.0 noun sense (encoded as a sense key) paired with its mapping to one or more 2.1 noun senses. We converted all the polysemous (nouns and verbs) and monosemous (nouns and verbs) to 2.1. Then lastly, we converted 2.1 synsets to 3.0. We used the 3.0 sense maps to convert all the synsets from 2.1 to 3.0. The synsets that are not in all the sense maps are used as is.

Algorithm 1 illustrates the steps taken during conversion of the sense maps. The algorithm was run twice, for first time to convert 2.0→2.1 then duplicate offset targets in 2.1 were removed. The second time to convert 2.1→3.0 then duplicate offset target in 3.0 were also removed. Table 1 shows a sample of the converted offsets that will later be used to match every synset in African WordNets from 2.0 to 3.0.

Table 1 shows a sample format of sense mapping that are later used to convert the WordNets from 2.0 to 3.0.

[7]https://wordnet.princeton.edu/documentation/senseidx5wn

Algorithm 1: Sense map conversion

Input: s: sense map file
Output: $\hat{s}$ list containing pair of source and target offset ID

def mono (s) **:**
  Let $F \leftarrow Open(s)$ be a to file reader;
  for $line$ **in** F **:**
    $SourceOffset \leftarrow$ use regular expression to match source offset ID from $line$;
    $TargetOffset \leftarrow$ use regular expression to match target offset ID from $line$;
    $\hat{s} \leftarrow [Sourceoffset, Targetoffset]$;
  return($\hat{s}$);

Table 1: Sample of the sense mapping

2.0	2.1	3.0
12976279-n	13571065-n	13752172-n
12976532-n	13571318-n	13752443-n

3.2 WordNets conversion

This section discusses conversion of African WordNets to PWN 3.0 and explain OMW format.

We collected the WordNets created by Bosch and Griesel (2017) from South African Centre for Digital Language Resources (SADiLaR)[8]. SADiLaR is a national center supported and funded by the South African Department of Science and Innovation. The WordNets are in the form of XML format based on PWN version 2.

We used a library called BeautifulSoup[9] to extract all the synset offset ID, part-of-speech tag, lemma, and word form since the WordNets are in XML format. Table 2 shows the number of synsets before and after conversion to 3.0 excluding the synsets that do not exists in PWN. There is an increase in number of synsets, isiZulu increased by 90, isiXhosa by 150, Sepedi by 101, Setswana by 240, and Tshivenda by 16. The increase is caused by synsets that have multiple mappings in PWN 3.0. We saved the new synsets in a format that is supported by OMW. The OMW format is as follows:

offset-pos langcode:lemma wordform

[8]https://www.sadilar.org/

[9]https://pypi.org/project/beautifulsoup4/

where *offset* is the unique ID (linking to the PWN), *langcode* is the universal language code[10], *wordform* is the written word, and *pos* is the part-of-speech.

Table 2: Conversion of synsets

Language	Original Synsets	New Synsets
isiZulu	9026	9116
isiXhosa	13731	13881
Sepedi	10647	10748
Setswana	22234	22474
Tshivenda	1581	1597

An example of the formatted synsets is depicted in Figure 1 that is compatible with OMW in NLTK. OMW consists of 29 languages in NLTK as shown in Table 3. There are 8 languages in OMW that contains lemmas less than that of Setswana, isiXhosa, and Sepedi. IsiZulu contains more lemmas than 7 languages in OMW while Tshivenda contains the smallest lemmas than all other languages.

Table 3: OMW in NLTK

Language	Lemma	Language	Lemma
eng	147306	glg	23124
fin	129839	ell	18225
jpn	89637	arb	17785
tha	80508	fas	17560
cmn	61532	**tsn**	**11972**
fra	55350	**xho**	**9460**
por	54069	**nso**	**7157**
cat	46531	bul	6720
pol	45387	**zul**	**6380**
nld	43077	als	5988
ita	41855	swe	5824
slv	41032	heb	5325
ind	36954	dan	4468
spa	36681	nob	4186
zsm	33932	nno	3387
hrv	29010	qcn	3206
eus	26240	**ven**	**1288**

3.3 Implementation

This section discuss implementation of African WordNets in NLTK.

Total of 5 files (sample shown in Figure 1) have been created that consists of the 5 languages to be added to NLTK. The files have been named according to the following format:

00002452-n	nso:lemma	selo
00003777-a	nso:lemma	hwago
00003777-a	nso:lemma	hwang
00004012-a	nso:lemma	felelago
00004012-a	nso:lemma	felelang
00004304-a	nso:lemma	khutsufaditšego
00004304-a	nso:lemma	khutsufaditšweng
00004304-a	nso:lemma	kopafaditšwego
00004304-a	nso:lemma	kopafaditšweng
00004492-v	nso:lemma	hupa

Figure 1: An extract of the converted WordNet for Sepedi using OMW format

- Sepedi: wn-data-nso.tab
- Setswana: wn-data-tsn.tab
- isiXhosa: wn-data-xho.tab
- isiZulu: wn-data-zul.tab
- Tshivenda: wn-data-ven.tab

where each file resides in a directory inside OMW corpus in NLTK and the directory name is named according to the ISO language code. The ISO language code for Sepedi is **nso**, Setswana is **tsn**, isiXhosa is **xho**, isiZulu is **zul**, and Tshivenda is **ven**.

A Python helper library[11] has been created to install these African WordNets to OMW in NLTK. The African WordNets can be used like other WordNets on OMW. For example, the library has to be imported to the environment then the following statements shows the lemma names of the word 'entity' in Setswana:

```
>>> from nltk.corpus import wordnet
>>> import africanwordnet
>>> wordnet.synset('entity.n.01').lemmas('tsn')
[Lemma('entity.n.01.selô'),
Lemma('entity.n.01.sengwe')]
```

Listing 1: Lemma example

The following statement is used to view the synsets of the isiZulu word 'iqoqo' (means collection).

```
>>> from nltk.corpus import wordnet
>>> import africanwordnet
>>> wordnet.synsets('iqoqo',lang=('zul'))
[Synset('whole.n.02'),
 Synset('conspectus.n.01'),
```

[10]https://www.loc.gov/standards/iso639-2/php/code_list.php

[11]https://pypi.org/project/africanwordnet

```
Synset('overview.n.01'),
Synset('sketch.n.03'),
Synset('compilation.n.01'),
Synset('collection.n.01'),
Synset('team.n.02'),
Synset('set.n.01')]
```

Listing 2: Synonym example

The following statement is used to view the hyponyms of the Sepedi word 'taelo' (means edict).

```
>>> from nltk.corpus import wordnet
>>> import africanwordnet
>>> synsets = wn.synsets('taelo',lang=('nso'))
>>> for synset in synsets:
...     for hypo in synset.hyponyms():
...         for lemma in hypo.lemmas("nso"):
...             print(lemma)
Lemma('behest.n.01.tlhalošo')
Lemma('commandment.n.01.molao')
Lemma('commandment.n.01.taelo')
Lemma('commission.n.06.taelo')
Lemma('injunction.n.01.taelo')
Lemma('order.n.01.taelo')
Lemma('summons.n.02.tagafalo')
```

Listing 3: Hyponym example

The following statement is used to view the hypernyms of the isiXhosa word 'omisa' (means dry).

```
>>> from nltk.corpus import wordnet
>>> import africanwordnet
>>> synsets = wn.synsets('omisa',lang=('xho'))
>>> for synset in synsets:
...     for hypo in synset.hypernyms():
...         for lemma in hypo.lemmas("xho"):
...             print(lemma)
Lemma('dry.v.01.omisa')
Lemma('change.v.01.guqula')
Lemma('change.v.01.tshintsha')
Lemma('change_integrity.v.01.guqula_imfezeko')
```

Listing 4: Hypernyms example

4 Conclusion and Future Work

This paper presented the implementation of African WordNets to be used in NLTK via OMW. We discussed the conversion of PWN sense maps from 2.0 to 2.1 to 3.0. There was an increase of synsets during conversion. We proposed an algorithm that helps to convert synsets from PWN 2.0 to 3.0. A Python library has been made available[12] to utilize the WordNets.

The future work will focus on

- improving conversion of PWN sense maps from 2.0 to 3.0 so that all synsets are available in 3.0. Kim et al. (2018) proposed automatic mapping of synsets using bilingual dictionaries. Due to limited bilingual dictionaries this method could not be utilized.
- evaluation of the African WordNets using various evaluation methods. Ramanand and Bhattacharyya (2007) proposed a method to evaluate synsets using dictionary definitions since currently there are no enough dictionaries for these languages this method could not be utilized.

[12]https://pypi.org/project/africanwordnet

Acknowledgments

We would like to thank SADILAR for making the datasets available for research. And we would like to thank Github for hosting the developed library.

References

Ahmed Abbache, Farid Meziane, Ghalem Belalem, Fatma Zohra Belkredim, et al. 2016. Arabic query expansion using WordNet and association rules. *International Journal of Intelligent Information Technologies (IJIIT)*, 12(3):51–64.

Hiteshwar Kumar Azad and Akshay Deepak. 2019. A new approach for query expansion using Wikipedia and WordNet. *Information sciences*, 492:147–163.

Stefano Baccianella, Andrea Esuli, and Fabrizio Sebastiani. 2010. Sentiwordnet 3.0: an enhanced lexical resource for sentiment analysis and opinion mining. In *Lrec*, volume 10, pages 2200–2204.

Francis Bond and Ryan Foster. 2013. Linking and extending an open multilingual wordnet. In *Proceedings of the 51st Annual Meeting of the Association for Computational Linguistics (Volume 1: Long Papers)*, pages 1352–1362.

Sonja E Bosch and Marissa Griesel. 2017. Strategies for building wordnets for under-resourced languages: The case of african languages. *Literator (Potchefstroom. Online)*, 38(1):1–12.

Sabry ElKateb, William Black, Horacio Rodríguez, Musa Alkhalifa, Piek Vossen, Adam Pease, and Christiane Fellbaum. 2006. Building a wordnet for arabic. In *Proceedings of the Fifth International Conference on Language Resources and Evaluation (LREC'06)*, pages 29–34.

Marissa Griesel, Sonja Bosch, and Mampaka L Mojapelo. 2019. Thinking globally, acting locally–progress in the African wordnet project. In *Proceedings of the Tenth Global Wordnet Conference*, pages 191–196.

Ali Muttaleb Hasan, Noorhuzaimi Mohd Noor, Taha Hussein Rassem, Shahrul Azman Mohd Noah, and Ahmed Muttaleb Hasan. 2020. A proposed method using the semantic similarity of wordnet 3.1 to handle the ambiguity to apply in social media text. In *Information Science and Applications*, pages 471–483. Springer.

Farkhund Iqbal, Benjamin CM Fung, Mourad Debbabi, Rabia Batool, and Andrew Marrington. 2019. Wordnet-based criminal networks mining for cybercrime investigation. *IEEE Access*, 7:22740–22755.

Jiseong Kim, Younggyun Hahm, Sunggoo Kwon, and Key-Sun Choi. 2018. Automatic wordnet mapping: from corenet to princeton wordnet. In *Proceedings of the Eleventh International Conference on Language Resources and Evaluation (LREC 2018)*.

Krister Lindén and Lauri Carlson. 2010. Finnwordnet-wordnet på finska via översättning. *LexicoNordica – Nordic Journal of Lexicography*, 17:119–140.

Vukosi Marivate and Tshephisho Sefara. 2020. Improving short text classification through global augmentation methods. In *International Cross-Domain Conference for Machine Learning and Knowledge Extraction*, pages 385–399. Springer.

George A Miller. 1995. Wordnet: a lexical database for english. *Communications of the ACM*, 38(11):39–41.

MC Postma, E Miltenburg, R Segers, A Schoen, and PTJM Vossen. 2016. Open dutch wordnet. In *Proceedings of the Eigth Global Wordnet Conference*.

J Ramanand and Pushpak Bhattacharyya. 2007. Towards automatic evaluation of wordnet synsets. *GWC 2008*, page 360.

Yasser Regragui, Lahsen Abouenour, Fettoum Krieche, Karim Bouzoubaa, and Paolo Rosso. 2016. Arabic wordnet: New content and new applications. In *Proceedings of the Eighth Global WordNet Conference*, pages 330–338.

Tshephisho Sefara, Tumisho Mokgonyane, and Vukosi Marivate. 2020. Wordnets for South African languages. Zenodo, December.

Advaith Siddharthan, Nicolas Cherbuin, Paul J Eslinger, Kasia Kozlowska, Nora A Murphy, and Leroy Lowe. 2018. WordNet-feelings: a linguistic categorisation of human feelings. *arXiv preprint arXiv:1811.02435*.

Piek Vossen, 1998. *Introduction to EuroWordNet*, pages 1–17. Springer Netherlands, Dordrecht.

Xiang Zhang, Junbo Zhao, and Yann LeCun. 2015. Character-level convolutional networks for text classification. In *Advances in neural information processing systems*, pages 649–657.

Homonymy and Polysemy Detection with Multilingual Information

Amir Ahmad Habibi, Bradley Hauer, Grzegorz Kondrak
Alberta Machine Intelligence Institute, Department of Computing Science
University of Alberta, Edmonton, Canada
{amirahmad,bmhauer,gkondrak}@ualberta.ca

Abstract

Deciding whether a semantically ambiguous word is homonymous or polysemous is equivalent to establishing whether it has any pair of senses that are semantically unrelated. We present novel methods for this task that leverage information from multilingual lexical resources. We formally prove the theoretical properties that provide the foundation for our methods. In particular, we show how the *One Homonym Per Translation* hypothesis of Hauer and Kondrak (2020a) follows from the synset properties formulated by Hauer and Kondrak (2020b). Experimental evaluation shows that our approach sets a new state of the art for homonymy detection.

1 Introduction

A word with multiple senses considered to be semantically ambiguous. In WordNet (Fellbaum, 1998), a word is semantically ambiguous if and only if it occurs in more than one synset. There are two types of word ambiguity: Two senses of a word are in the relation of *polysemy* if they are semantically related. For example, the WordNet senses `bank#n#2` "financial institution" and `bank#n#9` "financial building" are semantically related. Two senses of a word which are not semantically related are in the relation of *homonymy*. Continuing the example, `bank#n#1` "sloping land" is not related to `bank#n#2` "financial institution." A word is *homonymous* if and only if it has a pair of senses in the homonymy relation. A word which is ambiguous, but not homonymous, is *polysemous*. *Polysemy classification* (Utt and Padó, 2011), or *homonym detection*, is the task of automatically deciding whether a given ambiguous word is homonymous or polysemous. In this paper, we develop and present novel methods for this task.

Homonymy detection is vital to the tasks of defining sense inventories and clustering fine-grained senses (Navigli, 2006; Hovy et al., 2006). Distinguishing between homonymous and polysemous words is a core problem in lexicography (Mel'čuk, 2013). It has also been a subject of study in psycholinguistics (Brown, 2008). Consistent with the well-known tendency for distinct senses of a word to translate differently in other languages (Resnik and Yarowsky, 1999), Liu et al. (2018) show that special processing of homonymous words can improve neural machine translation.

Deciding whether a given word is homonymous or polysemous typically requires extensive manual effort and consultation of hand-crafted resources, as the intuitions of native speakers alone are not sufficient. WordNet does not contain homonymy information. Liu et al. (2018) rely upon a list of homonymous words obtained from a Wikipedia article, which is not reliable. Rice et al. (2019) manually identify a set of homonyms using a dictionary. Noting the lack of of any existing homonymy resources of sufficient quality and coverage, Hauer and Kondrak (2020a) manually construct a list of homonyms from English etymological dictionaries, and map these homonyms to WordNet senses. While the list is not exhaustive, it provides a benchmark to evaluate homonymy detection methods.

We adopt a graph-based approach, constructing a sense graph for an input word using WordNet, and a multilingual extension, BabelNet (Navigli and Ponzetto, 2012). In such a graph, vertices are senses, while edges represent semantic relatedness. We make the simplifying assumption that the polysemy relation is transitive. Thus, any pair of senses which are connected in the sense graph are semantically related. Furthermore, if the graph has more than one connected component, the word is homonymous, as it has at least one pair of unrelated senses. Thus, the task of identifying homonymous words is reduced to task of deciding the pairwise semantic relatedness of senses. We present a variety of methods for this sub-task, which leverage both monolingual and multilingual information. We formally prove the theoretical properties that provide the foundation for our methods. In particular, we show how the *One Homonym Per Translation* (OHPT) hypothesis of Hauer and Kondrak (2020a) follows from the synset properties formulated by Hauer and Kondrak (2020b).

The results of our experiments set a new state of the art for the task of homonym detection, outperforming the prior work of van den Beukel and Aroyo (2018). On a balanced dataset of homonymous and polysemous words, we achieve a 12% improvement in F_1 score. We also investigate which combination of translation languages yields the best overall results.

2 Related Work

Homonymy detection has been investigated in natural language processing. Utt and Padó (2011) propose a statistical model which computes a polysemy index on the scale between homonymy and polysemy. Their work is not comparable to ours, as it depends upon an additional sources of ontological information. More recently, van den Beukel and Aroyo (2018) detect homonymous words for the task of humor recognition. Their method uses WordNet path similarity (Pedersen et al., 2005) and the textual similarity between synset definitions. Their definition of homonyms is broader than ours, including distinct word forms with identical pronunciations (homophones).

Homonymy detection has also been studied in psycholinguistics. Beekhuizen et al. (2018) distinguish between monosemous, polysemous, and homonymous words using word embeddings and contextual embeddings. The idea is that the embedding of a monosemous word should be closer to the embedding of its context than a polysemous word, which should in turn exhibit greater similarity to its context compared to a homonymous word. Rice et al. (2019) extract a list of 534 homonymous words from the Wordsmyth dictionary, and annotate them manually in sentential contexts. These resources are then used to analyze the relative frequencies of these homonyms.

As homonymous words are exactly those with semantically unrelated senses, the study of homonymy is closely related to the study of semantic relatedness between word senses. To this end, Dyvik (2004) presents methods aimed at automatic construction of a WordNet-like resource using information extracted from parallel text corpora. This involves the use of translation information to induce semantic fields, which partition senses according to their semantic relatedness. Van der Plas and Tiedemann (2006) identify semantic relations between words using distributional information extracted from corpora, and show that leveraging multilingual data yields substantial improvements for the task of detecting synonymous words.

3 Background

Our work builds upon recent investigations into the linguistic phenomena of sense, homonymy, polysemy, synonymy, and translation. Therefore, we begin with a review of the relevant terminology, definitions, and general background knowledge.

3.1 Homonyms and Homonymous Words

Hauer and Kondrak (2020a) provide definitions of terms relevant to homonym detection. A *lexeme* is a single entry of a word in a lexicon (Jurafsky and Martin, 2008). A *word* is a basic written form which represents one or more lexemes. Each lexeme has at least one *sense*, corresponding to a use of the associated word to express a single lexicalized concept. The senses of a lexeme all relate to a single general meaning, and therefore they are all semantically related and so polysemous (Murphy and Koskela, 2010). Contrariwise, senses of a single word, but of distinct lexemes, are unrelated; the fact that a single word represents both lexemes may be entirely coincidental. Unrelated senses of a single word are *homonymous*; a word with a pair of homonymous senses is likewise called *homonymous*, and the lexemes it represents are called *homonyms*. Equivalently, a word is homonymous if it represents more than one lexeme. When it is clear that we are referring to a word, we can refer to a homonymous word simply as a homonym.

A classic example of a homonym is *bank*. This word represents two lexemes, referring generally to a repository (as in "bank account"), or to a slope (as in "river bank"). Each lexeme has multiple senses; for example the "slope" lexeme has senses expressing the concept of a shore, and that of an aircraft maneuver. A word is polysemous if it has multiple senses, but only one lexeme, i.e. if all of its senses are semantically related.

Parallel homonymy exists when two different words lexicalize the same pair of unrelated concepts. Parallel homonymy may exist between words in the same language, or in different languages. For example, both the English words *set up*[1] and *rig* have a pair of homonymous senses expressing the meanings "equip" and "manipulate". A cross-lingual example involves the English *band* and Italian *banda*; each has a pair of homonymous senses expressing the meanings "ring" and "group". Where cross-lingual parallel homonymy exists, two homonyms share at least one translation, which violates the OHPT hypothesis of Hauer and Kondrak (2020a).

3.2 Synsets, Wordnets, and Multi-Wordnets

Hauer and Kondrak (2020b) define synonymy as the relation of sameness of meaning. They note that it can be applied to various linguistic types – we can speak of synonymous words, synonymous senses, etc. – and that it can be conditional (*near-synonymy*) or absolute. The Princeton WordNet (Fellbaum, 1998) is composed of synonym sets, or *synsets*. Following prior work, we use the common noun *wordnet* to refer to any resource structured analogously to Princeton WordNet. A synset is a set of words which are all pairwise near-synonyms; each synset corresponds to a lexicalized concept, which each word in the synset can be used to express. There exists a one-to-one correspondence between the senses of a word, and the synsets which contain it; therefore, synsets induce a sense inventory. Synsets have the following properties (Hauer and Kondrak, 2020b):

1. *A word is monosemous iff it is in a single synset. A word is polysemous iff it is in multiple synsets.*
2. *Words are near-synonyms iff they share at least one synset. Words are absolute synonyms iff they share all their synsets.*
3. *Word senses are synonymous iff they are in the same synset.*
4. *Every word sense belongs to exactly one synset.*
5. *Every sense of a polysemous word belongs to a different synset.*

Multilingual wordnets (multi-wordnets) consist of multi-lingual synsets (multi-synsets). They are constructed either by adding words from other languages to the (monolingual) synsets of a pre-existing wordnet, or linking synsets from multiple wordnets in different languages (Vossen, 1996). In any case, a multilingual synset can be viewed as set of words, each associated with a language, and capable of representing the lexicalized concept to which the multi-wordnet corresponds.

A wordnet facilitates the enumeration of the senses of a word, by identifying the concepts associated with the synsets containing the word. A multi-wordnet further enables the enumeration of the translations of a specific sense of a word, by retrieving the elements of the corresponding synset, excluding those from the same language as the word to be translated. Hauer and Kondrak (2020b) refer to this property as the *multi-wordnet assumption*: senses share a synset if and only if they are semantically equivalent.

4 Methods

In this section, we present our graph-based method for deciding whether a given word is homonymous or not. Under our definitions, this is equivalent to deciding whether the word has any senses that are semantically unrelated. Operating under the assumption that semantic relatedness of senses is symmetric and transitive, our strategy is as follows:

1. Enumerate the senses of the word.
2. If the word has only one sense, classify it as monosemous (and therefore not a homonym).
3. Identify pairs of senses that are semantically related.
4. Construct a graph whose vertices are senses of the input word, which are connected by an edge if they are semantically related.
5. Classify the word as homonymous if its graph has more than one connected component; otherwise, classify the word as polysemous.

In the semantic graph constructed by this procedure, adjacent senses are semantically related by definition, and connected senses are semantically related by transitivity. Therefore, the existence of more than one connected component implies that the word has semantically unrelated senses, and so is homonymous. Any sense inventory can be used to enumerate senses, and graph connectivity can be decided using a simple breadth-first search. All that remains is to establish methods of detecting whether two senses of a word are semantically related. We present five sufficient conditions for semantic relatedness between senses, one in each

[1] Following the example of WordNet, non-compositional multi-word units are considered words.

of the following five subsections. For each of these criteria, we describe the circumstances under which it detects semantic relatedness, and provide a theoretical argument for its soundness.

One strength of this method is its lack of dependence on any hyperparameters or additional training data. A vector-based method leveraging distributional semantics, for example, would necessarily depend on some continuous measure of semantic similarity. This in turn would require access to a large text corpus to learn distributional embeddings. In addition, a threshold value would need to be tuned, which would depend on the embeddings and the corpus. By avoiding such requirements, our method is easier to apply to arbitrary domains, and can be applied to any language which is represented in a multi-wordnet.

4.1 Two Senses, One Translation (OHPT)

Our first method is an application of the OHPT hypothesis of Hauer and Kondrak (2020a). OHPT states that semantically unrelated senses of a word do not share any translations. It follows that if two senses of a word can be translated by a single word in another language, those senses are semantically related. We refer to this approach to detecting semantic relatedness as "two senses, one translation" or simply as OHPT.

The following theorem generalizes the OHPT hypothesis to account for the few exceptions found by Hauer and Kondrak (2020a):

Theorem 1 (Two Senses, One Translation). *If two distinct senses x_1 and x_2 of a word x in one language can be translated by a word y in another language, then one and only one of the following condition holds:*

1. *x_1 and x_2 are polysemous.*
2. *x and y exhibit parallel homonymy.*

Proof. Distinct senses x_1 and x_2 belong to different multi-synsets (by synset property #5). Since they both can be translated by y, the two multi-synsets also contain senses y_1 and y_2 of y, respectively (by the multi-wordnet assumption). x_1 and x_2 are unrelated if and only if y_1 and y_2 are unrelated, as they express the same pair of concepts. Therefore, either all four senses are related, or x and y exhibit parallel homonymy. □

Theorem 1 is the principal theoretical result in this work, which provides a theoretical foundation

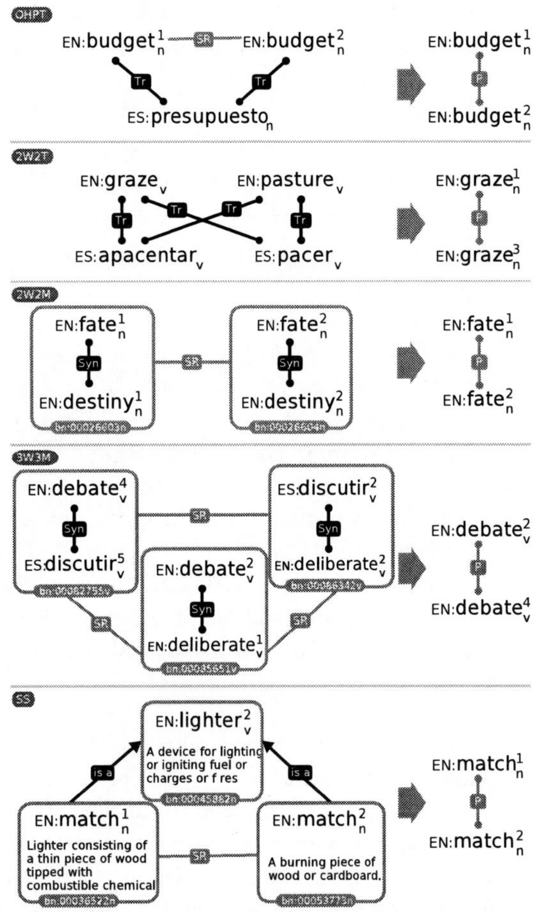

Figure 1: Examples that illustrate our methods. The semantic relations in black are provided by the resources. The polysemy relations in red are inferred by the methods.

for the OHPT hypothesis. In fact, all actual English-Italian exceptions to the hypothesis that Hauer and Kondrak (2020a) identify in their experiments involve parallel homonymy.

Operating under the assumption that parallel homonymy is rare[2], we arrive at the criterion described above: senses which share a translation are related. The first part of Figure 1 shows an example application of OHPT.

4.2 Two Words in Two Multi-synsets (2W2M)

Theorem 1 can be generalized to include pairs of words from the same language. This follows from the observation of Hauer and Kondrak (2020b)

[2]Hauer and Kondrak (2020a) find only three cases of parallel homonymy, across two languages of translation, using a database of 2759 homonyms.

that intra-lingual synonymy and cross-lingual synonymy are two views of the same phenomenon: semantic equivalence. As words in different languages share multi-synsets if they are mutual translations, so words in the same language share multi-synsets if they are near-synonymous. The following theorem captures this insight:

Theorem 2 (Two Words in Two Multi-synsets). *If two distinct words x and y (either in the same or different languages) share two multi-synsets, then one and only one of the following condition holds:*

1. *The two pairs of senses of x and y, which correspond to those synsets, are polysemous.*
2. *x and y exhibit parallel homonymy.*

Proof. Senses that share a multi-synset are in the relation of absolute synonymy (Property 3). Thus, the two senses of x are unrelated if and only if the two senses of y are unrelated. Therefore, either all four senses are related, or x and y exhibit parallel homonymy. □

Interestingly, Theorem 2 provides a theoretical foundation for Heuristic #3 of Pericliev (2015) which states that the presence of distinct synonymous colexifiers in one language indicates polysemy rather than homonymy. Our theorem establishes that the only reason for the heuristic to fail is parallel homonymy. Since parallel homonymy is rare, we will assume that two senses of a given word are semantically related whenever their respective synsets or multi-synsets share another word. See Figure 1 for an example.

4.3 Three Words in Three Multi-synsets (3W3M)

Theorem 1, implies that, in the absence of parallel homonymy, if two senses of a word share a synset with a single word from another language, they are related. Theorem 2 removed the "from another language" clause. Theorem 3 extends this further, from two words sharing two multi-synsets to three words (in any combination of languages) sharing three multi-synsets.

Theorem 3 (Three Words in Three Multi-synsets). *If three pairs of senses (x_1, y_1), (x_2, z_2), and (y_3, z_3) of three different words x, y, and z share three multi-synsets, respectively, then one and only one of the following conditions holds:*

1. *The three pairs of senses of x, y, and z are polysemous.*
2. *At least two of the three words are homonymous.*

Proof. Without loss of generality, suppose that x_1 and x_2 are not semantically related, and that the words y and z are not homonymous. Then both y_1 and y_3, and z_2 and z_3 are semantically related. By transitivity of semantic relatedness, this implies that x_1 and x_2 are also semantically related. Contradiction. □

This gives us our third criterion for establishing the semantic relatedness of a pair of senses of a word. As with the previous two theorems, given the rarity of homonymy, if the antecedent condition of the theorem is satisfied, the senses of each word involved are taken to be related. See Figure 1 for an example.

4.4 Two Words, Two Translations (2W2T)

Our next theorem is defined on words rather than senses.

Theorem 4 (Two Words, Two Translations). *If two distinct words x and y in one language E both translate into two different words w and z in another language, then one and only one of the following conditions holds:*

1. *All senses involved in all those translation instances are semantically related.*
2. *At least two of the four words are homonymous.*

Proof. Without loss of generality, suppose senses x_1 and w_1 are mutual translations, and that neither is semantically related to any senses of y or z. Then, since x can also be translated as z, there exists a translation instance between another sense of x, call it x_2, and a sense of z, call it z_2. Since x_1 and w_1 are not semantically related to z_2, x_1 and x_2 are not semantically related to each other (otherwise x_1 and w_1 would be related to z_2 by transitivity through x_2). So x is a homonymous word. A symmetrical reasoning leads to the conclusion that w_1 and w_2 are not semantically related to each other, so w is also a homonymous word. □

Given the rarity of homonymy (most ambiguous words are not homonymous), we again create a condition for semantic relatedness which assumes that the antecedent implies the first condition. Figure 1 shows an example application of this theorem.

4.5 Sibling Synsets (SS)

So far, the only semantic relations leveraged in our method are synonymy and translational equivalence. However, WordNet and comparable resources contain various other semantic relations between synsets, which could be used to infer semantic relatedness. In particular, we hypothesize that synsets which share a common hypernym or holonym are semantically related. We call this method Sibling Synsets (**SS**). Figure 1 illustrates an example of this method, with three synsets and their definitions.

4.6 UNION

We began this section by describing a method which classifies an ambiguous word as homonymous or polysemous by constructing a graph of its senses. In this graph, senses have an edge between them if and only if they are semantically related. This reduces the task of homonym detection to detecting pairwise semantic relatedness between senses of a single word. That is, given two senses of a word, are they senses of a single lexeme, or distinct lexemes?

We have presented five sufficient conditions for the semantic relatedness of senses: OHPT, 2W2M, 3W3M, 2W2T, and SS. Each of these criteria can be seen as adding a set of edges to the sense graph created by our method. It is, of course, possible to combine these methods by simply taking the union of the edge sets they return. This leads to a final criterion, **UNION**, which finds a pair of senses to be semantically related if any of the aforementioned five criteria do.

5 Experiments

Having provided theoretical support for our homonym detection methods in Section 4, we now empirically evaluate their ability to distinguish between homonymous and polysemous words. We start by describing our datasets and resources, as well as the method for obtaining translations of senses. We then present our results on both words and senses.

5.1 Data and Resources

To test our method, we create a balanced benchmark dataset for homonym detection consisting of 948 words, with 474 in each class. Note that the hand-crafted English resources described below are used for evaluation only, as our methods are largely language-independent, being based on the BabelNet's sense translation information.

We extract the positive instances, from the list of homonymous words released by Hauer and Kondrak (2020a). For each homonymous word, the list includes a partial mapping of its WordNet 3.0 senses to the individual homonyms. The original homonym-based sense clustering is both incomplete and noisy, due to the use of an automated pre-clustering procedure (Navigli, 2006) in the mapping process. We completed this mapping, ensuring that *all* senses of the included words are mapped to homonyms. We also manually corrected a number of errors in the mapping, where necessary. This new version of the resource has 474 homonymous words with a total of 1017 homonyms.[3] We make the corrected resource publicly available.

We also carefully select the negative (non-homonymous) instances. Strictly speaking, any word which has more than one sense, and which is not in any homonym list known to us, could be labeled a polysemous word and used as a negative example. However, to make the dataset more challenging, we take advantage of the manually-crafted and validated clustering of WordNet 3.0 senses released as part of the OntoNotes project (Hovy et al., 2006). We select 474 words at random from among the 3232 words which have more than one sense cluster in OntoNotes, but which are not among the homonyms described above. Thus, the dataset requires a homonym detection method to distinguish homonyms from words which not only have multiple senses in the fine-grained WordNet sense inventory, but also in the coarse-grained OntoNotes sense inventory.

We set aside 20% of these words (95 homonymous and 95 polysemous) as a test set, and use the rest for development. We compare our method to a simple baseline which simply predicts every word to be homonymous. We experimented with other baselines which threshold the number of WordNet senses of the input word, but they failed to consistently outperform this simple baseline.

5.2 Language Selection

Our criteria for semantic relatedness crucially depend upon sense translation information: words in other languages that can be used to express a given concept. We obtain this information from

[3]We exclude words whose homonyms have entirely disjoint parts of speech, e.g. *bear*, and words with only one homonym represented in WordNet 3.0, e.g. *wit*.

BabelNet multi-synsets. However, BabelNet is not a hand-crafted resource, and as such suffers from both coverage and accuracy problems. Specifically, many languages are only sparsely represented, and many automatically-generated translations are simply incorrect for a given sense. Since our method is based exclusively on the positive evidence for polysemy, considering more languages of translations improves the precision of homonymy detection, but decreases the recall, as many sense pairs are incorrectly identified as related. Thus, we attempt to identify a set of languages that yields the best trade-off in terms of F_1 score on our development set.

Since it would be infeasible to test all possible combinations of hundreds of languages, we instead perform a heuristic search for a reasonably well-performing set of languages. We select our languages of translation from the 50 languages with the highest overall synset coverage in BabelNet. We then evaluate the performance of the OHPT method using each of these 50 languages. The resulting F_1 scores of these development experiments provide a ranking of the languages, which we interpret as an estimate of its usefulness for our task. The top ten languages, in order, are Indonesian, Malay, Spanish, Catalan, Slovenian, Portuguese, Finnish, Italian, Romanian, and Croatian. It is difficult to interpret this ranking without language-specific knowledge, but we note that Indonesian and Malay are standardized varieties of an Asian *lingua franca*, while the others are European languages that share a substantial number of Greek and Latin roots.

We also experimented with combining translation information from multiple languages, whereby the evidence from any of them is accepted for establishing semantic relatedness of senses. In our development experiments, we found that the combination of Indonesian and Spanish yielded the best F_1 score. Therefore, for our remaining experiments, when a criterion requires translation information, senses are considered semantically related if translation into Indonesian or Spanish provides evidence for semantic relatedness. We speculate that this combination is effective because they represent two very different languages that may complement each other.[4] It is likely that adding Malay or other European languages to the mix provides

[4]Resnik and Yarowsky (1999) note that distantly related languages seem to provide greater ability to resolve sense distinctions.

Method	Pre	Rec	F_1	Acc
Baseline	50.0	**100**	66.7	50.0
BA-2018	51.1	99.0	67.4	52.1
OHPT	74.5	83.2	**78.6**	**77.4**
UNION	**79.1**	71.6	75.1	76.3

Table 1: Homonym detection results on our test set, in terms of precision, recall, F_1 score, and accuracy.

only a minimal gain in terms of diversity, at the cost of increasing the level of noise in the data.

5.3 Homonymy Detection

In our main evaluation experiment, we test two variants of our method, OHPT (Section 4.1) and UNION (Section 4.6), on our balanced test set of 190 words (95 homonymous, 95 polysemous). In addition to our naive baseline (Section 5.1), we compare our results against the method of van den Beukel and Aroyo (2018), which we denote as BA-2018.

The results are shown in Table 1. The baseline yields 100% recall and 50% precision and accuracy. Surprisingly, the BA-2018 method classifies almost all words as homonyms, which translates into only a small improvement in accuracy over the baseline. This attests to the difficulty of our dataset: highly-polysemous words with coarse-grained sense distinctions are not easy to distinguish from true homonyms.

Both OHPT and UNION easily outperform BA-2018. They identify far fewer false homonyms, resulting in a much higher precision. Interestingly, the OHPT criterion by itself gives better F_1 score and accuracy than the UNION criterion. As UNION encompasses OHPT, the higher precision and lower recall of the latter are expected. This is because considering multiple criteria can only increase the connectivity of the sense graph. However, the higher F_1 score of the simpler method is surprising. Based on these results, we conclude that the UNION criterion is best when precision is more important than recall, while the OHPT criterion is best when overall accuracy is desired.

5.4 Sense-Level Polysemy Detection

In our second experiment, we conduct a direct evaluation of the polysemy detection at the level of sense pairs. The task is deciding whether two senses of a single word are semantically related (positive classification) or unrelated (negative classification). This is different from our previous eval-

	Pre	Rec	F_1	Acc
BA-2018	**92.2**	22.3	35.9	44.3
OHPT	86.5	65.8	74.7	68.8
UNION	81.8	**80.5**	**81.1**	**73.8**

Table 2: Sense-level SRC results on our test set, in terms of precision, recall, F_1 score, and accuracy.

uation on a word-level task of homonymy detection, where we used sense-level polysemy detection to create edges in the sense graph.

Table 2 presents the results on the same test set as in Section 5.3. Both OHPT and UNION substantially outperform the BA-2018 method in terms of F_1 and accuracy. This is consistent with our homonym detection results in Section 5.3: spurious positive classification at the sense level may lead to spurious *negative* classification on word-level homonym detection. Compared to OHPT and UNION, BA-2018 produces slightly fewer false positives, but many more false negatives. Consequently, our methods attain much higher recall for this task, which is in accordance with their much higher precision for homonym detection.

Unlike in the word-level experiment, UNION achieves better results than OHPT, because its much higher recall offsets its reduced precision. This establishes the utility of the various criteria developed in Section 4 for inclusion in UNION.

5.5 Error Analysis

The errors made by our homonymy detection methods can be divided into false positives and false negatives. While we used only Indonesian and Spanish translations in our English evaluation experiments, here we provide examples from languages with which we are more familiar.

False-positives, i.e. words incorrectly classified as homonymous, arise when two semantically related senses remain disconnected in the sense graph constructed by our method. We find that such cases are generally caused by data sparsity in BabelNet, which lacks many valid translations that could connect related senses in the graph. Another type of false positives is caused by *lexical gaps*, which occur when a language has no word or non-compositional phrase to express a given concept. For example, the sense of the polysemous adjective *seamless* glossed as "not having seams" corresponds to a lexical gap in Italian. Therefore, there is no translation in Italian that could relate this sense to any other sense of *seamless*. An example of a lexical gap in English is the concept lexicalized by the Persian word پریروز (/pæriːˈruːz/) "the day before yesterday."

False-negatives are homonymous words for which our method finds evidence of relatedness between two unrelated senses. Such errors can be divided into three categories: spurious translation, incorrect sense-to-homonym mapping, and parallel homonymy. Below, we provide examples for each category.

First, many translations in BabelNet are incorrect because they were obtained from machine translation models. This spurious translation information, under criteria such as OHPT, can result in unrelated senses being classified as related. For example, the homonymous verb *shark* has two senses in BabelNet: "to act with trickery" and "to hunt sharks." The French word *requin* shares both of the corresponding multi-synsets, which incorrectly implies that it translates both senses of *shark*. As a consequence, our method misclassifies these two senses as related.

Second, our homonym resource, even after manual cleaning, still contains some incorrect sense-to-homonym mappings, which are inherited from the automatic clustering of WordNet senses. For example, two unrelated senses of the noun *content*, ("the sum of what has been perceived" and "the state of being contented") are incorrectly mapped to a single lexeme.

Finally, while parallel homonymy is rare, it does occur. As discussed in Section 4, parallel homonymy can create exceptions to our translation-based criteria for semantic relatedness, resulting in misclassifications. For example, two semantically unrelated senses of the English word *boil*, glossed as "the temperature of boiling" and "a painful sore," can both be translated by the Persian word جوش/d͡ʒuːʃ/.

6 Conclusion

We have presented a novel approach to the problem of distinguishing between homonymy and polysemy. Our methods for establishing semantic relatedness leverage sense translation information from a multi-wordnet, and are supported by proofs constructed upon a formal theory of senses, synonymy, and translation. Our approach sets a new state of the art for the task of homonym detection. In the future, we would like to investigate stochastic methods for this task, including random walks on semantic graphs, as well as the use of graph embeddings to compute the similarity of concepts in a dense vector space. To facilitate further research on homonymy detection, we make the augmented homonymy resource publicly available.[5]

Acknowledgments

This research has been supported by the Natural Sciences and Engineering Research Council of Canada (NSERC), and the Alberta Machine Intelligence Institute (Amii).

References

Barend Beekhuizen, Sasa Milic, Blair C Armstrong, and Suzanne Stevenson. 2018. What company do semantically ambiguous words keep? insights from distributional word vectors. In *Proceedings of the 40th Annual Conference of the Cognitive Science Society*, pages 1347–1352.

Susan Windisch Brown. 2008. Choosing sense distinctions for WSD: Psycholinguistic evidence. In *Proceedings of ACL-08: HLT, Short Papers*, pages 249–252, June.

Helge Dyvik. 2004. Translations as semantic mirrors: from parallel corpus to wordnet. In *Advances in corpus linguistics*, pages 309–326. Brill Rodopi.

Christiane Fellbaum. 1998. WordNet: An on-line lexical database and some of its applications. *MIT Press*.

Bradley Hauer and Grzegorz Kondrak. 2020a. One homonym per translation. In *Proceedings of the AAAI Conference on Artificial Intelligence*, volume 34, pages 7895–7902.

Bradley Hauer and Grzegorz Kondrak. 2020b. Synonymy= translational equivalence. *arXiv preprint arXiv:2004.13886*.

Eduard Hovy, Mitchell Marcus, Martha Palmer, Lance Ramshaw, and Ralph Weischedel. 2006. OntoNotes: The 90% solution. In *Proceedings of the Human Language Technology Conference of the NAACL, Companion Volume: Short Papers*, pages 57–60.

Daniel Jurafsky and James H Martin. 2008. *Speech and Language Processing*. Prentice Hall.

Frederick Liu, Han Lu, and Graham Neubig. 2018. Handling homographs in neural machine translation. In *Proceedings of the 2018 Conference of the North American Chapter of the Association for Computational Linguistics: Human Language Technologies, Volume 1 (Long Papers)*, pages 1336–1345. Association for Computational Linguistics.

Igor Mel'čuk. 2013. *Semantics: From meaning to text*, volume 2. John Benjamins.

M. Lynne Murphy and Anu Koskela. 2010. *Key terms in semantics*. London: Continuum.

Roberto Navigli and Simone Paolo Ponzetto. 2012. BabelNet: The automatic construction, evaluation and application of a wide-coverage multilingual semantic network. *Artificial Intelligence*, 193:217–250.

Roberto Navigli. 2006. Meaningful clustering of senses helps boost word sense disambiguation performance. In *Proceedings of the 21st International Conference on Computational Linguistics and 44th Annual Meeting of the Association for Computational Linguistics*, pages 105–112, July.

Ted Pedersen, Satanjeev Banerjee, and Siddharth Patwardhan. 2005. Maximizing semantic relatedness to perform word sense disambiguation. Technical report, Research Report UMSI 2005/25, University of Minnesota Supercomputing Institute.

Vladimir Pericliev. 2015. On colexification among basic vocabulary. *Journal of Universal Language*, 63-93.

Philip Resnik and David Yarowsky. 1999. Distinguishing systems and distinguishing senses: New evaluation methods for word sense disambiguation. *Natural language engineering*, 5(2):113–133.

Caitlin A Rice, Barend Beekhuizen, Vladimir Dubrovsky, Suzanne Stevenson, and Blair C Armstrong. 2019. A comparison of homonym meaning frequency estimates derived from movie and television subtitles, free association, and explicit ratings. *Behavior research methods*, 51(3):1399–1425.

Jason Utt and Sebastian Padó. 2011. Ontology-based distinction between polysemy and homonymy. In *Proceedings of the Ninth International Conference on Computational Semantics (IWCS 2011)*, pages 265–274.

Sven van den Beukel and Lora Aroyo. 2018. Homonym detection for humor recognition in short text. In *Proceedings of the 9th Workshop on Computational Approaches to Subjectivity, Sentiment and Social Media Analysis*, pages 286–291.

Lonneke Van der Plas and Jörg Tiedemann. 2006. Finding synonyms using automatic word alignment and measures of distributional similarity. In *Proceedings of the COLING/ACL on Main conference poster sessions*, pages 866–873. Association for Computational Linguistics.

PJTM Vossen. 1996. Right or wrong: Combining lexical resources in the EuroWordNet project. In *M. Gellerstam, J. Jarborg, S. Malmgren, K. Noren,*

[5]`https://webdocs.cs.ualberta.ca/~kondrak/homonyms.html`

L. Rogstrom, CR Papmehl, Proceedings of Euralex-96, Goetheborg, 1996, pages 715–728. Vrije Universiteit.

Taboo Wordnet

Merrick Choo Yeu Herng and **Francis Bond**
School of Humanities
Nanyang Technological University
bond@ieee.org,merrick.emrys@gmail.com

Abstract

This paper describes the development of an online lexical resource to help detection systems regulate and curb the use of offensive words online. With the growing prevalence of social media platforms, many conversations are now conducted online. The increase of online conversations for leisure, work and socializing has led to an increase in harassment. In particular, we create a specialized sense-based vocabulary of Japanese offensive words for the Open Multilingual Wordnet. This vocabulary expands on an existing list of Japanese offensive words and provides categorization and proper linking to synsets within the multilingual wordnet. This paper then discusses the evaluation of the vocabulary as a resource for representing and classifying offensive words and as a possible resource for offensive word use detection in social media.

Content Warning: this paper deals with obscene words and contains many examples of them.

1 Introduction

The aim of this paper is to create a sense-based lexicon of offensive and potentially inappropriate terms linked to the Open Multilingual Wordnet (Bond and Foster, 2013). As well as adding new terms, we will categorize existing terms. The categorization is designed to be useful for both human and machine users. We distinguish between offensive terms, where the word itself has a negative connotation, and inappropriate terms, which may fine in some contexts, but not in others.

Real-life communication and socializing are rapidly being replaced by their online counterparts due to the overwhelming popularity and exponential growth of the use of social media platforms. Social media platforms allow people to express their opinions and feelings on various topics, including social, cultural and political issues, mirroring tensions that are relevant in real-life conversations. While social media connects people instantly on a global scale, it also enables a wide-reaching and viral dissemination of harassing messages filled with inappropriate words. With more online conversations, the use of inappropriate words to express hostility and harass others also increases accordingly, and this is further amplified by the globalization of the internet where inappropriate words in different languages and cultures are utilized and manipulated to attack and offend. Anonymity on social media platforms enables people to be crueler and less restrained by social conventions when they use inappropriate words in these conversations. As such, the development of new linguistic resources and computational techniques for the detection, analysis and categorization of large amounts of inappropriate words online becomes increasingly important.

Machine learning from annotated corpora is a very successful approach but does not provide a general solution that can be used across domains. Our goal is to make multilingual online lexicons of inappropriate word meanings that can then be utilized in hate speech detection systems. Due to an inadequate representation and classification of inappropriate words in physical dictionaries, these online resources and systems are essential in empowering the regulation and moderation of the use of inappropriate words online. Additionally, online lexicons can be updated and edited at any time while being easily shared across the world.

This paper presents the development of a lexicon of Japanese inappropriate words that will be added to the Open Multilingual Wordnet (OMW) with links to existing synsets and the creation of new synsets to define new inappropriate words. These words in the OMW can then be used as an online lexical resource to build awareness while analyzing and identifying inappropriate words in a multilingual context.

2 Background

While there is much relevant work on the detection of offensive language (Zampieri et al., 2019, 2020) [1] lexicons of abusive words receive little attention in literature, especially for lexicons in languages other than English. Lexicons of abusive words are often manually compiled and processed specifically for a task and are not reusable in other contexts or tasks and are rarely updated once the task it was created for has been completed.

One exception is Hurtlex (Bassignana et al., 2018). It was created as a multilingual lexicon that is reusable and not task-specific or limited by context of its development. The creators of Hurtlex expanded on the lexicon of *Le parole per ferire* "words that hurt" (Mauro, 2016) and linked the words to lexical resources such as MultiWordNet and BabelNet, while translating Hurtlex into a multilingual lexicon with a combination of semi-automatic translation and expert annotation. Unfortunately, the Hurtlex release[2] does not include the links to the wordnets, only lists of words. It has been updated twice, with versions 1.0, 1.1 and 1.2.

There are certain criteria that a lexicon needs to fulfil in order to be effective in classifying and representing inappropriate words, let alone function as a resource for hate speech detection. The lexicon needs to be accessible, tractable, comprehensive and relevant. While Hurtlex is both tractable and accessible, it cannot be considered as truly comprehensive as much of the lexicon was translated from the original French resource. This may result in a loss of semantics and nuance, especially with regards to euphemisms and cultural expressions and has no way of adding culturally specific terms. We discuss Hurtlex more in the evaluation.

Vulgar words in dictionaries for humans are normally marked with a usage note. The naming of the note varies considerably from dictionary to dictionary, and even from edition to edition of the same dictionary (Uchida, 1997). Typically dictionaries have two or three levels, a sample is shown in Table 1.

The definitions for the terms for the American Heritage Dictionary (AHD) are shown below (cited in Uchida, 1997, p41). Note that fewer than ten words are in the classes ⟪obscene⟫ or ⟪usually considered vulgar⟫.

Vulgar The label ⟪vulgar⟫ warns of social taboos attached to a word; the label may appear alone or in combination as ⟪vulgar slang⟫.

Obscene A term that is considered to violate accepted standards of decency is labeled ⟪obscene⟫

Offensive This label is reserved for terms such as racial slurs that are not only insulting and derogatory, but a discredit to the user as well.

The lack of consistency in terminology, definitions of the terminology and which word is in which class show the inherent subjectivity of the decisions.

Interestingly, generally **insulting** words, such as ***idiot*** or ***slacker***, are not normally marked in the lexicons: the only indication that a word denigrates its referent is through understanding the definition. For work on cyberbullying, such words are perhaps even more important than vulgar words.

3 Resources

To extend the wordnets, we looked at a couple of resources.

3.1 Princeton WordNet

Princeton WordNet version 3.0 (Fellbaum, 1998) has 29 different usage categories for synsets, of which we consider three to be relevant, shown in Table 2. Irrelevant categories include ⟪synecdoche⟫, ⟪plural⟫ and ⟪trope⟫.

The categorization is fairly hit and miss: ***jap*** is in **disparagement** but not **ethnic slur**, ***cock*** is in **obscenity** but ***cunt*** is not, and so forth. The same variation also occurs in the definitions. Sometimes the fact that a word is obscene is marked in other ways in the lexicon: the synset for ***cock*** has the definition "obscene terms for penis". However ***bugger all*** is just "little or nothing at all" and while ***cunt*** "obscene terms for female genitals" is marked as obscene in the definition it does not have the usage category. One of the goals of this research is to create a more comprehensive list of potentially offensive words and mark them more consistently.

Pullum (2018) suggests that the fact that a slur is offensive should only be encoded in the metadata,

[1] See also the OffensEval series of shared tasks: `https://sites.google.com/site/offensevalsharedtask/home`.

[2] `https://github.com/valeriobasile/hurtlex`

AHD	Examples	MWCD	Examples
vulgar	ass, dick	sometimes considered vulgar	piss, turd
obscene	fuck, cunt, shit, motherfucker	often considered vulgar	ass, balls
offensive	Polack, Jap	usually considered vulgar	fuck, cunt, dick

Table 1: Usage Notes from Dictionaries

AHD is the American Heritage Dictionary (Ed 3); MWCD is Merriam Webster's Collegiate Dictionary (Ed 8)

Category	Frequency	Example
《disparagement》	40	suit, tree-hugger, coolie
《ethnic slur》	12	coolie, paddy, darky
《obscenity》	9	cock, bullshit, bugger all

Table 2: Princeton Wordnet Offensive Categories

not the definition itself. So something like ***cock*** should just be "a penis" 《vulgar》.[3]

In addition to the explicit marking, there is implicit marking in the hypernymy hierarchy: PWN has a synset ***unwelcome person***, and most all of its hyponyms are insults, for example ***ingrate***, ***pawer***, ***cad*** and ***sneak***.

The criteria for separating synsets is not always transparent. Maks and Vossen (2010) note that in the Dutch Wordnet, words with different connotation often appeared in the same synset. In the English wordnet, words with a different connotation are generally split into a different synset, so we have ***Kraut, Boche, Jerry, Hun*** "offensive term for a person of German descent" as a hyponym of ***German*** "a person of German nationality". They noted that this structure, while allowing one to mark sentiment/connotation, is unintuitive and suggest a solution using roles. We suggest a similar solution using **Inter Register Synonymy** in Section 6.

3.2 J-lex: a list of Japanese inappropriate words

We had available a dictionary of Japanese words produced by researchers in Japan. Because they were unable to release the data themselves, they offered it to us so that we could incorporate it into the Japanese wordnet. Interestingly, the main reason they could not release the data was that they did not want their organization to be associated with a dictionary of abusive terms. However, they did want to make their lexicon available to help other researchers work on cyber-bullying. They therefore offered it to the Japanese wordnet project (Isahara et al., 2008), a richly structured open source lexicon which is linked to wordnets in many other languages. This makes it a good means of distributing the data. The data in J-Lex was originally taken from words marked as `X`, "rude or X-rated term (not displayed in educational software)" by the WWW-JDICT project[4] Breen (1995); Breen et al. (2020) with some additions by researchers on cyberbullying including Ptaszynski et al. (2010).

The list includes more than 1,600 Japanese words that are prevalent in both formal and informal speech and the words were categorized into 4 macro-categories: words related to sex, words related to bodily fluids and excrement, insulting words (used to attack and hurt) and words related to controversial topics. These macro-categories and the following sub-categories under them are not exclusive and a single word can be under multiple sub-categories. Of these 1,688 words, 1,207 are related to sex, 117 are related to bodily fluids and excrement, 468 are general insulting words while 220 are words related to controversial topics. The list of words is then further divided into 53 more specific and fine-grained sub-categories.

Looking at them, it becomes clear that not all the words are necessarily offensive: neutral words in the domain of 《sex》 and 《excrement》, like ***nipple*** or ***urine*** are fine in context but may be inappropriate out of context.

3.3 Hurtlex

Looking at the English and Japanese versions of Hurtlex,[5] we were impressed by its size. There was a big improvement in quality from version 1.1 to 1.2,

[3]Metadata such as usage information will be shown encased in double angle brackets: 《vulgar》 while domains will be shown in single angle brackets: ⟨linguistics⟩.

[4]`http://www.edrdg.org/wwwjdic/wwwjdicinf.html#code_tag`

[5]`https://github.com/valeriobasile/hurtlex`

but especially in Japanese, we found many entries we considered to be errors: words that were left as English, words that were clearly mistranslated and so on.

3.3.1 Comparing J-lex and Hurtlex

While Hurtlex is a lexicon of words used in hate speech to attack and harass and J-lex is a general lexicon of taboo and offensive Japanese words, we expected that these lexicons about Japanese taboo and offensive words would have considerable overlap. However, despite the Japanese version of Hurtlex having 5,428 unique items and J-lex having 1,688 unique items, only 154 unique words appear in both of them.

One major reason is that Hurtlex is a translated lexicon, and thus is missing many native Japanese expressions. In addition, there are 758 non-translated items in the Japanese version of Hurtlex. These 758 words are presented in the ISO basic Latin alphabet and examples include *animalia*, *arsehole* and *ballock*. Some of these words are neither English nor Japanese. Furthermore, translating words used in hate speech that are often lexicalized and require nuance causes words like 鳥肉 *toriniku* "chicken meat" and 小鳥 *kotori* "small bird"to be classified as hate speech despite their neutral connotations in the Japanese's language and culture: we guess the first is a mistranslation of *chicken* "coward", we have no idea why the second one is there.

3.4 Vulgar words

We also accessed a list of vulgar words curated by Cachola et al. (2018) from `https://www.noswearing.com/`.[6] This had 267 English swear words, divided into 《general》, 《homosexual》 and 《slur》.

4 Building the Taboo Wordnet

4.1 Linking J-lex to the Japanese wordnet

In order to make the J-lex data available to the wordnets we first had to link words to senses. The first step of development consisted of linking the 1,688 unique items extracted from the Japanese lexicon J-lex to existing synsets in the Open Multilingual Wordnet. First we did this through looking up words in the Japanese wordnet, and were able to link 397 (23%) of all unique words. An example is given in (1).[7]

(1)

`lem:ja`	し尿, 屎尿
`pron:ja`	しにょう *shinyou*
`class`	shit01
`synset`	OMW `14855635-n`
`def:ja`	人間の体内からの排出物
`def:en`	the body wastes of human beings

This matching was done even on low confidence Japanese entries: that is those that were automatically created but not hand-checked (Bond et al., 2008). If we got a match then we raised the confidence. Having the automatically generated low confidence entries proved to save some time. In Princeton Wordnet 3.0 this is not marked as a taboo word in any way, and the word does not appear in Hurtlex.

As a second step, the remaining 1,291 words were analyzed manually with the help of other Japanese online dictionaries such as WWWJDIC. A further 421 unique words could be linked to existing synsets for a total of 818 (46%). We give some examples in (2), (3) and (4).

(2)

`lem:ja`	手こき
`pron:ja`	てこき *tekoki*
`class`	sex02
`synset`	OMW `00856193-n`
`def:ja`	マスターベーションを意味する俗語
`def:en`	slang for masturbation

(3)

`lem:ja`	けばい
`pron:ja`	けばい *kebai*
`class`	insult09
`synset`	OMW `02393791-a`
`def:ja`	目を引く趣味悪さの
`def:en`	tastelessly showy

(4)

`lem:ja`	支那人
`pron:ja`	しなじん *shinajin*
`class`	insult15
`synset`	OMW `09698337-n`
`def:ja`	中国系の人にとっては不快な言葉
`def:en`	offensive term for a person of Chinese descent

Of the remaining 870 unique words, 71 were judged to be compositional and did not need to be included into the Japanese Wordnet. 226 words were considered as genuinely inappropriate and still relevant and thus require new synsets to encompass

[6] Taken from `https://github.com/ericholgate/vulgartwitter`.

[7] `lem` is the lemma, `pron` is the pronunciation (in hiragana, we also give the transliteration here), `synset` is the ID in the Japanese wordnet (normally the same as the synset offset in PWN 3.0, `def` is the definition.

their lemmas. The final 573 words need to be reviewed by native Japanese speakers as to whether they are truly inappropriate and whether they are used widely enough to be entered into the lexicon. A majority of the 226 new synsets are related to the domain of sexual activity rather than disparagement while there are no synsets related to the usage note of vulgar.

Examples of words deemed compositional include 変態オヤジ *hentai oyaji* "pervert old man" and 性格わるい *seikaku warui* "personality bad". The former expression is used to describe a perverted old man and is a combination of the word 変態 *hentai* "perverted" and オヤジ *oyaji* "middle aged/old man" or "one's own father". Similarly, 性格わるい *seikaku warui* "personality bad" is used to describe someone who has a bad character or personality and is a combination of the word 性格 *seikaku* "character/personality" and わるい *warui* "bad".

On the other hand, it is not as clear cut to differentiate whether words are genuinely inappropriate. For example 巨乳 *kyonyu* "huge breasts" is generally used positively but would be inappropriate in a work place. 短足 *tansoku* "short-legs" is generally insulting, but does not absolutely have to be. Words like ブヨブヨ (buyobuyo) meaning soft and flabby is generally offensive while 同和地区 (dowa chiku) meaning "untouchable area, slums" is always offensive.

We made a new Japanese extension of wordnet, that adds the new lexical entries from J-Lex to the appropriate synsets. It will be made available at `https://github.com/bond-lab/taboown` and shared with the Japanese Wordnet Project (Isahara et al., 2008).

4.2 Re-Labeling Wordnet

We decided to mark words in two different ways. First, we use the general domain category link to link words into topic domains, that are not necessarily taboo, but may be of interest to research into taboo terms. Existing topic domains include things like ⟨law⟩, ⟨music⟩ or ⟨terrorism⟩. To these we will add: ⟨***sexual activity***⟩, ⟨***excrement***⟩ and ⟨LGBTQ+⟩ (a new synset). At least in English and Japanese, these domains are potentially inappropriate without being necessarily offensive. In general, anything marked in J-Lex with sex* will be put into the ⟨***sexual activity***⟩ topic, anything marked shit* into ⟨***excrement***⟩ and controversial07 will be marked as ⟨LGBTQ+⟩.[8]

Tag	Number	Example
⟨excrement⟩	33	shit, toilet bowel
⟨LGBTQ+⟩	9	gay, lesbian
⟨sexual⟩	274	promiscuous, arouse
⟪disparagement⟫	630	lunatic, bimbo
⟪ethnic slur⟫	14	gringo, redneck
⟪obscenity⟫	48	chickenshit, butch

Table 3: Usage and Domain tags in the Taboo Wordnet

For usage notes, there is very little agreement as to what should be marked in dictionaries (Sakwa, 2012). So we decided to keep the three broad categories already used by wordnet: ⟪disparagement⟫ for words which are basically insulting; ⟪obscenity⟫ for words that are considered inappropriate in many circumstances, typically because of their association with a taboo subject and ⟪ethnic slur⟫ for ethnic slurs.

We took advantage of both J-Lex and the structure of wordnet to mark offensive words. We marked with ⟪disparagement⟫ everything labelled in J-Lex as insult* or controversial99 as well as all hyponyms of ***criminal***, ***unpleasant person*** or ***bad person*** as ⟪disparagement⟫.

Finally, we were still were missing information about which terms should be marked as ⟪obscenity⟫. To increase our coverage, we manually checked the English wordnet against the terms in `https://www.noswearing.com/` which gave another 38 vulgar synsets.

We end up with a total of 912 synsets marked in some way, with many being marked with multiple tags. The breakdown per tag is given in Table 3.

These categorizations will be made available as a stand-alone file at `https://github.com/bond-lab/taboown`, along with links to the original J-Lex categories. In addition, we will share them with the English Wordnet Project (McCrae et al., 2020). We will also release scripts to use the Open Multilingual Wordnet to generate offensive word lists for any language in the OMW using the Wn Python Library (Goodman and Bond, 2021).

[8] We also added some new words to this domain as part of a separate project by our annotators to improve the coverage of LGBTQ+ terms.

Lexicon	# Words	Comment
Wordnik	1,282	
Wordnet Original	50	
Wordnet Offensive	1,512	645 synsets
Wordnet Extended	2,095	912 synsets
HurtLex Conservative	2,228	
HurtLex Inclusive	5,965	

Table 4: Offensive Word Lists

5 Evaluation

We used a curated list to test the coverage of our enhanced wordnet. It is the list of 1,285 offensive words from the Wordnik online English dictionary.[9] Note that, while we had originally worked on adding Japanese senses, we are using the multilingual wordnet links to produce English data here.

We compare three versions of the wordnet: **Original** which just has those entries marked as 《disparagement》, 《ethnic slur》 or 《obscenity》 in the original PWN 3.0; **Offensive** which has those marked as such in the Taboo Wordnet; and **Extended**, which also includes everything from the domains of ⟨excrement⟩, ⟨sexuality⟩ and ⟨LGBTQ+⟩. We also compared the results to the Hurlex (1.2), using both the Conservative and Inclusive lists. The resources are summarized in Table 4.

The comparison in Table 5 shows a surprisingly small overlap. The original wordnet does very badly. The Taboo wordnet matches with roughly the same accuracy as Hurtlex, with far less noise. The resources differ in their use of number. When we did error analysis, we noticed that both Wordnik and Hurtlex often had both singular and plural forms of terms (e.g. *gringo* and *gringos*) or sometimes only plural forms. We automatically lemmatized everything to singular (results shown in the final column). This improves wordnet's coverage but degrades hurtlex (as plural forms are not longer being counted separately).

An analysis of errors shows three main causes for the lack of cover. The first is that wordnik's entries are not necessarily lemmatized in the same way as wordnet: ***beating your meat*** rather than ***beat one's meat*** "masturbate", respectively. The second is that many existing synsets do not have all the possible variants, especially colloquial entries: e.g. ***nut sack*** for "scrotum". Finally, there is still a long tail of new

[9] `https://www.wordnik.com/lists/offensive`, we removed a couple of non-offensive entries.

Lexicon	in Wordnik	singular
Wordnet Original	18	18
Wordnet Offensive	82	86
Wordnet Extended	163	172
HurtLex Conservative	98	95
HurtLex Inclusive	139	137

Table 5: Comparison with Wordnik

synsets: e.g., ***happy ending*** "A handjob, especially one after a massage". We estimate that around 80% of the missing entries could go into existing synsets, and around 20% would need new ones (approximately 200).

6 Discussion and Future Work

The Taboo Wordnet is based on synsets, not words. This is important as words such as しゃくはち which could either mean しゃくはち *shakuhachi* "a Japanese and ancient Chinese longitudinal, end-blown bamboo-flute" or しゃくはち *shakuhachi* "fellatio or oral stimulation of the penis". A word based lexicon such as HurtLex will confuse such uses.

In future work, we intend to:

- Help upstream wordnets integrate this data
- Add missing senses for existing synsets in English (as we have done for Japanese): the coverage of colloquial expressions is still low
- Create new synsets for missing concepts from J-Lex and Wordnik
- Reorganize the wordnet structures: currently a synset with offensive terms is normally linked as a hyponym of the neutral term. However, it shares the same denotation, with a different connotation. This is the relation of Inter Register Synonymy, described in Maziarz et al. (2015), and now added in the Global Wordnet Association format (McCrae et al., 2021). We will replace hyponym with inter register synonymy where appropriate.
- Add exclamatives, like *fuck off* "go away", using the extension of Morgado da Costa and Bond (2016). In Japanese, a typical equivalent is 消えろ *go away* "disappear".
- Decide how to deal with reclaimed slurs, those historically derogatory names or term that are

used or reinterpreted in a positive way, as in pride for one's social group. As slurs are generally only partly reclaimed it is important to make sure that this is clear to the dictionary user.

- Decide how to deal with expressions that were not inappropriate in the past but are currently inappropriate due to new contexts that have emerged in the recent years. As these expressions may not be unacceptable for all, it is important for the dictionary user to understand that there are two separate but related versions of the expressions.

As the Taboo Wordnet is an online resource, it can be updated frequently, and this allows for the Taboo Wordnet to reflect the ever changing status of words and expressions. Such changes in status may be due to reclamation of offensive words for in-group social pride or due to new contexts that have emerged in recent years causing some neutral words to take on a new meaning. We welcome contributions.

7 Conclusion

The main contribution of this paper is the categorization of offensive and potentially inappropriate synsets. We have also added many Japanese for these words. Through the collaborative interlingual index, they can be used for future categorization and analysis of words in other languages. These additions will be made available in the OMW as a resource for future studies on inappropriate words and may function as a sense-tagging tool for these words as well.

Acknowledgements

We would like to thank the anonymous providers of the Japanese lexical data. This research was mainly carried out during NTU's Undergraduate Research Experience on Campus Programme (URECA).

References

Elisa Bassignana, Valerio Basile, and Viviana Patti. 2018. Hurtlex: A multilingual lexicon of words to hurt. In *5th Italian Conference on Computational Linguistics, CLiC-it 2018*, volume 2253, pages 1–6. CEUR-WS. URL `http://ceur-ws.org/Vol-2253/paper49.pdf`.

Francis Bond and Ryan Foster. 2013. Linking and extending an open multilingual wordnet. In *51st Annual Meeting of the Association for Computational Linguistics: ACL-2013*, pages 1352–1362. Sofia. URL `http://aclweb.org/anthology/P13-1133`.

Francis Bond, Hitoshi Isahara, Kyoko Kanzaki, and Kiyotaka Uchimoto. 2008. Boot-strapping a WordNet using multiple existing WordNets. In *Sixth International Conference on Language Resources and Evaluation (LREC 2008)*. Marrakech.

James Breen, Timothy Baldwin, and Francis Bond. 2020. The Japanese dictionary entry: Lexicographic issues and terminology. In *Globalex Workshop on Lexicography and Neologism at Euralex 2020 (GWLN 2020)*. To appear.

James W. Breen. 1995. Building an electronic Japanese-English dictionary. Japanese Studies Association of Australia Conference (`http://www.csse.monash.edu.au/~jwb/jsaa_paper/hpaper.html`).

Isabel Cachola, Eric Holgate, Daniel Preoţiuc-Pietro, and Junyi Jessy Li. 2018. Expressively vulgar: The socio-dynamics of vulgarity and its effects on sentiment analysis in social media. In *Proceedings of the 27th International Conference on Computational Linguistics*, pages 2927–2938. URL `http://aclweb.org/anthology/C18-1248`.

Christine Fellbaum, editor. 1998. *WordNet: An Electronic Lexical Database*. MIT Press.

Michael Wayne Goodman and Francis Bond. 2021. Intrinsically interlingual: The Wn Python library for wordnets. In *11th International Global Wordnet Conference (GWC2021)*. (this volume).

Hitoshi Isahara, Francis Bond, Kiyotaka Uchimoto, Masao Utiyama, and Kyoko Kanzaki. 2008. Development of the Japanese WordNet. In *Sixth International conference on Language Resources and Evaluation (LREC 2008)*. Marrakech.

Isa Maks and Piek Vossen. 2010. Modeling attitude, polarity and subjectivity in wordnet. In *In Proceedings of Fifth Global Wordnet Conference, Mumbai, India*.

Tullio De Mauro, editor. 2016. *Le parole per ferire*. 'Joe Cox' Committee on intolerance, xenophobia, racism and hate phenomena, of the Italian Chamber of Deputies.

Marek Maziarz, Maciej Piasecki, Stan Szpakowicz, and Joanna Rabiega-Wisniewska. 2015. Semantic relations among nouns in polish wordnet grounded in lexicographic and semantic tradition. *Cognitive Studies*, 11:161–182.

John P. McCrae, Michael Wayne Goodman, Francis Bond, Alexandre Rademaker, Ewa Rudnicka, and Luis Morgado da Costa. 2021. The global wordnet formats: Updates for 2020. In *11th International Global Wordnet Conference (GWC2021)*. (this volume).

John P. McCrae, Ewa Rudnicka, and Francis Bond. 2020. English wordnet: A new open-source wordnet for English. Technical report, K Lexical News. URL `https://kln.lexicala.com/kln28/mccrae-rudnicka-bond-english-wordnet/`.

Luís Morgado da Costa and Francis Bond. 2016. Wow! what a useful extension to wordnet! In *10th International Conference on Language Resources and Evaluation (LREC 2016)*. Portorož.

Michal Ptaszynski, Pawel Dybala, Tatsuaki Matsuba, Fumito Masui, Rafal Rzepka, and Kenji Araki. 2010. Machine learning and affect analysis against cyber-bullying. In *Proceedings of the Linguistic And Cognitive Approaches To Dialog Agents Symposium, Rafal Rzepka (Ed.), at the AISB 2010 convention*. AISB 2010 Organizing Committee, De Montfort University, Leicester, UK. URL `https://www.researchgate.net/publication/228791020_Machine_Learning_and_Affect_Analysis_Against_Cyber-Bullying`.

Geoffrey K. Pullum. 2018. *Bad Words: Philosophical Perspectives on Slurs*, chapter Slurs and Obscenities: Lexicography, Semantics, and Philosophy. OUP.

Lydia Sakwa. 2012. Problems of usage labelling in English lexicography. *Lexikos*, 21(1). URL `https://lexikos.journals.ac.za/pub/article/view/47`.

Hiroaki Uchida. 1997. The treatment of vulgar words in major English dictionaries. *Lexicon*, 27:152–168.

Marcos Zampieri, Shervin Malmasi, Preslav Nakov, Sara Rosenthal, Noura Farra, and Ritesh Kumar. 2019. Semeval-2019 task 6: Identifying and categorizing offensive language in social media (offenseval). In *Proceedings of the 13th International Workshop on Semantic Evaluation*, pages 75–86.

Marcos Zampieri, Preslav Nakov, Sara Rosenthal, Pepa Atanasova, Georgi Karadzhov, Hamdy Mubarak, Leon Derczynski, Zeses Pitenis, and Çağrı Çöltekin. 2020. SemEval-2020 Task 12: Multilingual Offensive Language Identification in Social Media (OffensEval 2020). In *Proceedings of SemEval*.

Ask2Transformers: Zero-Shot Domain labelling with Pre-trained Language Models

Oscar Sainz and **German Rigau**

HiTZ Center - Ixa Group,
University of the Basque Country (UPV/EHU)
{oscar.sainz, german.rigau}@ehu.eus

Abstract

In this paper we present a system that exploits different pre-trained Language Models for assigning domain labels to WordNet synsets without any kind of supervision. Furthermore, the system is not restricted to use a particular set of domain labels. We exploit the knowledge encoded within different off-the-shelf pre-trained Language Models and task formulations to infer the domain label of a particular WordNet definition. The proposed zero-shot system achieves a new state-of-the-art on the English dataset used in the evaluation.

1 Introduction

The whole Natural Language Processing (NLP) research area have been accelerated with the advent of the unsupervised pre-trained Language Models. First with ELMo (Peters et al., 2018) and then with BERT (Devlin et al., 2019) the paradigm of using pre-trained Language Models for fine-tuning on a particular NLP task has became the new standard approach, replacing the more traditional knowledge-based and fully supervised approaches. Currently, as the size of the corpus and models increase, the research community has observed that the Transfer Learning approach has the capacity to work without any or with a very small fine-tuning. Some examples of the strength of this approach are GPT-2 (Radford et al., 2019) or more recently GPT-3 (Brown et al., 2020) that shows the ability of these huge pre-trained Language Models to solve tasks for which have not even trained.

Recently, with the arrival of the GPT-3 new ways to perform zero and few shot approaches have been discovered. These approaches propose the inclusion of a small number of supervised examples in the input as a hint for the model. The model then, just by looking a small set of examples, is able to complete successfully the task at hand. Brown et al. (2020) report that they solve a wide range of NLP tasks just following the previous approach. However, this approach only looks appropriate when the model is large enough.

In this paper we exploit the domain knowledge already encoded within the existing pre-trained Language Models to enrich the WordNet (Miller, 1998) synsets and glosses with domain labels. We explore and evaluate different pre-trained Language Models and pattern objectives. For instance, consider the example shown in Table 1. Given a WordNet definition such as the one of <hospital, infirmary> and the knowledge encoded in a pre-trained Language Model, the task is to assess which is its most suitable domain label. Thus, we create an appropriate pattern in natural language adapted to the objective of the Language Model. In the example, we use a Language Model fine-tuned on a general task such as Natural Language Inference (NLI) (Bowman et al., 2015). The NLI objective is to train a model able to classify the relation between two sentences as entailment, contradiction or neutral. Having four domains such as *medicine*, *biology*, *business* and *culture*, our system performs four queries to the model, each one with one of the four domains. Each query takes as a first sentence the WordNet definition and as a second sentence *The domain of the sentence is about [domain-label]*. As expected, the most suitable domain label in this example is *medicine* with a confidence of 0.77. As shown, an off-the-shelf Language Model which have been fine-tuned on a general NLI task is able to infer the most appropriate domain label for the WordNet definition without any further training. Also note that the approach can use any given set of domain labels.

Interestingly, without any training on the task at hand, the proposed zero-shot system obtains an F1 score of 92.4% on the English dataset used in the evaluation.

All the implementation code along with the experiments is freely available on a GitHub repository [1].

After this short introduction, the next section presents previous work on domain labelling of WordNet. Section 3 presents our approach, Section 4 the experimental setup and Section 5 the results from our experiments. Finally, Section 6 revises the main conclusions and the future work.

2 Related Work

Building large and rich lexical knowledge bases is a very costly effort which involves large research groups for long periods of development. Starting from version 3.0, Princeton WordNet has associated topic information with a subset of its synsets. This topic labeling is achieved through pointers from a source synset to a target synset representing the topic. WordNet uses 440 topics and the most frequent one is <law, jurisprudence>.

In order to reduce the manual effort required, a few semi-automatic and fully automatic methods have been applied for associating domain labels to synsets. For instance, WordNet Domains[2] (WND) is a lexical resource where synsets have been semi-automatically annotated with one or more domain labels from a set of 165 hierarchically organized domains (Magnini, 2000; Bentivogli et al., 2004). The uses of WND include the possibility to reduce the polysemy degree of the words, grouping those senses that belong to the same domain (Magnini et al., 2002). But the semi-automatic method used to develop this resource was far from being perfect. For instance, the noun synset <diver, frogman, underwater diver> defined as *some-one who works underwater* has domain *history* because it inherits from its hypernym <explorer, adventurer> also labelled with *history*. Moreover, many synsets have been labelled as *factotum* meaning that the synset cannot be labelled with a particular domain. WND also provides mappings to WordNet Topics and also to Wikipedia categories.

eXtended WordNet Domains[3] (XWND) (Gonzalez-Agirre et al., 2012; González et al., 2012) applied a graph-based method to propagate the WND labels through the WordNet structure.

Domain information is also available in other lexical resources. For instance, IATE[4], a European Union inter-institutional terminology database. The domain labels of IATE are based on the Eurovoc thesaurus[5] and were introduced manually.

More recently, BabelDomains[6] (Camacho-Collados and Navigli, 2017) propose an automatic method that propagates the knowledge categories from the Wikipedia to WordNet by exploiting both distributional and graph-based clues. As domains of knowledge, BabelDomains opted for domains from the Wikipedia featured articles page[7]. This page contains a set of thirty-two domains of knowledge. When labelling WordNet synsets with these domains, BabelDomains reports a precision of 81.7, a recall of 68.7 and an F1 score of 74.6. Unfortunately, as these numbers suggest not all WordNet synsets have been labelled with a domain. For instance, the synset <hospital, infirmary> with a gloss definition *a health facility where patients receive treatment* has no Babeldomain assigned.

It is worth to note that all these methods depart from a particular set of domain labels (or categories) manually assigned to a set of WordNet synsets (or Wikipedia pages). Then, these labels are propagated through the WordNet structure following automatic or semi-automatic methods. In contrast, our zero-shot method does not require an initial manual annotation. Furthermore, it is not designed for a particular set of domain labels. That is, it can be applied to label from scratch any dictionary or lexical knowledge base (or wordnet) with distinct sets of domain labels.

3 Using pre-trained LMs for domain labelling

Recent studies such as the one of GPT-3 (Brown et al., 2020) shows that when increasing the size of the model, the capacity to solve different tasks with just a few positive examples also increases (few-shot learning). However, very large Language Models also have important hardware requirements (i.e. large RAM GPUs). Thus, we decided to keep the size of the models used manage-

[1] `https://github.com/osainz59/Ask2Transformers`

[2] `http://wndomains.fbk.eu/`

[3] `https://adimen.si.ehu.es/web/XWND`

[4] `http://iate.europa.eu/`

[5] `https://op.europa.eu/en/web/eu-vocabularies/th-dataset/-/resource/dataset/eurovoc`

[6] `http://lcl.uniroma1.it/babeldomains/`

[7] `https://en.wikipedia.org/wiki/Wikipedia:Featured_articles`

Definition:	hospital: a health facility where patients receive treatment.		
Pattern:	The domain of the sentence is about	**medicine**	**0.77**
		biology	0.08
		business	0.04
		culture	0.02

Table 1: An example of domain labelling.

able with small hardware requirements.

The task where we focused on is the domain labelling of WordNet glosses. This task consist in the following. Given a WordNet gloss g to predict the corresponding domain d of the WordNet concept defined. In this paper, the domains are taken from BabelDomains (Camacho-Collados and Navigli, 2017). Supervised domain labelling can be solved as any other multiclass problem, where the output of the model is a class probability distribution. In our zero-shot experiments we did not modify any of the pre-trained models. We just reformulate the domain labelling task to match with the LMs training objective.

3.1 Masked Language Modeling

The Masked Language Modeling (MLM) is a pre-training objective followed by models such as BERT (Devlin et al., 2019) and RoBERTa (Liu et al., 2019). This objective works as follows. Given a sequence of tokens $s = [t_1, t_2, ..., t_n]$, the sequence is first perturbed by replacing some of the tokens t with an special token [MASK]. Then, the model is trained to recover the original sequence s given the modified sequence $\hat{s}$. This denoising objective can be seen as an evolution for the contextual embeddings of the previous CBOW from word2vec (Mikolov et al., 2013).

For domain labelling, we have replaced the input for the model following the next pattern:

s: Context: [context] Topic: [MASK]

where we introduce the input sentence replacing the [context] tag. Then, we let the model predict the most probable token for the [MASK] tag. For instance, given the biological definition of *cell*, the model returns the following topics: *Biology*, *evolution*, *life*, etc.

This approach has been used to explore the knowledge of the model without any predefined set of domain labels in Section 5.7.

3.2 Next Sentence Prediction

Along with the MLM the Next Sentence Prediction (NSP) is the training objective used by the BERT models. Given a pair of sentences s_1 and s_2, this objective predicts whether s_1 is followed by s_2 or not.

To adapt the BERT objective to the domain labelling task, we propose the next strategy inspired in the work from Yin et al. (2019). We use the following input pattern:

s_1: [context]
s_2: Domain or topic about [domain-label]

where s_1 encodes a WordNet gloss as a context and s_2 is formed by a *template* and a domain-label. In order to make the classification, we run as many times as domain labels and then apply a softmax over the positive class outputs. We hypothesize that, no matter if any of the s_2 can really follow the given s_1, the most probable one should be the s_2 formed by the correct label. For instance, recall the *hospital* example shown in Table 1.

3.3 Natural Language Inference

In this case, we use a pre-trained LM that has been fine-tuned for a general inference task which is the Natural Language Inference (Williams et al., 2018a). Given two sentences in the form of a premise s_1 and an hypothesis s_2, the NLI task consists on redicting whether the s_1 *entails* or *contradicts* s_2 or if the relation between both is *neutral*.

We also used the input pattern shown in the previous NSP approach to adapt the NLI models to the domain labelling task. In this case, we just use the predictions of the *entailment* class. The predictions of the contradiction and *neutral* are not used. As in the previous case, no matter if any of the s_2 hypothesis entails the premise s_1 or not, the most probable entailment should be the correct domain label. For example, consider again the example presented in Table 1.

4 Experimental setting

This section describes our experimental setup. We introduce the pre-trained Language Models and the dataset used. For the case of the Language Models, we have tested BERT (Devlin et al., 2019), RoBERTa (Liu et al., 2019) and BART (Wang et al., 2019). For the dataset, we have used the one released by Camacho-Collados et al. (2016) based on WordNet.

4.1 Pretrained models

All the Language Models have been obtained from the Huggingface Transformers library (Wolf et al., 2019).

MLM For the objective we have used *roberta-large* and *roberta-base* checkpoints. These models have obtained state-of-the-art results on many NLP tasks and benchmarks.

NSP For this objective we use the BERT models as they are the only ones trained on that objective. For the sake of comparing the performance of more than one model of each objective we have selected the *bert-large-uncased* and *bert-base-uncased* checkpoints. They only differ on the size of the Language Model.

NLI For this objective we used a checkpoint based on RoBERTa *roberta-large-mnli* which have been fine-tuned with MultiNLI (Williams et al., 2018b). We also include *bart-large-mnli* for testing a generative model.

4.2 Dataset

We evaluate our approaches on a dataset derived from WordNet which have been annotated with Babeldomain labels (Camacho-Collados et al., 2016). This dataset consist of **1540** synsets manually annotated with their corresponding Babeldomain label. The distribution of domain labels in the dataset is shown in Figure 1. Note that the dataset is quite unbalanced. In fact, some important domains such as *Transport and travel* or *Food and drink* have no single labelled example. As our system is unsupervised, we use the whole dataset for testing.

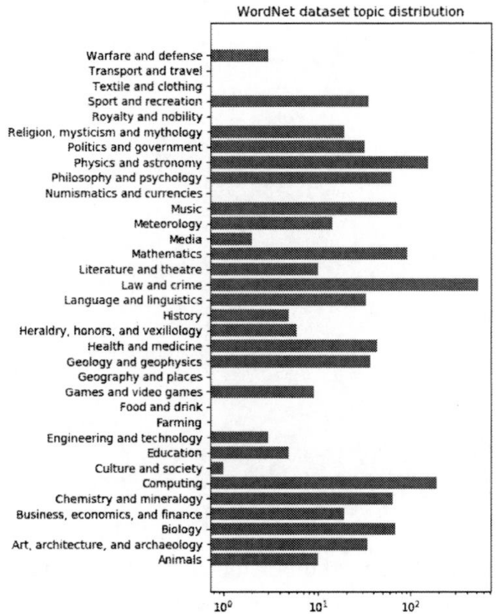

Figure 1: Distribution of domains in the WordNet dataset.

Method	Top-1	Top-3	Top-5
MNLI (roberta-large-mnli)	**78.44**	**87.46**	**89.74**
MNLI (bart-large-mnli)	61.81	79.85	87.59
NSP (bert-large-uncased)	2.07	8.57	16.49
NSP (bert-base-uncased)	2.85	10.32	16.88

Table 2: Top-K accuracy of different approaches.

5 Evaluation and Results

This section presents a quantitative and qualitative evaluation. One the one hand, the quantitative evaluation has been done incrementally in order to obtain the best-performing system. First, we have evaluated the different alternative models using the same objective pattern. Then, once the best approach was selected we have explored alternative patterns using the best model. When the best performing pattern was discovered we have focus on finding a better label representation. Finally, we have compared our best system against the previous state-of-the-art methods.

On the other hand, as one of our system is based on a generative approach (MLM) the applied restrictions may not show the real performance of the method. So, we decided to at least do an small qualitative review of the approach.

5.1 Approach comparison

Table 2 shows the Top-1, Top-3 and Top-5 accuracy of each system when using the same objective pattern. To understand better the behaviour of the systems we also present in the Figure 2 the Top-K

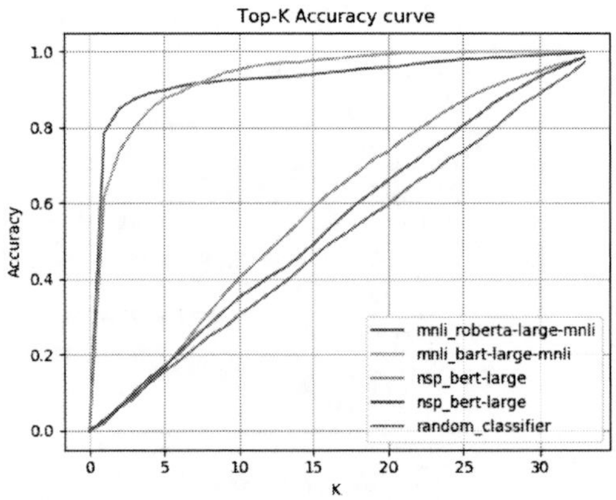

Figure 2: Top-K accuracy curve of the different approaches and a random classifier baseline.

accuracy curve comparing all the approaches and a random baseline. As expected the systems that follow the same approaches perform similarly and share a similar curve. The best performing system is the MNLI based *roberta-large-mnli*, followed by the *bart-large-mnli* checkpoint. We observe a large difference between the different models. For instance, the models pre-trained on the NLI task perform much better than those pre-trained on the general NSP task. The NSP approaches perform slightly better than the random classifier which can be a signal of a non appropriated objective model to use.

5.2 Input representation

Once selected the pre-trained Language Model, we evaluate different input patterns for the *roberta-large-mnli* checkpoint. As mentioned before, the MNLI approaches follow the same structure as NSP, where s_1 is the gloss of the synset and s_2 the sequence formed by a textual template plus the label.

Table 3 shows the results obtained by testing different textual patterns. Very short patterns obtain low results. The best performing textual template is obtained with *The domain of the sentence is about [label]*.

5.3 Label descriptors / Mapping

As important as the input patterns is the set of domain labels used. Actually, BabelDomains uses labels that refers to one or several specific domains. For instance, *Art, architecture and archaeology*. Although these coarse-grained labels can be useful when clustering close-related domains, we also implemented a two-step labelling procedure taking into account those specific domains. First, we run the system over a set of specific domains or descriptors. Second, we apply a function that maps the descriptors to the original BabelDomains.

Descriptors The descriptors defined in this work are quite simple. Given a composed domain label such us *Art, architecture and archaeology*, we define the set of descriptors as each of the components of the label. For instance, in this case *Art*, *Architecture* and *Archaeology*. In the case of labels that consist on a single domain, the descriptors are just the labels. For example, in the case of *Music* the descriptor is also *Music*.

Mapping function The mapping function that we use in this work consists on taking the maximum result of the descriptors as the result of the original domain label, i.e. $l_i = \max(d_{i1}, d_{i2}, ..., d_{in})$.

5.4 Training a specialized student

The inference time increases linearly with the number of labels. That is, for each example we need to test all the different domain labels. To speed-up the labelling process we annotate automatically the rest of WordNet glosses (around 79.000 glosses) using our best zero-shot approach. Then, we use that automatically annotated dataset to train a much smaller Language Model for the task. For instance, to label new definitions or new lexicons. We have fine-tuned two different models, the first one based with DistilBert (Sanh et al., 2019) which is 5 times smaller than the *roberta-large-mnli* and a XLM-RoBERTa (Conneau et al., 2020) *base* which is 2 times smaller and is trained in a multilingual fashion. We called them A2T$_{\text{FT-small}}$ and A2T$_{\text{FT-xlingual}}$ respectively. The first one achieve a **x425** faster inference (5 times smaller and 85 times less inferences) while the second one a speed boost of **x170**.

5.5 Results

In order to know how good is our final approach we compare our new systems with the previous ones. The results are reported on the Table 4 in terms of Precision, Recall and F1 for comparison purposes. We also include the results from two previous state-of-the-art systems. As we can see, the new systems based on pre-trained Language Models obtain much better performance (from a

Input pattern	Top-1	Top-3	Top-5
Topic: [label]	59.61	69.48	74.02
Domain: [label]	58.50	67.40	72.27
Theme: [label]	59.67	73.96	81.36
Subject: [label]	60.58	69.74	74.35
Is about [label]	73.37	87.72	91.94
Topic or domain about [label]	78.44	87.46	89.74
The topic of the sentence is about [label]	80.71	92.92	95.77
The domain of the sentence is about [label]	**81.62**	**93.96**	**96.42**
The topic or domain of the sentence is about [label]	76.62	88.63	91.23

Table 3: Some of the explored *input patterns* for the MNLI approach and their Top-1, Top-3 and Top-5 accuracy.

previous best result with an F1 of 74.6 to the new one of 82.10). We also obtain an small improvement when establishing a threshold to decide whether a prediction is taken into consideration or not. Our system performs slightly better with a confidence score greater than 5% (A2T$_{(>0.05)}$). Figure 3 reports the Precision/Recall trade-off of the A2T system. As mentioned before labels composed of multiple domains can make the prediction harder for the zero-shot system. As a result, a simple system using the label descriptors boosts the performance of the system reaching a final **92.14** F1 score (A2T$_{+\text{ descriptors}}$). Finally, we also include the results of both the fine-tuned student versions which still obtain very competitive results while drastically reducing the inference time of the original models.

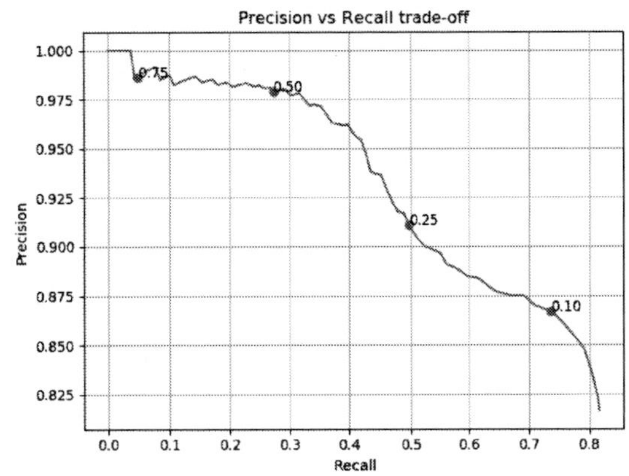

Figure 3: Precision/Recall trade-off of A2T system. Annotations indicates the probability thresholds.

Method	Precision	Recall	F1
Distributional	84.0	59.8	69.9
BabelDomains	81.7	68.7	74.6
A2T	81.62	81.62	81.62
A2T$_{(>0.05)}$	83.20	81.03	82.10
A2T$_{+\text{ descriptors}}$	**92.14**	**92.14**	**92.14**
A2T$_{\text{FT-small}}$	91.42	91.42	91.42
A2T$_{\text{FT-xlingual}}$	90.58	90.58	90.58

Table 4: Micro-averaged precision, recall and F1 for each of the systems. Distributional (Camacho-Collados et al., 2016) and BabelDomains (Camacho-Collados and Navigli, 2017) measures are the ones reported by them.

5.6 Error analysis

Figure 4 presents the confusion matrix of our best system. The matrix is row wise normalized due to the imbalance of the dataset label distribution. Looking at the figure there are 4 classes that are misleading. The "Animals" domain is confused with the related domains "Biology" and "Food and drink". For instance, this is the case of the synset <diet> with the definition *the usual food and drink consumed by an organism (person or animal)* which is labelled by our system as "Food and drink". The "Games and video games" domain is confused with the related domain "Sport and recreation". For example the sense referring to *game: a single play of a sport or other contest; "the game lasted two hours"* which is labelled by our system as "Sport and recreation". The third one, "Heraldry, honors and vexillology" is also confused with a very close domain "Royalty and nobility". Obviously, close-related domains can be very difficult to distinguish even for humans. For example, the sense <audio cd, audio compact disc> annotated in the gold standard as "Music" is labelled by our system as "Media". Finally,

Synset	cell	phase space	rounding error	wipeout
Label	Biology	Physics and astronomy	Mathematics	Sports and Recreation
Top predictions	**Biology** EOS biology evolution life	EOS physics **Physics** geometry relativity	rounding EOS math taxes **Math**	sports EOS sport accident **Sports**

Table 5: Top predictions of the MLM approach using the *roberta-large* checkpoint.

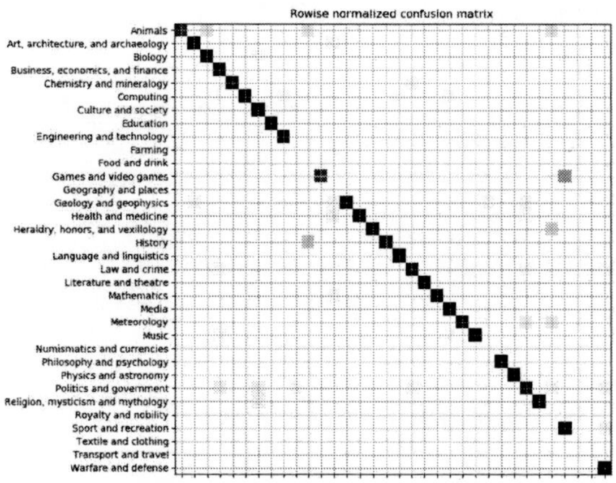

Figure 4: Rowise normalized confusion matrix of the $A2T_{+\text{ descriptors}}$ system.

sometimes the "History" domain is confused with "Food and drink". A curious example of this case is the sense referring to the history event <Boston tea party> that is labelled as "Food and drink".

5.7 Qualitative analysis

Table 5 shows some of the top predictions obtained by a Masked Language Model (MLM) and the real label for 4 different synsets. In this case, the system is guessing its best predicted domain. That is, the system is not restricted to a select the best label from a pre-defined set of domain labels. Now, the system is free to return the word that best fit the masked term.

We can see in the table that the predictions of the model are close to the correct label although not always equal. Sometimes because of a different case. They can also be seen as fine-grained domains or domain keywords of the real domain.

6 Conclusions and Future Work

In this paper we have explored some approaches for domain labelling of WordNet glosses by exploiting pre-trained LM in a zero-shot manner. We have presented a simple approach that achieves a new state-of the art on the Babeldomain dataset.

Even if we have focused on domain labelling of WordNet glosses, our method seems to be robust enough to be adapted to work on tasks such as Sentiment Analysis or other type of text classification. In particular, we think that the approach can be very useful when no annotated data is available.

For the future, we have considered three main objectives. First, we plan to apply this approach to other sources of domain information such as WordNet topics and WordNet Domains. We will also explore how to deal with definitions with generic domains (with no BabelDomains labels or with WordNet Domains factotum label). Second, we also aim to explore the cross-lingual capabilities of pre-trained Language Models for domain labelling of non-English wordnets and other lexical resources. Finally, we also plan to explore the utility of these findings in the Word Sense Disambiguation task.

Acknowledgments

This work has been funded by the Spanish Ministry of Science, Innovation and Universities under the project DeepReading (RTI2018-096846-B-C21) (MCIU/AEI/FEDER,UE) and by the BBVA Big Data 2018 “BigKnowledge for Text Mining (BigKnowledge)” project. We also acknowledge the support of the Nvidia Corporation with the donation of a GTX Titan X GPU used for this research.

References

Luisa Bentivogli, Pamela Forner, Bernardo Magnini, and Emanuele Pianta. 2004. Revising the wordnet domains hierarchy: semantics, coverage and balancing. In *Proceedings of the workshop on multilingual linguistic resources*, pages 94–101.

Samuel Bowman, Gabor Angeli, Christopher Potts, and Christopher D Manning. 2015. A large annotated corpus for learning natural language inference. In *Proceedings of the 2015 Conference on Empirical Methods in Natural Language Processing*, pages 632–642.

Tom B Brown, Benjamin Mann, Nick Ryder, Melanie Subbiah, Jared Kaplan, Prafulla Dhariwal, Arvind Neelakantan, Pranav Shyam, Girish Sastry, Amanda Askell, et al. 2020. Language models are few-shot learners. *arXiv preprint arXiv:2005.14165*.

Jose Camacho-Collados and Roberto Navigli. 2017. BabelDomains: Large-scale domain labeling of lexical resources. In *Proceedings of the 15th Conference of the European Chapter of the Association for Computational Linguistics: Volume 2, Short Papers*, pages 223–228, Valencia, Spain. Association for Computational Linguistics.

José Camacho-Collados, Mohammad Taher Pilehvar, and Roberto Navigli. 2016. Nasari: Integrating explicit knowledge and corpus statistics for a multilingual representation of concepts and entities. *Artificial Intelligence*, 240:36 – 64.

Alexis Conneau, Kartikay Khandelwal, Naman Goyal, Vishrav Chaudhary, Guillaume Wenzek, Francisco Guzmán, Edouard Grave, Myle Ott, Luke Zettlemoyer, and Veselin Stoyanov. 2020. Unsupervised cross-lingual representation learning at scale. In *Proceedings of the 58th Annual Meeting of the Association for Computational Linguistics*, pages 8440–8451, Online. Association for Computational Linguistics.

Jacob Devlin, Ming-Wei Chang, Kenton Lee, and Kristina Toutanova. 2019. BERT: Pre-training of deep bidirectional transformers for language understanding. In *Proceedings of the 2019 Conference of the North American Chapter of the Association for Computational Linguistics: Human Language Technologies, Volume 1 (Long and Short Papers)*, pages 4171–4186, Minneapolis, Minnesota. Association for Computational Linguistics.

Aitor González, German Rigau, and Mauro Castillo. 2012. A graph-based method to improve wordnet domains. In *International Conference on Intelligent Text Processing and Computational Linguistics*, pages 17–28. Springer.

Aitor Gonzalez-Agirre, Mauro Castillo, and German Rigau. 2012. A proposal for improving wordnet domains. In *LREC*, pages 3457–3462.

Yinhan Liu, Myle Ott, Naman Goyal, Jingfei Du, Mandar Joshi, Danqi Chen, Omer Levy, Mike Lewis, Luke Zettlemoyer, and Veselin Stoyanov. 2019. Roberta: A robustly optimized bert pretraining approach. *arXiv preprint arXiv:1907.11692*.

B Magnini. 2000. G. cavagli a. integrating subject field codes into wordnet. In *Proceedings of LREC-2000, 2nd International Conference on Language Resources and Evaluation*, pages 1413–1418.

Bernardo Magnini, Carlo Strapparava, Giovanni Pezzulo, and Alfio Gliozzo. 2002. The role of domain information in word sense disambiguation. *Natural Language Engineering*, 8(4):359–373.

Tomas Mikolov, Kai Chen, Greg Corrado, and Jeffrey Dean. 2013. Efficient estimation of word representations in vector space. *arXiv preprint arXiv:1301.3781*.

George A Miller. 1998. *WordNet: An electronic lexical database*. MIT press.

Matthew Peters, Mark Neumann, Mohit Iyyer, Matt Gardner, Christopher Clark, Kenton Lee, and Luke Zettlemoyer. 2018. Deep contextualized word representations. In *Proceedings of the 2018 Conference of the North American Chapter of the Association for Computational Linguistics: Human Language Technologies, Volume 1 (Long Papers)*, pages 2227–2237, New Orleans, Louisiana. Association for Computational Linguistics.

Alec Radford, Jeffrey Wu, Rewon Child, David Luan, Dario Amodei, and Ilya Sutskever. 2019. Language models are unsupervised multitask learners. *OpenAI blog*, 1(8):9.

Victor Sanh, Lysandre Debut, Julien Chaumond, and Thomas Wolf. 2019. Distilbert, a distilled version of bert: smaller, faster, cheaper and lighter. *arXiv preprint arXiv:1910.01108*.

Liang Wang, Wei Zhao, Ruoyu Jia, Sujian Li, and Jingming Liu. 2019. Denoising based sequence-to-sequence pre-training for text generation. In *Proceedings of the 2019 Conference on Empirical Methods in Natural Language Processing and the 9th International Joint Conference on Natural Language Processing (EMNLP-IJCNLP)*, pages 4003–4015, Hong Kong, China. Association for Computational Linguistics.

Adina Williams, Nikita Nangia, and Samuel Bowman. 2018a. A broad-coverage challenge corpus for sentence understanding through inference. In *Proceedings of the 2018 Conference of the North American Chapter of the Association for Computational Linguistics: Human Language Technologies, Volume 1 (Long Papers)*, pages 1112–1122. Association for Computational Linguistics.

Adina Williams, Nikita Nangia, and Samuel Bowman. 2018b. A broad-coverage challenge corpus for sentence understanding through inference. In *Proceedings of the 2018 Conference of the North American*

Chapter of the Association for Computational Linguistics: Human Language Technologies, Volume 1 (Long Papers), pages 1112–1122.

Thomas Wolf, Lysandre Debut, Victor Sanh, Julien Chaumond, Clement Delangue, Anthony Moi, Pierric Cistac, Tim Rault, R'emi Louf, Morgan Funtowicz, and Jamie Brew. 2019. Huggingface's transformers: State-of-the-art natural language processing. *ArXiv*, abs/1910.03771.

Wenpeng Yin, Jamaal Hay, and Dan Roth. 2019. Benchmarking zero-shot text classification: Datasets, evaluation and entailment approach. In *Proceedings of the 2019 Conference on Empirical Methods in Natural Language Processing and the 9th International Joint Conference on Natural Language Processing (EMNLP-IJCNLP)*, pages 3914–3923, Hong Kong, China. Association for Computational Linguistics.

Discriminating Homonymy from Polysemy in Wordnets: English, Spanish and Polish Nouns

Arkadiusz Janz, Marek Maziarz
Wrocław University of Science and Technology, Poland
{arkadiusz.janz|marek.maziarz}@pwr.edu.pl

Abstract

We propose a novel method of homonymy-polysemy discrimination for three Indo-European Languages (English, Spanish and Polish). Support vector machines and LASSO logistic regression were successfully used in this task, outperforming baselines. The feature set utilised lemma properties, gloss similarities, graph distances and polysemy patterns. The proposed ML models performed equally well for English and the other two languages (constituting testing data sets). The algorithms not only ruled out most cases of homonymy but also were efficacious in distinguishing between closer and indirect semantic relatedness.

1 Introduction

Lexical polysemy is the word property of being a signifier for different but semantically related senses. Homonymy, on the other hand, is the accidental identity of word-forms, with no traces of real semantic relatedness. Homonyms have different etymologies, while *polysemes* are the product of the sense extending diachronic processes (Lyons, 1995, pp. 54-60). In fact, homonymous words – as semantically unrelated – should be treated as separate words. For Natural Language Processing this task is completely valid since homonyms frequently appear in textual corpora. Wordnets suffer from the absence of explicit links between related meanings and do not distinguish between the two types of ambiguity, making the task harder (Freihat et al., 2013b; Mihalcea, 2003).

In this paper we present a machine learning approach to automatic discrimination of homonymy from polysemy in three languages: English, Spanish and Polish. We randomly drew samples of noun polysemous lemmas from each wordnet and generated all possible sense couplings. Then we cross-checked them in traditional dictionaries in search of their homonymy/polysemy status (Section 3.1). Each pair was annotated with four different groups of features, representing: lemma properties (Sec. 3.2.1), semantic similarities between glosses (3.2.2), graph properties of nodes (3.2.3) and polysemy patterns (3.2.4). Having trained ML models on English data, we checked their efficacy on Spanish and Polish sense pairs (Sec. 4.1). Then, we passed to the analysis of each model behavior on the subset of English words with known sense distances (we transformed macro- and microstructures of Oxford Lexico and Merriam-Webster Dictionary into graphs, Sec. 4.2). We also introduced a definitional guidelines for distinction between *close* and *indirect* polysemy relationship. At the end, we manually inspected 300 sense pairs to assess how well homonymy-polysemy discrimination served close polysemy recognition (Sec. 6).

We define *homonyms* or *homographs* as etymologically unrelated sets of senses, having the same part of speech (POS) category and signified by the same lemma. We abstract from other grammatical properties of nouns, such as the mass/countable noun distinction in English or gender differences in Spanish. We say that two nominal senses represent homonymy, if they share the same lemma and whose dictionary equivalents are noted under distinct entries (i.e., in disjoint entry microstructures).

2 Related Work

Polysemy and homonymy attracted huge researchers' attention. Approaches to dissolve the problem could be divided roughly into three main camps: (i) regular polysemy pattern recognition, (ii) polysemy instance recognition and (iii) ontology-based discrimination. Our method belongs to the second group.

(i) Numerous papers were devoted to recognising regular polysemy types (patterns), i.e. classes of polysemy instances (actual sense pairs), sharing the same two superordinate semantic categories (Apresjan, 1974). Those pairs of categories include *animal – food, container – content, institution – building* etc. To computational linguistics this approach was introduced first by Buitelaar (Buitelaar, 2000, 1998). Wordnets were searched for polysemy patterns since then by many scientific teams. Peters and Peters (2000) and Peters et al. (1998) tested WordNet unique beginners, as well as, different combinations of indirect hypernyms as representatives of semantic domains ("conceptual signposts") for English, Spanish, and Dutch, see also (Peters, 2003). Freihat et al. (2016), Freihat et al. (2013b) and Freihat et al. (2013a) identified polysemy patterns and homonymy through the automatic analysis of WordNet taxonomy and logical-like inferences. They searched for parental semantic categories below the upper levels of WordNet hierarchy. Precisions as high as 90% were reported by different research groups. Since the automatic assessment of recall was impossible in this methodology (cf. Barque and Chaumartin (2009)), instead, the coverage ratio for wordnets was often given.

(ii) Regular polysemy does not exhaust the possible polysemous link types, since polysemous senses might be related irregularly, according to metonymy or metaphor paths specific to one or very few pairs. This topic is of high interest for Word Sense Disambiguation, because finding precise semantic links between senses may lead directly to sense merging and – the so called – polysemy reduction (Palmer et al., 2007; Navigli, 2009; Mihalcea, 2003). Some general kinds of polysemy are being distinguished, like metaphor, metonymy or specialisation/generalisation (Peters et al., 1998). Barque and Chaumartin (2009) and Peters (2006) constructed rules and imposed keyword constrains on glosses. Veale (2004) investigated the broader range of possible rules relying not only on glosses but also on local graph topological properties. New models/algorithms may be used to adding new instances of polysemy to WordNet, cf. for instance a metonymy enrichment in (Hayes et al., 2004).

(iii) Instead of investigating sense pair status, Utt and Padó (2011) carried out the division at the *lemma* level. They made use of polysemy patterns, based on basic types of Buitelaar's CoreLex, and looked for *n* most frequent polysemy types. They found the fact that polysemous words tended to have more frequent patterns than homonyms useful in homonymy-polysemy discrimination.

3 Method

3.1 Resources and Samples

In discriminating homonymy from polysemy we relied on traditional dictionaries. For English they were Oxford *Lexico*[1] and American English *Merriam-Webster Dictionary*[2]. For Spanish we utilised *Diccionario de la lengua española* of Real Academia Española[3] and Lexico *Spanish Dictionary* of Oxford University Press[4]. Polish dictionaries included *Uniwersalny słownik języka polskiego*[5], Doroszewski's *Słownik języka polskiego*[6] and *Słownik języka polskiego*[7], all published by Wydawnictwo Naukowe PWN.

We used Open Multilingual WordNet (version 1, Bond and Paik (2012); Bond and Foster (2013)) as the source of polysemous lemmas. We focused on English WordNet (Fellbaum, 1998), Spanish part of the Multilingual Central Repository (Atserias et al., 2004; Gonzalez-Agirre et al., 2012) and Polish WordNet (Maziarz et al., 2016). For each wordnet we randomly sampled a set of polysemous noun lemmas. Then each lemma was checked in the dictionaries in order to find whether it was homonymous or not. If so, we carefully checked all couplings of lemma senses and decided their homonymy/polysemy status. For lemmas that were considered polysemous we automatically assumed polysemy of their sense pairs. Then we added a couple dozen potentially homonymous nouns to increase the number of homonymy cases.[8] We searched the potential homonyms in the literature on homonymy. These new nouns were then cross-checked with dictionaries, pair by pair. In

[1] `https://www.lexico.com/`

[2] `https://www.merriam-webster.com/`

[3] `https://dle.rae.es/`

[4] `https://www.lexico.com/es/`

[5] `https://usjp.pwn.pl/`

[6] `http://doroszewski.pwn.pl/`

[7] `https://sjp.pwn.pl/`

[8] Having added new homonymy cases to our data sets, we must have distorted the real proportion between homonymy and polysemy. This choice affected the subsequent measurements of precision and recall. Consequently, the calculated homonymy recognition precision will be treated as the upper bound for the real homonymy precision, while the obtained polysemy precision will be regarded as the lower bound for the real polysemy precision. Random sampling enables us to directly assess recall of ML models, which is an obvious advantage.

the case of English we simply borrowed 25 English homonymous lemmas from a previously made resource,[9] see Sec. 4.2 for details. Table 1 presents statistics of final data sets. As could be seen the data set was unbalanced.

wordnet		sample		# sense pairs		
lang	#nS	#L	#S/L	H	P	$\sum$
eng	82k	159	4.1	325	1,241	1,566
spa	26k	135	4.0	87	1,060	1,147
pol	29k	111	2.5	39	232	271

Table 1: English, Spanish and Polish polysemous wordnet nouns with annotated homonymy cases. Symbol: #nS – number of noun synsets in a wordnet, #L – number of lemmas in a sample, #S/L – an average number of senses per lemma.

3.2 Features

We used a set of 19 features, representing different properties of sense pairs (Fig. 1). We started from Open Multilingual Wordnet and its language-dependent lemma-synset pairings. Having obtained the set of – let's say – n noun senses, we generated all possible $\frac{n\times(n-1)}{2}$ combinatorial pairs of senses. We treated PWN network structure, synset glosses, synset semantic domains etc. as means of meaning description. English served as the metalanguage for language specific lemma-sense pairs, not only in the case of Spanish and Polish, but also in the case of English itself. Thus English language was used in a two-fold way: as a semantic metalanguage (via PWN), and also as the object of semantic description (via OMW). Thanks to such an approach, our analysis and developed statistical models hopefully could be applicable to virtually any OMW language.

The features that we used could be roughly divided into four main groups: (a) lemma properties (standardised to obtain language independent measures), (b) gloss similarities, (c) graph measures and (d) polysemy patterns. We give them a sharp description below.

[9] https://github.com/MarekMaziarz/PolysemyTheories/blob/master/LEX-MW-merged-graph-distances.txt

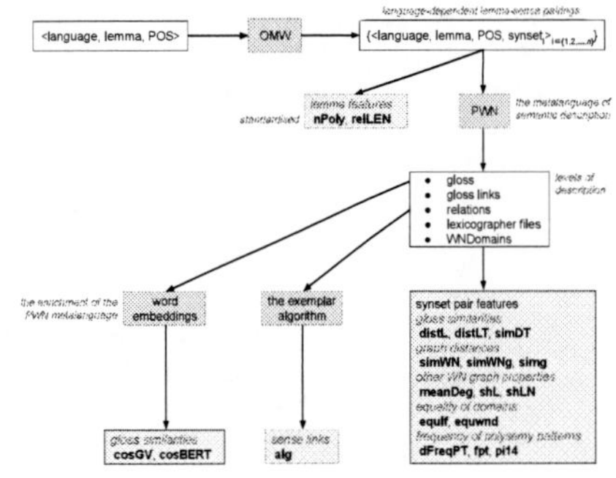

Figure 1: Feature calculation stages.

3.2.1 Lemma properties

nPoly – is a standardised number of senses of a given lemma l:

$$nPoly(l) := \frac{nsen(l) - m}{s}, \quad (1)$$

where $nsen(l)$ is the number of lemma l senses, m – a mean lemma sense number in a language and s – a standard deviation of lemma sense number in the language.

relLEN – is a standardised length of a given lemma l in characters, given by the formula:

$$relLEN(l) := \frac{nchar(l) - m}{s}, \quad (2)$$

where $nchar(l)$ is the lemma l length in characters, m – a mean lemma length in a language and s – a standard deviation of lemma length in the language.

3.2.2 Gloss similarities

distL – is a synset gloss dissimilarity measured on strings of letters through Levensthein edition distance:

$$distL(g(s_1), g(s_2)) := \frac{L(g(s_1), g(s_2))}{max(nchar(g(s_1)), nchar(g(s_2)))}, \quad (3)$$

where s_1, s_2 are synsets, $g(s)$ - is a gloss of synset s, $nchar(\cdot)$ - is a string length in characters, $L(\cdot, \cdot)$ - is a Levensthein edition distance between two strings.

distLT – is a synset gloss dissimilarity measured on sequences of tagged glosses through Levens-

their edition distance:

$$distLT(g(s_1), g(s_2)) := \frac{L(T(g(s_1)), T(g(s_2)))}{max(nchar(T(g(s_1))), nchar(T(g(s_2))))}, \quad (4)$$

where $T(\cdot)$ denotes a sequence of glosses lemmatised by the Stanford Tagger, and all other symbols defined exactly as in the definition of $distL$.

simOV – is a synset gloss similarity measured as the overlap between two sets of gloss lemmas. Let $V = (v_1, ..., v_n)$ and $W = (w_1, ..., v_m)$ be the sequences of words constituting glosses $g(s_1) = V$ and $g(s_2) = W$, respectively. Let then $ST(X)$ denotes the set of tagged words constituting the gloss sequence $X = (x_1, ..., x_n)$, i.e., $ST(X) = ST(x_1, ..., x_n) = \{T(x_1), ..., T(x_n)\}$. Thus we define $simOV$ similarity as follows:

$$simOV(g(s_1), g(s_2)) := \frac{|ST(V) \cap ST(W)|}{min(|ST(V)|, |ST(W)|)}, \quad (5)$$

where $|A|$ denotes a cardinality of the set A.

cosGV – is a cosine of two 50D vectors representing mean of GloVe vectors for all words constituting a gloss of a synset. Let $GV(w)$ be a 50D GloVe vector of the word w. We define $\overline{GV(g(s))} = \overline{GV(W)}$ as a mean vector of all words constituting the sequence W of length n, i.e.

$$\overline{GV(W)} = \frac{GV(w_1) + ... + GV(w_n)}{n}. \quad (6)$$

Then, if $V = g(s_1)$ and $W = g(s_2)$,

$$cosGV(V, W) := cos(\overline{GV(V)}, \overline{GV(W)}). \quad (7)$$

cosBERT – cosine of BERT vectors representing two glosses of paired synsets.

3.2.3 Graph properties

Six measures were based on graph properties:

simWN – was measured on the bidirectional graph of sole WordNet relations:

$$simWN(s_1, s_2) := \frac{1}{dist_{WN}(s_1, s_2)^2 + 1}. \quad (8)$$

Here $dist_{WN}(s_1, s_2)$ describes Dijkstra's distance on WordNet graph.

simWNg – was defined on WordNet graph expanded with bidirectional gloss relations:

$$simWNg(s_1, s_2) := \frac{1}{dist_{WNg}(s_1, s_2)^2 + 1}. \quad (9)$$

simg – was defined accordingly on the graph of gloss relations:

$$simg(s_1, s_2) := \frac{1}{dist_g(s_1, s_2)^2 + 1}. \quad (10)$$

meanDeg – is a mean degree of two synsets measured in bidirectional WordNet graph as follows:

$$meanDeg(s_1, s_2) := \frac{F(s_1) + F(s_2)}{2}, \quad (11)$$

where $F(s)$ is a geometric mean of a square root of the instance degree $\sqrt{deg_i(s)}$ of the synset s (total number of instance relations coming to and from the node s) and the type degree $deg_t(s)$ (total number of relation types the node s is involved within), i.e.

$$F(s) := \frac{2 \cdot deg_t(s) \cdot \sqrt{deg_i(s)}}{deg_t(s) + \sqrt{deg_i(s)}}, \quad (12)$$

shL – is a shared lemma index, i.e. the intersection of sets of lemma synsets divided by the cardinality of the smallest lemma set:

$$shL(s_1, s_2) := \frac{|lem(s_1) \cap lem(s_2)|}{min(|lem(s_1)|, |lem(s_1)|)}, \quad (13)$$

$lem(s)$ being the set of all lemmas of the synset s.

shLN – is a shared lemma neighborhood index. Let $Nb(s) = \{s_1, ..., s_m\}$ be the set of all m synsets that are one step apart from the synset s in bidirectional WordNet graph. Let Lem be a function such that

$$Lem(Nb(s)) = lem(s_1) \cup ... \cup lem(s_m). \quad (14)$$

The shLN measure is given by the formula:

$$shLN(s_1, s_2) := \frac{|Lem(Nb(s_1)) \cap Lem(Nb(s_2))|}{min(|Lem(Nb(s_1))|, |Lem(Nb(s_1))|)}. \quad (15)$$

3.2.4 Polysemy patterns

The last group of features relies on our ability to capture polysemy patterns and relations.

alg – is a binary function which checks whether a given sense pair is predicted by a sense linking algorithm, called *exemplar* algorithm (cf. Ramiro et al. (2018)). The exemplar algorithm links word senses into a polysemy net according to their proximity in WordNet+glosses graph. At each step we join a new sense that is the closest to all already linked senses. The algorithm starts from the synset with the highest vertex degree (given by the formula (12)).

equlf – is a binary function that checks equality of semantic domains as defines by lexicographer files. Let $LF(s)$ be a semantic domain of the synset s given in lexicographer files.

$$equlf(s_1, s_2) = \begin{cases} 1 & \text{if } LF(s_1) = LF(s_2) \\ 0 & \text{otherwise.} \end{cases} \quad (16)$$

equwnd – is a binary function that checks equality of semantic domains as defined by WordNet Domains.[10] Let $WND(s)$ be a semantic domain of the synset s given by WND, then

$$equlf(s_1, s_2) = \begin{cases} 1 & \text{if } WND(s_1) = WND(s_2) \\ 0 & \text{otherwise.} \end{cases} \quad (17)$$

fpt – is a binary function that checks whether a given sense pair belongs to the 5% of the most frequent polysemy patterns. Let's define a polysemy type PT as a pair of semantic domains, i.e. $PT(s_1, s_2) = (LF(s_{\tilde{1}}), LF(s_{\tilde{2}}))$ (ordered alphabetically from left to right, which we mark symbolically with a tilde mark). If we arrange PTs into a ranking list according to their frequency in WordNet (that is in the set of all possible pairs of polysemous senses) and establish the set $FreqPT$ of most frequent PTs which accounts altogether for at most 5% of PT occurrences in WordNet, then

$$fpt(s_1, s_2) = \begin{cases} 1 & \text{if } PT(s_1, s_2) \in FreqPT \\ 0 & \text{otherwise.} \end{cases} \quad (18)$$

dFreqPT – is a cumulative distribution of a given polysemy pattern. Let N be the total number of all polysemy pairs in a wordnet, m be the total number of polysemy patterns, i be the rank of the polysemy type PT_i and $Freq(PT_i)$ be the count of all occurrences of PT in the wordnet.

$$N = \sum_{i=1}^{m} Freq(PT_i). \quad (19)$$

Then

$$dFreqPT(s_1, s_2) = \frac{\sum_{i=1}^{p} Freq(PT_i)}{N}, \quad (20)$$

where $PT_p = PT(s_1, s_2), p \leq m$.

pi14 – is the measure inspired by the π_{81}-score from (Utt and Padó, 2011). Let $FreqPT$ be the set of most frequent polysemy patterns, as defined above, P_w be the set of polysemy patterns PT of a given lemma l, then

$$pi14(l) := \frac{|FreqPT \cap P_w|}{|P_w|}, \quad (21)$$

i.e., it is the ratio of language most frequent PTs in the set of PT characteristic for a given l.

4 Results

4.1 Polysemy vs. Homonymy

To cope with the unbalanced data problem a resampling methodology was applied for the smaller 'H' class.[11] Data were divided into 10 folds according to their *lemmas*.[12] Models were presented iteratively 9 training folds and then evaluation was performed on the 10th fold. The final tests were performed on Spanish and Polish (broken down into 5 folds for the comparison with baselines). LR was optimised through LASSO methodology (with 1 SE optimisation).[13] SVM was run with default parameters. Tables 2, 3 and 4 present the results for English, Spanish and Polish, respectively.

The obtained results prove that our two classes are not easily separable. This is caused not only by the choice of particular features, but also by the actual nature of polysemy. As soon as we matched various sense pairs of polysemous words, we had to deal with different parts of polysemy nets. Some

[10] If there were more than one category ascribed to a synset, we manually picked the most representative.

[11] We presented a ML model each homonymy pair four times.

[12] Sense pairs representing the same lemma landed in the same fold

[13] We optimalised λ parameter of the LASSO logistic regression on each training data set, then for the whole training data set the optimalised λ (corresponding to the most parsimonious model within 1 SE from the minimal error model) was established. The number of features was reduced to 13, with the most prominent being relLEN, simWN, simWNG, cosBERT, equlf, meanDeg, nPoly, pi14 and shL.

English	class	prediction P	H	efficiency Prec.	Recall
SVM	P	716	525	$\mathbf{.94}^{*}_{*}$	$\mathbf{.58}_{*}$
	H	43	282	$\mathbf{.35}_{*}$	$\mathbf{.87}^{*}_{*}$
LR	P	661	580	$\mathbf{.97}^{*}_{*}$	.53
	H	19	306	$\mathbf{.34}_{*}$	$\mathbf{.94}^{*}_{*}$
mBL	P	1241	0	.79	1^{*}_{*}
	H	325	0	–	0
rBL	P	620.5	620.5	.79	.50
	H	162.5	162.5	.21	.50

Table 2: Confusion matrices for English test set, 10-fold cross-validation. Baselines: 'mBL' – the majority class, 'rBL' – random (uniform distribution). Results significant at 5% significance level are marked with an asterisk (Holm's correction for multiple comparisons was applied, see Holm (1979)). In superscripts we give the comparison with mBL, while in subscripts – to rBL. In the case of mBL baseline, in superscript we present comparison to SVM and in subscript – to LR.

Spanish	class	prediction P	H	efficiency Prec.	Recall
SVM	P	600	460	$\mathbf{.98}^{*}_{*}$	.57
	H	10	77	$\mathbf{.14}_{*}$	$\mathbf{.88}^{*}_{*}$
LR	P	525	535	$\mathbf{1}^{*}_{*}$	.50
	H	0	87	$\mathbf{.14}_{*}$	$\mathbf{1}^{*}_{*}$
mBL	P	1060	0	.92	1^{*}_{*}
	H	87	0	–	0
rBL	P	530	530	.92	.50
	H	47.5	47.5	.08	.50

Table 3: Confusion matrices for Spanish test set. 5-fold cross-validation (with Benjamini-Hochberg correction, see Benjamini and Hochberg (1995)).

pairs were semantically as close as an extended sense and its base sense. Another represented distant relationships, i.e. indirect links. Although the polysemy class contained only related senses, the real nature of their semantic proximity was not determined. As a result the polysemy relationship class might have been torn apart between closer relationships and the heavy body of (resampled) homonymy class – representing the opposite poles of the polysemy-homonymy axis.[14]

[14]Lyons (1977, p. 550) perceived polysemy as a non-binary relation ranging from vagueness of meaning shades to total unrelatedness of homonymy.

Polish	class	prediction P	H	efficiency Prec.	Recall
SVM	P	149	83	$\mathbf{.96}^{*}_{*}$	$\mathbf{.64}_{*}$
	H	6	33	$\mathbf{.28}_{*}$	$\mathbf{.85}^{*}_{*}$
LR	P	116	116	$\mathbf{.96}^{*}_{*}$	.50
	H	5	34	$\mathbf{.23}_{*}$	$\mathbf{.87}^{*}_{*}$
mBL	P	232	0	.86	1^{*}_{*}
	H	39	0	–	0
rBL	P	116	116	.86	.50
	H	19.5	19.5	.14	.50

Table 4: Confusion matrices for Polish test set. 5-fold cross-validation (Benjamini-Hochberg correction).

It seems that both SVM and logistic regression aimed at capturing as many cases of homonymy as possible, with slight predominance of the logistic regression in this task. Both models led to ruling out many semantically related pairs, thus as a result we obtained a heterogeneous class of homonymy predictions and homogeneous polysemy class. Despite these weaknesses both models easily outperformed majority baselines, as well as random ones.

4.2 Close vs. Distant Polysemy

To check how well the two models cope with close (direct) and distant (indirect) polysemy, we contrasted their outputs with external data from Lexico and Merriam-Webster Dictionary. We analysed 57 nominal lemmas.[15] Onto each noun and its senses we mapped corresponding Princeton WordNet synsets. Then we transformed dictionary microstructures into graphs – according to sense ordering and polysemy hierarchy. It enabled us to measure distances between PWN senses in both dictionary-based graphs.[16]

Figure 2 presents both prediction classes "P" and "H" projected onto the plane of semantic distances measured either in Lexico graph ("distLEX"), or in Merriam-Webster ("distMW"). Homonymy resides in the top right most corner

[15]This comprised following nouns: *angle, band, bank, bark, bat, board, can, chapter, chop, clip, concealment, crest, cylinder, date, degree, duck, fall, fame, file, fly, gloss, intellect, lump, master, match, palm, pasturage, plant, ring, rock, rose, saw, scale, score, sentence, shilling, sink, skimmer, spring, stage, stalk, table, term, tie, tongue, trepan, trip, tune, veneer, vermin, victim, voucher, well, whirl, wrapping* and *wreck*.

[16]The transformation followed two main rules: (1) link main senses into a chain according to their ordering, (2) link a subsense to its superordinate.

of the plane, while direct polysemy occupies the area close to the origin of the coordinate system, i.e. the point $(0, 0)$. Graph distances themselves are highly correlated if we include homonymy cases.[17]. Spearman's rank correlation $\rho = 0.771$. If we exclude homonymy the correlation drops to the moderate values, $\rho = 0.453$ (sole polysemy cases). Intuitively, we could define *close polysemy* as a pair of senses which are (at least in one dictionary graph):

- either adjacent nodes in the chain of ordered senses,
- or a main sense and its subsense.

More formally we would say that two senses s_i and s_j of the same word represents the relation of close polysemy (cP) if the following condition holds:

$$cP := \{(s_i, s_j) \in S \times S : dist_{LEX}(s_i, s_j) \leq 1 \vee dist_{MW}(s_i, s_j) \leq 2\}, \quad (22)$$

where $S = s_1, ..., s_n$ is the set of n senses of the same word, while $dist_{LEX}$ and $dist_{MW}$ are measured on Lexico and Merriam-Webster graphs, respectively.[18] The 'dP' class was a set-theoretic complement of the 'cP' set to the 'P' class, i.e.

$$dP := \{(s_i, s_j) \in S \times S : (s_i, s_j) \notin H \wedge dist_{LEX}(s_i, s_j) > 1 \wedge dist_{MW}(s_i, s_j) > 2\}, \quad (23)$$

where H is the set of homonymy cases.

Figure 3 and Table 5 illustrate how well the logistic classifier and the SVM model deal with the two different types of polysemy: close, 'cP', and distant, 'dP', as well as with homonymy pairs, 'H'. As could be seen, the prediction class 'H' comprises almost all homonymy cases and most cases of distant polysemy. Almost half cases of close polysemy belongs there also. When one looks at the prediction 'P' class, the reversed picture is revealed. It contains nearly no cases of homonymy, and 2 times more close polysemy pairs than distant polysemy. It seems that the prediction class 'P' approximates close polysemy (with 67% precision and 50% recall), although we did not teach models the direct recognition of this class.

[17]Transforming infinities to maximum values for homonymy, i.e. $Inf \longrightarrow max(dist) + 1$.

[18]Since Merriam-Webster has more fine-grained sense distinctions, we used different thresholds for both dictionaries.

English		prediction		efficiency	
	class	P	H	P	R
SVM	cP	170	125	**.59**$^*_*$	.58$_*$
	dP	105	172	**.67**$^*_*$	**.68**$^*_*$
	H	11	80		
LR	cP	157	138	**.66**$^*_*$	.53
	dP	80	197	**.67**$^*_*$	**.78**$^*_*$
	H	2	89		
mBL	cP	295	0	.44	**1**$^*_*$
	dPH	368	0	–	0
rBL	cP	147.5	147.5	.44	.50
	dPH	184	184	.56	.50

Table 5: The subset of LR and SVM confusion matrices presented in Table 2 limited to Lexico and Merriam-Webster data. Three grades of semantic similarity/dissimilarity represent: close polysemy ('cP') – distant polysemy ('dP') – homonymy ('H'), as cross-tabulated with binary logistic predictions ('P', 'H'). Efficiency measures were calculated for the 'cP' class and for the joint 'dP' + 'H' class. Two baselines were calculated: 'mBL', i.e., the majority class and 'rBL' – random baseline. Benjamini-Hochberg correction was applied in the comparison with baselines on 5 random folds (5% significance was marked with asterisks).

4.3 Manual evaluation

Table 6 presents results of the independent manual evaluation by the first (#1) and the second (#2) author of this paper. #2 annotated 300 sense pairs (100 for each language), randomly selected from the outcome 'P' class of the English logistic regression model. #1 evaluated a subset of 100 of those pairs. Sense pairs were judged against their PWN definitions. Two senses were considered a close polysemy pair ('cP') if only they could be classified as one of the following polysemy subtypes: (i) metaphor, (ii) metonymy (including situation-argument relationships), (iii) sense broadening/narrowing, (iv) co-hyponymy, (v) antonymy and (vi) near-synonymy (cf. (Cruse, 2006, pp. 133-4), (Taylor, 2000, pp. 128-9)). Otherwise they were considered 'dP' (if they were semantically related) or 'H' case (if there was no relationship at all).

The resulting agreement was moderate, with Cohen's $\kappa = 0.4$ ('dP' and 'H' class were identified). 24 remaining disagreement cases were then again independently rejudged, resulting a higher

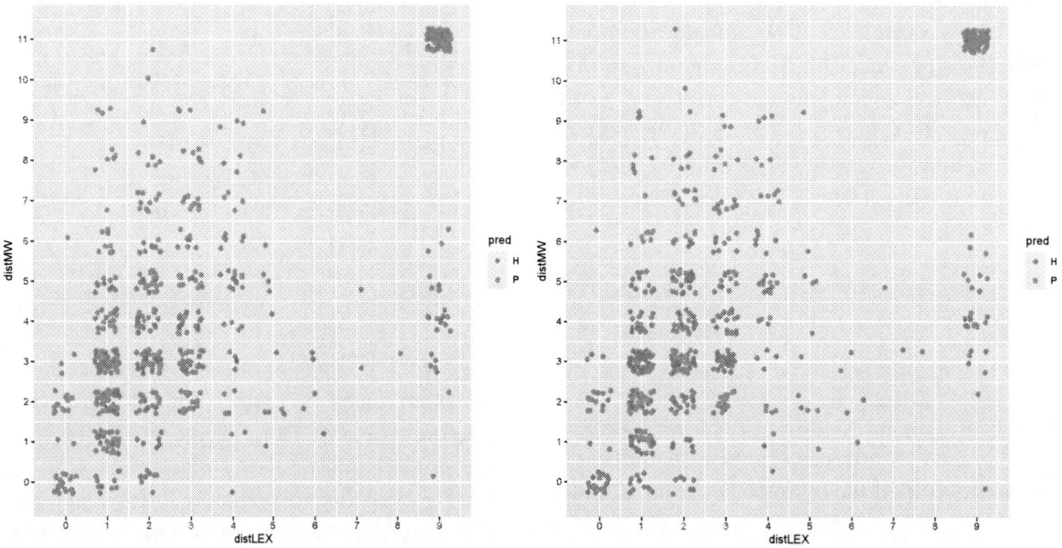

Figure 2: On the left – SVM, on the right: logistic regression. Prediction classes "P" and "H" compared with Lexico and Merriam-Webster distances (distLEX and distMW, respectively). Real homonymy cases occupy the top right corner, while direct polysemy cases take up the bottom left area. Please note, this is the subset of 10-fold cross-validation data (Table 2) limited to Lexico and Merriam-Webster lemmas.

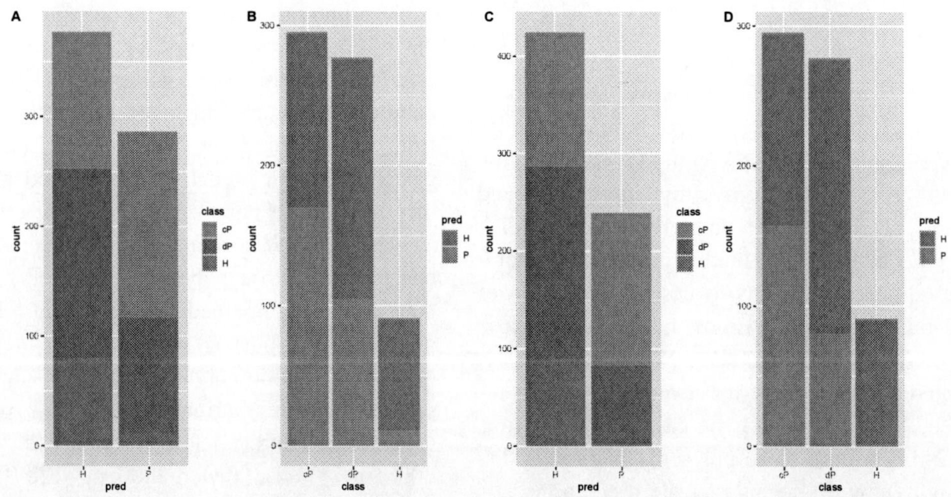

Figure 3: On the left (A, B) – SVM outcome, on the right (C and D) – LR model. Prediction classes 'P' and 'H' as compared to close and distant polysemy, 'cP', 'dP' and real homonymy 'H'. A, C – facets by prediction classes, B, D – facets by cP, dP and real homonymy.

pred. 'P' class		eng* n	spa n	pol n	in total $\sum$	CI [%]
#1	cP	24	26	28	78	69-86
	dPH	10	7	5	22	14-31
	$\sum$	34	33	33	100	100%
#2	cP	58	70	71	199	61-72
	dPH	42	30	29	101	28-39
	$\sum$	100	100	100	300	100%

Table 6: Manual evaluation of the prediction class 'P' given by the LR classifier with regard to 'cP', 'dP/H' classes. Symbols: * – cross-validation results, CI – a 95% confidence interval. The annotator #2 validated 300 cases, out of which the annotator #1 annotated 100. Cohen's $\kappa = 0.4$.

kappa, $\kappa = 0.6$, with the percentage IAA = 86%. Taking into account only the agreed 86 cases, we got CI for 'cP' equal to 68%-86%. Though the agreement was not perfect, the experiment proved that the majority of 'P' class instances was indeed close polysemy. The obtained confidence intervals are almost in perfect concordance with the automatic evaluation performed on the Lexico and Merriam-Webster graphs.

5 Conclusions

In a small-scale study of 400 nouns from three languages representing different branches of the Indo-European family we checked usefulness of two ML models (logistic regression and SVM) in discriminating homonymy from polysemy. We proposed a new set of 19 language-independent features, which comprised: lemma properties (like length), gloss similarities (including embeddings), graph properties (like graph distances) and frequent polysemy patterns. LR and SVM were trained on English data and tested on Spanish and Polish. The results were comparable, suggesting that our method could be transferred to non-congenial languages. Machine learning models performed above baselines for all languages.

Comparison with traditional dictionaries showed that trained classifiers preserved not only the polysemy-homonymy distinction, but also favoured direct polysemy over indirect relationships (in the prediction class 'P', with the reversed situation for 'H' predictions). Manual inspection of the LR 'P'-class outcome confirmed this finding: majority of sense pairs were classified as close rather than indirect semantic links.

Acknowledgments

This research was financed by the National Science Centre, Poland, grant number 2018/29/B/HS2/02919, and supported by the CLARIN-PL[19] research infrastructure.

References

Ju D Apresjan. 1974. Regular polysemy. *Linguistics*, 12(142):5–32.

Jordi Atserias, Luıs Villarejo, German Rigau, Eneko Agirre, John Carroll, Bernardo Magnini, and Piek Vossen. 2004. The meaning multilingual central repository. In *2nd International Global Wordnet Conference, January 20-23, 2004: proceedings*, pages 23–30. Masaryk University.

Lucie Barque and François Régis Chaumartin. 2009. Regular polysemy in wordnet. *Journal for Language Technology and Computational Linguistics*, 24(2):5–18.

Yoav Benjamini and Yosef Hochberg. 1995. Controlling the false discovery rate: a practical and powerful approach to multiple testing. *Journal of the Royal statistical society: series B (Methodological)*, 57(1):289–300.

Francis Bond and Ryan Foster. 2013. Linking and extending an open multilingual wordnet. In *Proceedings of the 51st Annual Meeting of the Association for Computational Linguistics (Volume 1: Long Papers)*, pages 1352–1362.

Francis Bond and Kyonghee Paik. 2012. A survey of wordnets and their licenses. In *Proceedings of the 6th International Global Wordnet Conference*, volume 8.

Paul Buitelaar. 1998. *CoreLex: systematic polysemy and underspecification*. Ph.D. thesis.

Paul Buitelaar. 2000. Reducing lexical semantic complexity with systematic polysemous classes and underspecification. In *NAACL-ANLP 2000 Workshop: Syntactic and Semantic Complexity in Natural Language Processing Systems*.

A. Cruse. 2006. *A Glossary of Semantics and Pragmatics*. Edinburgh University Press.

Christiane Fellbaum. 1998. Wordnet: An electronic lexical database.

[19] `http://clarin-pl.eu`

Abed Alhakim Freihat, Fausto Giunchiglia, and Biswanath Dutta. 2013a. Approaching regular polysemy in wordnet. In *proceedings of 5th International Conference on Information, Process, and Knowledge Management (eKNOW), Nice, France.*

Abed Alhakim Freihat, Fausto Giunchiglia, and Biswanath Dutta. 2013b. Regular polysemy in wordnet and pattern based approach. *International Journal On Advances in Intelligent Systems*, 6.

Abed Alhakim Freihat, Fausto Giunchiglia, and Biswanath Dutta. 2016. A taxonomic classification of wordnet polysemy types. In *Proceedings of the 8th GWC Global WordNet Conference.*

Aitor Gonzalez-Agirre, Egoitz Laparra, and German Rigau. 2012. Multilingual central repository version 3.0. In *LREC*, volume 2525, page 2529.

Jer Hayes, Tony Veale, and Nuno Seco. 2004. Enriching wordnet via generative metonymy and creative polysemy. In *LREC*. Citeseer.

Sture Holm. 1979. A simple sequentially rejective multiple test procedure. *Scandinavian journal of statistics*, pages 65–70.

John Lyons. 1977. *Semantics*, volume 1. Cambridge University Press: Cambridge.

John Lyons. 1995. *Linguistic semantics: An introduction*. Cambridge University Press.

Marek Maziarz, Maciej Piasecki, Ewa Rudnicka, Stan Szpakowicz, and Paweł Kędzia. 2016. PlWordNet 3.0 – a Comprehensive Lexical-Semantic Resource. In Nicoletta Calzolari, Yuji Matsumoto, and Rashmi Prasad, editors, *COLING 2016, 26th International Conference on Computational Linguistics, Proceedings of the Conference: Technical Papers, December 11-16, 2016, Osaka, Japan*, pages 2259–2268. ACL, ACL.

Rada Mihalcea. 2003. Turning wordnet into an information retrieval resource: Systematic polysemy and conversion to hierarchical codes. *International journal of pattern recognition and artificial intelligence*, 17(05):689–704.

Roberto Navigli. 2009. Word sense disambiguation: A survey. *ACM computing surveys (CSUR)*, 41(2):1–69.

Martha Palmer, Hoa Trang Dang, and Christiane Fellbaum. 2007. Making fine-grained and coarse-grained sense distinctions, both manually and automatically. *Nat. Lang. Eng.*, 13(2):137–163.

Wim Peters. 2003. Metonymy as a cross-lingual phenomenon. In *Proceedings of the ACL 2003 Workshop on the Lexicon and Figurative Language*, pages 1–9.

Wim Peters. 2006. In search for more knowledge: Regular polysemy and knowledge acquisition. *Proceedings of GWC2006.*

Wim Peters and Ivonne Peters. 2000. Lexicalised systematic polysemy in wordnet. In *Proceedings of LREC-2000.*

Wim Peters, Ivonne Peters, and Piek Vossen. 1998. Automatic sense clustering in eurowordnet. In *Proceedings of first international conference on language resource and evaluation: Granada, Spain, 28-30 May, 1998*, pages 409–416. ELRA.

Christian Ramiro, Mahesh Srinivasan, Barbara C. Malt, and Yang Xu. 2018. Algorithms in the historical emergence of word senses. *Proceedings of the National Academy of Sciences*, 115(10):2323–2328. URL `https://www.pnas.org/content/115/10/2323`.

John R. Taylor. 2000. *The Lexicon-Encyclopedia Interface*, chapter Approaches to word meaning: The network model (Langacker) and the two-level model (Bierwisch) in comparison, pages 115–142. Elsevier.

Jason Utt and Sebastian Padó. 2011. Ontology-based distinction between polysemy and homonymy. In *Proceedings of the Ninth International Conference on Computational Semantics (IWCS 2011).*

Tony Veale. 2004. Polysemy and category structure in wordnet: An evidential approach. In *LREC*. Citeseer.

Implementing ASLNet V1.0: Progress and Plans

Colin P. Lualdi[1,2,†] **Elaine Wright**[1,3,4] **Jack Hudson**[1] **Naomi K. Caselli**[5] **Christiane Fellbaum**[4,6]

[1]SignSchool Inc., Madison, Wisconsin, USA
[2]Department of Physics, University of Illinois, Urbana-Champaign, Illinois, USA
[3]Department of Electrical Engineering, Princeton University, Princeton, New Jersey, USA
[4]Program in Linguistics, Princeton University, Princeton, New Jersey, USA
[5]Programs in Deaf Studies, Boston University, Boston, Massachusetts, USA
[6]Department of Computer Science, Princeton University, Princeton, New Jersey, USA
†colin@signschool.com

Abstract

We report on the development of ASLNet, a wordnet for American Sign Language (ASL). ASLNet V1.0 is currently under construction by mapping easy-to-translate ASL lexical nouns to Princeton WordNet synsets. We describe our data model and mapping approach, which can be extended to any sign language. Analysis of the 390 synsets processed to date indicates the success of our procedure yet also highlights the need to supplement our mapping with the "merge" method. We outline our plans for upcoming work to remedy this, which include use of ASL free-association data.

1 Background and Motivation

First proposed in 2019 by Lualdi et al., ASLNet is an effort to extend the wordnet model pioneered by the Princeton WordNet (Miller, 1995; Fellbaum, 2010) to the visual-kinesthetic realm of sign languages. This endeavor is in part inspired by the creation of wordnets in dozens of other spoken languages, including those outside the Indo-European language family (Bond and Foster, 2013; Vossen, 2004), as well as images via ImageNet (Deng et al., 2009). It is only natural to develop wordnets for sign languages like American Sign Language (ASL) as they are unique languages in their own right.

There are many benefits to creating a wordnet representation of the ASL lexicon. The semantic relations encoded by a wordnet enable semantically-driven language acquisition (Miller and Fellbaum, 1992), resulting in a powerful first-language (L1) and second-language (L2) pedagogical resource that will also contribute to ASL linguistics. Furthermore, with the Princeton WordNet (PWN) serving as a hub linking multiple wordnets, connecting an ASL wordnet to PWN will bridge ASL to other languages (and ImageNet images), allowing for novel linguistic investigations. Lastly, with wordnets being invaluable to natural language processing (NLP), specifically word sense disambiguation (Navigli, 2009), an ASL wordnet will support burgeoning ASL machine translation efforts (Bragg et al., 2019).

The original ASLNet proposal (Lualdi et al., 2019) examined theoretical questions and strategies for extending the wordnet model to a sign language. The findings were synthesized into a proposed roadmap for creating ASLNet via a hybrid "map" and "merge" approach. ASLNet development would start with mapping straightforward ASL lexical nouns to PWN synsets, followed by creating ASLNet synsets with ASLNet-specific relations to be merged with PWN where appropriate.

In this paper, we report on the latest progress on implementing ASLNet V1.0 according to the prescription set forth by Lualdi et al. (2019). We describe the mapping procedure and evaluate its effectiveness. We also discuss how our work to date is informing the direction of subsequent ASLNet development.

2 ASLNet V1.0 Overview

As recommended by Lualdi et al. (2019), our objective for ASLNet V1.0 is to map ASL signs to their corresponding PWN synsets. For simplicity, we consider only lexical nouns, which often refer to concrete entities and hence are easier to represent; nouns also tend to map better crosslingually than verbs. Furthermore, most of the words in a lexicon (e.g., dictionaries, wordnets, etc.) are generally nouns, resulting in more data to work with. Therefore, ASLNet V1.0 is a table of noun PWN synsets and their mapped ASL sign(s). All semantic structure is directly derived from PWN, considerably simplifying the development work, albeit at the cost of (temporarily) ignoring aspects of ASL not present in English and therefore not encoded by PWN, such as classifier constructions, which lack a clear parallel in the English language.

While the "map" technique is not new to the wordnet community, this work presents a novel challenge in that, by working with a sign language, we are required to employ video exemplars. This stems from the lack of a conventional system for transcribing signs; there is no standardized writing system or even an International Phonetic Alphabet (IPA) for sign languages. Consequently, the signing community has no consensus on how to distinguish phonologically similar signs from one another, which complicates the isolation of particular signed forms for encoding in a sign language wordnet. By leaning on existing PWN synsets and structure during this initial stage of development, we therefore have more bandwidth for implementing an experimental model for organizing the sign data.

Difficulties with encoding signs are significant contributing factors to the resource-scarce nature of sign languages like ASL. They complicate the logistical challenges of gathering and processing video exemplars of signs, especially in the absence of practical computer vision, motion capture, and sign language machine translation technologies. Consequently, sign language lexical databases and corpora tend to be comparatively smaller than those of languages accompanied by robust orthographies. Accordingly, the challenges faced by the ASLNet team are not so different from those of teams working with other under-resourced languages. In fact, many of the techniques utilized in the development of ASLNet V1.0, such as the initial focus on mapping lexical nouns, are similar to those employed by the African Wordnet Project (AWN) in creating wordnets for five resource-scarce African languages (Bosch and Griesel, 2017).

2.1 Sign Data

In the original ASLNet proposal, it was suggested that the ASL sign data be drawn from SignStudy (www.signschool.org), a non-profit ASL research resource. SignStudy is supported by SignSchool Technologies LLC (www.signschool.com), a Deaf-led and owned ASL education company. While SignStudy's database size is respectable with 4,500+ sign videos, ASLNet V1.0 will function best as a wordnet when it possesses multiple clusters with a high density of sign-synset mappings. Furthermore, understanding how PWN structure lends itself to this small subset of ASL data will guide the ASLNet "merge" phase by highlighting any PWN deficiencies (in the context of ASL) that need addressing. So, to improve our ability to create such well-filled regions of PWN semantic hierarchy, we increase the number of documented signs available for mapping by also incorporating signs from two other ASL databases, ASL-LEX 2.0 (Sehyr et al., 2020; Caselli et al., 2017) with ~2,700 signs and ASL Signbank (Hochgesang et al., 2020) with ~3,500 signs.

As SignStudy, ASL-LEX, and ASL Signbank contain sign metadata[1], incorporating their signs not only improves ASLNet filling but also makes available linguistic data that will likely prove valuable for implementing ASLNet-specific relations and features during the upcoming "merge" stage of ASLNet development.

2.2 Data Model

To organize the ASLNet V1.0 data, we developed a tripartite model (Fig. 1). The first (lowest) level consists of "Signs", individual sign entries (including metadata) from the three sign databases[2]. Since these databases may overlap in coverage, we introduce a second (middle) level that combines identical-in-form Signs into "Combined Sign" objects. This merges complementary metadata for duplicate signs, resulting in a richly-annotated combined lexical database. Together, Signs and Combined Signs comprise the "Form Level", as they are strictly concerned with sign production; their organization is independent of semantics.

Note that determining whether two Signs should be grouped together in a Combined Sign (i.e., considered identical in form) or kept separate is not always a clear-cut process. One could adopt the strategy of considering signs identical if every phonological component is shared. However, the aforementioned lack of widely-used conventions for cod-

[1] SignStudy: Each sign is annotated with its constituent handshapes (~70 unique handshapes identified) as well as semantic category (~40) and subcategory (~200). ASL-LEX: Each sign is annotated for six phonological properties (sign type, selected fingers, flexion, major and minor location, and movement), four lexical properties (initialization, lexical class, compounding, and fingerspelling), and subjective frequency and iconicity ratings. ASL Signbank: Each sign is identified by a unique "ID gloss" and partially annotated with various phonological, morphological, semantic, and miscellaneous metadata.

[2] In this paper, "Sign" with a capital "S" refers to the sign data object while "sign" with a lowercase "s" refers to the actual sign itself.

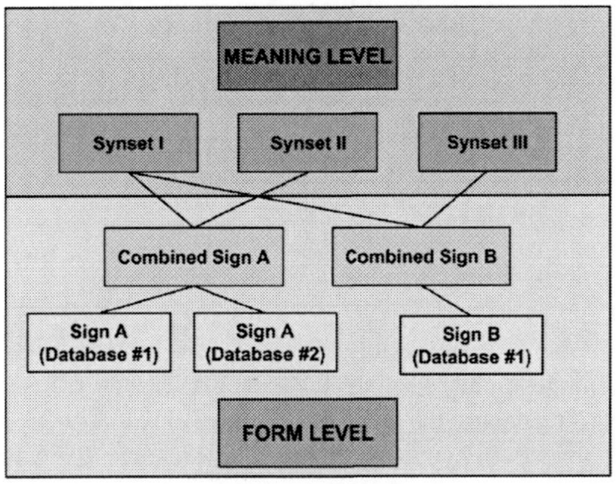

Figure 1: The ASLNet V1.0 data model. Sign A (Database #1) and Sign A (Database #2) are duplicates merged into Combined Sign A. Sign B is a distinct sign with its own Combined Sign object (B). Both Combined Sign A and B are polysemous and map to multiple synsets (I & II and I & III). They are also synonymous for a certain sense (Synset I) and thus both map to it.

ing ASL phonology makes it difficult to distinguish similar-in-form signs from one another. For the time being, we consider signs identical in form if they are treated as indistinguishable in use by native speakers. Any evidence of perceivable difference (e.g., one sign being a known regional variation of the other) is grounds for distinguishability. Since we expect this criteria to evolve as sign encoding conventions develop, our data model is designed to be flexible by allowing for easy rearrangement of Signs under Combined Signs without the need to drastically modify the entire system.

The third (top) level is the "Meaning Level", where we introduce semantics by linking Combined Signs to their corresponding PWN synsets. Due to polysemy, a Combined Sign may link to multiple PWN synsets. Similarly, synonymy results in individual synsets being associated to several Combined Sign objects.

3 Sign-Synset Mapping

To link the "Form" and "Meaning" levels of our data model, we developed a procedure to map signs to synsets with the objective of creating high-density synset clusters in ASLNet V1.0. While we are working with ASL signs, our procedure may be extended to any sign language with available lexical databases and corresponding wordnets.

3.1 Choosing Synset Clusters

With 10^4 signs and 10^5 synsets[3] available, it is challenging to identify the initial synset clusters to build. To condense our options, we imposed two criteria: relevance and efficiency.

We ensure relevance by considering only synsets belonging to common semantic domains (e.g., people, food, etc.) appearing frequently in everyday ASL discourse; their early incorporation will make ASLNet useful sooner.

To help us identify these synsets, we can utilize both the English equivalents of the signs in our combined ASL lexical database and the "Core" WordNet (CPWN), a collection of 5,000 more-frequently used word senses derived from British National Corpus (BNC) frequency data (Boyd-Graber et al., 2006). At high frequencies, BNC only differs by about 10% from the Corpus of Contemporary American English (Davies, 2011–), so the use of CPWN synsets to approximate frequently used word senses in American English is reasonable. While it would be ideal to use ASL frequency ratings, said data is limited due to the sign-coding challenges mentioned previously. However, since a large number of ASL speakers are bilingual ASL-English Americans, it is fair to assume frequency data for ASL and American English are comparable to a degree (Wright, 2020). Indeed, it was found that ASL-LEX subjective frequency data is moderately correlated with English frequency counts (Caselli et al., 2017). Furthermore, the small sizes of the sign databases we utilize imply that the included signs are relatively frequently used.

Therefore, instead of searching the entirety of PWN 3.0 for possible clusters of interest, we constrain ourselves to a smaller subset formed by the union of (A) all CPWN synsets and (B) PWN 3.0 synsets with at least one lemma matching sign data English equivalents[4]. The resulting synsets are favorable to our sign data while also identifying possible gaps worth filling during ASLNet development.

To achieve efficient use of the sign data supplied by SignStudy, ASL-LEX, and ASL Signbank, we chose domains from this subset that were very likely to achieve high sign-synset mapping densities. E.g., if our combined sign database is rich in

[3] PWN 3.0 synsets.

[4] Note that guessing signs' corresponding PWN synsets on the basis of the signs' manually annotated English equivalents is a crude heuristic; the listed translations may not be comprehensive or capture all of a sign's meanings.

"vegetables" signs but lean in "fruits", it is in our interest to perform the mapping work in the former.

We devised a computerized screening process incorporating the two criteria above to identify candidate clusters. First, we generated the union subset. Then, we checked if any synset in this set was a direct PWN hypernym of another set element, and if so, we added the hypernym to the candidate list. Synsets with a common 1st- or 2nd-level hypernym were also identified, with the shared hypernym added to the candidate list. After filtering for duplicates, we generated a list of existing 1st- and 2nd-generation hyponyms for each candidate list synset[5].

Each of these lists were scored by the proportion of constituent synsets with at least one lemma matching signs' English equivalents. The clusters (labeled by their "parent" synset from the candidate list) with the highest scores (closer to 1) were therefore recognized as optimal starting points.

Results from the screening process are summarized in Fig. 2 and Table 1. Smaller clusters, for the most part, score better than larger clusters. Overall, 3606 candidates with nonzero scores were identified, with an average score of 0.33 ($\sigma = 0.24$).

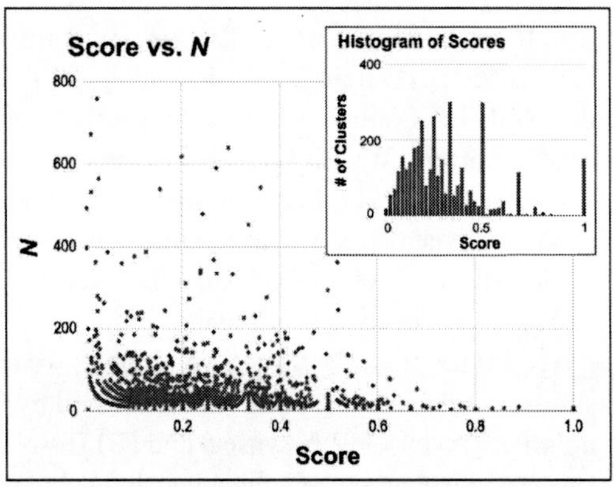

Figure 2: Candidate cluster score versus size (N). High-scoring clusters tend to be smaller. Plot excludes two $N > 1,000$ outliers [(0.002, 2532), (0.19, 1615)]. Inset: Histogram of candidate cluster scores.

3.2 Mapping Protocol and Tool

With the target synset clusters identified, the next step is to map signs to the synsets belonging to these clusters. A team of 3 ASL-English bilingual

Candidate Synset	Score	N
contact.n.04	0.89	9
kinsman.n.01	0.67	6
hair.n.01	0.40	43
jewelry.n.01	0.31	36
vegetable.n.01	0.15	75
pasta.n.02	0.08	26

Table 1: Select results of the screening process to determine possible starting clusters for ASLNet V1.0. Score (N) denotes the proportion (number) of 1st- or 2nd-generation hyponyms in the cluster that can likely map to one or more available signs.

lexicographers[6] was assembled for the mapping.

As a preliminary step, one of the lexicographers manually generated correspondence tables linking SignStudy, ASL-LEX, and ASL Signbank, grouping duplicate signs into Combined Sign objects. Since combining Signs into Combined Signs can be a difficult task for reasons mentioned previously, Sign objects (rather than Combined Signs) are currently being mapped directly to the synsets; at a later time the Signs will be condensed into Combined Signs on a synset-by-synset basis and the results checked against the manually-prepared Combined Signs.

For the mapping, we developed an online tool ("Synset Mapper") to guide the lexicographers through the mapping protocol as follows:

Step 1: Lexicographer searches for a PWN synset. Search returns a list containing the query synset and all of its existing 1st-generation hyponyms[7].

Step 2: Clicking on any of these synsets opens up its review page displaying the synset's name, definition, status, review state, notes, mapped Signs, computer-suggested Signs, and a Sign search. Each Sign is presented as a user-playable video accompanied by its associated English equivalent(s) and source (i.e., SignStudy, ASL-LEX, or ASL Signbank).

Step 3: Lexicographer reviews the synset definition and selects the appropriate Sign(s) from either the suggestions or a manual gloss search. See Fig. 3 (located at the end of the paper, after the references section) for a screenshot of this step.

[5]CPWN is a disjointed list with no internal navigation functionality. Since we intend to map to well-filled clusters, we elect to generate the hyponym lists from PWN.

[6]The team consisted of two deaf individuals with graduate-level education and one hearing ASL interpreter with a MA in Linguistics.

[7]From the full PWN 3.0.

Step 4: Lexicographer updates the synset status and review state according to the mapping outcome. Clicking on "save" closes the synset review page and brings back the hyponym list from Step 1.

Step 5: Lexicographer repeats Steps 2 - 4 for all existing synsets in the hyponym list.

Step 6: Lexicographer repeats Steps 1-5 with each existing 1st-generation hyponym as the query synset. The cluster is complete once all of its existing 1st and 2nd-generation hyponyms have been reviewed.

As the effectiveness of the Synset Mapper tool and its accompanying mapping protocol is still being evaluated via our preliminary mapping work, the tool is not yet publicly available. However, the video-centered design of Synset Mapper will likely make it very applicable to wordnet-development efforts for languages where a video-based lexical database is an efficient means of documenting individual units of meaning, such as for other signed or spoken languages without robust orthographies. For this reason, we hope to make our tool accessible for this purpose in the near future once it is fully developed.

3.2.1 Synset Status and Review State

The synset status indicates the status of a synset's mapping, with four options to choose from:

- **Unreviewed:** The default status.
- **Incomplete:** Mapping incomplete due to a gap in the sign data.
- **Approved:** Mapping complete; all appropriate Signs have been linked.
- **Deferred:** Mapping is non-trivial, reserve for future analysis.

The review state indicates if the mapping has been finalized by the lexicographers. To ensure consistency and limit individual subjectivity, we adopted a measure-twice-and-cut-once protocol, where each lexicographer's mappings ("Tentative" state) are verified by a second lexicographer ("Final" state). The default state is "not started".

3.2.2 Computer-Suggested Signs

To expedite the mapping task, Synset Mapper can function in a computer-assisted mode by providing "recommended signs" and "corresponding signs".

A Sign appears in "recommended signs" if any of its English equivalents satisfies a "string contains" regular expression match with at least one of the lemmas of the synset under review, or of its hypernym(s) and hyponym(s) (when they exist).

The "corresponding signs" list utilizes the manually-prepared Combined Sign correspondence tables. When a Sign is mapped to a synset, Synset Mapper checks if this Sign belongs to a Combined Sign containing other Signs. Any associated Signs are then added in real time to the "corresponding signs" list for the lexicographer to map (if suitable). This serves as an effective means of verifying our preliminary Combined Sign groupings.

4 Mapping Progress

The lexicographers are currently performing preliminary mapping work to evaluate the strategy described in Sections 2 and 3, paving the way for large-scale development. To date, we have processed 390 synsets (including both "Tentative" and "Final" states) in 14 randomly-selected clusters with scores in vicinity of the average from the cluster screening process (Table 2). As the optimal score threshold for mapping in practice is unknown due to a lack of data, the "in the vicinity of the average" criteria was arbitrarily selected. Variety in the scores of the selected clusters will allow evaluation of correlations between their score and actual completeness upon the conclusion of mapping as a test of our cluster screening procedure.

A total of 271 signs[8] have been mapped to synsets. On average, each cluster contains ~184 synsets with ~50% of its synsets processed (e.g., reviewed by the lexicographers) and ~13% mapped to at least one Sign. These statistics, along with these reported in the remainder of this paper, consider all processed synsets (i.e., both the "Tentative" and "Final" states) unless otherwise noted.

As indicated by Table 3, the fact that the processed synsets are not overly dominated by those with "Incomplete" status is a testament to the success of our cluster screening and the coverage of the combined ASL lexical database. This is further supported by observing that 30% of the "Incomplete Synsets" have at least one mapped sign (i.e., they still need additional ASL forms not present in the sign data to achieve "Approved" status).

Of the synsets with mapped signs, 13 had 1 sign, 18 had 2 signs, and 62 had 3+ signs. The apparent propensity of these synsets to have a large number of mapped signs is likely due to the fact we

[8] 104 from SignStudy, 88 from ASL-LEX, and 79 from ASL Signbank.

Cluster	Size	Score	Fraction Processed	Fraction Mapped	# of Signs
baseball_equipment.n.01	18	0.47	0.67	0.05	2
clock_time.n.01	20	0.42	1.00	0.50	36
hair.n.01	44	0.40	1.00	0.34	10
sports_equipment.n.01	69	0.34	0.46	0.04	4
jewelry.n.01	37	0.31	0.35	0.16	20
head_of_state.n.01	15	0.29	0.40	0.20	7
starches.n.01	43	0.24	0.95	0.14	17
furniture.n.01	83	0.23	0.96	0.12	45
building.n.01	176	0.21	0.01	0.01	4
person.n.01	1616	0.19	0.02	0.01	48
woman.n.01	126	0.18	0.02	0.02	8
vegetable.n.01	79	0.15	0.36	0.07	17
edible_fruit.n.01	136	0.12	0.35	0.07	45
beverage.n.01	112	0.11	0.38	0.11	39

Table 2: The 14 randomly-selected clusters (with scores in vicinity of the average) for preliminary ASLNet V1.0 mapping work. Mapping is underway; "Fraction Processed", "Fraction Mapped", and "# of Signs" indicates the fraction of cluster synsets having been reviewed by lexicographers, the fraction of cluster synsets having at least one mapped Sign, and the number of Signs mapped to the cluster's synsets, respectively. In the ideal case (i.e., where our cluster screening process is indeed reliable), as "Fraction Processed" approaches 1.0 for a given cluster, its "Fraction Mapped" value will approach the cluster's "Score". Based on our progress so far, this seems to be the case. However, our mapping work is still too preliminary to draw a definitive conclusion on the predictive ability of our cluster screening process.

Synset Status	Tentative	Final	Overall
Incomplete	44	69	113
Approved	8	50	58
Deferred	188	31	219
Total	**240**	**150**	**390**

Table 3: Status and review states of processed synsets.

have yet to collapse Signs over Combined Signs, especially since the three sign databases used are known to have some overlap. However, this may also be explained by a high incidence of synonymous signs, which might be an interesting metric to compare against other languages. The actual cause will be revealed when the Signs for each synset are reviewed and condensed into Combined Signs as appropriate.

Comparing the number of synsets in each of the "Tentative" and "Final" review state suggests the presence a processing bottleneck introduced by the measure-twice-cut-once protocol. While this is a worthwhile trade-off for early mapping efforts due to the lexicographers' inexperience, it is not for large-scale work. Mapping quality will instead be maintained via a training regimen for future lexicographers along with the development of a mapping guide with instructions for common cases such as whether to incorporate signs of foreign origin.

Some of the "Deferred" synsets correspond to ASL lexical gaps. Yet it is difficult to disambiguate between gaps and certain signs (e.g., classifier constructions) that differ from basic lexicalized forms. Others are technical concepts (present due to the taxonomic depth of PWN) unfamiliar to our lexicographers. The latter will be addressed by querying relevant experts who are also native ASL signers. Altogether, the non-triviality of the "Deferred" synsets relegate their analysis to future work.

The question of ASL lexical gaps also spotlights a serious limitation of the "map" approach. Despite having $N_{\text{Signs}} << N_{\text{Synsets}}$, we elected to map Signs to synsets rather than vice versa as it is easier for the lexicographers to retrieve Signs corresponding to the definition of a given synset as opposed to searching for a synset matching a given Sign. While suitable for basic mapping work, this precludes identifying PWN gaps for concepts lexicalized in ASL. To find such signs, this deficiency must be addressed in upcoming work.

5 Next Steps

With the mapping infrastructure implemented and its evaluation underway, it is beneficial to identify next steps as we scale up mapping operations.

5.1 Supplementing Mapping with Merging

The challenges pertaining to the "Deferred" synsets and PWN lexical gaps described in Section 4 reveal the limitations of the "map" technique for crosslingual wordnet development. This conclusion is expected, and is similar to that of the AWN team, who realized that mapping PWN to African languages resulted in a translation of predominately European concepts rather than a true African resource (Bosch and Griesel, 2017). One part of the solution is to ramp up the "merge" phase of ASLNet development where a new wordnet is built solely for ASL (and eventually merged with PWN). This affords us the flexibility to include ASL-specific synsets as well as implement the ASLNet-specific structure proposed in (Lualdi et al., 2019). A new wordnet structure and understanding of the nature of ASL-only synsets may guide us in resolving many of the currently "Deferred" synsets.

For the ASL-specific synsets, we propose to start with two basic discovery techniques. First, we will begin by having our lexicographers select specific semantic domains for which they will then supply any ASL signs that come to mind. While some of these will overlap with existing PWN synsets, we anticipate that others will correspond to lexical gaps in English. Second, once the mapping work reaches a stage where a large percentage of the available sign data has been mapped to PWN synsets, the remaining unmapped signs will be reviewed, as chances are high that they represent lexical gaps in English. The signs identified by these techniques will then be incorporated into ASLNet either as a Collaborative Interlingual Index (Bond et al., 2016) synset if a suitable match exists, or as a new synset.

5.2 Free Association

A more involved technique to probe senses and relations unique to ASL is to perform free-association tests on native ASL speakers. The premise is that associated words may be semantically related and therefore inform "merge" ASLNet development.

Free-association has been well studied for the English language (Nelson et al., 2004) and extended to PWN via studies of evocation between synsets (Boyd-Graber et al., 2006). The ASL-LEX team is currently working to collect semantic free associations from native ASL users for all of the signs in ASL-LEX, which will be used to generate a semantic network of the ASL lexicon. Because ASLNet and its sign data will be cross-referenced with ASL-LEX, we will be able to compare the semantic structure of the lexicon as measured in these two different ways (e.g., like Steyvers and Tenenbaum (2005) did for English). Additionally, as has been done for other languages (e.g., (Sinopalnikova, 2004; Ma, 2013)), we will leverage the ASL-LEX semantic associations in building ASLNet (e.g., using the free associates as suggested items in a later version of the Synset Mapper tool, among other possibilities). Accordingly, the "map" ASLNet work will prioritize the linking of ASL-LEX signs in anticipation of ASL-LEX semantic association data.

This work has NLP benefits as well. Spoken-language wordnets are generally thought to model human mental lexicon organization to some extent, hence their utility for word sense disambiguation (Fellbaum, 2010; Navigli, 2009). It is an open question if this premise extends to ASL. By comparing the ASL free-association data against both the "map" and "merge" components of ASLNet, one can verify the suitability of the wordnet model for organizing the ASL lexicon. This has important implications for ASLNet design and its applicability to ASL NLP efforts. Along these lines, one of the major barriers to NLP efforts for sign languages is a lack of the datasets necessary to train models (Bragg et al., 2019). By offering a semantically-structured lexicon, ASLNet could serve as one of the resources for developing such models.

6 Conclusion

Overall, progress is being made with developing ASLNet V1.0, with a focus on mapping easy-to-translate lexical nouns. Our tripartite data model, cluster screening technique, Synset Mapper tool, and mapping protocol all have enabled successful linking of ASL signs to PWN synsets, and in fact can be easily extended to other sign languages. In particular, these tools so far have been helpful in solving the unique challenges of building a sign language wordnet, overcoming the fact that there is no conventional notation system for identifying and disambiguating signs. However, preliminary work has highlighted the need for the "merge" technique to incorporate aspects of ASL overlooked by our current mapping efforts such as ASL-only synsets. Moving forward, the "map" technique used so far will be supplemented by "merge" development work that include the utilization of ASL free-association data.

Acknowledgments

The authors would like to thank lexicographers Miriam Goldberg and Heidi Johnson for their work. Comments and feedback from the 2021 Global Wordnet Conference attendees as well as three anonymous reviewers are also greatly appreciated.

References

Francis Bond and Ryan Foster. 2013. Linking and Extending an Open Multilingual Wordnet. In *Proceedings of the 51st Annual Meeting of the Association for Computational Linguistics (Volume 1: Long Papers)*, pages 1352–1362, Sofia, Bulgaria. Association for Computational Linguistics.

Francis Bond, Piek Vossen, John P. McCrae, and Christiane Fellbaum. 2016. CILI: The Collaborative Interlingual Index. In *Proceedings of the Eighth Global WordNet Conference*, pages 50–57.

Sonja E. Bosch and Marissa Griesel. 2017. Strategies for building wordnets for under-resourced languages: The case of African languages. *Literator (Potchefstroom. Online)*, 38:1 – 12.

Jordan Boyd-Graber, Christiane Fellbaum, Daniel Osherson, and Robert Schapire. 2006. Adding Dense, Weighted Connections to Wordnet. In *Proceedings of the Third Global WordNet Conference*, pages 29–35.

Danielle Bragg, Oscar Koller, Mary Bellard, Larwan Berke, Patrick Boudreault, Annelies Braffort, Naomi Caselli, Matt Huenerfauth, Hernisa Kacorri, Tessa Verhoef, Christian Vogler, and Meredith Ringel Morris. 2019. Sign Language Recognition, Generation, and Translation: An Interdisciplinary Perspective. In *The 21st International ACM SIGACCESS Conference on Computers and Accessibility*, ASSETS '19, pages 16–31, New York, NY, USA. Association for Computing Machinery.

Naomi K. Caselli, Zed Sevcikova Sehyr, Ariel M. Cohen-Goldberg, and Karen Emmorey. 2017. ASL-LEX: A lexical database of American Sign Language. *Behavior Research Methods*, 49(2):784–801.

Mark Davies. 2011–. Most frequent 100,000 word forms in English (based on data from the COCA corpus). Available online at https://www.wordfrequency.info/.

J. Deng, W. Dong, R. Socher, L. Li, Kai Li, and Li Fei-Fei. 2009. ImageNet: A large-scale hierarchical image database. In *2009 IEEE Conference on Computer Vision and Pattern Recognition*, pages 248–255. ISSN: 1063-6919.

Christiane Fellbaum. 2010. WordNet. In Roberto Poli, Michael Healy, and Achilles Kameas, editors, *Theory and Applications of Ontology: Computer Applications*, pages 231–243. Springer Netherlands, Dordrecht.

Julie A. Hochgesang, Onno Crasborn, and Diane Lillo-Martin. 2020. ASL Signbank. New Haven, CT. Haskins Lab, Yale University.

Colin Lualdi, Jack Hudson, Christiane Fellbaum, and Noah Buchholz. 2019. Building ASLNet, a Wordnet for American Sign Language. In *Proceedings of the Tenth Global WordNet Conference*, pages 315–322.

Xiaojuan Ma. 2013. Evocation: analyzing and propagating a semantic link based on free word association. *Language Resources and Evaluation*, 47(3):819–837.

George A. Miller. 1995. WordNet: a lexical database for English. *Communications of the ACM*, 38(11):39–41.

George A. Miller and Christiane Fellbaum. 1992. WordNet and the Organization of Lexical Memory. In *Intelligent Tutoring Systems for Foreign Language Learning*, NATO ASI Series, pages 89–102, Berlin, Heidelberg. Springer.

Roberto Navigli. 2009. Word sense disambiguation: A survey. *ACM Computing Surveys*, 41(2):10:1–10:69.

Douglas L. Nelson, Cathy L. McEvoy, and Thomas A. Schreiber. 2004. The University of South Florida free association, rhyme, and word fragment norms. *Behavior Research Methods, Instruments, & Computers*, 36(3):402–407.

Zed Sevcikova Sehyr, Naomi K. Caselli, Ariel M. Cohen-Goldberg, and Karen Emmorey. 2020. Under review.

Anna Sinopalnikova. 2004. Word Association Thesaurus As a Resource for Building WordNet. In *Proceedings of the Second Global WordNet Conference*, pages 199–205.

Mark Steyvers and Joshua B. Tenenbaum. 2005. The Large-Scale Structure of Semantic Networks: Statistical Analyses and a Model of Semantic Growth. *Cognitive Science*, 29(1).

Piek Vossen. 2004. EuroWordNet: A multilingual database of autonomous and language-specific wordnets connected via an inter-lingual-index. *International Journal of Lexicography*, 17(2):161–173. Publisher: Oxford Academic.

Elaine Wright. 2020. From Intractable to Tractable: Simplifications and Strategies for Implementing ASLNet. Princeton, NJ. Princeton University Undergraduate Independent Work.

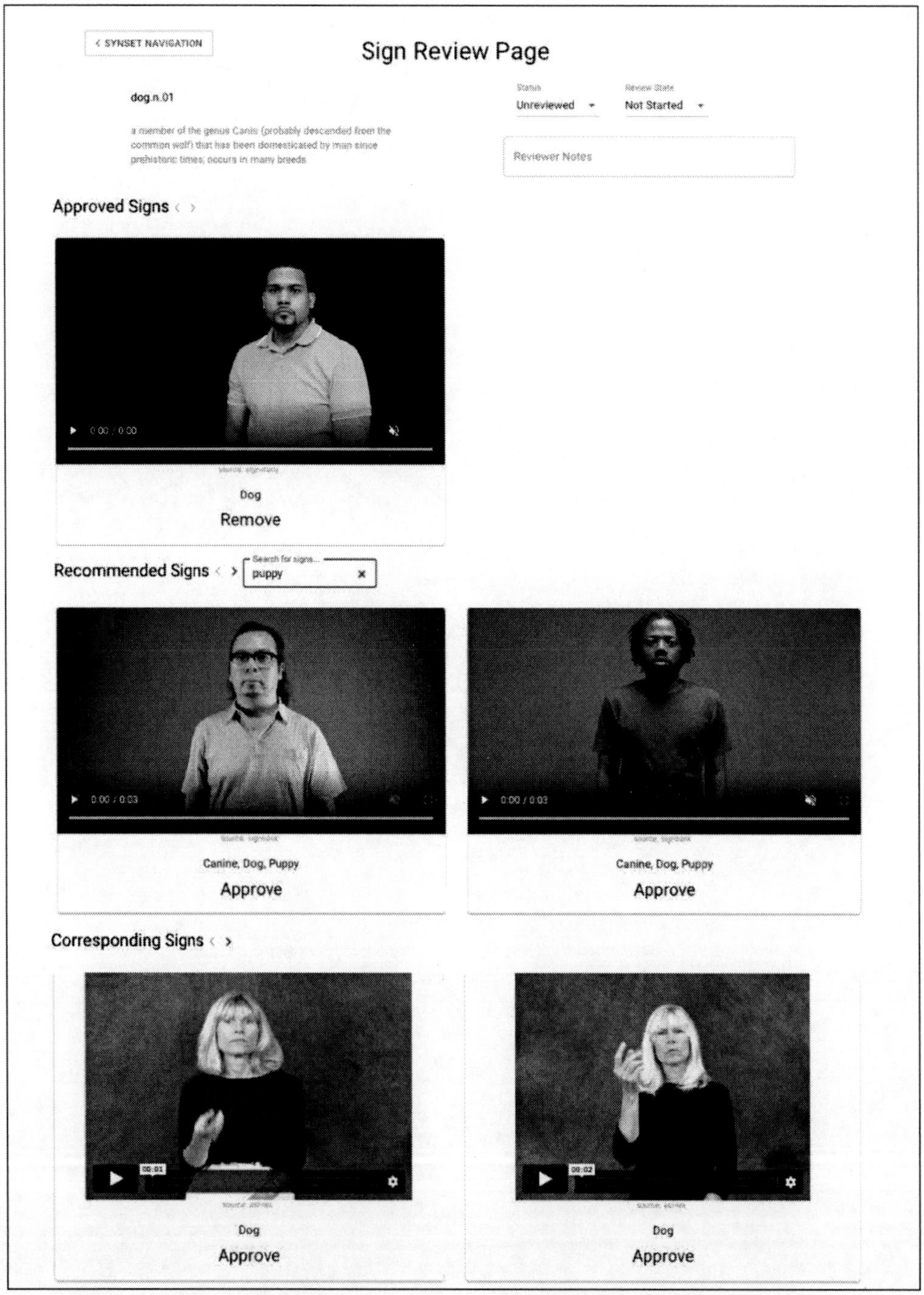

Figure 3: Synset Mapper tool Step 3: Synset review page displaying the synset's name, definition, status, review state, notes, mapped Signs, "recommended signs", "corresponding signs", and a Sign search.

Monolingual Word Sense Alignment as a Classification Problem

Sina Ahmadi, John P. McCrae
Insight Centre for Data Analytics
Data Science Institute, National University of Ireland Galway
{sina.ahmadi, john.mccrae}@insight-centre.org

Abstract

Words are defined based on their meanings in various ways in different resources. Aligning word senses across monolingual lexicographic resources increases domain coverage and enables integration and incorporation of data. In this paper, we explore the application of classification methods using manually-extracted features along with representation learning techniques in the task of word sense alignment and semantic relationship detection. We demonstrate that the performance of classification methods dramatically varies based on the type of semantic relationships due to the nature of the task but outperforms the previous experiments.

1 Introduction

Dictionaries are valuable resources which document the life of words in a language from various points of view. Creating and maintaining such resources for a constantly changing phenomenon like human language requires much time and effort. With the expansion of collaboratively-curated resources such as Wiktionary, processing lexicographical resources automatically and efficiently is of high importance recently in computational lexicography, computational linguistics and natural language processing (NLP).

Senses, or definitions, are important components of dictionaries where dictionary entries, i.e. lemmata, are described in plain language. Therefore, unlike other properties such as references, comparisons (*cf.*), synonyms and antonyms, senses are unique in the sense that they are more descriptive but also highly contextualized. Moreover, unlike lemmata which remain identical through resources in the same language, except in spelling variations, senses can undergo tremendous changes based on the choice of the editor, lexicographer and publication period, to mention but a few factors. Therefore, the task of word sense alignment (WSA) will facilitate the integration of various resources and the creation of inter-linked language resources.

Considering the literature, various components of the WSA task has been matters of research previously. However, a few of previous papers address WSA as a specific task on its own. In this paper, our focus is on providing explainable observations for the task of WSA using manually-extracted features and analyze the performance of traditional machine learning algorithms for word sense alignment as a classification problem. Despite the increasing popularity of deep learning methods in providing state-of-the-art results in various NLP fields, we believe that evaluating the performance of feature-engineered approaches is an initial and essential step to reflect the difficulties of the task and also, the expectations from the future approaches.

2 Related Work

The alignment of lexical resources has been previously of interest both to create resources and propose alignment approaches. In this section, we only focus on WSA techniques in the related literature.

Graph-based approaches have been widely used for the WSA task. Matuschek and Gurevych (2013) propose a graph-based approach, called Dijkstra-WSA, for aligning lexical-semantic resources, namely wordnet, OmegaWiki, Wiktionary and Wikipedia. In this approach, senses are represented as the nodes of a graph where the edges represent the semantic relation between them. Assuming that monosemous lemmata have a more specific meaning and therefore less ambiguous to match, a semantic relation is created among the senses of such lemmata when they appear in a sense of a polysemous lemma. Using

Dijkstra's shortest path algorithm along with semantic similarity scores and without requiring any external data or corpora, a set of possible sense matches are retrieved. In the same vein, Ahmadi et al. (Ahmadi et al., 2019) model the alignment task as a bipartite-graph where an optimal alignment solution is selected among the combination of possible sense matches in two resources. Although this algorithm performs competitively with the Dijkstra-WSA technique on the same datasets, no viable solution is provided regarding the tuning of the matching algorithm. Similarly, other authors (Nancy and Véronis, 1990; Pantel and Pennacchiotti, 2008; Meyer and Gurevych, 2010; Pilehvar and Navigli, 2014) focus on linking senses without considering semantic relationships.

Beyond aligning lexical resources, there has been much effort in inducing semantic relationships, particularly within more generic fields such as taxonomy extraction (Bordea et al., 2015), hypernym discovery (Camacho-Collados et al., 2018) and semantic textual similarity (Agirre et al., 2016). Although in these tasks the focus is on the relationship within words, there are a few works exploring how to induce semantic relationships between definitions. Heidenreich and Williams (2019) introduce an algorithm using a directed acyclic graph to construct a wordnet based on the Wiktionary data and enriched with synonym and antonym relationships. Using the semantic relationship annotations provided in Wiktionary, the method induces a semantic hierarchy by identifying a subset within each sense that can relate two lemmas together. In addition to graph-based methods, there are various other closely-related fields, such as word sense disambiguation (Maru et al., 2019) and sense embeddings (Iacobacci et al., 2015), which can potentially contribute to the task of WSA. However, we could not find any previous work exploring those approaches.

One major limitation regarding previous work is with respect to the nature of the data used for the WSA task. Expert-made resources, such as the Oxford English Dictionary, require much effort to create and therefore, are not as widely available as collaboratively-curated ones like Wiktionary[1] due to copyright restrictions. On the other hand, the latter resources lack domain coverage and descriptive senses. To address this, Ahmadi et al. (2020) present a set of 17 datasets containing monolingual dictionaries in 15 languages, annotated by language experts with five semantic relationships according to the simple knowledge organization system reference (SKOS) (Miles and Bechhofer, 2009), namely, broader, narrower, related, exact and none. Our objective within this project is to explore the alignment of these open-source datasets using classification methods.

3 Problem Definition

Ignoring the differences in dictionary structures and formats such as XML, LMF (Francopoulo et al., 2006) and Ontolex-Lemon (McCrae et al., 2017), there are different lexicographic and logical ways for describing senses in a dictionary (Solomonick, 1996). As an example, Table 3 provides the senses available for ENTIRE (adjective) in various lexical resources where the predominant sense of "whole" or "complete" is provided in all resources. However, all resources do not equally cover specific domains such as botany and mathematics. Therefore, there are differences in the number of provided senses, e.g. one sense is provided in MACMILLAN while the Oxford Dictionary provides five.

We define our task of WSA and semantic induction as the detection of the semantic relationship between a pair of senses in two monolingual resources, as follows:

$$rel = sem(p, s_i, s_j) \tag{1}$$

where p is the part-of-speech of the lemma, s_i and s_j are senses belonging to the same lexemes in two monolingual resources and rel is a semantic relation, namely exact, broader, narrower, related and none. Our goal is to predict a semantic relation, i.e. rel given a pair of senses. Therefore, we define three classification problems based on the relation:

- **Binary classification** which predicts if two senses can possibly be aligned together. Otherwise, none is selected as the target class.
- **SKOS classification** which predicts a label among `exact`, `broader`, `narrower` and `related` semantic relationships.
- **SKOS+none classification** which predicts a label given all data instances. This is similar to the previous classifier, with `none` as a target class.

[1] `www.wiktionary.org`

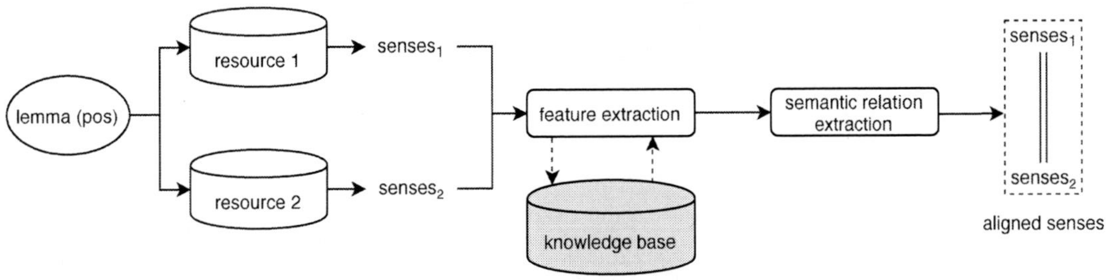

Figure 1: Our approach where features are extracted from word senses and external semantic resources

4 Approach

Assuming that the textual representation of senses as in definitions can be useful to align them, we define a few features which use the lengths of senses along with their textual and semantic similarities. In addition, we incorporate word-level semantic relationships to determine the type of relation that two senses may possibly have. To this end, we use CONCEPTNET (Speer et al., 2016), an openly-available and multilingual semantic network with relational knowledge from various other resources, such as Wiktionary and WordNet (Miller, 1995). A similar approach has been previously proposed for aligning bilingual with monolingual dictionaries (Saurí et al., 2019).

4.1 Feature Extraction

In this step, we extract sense instances from the MWSA datasets (Ahmadi et al., 2020), as $t = (p, s_i, s_j, r_{i_j})$. This instance is interpreted as sense s_i has relation r_{i_j} with sense s_j. Therefore, the order of appearance is important to correctly determine the relationship. It should also be noted that both senses belong to the same lemma with the part-of-speech p. Table 2 provides the basic statistics of the senses and their semantic relationships in various languages. # Entries and # SKOS refer to the number of entries and senses with a relationship within SKOS. In addition, the senses within the two resources which belong to the same lemma but are not annotated with a SKOS relationship, are included with a `none` relationship.

Given the class imbalance where senses with a `none` relationship are more frequent than the others, we carry out a data augmentation technique based on the symmetric property of the semantic relationships. By changing the order of the senses, also known as relation direction, in each data instance, a new instance can be created by semantically reversing the relationship. In other words, for each $t = (p, s_i, s_j, r_{ij})$ there is a $t' = (p, s_j, s_i, r'_{ij})$ where r'_{ji} is the inverse of r_{ij}. Thus, `exact` and `related` as symmetric properties remain the same, however, the asymmetric property of the `broader` and `narrower` relationships yields `narrower` and `broader`, respectively.

Once the senses extracted, we create data instances using the features in Table 1. Features 2 and 3 concern the length of senses and how they are different. Intuitively speaking, this regards the wordings used to describe two concepts and their semantic relationship. In features 4 to 11, we calculate this with and without function words, words with little lexical meaning. One additional step is to query CONCEPTNET to retrieve semantic relations between the content words in each sense pair. For instance, the two words "gelded" and "castrated" which appear in two different senses are synonyms and therefore, the whole senses can be possibly synonyms. In order to measure the reliability of the relationships, we sum up the weights, also known as *assertions*, of each relationship according to CONCEPTNET. Finally, features 12 and 13 provide the semantic similarity of each sense pair using word embeddings. For this purpose, we used GloVe (Pennington et al., 2014) and fastText[2]. The data instances are all standardized by scaling each feature to the range of [0-1].

4.2 Feature Learning

Restricted Boltzmann machine (RBM) is a generative model representing a probability distribution given a set of observations (Fischer and Igel, 2012). An RBM is composed of two layers, a visible one where the data instances according to the manually-created features are provided, and a latent one where a distribution is created by

[2]`https://fasttext.cc/`

#	feature	definition	possible values
1	POS_tag	part of speech of the headword	a one-hot vector of {N, V, ADJ, ADV, OTHER}
2	s_len_no_func_1/2	number of space-separated tokens in s_1 and s_2	$\mathbb{N}$
3	s_len_1/2	number of space-separated tokens in s_1 and s_2 without function words	$\mathbb{N}$
4	hypernymy	hypernymy score between tokens	sum of weights in CONCEPTNET
5	hyponymy	hyponymy score between tokens	sum of weights in CONCEPTNET
6	relatedness	relatedness score between tokens	sum of weights in CONCEPTNET
7	synonymy	synonymy score between tokens	sum of weights in CONCEPTNET
8	antonymy	antonymy score between tokens	sum of weights in CONCEPTNET
9	meronymy	meronymy score between tokens	sum of weights in CONCEPTNET
10	similarity	similarity score between tokens	sum of weights in CONCEPTNET
11	sem_sim	semantic similarity score between senses using word embeddings	averaging word vectors and cosine similarity [0-1]
12	sem_sim_no_func	semantic similarity score between senses without function words	averaging word vectors and cosine similarity excluding function words [0-1]
13	sem_bin_rel	target class	1 for alignable, otherwise 0
14	sem_rel_with_none	target class	{exact, narrower, broader, related, none}
15	sem_rel	target class	{exact, narrower, broader, related}

Table 1: Manually extracted features for semantic classification of sense relationships

the model by retrieving dependencies within variables. In other words, the relation of the features in how the target classes are predicted is learned in the training phase. We follow the description of (Hinton, 2012) in implementing and using an RBM for learning further features from our data instances. Regarding the classification problem, instead of training our models using the data instances described in the previous section, we train the models using the latent features of an RBM model. These new features have binary values and can be configured and tuned depending on the performance of the models.

4.3 Classification Method

For this supervised classification problem, we use support vector machines (SVMs) using various hyper-parameters, as implemented in Scikit[3] (Pedregosa et al., 2011). After a preprocessing step, where the datasets are shuffled, normalized and scaled, we split them into train, test and validation sets with 80%, 10% and 10% proportions, respectively.

[3]https://scikit-learn.org

5 Experiments

Table 2 presents the best performance of the models trained for each language. In addition to an SVM, we also evaluated the usage of an RBM to learn features and classify them similarly using an SVM. Our baseline is based on the evaluation of Kernerman et al (2020) on the same datasets. The baseline provides accuracy for classifying sense pairs with a semantic relationship or none, i.e. SKOS+none, and precision, recall and F_1-measure for predicting whether two senses should be matched, i.e. binary classification. In the same vein, our evaluation is carried out using accuracy, precision, recall and as defined in (Powers, 2011), but for all classification setups.

Despite the high accuracy of the baseline systems for most languages, they do not perform equally efficiently for all languages in terms of precision and recall. Although our classifiers outperform the baselines for all the relation prediction tasks and perform competitively when trained for the binary classification and also given all data instances, there is a significant low performance when it comes to the classification of SKOS relationships. This can be explained by the lower number of instances available for these relations.

Language	# Entries	# SKOS	# SKOS+none	# All	Metric	Baseline	Binary	All	SKOS	RBM-Binary	RBM-all	RBM-SKOS
Basque	256	813	3661	4382	Accuracy	78.90	78.79	58.47	49.77	70.37	54.17	28.85
					Precision	21.10	71.40	59.21	43.65	62.14	59.08	20.73
					Recall	5.00	72.78	58.45	46.01	74.93	52.55	50.87
					F-measure	8.10	**72.08**	**58.83**	**44.80**	67.94	55.62	29.46
Bulgarian	1000	1976	3708	5656	Accuracy	72.80	70.60	65.91	34.05	73.51	63.38	36.47
					Precision	25.00	68.75	64.79	31.75	77.46	34.46	36.85
					Recall	1.10	69.32	65.44	31.83	72.91	49.87	24.86
					F-measure	2.00	69.03	**65.11**	**31.79**	**75.11**	40.76	29.69
Danish	587	1644	16520	18164	Accuracy	81.70	66.47	34.82	27.87	73.85	50.08	29.67
					Precision	3.00	74.54	23.70	36.49	60.59	60.96	30.47
					Recall	2.30	75.51	62.90	22.87	55.66	66.92	73.04
					F-measure	4.30	**75.02**	34.43	28.12	**58.02**	63.80	**43.00**
Dutch	161	622	20144	20766	Accuracy	93.60	82.55	59.99	24.75	83.90	51.47	36.34
					Precision	0.00	86.97	78.59	31.38	59.78	77.82	30.66
					Recall	0.00	88.24	79.22	33.10	67.33	39.65	66.03
					F-measure	0.00	**87.60**	**78.90**	32.22	63.33	52.54	41.88
English	684	1682	9269	10951	Accuracy	75.20	89.00	81.00	49.00	80.16	65.03	48.57
					Precision	0.00	82.35	73.03	39.31	64.36	63.67	55.53
					Recall	0.00	82.87	76.41	46.63	82.13	79.35	34.51
					F-measure	0.00	**82.61**	**74.68**	**42.66**	72.17	70.65	42.57
Estonian	684	1142	2316	3426	Accuracy	48.20	78.98	58.92	46.11	75.96	62.75	47.82
					Precision	54.50	76.06	68.83	40.81	63.53	60.67	36.63
					Recall	9.30	20.76	57.82	44.02	28.18	49.35	22.44
					F-measure	15.90	32.62	**62.85**	**42.35**	**39.05**	54.43	27.83
German	537	1211	4975	6185	Accuracy	77.77	73.14	61.99	49.58	77.97	43.23	44.21
					Precision	0.00	77.72	64.74	41.89	80.44	66.34	40.99
					Recall	0.00	54.41	59.95	43.73	22.88	27.92	48.99
					F-measure	0.00	**64.01**	**62.25**	42.79	35.63	39.30	**44.63**
Hungarian	143	949	15774	16716	Accuracy	94.00	79.65	58.40	22.95	81.46	36.27	15.20
					Precision	5.30	49.96	30.14	23.41	68.50	59.80	26.58
					Recall	1.20	54.47	37.95	68.08	56.72	73.85	29.23
					F-measure	2.00	52.12	33.60	**34.85**	**62.05**	**66.09**	27.84
Irish	680	975	2816	3763	Accuracy	58.30	75.00	55.75	26.27	79.61	60.84	24.75
					Precision	68.00	84.42	46.58	31.84	79.03	42.52	30.25
					Recall	18.50	84.46	39.85	46.15	52.47	54.65	25.40
					F-measure	29.10	**84.44**	42.95	37.68	63.06	**47.83**	27.61
Italian	207	592	2173	2758	Accuracy	69.30	59.08	55.43	44.48	77.23	46.26	43.01
					Precision	0.00	52.55	42.98	28.80	75.69	46.31	40.56
					Recall	0.00	66.47	52.64	42.16	45.05	68.67	31.27
					F-measure	0.00	**58.69**	47.32	**34.22**	56.49	**55.32**	35.32
Serbian	301	736	5808	6542	Accuracy	59.90	80.05	32.53	27.55	82.35	41.43	32.96
					Precision	19.00	76.78	48.57	43.06	73.51	37.70	21.49
					Recall	46.40	65.73	69.40	27.10	77.46	48.45	55.53
					F-measure	26.90	70.83	**57.15**	**33.26**	**75.43**	42.40	30.99
Slovenian	152	244	1100	1343	Accuracy	44.20	84.29	36.13	26.13	78.93	39.57	31.63
					Precision	17.30	73.08	23.19	46.98	78.62	38.59	20.97
					Recall	58.70	83.22	45.07	28.61	41.64	28.09	33.02
					F-measure	26.80	**77.82**	30.62	**35.56**	54.45	**32.51**	25.65
Spanish	351	1071	4898	5919	Accuracy	-	73.79	54.67	30.28	80.71	54.38	58.48
					Precision	-	79.78	55.07	33.21	79.40	42.54	39.57
					Recall	-	80.37	53.15	40.04	60.18	20.68	38.59
					F-measure	-	**80.07**	**54.10**	36.31	68.47	27.83	**39.07**
Portuguese	147	275	2062	2337	Accuracy	92.10	71.31	66.62	51.71	73.14	55.69	42.87
					Precision	8.30	49.29	58.23	53.52	77.72	69.41	40.45
					Recall	2.40	37.47	70.41	53.47	54.41	22.32	38.15
					F-measure	3.70	42.57	**63.74**	**53.49**	**64.01**	33.78	39.26
Russian	213	483	3376	3845	Accuracy	75.40	60.88	58.90	37.75	75.80	59.76	33.10
					Precision	43.80	72.92	63.83	27.28	73.38	73.77	32.71
					Recall	17.90	82.21	44.43	36.74	68.23	70.39	47.75
					F-measure	25.50	**77.29**	52.39	31.31	70.71	**72.04**	**38.82**

Table 2: Basic statistics of the datasets and the best classification results with and without an RBM. # refers to the number

Moreover, distinguishing certain types of relationships, such as `related` versus `exact`, is a challenging task even for an expert annotator. For instance, the relationship between two senses of ENTIRE in Table 3, "constituting the undiminished entirety" and "complete in all parts; undivided; undiminished; whole" is annotated as `narrower` and `exact` by two different annotators [4].

Regarding the performance of RBM, we do not observe a similar improvement in the results of all classifiers. The precision of the models which learn features with an RBM is higher in the majority of cases. Our optimal models where trained with 50 iterations, a learning rate within [0.05-0.2] and a hidden unit number within the range of 400 and 600.

6 Conclusion and Future Work

This paper presents a preliminary study on the task of word sense alignment using monolingual lexicographic datasets from 15 languages. The task is modeled as a classification task where data

[4]According to the datasets available at https://github.com/elexis-eu/MWSA

instances are extracted using various manually-defined features. The classification task aims at classifying sense matches across dictionaries and also, prediction of the semantic relationship between two given senses, namely narrower, broader, exact and related. The results indicate a better performance of the proposed approach with respect to the baselines reported previously.

One major limitation of the current approach is the usage of crafted features. We believe that as a future work further techniques can be used, particularly thanks to the current advances in word representations and neural networks. In addition, incorporating knowledge bases and external language resources such as corpora can be beneficial in improving to address sense ambiguity for polysemous entries.

Acknowledgements

The authors would like to thank the three anonymous reviewers for their insightful suggestions and careful reading of the manuscript. This work has received funding from the EU's Horizon 2020 Research and Innovation programme through the ELEXIS project under grant agreement No. 731015.

References

[Agirre et al.2016] Eneko Agirre, Aitor Gonzalez Agirre, Inigo Lopez-Gazpio, Montserrat Maritxalar, German Rigau Claramunt, and Larraitz Uria. 2016. Semeval-2016 task 2: Interpretable semantic textual similarity. In *SemEval-2016 Task 2: Interpretable semantic textual similarity. SemEval-2016. 10th International Workshop on Semantic Evaluation; 2016 Jun 16-17; San Diego, CA. Stroudsburg (PA): ACL; 2016. p. 512-24.* ACL (Association for Computational Linguistics).

[Ahmadi et al.2019] Sina Ahmadi, Mihael Arcan, and John McCrae. 2019. Lexical sense alignment using weighted bipartite b-matching. In *Proceedings of the LDK 2019 Workshops*. 2nd Conference on Language, Data and Knowledge (LDK 2019).

[Ahmadi et al.2020] Sina Ahmadi, John P McCrae, Sanni Nimb, Fahad Khan, Monica Monachini, Bolette S Pedersen, Thierry Declerck, Tanja Wissik, Andrea Bellandi, Irene Pisani, et al. 2020. A multilingual evaluation dataset for monolingual word sense alignment. In *Proceedings of the 12th Language Resource and Evaluation Conference (LREC 2020)*.

[Bordea et al.2015] Georgeta Bordea, Paul Buitelaar, Stefano Faralli, and Roberto Navigli. 2015. SemEval-2015 task 17: Taxonomy extraction evaluation (TExEval). In *Proceedings of the 9th International Workshop on Semantic Evaluation (SemEval 2015)*, pages 902–910, Denver, Colorado, June. Association for Computational Linguistics.

[Camacho-Collados et al.2018] Jose Camacho-Collados, Claudio Delli Bovi, Luis Espinosa-Anke, Sergio Oramas, Tommaso Pasini, Enrico Santus, Vered Shwartz, Roberto Navigli, and Horacio Saggion. 2018. SemEval-2018 task 9: Hypernym discovery. In *Proceedings of the 12th International Workshop on Semantic Evaluation (SemEval-2018); 2018 Jun 5-6; New Orleans, LA. Stroudsburg (PA): ACL; 2018. p. 712–24.* ACL (Association for Computational Linguistics).

[Fischer and Igel2012] Asja Fischer and Christian Igel. 2012. An introduction to restricted Boltzmann machines. In *Iberoamerican congress on pattern recognition*, pages 14–36. Springer.

[Francopoulo et al.2006] Gil Francopoulo, Monte George, Nicoletta Calzolari, Monica Monachini, Nuria Bel, Mandy Pet, and Claudia Soria. 2006. Lexical markup framework (LMF). In *Proceedings of the Fifth International Conference on Language Resources and Evaluation (LREC'06)*, Genoa, Italy, May. European Language Resources Association (ELRA).

[Heidenreich and Williams2019] Hunter Heidenreich and Jake Williams. 2019. Latent semantic network induction in the context of linked example senses. In *Proceedings of the 5th Workshop on Noisy User-generated Text (W-NUT 2019)*, pages 170–180.

[Hinton2012] Geoffrey E Hinton. 2012. A practical guide to training restricted Boltzmann machines. In *Neural networks: Tricks of the trade*, pages 599–619. Springer.

[Iacobacci et al.2015] Ignacio Iacobacci, Mohammad Taher Pilehvar, and Roberto Navigli. 2015. Sensembed: Learning sense embeddings for word and relational similarity. In *Proceedings of the 53rd Annual Meeting of the Association for Computational Linguistics and the 7th International Joint Conference on Natural Language Processing (Volume 1: Long Papers)*, pages 95–105.

[Kernerman et al.2020] Ilan Kernerman, Simon Krek, John P. McCrae, Jorge Gracia, Sina Ahmadi, and Besim Kabashi, editors. 2020. *Proceedings of the 2020 Globalex Workshop on Linked Lexicography*, Marseille, France, May. European Language Resources Association.

[Maru et al.2019] Marco Maru, Federico Scozzafava, Federico Martelli, and Roberto Navigli. 2019. SyntagNet: challenging supervised word sense disambiguation with lexical-semantic combinations. In

Proceedings of the 2019 Conference on Empirical Methods in Natural Language Processing and the 9th International Joint Conference on Natural Language Processing (EMNLP-IJCNLP), pages 3525–3531.

[Matuschek and Gurevych2013] Michael Matuschek and Iryna Gurevych. 2013. Dijkstra-WSA: A graph-based approach to word sense alignment. *Transactions of the Association for Computational Linguistics*, 1:151–164.

[McCrae et al.2017] John P McCrae, Julia Bosque-Gil, Jorge Gracia, Paul Buitelaar, and Philipp Cimiano. 2017. The Ontolex-Lemon model: development and applications. In *Proceedings of eLex 2017 conference*, pages 19–21.

[Meyer and Gurevych2010] Christian M Meyer and Iryna Gurevych. 2010. Worth its weight in gold or yet another resource—a comparative study of Wiktionary, OpenThesaurus and GermaNet. In *International Conference on Intelligent Text Processing and Computational Linguistics*, pages 38–49. Springer.

[Miles and Bechhofer2009] Alistair Miles and Sean Bechhofer. 2009. SKOS simple knowledge organization system reference. *W3C recommendation*, 18:W3C.

[Miller1995] George A Miller. 1995. WordNet: a lexical database for English. *Communications of the ACM*, 38(11):39–41.

[Nancy and Véronis1990] I Nancy and Jean Véronis. 1990. Mapping dictionaries: A spreading activation approach. In *6th Annual Conference of the Centre for the New Oxford English Dictionary*, pages 52–64. Citeseer.

[Pantel and Pennacchiotti2008] Patrick Pantel and Marco Pennacchiotti. 2008. Automatically Harvesting and Ontologizing Semantic Relations. In *Proceedings of the 2008 Conference on Ontology Learning and Population: Bridging the Gap between Text and Knowledge*, page 171–195, NLD. IOS Press.

[Pedregosa et al.2011] F. Pedregosa, G. Varoquaux, A. Gramfort, V. Michel, B. Thirion, O. Grisel, M. Blondel, P. Prettenhofer, R. Weiss, V. Dubourg, J. Vanderplas, A. Passos, D. Cournapeau, M. Brucher, M. Perrot, and E. Duchesnay. 2011. Scikit-learn: Machine Learning in Python. *Journal of Machine Learning Research*, 12:2825–2830.

[Pennington et al.2014] Jeffrey Pennington, Richard Socher, and Christopher D Manning. 2014. Glove: Global vectors for word representation. In *Proceedings of the 2014 conference on empirical methods in natural language processing (EMNLP)*, pages 1532–1543.

[Pilehvar and Navigli2014] Mohammad Taher Pilehvar and Roberto Navigli. 2014. A robust approach to aligning heterogeneous lexical resources. In *Proceedings of the 52nd Annual Meeting of the Association for Computational Linguistics (Volume 1: Long Papers)*, pages 468–478.

[Powers2011] David Martin Powers. 2011. Evaluation: from precision, recall and F-measure to ROC, informedness, markedness and correlation.

[Saurí et al.2019] Roser Saurí, Louis Mahon, Irene Russo, and Mironas Bitinis. 2019. Cross-Dictionary Linking at Sense Level with a Double-Layer Classifier. In *2nd Conference on Language, Data and Knowledge (LDK 2019)*. Schloss Dagstuhl-Leibniz-Zentrum fuer Informatik.

[Solomonick1996] Abraham Solomonick. 1996. Towards a comprehensive theory of lexicographic definitions. In *Euralex 1996 Conference Proceedings*, pages 1–8.

[Speer et al.2016] Robyn Speer, Joshua Chin, and Catherine Havasi. 2016. ConceptNet 5.5: An open multilingual graph of general knowledge. *arXiv preprint arXiv:1612.03975*.

Appendix

ENTIRE (adjective)	
WORDNET[5]	- (of leaves or petals) having a smooth edge; not broken up into teeth or lobes - constituting the full quantity or extent; complete - constituting the undiminished entirety; lacking nothing essential especially not damaged - (used of domestic animals) sexually competent
WEBSTER[6]	- complete in all parts; undivided; undiminished; whole; full and perfect; not deficient - without mixture or alloy of anything; unqualified; morally whole; pure; faithful - not gelded; – said of a horse - internal; interior.
WIKTIONARY[7]	- (sometimes postpositive) Whole; complete. - (botany) Having a smooth margin without any indentation. - (botany) Consisting of a single piece, as a corolla. - (complex analysis, of a complex function) Complex-differentiable on all of $\mathbb{C}$. - (of a male animal) Not gelded. - morally whole; pure; sheer
MACMILLAN[8]	- used for emphasizing that you mean all or every part of something
LONGMAN[9]	- used when you want to emphasize that you mean all of a group, period of time, amount etc
Oxford[10]	[attributive] - with no part left out; whole. - Without qualification or reservations; absolute. - Not broken, damaged, or decayed. - (of a male horse) not castrated. - Botany (of a leaf) without indentations or division into leaflets.
Cambridge[11]	- whole or complete, with nothing lacking, or continuous, without interruption

Table 3: Senses of ENTIRE (adjective) in various monolingual English dictionaries

Extraction of Common-Sense Relations from Procedural Task Instructions using BERT

Viktor Losing, Lydia Fischer, Joerg Deigmoeller

Honda Research Institute Europe
Carl Legien Strasse 17, Offenbach, Germany

Abstract

Manipulation-relevant common-sense knowledge is crucial to support action-planning for complex tasks. In particular, instrumentality information of what can be done with certain tools can be used to limit the search space which is growing exponentially with the number of viable options. Typical sources for such knowledge, structured common-sense knowledge bases such as ConceptNet or WebChild, provide a limited amount of information which also varies drastically across different domains. Considering the recent success of pre-trained language models such as BERT, we investigate whether common-sense information can directly be extracted from semi-structured text with an acceptable annotation effort. Concretely, we compare the common-sense relations obtained from ConceptNet versus those extracted with BERT from large recipe databases. In this context, we propose a scoring function, based on the WordNet taxonomy to match specific terms to more general ones, enabling a rich evaluation against a set of ground-truth relations.

1 Introduction

Lately, AI-based methods advanced rapidly in their capabilities leading to the tackling of ever more challenging tasks. This progress is expected to continue and to potentially culminate in general-purpose intelligence within a few decades (Müller and Bostrom, 2016). However, current systems are designed for highly specific tasks and lack crucial capabilities for their application in a broader context. In particular, they have insufficient common-sense knowledge and reasoning capabilities. Common-sense knowledge are essential facts humans acquire throughout our life and which are frequently applied for everyday tasks, mostly in a subconscious manner. However, such knowledge is rarely expressed as it is unnecessary to state the obvious, making it highly elusive. This paper addresses this challenge and focuses on the acquisition of common-sense knowledge. Concretely, we are interested in manipulation-relevant knowledge that can support action planning, answering questions such as "What do I need to cut a bread?" or "What can I do with a knife?". The acquisition is framed as a relation-extraction task where we focus on the instrumentality relations between tools, actions and objects in the kitchen domain.

The classical approach to acquire common sense knowledge is to query publicly available knowledge bases. However, since common-sense information is scarcely expressed, there exist only a few dedicated sources (Speer and Havasi, 2013; Tandon et al., 2017). The most prominent one is the ConceptNet knowledge graph (Speer and Havasi, 2013), which is widely used in various applications (Camacho-Collados et al., 2017; Bosselut et al., 2019; Mihaylov and Frank, 2018). It connects words and phrases of natural language with labeled assertions, so-called predicates. The main issue of ConceptNet and similar sources is that the provided amount of information is rather limited, due to the fact that crowd-sourcing is an ineffective strategy for collecting common-sense information. The incentive for the public to contribute is weak as the information by definition is common sense and widely known. Furthermore, the amount and granularity of the information varies substantially across different topics, making it rather unclear to assess its relevance for specific applications.

Recently published language models such as BERT or GPT2 (Devlin et al., 2018; Radford et al., 2018) constitute a drastic leap forward in the domain of natural language processing (NLP) as they distinctly improved benchmarks in the tasks of language translation, question answering, named entity recognition and many more. These large neural networks are pre-trained on a massive amount of unsupervised data and can be fine-tuned to different tasks based on comparably few labeled examples. Considering their success story, it is interesting to investigate their effectiveness in the extraction of common-sense information from widely available text databases. Such an approach is scalable as the models can easily process additional sources.

In this paper, we apply this concept to acquire instrumentality relations from procedural task instructions, more specifically recipes. Procedural task instructions are one of the few sources where common-sense knowledge is made explicit because they aim to instruct humans to perform a task they are potentially unfamiliar with. Concretely, we fine-tune BERT to learn the relation extraction using a few labeled examples and compare the yielded relation set against the one of ConceptNet. The evaluation is based on a set of ground-truth relations, which we collect in a study. In this context, we propose a scoring function to match specific terms to more general ones based on the WordNet taxonomy. The extensive evaluation underlines the effectiveness of BERT, leading to distinctly more relations with an acceptable proportion of false relations that can flexibly be adjusted with standard filtering techniques.

2 Related Work

The lack of common-sense knowledge and reasoning capabilities was recently addressed in DARPA's "Machine common sense" initiative (Gunning, 2018) and led to an increased attention within the research community. Various new sources for common-sense knowledge have been established since. ATOMIC (Sap et al., 2019), for example, provides a database with causes and effects of common everyday actions such as making a coffee. WebChild (Tandon et al., 2017) is a common-sense knowledge graph that provides in contrast to other sources also comparative knowledge using relations such as "larger than" between different concepts. It does not rely on crowd-sourcing, but instead uses different algorithms to accumulate the knowledge on the basis of large text corpora. Databases for visual common-sense have been recently proposed by Goyal et al. (2017).

Sources derived from Wikipedia such as DB-Pedia (Lehmann et al., 2015), Yago (Suchanek et al., 2007) or WikiData (Vrandecic and Krötzsch, 2014) have often been used to extract common-sense knowledge from. Jebbara et al. (2019) proposed multiple score-functions in to rank relations that encode prototypical locations of objects. They relied on crowd-sourcing, DBPedia and annotated image databases to generate ground truth relations to evaluate their methods. Manipulation-related knowledge is particularly interesting in the field of robotics, where explicit action representations are based on relations between one action and the manipulated object (Zech et al., 2019). Such relations are extracted from video (Yang et al., 2014), text data (Jebbara et al., 2019; Kaiser et al., 2014) or even multiple modalities (Yang et al., 2016).

Common-sense knowledge is tackled in a broad range of topics. Zhou et al. tackled temporal common-sense by proposing dedicated datasets and a specific language model that outperforms BERT on the task of classifying typical events according to their temporal properties (Zhou et al., 2019; Zhou et al., 2020). Common-sense properties of word embeddings were extracted by Yang et al. (2018) using a zero-shot learning approach. This enables a property-based comparison of entities to answer questions like "Is an elephant bigger than a tiger?". Hu et al. (2019) augmented the entities contained in the SQuAD dataset (Rajpurkar et al., 2016) with common-sense knowledge from ConceptNet and WordNet, allowing them to answer a variety of additional questions about the entities.

Recent work focuses on the extraction of action effects, i. e. how does the object state changes when certain actions are applied (Gao et al., 2018). In this regard, the action context is often encoded as well (Baker et al., 1998; Palmer et al., 2005; Yang et al., 2016; Chai, 2018), which is similar to the linguistic concept of verb semantics (Wu and Palmer, 1994). Verb semantics describe the meaning of a verb within a context depending on the "agent" (the one executing the action), the "patient" (here the object on which the action is applied on) and an instrument (the tool used for manipulation).

Fine-tuning BERT has been done for various tasks. Recently, Wang et al. (2019) proposed a two-step process for entity relation extraction from documents and argued for its adoption as new task baseline, since it clearly outperformed the current baseline approach (LSTM).

In contrast to the mentioned work, our contribution provides three novel aspects. First, it investigates the viability of common-sense relation extraction using pre-trained models that are fine-tuned with a very small amount of labeled examples for a specific application. Second, it measures the relevance of the extracted relations based on their coverage of a ground-truth relation set, thereby proposing a scoring function to consider the matching between specific and more general terms. Lastly, it compares the relation set against the one contained in ConceptNet, which provides insight into ConceptNet's practical relevance for the specific application.

3 Approach

We are interested in acquiring instrumentality relations for the kitchen domain. Specifically, we want to know the relevant tools for certain tasks. For instance, a knife can be used for cutting bread, but a cutting board may be helpful as well. A relation $r = (t, a, o)$ is a triplet consisting of three strings, where t encodes one tool and the associated task is described by action a and object o. Some examples for relevant relations are (knife, cut, bread), (fridge, cool, food), and (bowl, mix, salad).

We use BERT to extract such information from large text corpora, where the text is loosely structured. In the past, powerful models required a large amounts of labeled data to achieve a reasonable performance, making such approaches not applicable for most applications. However, pre-trained models have drastically reduced the label-burden and simultaneously increased their performance. The main advantage of this approach in comparison to the extraction from structured database is its scalability. Once the model is trained it can easily be applied on vast amounts of available text to harness the desired information. Hence, more relations can be extracted with a higher language variety as are contained in current common-sense databases. Furthermore, it can be applied on other domains as long as text corpora cover the relevant relations. The disadvantage is the necessity of annotating some examples for the specific application. In the following, we describe the approach in detail and also propose an evaluation metric to measure the match between two relation sets. This is crucial to determine the relevance of the extracted relations according to a set of ground-truth relations.

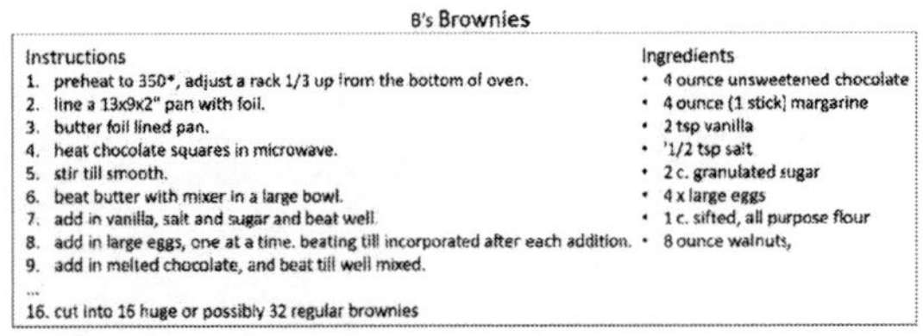
B's Brownies

Instructions	Ingredients
1. preheat to 350*, adjust a rack 1/3 up from the bottom of oven.	• 4 ounce unsweetened chocolate
2. line a 13x9x2" pan with foil.	• 4 ounce (1 stick) margarine
3. butter foil lined pan.	• 2 tsp vanilla
4. heat chocolate squares in microwave.	• '1/2 tsp salt
5. stir till smooth.	• 2 c. granulated sugar
6. beat butter with mixer in a large bowl.	• 4 x large eggs
7. add in vanilla, salt and sugar and beat well.	• 1 c. sifted, all purpose flour
8. add in large eggs, one at a time. beating till incorporated after each addition.	• 8 ounce walnuts,
9. add in melted chocolate, and beat till well mixed.	
...	
16. cut into 16 huge or possibly 32 regular brownies	

Figure 1: One recipe of *Recipe1M+*. Only a few instructions contain a complete relation.

3.1 Relation Extraction from Recipes

An obvious source for task-specific relations are procedural task instructions from the task domain. The instructions decompose the description of how to complete a task in a step-wise manner. Single steps are phrased in a brief way, only specifying the necessary information. Examples for procedural task instructions are do-it-yourself manuals or recipes. These are nowadays publicly available for a broad range of tasks and domains. WikiHow (Koupaee and Wang, 2018) for instance is a webpage that provides procedural-task description for a broad range of everyday tasks such as "How to clean a kitchen table?", but also very specific ones as "How to take the U.S. census?".

As we are interested in the kitchen domain, we rely on the large recipe database *Recipe1M+* (Marin et al., 2019). It contains over 1 Million cooking recipes covering a broad range of topics and themes with a high variety of used language. Figure 1 shows a recipe example consisting of the ingredients and the instructions. We only use the latter. Even though procedural task instructions are usually densely packed with relations, the extraction is still a challenging problem as these are phrased in a peculiar language, often neglecting a valid English grammar. Instructions can be very brief, use domain-specific terms and often require the context of previous steps for resolving ambiguous references.

3.1.1 Token Classification

We frame the relation extraction from instructions as a token-classification task, where tools, actions, and objects are mapped to their respective token labels. A set of labeled instructions is used to fine tune BERT. From each instruction at most one relation is extracted. The model solely accesses the single instruction, i. e. it does not consider previous instructions. In fact, most instructions do not explicitly name a complete relation as can be seen in the example of Figure 1. Only instructions 4 and

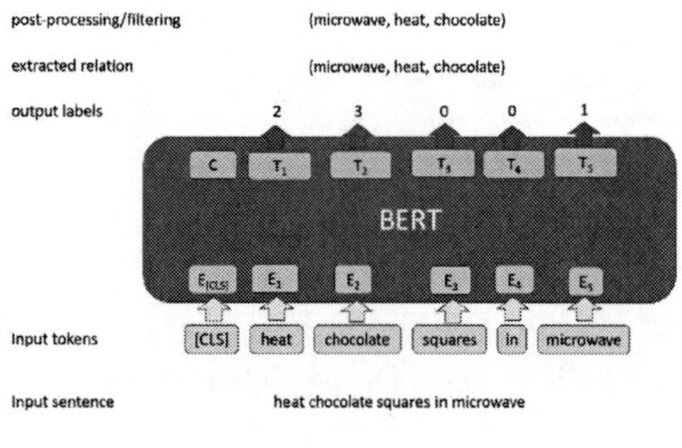

Figure 2: Overview of the processing pipeline.

6 contain a complete relation, whereas the others provide partial relations, requiring previous instructions or common-sense information to fill the gap. In such cases, all tokens are labeled as irrelevant. Conversely, there are instructions that contain more than one complete relation, if multiple or alternative tools are suggested to perform a task. For instance, instruction 6 of the exemplary recipe names a *mixer* and a *large bowl* as required tools to beat the butter. Here, we simply label the relation that gets mentioned first and ignore the other. This limitation of the token-classification was accepted in favour of its simplicity as our focus is to demonstrate easy-to-use alternatives to common-sense knowledge bases. Nonetheless, there is uncovered potential to increase the data efficiency of the models by applying more sophisticated architectures that are able to extract relations across instructions or consider multiple relations per instruction. Altogether, we annotated 400 instructions for fine-tuning of which 230 contain a valid relation.

Figure 2 shows the pipeline of the relation extraction. An instruction is tokenized and fed into the fine-tuned BERT model. The related output labels are concatenated to the relation structure and validated by a post-processing step.

3.2 Post-processing

Some of the extracted relations are filtered or modified to reduce the amount of false relations. Formally, let V be the set of all WordNet lemmas that are assigned to verb-synsets and N the ones assigned to noun-synsets. Furthermore, let T be the set of predefined tools. A given relation $r = (t, a, o)$ is only kept if:

$$a \in V \land o \in N \land \exists t_i \in T : substring(t_i, t),$$

where $substring(a, b)$ is a boolean function that determines whether a is a substring of b.

Figure 3: The set of predefined tools.

Assuming the relation is kept, we still have to map t to a concrete tool $\hat{t} \in T$. Here, our goal is to conserve the specificity of the extracted tool. For instance, assume t = "big fruit knife" than we prefer to map it to "fruit knife" over the more general term "knife". Therefore, we choose the $\hat{t} \in T$ that is the longest substring of t, i. e. $\hat{t} = \arg\max_{t_i \in T} \mathbb{1}(substring(t_i, t))|t_i|$.

3.3 Ground-Truth Relations

There are various possibilities to estimate the quality of common-sense relations. One viable approach is to estimate the number of "correct" relations, based on sampling and manual inspection. However, it neglects the quality aspect as some relations are clearly more common and intuitive than others. Instead, we count the amount of matched ground-truth relations, that were proposed in a study as common relations. We predefined 63 tools as depicted in Figure 3, and asked ten subjects to provide relations for those.

Neither the actions nor the corresponding objects were restricted, but we provided a few instructive examples. The subjects had 20 minutes to come up with as many relations as possible. Altogether, 539 relations were collected of which 386 are unique. Table 1 shows the most frequently named relations.

3.4 Relation Matching

Given a set of m ground-truth relations $G := \{(t_1, a_1, o_1), \ldots, (t_m, a_m, o_m)\}$ and a set of n candidate relations $C = \{(\hat{t}_1, \hat{a}_1, \hat{o}_1), \ldots, (\hat{t}_n, \hat{a}_n, \hat{o}_n)\}$ we want to measure the matching error $e(G, C)$. The naive approach is to use the intersection of both sets:

Table 1: The most common relations provided by the subjects.

Relation	Recurrence
can opener, open, can	9
masher, mash, potato	9
garlic press, press, garlic	8
bread knife, cut, bread	7
grater, grate, cheese	7
coffee maker, make, coffee	6
corkscrew, open, wine bottle	5
oven, bake, cake	5
pizza cutter, cut, pizza	5
bottle opener, open, bottle	4

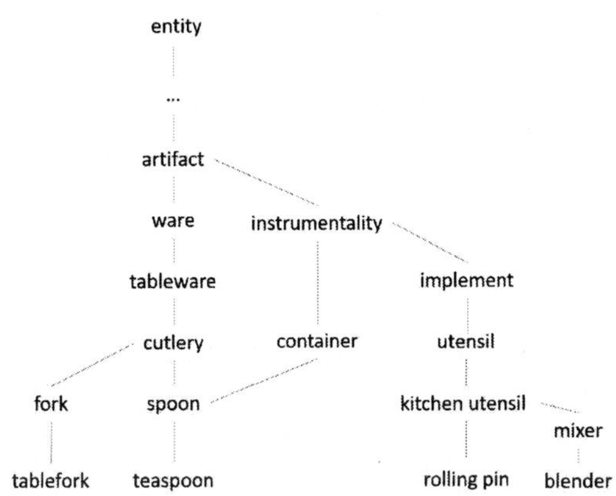

Figure 4: A fraction of the WordNet taxonomy covering a few of the predefined tools.

$e(G, C) = 1 - |G \cap C|/|G|$. However, such a measure accounts only for perfect matches, whereas it is reasonable to match against synonyms or semantically close terms. Hence, we propose a more informative matching function that utilizes the hypernym graph of WordNet. The intuition behind the matching is that a ground-truth relation can always be generalized, but never specialized. This is illustrated based on the depicted hypernym graph in Figure 4. The ground-truth relation (knife,cut,bread) can be generalized to (cutlery,cut,bread) or even (entity,cut,bread), as there is at least one hyponym of cutlery, knife itself, that is able to perform the task. In contrast, specialization entails that *all* instances can be used in such a context, which usually does not apply. In other words, if (cutlery,cut,bread) is the ground-truth relation we cannot conclude that all hyponyms of cutlery can be used as well, as spoon for instance is unsuitable. Consequently, the matching function between two relations cannot be symmetric, since it is crucial to distinguish between the ground-truth and the candidate. In other words, it is a pseudo-metric. Nonetheless, as the distance notion is quite intuitive we keep it throughout the paper. In the following, we first define the matching for single words and subsequently for whole relations.

3.4.1 Word Distance

Let each word w be assigned to a set of synsets S_w, where $S_w = \emptyset$ for words that are not represented in WordNet. The distance between the ground-truth word w and the candidate word $\hat{w}$ is the minimum distance between their synsets S_w, $S_{\hat{w}}$:

$$d(w, \hat{w}) = \min_{\forall s \in S_w, \forall \hat{s} \in S_{\hat{w}}} \hat{d}(s, \hat{s}) \quad (1)$$

Every synset s has a set of hypernym paths $P_s = \{p_1, \ldots, p_k\}$, where each path $p_i := [s_1, s_2, \ldots, s_k | s_1 = s \wedge s_k = r]$ connects s with the root synset r ("entity" is the root synset in WordNet). We denote the distance between a synset s and a path p as the index of s in p:

$$\tilde{d}(s, p) = \begin{cases} Index(s, p) & \text{if } s \in p \\ \infty & \text{otherwise.} \end{cases}$$

Finally, we are able to define the distance between a ground-truth synset s and a candidate synset $\hat{s}$

$$\hat{d}(s, \hat{s}) = \min_{\forall p \in P_s} \tilde{d}(\hat{s}, p).$$

3.4.2 Relation Distance

The distance between a ground-truth relation $r = (t, a, o)$ and the candidate $\hat{r} = (\hat{t}, \hat{a}, \hat{o})$ is simply the element-wise sum of word distances

$$D(r, \hat{r}) = d(t, \hat{t}) + d(a, \hat{a}) + d(o, \hat{o}).$$

The distance measure can be used to parameterize the error rate function with a maximum relation distance k:

$$e_k(S, \hat{S}) = \frac{1}{|S|} \sum_{i=1}^{m} \mathbb{1}(\min_{j \in \{1, \ldots n\}} D(S_i, \hat{S}_j) > k) \quad (2)$$

Varying k allows to control the matching granularity, i. e. $k = 0$ considers only perfect matches or those using the WordNet synonyms, whereas $k \to \infty$ uses the complete hypernympaths of each ground-truth word to match the candidates.

4 Experiments

Initially, we discuss the relation extraction from recipes using BERT. This evaluation is based on the small set of manually labeled instructions. Subsequently, we analyze how well these extracted relations match the set of ground-truth relations in comparison to those of ConceptNet.

4.1 Relation Extraction From Recipes

We assess BERT's relation-extraction performance based on the set of 400 annotated instructions. We use a 5-fold cross validation with 50 repetitions. Figure 5 depicts on the left the learning curves of the model regarding the classification of single tokens as well as complete relations. The correct classification of a single relation is equivalent to perfectly classifying all tokens of the corresponding instruction. Hence, an accurate token classification is required to achieve reasonable results for whole relations, as can be seen by the discrepancy in the error rates. Even with 320 training examples a very low token-classification error is achieved (7.2 %) and around half the triplets are perfectly extracted (51.5 %). Figure 5 also illustrates the effectiveness of the post-processing (see Section 3.2) as it significantly improves the relation extraction. The curve seems already to converge after 100 training instructions. However, the total amount of correctly extracted relations is further increasing (Figure 5 on the right). In other words, the post-processing rejects fewer relations and the approach becomes more efficient, extracting more relations from the same amount of data.

The error of the relation classification after post-processing (brown curve) can be interpreted as an upper bound for the proportion of false relations. However, in practice the proportion is significantly lower as can be seen by our estimates in Section 4.3.1. The small dataset naturally leads to a high variance in the performance across different repetitions. It can be expected that the error is further reduced with additional supervised data as no saturation has been reached yet. In particular, considering the discrepancy between the language type used to pre-train BERT, proper English from books and Wikipedia articles, and the one of recipes, compressed short sentences often neglecting a valid grammar, the performance is likely to improve when this mismatch is further minimized.

4.1.1 Processing the Whole Dataset

BERT is fine-tuned with all annotated instructions to extract the relation set of Recipe1M+. Overall, the dataset contains around 10 million instructions of from which our pipeline extracts 28729 unique relations. The mean recurrence rate of a triplet is 4.4 with a median of 1. Table 2 lists the most frequent relations. Relations using a mixer / blender are predominant, which is reasonable as they are used in most baking recipes.

Table 2: The most frequent relations extracted from the recipes.

Relation	Recurrence
mixer, beat, butter	3491
mixer, beat, cheese	2052
mixer, beat, egg	1082
blender, cut, butter	931
mixer, cream, butter	889
rolling pin, roll, dough	783
mixer, beat, cream	704
blender, blend, ingredients	676
blender, puree, soup,	670
mixer, beat, ingredients	603

4.2 Relation Extraction from ConceptNet

We briefly describe the straight-forward extraction from ConceptNet. Starting from our set of predefined tools we use only the relevant link-types "used for" and "capable of" to extract the relations. These link types connect the tools with single words or short phrases. We use the syntactic parsing of spaCy (Honnibal and Montani, 2017) to extract the action and object from the short phrases based on a few case-based rules. ConceptNet contains 2574 entries for our tool set and the considered link-types. However, such entries often lack an object as required for the type of relations we are aiming for, e. g. "knife-used for-cutting", "fork-used for-eating". Alltogether, we extracted 1322 complete relations that are in accordance with the WordNet vocabulary.

4.3 Relation Matching

We determine the matching rate between the ground-truth relations from the study and both extracted sets respectively. The rate is measured as defined by Equation 2. Figure 6 depicts how the matching improves when the maximum distance threshold k is increased. The recipe relations match distinctly more of the ground-truth relations. Concretely, they yield three times more "perfect" matches ($k = 0$). The relations of ConceptNet profit more from an increasing distance threshold. The probable explanation is that recipes usually use very specific terms to precisely describe the single steps, whereas ConceptNet contains information concerning more general terms that are more likely to match for larger distance thresholds. This hypothesis is supported by the fact that the average length of the hypernympaths assigned to the synsets within the ConceptNet triplets is smaller than those of the recipes (6.1 vs. 7.2). The structured data of ConceptNet facilitates the relation extraction,

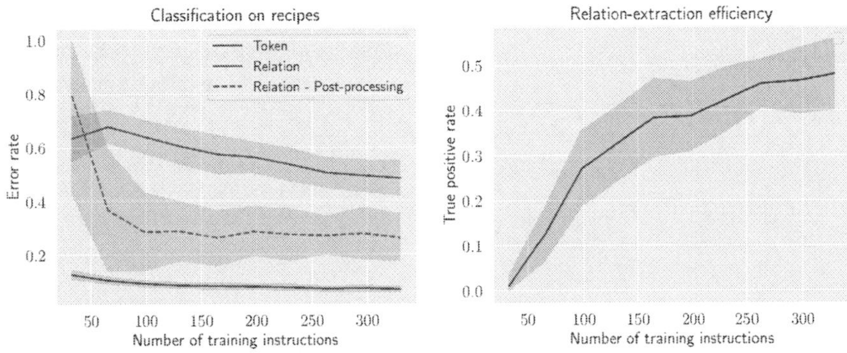

Figure 5: On the left: Learning curves of the token- and relation classification. The relation classification is depicted before (solid blue) and after post-processing(dashed brown).
On the right: Proportion of relations that are correctly extracted after post-processing.

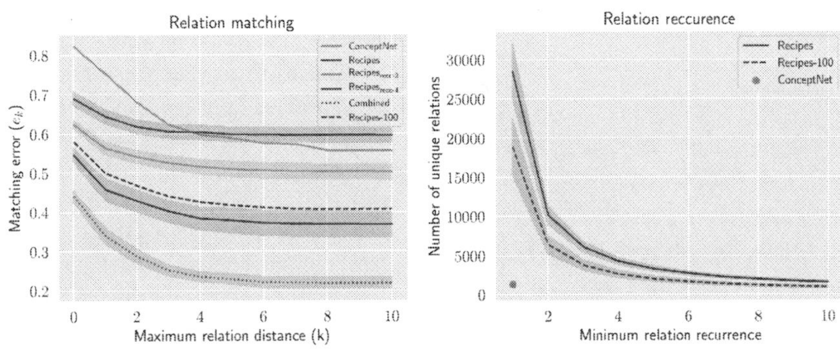

Figure 6: On the left: Matching error rate e_k for an increasing distance threshold k. The advantage of the extraction from recipes is particularly pronounced for exact matches (k=0). On the right: Amount of extracted unique relations when the minimum recurrence is varied.

leading to a naturally low rate of false relations, whereas the opposite applies for the extraction from recipes. However, the recurrence of the recipe relations can be used as confidence for their validity, providing a way to control the proportion of false relations against the number of extracted relations. Therefore, we also illustrate the performance for a minimum recurrence rate of two and four.

To assess the minimum amount of required labeled instructions, we trained another BERT model based using only 100 training instructions ("Recipe-100" in Figure 6). Its matching error is only slightly worse in comparison to the model using 400 labeled instructions, suggesting that even fewer examples may be sufficient to achieve comparable results.

Figure 6 depicts on the right the amount of unique relations amount depending on the minimum recurrence rate. Even a minimum recurrence rate of 10 yields more unique relations than ConceptNet. This graph points out the massive discrepancy in the amount of the relations yielded by BERT over those contained in ConceptNet. The BERT model trained with 100 examples extracts distinctly fewer relations, which is in line with the right plot of Figure 5 and confirms that more training examples in particular increase the data efficiency of the model. It is not surprising that the combination of both sets leads to the overall the best-performance as shown by the purple curve in Figure 6. However, it is noteworthy that the relations are complementary to some degree, since the improvement is significant (> 10 %), suggesting the fusion of both approaches.

4.3.1 Taking False Relations into Account

The correctness of common-sense relations is of utmost importance. In case of planning algorithms, false relations can prevent the generation of a plan or even result in incorrect ones, potentially leading to severe failures. In our case, false relations are

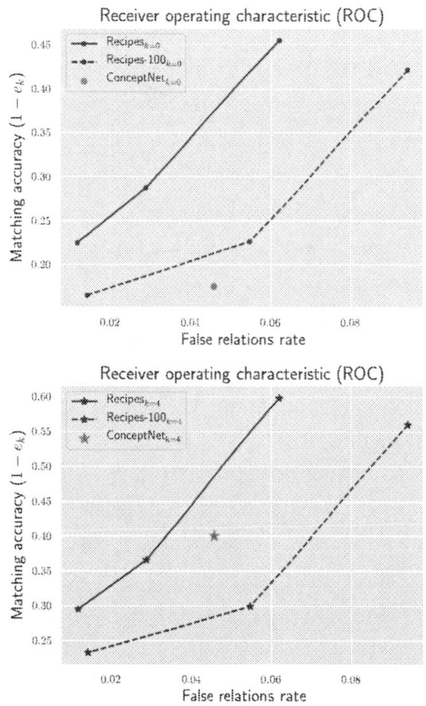

Figure 7: ROC curves for exact matches ($k = 0$, on the left) and for matches with a maximum distance of $k = 4$ (on the right). The false relation rates were determined based on sampling and manual inspection. The rates of the recipes are varied by adjusting the minimum recurrence rate.

mainly caused by the extraction process, as the relations in the recipes as well as ConceptNet generally are valid in some context.

We estimate the false relation rate based on multiple samples, thereby manually inspecting ~ 3000 relations[1]. Figure 7 shows the resulting ROC curves. Concretely, it provides ROC curves for maximum relation distances of $k \in \{0, 4\}$. In case of the recipes, we control the proportion of false relations by varying the minimum recurrence. We sampled the false relations rate for reccurence rates of $\{1, 5, 9\}$. The results of ConceptNet are represented by single points, since recurrence-based filtering is not applicable for its unique relations. The false relation rate of the recipes is reduced for higher recurrence rates. The corresponding curves yield superior results in compared to the values of ConceptNet, particularly for exact matches ($k = 0$). To put it in a nutshell, the relations extracted from recipes do not only match distinctly more relations that are naturally named by humans, but also yield a lower rate of false relations when the minimum recurrence is accordingly adjusted.

The analysis may seem to be biased, since we compare the relations of a general-purpose database with those of domain-specific procedural task instructions. Particularly, considering the fact that the kitchen domain is very popular with an abundance of publicly available data. This is a valid point and we are currently considering a comparison to sources providing procedural task instructions for a broad range of tasks such as wikiHow. However, our main point is not to stress the fact that more relations can be extracted from procedural task instructions. Instead, we demonstrate that with a relatively small effort BERT can be trained to extract these relations with a high precision leading to overall superior results.

5 Conclusion

We explored whether BERT can be used to extract common-sense relations from procedural task instructions as an alternative to querying public databases. We fine-tuned BERT for the relation extraction from recipes based on very few labeled instructions and extracted the relations from the large *Recipe1M+* dataset. To assess their relevance we collected a set of ground-truth relations in a study and proposed an evaluation measure that utilizes the WordNet hypernym graph to incorporate matches between specific and general terms. The matching granularity can naturally be adjusted, allowing a diverse analysis. The experiments highlight various advantages of the BERT based approach. It does not only yield a very large amount of unique relations (28k versus 1.3k) and correspondingly matches a large portion of the ground-truth relations, but the recurrence of the relations can also be used to reduce the proportion of false relations. Therefore, we regard the extraction of common-sense relations from text as a competitive and complementary approach, particularly considering the ongoing and rapid advance of NLP techniques.

References

Collin F. Baker, Charles J. Fillmore, and John B. Lowe. 1998. The berkeley FrameNet project. In *17th International Conference on Computational Linguistics*.

[1] The sample size for a confidence width of $w = 0.04$ is determined by the number of false relations within an initial sample of 100 relations.

Antoine Bosselut, Hannah Rashkin, Maarten Sap, Chaitanya Malaviya, Asli Celikyilmaz, and Yejin Choi. 2019. Comet: Commonsense transformers for automatic knowledge graph construction. *arXiv preprint arXiv:1906.05317*.

Jose Camacho-Collados, Mohammad Taher Pilehvar, Nigel Collier, and Roberto Navigli. 2017. Semeval-2017 task 2: Multilingual and cross-lingual semantic word similarity. In *SemEval@ACL*, pages 15–26.

Joyce Y. Chai. 2018. Language to action: Towards interactive task learning with physical agents. In *Proceedings of the 17th International Conference on Autonomous Agents and MultiAgent Systems*, AAMAS '18. International Foundation for Autonomous Agents and Multiagent Systems.

Jacob Devlin, Ming-Wei Chang, Kenton Lee, and Kristina Toutanova. 2018. Bert: Pre-training of deep bidirectional transformers for language understanding. *arXiv:1810.04805*.

Qiaozi Gao, Shaohua Yang, Joyce Chai, and Lucy Vanderwende. 2018. What action causes this? Towards naive physical action-effect prediction. In *ACL (1)*, pages 934–945.

Raghav Goyal, Samira Ebrahimi Kahou, Vincent Michalski, Joanna Materzynska, Susanne Westphal, Heuna Kim, Valentin Haenel, Ingo Fruend, Peter Yianilos, Moritz Mueller-Freitag, et al. 2017. The" something something" video database for learning and evaluating visual common sense. In *ICCV*, volume 1, page 5.

David Gunning. 2018. Machine common sense concept paper. *arXiv:1810.07528*.

Matthew Honnibal and Ines Montani. 2017. spaCy 2: Natural language understanding with Bloom embeddings, convolutional neural networks and incremental parsing. To appear.

Yidan Hu, Gongqi Lin, Yuan Miao, and Chunyan Miao. 2019. Commonsense knowledge+ bert for level 2 reading comprehension ability test. *arXiv preprint arXiv:1909.03415*.

Soufian Jebbara, Valerio Basile, Elena Cabrio, and Philipp Cimiano. 2019. Extracting common sense knowledge via triple ranking using supervised and unsupervised distributional models. *Semantic Web*, 10(1):139–158.

Peter Kaiser, Mike Lewis, Ronald P. A. Petrick, Tamim Asfour, and Mark Steedman. 2014. Extracting common sense knowledge from text for robot planning. In *ICRA*, pages 3749–3756.

Mahnaz Koupaee and William Wang. 2018. Wikihow: A large scale text summarization dataset. In *arXiv:1810.09305*.

Jens Lehmann, Robert Isele, Jakob, et al. 2015. DBpedia–a large-scale, multilingual knowledge base extracted from wikipedia. *Semantic Web*, 6(2):167–195.

Javier Marin, Aritro Biswas, Ferda Ofli, Nicholas Hynes, Amaia Salvador, Yusuf Aytar, Ingmar Weber, and Antonio Torralba. 2019. Recipe1m+: A dataset for learning cross-modal embeddings for cooking recipes and food images. *IEEE Trans. Pattern Anal. Mach. Intell.*

Todor Mihaylov and Anette Frank. 2018. Knowledgeable reader: Enhancing cloze-style reading comprehension with external commonsense knowledge. In *ACL (1)*.

Vincent C Müller and Nick Bostrom. 2016. Future progress in artificial intelligence: A survey of expert opinion. In *Fundamental issues of artificial intelligence*, pages 555–572.

Martha Palmer, Daniel Gildea, and Paul Kingsbury. 2005. The proposition bank: An annotated corpus of semantic roles.

Alec Radford, Karthik Narasimhan, Tim Salimans, and Ilya Sutskever. 2018. Improving language understanding by generative pre-training.

Pranav Rajpurkar, Jian Zhang, Konstantin Lopyrev, and Percy Liang. 2016. Squad: 100,000+ questions for machine comprehension of text. *arXiv preprint arXiv:1606.05250*.

Maarten Sap, Ronan Le Bras, Emily Allaway, Chandra Bhagavatula, Nicholas Lourie, Hannah Rashkin, Brendan Roof, Noah A Smith, and Yejin Choi. 2019. Atomic: An atlas of machine commonsense for if-then reasoning. In *Proceedings of the AAAI Conference on Artificial Intelligence*, volume 33, pages 3027–3035.

Robert Speer and Catherine Havasi. 2013. Conceptnet 5: A large semantic network for relational knowledge. In *The Peoples Web Meets NLP*, pages 161–176. Springer.

Fabian M. Suchanek, Gjergji Kasneci, and Gerhard Weikum. 2007. Yago: A core of semantic knowledge. In *International Conference on World Wide Web*, pages 697–706.

Niket Tandon, Gerard De Melo, and Gerhard Weikum. 2017. Webchild 2.0: Fine-grained commonsense knowledge distillation. In *Proceedings of ACL 2017, System Demonstrations*, pages 115–120.

Denny Vrandecic and Markus Krötzsch. 2014. Wikidata: A free collaborative knowledge base. *Communications of the ACM*, 57:78–85.

Hong Wang, Christfried Focke, Rob Sylvester, Nilesh Mishra, and William Wang. 2019. Fine-tune bert for docred with two-step process. *arXiv preprint arXiv:1909.11898*.

Zhibiao Wu and Martha Palmer. 1994. Verbs semantics and lexical selection. In *Proceedings of the 32nd annual meeting on Association for Computational Linguistics*, pages 133–138. Association for Computational Linguistics.

Yezhou Yang, Anupam Guha, Cornelia Fermüller, and Yiannis Aloimonos. 2014. Manipulation action tree bank: A knowledge resource for humanoids. In *Humanoids*, pages 987–992. IEEE.

Shaohua Yang, Qiaozi Gao, Changsong Liu, Caiming Xiong, Song-Chun Zhu, and Joyce Chai. 2016. Grounded semantic role labeling. In *HLT-NAACL*, pages 149–159.

Yiben Yang, Larry Birnbaum, Ji-Ping Wang, and Doug Downey. 2018. Extracting commonsense properties from embeddings with limited human guidance. In *Proceedings of the 56th Annual Meeting of the Association for Computational Linguistics (Volume 2: Short Papers)*, pages 644–649.

Philipp Zech, Erwan Renaudo, Simon Haller, Xiang Zhang, and Justus Piater. 2019. Action representations in robotics: A taxonomy and systematic classification. *International Journal of Robotics Research*, 38(5):518–562.

Ben Zhou, Daniel Khashabi, Qiang Ning, and Dan Roth. 2019. " going on a vacation" takes longer than" going for a walk": A study of temporal commonsense understanding. *arXiv preprint arXiv:1909.03065*.

Ben Zhou, Qiang Ning, Daniel Khashabi, and Dan Roth. 2020. Temporal common sense acquisition with minimal supervision. *arXiv preprint arXiv:2005.04304*.

The Global Wordnet Formats: Updates for 2020

John P. McCrae♣, **Michael Wayne Goodman**,♢ **Francis Bond**,♢
Alexandre Rademaker,♠ **Ewa Rudnicka**♡ and **Luís Morgado da Costa**♢
♣ Data Science Institute, NUI Galway, Ireland
♢ Nanyang Technological University, Singapore
♠IBM Research and FGV/EMAp, Brazil
♡Wrocław University of Science and Technology, Poland
john@mccr.ae, goodmami@uw.edu, bond@ieee.org
alexrad@br.ibm.com, ewa.rudnicka@pwr.edu.pl, lmorgado.dacosta@gmail.com

Abstract

The Global Wordnet Formats have been introduced to enable wordnets to have a common representation that can be integrated through the Global WordNet Grid. As a result of their adoption, a number of shortcomings of the format were identified, and in this paper we describe the extensions to the formats that address these issues. These include: ordering of senses, dependencies between wordnets, pronunciation, syntactic modelling, relations, sense keys, metadata and RDF support. Furthermore, we provide some perspectives on how these changes help in the integration of wordnets.

1 Introduction

The introduction of the Global WordNet Grid (Vossen et al., 2016) and the Collaborative Interlingual Index (Bond et al., 2016) presented a need for greater compatibility between individual wordnet projects through a common format for the representation of wordnets. As such the Global WordNet Association introduced a format with several serialization methods[1] that have been used by several projects, including the new open English WordNet (EWN; McCrae et al., 2020, 2019), the Open Multilingual Wordnet (OMW; Bond and Foster, 2013) and the Wn Python library (Goodman and Bond, 2021). Along with the increased adoption came the perception of shortcomings in the format as it was initially defined, such as the inability to capture all of the information present in Princeton WordNet (PWN; Miller, 1995; Fellbaum, 2012) or to capture some key information that other projects wished to use in their modelling. It was therefore deemed necessary to extend the model and, for this reason, we have introduced a new extended version (v1.1) of the format that covers some of these use cases.

[1] `https://globalwordnet.github.io/schemas`

In this paper, we describe the model as a reference for users and then describe the extensions that have been made to the format. In particular, there are several main areas that have been improved. Firstly, the order of words in a synset was not being captured explicitly within the model, which was information that was present in PWN, but did not have a clear semantics. Secondly, as many projects build on other projects, either by adding new information (McCrae et al., 2017) or by translating an existing wordnet, it was felt that it was important to capture the dependencies between projects. In addition, pronunciation information was something that some wordnets have or are in the process of adding, so modelling for this was added. Furthermore, we have added some new semantic relations (mainly inspired by plWordNet (Piasecki et al., 2009).

Finally, there were some technical issues to do with the modelling of syntactic behaviours, and while the current formats could capture the information, they did so in a way that was quite verbose and lead to bloated files. In addition, we fixed a few minor issues related to the representation of lexicographer files, sense keys and metadata.

2 Background

The Global WordNet Association's formats are a common data model with three(-plus) serializations in XML, JSON and various RDF formats.[2] The XML format is based on the Lexical Markup Framework (Francopoulo et al., 2006) and in particular on the version developed in the Kyoto project (Soria and Monachini, 2008). This represents the wordnet as a `LexicalResource` with a number of `Lexicons`, one for each language, along with multiple metadata elements about the lexicon, including identifiers, version, language, license, contact email,

[2] Any RDF serialization is valid, but for this paper we consider the Turtle form of RDF.

citation, etc. The format splits the data into two distinct elements, the LexicalEntry, which contains the syntactic information about the usage of individual words, and the Synset, which provides the semantic information about the synset and the relations to other synsets.

```
<LexicalEntry id="ex-rabbit-n">
  <Lemma writtenForm="rabbit"
         partOfSpeech="n"/>
  <Sense id="ex-rabbit-n-1"
         synset="ex-s1"/>
</LexicalEntry>

<Synset id="ex-s1">
  <Definition>Example
    definition</Definition>
  <SynsetRelation
    relType="hypernym"
    target="ex-s2"/>
</Synset>
```

The JSON schema is very close to this and is defined by means of both a JSON Schema description and also a JSON-LD context, that means that it can be easily interpreted as an RDF file as well. The same example in JSON is rendered as follows:

```
{
  "entry": [{
    "@id": "ex-rabbit-n",
    "lemma": {
      "writtenForm": "rabbit" },
    "partOfSpeech": "noun",
    "sense": [{
      "@id": "ex-rabbit-n-1",
      "synset": "ex-s1"
    }]
  }],
  "synset": [{
    "@id": "ex-s1",
    "definition": [{
      "gloss":
"Example definition"
    }],
    "relations": [{
      "relType": "hypernym",
      "target": "ex-s2"
    }]
  }]
}
```

The RDF version of this as serialized in Turtle is very similar and uses the OntoLex-Lemon vocabulary (Cimiano et al., 2016) to express most of the elements along with a small wordnet specific ontology that is published at https://globalwordnet.github.io/schemas/wn.

```
<#ex-rabbit-n>
  a ontolex:LexicalEntry ;
  ontolex:canonicalForm [
    ontolex:writtenRep "rabbit"@en
  ] ;
  wn:partOfSpeech wn:noun ;
  ontolex:sense <#ex-rabbit-n-1> .

<#ex-rabbit-n-1>
  a ontolex:LexicalSense ;
  ontolex:reference <#ex-s1> .

<#ex-s1>
  a ontolex:LexicalConcept ;
  wn:definition [
    rdf:value "Example definition"@en
  ] .

[] vartrans:source <#ex-s1> ;
 vartrans:category wn:hypernym ;
 vartrans:target <#ex-s2> .
```

3 Updates to the WordNet Schemas

3.1 Ordering within/of Synsets

The ordering of words in a synset and, correspondingly, the order of synsets (senses) of a word can be used to model the relative importance of synsets and words. While many wordnets do not systematically order their senses or synsets, the ordering is something that we would like the format to be able to capture. The latter issue, the order of senses of a word, has been captured in the XML by means of the order of the <Sense> tags. However, the converse information was being lost in the format. Resources such as the open English WordNet were preserving this by means of encoding it within the sense identifiers with a new attribute members. In the following example, we see that the order of the senses of 'rabbit' is ex-synset-1 followed by ex-synset-2, while the order of the lemmas in ex-synset-1 is 'rabbit', 'bunny'.

```
<LexicalEntry id="ex-rabbit-n">
  <Lemma writtenForm="rabbit"
         partOfSpeech="n"/>
  <Sense id="ex-rabbit-n-1"
    synset="ex-synset-1"/>
```

```
  <Sense id="ex-rabbit-n-2"
    synset="ex-synset-2"/>
</LexicalEntry>
<Synset id="ex-synset-1"
  members="ex-rabbit-n
           ex-bunny-n"/>
```

3.2 WordNet Dependencies and Extensions

Most wordnets are not built in isolation, but expect and depend upon the entities and relationships of other wordnets. We acknowledge two categories of such dependencies: concept-relation dependencies and lexicon extensions. The first is for wordnets built by the *expand* methodology (Vossen, 1998) whereby lexical entries and senses in the new language are defined around the concept structure of a larger wordnet which is almost always PWN. The second is for supplementary resources that build on top of an existing wordnet, for instance to add new lexical entries, senses, synsets, or relations. As this is a new feature, we are keeping it simple and only allowing monotonic effects. Destructive extensions that, for instance, remove entries or senses from a lexicon or selective dependencies that exclude certain relations are left to future work.

3.2.1 Concept-Relation Dependencies

Wordnets included in the Open Multilingual Wordnet (OMW; Bond and Foster, 2013) are linked together using CILI IDs. This linking allows for cross-lingual searches and the sharing of wordnet structure through synset relations, but it also means that most wordnets, particularly smaller ones, are dependent on the others for their structure. This approach works well when the OMW is taken as a holistic, multilingual resource but, as it is left implicit which structure-providing wordnets are required, it is not straightforward to use a wordnet in isolation of the full OMW, e.g., for experimental purposes. This issue is even more pronounced for wordnets that are not included in the OMW. What we need, then, is a way for a wordnet to specify what other resources are required, much as how software projects specify their dependencies. We therefore introduce a new `Requires` element which selects the `id` and `version` attributes of an external lexicon that should be loaded along with the current lexicon for it to behave as expected. For example, the following specifies that the Japanese Wordnet (Isahara et al., 2008; Bond et al., 2008) depends on the PWN for its synset relations:

```
<Lexicon id="wnja" id="2.0">
  <Requires id="pwn" version="3.0"/>
</Lexicon>
```

The purpose is to declare what, exactly, is required so that an application that hosts the wordnets can signal to the user if dependencies are unmet, or to limit the wordnets that may be used when traversing external synset relations. It is left implicit which elements or kinds of elements from the external wordnet become available to the dependent wordnet but, following the OMW's behaviour, an application may choose to only allow synset relations and not, say, synsets or lexical entries. The `Requires` declarations are not only for expand-wordnets, but whenever a lexicon wants to reuse synset relations from another, as discussed in the next section.

3.2.2 Lexicon Extensions

A lexicon extension is an augmentation of an existing resource. For instance, someone may want to publish an extension providing domain-specific jargon, a list of common misspellings, or neologisms that may soon fall out of use (McCrae et al., 2017). An extension could even just provide additional relations between synsets. These entries and relations may not be a good fit for inclusion in the primary project, or perhaps the release cadence of the project is too slow for the user to wait for the entries to be added to the wordnet.

These situations would be well-served by the use of a partial wordnet that could be loaded alongside the primary wordnet and queried together. Unlike the concept-relation dependencies described in Section 3.2.1 where linking was implicit through the CILI, extensions require mechanisms for linking into the actual structures of a resource. Therefore we introduce a new lexicon element, `LexiconExtension`, which is similar to the `Lexicon` element of LMF, but requires an `Extends` element which specifies the `id` and `version` of the lexicon it extends. Under a `LexiconExtension`, lexical entries and synsets can be defined as normal, but in order to link them with primary wordnet through sense or synset relations, we need to introduce the identifiers of the external entities.[3] For these, we allow `ExternalLexicalEntry`, `ExternalSense`, and `ExternalSynset` elements. In addition to estab-

[3]This requirement is partially just to satisfy XML validators, but can also serve as a check on the dependent lexicon's assumptions about the structure of the primary wordnet.

lishing IDs for linking, these elements allow for augmenting the elements themselves, such as for adding senses to an existing lexical entry or relations to a synset. However, these elements do not allow one to change information in the provider wordnet, so lemmas on lexical entries, ILIs on synsets, and other required information may not be specified on the corresponding external elements.

For example, the Geonames Wordnet (Bond and Bond, 2019) provides additional synset relations on top of the PWN as well as an extended lexical hierarchy of location names in the PWN and many other wordnets. The extension would specify that it extends the PWN as follows:

```
<LexiconExtension id="geonames-pwn"
                  version="1.0">
  <Extends id="pwn" version="3.0"/>
</LexiconExtension>
```

In some cases it might make sense to use both the `Extends` and `Requires` elements. For instance, if we want to extend the Japanese Wordnet with its entries from the Geonames Wordnet and reuse the relations from the English Geonames extension, we could specify the relationships as follows:

```
<LexiconExtension id="geonames-wnja"
                  version="1.0">
  <Extends id="wnja" version="2.0"/>
  <Requires id="geonames-pwn"
           version="1.0"/>
</LexiconExtension>
```

3.3 Pronunciation

One of the extensions that has been requested by other projects (Declerck et al., 2020) is the ability to represent phonetic information giving the pronunciation of lemmas in a schema such as the International Phonetic Alphabet. As well as giving the IPA text, it was also desired that we should be able to provide information about the specific variety, as well as further notes about the form of the pronunciation. In addition, we want to indicate whether the transcription is phonemic or phonetic, that is whether it includes expected features of the language such as aspiration. For 'variety', we decided to support the use of IETF language tags to indicate dialect, for example encoding British English in IPA as `en-GB-fonipa`, and an additional `notes` field that can encode further information such as indicating a particular British English dialect. We also added a field allowing a URL to give an audio file of the word being pronounced. An example of encoding is given below:

```
<LexicalEntry id="ex-rabbit-n">
  <Lemma writtenForm="rabbit"
         partOfSpeech="n"/>
    <Pronunciation
     variety="en-GB-fonxsamp
              en-US-fonxsamp">
     'r\{bIt</Pronunciation>
    <Pronunciation
     variety="en-AU-fonxsamp"
     notes="weak vowel merger">
     'r\{b@t</Pronunciation>
  </Lemma>
</LexicalEntry>
```

3.4 Syntactic Behaviours

One weakness of the current format was that the representation of syntactic behaviours was quite verbose and required that all of the information about the syntactic behaviour was repeated for each entry. This meant that, even for simple generic frames like transitive verbs, you would have a different frame for each entry. We changed this with the current version by allowing each frame to appear only once at the lexicon-level and have an identifier which can be referenced by individual senses. For example:

```
<Lexicon id="ex">
  <LexicalEntry id="ex-play-n">
    <Lemma writtenForm="play"
      partOfSpeech="n"/>
    <Sense id="ex-play-n-1"
      subcat="transitive"/>
    <Sense id="ex-play-n-1"
      subcat="transitive
        intransitive-with"/>
  </LexicalEntry>
  <SyntacticBehaviour
    id="transitive"
    subcategorizationFrame=
  "Somebody ----s something"/>
  <SyntacticBehaviour
    id="intransitive-with"
    subcategorizationFrame=
  "Somebody ----s with something"/>
</Lexicon>
```

3.5 New Relations

The original inventory of semantic relations (between synsets) and sense relations (between senses) were mainly drawn from the Princeton WordNet (PWN) and Euro WordNet (EWN) (Fellbaum, 1998; Vossen, 1998). Up-to-date documentation of these resources is available at `https://globalwordnet.github.io/gwadoc/`. This is important as there have been changes in the interpretation of the meanings of particular relations over the lifetime of the various projects, and of course between projects. By maintaining documentation through one of the Global Wordnet Association working groups, we hope to keep it up-to-date. To keep it accessible we use a version control system to store the documentation, and release it it under an open license, rather than in journals, books and technical documentation.

However, there are some relations used in several wordnets not currently in our inventory. In order to make the resource more useful across languages, we propose to add some of them. They are listed in Table 1. All of these are used in the innovative plWordNet project (Piasecki et al., 2009) and many of them in other projects as well.

The first two relations are to do with aspect. Most Slavic languages have two forms for most verbs: perfective and imperfective, and these are linked with the **simple_aspect** relation. This is the same as the "pure aspect" in plWordNet where the two members of a "pure" aspectual pair are located in distinct synsets with no change in meaning (Piasecki et al., 2009). The Bulgarian Wordnet (BulNet) also marks these pairs as different synsets, but links them to common hypernyms (Koeva, 2008). Apart from pure aspectual pairs, many Slavic languages have other productive verb alternations rendered by the addition of various prefixes. plWordNet groups them under a common label "secondary aspect". To represent these we would like to include **secondary_aspect** relation. In order to show the direction, the actual relations will be in pairs: **simple_aspect_ip** "simple aspect, imperfective to perfective" and **simple_aspect_pi** "simple aspect, perfective to imperfective", and similarly for **secondary_aspect**.

The next five are for specific relations, normally derivational in Slavic languages. PWN marks these relations (where they exist) as **hyponym**. plWordNet and BulNet specialize **feminine_form**, **young_form**, **diminutive** and **augmentative**. The Czech wordnet also suggested two relations here **X_HAS_MALE** and **X_HAS_FEMALE** (Pala and Smř, 2004). Although these relations are relatively rare in English (we estimate around a hundred), in plWordNet there are almost 10,000 of these (mainly feminine form and diminutives)![4] For the masculine, feminine and young relations, we wish to capture both derivative relations like ***prince/princess*** but also purely semantic ones (like ***king/queen*** or ***kangaroo/joey***). For this reason we allow them both at the sense level (when there is a dervational relation) and the synset level.

Because some wordnets use these as sense relations and some as synset relations, we propose to allow them for both. Here we will also have two forms of each: e.g., **female** and **has_female**.

Next we propose to introduce three specializations of **antonym**. These are used in the plWordNet, but we follow the naming convention of Saeed (2009). The first, and most common, is gradable antonyms. Then there are simple antonyms (also known as complementary or binary antonyms) where the negative of one entails the positive of the other. Finally we add **converse**: these are those which describe a relationship between two entities from different points of view. Piasecki et al. (2009) argues that the converse relation is different enough from the other antonyms that it should be kept separate. However, linguists such as Saeed (2009) consider converse to be antonymy and in other wordnets, such as PWN, converses are treated as antonyms, so we decided to group them together.

The last relation we introduce is inter-register synonymy (**ir_synonym**), introduced by Maziarz et al. (2015). This is for synsets where the denotation is the same, but the connotation is different, for example for informal terms or honorific variants. This is a very common relation: there are over 12,000 examples of these in the plWordNet. Antonyms and synonyms are reflexive: they are their own reverse relation.

3.6 Other improvements

3.6.1 Lexicographer files and sense keys

One concern was with the modelling of lexicographer files and sense keys. These two aspects are part of the development of Princeton WordNet and it is not clear how many other wordnet projects use them. For the lexicographer files, it was previously recommended that they be modelled using Dublin Core (Weibel and Koch, 2000) metadata properties, in particular with the 'subject' property. It was de-

[4] `http://plwordnet.pwr.wroc.pl/wordnet/stats`

Relation	Example	Lang
simple_aspect	***czytać*** "read/be reading (habitual/progressive)" → ***przeczytać*** "have read"	pl
secondary_aspect	***kopać*** "dig/be digging" → ***nakopać*** "have dug out a lot of sth"	pl
female	***pig*** → ***sow***	en
male	***pig*** → ***boar***	en
young	***pig*** → ***piglet***	en
diminutive	***pig*** → ***piggy***	en
augmentative	**дом** "house" → **домище** "great house"	ru
anto_gradable	***hot*** ↔ ***cold***, ***warm*** ↔ ***cool***	en
anto_simple	***complete*** ↔ ***incomplete***	en
anto_converse	***wife*** ↔ ***husband***, ***employer*** ↔ ***employee***	en
ir_synonym	***money*** ↔ ***dough***, ***loot*** ⟪informal⟫,	en
	食べる *taberu* "eat"↔ 召し上がる *meshiagaru* "honored person eats" ⟪honorific⟫	ja

Table 1: Proposed new relations

Examples are in English (en), Japanese (ja), Polish (pl) and Russian (ru).

cided that for the 1.1 version of the schema,[5] we should allow a special property for these values that can be used by Princeton and other projects that make use of lexicographer files. The second issue was that the sense keys used in Princeton WordNet are sometimes used to map between other wordnets. This is problematic, as the principal methodshould be through the InterLingual Index and the sense IDs are limited to particular senses of PWN. This issue principally came from English WordNet, which mapped back to Princeton WordNet using sense keys represented in another Dublin Core property (in this case 'identifier'). The English WordNet project is now removing its own sense key schema and using sense identifiers that correspond in a one-to-one manner with Princeton identifiers. In a few cases, the sense keys have had to been changed, due to either changes of spelling in a lemma, changing part-of-speech from satellite to head adjective or changes in the structure of the wordnet. For these cases, we recommend the use of a stand-off annotation to provide mapping if it is necessary.[6]

3.6.2 Metadata improvements

Metadata about elements is an important part of the schema and as such we allowed any Dublin Core property to be represented. It was noted that the XML format we published did not follow the Dublin Core recommendations, in that it specified that the properties should be attributes, rather than independent elements. In order to maintain backwards compatibility, we updated the namespace for Dublin Core to one on our repository so that there is no issue with clashing XML schemas, while not leading to any need for users of the schema to update the data except for the XML header. In addition, a further metadata property was added for projects to give a logo that can be displayed on the Open Multilingual Wordnet.

3.6.3 Further RDF schemas

Following the increasingly popular way of addressing the issue of interoperability, the use of Linked Data and Semantic Web standards such as RDF and OWL (McGuinness et al., 2004) have led to the emergence of a number of Linked Data projects for lexical resources (De Melo, 2015; Cimiano et al., 2020). The adoption of such standards not only allows both the data model and the actual data to be published in the same format, they also provide for instant compatibility with a vast range of existing data processing tools and storage systems, triple stores, providing query interfaces based on the SPARQL standard (W3C SPARQL Working Group, 2013).

To encode any data in RDF, one needs to decide which classes and properties (vocabulary) will be used. The adoption of already defined vocabularies helps with data interoperability since these makes data easily integrate with other resources.

The first RDF vocabulary for wordnets encoding proposed by Van Assem et al. (2006) was based on Princeton WordNet 2.0. Their work includes

[5] Princeton WordNet's schema cannot be used directly as a sense ID, due to the '%' character

[6] English WordNet's file is at `https://github.com/globalwordnet/english-wordnet/blob/master/src/sensekey-maps.csv`

(1) a mapping of WordNet 2.0 concepts and data model to RDF/OWL; (2) conversion scripts from the WordNet 2.0 Prolog distribution to RDF/OWL files; and (3) the actual WordNet 2.0 data. The suggested representation stayed as close to the original source as possible, that is, it reflects the original WordNet data model without interpretation. The WordNet schema proposed by Van Assem et al. (2006) has three main classes: *Synset*, *WordSense* and *Word*. The first two classes have subclasses for each lexical group present in WordNet. Each instance of Synset, WordSense and Word has its own URI, sharing the same prefix, a project-specific namespace. Another RDF vocabulary for wordnet encoding is the already cited OntoLex-Lemon vocabulary (Cimiano et al., 2016).

Since Van Assem et al. (2006) was based on Princeton WordNet 2.0, its use required adaptations. The first decision was regarding the URIs. Each wordnet project should have their own base URIs (namespace) for instances of synsets, senses and words. Second, additional relations were added in the RDF vocabulary available at `https://github.com/globalwordnet/schemas`. In RDF, the support the interoperability between wordnets (see Section 3.2) is very natural. For instance, a synsets of a particular wordnet can be connected to any other wordnet synset instances through *owl:sameAs* relations, estabilishing the mapping. That is the approach adopted in the OpenWordnet-PT (de Paiva et al., 2012). The code for converting Princeton WordNet 3.0 database files to RDF following this vocabulary is provided at `https://github.com/own-pt/wordnet2rdf`.

4 Discussion and Future Work

In order for wordnets to continue to grow, we have to allow for changes in their structure. In the past, each project has gone ahead on its own, which has led to divergence, with similar changes being implemented in slightly different ways. Through the release of a community-driven schema, we can help to harmonise the various projects. This should also lead to the development of interoperable tools, allowing for more rapid development.

Ideally, we do not just want to make the new format available, but to help projects take advantage of it. For example, the open English WordNet may wish to specify its antonym links using the three types (simple, gradable, converse) from plWordNet. We can use the CILI to suggest these changes automatically.

We would also like to help grow a collection of wordnets available in the new format, both through the Open Multilingual Wordnet or as individual wordnets and extensions.

The formats we are proposing fit well with the standardisation initiatives that are on-going around the representation of lexicographic data. As described in this paper we take advantage of both the Lexical Markup Framework (Francopoulo et al., 2006), being developed by ISO as well as the OntoLex model (Cimiano et al., 2016) from the W3C. In addition, we are looking at other standardisation efforts such as the LEXIDMA model[7] from the OASIS standardisation body. We are also aware of and taking account of other formats and tools in use in the community including DebVisDic (Horák et al., 2006), WordNetLoom (Piasecki et al., 2013) and Mill.[8]

5 Conclusion

The formats proposed by the Global WordNet Association have already been adopted by some projects and this has provided valuable feedback on the quality. We have found that the open methodology we have adopted has allowed us to quickly address these changes (with some spirited debate). The changes that we have made should ensure that the format continues to be useful and relevant and helps in the integration of wordnets through the collaborative interlingual index.

Acknowledgements

This work is supported by the EU H2020 programme under grant agreements 731015 (ELEXIS - European Lexicographic Infrastructure). John McCrae is also supported by a research grant from Science Foundation Ireland, co-funded by the European Regional Development Fund, for the Insight Centre under Grant Number SFI/12/RC/2289. Ewa Rudnicka is supported by the CLARIN-PL project, which is part of the investment in the CLARIN-PL research infrastructure funded by the Polish Ministry of Science and Higher Education. Documentation for the semantic relations was supported by the Google Season of Docs (2020).[9]

[7] `https://www.oasis-open.org/committees/lexidma`

[8] `https://github.com/own-pt/mill/`

[9] `https://developers.google.com/season-of-docs/`

References

Francis Bond and Arthur Bond. 2019. GeoNames wordnet (GeoWN): extracting wordnets from GeoNames. In *Proceedings of the 11th Global Wordnet Conference (GWC 2019)*.

Francis Bond and Ryan Foster. 2013. Linking and extending an open multilingual Wordnet. In *Proceedings of the 51st Annual Meeting of the Association for Computational Linguistics (Volume 1: Long Papers)*, pages 1352–1362, Sofia, Bulgaria. Association for Computational Linguistics.

Francis Bond, Hitoshi Isahara, Kyoko Kanzaki, and Kiyotaka Uchimoto. 2008. Boot-strapping a WordNet using multiple existing WordNets. In *Proceedings of the Sixth International Conference on Language Resources and Evaluation (LREC'08)*, Marrakech, Morocco. European Language Resources Association (ELRA).

Francis Bond, Piek Vossen, John P. McCrae, and Christiane Fellbaum. 2016. CILI: the Collaborative Interlingual Index. In *Proceedings of the Global WordNet Conference 2016*.

Philipp Cimiano, Christian Chiarcos, John P. McCrae, and Jorge Gracia. 2020. *Linguistic Linked Data: Representation, Generation and Applications*. Springer.

Philipp Cimiano, John P. McCrae, and Paul Buitelaar. 2016. Lexicon Model for Ontologies: Community Report.

Gerard De Melo. 2015. LexVo.org: Language-related information for the linguistic linked data cloud. *Semantic Web*, 6(4):393–400.

Thierry Declerck, Lenka Bajcetic, and Melanie Siegel. 2020. Adding pronunciation information to wordnets. In *Proceedings of the LREC 2020 Workshop on Multimodal Wordnets (MMW2020)*, pages 39–44.

Christiane Fellbaum. 2012. Wordnet. *The encyclopedia of applied linguistics*.

Christine Fellbaum, editor. 1998. *WordNet: An Electronic Lexical Database*. MIT Press.

Gil Francopoulo, Monte George, Nicoletta Calzolari, Monica Monachini, Nuria Bel, Mandy Pet, and Claudia Soria. 2006. Lexical markup framework (lmf). In *International Conference on Language Resources and Evaluation - LREC 2006*.

Michael Wayne Goodman and Francis Bond. 2021. Intrinsically interlingual: The Wn Python library for wordnets. In *11th International Global Wordnet Conference (GWC2021)*. (this volume).

Aleš Horák, Karel Pala, Adam Rambousek, and Martin Povolný. 2006. Debvisdic–first version of new client-server wordnet browsing and editing tool. In *Proceedings of the Third International WordNet Conference-GWC*, pages 325–328.

Hitoshi Isahara, Francis Bond, Kiyotaka Uchimoto, Masao Utiyama, and Kyoko Kanzaki. 2008. Development of the Japanese WordNet. In *Proceedings of the Sixth International Conference on Language Resources and Evaluation (LREC'08)*, Marrakech, Morocco. European Language Resources Association (ELRA).

Svetla Koeva. 2008. Derivational and Morphosemantic Relations in Bulgarian Wordnet. *Intelligent Information Systems*, XVI:359–389.

Marek Maziarz, Maciej Piasecki, Stan Szpakowicz, and Joanna Rabiega-Wisniewska. 2015. Semantic relations among nouns in Polish WordNet grounded in lexicographic and semantic tradition. *Cognitive Studies*, 11:161–182.

John P. McCrae, Alexandre Rademaker, Francis Bond, Ewa Rudnicka, and Christiane Fellbaum. 2019. English WordNet 2019 – An Open-Source WordNet for English. In *Proceedings of the 10th Global WordNet Conference – GWC 2019*.

John P. McCrae, Ian Wood, and Amanda Hicks. 2017. The Colloquial WordNet: Extending Princeton WordNet with Neologisms. In *Proceedings of the First Conference on Language, Data and Knowledge (LDK2017)*, pages 194–202.

John Philip McCrae, Alexandre Rademaker, Ewa Rudnicka, and Francis Bond. 2020. English WordNet 2020: Improving and Extending a WordNet for English using an Open-Source Methodology. In *Proceedings of the Multimodal Wordnets Workshop at LREC 2020*, pages 14–19.

Deborah L McGuinness, Frank Van Harmelen, et al. 2004. OWL web ontology language overview. W3c recommendation, World Wide Web Consortium.

George A Miller. 1995. WordNet: a lexical database for English. *Communications of the ACM*, 38(11):39–41.

Valeria de Paiva, Alexandre Rademaker, and Gerard de Melo. 2012. Openwordnet-pt: An open Brazilian Wordnet for reasoning. In *Proceedings of COLING 2012: Demonstration Papers*, pages 353–360, Mumbai, India. The COLING 2012 Organizing Committee. Published also as Techreport http://hdl.handle.net/10438/10274.

Karel Pala and Pavel Smř. 2004. Building Czech WordNet. *Romanian Journal of Information Science and Technology*, 7:79–88.

Maciej Piasecki, Michał Marcińczuk, Radosław Ramocki, and Marek Maziarz. 2013. Wordnetloom: a wordnet development system integrating form-based and graph-based perspectives. *International Journal of Data Mining, Modelling and Management*, 5(3):210–232.

Maciej Piasecki, Stan Szpakowicz, and Bartosz Broda. 2009. *A Wordnet from the Ground Up*. Wroclaw University of Technology Press. (ISBN 978-83-7493-476-3).

John I. Saeed. 2009. *Semantics*, 3 edition. Wiley-Blackwell.

Claudia Soria and Monica Monachini. 2008. Kyoto-LMF. Wordnet representation format. *KYOTO Working Paper WP02_TR002_V4_Kyoto_LMF*.

Mark Van Assem, Aldo Gangemi, and Guus Schreiber. 2006. Conversion of WordNet to a standard RDF/OWL representation. In *Language Resource and Evaluation Conference (LREC)*, pages 237–242.

Piek Vossen, editor. 1998. *Euro WordNet*. Kluwer.

Piek Vossen, Francis Bond, and John P. McCrae. 2016. Toward a truly multilingual Global Wordnet Grid. In *Proceedings of the Global WordNet Conference 2016*.

W3C SPARQL Working Group. 2013. SPARQL 1.1 overview. Technical report, World Wide Web Consortium.

Stuart L Weibel and Traugott Koch. 2000. The Dublin core metadata initiative. *D-Lib Magazine*, 6(12):1082–9873.

Intrinsically Interlingual: The Wn Python Library for Wordnets

Michael Wayne Goodman and Francis Bond
Nanyang Technological University
goodmami@uw.edu, bond@ieee.org

Abstract

This paper introduces Wn, a new Python library for working with wordnets. Unlike previous libraries, Wn is built from the beginning to accommodate multiple wordnets—for multiple languages or multiple versions of the same wordnet—while retaining the ability to query and traverse them independently. It is also able to download and incorporate wordnets published online. These features are made possible through Wn's adoption of standard formats and methods for interoperability, namely the WN-LMF schema (Vossen et al., 2013; Bond et al., 2020) and the Collaborative Interlingual Index (Bond et al., 2016). Wn is open-source, easily available,[1] and well-documented.[2]

1 Introduction

Wordnet is a popular tool for natural language processing, and there are interfaces in many programming languages. For Python alone, there are 99 packages that mention wordnet in the Python Package Index.[3] Many of them provide an interface to a single language, like Romanian (Dumitrascu et al., 2019), or multiple languages from the same project, like Panjwani et al. (2018) for the Indian languages. Of course, there are many interfaces for English, of which the Natural Language Tool Kit's implementation is very widely used (Bird et al., 2009). The NLTK has a very well documented and clear interface to the Princeton WordNet (PWN; Fellbaum, 1998), with several distance metrics also implemented. The interface makes some design decisions that simplify wordnet structure, such as treating the word ↔ sense ↔ synset triad as a lemma ↔ synset dyad.

The Wn library introduced by this paper differs from the existing Python packages in several ways. It is not tied to any particular wordnet and does not immediately include any wordnet data, but instead it can read and use any wordnet published in the WN-LMF format (Vossen et al., 2013; Bond et al., 2020). As a convenience, dozens of such wordnets hosted online are indexed by Wn (see Appendix A) for easy downloading. Wn also differs from the NLTK in that it uses the triadic structure, but in many ways it is deliberately similar to the NLTK's interface in order to help smooth the transition for new users.

In 2015, the NLTK was extended to cover the wordnets in the Open Multilingual Wordnet (OMW 1.0; Bond and Foster, 2013).[4] OMW 1.0 was made to deal with wordnets produced by the **expand** method which take the structure of an existing wordnet, in this case PWN 3.0, and extend it by adding lemmas in a new language to existing synsets (Vossen, 1998). Most wordnets are built in this manner (Bond and Paik, 2012). The main advancement of OMW 1.0 was in the production of multiple wordnets, all in the same format, under open licenses.[5]

This structure where all synsets are shared among all languages has several advantages, such as the straightforward translation of words and the implicit sharing of structure which makes smaller wordnets more useful. It also has immediate disadvantages, the most prominent being that synsets not in PWN cannot be included. Some disadvantages are more subtle: as the OMW structure is the union of the structure of all the wordnets, new paths could become available when another wordnet is added,

[1] `https://pypi.org/project/wn`

[2] `https://wn.readthedocs.io`

[3] `https://pypi.org/search/?q=wordnet`

[4] NLTK was built for teaching, and the first version of the OMW wordnet extension was actually built by students as a programming assignment in a computational linguistics class!

[5] To make its data available to Wn, OMW 1.0 now additionally publishes each wordnet as a WN-LMF file at `https://github.com/bond-lab/omw-data`. The many wordnets derived from Wiktionary data (Bond and Foster, 2013) are not published but can similarly be converted.

which has ramifications for reproducibility in research. In practice, for OMW 1.0, all structure came from PWN 3.0 and non-English wordnets contributed no relations so this was never an issue, but we are anticipating future developments to OMW which may cause such problems.

To allow for wordnets with different structures and synsets not in PWN, a new version of the OMW (2.0) is under development. It uses the Collaborative Interlingual Index (CILI; Bond et al., 2016) to link synsets. This allows wordnets to define their own synset structure while maintaining interlingual linking through the shared, resource-agnostic index. The software for the Open Multilingual Wordnet 2.0[6] is released as open-source software with the aim of making it easily available for everyone. However, its primary goals were to allow the browsing of the unified resource and to facilitate the validation, addition, and management of new and historical wordnets and CILI entries—not to assist the individual researcher with downloading and using particular wordnets from its collection. As such, the software is not optimized for loading just one or two wordnets, and while it can run locally, it is expected to run as a web service.

In contrast, Wn does fewer checks and assumes that the wordnets are generally well-formed. This assumption should hold if the wordnets come from a source that performs these checks, such as the OMW. Wn allows a user to only load the wordnets they need and to access them distinctly. It is designed for wordnet users running things locally.

This paper describes a new Python interface for modeling wordnet data, including those from OMW 2.0, designed to replace the existing NLTK interface in a researcher's workflow. Wn is the first Python module designed from the beginning to use the Collaborative Interlingual Index to link separate wordnets. We discuss the desiderata for the software further in Section 2. We then briefly discuss the design of the system in Section 3. In Section 4 we give a brief tour of Wn's functionality. Finally we discuss a couple of aspects of why we think Wn is an improvement over previous implementations in Section 5 and conclude in Section 6.

2 Desiderata

The main goals of Wn are as follows:

Resource Independence: Each lexicon loaded into Wn is treated as a distinct resource and may be added and removed without affecting other lexicons.

WN-LMF Compliance: Wordnets in the modern WN-LMF format are fully supported and information is not lost upon loading or exporting wordnets.

Precise Modeling: All information in a wordnet is available to and discoverable by the user through intuitive structures. Notably, word senses have first-class status, just like words and synsets.

Interlingual Queries: Queries may traverse multiple wordnets, or not, depending on what the user specifies.

User Convenience: Data sources and query results are readily available; the user does not need to comprehend the complexity of the software to use it.

3 Design

Here we discuss several aspects of Wn's design, from the low-level database design in Section 3.1 to the user-facing Python data structures in Section 3.2 and the methodology for performing interlingual queries in Section 3.3. To support the distribution of wordnets as individual resources or in collections, formats for packaging wordnets are described in Section 3.4.

3.1 Database Design

From the outset, Wn was designed to handle both monolingual and interlingual queries over a multitude of wordnets. All loaded lexicons are stored in the same database,[7] but the elements are keyed to the lexicon that contributed them. Identifiers that are unique within a single wordnet, such as for synsets, are not necessarily unique when multiple wordnets are present, so their uniqueness is not enforced in the database. Instead, relationships between elements are linked via globally-unique table row identifiers and the original wordnet identifiers are only used for direct lookups within a lexicon. No identifiers are shared across lexicons except for CILI IDs, which are the only way to perform interlingual queries.

[6] `https://github.com/globalwordnet/OMW/`

[7] In the current implementation, the database engine is SQLite (`https://www.sqlite.org/`) but this detail should not concern most users as all operations in the public API are abstracted from the underlying infrastructure.

3.2 Class Modeling

The primary entities in WN-LMF wordnets are the lexical entries (i.e., words) and synsets. Word senses are essentially the link between words and synsets, but as they may be assigned metadata, take part in sense relations, and contain examples, they are given status as first-class entities in Wn. Each of these gets a Python class—`Word`, `Sense`, and `Synset`—that models its data and relationships. Figure 1 illustrates these entities and their relationships to each other. In addition, a `Wordnet` class represents a selection of lexicons used to filter queries.

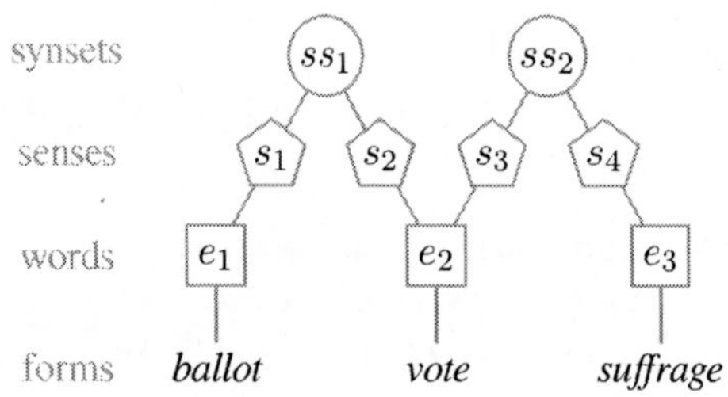

Figure 1: Modeling wordnet entities

All queries to the database are made through instances of these classes, which act as database abstraction layers. The primary queries, for words, senses, or synsets, are made through the `Wordnet` objects. Secondary queries, such as for word forms, synset or sense relations, definitions, examples, etc., are made through the `Word`, `Sense`, or `Synset` objects. These entity objects each contain a reference to the `Wordnet` object that was used to find them. This reference allows for the secondary queries to make use of the same lexicon filters. We give examples of querying the senses in Section 4.3 and Section 4.4.

3.3 Interlingual Queries

All interlingual queries must go through shared ILI links. Figure 2 illustrates how Wn translates a synset ss^f in lexicon f to other lexicons through shared ILI links. Every ILI has a synset in a queried language. If no synset is explicitly given in the lexicon, an implicit, empty synset is used instead.

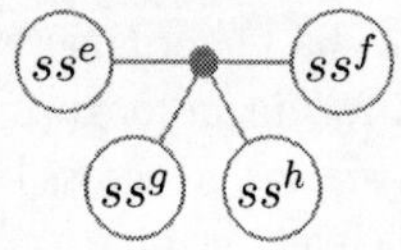

Figure 2: Translating synsets via ILI
The gray node is the ILI link.

Figure 3 illustrates how Wn can find synset relation paths from a synset ss_1^f, even when there are no relations defined in its lexicon, by sharing relations from a second lexicon e. From synset ss_1^f, Wn expands the search to ss_1^e via a shared ILI link. As ss_1^e has a relation to ss_2^e, Wn first traverses it and then attempts to find a corresponding synset in the original lexicon f. Since there is no synset in f for the ILI, it instead returns an inferred (and empty) synset. An inferred synset contains no information except its ILI link and the lexicon filters in force, but this is enough information to allow Wn to search for the next relation. Wn can then cross the ILI to ss_2^e, traverse the relation to ss_3^e, and cross the ILI again to ss_3^f, which is in the target lexicon.

This situation is common in OMW lexicons which only provide words and senses for a subset of PWN's synsets but offer no synset relations of their own. In this process, the synsets that may be the result of the relation traversal, such as ss_1^f and ss_3^f, are called the *target* set, while the synsets that may be used via ILI links for their relations are called the *expand* set.

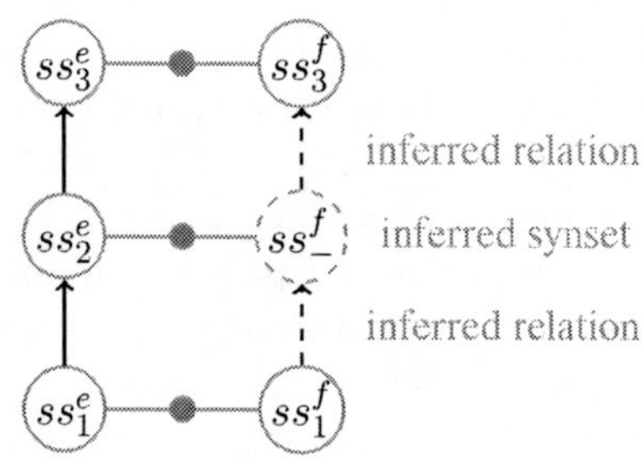

Figure 3: Traversing external relations via ILI

The inferred synsets are only necessary for relation traversal with expand lexicons. Standalone wordnets that do not require an expand lexicon have no use for inferred synsets.

3.4 Packaging Wordnets

As will be shown in Section 4.1, Wn is able to download and add wordnets from the web as well as from local files. Some wordnets, such as the English WordNet, are distributed just as the WN-LMF XML file, while others, such as the Open German WordNet (Siegel and Bond, 2021), include the full text of the license and the canonical citation as accompanying files, and the full OMW is distributed as a collection of multiple wordnets. In order to accommodate these different modes of distribution, we have designed three levels of packaging for wordnets. Each of these three may be distributed uncompressed or compressed with gzip or LZMA compression.

Resource A file containing lexicon data is called a resource. While future versions of Wn may allow multiple formats, such as the JSON or RDF variants of WN-LMF (McCrae et al., 2021), currently only the XML format is supported.

Package A package is a directory containing a resource and optionally metadata files containing the license (LICENSE), basic documentation (README), or the canonical citation (citation.bib). Exactly one resource file is allowed in a package and at most one of each of the metadata files. Other files are allowed, but they will be ignored by Wn. A package directory, when distributed over the web, should be archived as a tarball.

Collection Multiple packages may be distributed in a directory called a collection. Wn will only search for packages in the collection's top directory and not under subdirectories, so a collection is a flat list of packages. In order for Wn to better distinguish between packages and collections, which are both directories, resource files may not appear in the collection without being in a package directory. A collection may optionally contain the same metadata files as packages, where any license, documentation, or citation pertains to the collection itself and not the individual packages. Any other files or directories in a collection will be ignored by Wn. As with packages, collections should be distributed as a tarball.

4 Usage

In this section we give a brief tour of Wn's programming interface.

4.1 Loading Wordnets

Wn was created for wordnets following the WN-LMF schema (Vossen et al., 2013; Bond et al., 2020) as this format requires synsets to declare their association with a CILI ID, if any. Older formats, such as WNDB,[8] are not directly supported, but conversion tools exist.[9]

The Wn project keeps an index of publicly available and open wordnets in the WN-LMF format, such as the English WordNet (McCrae et al., 2020) and OdeNet, the Open German WordNet (Siegel and Bond, 2021).[10] They can be listed with Wn's `wn.projects()` function as shown in Figure 4, which shows an abbreviated list. The full list of the current release is given in Table 1 (Appendix A).

Users can install wordnets from this list with Wn's `wn.download()` function, for instance by specifying the project's identifier and version:

```
>>> import wn
>>> wn.download('ewn:2020')
Download complete (13643357 bytes)
Added ewn:2020 (English WordNet)
```

As a convenience, if the user only specifies the project identifier (e.g., `'ewn'`), Wn will get the latest known version. For wordnets not indexed by Wn, users can provide an explicit URL as the first argument, and the lexicon ID and version will be extracted from the downloaded file. For instance, if OdeNet were not indexed by Wn, we could download it directly by the URL of its resource file:

```
>>> wn.download(url_of_odenet)
Download complete (2001396 bytes)
Added odenet:1.3 (Offenes Deutsches WordNet)
```

We encourage more wordnets to provide a persistent URL for this usage. Wordnets from OMW 1.0 (or in that format) can be automatically converted to the 2.0 (WN-LMF) format and loaded. Since there is a mapping from PWN synsets to CILI, synsets in wordnets that are built from PWN can be automatically linked to CILI as well.

Wordnets can be installed from a local WN-LMF file using the `wn.add()` function:

```
>>> wn.add('wnja.xml')
Added wnja:2.0 (Japanese Wordnet)
```

Wn is robust to small errors in the wordnet file (like different parts of speech in the synset and word or a confidence less than 0 or greater than 1) but will generally warn the user when they occur.

The `wn.lexicons()` function lists all installed lexicons. The objects returned by this function can be inspected to find the name, version, language, license, contact email, and other kinds of metadata of a lexicon:

```
>>> for l in wn.lexicons():
...     print(l.id, l.version, l.label)
...
ewn 2020 English WordNet
wnja 2.0 Japanese Wordnet
odenet 1.3 Offenes Deutsches WordNet
```

[8] https://wordnet.princeton.edu/documentation/wndb5wn

[9] https://github.com/jmccrae/gwn-scala-api

[10] https://github.com/hdaSprachtechnologie/odenet

```
>>> some_projects = wn.projects()[:6]
>>> [(p['id'], p['label'], p['version'], p['language']) for p in some_projects]
[('ewn', 'Open English WordNet', '2019', 'en'),
('ewn', 'Open English WordNet', '2020', 'en'),
('pwn', 'Princeton WordNet', '3.0', 'en'),
('pwn', 'Princeton WordNet', '3.1', 'en'),
('odenet', 'Open German WordNet', '1.3', 'de'),
('omw', 'Open Multilingual Wordnet v1.3', '1.3', 'mul')]
```

Figure 4: Listing indexed projects with Wn; see Appendix A for the full list

4.2 Selecting Lexicons

As mentioned, primary queries go through a `Wordnet` object, so one must be instantiated first. To motivate this step, consider a user who has installed both the English WordNet and the French wordnet WOLF (Sagot and Fišer, 2008). If they search for synsets for the word form *chat*, the `Wordnet` object determines if they receive synsets related to the English verb meaning *to talk*, those related to the French word for a cat, or both.

```
# Instantiation                  Results
wn.Wordnet()                     # all
wn.Wordnet(lang='fr')            # only French
wn.Wordnet(lexicon='ewn')        # only EWN
```

Also, since it is possible to load multiple versions of the same wordnet, filtering on the lexicon ID only (ewn) only uses the most recently installed version (whether or not it's a newer release). A version specifier on the `lexicon` argument may be necessary to precisely differentiate:

```
wn.Wordnet(lexicon='ewn')        # recent
wn.Wordnet(lexicon='ewn:2020')   # 2020 only
wn.Wordnet(lexicon='ewn:*')      # all EWN
```

A user may wish to search a subset of the installed lexicons at once, such as when they have installed an extension lexicon containing additional words. In this case, the `lexicon` argument may take a space-separated list of lexicon specifiers. Finally, users may choose the lexicons to use for the *expand* set of interlingual queries, as described in Section 3.3, with the `expand` parameter:

```
wn.Wordnet(lexicon='wnja', expand='ewn')
```

If the `expand` parameter is not given, Wn allows any installed lexicon to be used in the expand set, in order to mimic the behavior of the OMW. A user may also specify an empty expand set (`expand=''`) to block ILI traversals when exploring relations.

Once a `Wordnet` object has been instantiated as described above, any queries performed on the object will restrict the search to the matching lexicons.

4.3 Primary Queries

All primary queries have several optional parameters which are used to narrow down the results. The first parameter is for a matching wordform and the second is for part-of-speech. Synsets also have a parameter for selecting by ILI ID. Below, assume `w` is a `Wordnet` object instantiated as above.

```
w.words()               # all words
w.words('犬')           # words w/ form '犬'
w.words(pos='n')        # all nominal words
w.senses()              # all senses
w.synsets()             # all synsets
w.synsets(ili='i1')     # synsets w/ ili 'i1'
```

Here is an example of getting synsets for the Japanese noun 犬 *inu* "dog":

```
>>> ja = wn.Wordnet(lang='ja')
>>> ja.synsets('犬', pos='n')
[Synset('wnja-02084071-n'),
 Synset('wnja-10641755-n')]
```

4.4 Secondary Queries

Secondary queries happen on the objects returned by primary queries. Below, assume `e` is a `Word` object, `s` is a `Sense` object, and `ss` is a `Synset` object. The list of secondary queries below is not exhaustive.

```
e.senses()              # senses for e
e.lemma()               # canonical lemma for e
e.forms()               # all word forms for e
s.word()                # the sense's word
s.synset()              # the sense's synset
s.derivations()         # derivation relation
ss.senses()             # synset's senses
ss.hypernyms()          # synset's hypernyms
ss.definition()         # synset definition
```

In the following example, we find the hypernyms of one synset for 犬 *inu* "dog":

```
>>> inu = ja.synsets('犬', pos='n')[0]
>>> inu.hypernyms()[0]
Synset('wnja-01317541-n')
```

4.5 Shortcut Functions

As a convenience to the user, Wn provides functions for primary queries that do not require them to first instantiate a `Wordnet` object:

```
wn.words()
wn.senses()
wn.synsets()
```

Each of these functions will create a `Wordnet` object when it is called and use it for the query. As such, these functions additionally take the `lang` and `lexicon` parameters which are passed on to the `Wordnet` object.

Additionally, there are shortcut secondary queries to go directly from words to synsets and vice-versa:

```
e.synsets()   # all synsets for e
ss.words()    # all words for ss
ss.lemmas()   # lemmas of all words for ss
```

The following lists the lemmas for the hypernym found in the previous example:

```
>>> hyp = inu.hypernyms()[0]
>>> hyp.lemmas()
['家畜']
```

4.6 Translating via ILI

Words, senses, and synsets can all be translated to some other lexicon via a synset's ILI link. The most natural object to translate is a sense, as it links a specific word to a specific concept, but all translation go through the ILI and thus through a synset. Translations of a synset will return at most one translated synset per target lexicon,[11] but the function returns a list because there may be multiple target lexicons. Translations of a sense return a list of senses in the target lexicon(s) shared by the sense's translated synset. Translations of a word return a mapping of senses to lists of sense translations, and this is because a word may have multiple unrelated concepts so it wouldn't make sense to group them in a flat list. The `translate()` methods below all take a `lang` or `lexicon` parameter to filter the target lexicons.

```
e.translate()    # translate a word
s.translate()    # translate a sense
ss.translate()   # translate a synset
```

Continuing the example from above, here are lemmas of translations for the found hypernym:

```
>>> hyp.translate(lang='en')[0].lemmas()
['domestic animal', 'domesticated animal']
```

5 Discussion

Here we discuss how Wn improves over previous offerings for users and researchers.

[11]Every ILI should have only one synset in a lexicon.

5.1 Query Language Persistence

One common point of confusion with the NLTK's interface is that the default language is English regardless of the operations used previously, and this is confounded by the fact that synsets for all languages in the OMW 1.0 (which the NLTK distributes) use the same PWN set. This problem is illustrated in Figure 5.

```
>>> from nltk.corpus import wordnet
>>> ss1 = wordnet.synsets("door")[0]
>>> ss1.lemma_names()
['door']
>>> ss2 = wordnet.synsets("pintu",
...                       lang="zsm")[0]
>>> ss2.lemma_names()
['door']
>>> ss2.lemma_names(lang="zsm")
['laluan', 'pintu']
```

Figure 5: The NLTK's interface defaults to English language queries.

In Wn, each lexicon has its own synset structure, and the results of primary queries keep a reference to the `Wordnet` object that was used, so the lexicon restrictions of the first query persist for follow-up queries.

5.2 Reproducibility

The OMW, both 1.0 and 2.0, is considered one large, multilingual wordnet, but it is not versioned as a single resource. Individual lexicons may be added or get updated without changing the OMW's version number. Also, changes to the structure of OMW through such updates can affect the results of queries on completely different lexicons, as synset relations are always implicitly shared. This means that a researcher performing an experiment using OMW data cannot guarantee reproducibility unless they can somehow recreate the exact database used. The OMW 2.0 database stores the information about which relations come from which wordnet, but the current OMW web interface does not allow you to filter on this.

Wn, in contrast, versions each individual lexicon and allows queries to specify which lexicons are used in the queries. This allows them to much more precisely state the requirements of their research product and thereby better describe a reproducible experiment.

6 Conclusions

This paper describes Wn: software for accessing wordnets in the global wordnet associations LMF format, linked by the collaborative interlingual index. Wn is built from the beginning to accommodate multiple wordnets while retaining the ability to query and traverse them independently. NLTK is already widely used amongst NLP researchers; we provide an enhanced functionality that goes beyond the current English based mapping.

Wn is open-source and available on GitHub.[12] We strongly encourage everybody to download, use, and, if possible, contribute back to the project. In future work, we intend to add the following capabilities:

(i) unloading wordnets from the database

(ii) exporting wordnets

(iii) modifying wordnet data locally

(iv) supporting information content (Resnik, 1995) and related similarity measures

(v) supporting new features in recent updates to the WN-LMF format (McCrae et al., 2021), such as wordnet dependencies and extensions

(vi) enabling morphological normalization for word lookup, similar to the use of Morphy in Princeton WordNet, but with hooks for external resources in other languages

Acknowledgments

Thanks to Liling Tan for the initial inspiration and early discussions and to three anonymous reviewers, Andrew Devadason, and Merrick Choo for comments on the paper. We would also like to thank the Google Season of Docs (2020), especially Yoyo Wu, for their contributions to the documentation.

References

Steven Bird, Edward Loper, and Ewan Klein. 2009. *Natural Language Processing with Python*. O'Reilly Media Inc.

Francis Bond, Luis Morgado da Costa, Michael Wayne Goodman, John P. McCrae, and Ahti Lohk. 2020. Some issues with building a multilingual wordnet. In *Proceedings of the 12th Language Resource and Evaluation Conference (LREC 2020)*, pages 3189–3197.

Francis Bond and Ryan Foster. 2013. Linking and extending an open multilingual Wordnet. In *Proceedings of the 51st Annual Meeting of the Association for Computational Linguistics (Volume 1: Long Papers)*, pages 1352–1362, Sofia, Bulgaria. Association for Computational Linguistics.

Francis Bond and Kyonghee Paik. 2012. A survey of wordnets and their licenses. In *Proceedings of the 6th Global WordNet Conference (GWC 2012)*, Matsue. 64–71.

Francis Bond, Piek Vossen, John P. McCrae, and Christiane Fellbaum. 2016. CILI: the Collaborative Interlingual Index. In *Proceedings of the Global WordNet Conference 2016*.

Stefan Dumitrascu, Avram Andrei, Morogran Luciana, and Stefan-Adrian Toma. 2019. Rowordnet –a python api for the romanian wordnet. In *10th International Conference on Electronics, Computers and Artificial Intelligence (ECAI)*.

Christine Fellbaum, editor. 1998. *WordNet: An Electronic Lexical Database*. MIT Press.

John P. McCrae, Michael Wayne Goodman, Francis Bond, Alexandre Rademaker, Ewa Rudnicka, and Luis Morgado da Costa. 2021. The global wordnet formats: Updates for 2020. In *11th International Global Wordnet Conference (GWC2021)*. (this volume).

John Philip McCrae, Alexandre Rademaker, Ewa Rudnicka, and Francis Bond. 2020. English WordNet 2020: Improving and Extending a WordNet for English using an Open-Source Methodology. In *Proceedings of the Multimodal Wordnets Workshop at LREC 2020*, pages 14–19.

Ritesh Panjwani, Diptesh Kanojia, and Pushpak Bhattacharyya. 2018. pyiwn: A python-based api to access indian language wordnets. In *Proceedings of the Global WordNet Conference*, volume 2018.

Philip Resnik. 1995. Using information content to evaluate semantic similarity. In *Proc. 14th International Joint Conference on Artificial Intelligence (IJCAI-95), Montreal, Canada*, pages 448–453.

Benoît Sagot and Darja Fišer. 2008. Building a free French wordnet from multilingual resources. In *Proceedings of the Sixth International Language Resources and Evaluation (LREC'08)*, Marrakech, Morocco.

Melanie Siegel and Francis Bond. 2021. Compiling a German wordnet from other resources. In *11th International Global Wordnet Conference (GWC2021)*. (this volume).

Piek Vossen. 1998. Introduction to EuroWordNet. *Computers and the Humanities*, 32(2):73–89.

Piek Vossen, Claudia Soria, and Monica Monachini. 2013. Wordnet-LMF: A standard representation for multilingual wordnets. *LMF Lexical Markup Framework*, pages 51–66.

[12] `https://github.com/goodmami/wn`

A Indexed Wordnets

Name	ID	Versions	Language
English WordNet	ewn	2020	English [en]
		2019	
Princeton WordNet	pwn	3.1	English [en]
		3.0	
Open German WordNet	odenet	1.3	German [de]
Open Multilingual Wordnet	omw	1.3	multiple [mul]
Albanet	alswn	1.3+omw	Albanian [als]
Arabic WordNet (AWN v2)	arbwn	1.3+omw	Arabic [arb]
BulTreeBank Wordnet (BTB-WN)	bulwn	1.3+omw	Bulgarian [bg]
Chinese Open Wordnet	cmnwn	1.3+omw	Mandarin (Simplified) [zh]
Croatian Wordnet	hrvwn	1.3+omw	Croatian [hr]
DanNet	danwn	1.3+omw	Danish [da]
FinnWordNet	finwn	1.3+omw	Finnish [fi]
Greek Wordnet	ellwn	1.3+omw	Greek [el]
Hebrew Wordnet	hebwn	1.3+omw	Hebrew [he]
IceWordNet	islwn	1.3+omw	Icelandic [is]
Italian Wordnet	iwn	1.3+omw	Italian [it]
Japanese Wordnet	jpnwn	1.3+omw	Japanese [jp]
Lithuanian WordNet	litwn	1.3+omw	Lithuanian [lt]
Multilingual Central Repository	catwn	1.3+omw	Catalan [ca]
Multilingual Central Repository	euswn	1.3+omw	Basque [eu]
Multilingual Central Repository	glgwn	1.3+omw	Galician [gl]
Multilingual Central Repository	spawn	1.3+omw	Spanish [es]
MultiWordNet	itawn	1.3+omw	Italian [it]
Norwegian Wordnet	nobwn	1.3+omw	Norwegian (Bokmål) [nb]
Norwegian Wordnet	nnown	1.3+omw	Norwegian (Nynorsk) [nn]
Open Dutch WordNet	nldwn	1.3+omw	Dutch [nl]
OpenWN-PT	porwn	1.3+omw	Portuguese [pt]
plWordNet	polwn	1.3+omw	Polish [pl]
Romanian Wordnet	ronwn	1.3+omw	Romanian [ro]
Slovak WordNet	slkwn	1.3+omw	Slovak [sk]
sloWNet	slvwn	1.3+omw	Slovenian [sl]
Swedish (SALDO)	swewn	1.3+omw	Swedish [sv]
Thai Wordnet	thawn	1.3+omw	Thai [th]
WOLF (Wordnet Libre du Français)	frawn	1.3+omw	French [fr]
Wordnet Bahasa	indwn	1.3+omw	Indonesian [id]
Wordnet Bahasa	zsmwn	1.3+omw	Malaysian [zsm]

Table 1: A listing of wordnets indexed by Wn; all with `1.3+omw` as a version are included in the Open Multilingual Wordnet and are also available individually.

Semantic Analysis of Verb-Noun Derivation in Princeton WordNet

Verginica Barbu Mititelu
Research Institute for Artificial Intelligence
Romanian Academy
vergi@racai.ro

Svetlozara Leseva
Institute for Bulgarian Language
Bulgarian Academy of Sciences
zarka@dcl.bas.bg

Ivelina Stoyanova
Institute for Bulgarian Language
Bulgarian Academy of Sciences
iva@dcl.bas.bg

Abstract

We present here the results of a morphosemantic analysis of the verb-noun pairs in the Princeton WordNet as reflected in the standoff file containing pairs annotated with a set of 14 semantic relations. We have automatically distinguished between zero-derivation and affixal derivation in the data and identified the affixes and manually checked the results. The data show that for each semantic relation an affix prevails in creating new words, although we cannot talk about their specificity with respect to such a relation. Moreover, certain pairs of verb-noun semantic primes are better represented for each semantic relation, and some semantic clusters (in the form of WordNet subtrees) take shape as a result. We thus employ a large-scale data-driven linguistically motivated analysis afforded by the rich derivational and morphosemantic description in WordNet to the end of capturing finer regularities in the process of derivation as represented in the semantic properties of the words involved and as reflected in the structure of the lexicon.

1 Introduction

The focus of this paper is the study of the derivational patterns between English verb-noun pairs. The perspective adopted is semantic, with two correlated aims: identifying semantic regularities involved in derivation (i.e., semantic relations between the members of a derivational pair) and establishing the semantic conditions in which it occurs (the semantic classes to which the nouns and verbs belong expressed in terms of semantic primitives, or primes (Miller et al., 1990), i.e. language-independent semantic classes).

The study is based on the semantically-labeled derivational pairs identified in the Princeton WordNet (PWN) (Fellbaum, 1998) presented in a standoff file (Fellbaum et al., 2009).

An in-depth study of the regularities will help paint a more detailed picture of the distribution of derivation, be it affixal or zero derivation. Based on the perspective adopted in this work, conclusions will highlight similarities and differences between the so-called "zero" morpheme conversion and the affixes involved in derivation.

Throughout this paper we use the terms *conversion* and *zero derivation* interchangeably to refer to the process of creating new words without any lexical material or, in other words, with the zero affix; *affixal derivation* refers to the morphological process involving the attachment of a non-zero affix to a base form to create a new word; *derivation* is their hypernym, a general term designating the morphological process whereby new words are created either involving affixes or not[1].

2 Related work

Zero derivation has been widely debated and discussed by linguists. Its high productivity in English specifically for creating verbs from words of other parts of speech was noted by researchers (Plag, 1999), as well as the fact that derivatives with overt suffixes are a subset of the possible meanings of converted verbs (Plag, 1999). A variety of meanings involved in conversion was noticed by Clark and Clark (1979), by Cetnarowska (1993), Plag (1999), Lieber (2004), Bauer et al. (2013), to mention but a few. Criteria for establishing the direction of conversion were identified and discussed (Bauer et al., 2013): semantic dependency, frequency, order of coining in the lan-

[1] Besides *conversion* or *zero derivation* and *affixal derivation*, another hyponym of *derivation* is *backformation*, which involves subtracting an affix from a word in order to create a new one.

guage. All studies consider words as entities involved in the process; however, our analysis here is done at the word sense level and is facilitated by the organizing principle of PWN, which takes the word sense as the minimal analysis unit.

3 Morphosemantic Relations in WordNet

The standoff file[2] consists of 16,812 [3] unique verb-noun pairs of which 53.57% represent patterns of affixal derivation and 46.43% are conversions. Each pair is annotated with a morphosemantic relation (out of a set of 14 such relations).

Although not explicitly defined, the meaning of these relations may be inferred from the observation of the data. Below, we sketch out a revised version of a description of these relations proposed by Koeva et al. (2016). Many of the relations have a more or less direct correspondence in the domain of thematic relations; in fact, in the lexicalist approaches in the Generative grammar of the 1980s, V-to-N derivation was accounted for as theta-role assignment from the predicate argument structure of the verb within the word structure of the noun (Müller, 2016), but this is not a one-to-one correspondence as the overview below shows.

3.1 Describing Morphosemantic Relations

An **Agent** is a person (noun.person), a social entity, such as organisations (noun.group), an animal (noun.animal) or a plant (noun.plant) that is capable of acting so as to bring about a result.

An **Instrument** is either a concrete, usually man-made object (noun.artifact), or something abstract, such as a noun with the prime noun.communication, e.g. *debug*:1 – *debugger*:1 ('a program that helps in locating and correcting programming errors') or noun.cognition, e.g. *stem*:4 – *stemmer*:3 ('an algorithm for removing inflectional and derivational endings in order to reduce word forms to a common stem'). It is always implied that the Instrument acts under the volition of an Agent.

A **Body-part** is an inalienable part of the body of an Agent expressed by nouns with the prime noun.body (rarely noun.animal or noun.plant).

The relation **Material** may denote a type of inanimate cause (Fellbaum et al., 2009) – substances that may bring about a certain effect: e.g. *inhibit*:2 – *inhibitor*:1 ('a substance that retards or stops an activity'). Besides noun.substance, noun.artifacts (synthetic substances or products) also qualify for the relation, e.g. *depilate*:1 – *depilatory*:2 ('hair removal cosmetics'). In addition, the relation may also express function or purpose, as in *sweeten*:1 – *sweetener*:1 ('something added to foods to make them taste sweeter').

The relation **Vehicle** represents a subclass of artifacts (means of transportation), so the respective synsets have the prime noun.artifact and are generally hyponyms of the synset *conveyance*:3; *transport*:8. Vehicles are distinguished from Instruments as their semantic and syntactic behaviour is more similar to Agents.

The relation **By-means-of** is also associated with two subtypes: on the one hand, it may be thought of as a kind of inanimate cause, e.g. *geyser*:1 ('to overflow like a geyser') – *geyser*:1 ('a spring that discharges hot water and steam') (noun.object), while on the other, it is found in cases where the semantics is not so much causative as enabling or facilitating: consider the pair *certify*:2 ('guarantee payment on; of checks') and *certificate*:2 ('a formal declaration that documents a fact of relevance to finance and investment').

The relation **Event** denotes a processual nominalization and involves nouns such as noun.act, noun.event, noun.phenomenon, noun.process, while ruling out concrete entities such as animate beings, natural (noun.object) or man-made (noun.artifact) objects, etc.

The relation **State** denotes abstract entities: feelings (noun.feeling), cognitive (noun.cognition) and other non-dynamic state-of-affairs, such as synsets with the prime noun.state.

The relation **Undergoer** denotes entities affected by the situation described and roughly corresponds to the thematic role of Patient/Theme.

The relation **Result** involves entities that are produced or come into existence as a result of the situation described by the verb.

The relation **Property** denotes various attributes and qualities. This relation involves primarily nouns with the prime noun.attribute and more rarely noun.location.

The relation **Location** denotes a concrete (natural or man-made) or an abstract location where an event takes place and therefore relates verbs with nouns with various primes – most typically noun.location, but also noun.object, noun.plant,

[2] https://wordnet.princeton.edu

[3] The actual size is 17,739 pairs, but we worked on an improved, more consistent version of the file (Koeva et al., 2016) and report cleaned data.

noun.artifact, noun.cognition, etc.

The relation **Destination** is associated with the primes noun.person, noun.location and noun.artifact, corresponding to two distinct interpretations in terms of the thematic role theory – as a Recipient (noun.person) or as a Goal (noun.artifact, noun.location).

The relation **Uses** denotes a function or purpose of an entity. In many cases, especially with verbs of putting, the entity is directly involved as the Theme of the verb, e.g. *lipstick*:2 ('apply lipstick to') – *lipstick*:1 ('makeup that is used to color the lips'). The relation allows nouns with various primes, both concrete and abstract.

A number of procedures towards the trimming of the morphosemantic relations in the standoff file were carried out previously (Koeva et al., 2016). These involved the disambiguation of 450 cases of multiple assignment, which included both very clear-cut 'bugs', such as the assignment of both Agent and Event to a pair of synsets, as well as ambiguous cases of relations that may be considered as overlapping in scope, such as Instrument and Uses or By-means-of and Instrument. The leading principle in choosing one relation over another was the consideration for the overall logic of the relations' assignment as reflected in the typical attested combinations of semantic primitives (of both verbs and nouns) and relations. Other inconsistencies were also removed following the same guidelines.

The analysis of the morphosemantic relations in light of their correspondence in the domain of thematic roles and their semantic grounding gives insights into the linguistic motivation behind the semantic description of the participants in the semantic structure of verbs and serves as a point of departure for a more fine-grained analysis of the semantics of derivation with respect to classes of words with certain properties, cf. Section 6.

3.2 Relations' Independence and Overlap

As the analysis of the data presented in the previous subsection reveals, some relations cover two distinct meanings: a causative one and a means-or-function-oriented one (consider the examples given for the relations Material and By-means-of). A more detailed approach would thus involve the redefinition and reassignment of relations so that they satisfy uniform criteria, a question which we leave aside for the time being.

On the other hand, not all relations seem to be equally justified. Indeed, Vehicle, as well as Body-part, may qualify as kinds of Instruments. However, both relations are very specifically defined, and the relevant nouns fall into clear-cut semantic classes and combine syntactically with very coherent classes of verbs, such as verbs of controlled motion or vehicle operation (Vehicle) or verbs of gestures and bodily movements (Body-part). Thus, we would rather recognise these relations' membership to a more comprehensive class of relations, rather than discarding them in favour of a greater generalisation by reassigning them as Instruments.

4 Distribution of Morphosemantic Relations between Affixal and Zero Derivation

The theoretical findings sketched in Section 2 and based on empirical analyses are reflected by the data we work with: on the one hand, zero derivation is found across all the relations under discussion; on the other, conversion is the prevalent process of creating new words for 8 relations (By-means-of, Undergoer, Vehicle, Result, Property, Location, Uses, Body-part), while suffixation is the dominant word-formation technique for 4 relations (Agent, Destination, Material, State); for 2 semantic relations (Instrument, Event) conversion and derivation are in quite strong competition. These data are shown in Table 1 and Figure 1.

For all morphosemantic pairs we analyzed, besides deciding upon the formation process (zero or affixal derivation), we have also automatically identified the affix (and manually validated the data) in the latter case. Thus we were able to establish the frequency of each occurring affix, as well as of the zero affix (Ø henceforth). For a number of relations Ø is not prevalent, but is the major competitor of the most productive suffix. In Table 1 a comparison between the proportion of Ø (column 3) and the most frequent affix (column 6) shows four relations clearly dominated by affixal derivation (State, Agent, Destination, and Material); however, for two relations (State and Agent) Ø is the second most frequent affix. Further, the results for Instrument and Event demonstrate balance between conversion and affixation.

An interesting case is that of the Vehicle relation which is morphologically represented either by Ø (57 cases) or by the suffix *-er* (37 cases). Sim-

Relation name	No. of Ø-deriv.	%	Most freq. aff.	No.	%	2nd most freq. aff.	No.	%	Rest, %	Total
Uses	655	87.92	-ation	31	4.16	-ify	19	2.55	5.37	745
Location	220	80.88	-ation	23	8.46	-er	14	5.15	5.51	272
Undergoer	664	76.85	-ation	87	10.07	-ee	36	4.17	8.91	864
Result	882	63.59	-ation	301	21.70	-ify	60	4.33	10.38	1,387
Property	190	62.09	-ation	58	18.95	-ence	25	8.17	10.78	306
Vehicle	57	60.64	-er	37	39.36	-	-	-	0.00	94
By-means-of	677	59.54	-er	155	13.63	-ation	195	17.15	9.67	1,137
Body-part	40	57.14	-er	28	40.00	-ate	2	2.86	0.00	70
Event	3,544	46.34	-ation	3,328	43.52	-ment	387	5.06	5.07	7,647
Instrument	352	45.30	-er	403	51.87	-ise	14	1.80	1.03	777
State	168	32.75	-ation	237	46.20	-ment	61	11.89	9.16	513
Agent	351	12.10	-er	2,491	85.90	-ation	19	0.66	1.34	2,900
Destination	2	6.90	-ee	25	86.21	-ify	2	6.90	0.00	29
Material	3	4.23	-er	58	81.69	-ise	5	7.04	7.04	71
TOTAL	**7,805**	**46.43**								

Table 1: Distribution of conversion and affixal derivation in PWN after changes were performed. The number of unique verb-noun derivational pairs labeled with morphosemantic relations totals 16,812.

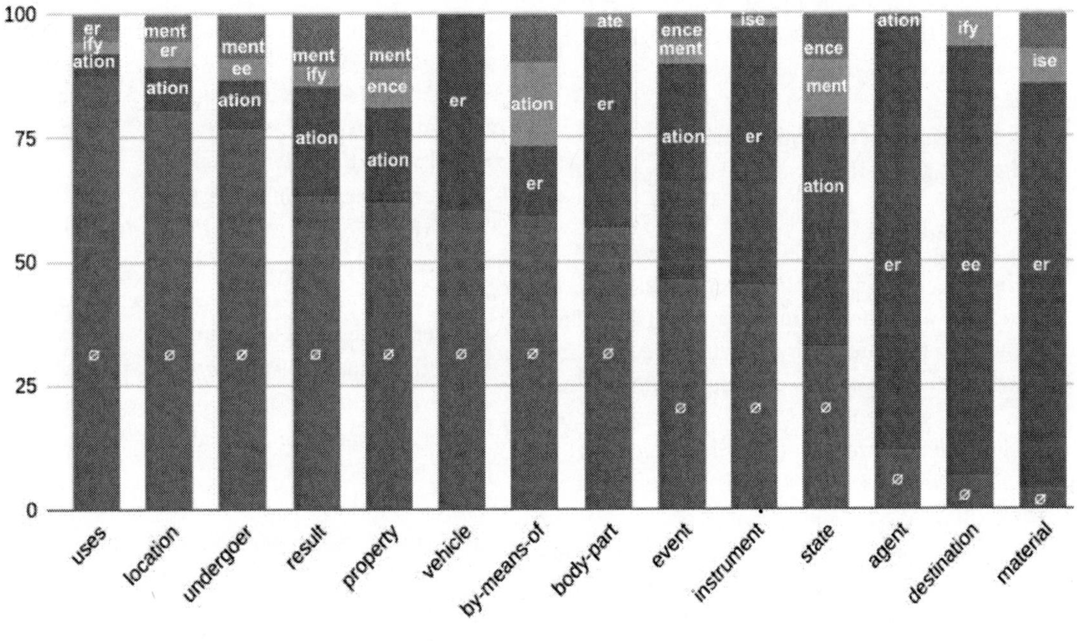

Figure 1: Competition between conversion (blue), the most frequent affix for each relation (red), the second most frequent affix (orange), the third most frequent one (green) and other affixes (purple).

ilarly, the relation Destination displays the suffix *-ee* (in 25 cases), Ø (in 2 cases) and verb suffix *-ify* (in other 2 cases). Both relations are scarce in the data under study, as the figures show.

The data presented clearly show that each relation is dominated by one or two affixes at most (including Ø), and that zero derivation plays an important role in creating new nouns and verbs, at least in the dataset under discussion. Based on our findings, *-er* and *-ation* are the most productive suffixes in these pairs, followed by Ø.

5 Morphosemantic Relations and Derivational Models

Besides the semantic perspective already incorporated by the morphosemantic relations (see Section 3), another perspective relevant for the process of creating new words is the tendency of certain semantic primes of serving either as derivation bases or as derivation results. We illustrate these trends below for each of the 14 relations.

5.1 Agent

The prevalent semantic prime of the nouns acting as Agents is noun.person, and this is no surprise. As opposed to the homogenous semantics of nouns, the verbs in these pairs belong to 14 (out of the 15) primes: the most productive ones with affixal derivation are:

• verb.communication (454[4]): *accuse*:1 – *accuser*:1, *announce*:1 – *announcer*:1;

• verb.contact (326): *carve*:1 – *carver*:1, *butt*:1 – *butter*:3;

• verb.social (318): *betray*:5 – *betrayer*:2;

while the most productive with conversion are:

• verb.social (97): *chairman*:1 – *chairman*:2, *knight*:1 – *knight*:3, *emcee*:1 – *emcee*:2;

• verb.communication (52): *blabber*:1 – *blabber*:2, *advocate*:1 – *advocate*:3;

• verb.possession (32): *auctioneer*:1 – *auctioneer*:2;

Some primes occur with both types of derivation, as noticed in these examples.

5.2 By-means-of

In the case of this morphosemantic relation, diverse verb and noun primes (11 and 10, respectively) are encountered in the data. The most frequent prime pair is verb.contact – noun.artifact, with 153 occurrences, 125 of them with conversion: *barricade*:3 – *barricade*:5, *chain*:1 – *chain*:3, *cushion*:1 – *cushion*:4. Other frequent pairs with conversion are:

• verb.communication – noun.communication (93): *alibi*:1 – *alibi*:3, *email*:2 – *email*:3, *gesture*:2 – *gesture*:4;

• verb.motion – noun.artifact (30): *bridge*:3 – *bridge*:5, *railroad*:1 – *railroad*:5, *sluice*:2 – *sluice*:5;

• verb.creation – noun.artifact (26): *festoon*:1 – *festoon*:2, *ornament*:1 – *ornament*:3, *cantilever*:1 – *cantilever*:3.

In the case of affixal derivation, the dominant prime pairs are:

• verb.communication – noun.communication (70): *impeach*:2 – *impeachment*:1, *confess*:1 – *confession*:2;

• verb.contact – noun.artifact (28): *decorate*:1 – *decoration*:2, *stop*:7 – *stopper*:2.

[4]The numbers in brackets indicate the number of synset pairs.

5.3 Destination

This relation is represented in the data with only 17 pairs. It is interesting that the prime noun.person is very well represented in combination with several verb primes and that the V-to-N derivation is dominated by the *-ee* suffix:

• verb.possession – noun.person (5): *grant*:5 – *grantee*:2, *trust*:5 – *trustee*:2;

• verb.communication – noun.person (4): *promise*:1 – *promisee*:1, *send*:2 – *sendee*:1;

• verb.social – noun.person (2): *patent*:5 – *patentee*:1, *retire*:7 – *retiree*:1;

• verb.motion – noun.person (2): *refer*:6 – *referee*:3.

5.4 Instrument

The prevalent prime pair is verb.contact – noun.artifact (398). Whereas nouns are mostly artifacts, the verbs are diverse: all 15 primes occur with this morphosemantic relation; some primes prevail with affixal derivation:

• verb.change (97): *deice*:1 – *deicer*:1;

• verb.motion (32): *elevate*:2 – *elevator*:1;

• verb.communication (24): *prompt*:2 – *prompter*:1, *buzz*:1 – *buzzer*:1, *page*:1 – *pager*:1.

Other primes tend to occur with conversion:

• verb.contact (239): *catapult*:2 – *catapult*:4;

• verb.creation (25): *crayon*:1 – *crayon*:2;

• verb.competition (14): *seine*:1 – *seine*:2.

5.5 Undergoer

Diverse noun and verb primes are implicated in pairs labeled with this morphosemantic relation, but the most frequent one is verb.communication – noun.communication: 77 occurrences out of which 42 are conversions (*compliment*:1 – *compliment*:3) and 35 are affixal derivations (*communicate*:1 – *communication*:1). Other prevalent prime pairs with conversion are:

• verb.possession – noun.possession (50): *store*:1 – *store*:6;

• verb.contact – noun.artifact (36): *veneer*:1 – *veneer*:3.

There are primes occurring only with conversion, never with affixal derivation:

• verbal primes: verb.competition: 17 with noun.animal (*rabbit*:1 – *rabbit*:2), 11 with noun.artifact (*bomb*:1 – *bomb*:3), 5 with noun.food (*prawn*:1 – *prawn*:3); verb.stative: 6 with noun.artifact (*overhang*:1 – *overhang*:3), etc.;

• noun primes: noun.animal: 17 with verb.competition (see above); 11 with verb.contact (*snail*:1 – *snail*:2); noun.plant: 11 with verb.change (*burr*:1 – *burr*:5), 7 with verb.contact (*mushroom*:2 – *mushroom*:7); noun.body: 10 with verb.body (*spit*:1 – *spit*:7), 6 with verb.contact (*transplant*:4 – *transplant*:7), etc.

Noun.person is the only noun prime for which derivation is more productive than conversion in the case of this morphosemantic relation: *address*:2 – *addressee*:1 (verb.communication), *employ*:2 – *employee*:1 (verb.social), *pay*:4 – *payee*:1 (verb.possession).

5.6 Vehicle

The prime pair verb.motion – noun.artifact is unsurprisingly the most frequent one among the pairs annotated as Vehicle: *baloon*:2 – *balloon*:3, *taxi*:2 – *taxi*:3. In the case of affixal derivation, another pair is notable: verb.competition – noun.artifact: *fight*:3 – *fighter*:1, *bomb*:1 – *bomber*:1.

5.7 Result

This relations involves great diversity in terms of both verb and noun primes. Among the most frequent prime pairs we find verb.creation – noun.artifact (82 occurrences, mostly conversions): *corduroy*:1 – *corduroy*:3. Other typical prime pairs with conversion include:

• verb.contact – noun.artifact (66): *bale*:1 – *bale*:2;

• verb.communication – noun.communication (36): *petition*:1 – *petition*:2;

Affixal derivation is frequently found with:

• verb.change – noun.substance (42): *calcify*:2 – *calcium*:1;

• verb.change – noun.attribute (37): *pinkify*:1 – *pink*:5;

• verb.change – noun.state (32): *calcify*:2 – *calcification*:3.

5.8 Body-part

This relation offers a fragmented picture in which 9 verb primes combine with 4 noun primes. As the relation is poorly represented, these prime pairs display only less than a handful of examples and we do not exemplify nor discuss them here.

5.9 Material

This relation displays the conglomeration of the pairs under 3 verb primes (verb.change, verb.contact, verb.body) and 2 noun primes (noun.artifact, noun.substance). The combination verb.change – noun.substance is the best represented (49 pairs): *opalize*:1 – *opal*:1.

5.10 Property

A relatively diverse set of 8 verb primes, the most productive of them being verb.change, verb.motion, verb.stative, combine with 2 noun primes, mostly with the prime noun.attribute and only a few pairs with noun.location. The most frequent prime pair is verb.change – noun.attribute (63, evenly distributed between zero and affixal derivation): *black*:4 – *black*:18, *cool*:1 – *cool*:11, *appear*:1 – *appearance*:4. Other frequent pairs with conversion are:

• verb.motion – noun.attribute (20): *slant*:3 – *slant*:5;

• verb.cognition – noun.attribute (14): *distrust*:1 – *distrust*:2;

• verb.contact – noun.attribute (11): *polish*:3 – *polish*:4.

Affixal derivation is more productive with the pairs:

• verb.change – noun.attribute (32): *align*:1 – *alignment*:2;

• verb.stative – noun.attribute (16): *abound*:1 – *abundance*:1.

5.11 Location

Diverse verb primes, among which the most productive ones are verb.motion, verb.contact, verb.stative, combine with nouns with primes such as noun.artifact, noun.location, noun.object, to express this relation. The most frequent prime pair is verb.contact – noun.artifact (39, mostly conversions[5]): *cabin*:1 – *cabin*:3, *closet*:1 – *closet*:2. Other frequent pairs are:

• verb.motion – noun.location (24): *port*:6 – *port*:14;

• verb.contact – noun.location (23): *park*:1 – *park*:7;

• verb.motion – noun.artifact (19): *corner*:1 – *corner*:4;

• verb.stative – noun.location (17): *bivouac*:1 – *bivouac*:3;

• verb.stative – noun.artifact (16): *lodge*:4 – *lodge*:5.

[5]Actually, examples of affixal derivation are very sparse with this relation.

5.12 Uses

Diversity of verb and noun primes characterizes this relation. The most frequent prime pair is verb.contact – noun.artifact (with over a hundred conversions and no affixal derivation): *carpet*:1 – *carpet*:4, *girth*:1 – *girth*:2. Other frequent pairs involve mainly conversion and they are:

• verb.possession – noun.artifact (57): *armor*:2 – *armor*:3;

• verb.contact – noun.substance (55): *asphalt*:1 – *asphalt*:3;

• verb.communication – noun.communication (44): *autograph*:1 – *autograph*:2;

• verb.body – noun.artifact (39): *bonnet*:1 – *bonnet*:2.

With affixal derivation a relatively frequent pair is verb.communication – noun.communication (13): *attest*:3 – *attestation*:1, while other pairs have only a few examples.

5.13 State

Many of the verb primes are involved in this relation, the most productive ones being: verb.change, verb.emotion, verb.social, verb.stative. Out of the several abstract noun primes, 2 occur more often: noun.state, noun.feeling. Affixation is more productive than conversion, but the dominant prime pairs are the same for both types of derivation:

• verb.emotion – noun.feeling (80): *abash*:1 - *abashment*:1, *joy*:2 – *joy*:4;

• verb.change – noun.state (86): *afflict*:1 – *affliction*:3, *decay*:1 – *decay*:8;

• verb.emotion – noun.state (48): *deject*:1 – *dejection*:1, *despair*:1 – *despair*:3.

5.14 Event

The most frequent prime pair is verb.communication – noun.communication and with this, the competition between derivation and conversion is the strongest (363 vs. 361). The most productive pairs differ for the two types of derivation. With affixal derivation they are:

• verb.change – noun.act (593): *alter*:3 – *alteration*:1;

• verb.social – noun.act (421): *abolish*:1 – *abolition*:1;

• verb.change – noun.process (283): *adapt*:1 – *adaptation*:3;

The most frequent pairs with conversion are:

• verb.motion – noun.act (423): *amble*:2 – *amble*:1;

• verb.contact – noun.act (337): *clasp*:2 – *clasp*:1;

• verb.competition – noun.act (126): *cricket*:2 – *cricket*:1.

6 Discussion

The presented data must be interpreted with a view to the PWN organization principles: all pairs contain words considered with only one of their possible meanings; i.e. the same pair of words may be found several times, labeled either with the same semantic relation or with a different one: e.g., the verb *net* and the noun *net* occur as a pair three times: once labeled as Instrument (for the meanings 'catch with a net' and 'a trap made of netting to catch fish or birds or insects', respectively), and twice as Result: the verb meaning 'yield as a net profit' and the noun denoting 'the excess of revenues over outlays in a given period of time (including depreciation and other non-cash expenses)', and the verb meaning 'construct or form a web, as if by weaving' with the noun denoting 'an open fabric of string or rope or wire woven together at regular intervals'. Not all senses of the words can enter a morphosemantic relation with all senses of another word: e.g., the verb *net* has four senses in PWN, the homonymous noun has six senses, but the only morphosemantic relations between them are the three mentioned above.

On the other hand, the PWN files include 4,520 noun-verb derivational pairs that do not occur in the standoff file: e.g.: *carbon* and *carbonate* are linked by a derivational relation in the PWN, but they were not included in the standoff file.

Some pairs in the data are not direct derivatives: consider the homonymous verbs and nouns *black* or *green*, where both are derived from the corresponding adjectives. This is not the case with colors only: e.g. the verb and the noun *equal* are both derived from the respective adjective, too[6].

An interesting topic for research is the direction of conversion. There are examples of each direction among the pairs labeled with the same semantic relation: e.g. among the pairs labeled as Agent, we find nouns created from verbs by means of conversion, such as *snoop*, as well as verbs converted from nouns, such as *mouth*. There are cases when, for the same pair of primes, affixation goes in one direction, while zero derivation goes in the opposite one: e.g. for the prime pair verb.possession –

[6]According to data in https://www.etymonline.com

noun.person, nouns are derived from verbs (*auctioneer* from *auction*) and verbs are created from nouns via zero derivation (*auctioneer*). These observations need to be explored in more detail.

Researchers, see mainly Clark and Clark (1979) and Plag (1999), have aligned derivational semantics (zero derivation in particular) with the semantics of verb classes. Bauer et al. (2013) discuss the predictability of the semantics of nominalizations especially those denoting "an instance or a state aspectual meaning". Such information can also be drawn from our data, but taking the form of clusters of hyponyms that belong to the same region of the wordnet structure (the same subtree). The more detailed analysis of the data leads us to conclude that the clusters give a more profound insight into the semantic conditions on derivation than general classes as it is clusters that provide the structured part of the lexicon involved.

Relation: V prime – N prime pair (total #)		
Cluster root	**No. cases**	**%**
Agent: verb.body – noun.person (109)		
{change:1}	24	22.02
{act:1}	14	12.84
Agent: verb.change – noun.person (140)		
{change:1}	69	49.29
Agent: verb.cognition – noun.person (168)		
{think:3}	71	22.26
Agent: verb.communication – noun.person (506)		
{act:1}	234	46.25
{express:2}	66	13.04
{think:3}	46	9.09
Agent: verb.consumption – noun.person (69)		
{consume:2}	39	56.52
Agent: verb.creation – noun.person (205)		
{make:3}	127	61.95
Agent: verb.motion – noun.person (286)		
{go:1}	149	52.10
{move:3}	34	11.89
Agent: verb.perception – noun.person (74)		
{perceive:1}	18	24.32
{watch:1}	15	20.27
{show:4}	7	9.46
Agent: verb.possession – noun.person (250)		
{transfer:5}	82	32.80
{take:21}	25	10.00
{show:4}	7	9.46

Table 2: Some significant clusters within the morphosemantic relation of Agent.

Table 2 shows the overall number of occurrences for the most numerous combinations of verb primes with the prime noun.person for the relation Agent. The most meaningful clusters are represented as the root verb synsets to whose tree the verbs in the clusters belong, the nouns being in the subtree of *person*:1. The table shows each

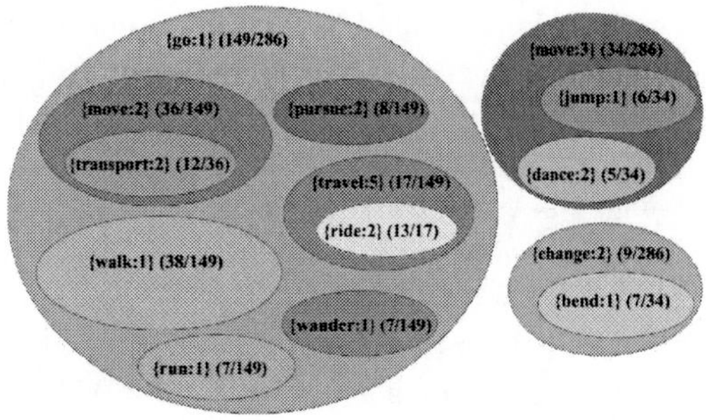

Figure 2: Clusters of verbs for the relation of Agent within the prime of verb.motion.

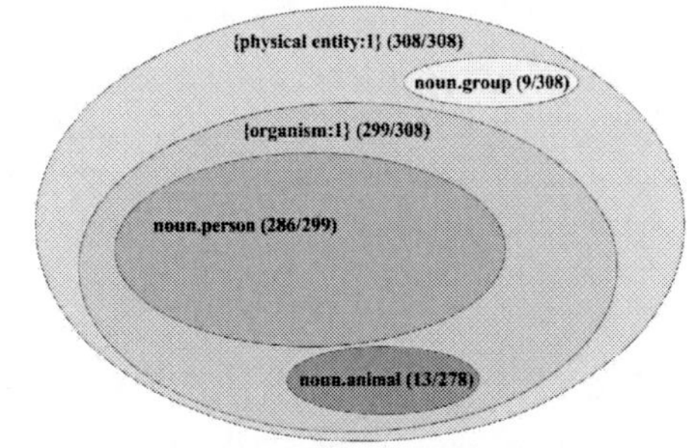

Figure 3: Clusters of nouns for the relation of Agent within the prime of verb.motion.

cluster's share as absolute numbers and as percentage of the number of the prime pair occurrences.

Figure 2 exemplifies the distribution of synsets belonging to the prime verb.motion which are involved in the relation Agent (see Table 2). More than half of the synsets (149 out of 286) are hyponyms of the synset *travel*:1; *go*:1; *move*:1; *locomote*:1 (the embedded bubbles). Each of these bubbles is the root of a smaller subtree and is also represented numerically. The blue and green bubbles exemplify outliers in other subtrees.

Figure 3 provides a similar representation of the noun synsets involved in the Agent relation with verbs of motion (verb.motion). Most of them are nouns designating persons (286 out of 308), with a very small number of synsets from other primes.

As not all derivational relations are assigned a morphosemanticl label (see above, this Section), the question of the predictability of the morphosemantic relations arises. Our analysis of several samples of the data shows that the relations are predictable only to a certain extent. A semantic relation of one of the 14 types could be automatically assigned to pairs of word senses that are derivationally related in PWN but lack a semantic label (as in the standoff file) if they occur in subtrees where a certain relation is already assigned to other pairs: consider the pairs in the standoff file: *nickel*:1 – *nickel*:1 , *silver*:1 – *silver*:1, *copper*:1 – *copper*:1 and *chrome*:1 – *chrome*:1. These four verbs are hyponyms of *cover*:1, while the nouns are hyponyms of *metal*:1; the semantic relation these pairs are annotated with is Uses. However, there are other such pairs in PWN, e.g.: *aluminium*:1 – *aluminize*:1, where the verb is a hyponym of *cover*:1 and the noun is a hyponym of *metal*:1 and there is a derivational relation between them, but it is not labeled morphosemantically. Given the four examples above, we can infer that the right semantic label for this pair (and other similar ones) is Uses. In other cases inferring a semantic relation may not be so trivial, but at least the number of possibilities will be greatly reduced and manual validation will be facilitated. Besides labeling new pairs, such regularities can also help to easily spot oddities in the data and correct them.

Regular polysemy is reflected in morphosemantic relations, especially as from a contemporary point of view a verb's sense may be considered to be related to more than one (closely) related noun senses or vice versa. Such an example is found with nouns of the class noun.artifact (mostly containers) and nouns denoting the quantity that the respective container holds, e.g. *barrel*:2, *cask*:2 ('a cylindrical container that holds liquids') and *barrel*:4, *barrelful*:1 ('the quantity that a barrel (of any size) will hold'). Each of the two synsets is related to *barrel*:1 ('put in barrels') by means of the relations Location and Undergoer, respectively. Regular polysemy reveals how regularities between related meanings in the nominal or the verbal domain are reflected in the semantics of the relation in verb-noun pairs.

Observations on structured parts of the lexicon such as the ones discussed above enable us also to predict missing relations, both morphosemantic and derivational. Consider *jar*:5 ('place in a cylindrical vessel') and the noun synsets *jar*:1 ('a vessel (usually cylindrical') and *jar*:2, *jarful*:1 ('the quantity contained in a jar'). Although only the Undergoer relation is encoded, the Location relation is easily predictable on the basis of the *barrel* example above. Exploring further the hyponyms of the synset *containerful*:1 ('the quantity that a container will hold'), we discover that 25 out of its 67 hyponyms have corresponding verbs, but only 3 of the verbs are appropriately linked to the noun synsets denoting the respective quantity and artifact (in a like manner to *barrel*) – the remaining verbs lack one or both morphosemantic relations or even the derivational ones. In such a way, we are able to tackle the inconsistencies in derivational and morphosemantic relations throughout this and other parts of the PWN structure.

7 Conclusions

Our study based on the PWN standoff file consisting of noun-verb pairs labeled with one of a set of 14 semantic relations shows the distribution of zero and affixal derivation within the data, at a general level, as well as with respect to each such relation. We have also presented the most frequent affixes by means of which words are created in the subgroups represented by relations labeled identically and showed that the zero affix is among the most frequent ones for each such subgroup: for some relations it is the prevalent affix and for others it competes with the prevalent one. The semantics of these pairs was further enriched with information about the semantic primes of each word in the pair and several noun-verb prime combinations proved more frequent in some subgroups, with some of the combinations even being specialised for a certain type of derivation.

We intend to augment the work with other pairs extracted from the PWN files and already linked by a derivational relation. We envisage a better representation of certain affixes (especially verbal ones) that are sparse in the standoff file.

Our work can be extended to derivational relations for other languages using the corresponding wordnets. Since the semantic dimension of morphosemantic relations is transferable across languages using the interlingual indexing within PWN, it facilitates the study of derivation across languages and possibly in comparison as well.

Acknowledgments

This work was carried out in the project *Enhancing Multilingual Language Resources with Derivationally Linked Multiword Expressions* between the Institute for Bulgarian Language of the Bulgarian Academy of Sciences and the Research Institute for Artificial Intelligence of the Romanian Academy.

References

L. Bauer, R. Lieber, I. Plag. 2013. The Oxford Reference Guide to English Morphology. Oxford University Press.

B. Cetnarowska. 1993. The Syntax, Semantics and Derivation of Bare Nominalisations in English. Katowice. Uniwersytet Slaski.

E. Clark, and H. H. Clark. 1979. When Nouns Surface as Verbs. *Language*. 55 (4).

Ch. Fellbaum (ed.). 1998. *WordNet: An Electronic Lexical Database*. Cambridge, MA: MIT Press.

Ch. Fellbaum, A. Osherson, and P. E. Clark. 2009. Putting Semantics into WordNet's 'Morphosemantic' Links. In: Z. Vetulani, H. Uszkoreit (eds) *Human Language Technology. Challenges of the Information Society. LTC 2007.* Lecture Notes in Computer Science, vol 5603. Springer, Berlin, Heidelberg.

S. Koeva, S. Leseva, I. Stoyanova, T. Dimitrova, M. Todorova. Automatic Prediction of Morphosemantic Relations. In: *Proceedings of GWC 2016.* Bucharest.

R. Lieber. 2004. Morphology and Lexical Semantics. Cambridge University Press.

G. A. Miller, R. Beckwith, C. Fellbaum, D. Gross, K.J. Miller. 1990. Introduction to WordNet: An Online Lexical Database. *International Journal of Lexicography,* 3 (4), pp. 235 – 244.

P. O. Müller 2016. Rules and Restrictions in Word-Formation I. General Aspects. *Word-Formation. An International Handbook of the Languages of Europe* De Gruyter Mouton.

I. Plag. 1999. *Morphological productivity: structural constraints in English derivation.* Berlin, New York: Mouton de Gruyter.

Building the Turkish FrameNet

Büşra Marşan
Starlang Yazılım Danışmanlık
busra@starlangyazilim.com

Neslihan Kara
Starlang Yazılım Danışmanlık
neslihan@starlangyazilim.com

Merve Özçelik
Starlang Yazılım Danışmanlık
merve@starlangyazilim.com

Bilge Nas Arıcan
Starlang Yazılım Danışmanlık
bilge@starlangyazilim.com

Neslihan Cesur
Starlang Yazılım Danışmanlık
nesli@starlangyazilim.com

Aslı Kuzgun
Starlang Yazılım Danışmanlık
asli@starlangyazilim.com

Ezgi Sanıyar
Starlang Yazılım Danışmanlık
ezgi@starlangyazilim.com

Oğuzhan Kuyrukçu
Starlang Yazılım Danışmanlık
oguzhan@starlangyazilim.com

Olcay Taner Yıldız
Özyeğin University
olcay.yildiz@ozyegin.edu.tr

Abstract

FrameNet (Lowe, 1997; Baker et al., 1998; Fillmore and Atkins, 1998; Johnson et al., 2001) is a computational lexicography project that aims to offer insight into the semantic relationships between predicate and arguments. Having uses in many NLP applications, FrameNet has proven itself as a valuable resource. The main goal of this study is laying the foundation for building a comprehensive and cohesive Turkish FrameNet that is compatible with other resources like PropBank (Kara et al., 2020) or WordNet (Bakay et al., 2019; Ehsani, 2018; Ehsani et al., 2018; Parlar et al., 2019; Bakay et al., 2020) in the Turkish language.

1 Introduction

Introduced in 1997, FrameNet (Lowe, 1997; Baker et al., 1998; Fillmore and Atkins, 1998; Johnson et al., 2001) has been developed by the International Computer Science Institute in Berkeley, California. It is a growing computational lexicography project that offers in-depth semantic information on English words and predicates. Based on the theory of Frame Semantics by Fillmore (Fillmore and others, 1976; Fillmore, 2006), FrameNet offers semantic information on predicate-argument structure in a way that is loosely similar to wordnet (Kilgarriff and Fellbaum, 2000).

In FrameNet, predicates and related lemmas are categorized under frames. The notion of frame here is thoroughly described in Frame Semantics as a schematic representation of an event, state or relationship. These semantic information packets called frames are constituted of individual lemmas (also known as Lexical Units) and frame elements (such as the agent, theme, instrument, duration, manner, direction etc.). Frame elements can be described as semantic roles that are related to the frame. Lexical Units, or lemmas, are linked to a frame through a single sense. For instance, the lemma "roast" can mean to criticise harshly or to cook by exposing to dry heat [1]. With its latter meaning, "roast" belongs to the Apply_Heat frame.

With this study, we aimed to recreate a comprehensive FrameNet in Turkish language following Fellbaum's notions related to Frame Semantics theory. For this purpose, we referred to English FrameNet's frames and Turkish WordNet's properties. In order to ensure compatibility with Turkish WordNet (KeNet) and Turkish PropBank (TRopBank), we used the same lemma IDs.

In this paper, we present our attempt at building a Turkish FrameNet. In Section 2 titled Towards a Turkish FrameNet, we explain our motivation,

[1] Definitions are taken from Merriam-Webster Dictionary at https://www.merriam-webster.com/dictionary

methodology and processes along with the challenges we faced during this study. In Section 3 we present our results and discuss these results in Section 4. Finally, we conclude with our suggestions regarding further study in Section 5.

2 Towards a Turkish FrameNet

2.1 Motivation

With this study, we aim to take the first step towards creating a comprehensive and coherent Turkish FrameNet that is able to illustrate the semantic richness and the typological properties of Turkish language. We intend to provide a certain level of correspondence between Turkish FrameNet and English FrameNet to allow using Turkish FrameNet in machine translation tasks and various other multilingual NLP processes. Another aspiration of ours is to build a FrameNet for Turkish that can be interconnected with other NLP resources in Turkish like PropBank (Kara et al., 2020) and WordNet (KeNet) (Bakay et al., 2019; Ehsani, 2018; Ehsani et al., 2018; Parlar et al., 2019; Bakay et al., 2020) in order to create state-of-the-art parsers, semantic role labelling tools and similar NLP applications with high accuracy and speed.

In many languages, the teams behind creating these resources are different. That is why finding a way to use more than one of them at the same time or in the same NLP application is a very challenging task which requires additional steps and many resources including time. In Turkish the same team created PropBank, WordNet and FrameNet. Moreover, same lemmas and synsets across these resources have the same IDs. As a result, it is possible to find the WordNet entry, PropBank entry or FrameNet frame of the same predicate only by using its ID number. In other words, combining these resources does not require an additional step or extra effort. We believe that such a coordination and compatibility would make it significantly easier to create NLP solutions that employ two or all three of these resources for increased accuracy.

2.2 Methodology

In this section, two different aspects of the methodology will be discussed: First the strategy, then the annotator team and their roles.

When examined closely, FrameNet projects of different languages adopt one of the two main strategies (Candito et al., 2014):

- A frame-by-frame approach that first creates frames and then fills them with Lexical Units. This approach is very prominent in FrameNet studies and employed by the vast majority.

- A lemma-by-lemma approach that brings together semantically similar Lexical Units to create their corresponding frame. This approach is fully adopted by the German FrameNet project SALSA (Burchardt et al., 2006; Burchardt et al., 2009) (and partially employed by Japanese FrameNet (Ohara et al., 2004; Ohara et al., 2003; Ohara et al., 2009; Ohara, 2008)).

Both strategies propose a set of advantages and challenges. As stated by Candito et al. (2014), the frame-by-frame approach ensures the coherency within the frames while lemma-by-lemma approach allows the annotators to unveil the full semantic range of a given lemma by discovering rarer senses and larger units encompassing many lemmas (Burchardt et al., 2009). Although a lemma-by-lemma approach leads to a more comprehensive analysis of the Lexical Units, it also creates a "biased" lexicon for "only senses pertaining to covered frames will appear in the lexicon, and these senses are not necessarily the most frequent senses of that lemma (Candito et al., 2014)." Moreover, a lemma-by-lemma approach makes it considerably more difficult to develop frames and build parent-child, inheritance and lateral relationships between these frames.

As neither of these strategies is objectively and ultimately "better," we turned to our data in order to choose the most viable strategy for building a Turkish FrameNet. Since a comprehensive Turkish PropBank (Kara et al., 2020) and Turkish WordNet (Bakay et al., 2019; Ehsani, 2018; Ehsani et al., 2018; Parlar et al., 2019; Bakay et al., 2020) was already available for Turkish, a quick research can show that Turkish has more than 18,000 documented predicates. Adopting a frame-by-frame approach to incorporate them all in a Turkish FrameNet would be unrealistic, if not impossible. On the other hand, choosing a lemma-by-lemma approach would take a painstakingly long time. As a low-resource language, Turkish's need for a FrameNet is very evident and rather urgent -especially when it is considered that an attempt for creating a Turkish FrameNet is made more than two decades after the English

FrameNet. That is why the best solution was opting for a hybrid strategy put forward by Candito et al. (2014) for building French FrameNet.

Our motivation for choosing a hybrid strategy was mostly related to efficiency: We aimed to release a version of Turkish FrameNet that captures at least a considerable majority of the most frequent predicates, thus offering a valuable and practical resource from day one. Because Turkish is a low-resource language, it was important to ensure that FrameNet had enough coverage that it could be incorporated into NLP solutions as soon as it is released to the public.

Following the footsteps of French FrameNet, we took a closer look at Turkish WordNet and designated 8 domains that would possibly contain the most frequent predicates in Turkish: Activity, Cause, Change, Motion, Cognition, Perception, Judgement and Commerce.

For the first phase, the focus was on the thorough annotation of these domains. Frames from English FrameNet were adopted when possible and new frames were created when needed. In the next phase[2], our team of annotators will attack the Turkish predicate compilation offered by TRopBank and KeNet for a lemma-by-lemma annotation process. This way, both penetration and coverage of the Turkish FrameNet will be increased.

Following the annotation strategy, we decided upon the roles of annotators. In the development process of the English FrameNet, 3 different teams worked (Baker et al., 1998): Vanguards who come up with frames, Annotators who match Lexical Units and Frame Elements with frames, and Rearguards who review lexical records and create lexical entries for lemmas and frames. In our study, we opted out of this workflow. Instead, we divided annotators to four teams of two. Each annotator was given a domain. Their duty was creating frames within that domain by translating and adopting related frames from English FrameNet. Then they had to extract lexical units from TRopBank and KeNet, annotate their frame elements, write sample sentences and annotate these sentences. During these processes, members of each team kept in touch and reviewed one another's annotations. Moreover, all teams and annotators met weekly for discussions and decision-making processes. After the annotation process was finished, a member of the team carefully went through all frames, sentences, LUs and FEs to ensure coherency and agreement. After disputable cases were discussed among the team, she fixed all issues.

The sample sentences in Turkish FrameNet were extracted from TDK Dictionary [3] when possible. Otherwise, annotators came up with novel sentences. Refer to Figure 1 for an annotated frame.

As stated in the previous section, one of our main goals was to create a Turkish FrameNet that is compatible with other NLP resources like TRopBank and KeNet in Turkish. That is why we used KeNet's synsets and lemma IDs in Turkish FrameNet. In other words, we did not annotate single lemmas as Lexical Units, instead we annotated synsets that share the same semantic and syntactic properties. For instance, wordnet synset with TUR10-0354260 ID number contains two predicates: "ısıtmak" and "sıcaklaştırmak." Both predicates:

- Literally mean "to heat,"
- Share a definition,
- Assign the same case to their internal argument,
- Give the Agent role to their external argument,
- Can be used interchangeably without any loss to the sense.

Thus, we added this synset in Apply_Heat frame (See Table 1)

Since both syntactic and semantic criteria was considered while creating synsets in KeNet, TRopBank uses these synsets as lemmas. As we aimed to make FrameNet as compatible as possible with both TRopBank and KeNet, we decided to use these existing synsets as well. Considering the fact that items in a synset share the same meaning, have the same number of arguments and assign the same theta roles to these arguments, we believe that taking them as Frame Units does not conflict with the theory behind FrameNet and does not negatively affect the accuracy. Moreover, it can even be argued that annotating synsets in their related frames provides additional information regarding the synonymy.

[2]Only the first phase is within the scope of this paper.

[3]https://sozluk.gov.tr

Frame	Definition	Lexical Unit Id	Lexical Unit Synset	Lexical Unit Definition	Frame Elements
Attempt	An Agent attempts to achieve a Goal. The Outcome may also be mentioned explicitly.	TUR10-0192570	denemek	Bir işe, başarmak amacıyla başlamak, girişimde bulunmak, teşebbüs etmek	Agent, Goal, Circumstances, Effort
		TUR10-1160410	teşebbüse geçmek	bir işi yapmak için davranmak, girişmek	Agent, Goal, Circumstances, Effort, Manners
		TUR10-1160420	teşebbüs etmek	girişmek, el atmak	Agent, Goal, Circumstances, Effort, Manners
		TUR10-0479350	koyulmak	Girişmek, başlamak, teşebbüs etmek	Agent, Goal, Manners
		TUR10-1032280	girişimde bulunmak	davranmak, teşebbüs etmek	Agent, Goal, Circumstances, Effort, Manners
		TUR10-1183220	yerini yapmak	bir şey elde etmek amacıyla girişimde bulunmak	Agent, Goal, Circumstances, Effort, Manners
		TUR10-0298660	girişmek	Kalkışmak	Agent, Goal, Manners

Figure 1: Attempt frame

Table 1: Apply_Heat Frame

Frame	Lexical Unit ID	Synset	Definition
Apply_Heat	TUR10-0354260	ısıtmak, sıcaklaştırmak	Sıcak duruma getirmek
Apply_Heat	TUR10-1154650	tava getirmek	Gereği kadar ısıtmak
Apply_Heat	TUR10-0810920	ütmek	Taze buğday veya mısırı ateşe tutup pişirmek
Apply_Heat	TUR10-0810910	ütmek	Bir şeyi, tüylerini yakmak için alevden geçirmek

2.3 Maintaining Inter-Annotator Agreement

In order to ensure inter-annotator agreement, members of each group kept in touch and consulted one another regarding debatable Lexical Units and frames. Moreover, the annotation interface allowed annotators to see, comment on and mark each other's annotations. Each week, all annotators had a meeting where they discussed ambiguities, marked annotations and challenging Lexical Units.

After the annotation process was completed, a team member took on the role of controller and went through every frame, Lexical Unit and its annotation to look for inconsistencies. The inconsistencies or potential issues detected by her were thoroughly discussed by the entire team. Afterwards, she fixed these issues and changed annotations when necessary.

Amongst all domains, Change posed most problems. A significant amount of predicates annotated in this domain were also present in frames that belonged to other domains. For instance, many predicates that implied a deliberate change of location by an Agent were annotated in both Change and Motion domain. Considering the nature and theoretical background of FrameNet, it is not surprising to find out that some predicates belong in two different frames (e.g. "koşmak" *(run)*, see 2), but a significant overlap is often an indicator of a serious problem. That is why the team of annotators discussed the common predicates in Change domain and other domains like Motion and Cognition. Since Change denotes a massive domain, team members almost scrutinised it to ensure that only both semantically and syntactically related predicates were annotated in the frames of this domain.

After careful inspection, some predicates were removed from this domain and some new subframes like Cognitive Change were created.

2.4 Challenges

For we took English FrameNet's frames as the guideline in this study, significant issues we faced were related to the typological differences between these two languages. As thoroughly discussed by Kara et al. (2020), Turkish has significantly more unaccusative verbs and lexicalized, figurative multi-word predicates. Thus, categorization of these Lexical Units posed a serious challenge. Unaccusative verbs do not take an agent or patient per se. Often they are used with expletives. That is why they are syntactically different from other verbs but from a semantic point of view, they are very similar with many accusative, transitive and ditransitive verbs. A perfect example of this phenomena can be seen in Activity_Paused_State frame. "dinmek" *(stop)* is only used for precipitation and takes no internal arguments (objects) while "dondurmak" *(freeze)* can be used for individuals and takes internal arguments (objects). Although their valency and argument structure differs significantly, both verbs conform to the definition of Activity_Paused_State frame[4]. After thorough discussions, our team of annotators decided upon including unaccusative verbs or lexicalized, figurative multi-word predicates. The reasoning behind this decision is the fact that FrameNet is a resource whose primary focus is on semantic properties of the Lexical Units. That is why even nominal forms like "moratorium" or "to freeze" are included in related frames in English FrameNet. Such unaccusative verbs are marked in their definition. If they are used only with an expletive or a certain lexical element, this is mentioned in the definition, e.g. "dinmek" *(stop)*. It is used only for precipitation, thus its external arguments can only be "kar" *(snow)*, "yağmur" *(rain)*, "dolu" *(hail)* or "tipi" *(blizzard)*. This is explicitly mentioned in the definition of this lexical entry, which can be found in Turkish FrameNet, WordNet and PropBank.

Another challenge was posed by the fact that some English Lexical Units have no correspondent in Turkish. As a result, it was not possible to recreate some English frames in Turkish, such as Activity_Ready_State. As a solution, we simply abandoned such frames. In contrast, some frames like Frugality were much richer than their English counterparts. For such instances, we divided those frames into subframes in accordance with the semantic properties of their Lexical Units. For the Frugality case, we introduced 3 subframes: Frugality_Time, Frugality_Waste and Frugality_Money (see Table 2 for frame statistics). The reason behind was the mere pattern displayed by Turkish predicates. When we brought together all predicates that belong to the Frugality frame, we noticed a pattern: From a semantic and syntactic point of view, it was possible to divide these Frugality predicates into 3 subcategories. While creating such sub-categories or creating new frames, we considered argument number and structure along with case and thematic role assignment of the predicates.

In addition to dividing richer and broader frames, we also needed to create new frames like Games_Jargon[5] in order to properly illustrate the intricate semantics of Turkish. The decision to create a new frame for Turkish was taken when there were multiple predicates that share at least one intrinsic semantic or syntactic feature that sets them apart from the closest English frame. A good example is Deprivation frame, created for Turkish FrameNet. Similar frames from English FrameNet are Deny_or_Grant_Permission, Preventing_or_Letting and Change_Access. In Deny_or_Grant_Permission frame, the focus is on allowing or disallowing a protagonist to engage in an action. Preventing_or_Letting frame refers to the situations where an agent can hinder something from happening. And finally, Change_Access frame refers to the access to a physical location. In Deprivation frame, an Agent or Authority deprives an entity or a group of entities of things they require for staying alive or completing a task. Although similar to the existing frames in English, Deprivation frame refers to a novel notion. Since there are multiple predicates in Turkish that correspond to this notion (7, to be exact), our team of annotators decided that creating such a frame was appropriate.

The main motivation behind our responses to the challenges we faced was being able to offer a coherent FrameNet for Turkish instead of a mere translation of English frames and Lexical Units. Although this adaptation based approach lowers the correspondence with English to some degree, the vast majority of the frames are parallel. That is why Turkish FrameNet is a resource fit for both Turkish NLP projects and bilingual NLP projects like machine translation.

3 Results

In this study, a total number of 139 Frames in 8 domains were created[6]. 16 of these frames were created specifically for Turkish while the remaining 123 are translated from English FrameNet. These frames include a total number of 2769 synsets (See Table 2). As we used Turkish WordNet and PropBank's repositories, the Lexical Units were made

[4]An Agent pauses in the course of an Activity.

[5]This frame contains Lexical Units related to tabletop games and board games.

[6]https://github.com/StarlangSoftware/TurkishFrameNet
https://github.com/StarlangSoftware/TurkishFrameNet-Py
https://github.com/StarlangSoftware/TurkishFrameNet-Cy
https://github.com/StarlangSoftware/TurkishFrameNet-C#
https://github.com/StarlangSoftware/TurkishFrameNet-CPP

Table 2: Statistics

Total Frames	139
Unique Frames	16
Synsets (LUs)	2561
Individual Predicates	4080
Frame Elements	203

Table 3: A comparison with initial versions of other FrameNets

Language	Frames	LUs
French	98	662
Chinese	322	3947
Swedish	51	2300

of wordnet synsets. Thus some LUs contain more than one predicate. The total number of predicates annotated in this study is 4080. In other words, 4080 predicates were annotated into their respective frames. Sample sentences of all were marked up for the specific roles in them.

Compared to initial versions of French FrameNet, Chinese FrameNet and Swedish FrameNet, the Turkish FrameNet developed by this study offers a promising coverage (see Table 3). It must be noted that French, Chinese and Swedish FrameNets have been being developed further, thus their current coverage is better than their initial versions.

4 Discussion

The aim of this study was creating a useful resource for Natural Language Processing studies in Turkish. Offering 139 frames, 2561 synsets and 4080 Lexical Units, this study can be considered as a very satisfactory first step towards this goal. In addition, Turkish FrameNet is created in correspondence with English FrameNet. Rather than being a mere translation, Turkish FrameNet employs new frames when necessary but maintains its close ties with English FrameNet. That is why it can be used in both Turkish NLP studies and English-Turkish translation applications. Moreover, this close correspondence to English FrameNet makes it possible to introduce cross-correspondence between Turkish and various other FrameNets that use same or similar frames as English FrameNet.

In many other languages, NLP resources like PropBank, WordNet and FrameNet use different identification and processing systems for their lemmas. That is why it is rather challenging to integrate them and create enhanced, state of the art NLP solutions. On the other hand, Turkish PropBank TRopBank, Turkish WordNet KeNet and Turkish FrameNet use the same set of lemmas. As a result, individual synsets have the same IDs across all platforms. That is why it is possible and relatively easier to integrate these three resources and create cutting edge NLP tools or train highly accurate semantic annotators. Such streamlined databanks and corpora offer a great value to NLP studies in low resource languages like Turkish.

Due to being able to easily correlate, TRopBank and Turkish FrameNet can be used together to empower NLP solutions. Because of its characteristic features, PropBank offers syntactic information regarding the predicates while fails to capture the semantic layer. On the other hand, FrameNet does not offer much information about the valency of a predicate. That is why the combination of these two offer a coherent and thorough analysis for NLP applications. Since the same team is behind creating KeNet, TRopBank and Turkish FrameNet, these three resources share same synsets and lemmas. Thus, they can be used together in the same NLP solution without spending much effort on making them compatible.

5 Further Studies

This study is the very first attempt to a Turkish FrameNet. That is why the primary aim was laying the foundation. In order to create initial frames and include at least some portion of the most commonly used predicates in Turkish, we opted for a top-down approach. In other words, we created 139 frames in 8 domains and added related lexical units into these frames. For the next step, a bottom-up approach may be more appropriate in order to extend the coverage of FrameNet. For this purpose, Turkish WordNet KeNet (Bakay et al., 2019; Ehsani, 2018; Ehsani et al., 2018; Parlar et al., 2019; Bakay et al., 2020) can provide a very useful resource. Annotators can start from the terminal branches and work their way up, creating new frames and building inheritance and/or lateral relationships between frames. In this step, KeNet's own hierarchy can be a guide for creating new frames.

Since this study consists of only 139 frames, the lateral and hierarchical (inheritance) relations between frames are significantly limited. For in-

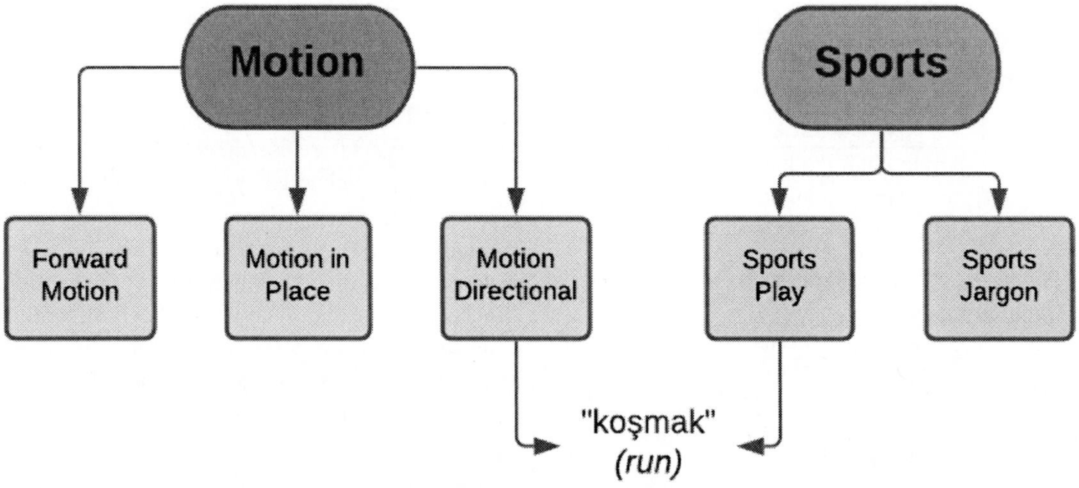

Figure 2: Frame relations

stance, frames within the Motion domain have a strong hierarchical relationship (See Figure 2). For instance, "kaçmak" *(run away)* LU is a member of Forward_Motion frame and its parent frame, Motion.

Yet some Lexical Units in Motion domain also correspond to Sports_Play frame (See Figure 2). The lateral relationship between these two overlapping frames is not strictly defined. Since the number of frames are relatively low at the moment, such refinements are not crucial but as the Turkish FrameNet grows, the necessity of defining both hierarchical and lateral relationships will be indispensable. Again, the relationships determined in KeNet can and should play a pivotal role for such definitions for the sake of coherence.

In this study, English FrameNet (Lowe, 1997; Baker et al., 1998; Fillmore and Atkins, 1998; Johnson et al., 2001) was taken as the baseline. That is why the vast majority of the frames correspond to English ones despite some necessary deviations due to the typological characteristics of Turkish. In the follow-up works, the correspondence between lexical units should be built, so that a cross-language resource that can be used in various NLP applications like machine translation is created.

References

Ö. Bakay, Ö. Ergelen, and O. T. Yıldız. 2019. Integrating Turkish wordnet kenet to princeton wordnet: The case of one-to-many correspondences. In *2019 Innovations in Intelligent Systems and Applications Conference (ASYU)*, pages 1–5.

O. Bakay, O. Ergelen, E. Sarmis, S. Yildirim, A. Kocabalcioglu, B. N. Arican, M. Ozcelik, E. Saniyar, O. Kuyrukcu, B. Avar, and O. T. Yıldız. 2020. Turkish WordNet KeNet. In *Proceedings of GWC 2020.*

Collin F. Baker, Charles J. Fillmore, and John B. Lowe. 1998. The Berkeley FrameNet project. In *36th Annual Meeting of the Association for Computational Linguistics and 17th International Conference on Computational Linguistics, Volume 1*, pages 86–90, Montreal, Quebec, Canada, August. Association for Computational Linguistics.

Aljoscha Burchardt, Katrin Erk, Anette Frank, Andrea Kowalski, Sebastian Padó, and Manfred Pinkal. 2006. The SALSA corpus: a German corpus resource for lexical semantics. In *Proceedings of the Fifth International Conference on Language Resources and Evaluation (LREC'06)*, Genoa, Italy, May. European Language Resources Association (ELRA).

Aljoscha Burchardt, Katrin Erk, Anette Frank, Andrea Kowalski, Sebastian Padó, and Manfred Pinkal, 2009. *Using FrameNet for the Semantic Analysis of German: Annotation, Representation, and Automation.* 01.

Marie Candito, Pascal Amsili, Lucie Barque, Farah Benamara, Gaël de Chalendar, Marianne Djemaa, Haas Pauline, Richard Huyghe, Yvette Yannick, Mathieu bullet, Philippe Muller, Benoît Sagot, and Laure Vieu. 2014. Developing a French framenet: Methodology and first results. 05.

Elin Ehsani, Ercan Solak, and Olcay Yildiz. 2018. Constructing a wordnet for Turkish using manual and automatic annotation. *ACM Transactions on Asian Language Information Processing*, 17:1–15, 04.

Elin Ehsani. 2018. *KeNet: A Comprehensive Turkish Wordnet And Its Applications In Text Clustering*. Ph.D. thesis, 01.

Charles J. Fillmore and B. T. S. Atkins. 1998. FrameNet and lexicographic relevance. In *Proceedings of the First International Conference On Language Resources And Evaluation, Granada, Spain, 28-30 May 1998.*

Charles J Fillmore et al. 1976. Frame semantics and the nature of language. In *Annals of the New York Academy of Sciences: Conference on the Origin and Development of Language and Speech*, volume 280, pages 20–32. New York.

Charles Fillmore. 2006. Frame semantics and the nature of language. *Annals of the New York Academy of Sciences*, 280:20 – 32, 12.

Christopher Johnson, Charles J Fillmore, E Wood, Josef Ruppenhofer, Margaret Urban, Miriam Petruck, and Collin Baker. 2001. The framenet project: Tools for lexicon building. *Manuscript. Berkeley, CA, International Computer Science Institute.*

Neslihan Kara, Busra Marsan, Deniz Aslan, Ozge Bakay, Koray Ak, and Olcay Taner Yildiz. 2020. Tropbank: Turkish propbank v2.0. 05.

Adam Kilgarriff and Christiane Fellbaum. 2000. Wordnet: An electronic lexical database. *Language*, 76:706, 09.

John B Lowe. 1997. A frame-semantic approach to semantic annotation. In *Tagging Text with Lexical Semantics: Why, What, and How?*

Kyoko Hirose Ohara, Seiko Fujii, Hiroaki Saito, Shun Ishizaki, Toshio Ohori, and Ryoko Suzuki. 2003. The Japanese FrameNet project: A preliminary report. In *Proceedings*. Pacific Association for Computational Linguistics, Pacific Association for Computational Linguistics.

Kyoko Ohara, Seiko Fujii, Shun Ishizaki, Toshio Ohori, Hiroaki Saito, and Ryoko Suzuki. 2004. The Japanese FrameNet project; an introduction. In Charles J. Fillmore, Manfred Pinkal, Collin F. Baker, and Katrin Erk, editors, *Proceedings of the Workshop on Building Lexical Resources from Semantically Annotated Corpora*, pages 9–12, Lisbon. LREC 2004, LREC 2004.

Kyoko Ohara, Seiko Fujii, Toshio Ohori, Ryoko Suzuki, Hiroaki Saito, and Shun Ishizaki, 2009. *Frame-Based Contrastive Lexical Semantics and Japanese FrameNet: The Case of RISK and Kakeru.* 01.

Kyoko Ohara. 2008. Lexicon, grammar, and multilinguality in the Japanese framenet. 01.

Selen Parlar, Bilge Nas Arican, Mehmet Erkek, Kamil Cayirli, and Olcay Taner Yildiz. 2019. Domain dependent wordnet for real estate. pages 1–4, 04.

Exploring Graph-based Representations for Taxonomy Enrichment

Irina Nikishina[‡], **Natalia Loukachevitch**[†], **Varvara Logacheva**[‡], and **Alexander Panchenko**[‡]

[‡]Skolkovo Institute of Science and Technology, Moscow, Russia
[†]Research Computing Center, Lomonosov Moscow State University, Moscow, Russia
{Irina.Nikishina,A.Panchenko,V.Logacheva}@skoltech.ru
louk_nat@mail.ru

Abstract

The vast majority of the existing approaches for *taxonomy enrichment* apply word embeddings as they have proven to accumulate contexts (in a broad sense) extracted from texts which are sufficient for attaching orphan words to the taxonomy. On the other hand, apart from being large lexical and semantic resources, taxonomies are graph structures. Combining word embeddings with graph structure of taxonomy could be of use for predicting taxonomic relations. In this paper we compare several approaches for attaching new words to the existing taxonomy which are based on the graph representations with the one that relies on fastText embeddings. We test all methods on Russian and English datasets, but they could be also applied to other wordnets and languages.

1 Introduction

Taxonomic structures are often used for the downstream tasks like lexical entailment (Herrera et al., 2005), entity linking (Moro and Navigli, 2015), named entity recognition (Negri and Magnini, 2004). Therefore, they always need to be up-to-date and to keep up with the language change. Moreover, with the rapid growth of lexical resources for specific domains it becomes more and more important to develop systems that could automatically enrich the existing knowledge bases with new words or at least facilitate the manual taxonomy extension process.

In this paper we tackle the taxonomy enrichment task which aims at associating new words (words not present in a taxonomy) with the appropriate hypernym synsets from the taxonomy. For instance, the word "foster-child" should be attached to the hypernym synset "child.n.1" (which refers to "child", "kid", "youngster") from WordNet, and the word "cactus" – to the synset "succulent.n.1". A word may have multiple hypernyms. The task of finding a single suitable synset is difficult for a machine, and a model trained to solve this task will inevitably return many false answers if asked to provide only one synset candidate. On the other hand, if we relax the requirement of uniqueness and ask instead to provide N (for example, 10 or 15) most suitable candidates, this list can contain correct synsets with higher probability. This setting is also suitable for the manual annotation: presenting an annotator with a small list of candidates will facilitate the annotation process, because the annotator will not need to look through all synsets of the taxonomy. Thus, the task is usually formulated as the soft ranking problem, where we need to rank all the synsets according to their suitability for a given word.

While word embeddings demonstrate decent results for predicting hypernyms (Arefyev et al., 2020; Dale, 2020), much less attention is paid to the approaches based on graph representations. We assume that graph-based representations are complementary to the distributional word embeddings, as they capture the hypo-hypernymy relations from graphs. We expect that models using graph representations could be beneficial for the taxonomy enrichment task in combination with distributed word vector representations or on their own. We check our hypothesis on several models which make use of graph structures: node2vec (Grover and Leskovec, 2016), Poincaré embeddings (Nickel and Kiela, 2017) and GCN autoencoder (Kipf and Welling, 2016a) and compare it with an approach of Nikishina et al. (2020b) which applies fastText (Bojanowski et al., 2017) and features from Wiktionary. All in all, our contribution is the exploration of graph-based representation for the taxonomy enrichment task and its combination with the word distributed representations.

2 Related Work

The existing studies on the taxonomies can be divided into three groups. The first one addresses the *Hypernym Discovery* problem (Camacho-Collados et al., 2018): given a word and a text corpus, the task is to identify hypernyms in the text. However, in this task the participants are not given any predefined taxonomy to rely on. The second group of works tackles *Taxonomy Induction* problem (Bordea et al., 2015; Bordea et al., 2016; Velardi et al., 2013), where the goal is to create a taxonomy automatically from scratch. The third group deals with the *Taxonomy Enrichment* task: the participants need to extend a given taxonomy with new words (Jurgens and Pilehvar, 2016; Nikishina et al., 2020a). Both word and graph representations can be applied to any of these tasks.

2.1 Approaches using word vector representations

Approaches using word vector representations are the most popular choice for all tasks related to taxonomies. When solving the *Hypernym Discovery* problem in SemEval-2018 Task 9 (Camacho-Collados et al., 2018) word embeddings are used by most of participants. Bernier-Colborne and Barrière (2018) predict the likelihood of the relationship between an input word and a candidate using word2vec (Mikolov et al., 2013) embeddings. Word2vec is used by Berend et al. (2018) to compute features to train a logistic regression classifier. Maldonado and Klubička (2018) simply consider top-10 closest associates from the Skip-gram word2vec model as hypernym candidates. Pre-trained GloVe embeddings (Pennington et al., 2014) are also used by Shwartz et al. (2016) to initialize embeddings for their LSTM-based Hypernymy Detection model.

Pocostales (2016) also solve the SemEval-2016 Task 13 on taxonomy induction with word embeddings: they compute the vector offset as the average offset of all the pairs generated and exploit it to predict hypernyms for the new data. Afterwards, Aly et al. (2019) apply word2vec embeddings similarity to improve the approaches of the SemEval-2016 Task 13 participants.

The vast majority of participants of SemEval-2016 task 14 (Jurgens and Pilehvar, 2016) and RUSSE'2020 (Nikishina et al., 2020a) also apply word embeddings to find the correct hypernyms in the existing taxonomy. For instance, Tanev and Rotondi (2016) compute a definition vector for the input word by comparing it with the definition vectors of the candidates from a wordnet using cosine similarity. Kunilovskaya et al. (2020) train word2vec embeddings from scratch and cast the task as a classification problem. Arefyev et al. (2020) compare the approach based on XLM-R model (Conneau et al., 2020) with the word2vec "hypernyms of co-hyponyms" method. It considers nearest neighbours as co-hyponyms and takes their hypernyms as candidate synsets.

Summing up, the usage of distributed word vector representations is a simple yet efficient approach to the taxonomy-related tasks and can be considered a strong baseline (Camacho-Collados et al., 2018; Nikishina et al., 2020a).

2.2 Graph-based representations for taxonomies

Graph-based representations for taxonomies have already been tested on other tasks related to the taxonomy enrichment. For instance, node2vec embeddings (Grover and Leskovec, 2016) are used by Liu et al. (2018) for taxonomy induction among other network embeddings.

Another work on Taxonomy Induction which benefits from graphs-based representations is the one by Aly et al. (2019) who achieve state-of-the-art results on all domains. The authors use hyperbolic Poincaré embeddings to enhance automatically created taxonomies. The subtask of reattaching orphan words to the taxonomy is quite similar to taxonomy enrichment. However, the datasets of the SemEval-2016 Task 13 are restricted to specific domains, which leaves an open question of the efficiency of Poincaré embeddings for the general domain and larger datasets. Moreover, Aly et al. (2019) use Hearst Patterns to discover hyponym-hypernym relationships. This technique operates on words, and cannot be transferred to word-synset relations without extra manipulation.

Graph convolutional networks (GCNs) (Kipf and Welling, 2016a) as well as graph autoencoders (Kipf and Welling, 2016b) are mostly applied to the link prediction task on large knowledge bases. Rossi et al. (2020) present an expanded review of the field and compare a wide variety of existing approaches. Graph embeddings are also often used for other taxonomy-related tasks, e.g. entity linking (Pujary et al., 2020). To the best of our knowledge, GCN embeddings have never been used for enhancing taxonomies like wordnets.

Thus, to the best of our knowledge, our work is the first work on Taxonomy enrichment task which considers wordnets from the prospective of graph structure instead of lexico-semantic resource and makes use of graph-based representations computed from the synsets and hypo-hypernym relations for hypernym prediction.

3 Diachronic WordNet Datasets

For this task we use two diachronic datasets described by Nikishina et al. (2020b): one for English, another one for Russian based respectively on Princeton WordNet (Miller, 1995) and RuWordNet taxonomies. Each dataset consists of a taxonomy and a set of novel words to be added to this resource. The statistics are provided in Table 1.

Dataset	Nouns	Verbs
WordNet1.6 - WordNet3.0	17 043	755
WordNet1.7 - WordNet3.0	6 161	362
WordNet2.0 - WordNet3.0	2 620	193
RuWordNet1.0 - RuWordNet2.0	14 660	2 154
RUSSE'2020	2 288	525

Table 1: Datasets statistics.

3.1 English Dataset

This dataset is created by selecting words which appear in a newer WordNet version, but do not appear in an older one. The words are added to the dataset if only their hypernyms appear in both snippets. Adjectives and adverbs are excluded, as they often introduce abstract concepts and are difficult to interpret by context. Besides, the taxonomies for adjectives and adverbs are worse connected than those for nouns and verbs, thus making the task more difficult.

3.2 Russian Dataset

For the Russian language we test methods on the RUSSE'2020 (Nikishina et al., 2020a) and non-restricted dataset by Nikishina et al. (2020b) which are based on RuWordNet (Loukachevitch et al., 2016), a taxonomy analogous to English WordNet. The RUSSE dataset was filtered from short words (<4 symbols), diminutives, named entities and other words that can distort the results of the competition. In contrast to this data, the non-restricted dataset did not undergo this preprocessing and contains all new words from RuWordNet2.0.

3.3 Evaluation Metric

The goal of diachronic taxonomy enrichment is to build a newer version of a wordnet given its older version and a list of new terms to be added to the wordnet. We cast this task as a soft ranking problem and use Mean Average Precision (MAP) score for the quality assessment:

$$\begin{aligned} MAP &= \tfrac{1}{N}\textstyle\sum_{i=1}^{N} AP_i; \\ AP_i &= \tfrac{1}{M}\textstyle\sum_{i}^{n} prec_i \times I[y_i = 1], \end{aligned} \quad (1)$$

where N and M are the number of predicted and ground truth values, respectively, $prec_i$ is the fraction of ground truth values in the predictions from 1 to i, y_i is the label of the i-th answer in the ranked list of predictions, and I is the indicator function.

This metric is widely used in the Hypernym Discovery shared tasks, where systems are also evaluated over the top candidate hypernyms (Camacho-Collados et al., 2018). Following Nikishina et al. (2020b), we use as gold standard hypernyms not only the immediate hypernyms of each lemma, but also the second-order hypernyms(hypernyms of the hypernyms). Finding the region where a word belongs can already be considered a success. Otherwise, the task of automatically identifying the exact hypernym is too challenging.

The MAP score takes into account the whole range of possible hypernyms and their rank in the candidate list. We use the MAP computation strategy as presented by Nikishina et al. (2020b). It transforms a list of gold standard hypernyms into a list of connectivity components, as new word may have more than one candidate and they could and could not be related directly.

4 Taxonomy Enrichment Methods

We test a number of methods that make use of taxonomy structure to predict hypernyms for the unseen words and compare their performance with the existing approach that is based on fastText embeddings. We describe each method in the corresponding section.

4.1 Word Embeddings with Features Extracted from Wiktionary

We consider approach by Nikishina et al. (2020b) as our baseline. There, a vector representation for a synset in the taxonomy is created by averaging vectors of all words from this synset. Then, for each new word top 10 closest synset vectors are retrieved (we refer to them as *synset associates*). For each of these associates, we extract its immediate hypernyms and hypernyms of all hypernyms (second-order hypernyms). This list of first- and second-order hypernyms forms our candidate set. We rank the candidate set using the following features:

- $n \times sim(v_i, v_{h_j})$, where v_x is a vector representation of a word or a synset x, h_j is a hypernym, n is the number of occurrences of this hypernym in the merged list, $sim(v_i, v_{h_j})$ is the cosine similarity of the vector of the input word i and hypernym vector h_j.
- candidate presence in the Wiktionary hypernyms list for the input word (binary feature),
- candidate presence in the Wiktionary synonyms list (binary feature),
- candidate presence in the Wiktionary definition (binary feature),
- average cosine similarity between the candidate and the Wiktionary hypernyms of the input word.

Finally, feature weights are computed by training a Linear Regression model with L2-regularisation on a training dataset from the previous WordNet/RuWordNet version. Candidate hypernyms are ranked by their model output score and are limited to the $k = 10$ best candidates.

4.2 Candidate Generation Using Poincaré Embeddings

Poincaré embeddings is an approach for "learning hierarchical representations of symbolic data by embedding them into hyperbolic space — or more precisely into an n-dimensional Poincaré ball" (Nickel and Kiela, 2017). Poincare models are trained on hierarchical structures and simultaneously capture hierarchy and similarity due to the underlying hyperbolic geometry. According to the authors, hyperbolic embeddings are more efficient on the hierarchically structured data and may outperform Euclidean embeddings on several tasks, e.g, in Taxonomy Induction (Aly et al., 2019).

Therefore, we use Poincaré embeddings of our wordnets for the taxonomy enrichment task. We train Poincaré ball model for our wordnets using the default parameters and the dimensionality of 10, which yields the best results on the link prediction task (Nickel and Kiela, 2017).

However, applying these embeddings to the task is not straightforward, because Poincaré model's vocabulary is non-extensible. It means that new words that we need to attach to the existing taxonomy will not have any Poincaré embeddings at all and we cannot make use of the embeddings similarity. To overcome this limitation, we compute top-5 fastText nearest synsets (analogously to the procedure described in Section 4.1) and then aggregate embeddings in hyperbolic space using Einstein midpoint following Gülçehre et al. (2019). The resulting vector is considered as an embedding of the input word in the Poincaré space.

Then, we search for the word's top-10 Poincaré nearest neighbours and consider them as candidates. We also try to extend the candidate list with the hypernyms of each Poincaré associate and rank them according to their frequency and similarity to the input word.

4.3 Candidate Generation Using Node2vec Embeddings

The hierarchical structure of the taxonomy is a graph structure, and we may also consider taxonomies as undirected graphs and apply random walk approaches to compute embeddings for the synsets. For this purpose we apply node2vec (Grover and Leskovec, 2016) approach which represents a "random walk of fixed length l" and "two parameters p and q which guide the walk in breadth of in depth". Node2vec randomly samples sequences of nodes and then applies a Skip-gram model to train their vector representations. We train node2vec representations of all synsets in our wordnets with the following parameters: $dimensions = 300$, $walk\_length = 30$, $num\_walks = 200$. The other parameters are taken from the original implementation.

However, analogously to Poincaré vector space, node2vec model has no technique for representing out-of-vocabulary words. Thus, it is unable to map new words to the vector space. To overcome this limitation, we apply the same technique of averaging top-5 nearest neighbours from fastText and considering their mean vector as the new word embedding and search for the most similar synsets.

We also use an alternative approach to computing out-of-vocabulary node2vec embeddings. Namely, we apply linear transformation from the source fastText to the target node2vec embeddings. For this purpose we train a matrix which is used to project fastText embeddings of the input words to the target node2vec space.

4.4 Link Prediction Using GCN Autoencoder

The models described above have a major shortcoming: the resulting vectors for the input words heavily depend on their representations in fastText model. This can lead to incorrect results if the word's nearest neighbour list is noisy and does not reflect its meaning. In this case the noise will propagate through the Poincaré model and result in inaccurate output even if the Poincaré model is of high quality.

Therefore, we test graph convolutional network architecture (Kipf and Welling, 2016a) that makes use of both fastText embeddings and the graph structure of the taxonomy. In particular, we use graph autoencoder model (Kipf and Welling, 2016b) whose encoder is a graph convolutional network architecture. This model learns vector representations in a completely unsupervised way: it encodes the nodes in the network in a low-dimensional space in such a way that the embeddings can be decoded into a reconstruction of the original network. FastText embeddings are used as input node features. Even though new words are not connected to the taxonomy, it is still possible to compute their embeddings according to their input node features.

For each new node we get its vector representation from the encoder and then predict the probability of the link between the new node and all other nodes in the graph. The top-10 synsets from the existing taxonomy with highest probabilities are considered as final candidates.

4.5 Combining Word and Graph Representations

Additionally, we extend the above model with features based on node2vec and Poincaré embeddings. Namely, we use two extra features: cosine similarity between the candidate and the input word in node2vec vector space and similarity between the candidate and the input word in Poincaré ball model. The overall formula is the following:

$$score_{h_j} = w \cdot m = \sum_{i=1}^{n} w_i m_i \tag{2}$$

Feature weights from the Logistic Regression model are denoted as vector w, m is the feature vector.

5 Experiments

In this section, we report the performance of our models on the Taxonomy Enrichment task and discuss reasons of low performance of methods exploiting hierarchical structure of the taxonomy.

5.1 Results

We test the models suggested in Section 4 on both English (Table 2) and Russian (Table 3) datasets. It is clearly seen that distributed word vector representations outperform graph-based approaches by a large margin.

Even though Poincaré ball model is designed for the taxonomic structures, the absence of vector representations for the OOV words dramatically affects the results. The aggregated vector of top-5 nearest neighbours retrieved from fastText can often provide a noisy or an overly general representation. Such representation is likely to yield incorrect hypernyms even if the Poincaré embeddings for the taxonomy are of perfect quality.

Likewise, node2vec model also possesses a non-extensible set of embeddings for the taxonomic synsets and uses averaging of fastText associates for representing the new words which negatively affects the results. However, the approach which uses node2vec embeddings and averages top-5 fastText associates is the best-performing approach across methods with graph representations. Moreover, node2vec embeddings perform much better than the Poincaré embeddings. Einstein midpoint aggregation used in our Poincaré-based model makes generalisation of the associate synsets, which results in too abstract synset candidates. On the other hand, averaging node2vec vectors does not have such an effect. The differences between the two models are illustrated by the examples in Table 5.

However, node2vec embeddings still rely on the fastText similarities of the closest embeddings to

method	nouns			verbs		
	1.6-3.0	1.7-3.0	2.0-3.0	1.6-3.0	1.7-3.0	2.0-3.0
Poincaré embeddings	0.0593	0.0658	0.1013	0.1255	0.0656	0.1092
node2vec (top-5 fastText associates)	0.1938	0.2187	0.1554	0.1514	0.1091	0.1469
node2vec (projection)	0.0400	0.0273	0.0218	0.1041	0.0517	0.0377
GCN autoencoder	0.1570	0.1751	0.1677	0.1088	0.0937	0.1173
Nikishina et al. (2020b)	**0.3372**	**0.3800**	**0.3443**	**0.2696**	**0.2002**	0.2366
Nikishina et al. (2020b) + node2vec	0.3130	0.3797	0.3402	0.2591	0.1948	0.1999
Nikishina et al. (2020b) + node2vec + Poincaré	0.3112	0.3498	0.2995	0.2508	0.1770	**0.2482**

Table 2: MAP scores for the taxonomy enrichment methods for the non-restricted English datasets of different WordNet versions.

method	nouns		verbs	
	non-restricted	restricted	non-restricted	restricted
Poincaré embeddings	0.1431	0.2517	0.1050	0.1397
node2vec (top-5 fastText associates)	0.2660	0.3659	0.1681	0.2518
node2vec (projection)	0.1854	0.2527	0.1800	0.2531
GCN autoencoder	0.1826	0.2605	0.0948	0.1406
Nikishina et al. (2020b)	0.4132	0.5515	0.2973	0.3889
Nikishina et al. (2020b) + node2vec	0.4095	0.5575	0.2931	0.3834
Nikishina et al. (2020b) + node2vec + Poincaré	**0.4141**	**0.5587**	0.3056	0.3910
Top-1 for nouns: *Yuriy*	0.3932	0.5522	0.2925	0.4355
Top-1 for nouns: *Yuriy*, no search engine features	0.3692	0.5071	0.2665	0.3888
Top-1 for verbs: Dale (2020)	0.2878	0.4178	**0.3398**	**0.4483**

Table 3: MAP scores for the taxonomy enrichment methods for the Russian datasets non-restricted and restricted (short words, named entities, diminutives excluded) datasets from (Nikishina et al., 2020a)

the input word vector and propagate the fastText inaccuracies. Linear projection which is an alternative option for the computation of node2vec vectors for out-of-vocabulary words, does not solve the problem either. As it can be seen in Table 5, candidates generated using node2vec with the linear projection come from completely irrelevant domains.

GCN autoencoder does not outperform the majority of the approaches for neiter of languages despite being a holistic and self-sufficient approach aimed at combining word representations with the graph structure of taxonomy. The model assigns high probabilities to all synsets in the word's neighbourhood in the graph, whereas only direct and second-order hypernyms are the correct answer. Taxonomic "uncles", "siblings", "cousins", and other distant "relatives" are not welcome.

The combined approach is not very consistent: incorporating graph-based features leads to an increase in scores for the Russian nouns and verbs datasets, whereas for the English dataset the approach does not yield any improvement except for the WordNet 2.0-3.0 dataset. Nevertheless, the combined method performs on par with the best RUSSE'2020 system for nouns track. Despite the close scores, our model can be considered superior to the winner of RUSSE'2020, because it is more stable across languages and easier to replicate.The best RUSSE'2020 approach for nouns extensively uses external tools such as online Machine Translation (MT) and search engines. This approach is difficult to replicate, because its performance for different languages can vary significantly, and we have no means for quantifying this difference.

Francis_Joseph_I emperor.n.01, sovereign.n.01		
Poincaré	node2vec	node2vec projection
person.n.01	king.n.01	fish_genus.n.01
entity.n.01	edward.n.02	genus.n.02
life_form.n.01	herod.n.01	mammal_genus.n.01
causal_agent.n.01	arthur.n.02	city.n.01
worker.n.01	messiah.n.03	municipality.n.01
european.n.01	louis_xiii.n.01	arthropod_genus.n.01
leader.n.01	louis_xiv.n.01	dicot_genus.n.01
object.n.01	frederick_ii.n.01	asterid_dicot_genus.n.01
ruler.n.01	belshazzar.n.01	animal_order.n.01
animal.n.01	pyrrhus.n.01	asterid_dicot_genus.n.01
GCN	fastText	combined (best)
day.n.04	king_of_england.n.01	king_of_england.n.01
metallic_element.n.01	king.n.01	king.n.01
large_integer.n.01	pope.n.01	holy_roman_emperor.n.01
semitic_deity.n.01	islamic_calendar_month.n.01	pope.n.01
hindu_deity.n.01	holy_roman_emperor.n.01	deliberation.n.02
hindu_calendar_month.n.01	general.n.01	islamic_calendar_month.n.01
month.n.02	calendar_month.n.01	**emperor.n.01**
anomalistic_month.n.01	**emperor.n.01**	missionary.n.02
chemical_element.n.01	frank.n.01	frank.n.01
religionist.n.01	jew.n.01	gravida.n.01

Table 4: Prediction noun examples from the English v 1.6-3.0 dataset. Underlined bold text denotes predictions of the model from the ground truth.

5.2 Error Analysis

In order to better understand the difference in systems performance and their main difficulties, we performed quantitative and qualitative analysis of the results on the English nouns subset.

First of all, we wanted to know to what extent the set of correct answers of graph-based models overlaps with the one of fastText-based models. In other words, we would like to know if the graph representations are able to discover hypernymy relations which could not be identified by word embeddings.

Therefore, for each new word we computed average precision (AP) score and compared those scores across different approaches. We found that at least 90% words for which fastText failed to identify correct hypernyms (i.e. words with AP=0) also have the AP of 0 in all the graph-based models. This means that if fastText cannot provide correct hypernyms for a word, other models cannot help either. Moreover, only 8% to 55% words correctly predicted by fastText are also correctly predicted by any of the graph-based models. At the same time, the number of cases where graph-based models perform better than fastText is very low (3–5% cases). Thus, combining them cannot improve the performance significantly. This observation is corroborated by the scores of the combined models.

We list the candidate synsets predicted by different methods in Table 5. They demonstrate the main features of the tested approaches. As we can see, the Poincaré embeddings retrieved by aggregating words from fastText provide too broad concepts which are clearly too far from the correct answers (“object”, “person”, “element”). GCN is too far from the correct answers in general, whereas node2vec results depend on the fastText embeddings and are semantically close to the ground truth synsets.

The candidates provided by fastText model combined with graph-based models features are

	overreact react.v.01, act.v.01	
Poincaré	node2vec	node2vec projection
change.v.01	react.v.02	play.v.01
act.v.01	**react.v.01**	compete.v.01
touch.v.01	pursue.v.04	utter.v.02
judge.v.02	**act.v.01**	change.v.01
change_magnitude.v.01	run_down.v.01	shape.v.03
interact.v.01	backfire.v.01	compete.v.01
think.v.03	buck.v.02	adjust.v.01
affect.v.01	marry.v.02	correct.v.01
tell.v.02	answer.v.02	fast.v.02
participate.v.01	wrench.v.01	travel.v.01
GCN	fastText	combined (best)
retaliate.v.02	**act.v.01**	**act.v.01**
exacerbate.v.02	react.v.02	**react.v.01**
cramp.v.01	**react.v.01**	react.v.02
respond.v.03	change.v.01	make.v.01
upset.v.01	affect.v.05	change.v.01
upset.v.06	make.v.01	fear.v.02
dictate.v.02	dramatize.v.02	terrify.v.01
irritate.v.02	misjudge.v.01	take.v.06
hurt.v.04	change_state.v.01	misjudge.v.01
sedate.v.01	right.v.01	burn.v.01

Table 5: Prediction verb examples from the English v 1.6-3.0 dataset. Underlined bold text denotes predictions of the model from the ground truth.

quite similar to those generated by the fastText model without additional features. Therefore, it is reasonable that the difference in scores is minor. However, for some cases (like "emperor.n.01" and "react.v.01" in Table 5) graph vector representations slightly improve the ranking.

6 Conclusion

In this work, we experimented with the graph-based representations for the taxonomy enrichment task and compared them to word vector representations. We tested approaches based on Poincaré and node2vec embeddings along with the approach based on graph autoencoder to predict hypernym synsets for the input word.

Our results show that the use of word vector representations is much more efficient than any of the tested graph-based approaches. Moreover, our baseline method (candidates retrieved from fastText nearest neighbour list and ranked with features extracted from Wiktionary) does not benefit from graph-based methods. Namely, combining the baseline scoring function with Poincaré and node2vec similarities results in marginal improvements for some datasets, but this does not hold for all of them.

According to our experiments, word vector representations are simple, powerful, and extremely effective instrument for taxonomy enrichment, as the contexts (in a broad sense) extracted from the pre-trained fastText embeddings are sufficient to attach new words to the taxonomy.

Error analysis also reveals that the correct synsets identified by graph-based models are usually retrieved by the fastText-based model alone. This makes graphs representations irrelevant and excessive. Nonetheless, there exist cases where graph representations were able to identify correctly some hypernyms which were not captured by fastText.

Despite the discouraging first results of the application of graph-based methods, we suggest that the taxonomy enrichment task could still benefit from them. In order to improve their performance, we plan to switch from linear transformation to non-linear to project fastText embeddings to node2vec and to apply recently published unsupervised graph word representations GraphGlove (Ryabinin et al., 2020). Moreover, we find it promising to experiment with temporal embeddings such of those of Goel et al. (2020) for the taxonomy enrichment task.

Acknowledgments

The work of Natalia Loukachevitch in the current study (preparation of data for the experiments) is supported by the Russian Science Foundation (project 20-11-20166). We thank Yuriy Nazarov and David Dale for running their approaches from RUSSE'2020 shared task on the English datasets.

References

Rami Aly, Shantanu Acharya, Alexander Ossa, Arne Köhn, Chris Biemann, and Alexander Panchenko. 2019. Every child should have parents: A taxonomy refinement algorithm based on hyperbolic term embeddings. In *Proceedings of the 57th Annual Meeting of the Association for Computational Linguistics*, pages 4811–4817, Florence, Italy, July. Association for Computational Linguistics.

Nikolay Arefyev, Maksim Fedoseev, Andrey Kabanov, and Vadim Zizov. 2020. Word2vec not dead: predicting hypernyms of co-hyponyms is better than reading definitions. In *Computational Linguistics and Intellectual Technologies: papers from the Annual conference "Dialogue"*.

Gábor Berend, Márton Makrai, and Péter Földiák. 2018. 300-sparsans at SemEval-2018 task 9: Hypernymy as interaction of sparse attributes. In *Proceedings of The 12th International Workshop on Semantic Evaluation*, pages 928–934, New Orleans, Louisiana, June. Association for Computational Linguistics.

Gabriel Bernier-Colborne and Caroline Barrière. 2018. CRIM at SemEval-2018 task 9: A hybrid approach to hypernym discovery. In *Proceedings of The 12th International Workshop on Semantic Evaluation*, pages 725–731, New Orleans, Louisiana, June. Association for Computational Linguistics.

Piotr Bojanowski, Edouard Grave, Armand Joulin, and Tomas Mikolov. 2017. Enriching word vectors with subword information. *Transactions of the Association for Computational Linguistics*, 5:135–146.

Georgeta Bordea, Paul Buitelaar, Stefano Faralli, and Roberto Navigli. 2015. SemEval-2015 task 17: Taxonomy extraction evaluation (TExEval). In *Proceedings of the 9th International Workshop on Semantic Evaluation (SemEval 2015)*, pages 902–910, Denver, Colorado, June. Association for Computational Linguistics.

Georgeta Bordea, Els Lefever, and Paul Buitelaar. 2016. SemEval-2016 task 13: Taxonomy extraction evaluation (TExEval-2). In *Proceedings of the 10th International Workshop on Semantic Evaluation (SemEval-2016)*, pages 1081–1091, San Diego, California, June. Association for Computational Linguistics.

Jose Camacho-Collados, Claudio Delli Bovi, Luis Espinosa-Anke, Sergio Oramas, Tommaso Pasini, Enrico Santus, Vered Shwartz, Roberto Navigli, and Horacio Saggion. 2018. SemEval-2018 task 9: Hypernym discovery. In *Proceedings of The 12th International Workshop on Semantic Evaluation*, pages 712–724, New Orleans, Louisiana, June. Association for Computational Linguistics.

Alexis Conneau, Kartikay Khandelwal, Naman Goyal, Vishrav Chaudhary, Guillaume Wenzek, Francisco Guzmán, Edouard Grave, Myle Ott, Luke Zettlemoyer, and Veselin Stoyanov. 2020. Unsupervised cross-lingual representation learning at scale. In *Proceedings of the 58th Annual Meeting of the Association for Computational Linguistics*, pages 8440–8451, Online, July. Association for Computational Linguistics.

David Dale. 2020. A simple solution for the taxonomy enrichment task: Discovering hypernyms using nearest neighbor search. In *Computational Linguistics and Intellectual Technologies: papers from the Annual conference "Dialogue"*.

Rishab Goel, Seyed Mehran Kazemi, Marcus Brubaker, and Pascal Poupart. 2020. Diachronic embedding for temporal knowledge graph completion. *Proceedings of the AAAI Conference on Artificial Intelligence*, 34(04):3988–3995, Apr.

Aditya Grover and Jure Leskovec. 2016. node2vec: Scalable feature learning for networks. In *Proceedings of the 22nd ACM SIGKDD International Conference on Knowledge Discovery and Data Mining*.

Çaglar Gülçehre, Misha Denil, Mateusz Malinowski, Ali Razavi, R. Pascanu, K. Hermann, P. Battaglia, V. Bapst, D. Raposo, Adam Santoro, and N. D. Freitas. 2019. Hyperbolic attention networks. *ArXiv*, abs/1805.09786.

Jesús Herrera, Anselmo Penas, and Felisa Verdejo. 2005. Textual entailment recognition based on dependency analysis and wordnet. In *Machine Learning Challenges Workshop*, pages 231–239. Springer.

David Jurgens and Mohammad Taher Pilehvar. 2016. SemEval-2016 task 14: Semantic taxonomy enrichment. In *Proceedings of the 10th International Workshop on Semantic Evaluation (SemEval-2016)*, pages 1092–1102, San Diego, California, June. Association for Computational Linguistics.

Thomas N Kipf and Max Welling. 2016a. Semi-supervised classification with graph convolutional networks. *arXiv preprint arXiv:1609.02907*.

Thomas N Kipf and Max Welling. 2016b. Variational graph auto-encoders. *NIPS Workshop on Bayesian Deep Learning*.

Maria Kunilovskaya, Andrey Kutuzov, and Alister Plum. 2020. Taxonomy enrichment: Linear hyponym-hypernym projection vs synset id classification. In *Computational Linguistics and Intellectual Technologies: papers from the Annual conference "Dialogue"*.

Ninghao Liu, Xiao Huang, Jundong Li, and Xia Hu. 2018. On interpretation of network embedding via taxonomy induction. In *Proceedings of the 24th ACM SIGKDD International Conference on Knowledge Discovery & Data Mining*, pages 1812–1820.

Natalia V Loukachevitch, German Lashevich, Anastasia A Gerasimova, Vladimir V Ivanov, and Boris V Dobrov. 2016. Creating russian wordnet by conversion. In *Computational Linguistics and Intellectual Technologies: papers from the Annual conference "Dialogue*, pages 405–415.

Alfredo Maldonado and Filip Klubička. 2018. ADAPT at SemEval-2018 task 9: Skip-gram word embeddings for unsupervised hypernym discovery in specialised corpora. In *Proceedings of The 12th International Workshop on Semantic Evaluation*, pages 924–927, New Orleans, Louisiana, June. Association for Computational Linguistics.

Tomas Mikolov, Ilya Sutskever, Kai Chen, Greg S Corrado, and Jeff Dean. 2013. Distributed representations of words and phrases and their compositionality. In C. J. C. Burges, L. Bottou, M. Welling, Z. Ghahramani, and K. Q. Weinberger, editors, *Advances in Neural Information Processing Systems 26*, pages 3111–3119. Curran Associates, Inc.

George A Miller. 1995. Wordnet: a lexical database for english. *Communications of the ACM*, 38(11):39–41.

Andrea Moro and Roberto Navigli. 2015. SemEval-2015 task 13: Multilingual all-words sense disambiguation and entity linking. In *Proceedings of the 9th International Workshop on Semantic Evaluation (SemEval 2015)*, pages 288–297, Denver, Colorado, June. Association for Computational Linguistics.

Matteo Negri and Bernardo Magnini. 2004. Using wordnet predicates for multilingual named entity recognition. In *Proceedings of The Second Global Wordnet Conference*, pages 169–174.

Maximilian Nickel and Douwe Kiela. 2017. Poincaré embeddings for learning hierarchical representations. In I. Guyon, U. V. Luxburg, S. Bengio, H. Wallach, R. Fergus, S. Vishwanathan, and R. Garnett, editors, *Advances in Neural Information Processing Systems 30*, pages 6341–6350. Curran Associates, Inc.

Irina Nikishina, Varvara Logacheva, Alexander Panchenko, and Natalia Loukachevitch. 2020a. RUSSE'2020: Findings of the First Taxonomy Enrichment Task for the Russian Language. In *Computational Linguistics and Intellectual Technologies: papers from the Annual conference "Dialogue"*.

Irina Nikishina, Alexander Panchenko, Varvara Logacheva, and Natalia Loukachevitch. 2020b. Studying taxonomy enrichment on diachronic wordnet versions. In *Proceedings of the 28th International Conference on Computational Linguistics*, Barcelona, Spain, December. Association for Computational Linguistics.

Jeffrey Pennington, Richard Socher, and Christopher Manning. 2014. GloVe: Global vectors for word representation. In *Proceedings of the 2014 Conference on Empirical Methods in Natural Language Processing (EMNLP)*, pages 1532–1543, Doha, Qatar, October. Association for Computational Linguistics.

Joel Pocostales. 2016. NUIG-UNLP at SemEval-2016 task 13: A simple word embedding-based approach for taxonomy extraction. In *Proceedings of the 10th International Workshop on Semantic Evaluation (SemEval-2016)*, pages 1298–1302, San Diego, California, June. Association for Computational Linguistics.

Dhruba Pujary, Camilo Thorne, and Wilker Aziz. 2020. Disease normalization with graph embeddings. In *Proceedings of SAI Intelligent Systems Conference*, pages 209–217. Springer.

Andrea Rossi, Donatella Firmani, Antonio Matinata, Paolo Merialdo, and Denilson Barbosa. 2020. Knowledge graph embedding for link prediction: A comparative analysis. *arXiv preprint arXiv:2002.00819*.

Max Ryabinin, Sergei Popov, Liudmila Prokhorenkova, and Elena Voita. 2020. Embedding words in non-vector space with unsupervised graph learning. *arXiv preprint arXiv:2010.02598*.

Vered Shwartz, Yoav Goldberg, and Ido Dagan. 2016. Improving hypernymy detection with an integrated path-based and distributional method. In *Proceedings of the 54th Annual Meeting of the Association for Computational Linguistics (Volume 1: Long Papers)*, pages 2389–2398, Berlin, Germany, August. Association for Computational Linguistics.

Hristo Tanev and Agata Rotondi. 2016. Deftor at SemEval-2016 task 14: Taxonomy enrichment using definition vectors. In *Proceedings of the 10th International Workshop on Semantic Evaluation*

(SemEval-2016), pages 1342–1345, San Diego, California, June. Association for Computational Linguistics.

Paola Velardi, Stefano Faralli, and Roberto Navigli. 2013. OntoLearn reloaded: A graph-based algorithm for taxonomy induction. *Computational Linguistics*, 39(3):665–707.

A (Non)-Perfect Match: Mapping plWordNet onto Princeton WordNet

Ewa Rudnicka, Wojciech Witkowski, Maciej Piasecki
G4.19 Research Group, Department of Computational Intelligence
Wrocław University of Technology, Wrocław, Poland
University of Wroclaw, Wroclaw, Poland
{ewa.rudnicka,maciej.piasecki}@pwr.edu.pl;wojciech.witkowski@uwr.edu.pl

Abstract

The paper reports on the methodology and final results of a large-scale synset mapping between plWordNet and Princeton WordNet. Dedicated manual and semi-automatic mapping procedures as well as interlingual relation types for nouns, verbs, adjectives and adverbs are described. The statistics of all types of interlingual relations are also provided.

1 Introduction

The goal of this paper is to present the machinery and guiding ideas behind a large-scale synset mapping between the Polish plWordNet (henceforth, plWN) and the English Princeton WordNet (henceforth, PWN). The resulting mapping is unique in terms of its character, scale and methodology. First, it is probably the only mapping built between the two very large wordnets constructed completely independently of each other (Fellbaum, 1998), (Piasecki et al., 2009), that is with no form of PWN content (synset) translation or structure mapping (in plWN construction)[1]. Second, it employs and further extends the whole array of inter-lingual inter-wordnet relations proposed for EuroWordNet by Vossen (2002), yet never fully implemented. Third, it is a manual mapping partially enhanced by automatic prompt systems yet not relying on them (Kędzia et al., 2013), (Rudnicka et al., 2015).

As such, the mapping had a lot of challenges: (partially) different wordnet construction methodologies of plWN and PWN; profound cross-linguistic differences between the synthetic Polish and the analytic English language; numerous cultural, sociological and historical differences between the two language communities affecting their lexicons to a large extent. Still, it seems the above challenges have been successfully met, proven by a number of cross-linguistic applications of the bilingual Polish-English wordnet.

In the paper we describe the systems of interlingual relations proposed and implemented for noun, adjective, adverb and verb synsets, presented in a chronological order motivated by the increasing difficulty of the milestones of the project. We close with the current statistics of interlingual synset relations.

2 Related works

WordNet started off as a lexico-semantic network for English (Fellbaum, 1998). With a quickly manifested potential both for linguistics and NLP research, it soon found its followers for other languages, e.g. GermaNet for German, (Hamp and Feldweg, 1997). Since cross-linguistic applications are always welcome, the idea of linking monolingual wordnets into a multilingual network naturally arose. It was put into practice in the EuroWordNet project (Vossen, 1998, 2002) and more recently in the OpenMultilingualWordnet project (Bond and Foster, 2013). Even before the start of EuroWordNet project, it was clear that constructing a wordnet from scratch and later linking it to similar resources is time and money-consuming. Few teams could afford it. On the other hand, taking Princeton WordNet as a basic template and expanding on it proved much more economical in terms of the investment needed. The two approaches were called merge and expand, respectively. Yet, science does not operate on a simple win-lose model. The expand approach rests on a

[1]The very model of plWordNet, clearly wordnet-like, is unique in several aspects in comparison to Princeton WordNet, cf Maziarz et al. (2013a)

long-abandoned assumption of the universality of mental lexicon (von Fintel and Matthewson, 2008). Thus, expand wordnets are useful language resources, but the accuracy of the specific language structure of the internal relation network may be arguable. Examples of expand wordnets are MultiWordNet (Bentivogli and Pianta, 2004), AsianWordNet (Robkop et al., 2009), IndoWordNet (Sinha et al., 2006), Open Dutch WordNet (Postma et al., 2016), and sloWNet for Slovenian (Fišer and Sagot, 2015). The few wordnets built through the merge approach are GermaNet (Hamp and Feldweg, 1997), DanNet, built on the basis of a Danish dictionary (Pedersen et al., 2009), and RuWordNet, constructed by a semi-automatic transformation of a Russian thesaurus (Loukachevitch et al., 2016).

plWordNet was constructed from scratch with a method exceptional in the wordnet world. It relied on the extraction of information about lexico-semantic relations from large text corpora (Piasecki et al., 2009). Automatically extracted relations and structures were presented as prompts to trained and supervised lexicographers who verified them with the help of reliable language resources for Polish (such as dictionaries, encyclopedia etc.) Thus, the method can be classified as a variant of the merge approach. As a consequence, the link to PWN had to be provided independently of plWN construction.

3 Nouns – bottom up

The prerequisite for mapping plWordNet onto Princeton WordNet was a reasonably advanced state of development of the former. Thus, we started with plWN 2.0 (Maziarz et al., 2013a) and PWN 3.1, see Table 1. Despite the bigger number of lemmas and lexical units in PWN, the number of synsets was comparable. It was especially visible for nouns, see Table 2.

The first challenge of mapping were partly different philosophies behind the construction of plWN and PWN (Maziarz et al., 2013a). In plWN, synset is rigidly defined as a set of lexical units sharing a set of constitutive relations (hypo/hypernymy, mero/holonymy, antonymy) (Maziarz et al., 2013b). This explains more fine-grained sense differentiation in plWN than in PWN, where synset membership is more arbitrary (Fellbaum, 1998). The second challenge of mapping were substantial cross-linguistic differences between English and Polish that also found its reflection in relation structures of the two wordnets. To explore the synthetic character of Polish, new types of lexical unit relations (PWN morphosemantic links) were added to plWN, such as, for instance, *diminutivity* (e.g. *pies* 2 - 'a dog' - *piesek* 1 - 'a small or young dog'), or *cross-categorial synonymy* (e.g. *piesek* 1 - *pieskowy* 1 - '[ADJ] related to a small dog'. The latter relation is established between a base and its derivative of a different POS when they relate to the same concept. In addition, PWN provided short definitions called *glosses*, sometimes followed by examples, for every synset, while plWN started adding glosses for lexical units (not for synsets) only at a later stage[2] of its development around the 3.0 version.

With the above challenges in mind, the guiding idea of the mapping was to link nodes of wordnet graphs that would mainly correspond in terms of relation structures (and possibly also with respect to glosses). This turned out a non-trivial task. Often, even for closely related concepts, their relation structures were partially or wholly different (Rudnicka et al., 2012). This explains the use of different types of interlingual relations (I-relations) going far beyond interlingual synonymy defined as *Simple Equivalence* by (Vossen, 2002). Most of Vossen's *Complex Equivalence* relations were adopted (e.g. I-hypo/hypernymy, I-near-synonymy, or I-mero/holonymy). Some new ones were added too, such as, for instance, *interlingual inter-register synonymy*.

Of the four parts of speech described by plWN and PWN, nouns share the most in terms of the fundamentals of their internal synset relation structure (Maziarz et al., 2013a). The basic relation is hypo/hypernymy, followed by mero/holonymy and near-synonymy. Therefore, the set of I-relations and the mapping procedure were first defined for and applied to noun synsets. It consisted of I-synonymy, I-partial-synonymy,

[2]However, even at the earlier stages of plWN development editors could add comments that were visible to other editors and facilitated the identification of the intended meaning of lexical units. Such comments were later transformed into the first version of glosses.

Elements	plWordNet 2.0	Princeton WordNet 3.1
Synsets	116 323	117 659
Lexical units	160 100	206 978
Lemmas	106 438	155 593

Table 1: Basic statistics for plWordNet 2.0 and Princeton WordNet 3.1

Elements	plWordNet 2.0	Princeton WordNet 3.1
Synsets	80 037	82 115
Lexical units	109 967	146 347
Lemmas	77 662	117 798

Table 2: Basic statistics for nouns in plWordNet 2.0 and Princeton WordNet 3.1

I-inter-register synonymy, I-hypo/hypernymy and I-mero/holonymy (Rudnicka et al., 2012). Later, it was supplemented by *I-type/instance* to link proper names, especially from PWN (Dziob et al., 2019).

For the first stage of mapping, we chose nouns from semantic domains (PWN lexicographer files) such as person, artefact, food, place, time, and names connected with thinking and communication, so as to start with concrete nouns, more likely to have unique referents regardless of a language, and then move to abstract nouns, for which the reference is often more culturally and socially dependent. We decided to go 'bottom up' in a wordnet graph. Such a move was motivated by the idea to start with the most specific, possibly unambiguous part of plWN which would form a basis for the further mapping. Also, we were trying to cover the whole branches of the hyponymy tree. The mapping direction was plWN-PWN.

4 Adjectives and adverbs – from hierarchy to dumbbell and island

With the mapping of nouns in progress, we proceeded to adjectives. The biggest challenge of adjective mapping were very different models of their internal synset relation structure in plWordNet and Princeton WordNet, shown in Table 4. As for numbers, plWN had approximately twice as much adjective synsets as PWN at the start of mapping, see Table 3.

Adjectives in plWN follow the same hierarchical, hyponymy-based model as nouns[3]. The subsidiary relations are: *gradability*, *near-synonymy* and *modifier* (Maziarz et al., 2012). On the contrary, adjectives in PWN are organized around *Similar to* relation with central and peripheral adjectives in the so called dumbbell model (Miller, 1998, Sheinman et al., 2013). *Similar to* relation is rather vague, but can be re-interpreted as one level hyponymy with a central adjective functioning as a hypernym of its peripheral adjectives. A subsidiary relation is *Member of this domain*. These profound differences in synset relation structures made us look into lexical unit relations. The latter exhibit more correspondence: antonymy/antonym, cross-categorial synonymy/pertainym, derivativity/derivationally related form. Therefore, in the mapping process we decided to consider both types of internal relations as well as the already existing I-relations between noun synsets, because some of the adjective relations are cross-categorial relations to nouns (e.g. cross-categorial synonymy, derivativity, Member of this domain). We proposed the following set of I-relations for adjective synsets: I-synonymy, I-hypo/hypernymy, I-partial synonymy, I-inter-register synonymy, and I-cross-categorial synonymy (Rudnicka et al., 2015), (Rudnicka et al., 2016). The latter relation was always used together with I-hyponymy to keep the POS information, and, in the case of very general I-hyponyms, to give more specification to the meaning of a mapped adjective. The use of such a pair of relations also allowed us to make up for the difference in size between plWN and PWN.

Having mapped a substantial part of adjective synsets, we moved to adverbs. Again, adverbs are more numerous in plWordNet than in Princeton WordNet, with twice as much lemmas, almost three times more lexical units and almost four times more synsets, as illustrated

[3]The placement of adjectives within specific hyponymy trees is conditioned on substitution tests and verified in corpora.

Elements	plWordNet 2.2	Princeton WordNet 3.1
Synsets	38 868	18 185
Lexical units	45 514	30 072
Lemmas	26 961	21 808

Table 3: Basic statistics for adjectives in plWordNet 2.2 and Princeton WordNet 3.1

Relation	plWordNet 2.2	Princeton WordNet 3.1
Value (of the attribute)	9658	639
Modifier	2 108	—
Hyponymy	18 225	—
Gradability	991	—
Near-synonymy	1 308	—
Similar to	—	21 434
Member of this domain	—	1 418

Table 4: Counts for adjective synset relations in plWordNet 2.2 and Princeton WordNet 3.1

in Table 5. Adverbs are unique in Princeton WordNet in that they have no synset relations. On the other hand, in plWordNet many adverbs were systematically derived from adjectives (Maziarz et al., 2016), hence they have a similar set of synset relations as adjectives (apart from Modifier), see Table 6. Therefore, we decided to take advantage of a previously established network of I-relations between adjectives in plWN and PWN and constructed automatic prompts for adverb synsets on the basis of internal relations between adjectives and adverbs and I-relations between adjectives. Those automatic prompts were later manually verified by lexicographers, for details see Section 6. The I-relations used were I-synonymy, I-hypo/hypernymy, I-partial synonymy, and I-inter-register synonymy.

5 Verbs – from lexico-grammatical hierarchy to semantic fields

Verbs were the last category to map due to their most complex and divergent relation structures resulting from substantial differences in rendering aspect and other verbal categories in English and Polish. Polish lexicalises aspect and in plWN perfective and imperfective verb forms always land in separate synsets (even in the case of pure aspectual pairs e.g. *czytać* - 'read/be reading' vs *przeczytać* - 'have read'). This partly accounts for bigger number of verbal elements in plWordNet 3.1 in comparison to Princeton WordNet 3.1 (see Table 7).

Similarly to nouns, verb synsets are organised around hypo/hypernymy relation both in plWN and in PWN. Other PWN verb relations include Verb group, Member of this domain (mainly Topic), and, relatively sparse, Entailment and Cause. At the start of verb mapping, plWN 3.1 used Causation, Processuality, and less numerous Distributivity, Inchoativity and Iterativity (Table 8). plWN verbs are also grouped into verb classes. These are drawn from situation types (Aktionsart (Vendler, 1967)) the verbs denote and their grammatical aspect. Class assignment is based on verb's meaning as it is evoked by a clausal context. Vendlerian classification served as the basis for creating artificial synsets whose function is to provide systematic hierarchical organization of verb synsets in plWN. Vendlerian *Activities, Achievements, and Accomplishments* are subsumed under Dynamic verbs. These are further subdivided into: distributive, cumulative, perdurative and delimitive, based on the meaning of the prefixes that attach to verbal roots. Vendler's *States* correspond to Stative verbs in plWN. Additionally, plWN distinguishes Action verbs which include: perfective forms of non-distributive, non-cumulative, non-perdurative, and non-delimitive verbs; imperfective forms of distributive, cumulative, perdurative, and delimitive verbs, and imperfective verbs with causative, procesual, inchoative, and completive meanings.

Thus, verb mapping had to overcome (partly) non-congruent internal relation networks and specific linguistic differences. Therefore, we decided to use I-synonymy, I-inter register synonymy, and I-hypo/hypernymy and introduce new interlingual relations specific to verb mapping. They were based on (Wiland, 2011) and include: I-attenuativity (to V to a lesser

Elements	plWordNet 3.1	Princeton WordNet 3.1
Synsets	11 396	3 625
Lexical units	14 207	5 592
Lemmas	8 113	4 475

Table 5: Basic statistics for adverbs in plWordNet 3.1 and Princeton WordNet 3.1

Relation	plWordNet 3.1	Princeton WordNet 3.1
Value (of the attribute)	4302	—
Fuzzynymy	9280	—
Hyponymy	10 082	—
Gradability	690	—
Near-synonymy	647	—

Table 6: Counts for adverb synset relations in plWordNet 3.1 and Princeton WordNet 3.1.

extent), e.g. *podczytać* 1 'to read a little' - *read* 1 'to interpret something that is written or printed', I-iterativity (to V repeatedly), e.g. *czytywać* 1 - 'to read from time to time' - *read* 1, I-perdurativity (to V for a period of time), e.g. *zaczytać się* 1 'to be continuously engaged in reading' - *read* 1, I-delimitivity (to V to a point in time), e,g, *poczytać* 2 'to spend some time reading' - *read* 1, I-inchoativity (onset of an action or state), e.g. *zaczytać* 2 ' to start reading' - *read* 1, I-completivity (completion of an action), e.g. *doczytać* 1 'to read to the end' - *read* 1, I-cumulativity (to V to a satisfying extent), e.g. *naczytać się* 1 'to read a lot, so that one does not want to read anymore' - *read* 1, I-distributivity (to V among many recipients), I-excessivity (to V to an excessive extent), I-causativity (to cause V), I-processuality (to become V), I-terminativity (termination of an action), I-anticausativity (be in a state caused by V), I-stativity (be in a state denoted by V), I-ablativity (V from), and I-allativity (V to). In addition, we proposed three types of cross-categorial relations: I-cross-categorial processuality, I-cross-categorial stativity, and I-cross-categorial causativity, which are always coupled with I-hyponymy relation. The function of verb-specific I-relations is to render the meaning correspondence as accurate as possible.

6 Procedures and tools

The entire mapping has been performed manually by a team of trained bilingual lexicographers supervised by senior lexicographers (Rudnicka et al., 2012). The actual mapping has been taking place in a custom-designed wordnet editing system called WordNetLoom which allows to visualise wordnet graphs for different languages on the same screen, manipulate them, compare their fragments and establish relations (Piasecki et al., 2010, Naskręt et al., 2018). The fact that an editor can see the relation structures for both languages[4], interactively explore them in any direction and depth, and make changes, e.g. by adding I-relation links directly to the graphs, noticeably facilitated the mapping process. Moreover, lexicographers' work has been monitored via another custom-designed tool, namely the WordNet Tracker system (Naskręt et al., 2018) documenting every action of a lexicographer in real time. Due to the scale of the project and its financing conditions, we worked in 1+1 model (a lexicographer establishing I-links plus a supervisor checking their adequacy).

The manual mapping procedure was first designed for nouns, but its basics have been kept for other parts of speech as well (Rudnicka et al., 2012, 2016). It consists of three main stages: (1) recognising the sense of a source synset, (2) searching candidates for a target synset, and (3) choosing a target synset and a type of interlingual relation. In the first stage, we carefully analyse the source synset internal relation structure, gloss, examples as well as interlingual relations if there are any within the close nodes in its hyponymy tree. In the second stage, candidates for a target synset are nominated on the basis of a bilingual linguist's intuition and information found in Polish-English language resources. Next, candidates for a tar-

[4] Automatically generated suggestions for I-relation links are also presented on the same screen, but marked as different kinds of relations – 'generated'.

Elements	plWordNet 3.1	Princeton WordNet 3.1
Synsets	29 110	13 789
Lexical units	40 181	25 061
Lemmas	19 836	11 540
Monosemous lemmas	11 265	6 284
Polysemous lemmas	8 571	5 256

Table 7: Basic statistics for verbs in plWordNet 3.1 and Princeton WordNet 3.1

Relation	plWordNet 3.1	Princeton WordNet 3.1
Hyponymy	31 784	13 251
Hypernymy	31 784	13 251
Causation	3 427	—
Processuality	1 204	—
Distributivity	676	—
Inchoativity	519	—
Iterativity	148	—
Entailment	—	406
Cause	—	214

Table 8: Counts for verb synset relations in plWordNet 3.1 and Princeton WordNet 3.1

get synset are analysed in a similar fashion as it is done for a source synset. In the third stage, the target synset is chosen, and depending on the degree and type of correspondence between the source and target synset, an interlingual relation is chosen and the two synsets get linked.

The results of the first stage of mapping of nouns were used as the input to an automatic prompt system developed for further stages of noun mapping (Kędzia et al., 2013). The system was based on the Relaxation Labeling algorithm of (Daudé et al., 1999). It mirrors the manual mapping procedure to the extent that it compares parts of a wordnet graph and suggests the closely related fragments. Next, Polish-English synset pairs produced by the algorithm were filtered by the so called cascade Polish-English dictionary[5] and pairs of synsets whose lemmas appear as dictionary equivalents were given the status of automatic prompts and presented to lexicographers as special links in the WordNetLoom system.

Moving to the mapping of adjectives, we could not resort to the automatic prompt system developed for nouns, because Relaxation Labeling algorithm used there requires parallel hierarchical structures to operate. Such structures are missing in the case of PWN adjectives. That made us look for other solutions. Despite superficially divergent models in plWN and PWN, we searched for common points in the relation structure both at synset and lexical unit level. As a consequence, two rule-based algorithms were designed that produced automatic prompts for the first stage of adjective mapping (Rudnicka et al., 2015). The first one relied on synset relations exclusively, the second one on synset and lexical unit relations. Both also took advantage of I-synonymy relations between noun synsets (provided the latter were internally linked to adjectives). Pairs of Polish-English lemmas (from the pairs of adjective synsets generated by the algorithms) were automatically verified by the cascade dictionary. Those recorded in the dictionary were presented to lexicographers in the form of prompts for manual mapping, (Rudnicka et al., 2015).

The procedures and relations developed for adjectives also found its use in the mapping of adverbs (Maziarz et al., 2016). In plWN many adverbs were automatically derived from adjectives. That allowed to generate automatic prompts for adverb mapping on the basis of adjective mapping. It consisted in copying interlingual relations established for adjective synsets to adverb synsets provided that the latter were systematically derived from the former in plWN. Another necessary condition was that target PWN adverbs were also derived from PWN adjectives already linked by an interlingual relation to plWN adjectives. Next, the prompts were verified by lexicographers and manual links were established. At

[5]Bilingual Cascade Dictionary is a collection of dictionaries organised in a cascade with the top-most dictionaries having the highest priority in applications.

the same time, adjective links were critically evaluated and modified, when necessary. In the overwhelming majority of cases automatic prompts were valid and a manual relation was established. More work was required for cases of one-to-many mapping (e.g. one synset serving as a hypernym for several other wordnet's synsets), while the most difficult cases constituted adverbs that were not derived from plWN adjectives holding I-relations to PWN adjectives. These required independent search for target synsets.

As for verb mapping, no automatic prompt system was designed. Although both plWN and PWN verb relation networks are hierarchical, these hierarchies are based on non-congruent prerequisites. Moreover, verb synsets are also linked via non-hierarchical relations, different in both wordnets. These differences combined with linguistic differences between Polish and English aspect morphology enforced a fully manual mapping procedure. The main focus in the procedure was put on providing as close meaning correspondence as possible. This was achieved by finding the most suitable plWN – PWN synset pair and choosing the I-relation that most adequately captures the meaning relation. The selection of I-relations was hierarchical. I-synonymy and I-inter register synonymy were prioritized. For verbs, we have exceptionally allowed for double synonymy in the case of pure aspectual pairs of verbs in Polish linked to aspectually unmarked English verbs (creating 2 – to – 1 mapping). Verb-specific relations were selected if I-synonymy and I-inter register synonymy relations could not be established and the prefix of the plWN verb carried a relevant facet of meaning. I-hyponymy relation was treated a 'last resort' relation, as it provided the most general meaning correspondence. In the cases in which PWN lacked a relevant verb synset, but a noun or adjective synset which would be used in a copula-construction in English was present, I-cross-categorial relations coupled with I-hyponymy relation linking plWN and PWN verb synsets were selected.

7 Result: a bilingual network and its applications

The result of bidirectional mapping of plWordNet and Princeton WordNet is a large Polish-English wordnet with almost 300k of unique interlingual relations. The counts of all types of I-relations are shown in Table 9. We can see that despite the priority of I-synonymy in the mapping procedure it is strongly overruled by I-hyponymy for all parts of speech. This tendency has been observed since the beginning of mapping, e.g. (Rudnicka et al., 2012, Maziarz et al., 2016), and is caused by independent methodologies and times of the two wordnets' construction leading to partly different relation structures and vocabulary coverage. Moreover, plWordNet currently outgrows Princeton WordNet in the number of synsets (and other basic elements) for all parts of speech [6]. Another reason are profound lexicogrammatical differences between English and Polish (e.g. systematic lexicalisation of aspect, gender and other grammatical categories) and socio-cultural differences between the two language communities resulting in lexical gaps (such as names of meals, administrative divisions and posts, or related to history (e.g. the Communist period or the WWII)).

The quality of the created resource has been confirmed by a number of applications, fostered by its open wordnet licence [7]. These include language learning and teaching (e.g. the creation of didactic tools such as CloudNet Word Cloud Generator [8]), dictionary making and machine translation (a component for PONS, Glosbe, Kamusigold, Ling.pl, BabelNet, Open Multilingual Wordnet, Google Translate), semi-automatic mapping of a number of domain thesauri as well as SUMO ontology on plWN, bilingual word sense disambiguation (Sherlock Holmes corpus?), multilingual wordnet construction and contrastive studies (Open Multingual Wordnet, the Yiddish project[9],[10]).

[6] `http://plwordnet.pwr.wroc.pl/wordnet/stats`
[7] http://nlp.pwr.wroc.pl/plwordnet/license/
[8] www.cloud-net.pl
[9] http://polonjid-dictionary.clarin-pl.eu/
[10] https://polonjid.wn.uw.edu.pl/?lang=en

I-relation	V		N		Adv		Adj		Total	
I-relation	pl	en	pl	en	pl	en	pl	en	pl	en
I-synonymy	3933	3933	38056	38056	1002	1002	4156	4156	47147	47147
I-partial syn.	—	—	6602	6601	330	330	1373	1373	8305	8304
I-int.-reg. syn.	602	602	1983	1983	53	53	98	98	2736	2736
I-meronymy	—	—	10946	8109	—	—	—	—	10946	8109
I-hypernymy	264	11274	34651	83355	182	9910	383	44613	35480	149152
I-hyponymy	11277	264	83359	34656	9910	182	44613	383	149159	35485
I-holonymy	—	—	8106	10946	—	—	—	—	8106	10946
I-Type	—	—	7930	707	—	—	—	—	7930	707
I-Instance	—	—	707	7930	—	—	—	—	707	7930
I-allative	90	—	—	—	—	—	—	—	90	—
I-delimitive	461	—	—	—	—	—	—	—	461	—
I-excess	72	—	—	—	—	—	—	—	72	—
I-perdurative	24	—	—	—	—	—	—	—	24	—
I-anticausative	1717	—	—	—	—	—	—	—	1717	—
I-atenuative	233	—	—	—	—	—	—	—	233	—
I-cumulative	360	—	—	—	—	—	—	—	360	—
I-procesuality	16	—	—	—	—	—	—	—	16	—
I-completive	78	—	—	—	—	—	—	—	78	—
I-inchoative	215	—	—	—	—	—	—	—	215	—
I-distributive	840	—	—	—	—	—	—	—	840	—
I-iterative	82	—	—	—	—	—	—	—	82	—
I-terminative	12	—	—	—	—	—	—	—	12	—
I-ablative	42	—	—	—	—	—	—	—	42	—
I-causative	297	—	—	—	—	—	—	—	297	—
I-c-c-made-of	—	—	—	—	—	—	1059	—	1059	—
I-c-c-resembling	—	—	—	—	—	—	938	—	938	—
I-c-c-related-to	—	—	—	—	93	—	22694	—	22787	—
Total	20615	16074	192341	192343	11570	11477	75315	50623	299841	270571

Table 9: Interlingual relation counts

8 Conclusion and Further works

The created resource is unique not only because of its scale and method of construction, but mainly due to the fact that it uses a rich network of interlingual relations which had not been done before. Such approach has its pluses and minuses. It shows the complexity of a bilingual lexicon, yet it does not offer that many simple equivalents (often very much wanted by dictionary users). This is also partly due to the fact that wordnet mapping is synset mapping. However, we saw a significant potential for future development of the created bilingual resource.

Thus, we have started a project (Rudnicka et al., 2017) on converting the synset level mapping to an interlingual mapping between lexical units based on the concept of translational equivalence (Rudnicka et al., 2019). Three types of equivalence links were identified: strong, regular and weak, in addition to the lack of equivalence. The recognition of a type of equivalence was based on the manual verification of values of equivalence features, cf (Rudnicka et al., 2019). In a pilot study, equivalence links were manually described for ≈10 000 bilingual pairs of senses (lexical units) coming mostly from noun synsets linked by I-synonymy. On average, only 1-2 strong equivalence links were identified for a pair of synsets (Rudnicka and Naskręt, 2020). As a result, a precise bilingual sense-level dictionary that can be used in translation, but also in many bilingual wordnet application was developed. We plan to expand this mapping both to remaining noun pairs and to other parts of speech.

Acknowledgements

The work co-financed as part of the investment in the CLARIN-PL research infrastructure funded by the Polish Ministry of Science and Higher Education.

References

Luisa Bentivogli and Emanuele Pianta. Extending wordnet with syntagmatic information. In *Proceedings of the Second Global WordNet Conference*, pages 47–53, Brno, Czech Republic, January, 20th-23rd 2004.

Francis Bond and Ryan Foster. Linking and extending an open multilingual wordnet. In *Proc. 51st Annual Meeting of the Association for Computational Lin-*

guistics (Volume 1: Long Papers), pages 1352–1362, 2013.

Jordi Daudé, Lluís. Padró, and German Rigau. Mapping multilingual hierarchies using relaxation labeling. *ArXiv*, cs.CL/9906025, 1999.

Agnieszka Dziob, Maciej Piasecki, and Ewa K. Rudnicka. plwordnet 4.1 - a linguistically motivated, corpus-based bilingual resource. In *Proceedings of the Tenth Global Wordnet Conference : July 23-27, 2019, Wrocław (Poland)*, pages 353–362, 2019. URL `https://clarin-pl.eu/dspace/handle/11321/718`.

Christiane Fellbaum, editor. *WordNet – An Electronic Lexical Database*. The MIT Press, 1998.

Darja Fišer and Benoît Sagot. Constructing a poor man's wordnet in a resource-rich world. *Language Resources and Evaluation*, 49(3):601–635, 2015. ISSN 1574-0218. doi: 10.1007/s10579-015-9295-6. URL `http://dx.doi.org/10.1007/s10579-015-9295-6`.

Birgit Hamp and Helmut Feldweg. GermaNet – a Lexical-Semantic Net for German. In *Proc. ACL Workshop on Automatic Information Extraction and Building of Lexical Semantic Resources for NLP Applications*, pages 9–15. Madrid, 1997.

Paweł Kędzia, Maciej Piasecki, Ewa Rudnicka, and Konrad Przybycień. Automatic Prompt System in the Process of Mapping plWordNet on Princeton WordNet. *Cognitive Studies*, 2013.

Natalia V. Loukachevitch, German Lashevich, Anna. A. Gerasimova, Vladimir V. Ivanov, and Boris. Dobrov. Creating russian WordNet by conversion. In *Proceedings of Conference on Computational Linguistics and Intellectual Technologies Dialog-2016*, pages 405–415, 2016.

Marek Maziarz, Stanisław Szpakowicz, and Maciej Piasecki. Semantic relations among adjectives in polish wordnet 2.0: a new relation set, discussion and evaluation. *Cognitive Studies*, (12), 2012.

Marek Maziarz, Maciej Piasecki, Ewa Rudnicka, and Stan Szpakowicz. Beyond the transfer-and-merge wordnet construction: plWordNet and a comparison with WordNet. In G. Angelova, K. Bontcheva, and R. Mitkov, editors, *Proc. International Conference Recent Advances in Natural Language Processing RANLP 2013*, pages 443–452. INCOMA Ltd. Shoumen, BULGARIA, 2013a.

Marek Maziarz, Maciej Piasecki, and Stanisław Szpakowicz. The chicken-and-egg problem in wordnet design: synonymy, synsets and constitutive relations. *Language Resources and Evaluation*, 47(3): 769–796, 2013b. doi: 10.1007/s10579-012-9209-9.

Marek Maziarz, Maciej Piasecki, Ewa Rudnicka, Stan Szpakowicz, and Paweł Kędzia. plwordnet 3.0 – a comprehensive lexical-semantic resource. In Nicoletta Calzolari, Yuji Matsumoto, and Rashmi Prasad, editors, *COLING 2016, 26th International Conference on Computational Linguistics, Proceedings of the Conference: Technical Papers, December 11-16, 2016, Osaka, Japan*, pages 2259–2268. ACL, ACL, 2016. URL `http://aclweb.org/anthology/C/C16/`.

George A. Miller. *A Semantic Network of English Verbs*, chapter 2, pages 47–68. In Fellbaum (1998), 1998.

Tomasz Naskręt, Agnieszka Dziob, Maciej Piasecki, Chakaveh Saedi, and António Branco. WordnetLoom–a Multilingual Wordnet Editing System Focused on Graph-based Presentation. In Francis Bond, Christiane Fellbaum, and Piek Vossen, editors, *Proceedings of the 9th Global Wordnet Conference, Singapore, 8-12 January 2018*. Global WordNet Association, 2018. URL `http://compling.hss.ntu.edu.sg/events/2018-gwc/pdfs/GWC2018_paper_57.pdf`.

Bolette S. Pedersen, Sanni Nimb, Jørg Asmussen, Nicolai H. Sørensen, Lars Trap-Jensen, and Henrik Lorentzen. DanNet – the challenge of compiling a WordNet for Danish by reusing a monolingual dictionary. *Language Resources and Evaluation*, 43: 269–299, 2009.

Maciej Piasecki, Stan Szpakowicz, and Bartosz Broda. *A Wordnet from the Ground Up*. Oficyna Wydawnicza Politechniki Wroclawskiej, Wroclaw, 2009. URL `http://www.dbc.wroc.pl/Content/4220/Piasecki_Wordnet.pdf`.

Maciej Piasecki, Michał Marcińczuk, Adam Musiał, Radosław Ramocki, and Marek Maziarz. Wordnet-Loom: a Graph-based Visual Wordnet Development Framework. In *Proceedings of the 2010 International Multiconference on Computer Science and Information Technology (IMCSIT)*, 2010. URL `http://ieeexplore.ieee.org/document/5679686/`.

Marten Postma, Emiel van Miltenburg, Roxane Segers, Anneleen Schoen, and Piek Vossen. Open Dutch WordNet. In *Proceedings of the Eight Global Wordnet Conference*, Bucharest, Romania, 2016.

Kergrit Robkop, Sareewan Thoongsup, T. Charoenporn, Virach Sornlertlamvanich, and H. Isahara. Wnms: Connecting the distributed wordnet in the case of asian wordnet. the 5th international conference of the global wordnet association (gwc-2010). 2009.

Ewa Rudnicka and Tomasz Naskręt. A dataset of translational equivalents built on the basis of plWordNet-Princeton WordNet synset mapping. In *Proceedings of the 12th Language Resources and Evaluation Conference*, pages 3260–3264, Marseille, France, May 2020. European Language Resources Association. URL `https://www.aclweb.org/anthology/2020.lrec-1.398`.

Ewa Rudnicka, Marek Maziarz, Maciej Piasecki, and Stan Szpakowicz. A Strategy of Mapping Polish WordNet onto Princeton WordNet. In *Proc. COLING 2012, posters*, pages 1039–1048, 2012.

Ewa Rudnicka, Wojciech Witkowski, and Michał Kaliński. A Semi-automatic Adjective Mapping Between plWordNet and Princeton WordNet. In *Text, Speech, and Dialogue*, pages 360–368. Springer, 2015. URL `https://link.springer.com/chapter/10.1007/978-3-319-24033-6_41`.

Ewa Rudnicka, Wojciech Witkowski, and Katarzyna Podlaska. Challenges of Adjective Mapping between plWordNet and Princeton WordNet. In Nicoletta Calzolari (Conference Chair), Khalid Choukri, Thierry Declerck, Sara Goggi, Marko Grobelnik, Bente Maegaard, Joseph Mariani, Helene Mazo, Asuncion Moreno, Jan Odijk, and Stelios Piperidis, editors, *Proceedings of the Tenth International Conference on Language Resources and Evaluation*

(LREC 2016). European Language Resources Association (ELRA), 2016. ISBN 978-2-9517408-9-1. URL http://www.lrec-conf.org/proceedings/lrec2016/pdf/481_Paper.pdf.

Ewa Rudnicka, Francis Bond, Łukasz Grabowski, Maciej Piasecki, and Tadeusz Piotrowski. Towards equivalence links between senses in plWordNet and princeton WordNet. *Lodz Papers in Pragmatics*, 13 (1):3–24, 2017.

Ewa K. Rudnicka, Maciej Piasecki, Francis Bond, Łukasz Grabowski, and Tadeusz Piotrowski. Sense equivalence in plwordnet to princeton wordnet mapping. *International Journal of Lexicography*, 32:296–325, 2019. doi: 10.1093/ijl/ecz004. URL https://academic.oup.com/ijl/article/32/3/296/5382106.

Vera Sheinman, Christiane Fellbaum, Isaac Julien, Peter F. Schulam, and Takenobu Tokunaga. Large, huge or gigantic? identifying and encoding intensity relations among adjectives in wordnet. *Language Resources and Evaluation*, 47:797–816, 2013.

Manish Sinha, Mahesh Reddy, and Pushpak Bhattacharyya. An approach towards construction and application of multilingual indo-wordnet. 3rd global wordnet conference (gwc 06). jeju island, korea. 2006. URL www.cse.iitb.ac.in/~pb/papers/gwc06_IITB_IndoWN.pdf.

Zeno Vendler. *Linguistics in Philosophy*. Ithaca: N.Y., Cornell University Press, 1967.

Kai von Fintel and Lisa Matthewson. Universals in semantics. *The Linguistic Review*, 25(1-2):139 – 201, 2008. doi: https://doi.org/10.1515/TLIR.2008.004. URL https://www.degruyter.com/view/journals/tlir/25/1-2/article-p139.xml.

Piek Vossen, editor. *EuroWordNet. A multilingual Database with Lexical Semantic Networks*. Kluwer Academic Publishers, 1998.

Piek Vossen. EuroWordNet General Document Version 3. Technical report, Univ. of Amsterdam, 2002.

Bartosz Wiland. Prefix stacking, syncretism and the syntactic hierarchy. In Marketa Zikova and Mojmir Docekal, editors, *Slavic Languages in Formal Grammar*, pages 307–324. Peter Lang, Bern, Switzerland, 2011.

Persian SemCor: A Bag of Words Sense Annotated Corpus for the Persian Language

Hossein Rouhizadeh , Mehrnoush Shamsfard , Mahdi Dehghan , and Masoud Rouhizadeh

Shahid Beheshti University, Tehran, Iran
hrouhizadeh@gmail.com, m-shams@sbu.ac.ir
mahdi.dehghan551@gmail.com, mrouhizadeh@gmail.com

Abstract

Supervised approaches usually achieve the best performance in the Word Sense Disambiguation problem. However, the unavailability of large sense annotated corpora for many low-resource languages make these approaches inapplicable for them in practice. In this paper, we mitigate this issue for the Persian language by proposing a fully automatic approach for obtaining Persian SemCor (PerSemCor), as a Persian Bag-of-Word (BoW) sense-annotated corpus. We evaluated PerSemCor both intrinsically and extrinsically and showed that it can be effectively used as training sets for Persian supervised WSD systems. To encourage future research on Persian Word Sense Disambiguation, we release the PerSemCor in *nlp.sbu.ac.ir* .

1 Introduction

Word Sense Disambiguation (WSD) is the task of associating ambiguous context words with their most suitable meanings in a pre-defined sense inventory. WSD can be mentioned as a key area in Natural Language Processing (NLP) since it plays a crucial rule in multiple down-stream tasks such as Machine Translation (Neale et al., 2016). The main approaches of WSD can be grouped into two categories i.e., Knowledge-based and Supervised WSD (Raganato et al., 2017b). Knowledge-based WSD systems tend to exploit information from structure or content of lexical resources such as WordNet (Miller et al., 1990) and BabelNet (Ponzetto and Navigli, 2010). On the other hand, the latter approach utilizes machine learning techniques to train a model for automatic sense annotation (Zhong and Ng, 2010),(Raganato et al., 2017a),(Chaplot and Salakhutdinov, 2018). Thanks to the training phase, supervised systems usually outperform the knowledge-based alternatives (Raganato et al., 2017b). In fact, the main reason for the high performance of the supervised systems is the utilization of large manually sense annotated corpus through the training process. Unfortunately, obtaining manually sense annotated corpora such as SemCor (Miller et al., 1993) (i.e. the largest and the most predominant manually sense annotated corpus developed for English) is extremely hard and time-consuming and as a result only a limited number of languages can perform supervised WSD. To tackle this issue, in recent years, a line of research has focused on developing automatic or semi-automatic methodologies capable of producing annotated corpora (Pasini and Navigli, 2017) (Pasini et al., 2018) (Scarlini et al., 2019) (Scarlini et al., 2020a) (Scarlini et al., 2020a) (Barba et al., 2020). Although the developed annotated corpora are multi-lingual and lead the supervised systems to achieve a big improvement in WSD, as mentioned in Scarlini et al. (2019), they suffer from some limitations such as (1): strict dependency on the structure of the knowledge graph, (2): requiring huge parallel corpora. In addition, almost all developed corpora are only limited to nouns and provide no annotated instances for other parts-of-speech (POS) i.e., verbs, adjectives, and adverbs.

In this paper, we focus on developing a fully automatic approach for creating a sense annotated corpus for the Persian language. A key part of the former developed approaches for construction of automatic sense-annotated corpora is the use of high performance pre-processing tools i.e., lemmatizer, tokenizer and POS tagger. However, to the best of our knowledge, developed Persian pre-processing tools can not perform as well as their counterparts for English or other European languages. It could be problematic especially when we need to tokenize multi-words and obtain their lemma for exploiting sense candidates from FarsNet (the Persian WordNet) synsets. To deal with this, we designed our method in such a way that it requires no auto-

matic lemmatizer, tokenizer or PoS tagger.
Our proposed system takes English sense annotated corpora (SemCor, for instance) as input and utilizes inter-language semantic relations between English and Persian to obtain a Bag-of-Words (BOW) sense annotated corpus for Persian. It can be a step forward towards the development of sentence-level sense-annotated corpora for the Persian language. The main contributions of our proposed system are as follows:

- **Obtaining state-of-the-art performance on the SBU-WSD-Corpus**
  Our experiments on the standard Persian All-Words WSD test set, developed by Rouhizadeh et al. (2020), indicates that the supervised baselines, trained on PerSemCor, outperform knowledge-based alternatives and achieve state-of-the-art performance in Persian All-words WSD.

- **Providing sense tagged instances for words with different POS**
  In contrast to the almost all recent automatically developed sense-annotated corpora, PerSemCor is not limited to nominal instances and provide sense annotated samples for all parts-of-speech, i.e. nouns, verbs, adjectives, and adverbs.

- **Low dependency on the structure of knowledge-resource**
  We reduced the dependency on the structure of knowledge-resources by only utilizing one inter-language relation between FarsNet and WordNet (i.e, 'Equal-to relation')

- **No dependency to the performance of Persian pre-processing tools**
  In order to ignore the possible lexical or syntax-based errors in PerSemCor , i.e. the errors that can be generated by Persian tokenizers, lemmatizers or Pos taggers, we designed our approach in such a way that include no dependency on the Persian pre-processing tools.

2 Data and Resources

SemCor: English SemCor (Miller et al., 1993) is a subset of the English Brown corpus and include 352 documents with more than 220K sense annotations. The whole corpus is manually tagged with senses from WordNet 1.6. SemCor can be mentioned as the most widely used sense annotated corpus in the English WSD literature (Scarlini et al., 2020b), (Huang et al., 2019), (Luo et al., 2018b), (Luo et al., 2018a). In this paper, we used SemCor 3.0 which includes mapped sense annotations from WordNet 1.6 to WordNet 3.0. [1]

WordNet: WordNet (Miller et al., 1990) is one of the most widely used lexical resources in the WSD literature. It was initially developed for English at Princeton University. WordNet organizes words and phrases into synsets (sets of synonym words with the same POS) and provides a $gloss$ (descriptive definition of the synset words) and possibly an $example$ (a practical example of synset words) for each of them. WordNet synsets are linked via several lexical and semantic relationships. WordNet 3.0, covers around $155K$ English words and phrases organized in around $117K$ synsets.

FarsNet (The Persian WordNet): FarsNet (Shamsfard et al., 2010) is the first Persian lexical ontology which has been developed in the NLP lab of Shahid Beheshti University[2]. Over the past 12 years, numerous studies have been conducted to develop FarsNet (Rouhizadeh et al., 2007)(Rouhizadeh et al., 2010)(Mansoory et al., 2012) (Yarmohammadi et al., 2008) (Khalghani and Shamsfard, 2018). FarsNet 3.0, the last version of FarsNet, covers more than $100K$ Persian words and phrases. Similar to English WordNet, the basic components of FarsNet are synsets that are interlinked via several types of relations. FarsNet relations can be classified to two main classes: Inner-language and Inter-language relations.
Inner-Language Relations connect pairs of word senses and synsets of FarsNet. More in details, Inner-language relations of FarsNet include two major classes, i.e, Semantic and Lexical relations which are defined between FarsNet senses and synsets, respectively. The Inner-Language relations of FarsNet include all the WordNet 2.1 relations as well as some other relationships like 'patient-of', 'salient', and 'agent-of'.
On the other hand, Inter-Language Relations are held between FarsNet 3.0 and WordNet 3.0 synsets. 'Equal-to' and 'Near-equal-to' are two main classes of this kind of relation. 'Equal-to' indicates that words of two synsets (One in FarsNet and another one in WordNet) have the exactly same meaning and PoS. Whereas, the latter one is representative of the similar (not the same) meaning between two

[1] web.eecs.umich.edu/ mihalcea/downloads.html
[2] http://farsnet.nlp.sbu.ac.ir/Site3/Modules/Public/Default.jsp

synsets. It is worth noting that Inter-Language relations between FarsNet and WordNet are not necessarily pair-wise. In other words, one WordNet synset can be linked to one or more FarsNet synsets via 'Equal-to' relation.

Persian-news Corpus: A key component of our system is leveraging a large Persian raw corpus. Our main objectives to utilize such a corpus is to train word embedding models. Although Wikipedia dumps have shown to be useful for training such models [3] in a variety of languages, Persian Wikipedia articles are often short and are not the best choice for this end. To deal with this, we crawled around 1 M documents from several Iranian news agencies web sites [4] to train the word embedding models on that.

Google Translate: Google Translate is a neural machine translation, developed by Google, which provides both word-level and sentence-level translation tool for more than 100 languages. For each input word w of the source language, the word-level translation tool of Google Translate provides a translation table, consisting of three columns: 1) translation candidates, 2) synonyms of the input word with the same translation and 3) frequency of the translation candidates in the public documents [5].

Figure 1 shows the output of the English-Persian tool of Google Translate for the word 'research'. As can be seen, Google Translate suggests 9 translation candidates for the word 'research' in Persian. Additionally, according to the third column of the output schema, it can be concluded that the Persian words appeared in the first and the fifth row of the figure are the most common translations of 'research' in Persian.

In this paper, we used word-level English-Persian tool of Google Translate in the construction pipeline of the PerSemCor.

Persian all-words WSD test set: For evaluating the supervised systems, trained on PerSemCor, we use SBU-WSD-Corpus (Rouhizadeh et al., 2020) as the only available all-word WSD test set for the Persian language. SBU-WSD-Corpus include 16 documents (13 documents for training and 3 for tuning) covering different domains such as Sports, Medical, Science, Technology, etc. It is annotated with senses from FarsNet 3.0 sense inventory and includes 2784 sense-annotated instances (1764 nouns, 494 verbs, 515 adjectives ,and 111 adverbs).

Figure 1: Output of English-Persian Google Translate tool for the word 'research'.

3 Construction of PerSemCor

In this section, we present our proposed approach which aims at automatic construction of PerSemCor, a BoW sense-annotated corpus for the Persian language. The main idea of our proposed approach is inspired by the assumption presented in Bentivogli et al. (2004), i.e, sense annotations of a source language can be transferred to a target language. Given a sense annotated corpus (SemCor, in our case) as input, our proposed system utilizes inter-language semantic relations between English and Persian lexical graphs (WordNet and FarsNet) to obtain a Bag-of-Words(BoW) sense annotated corpus for Persian.

In the following, we first introduce a set of notations which have been used in our proposed approach and then provide details on the way we used the relations between WordNet and FarsNet to create PerSemCor.

3.1 Formal description of notations used in the proposed system

- $S = \{w_{en_1}, ..., w_{en_N}\}$: An English sentence including N English words $(w_{en_1}, ..., w_{en_N})$
- $S\prime = \{w_{p_1}, ..., w_{p_M}\}$: BoW translation of S in Persian including M Persian words $(w_{p_1}, ..., w_{p_M})$
- WN_{key}: Synset key in WordNet[6].

[3] www.dumps.wikimedia.org

[4] we only crawled the news-agencies websites that cover multiple news categories

[5] The length of the blue bar indicates the prevalence of each translation in Persian (see Figure1

[6] Each synset of WorNet is specified with a unique ID (key)

- FN_{key}: Synset key in FarsNet[7]
- $WnSyn_{key}$: The WordNet synset which is identified with the unique ID: key
- $FnSyn_{key}$ The FarsNet synset which is identified with the unique ID: key

3.2 Proposed Approach

Given the English sentence $s = \{w_1, ...w_n\}$ from SemCor, we first remove the stop words and divide the content words into three groups, i.e. C_1, C_2 and C_3. Next, we transfer the words and annotations of C_1, C_2 and C_3 into Persian, respectively.

C_1: The sense-annotated words with one connection with FarsNet

The words of C_1 only include one connection ('equal-to' relation) with FarsNet. For each $w_{en} \in C_1$ which is sense-labeled with WN_{key} (i.e, key of $WnSyn_{key}$), we first retrieve the FarsNet synset $FnSyn_{key}$ which is connected to $WnSyn_{key}$ via 'Equal-to' relation. Although all the present words in $FnSyn_{key}$ share the same meaning, we aim to choose the most suitable one, i.e, $w_p \in FnSyn_{key}$, to make PerSemCor approach to the real Persian texts. Among the synset words, we choose the most frequent one as the best one. To this end, we utilize Google Translate which provides frequency information about the translations of w_{en} (see section 2 for more details) and choose the word w_p with the highest frequency in translation candidates as the best translation.

The proposed approach can be considered as a hybrid approach as it uses semantic and statistical information to transfer (w_{en}, WN_{key}) to (w_p, FN_{key}). More in detail, the approach makes use of 'Equal-to' relations between FarsNet and WordNet which transfer lexical-semantic information from English to Persian. In addition, we employ Google Translate to obtain statistical information of translation candidates and choose the most frequent word one as the final choice.

C_2: The sense-annotated words with at least two connections with FarsNet

As mentioned in section 2, inter-language relations between FarsNet and WordNet are not necessarily pair-wise. Therefore, one annotation key of an English word may have more than one connection to FarsNet. It is worth noting that the FarsNet synsets with the same connection with one WordNet synset share the same meaning. Similar to the former hybrid approach, applied on C_1 words, the aim is to find the best synset which includes the best translation of w_{en} in Persian. To this end, for each $w_{en} \in C_2$, we utilize Google Translate and extract all the possible translations of w_{en} in Persian. Considering $T = \{t_1, ..., t_k\}$ as the possible translations of w_{en} in Persian, we extract the most frequent one $(tj, 0 \leqslant j \leqslant k)$ and choose the synset which include tj as the most suitable synset.

C_3: The words with no connection with FarsNet

These words either do not have a sense label in SemCor or their label does not have a connection to FarsNet. As a result, unlike the words of the former groups, we can not obtain any FarsNet synset to exploit translation candidates. In other words, no semantic information is available via lexical graph connections.

To deal with this, we first utilize the vector representation of former translated words of s (i.e. Persian translation of C_1 and C_2 words) to represent the Persian sentence in semantic space $(V_{s\prime})$. More formally, if the former Persian translated words in $s\prime$ are $\{w_{p_1}, ..., w_{p_k}\}$, $V_{s\prime}$ will be computed as follows:

$$V_{s\prime} = \frac{1}{k} \sum_{i=1}^{k} V(w_{p_i}) \qquad (1)$$

where $V(w_{p_i})$ is the vector representation of w_{p_i}.

Next, for each $w_{en} \in C_3$, we utilize Google Translate and extract $T = \{t_1, ..., t_m\}$ as the translation candidates of w_{en} in Persian. Then we compute the cosine similarity between vector representation of each $t_i \in T$ and $V_{s\prime}$ (Formula 2) and choose t_j $(0 \leqslant j \leqslant m)$ with highest similarity as the best translation of w_{en} in Persian.

$$t_j = \arg\max_{t \in T} Cos(V(t), V_{s\prime}) \qquad (2)$$

The result of the above steps is a Persian BoW sentence which is POS tagged, lemmatized, tokenized, and semantically-annotated. We perform the above steps for all the sentences of SemCor and provide PerSemCor as a BoW sense-annotated corpus for Persian. We also provide the general statistics of PerSemcor and compare them with English SemCor in Table 1. The statistics include the number of documents together with the number of sentences, number of annotations (divided per POS), number of distinct senses, number of distinct lemmas, and average polysemy of both PerSemCor and English SemCor.

[7] A unique ID (key) is assigned to each FarsNet synset

	Docs	Sentences	Noun Tags	Verb Tags	Adj Tags	Adv Tags	All tags	Distinct Senses	Distinct lemmas	Average polysemy
En SemCor	352	31176	87002	88334	31784	14787	226036	33,362	22436	6.8
Per SemCor	352	31176	56955	55972	19985	9078	141819	10381	7122	3.5

Table 1: General statistics of English and Persian SemCor.

POS	Noun	Verb	Adjective	Adverb
Coverage	74.0	76.0	82.3	84.7

Table 2: Coverage of PerSemCor on SBU-WSD-Corpus

4 Evaluation

We carried out a number of experiments on PerSemCor to evaluate it both intrinsically and extrinsically. More in detail, in our intrinsic evaluations, we assessed the quality of sense annotations of PerSemCor. In addition, we utilized PerSemCor for training a set of supervised WSD baselines to extrinsically evaluate it.

4.1 Intrinsic Evaluation

In order to assess the intrinsic quality of PerSemCor, i.e. evaluating the generated annotations, we created a golden standard by randomly sampling 100 sentences from English SemCor. As the next step, we translated the sentences into Persian and asked an Iranian linguist to semantically annotate them with FarsNet 3.0 senses. The result of our evaluation, i.e. comparison between manual and automatic sense tags, indicates that our strategy for transferring sense tags from English to Persian seems promising as more than 95% of automatic tags were the same with the manual counterparts. The high quality of the transmitted sense labels can be explained by the fact that all inter-language relationships between FarsNet and WordNet synsets are determined by expert linguists and therefore are very accurate and reliable.

4.2 Extrinsic Evaluation

We exploited the Word Sense Disambiguation task to assess the quality of our automatically- generated corpus. Therefore, we trained a reference WSD model on the data generated by OneSeC and compared the results against those achieved by the same model trained on other re- sources. In order to extrinsically asses the quality of PerSemCor, we employ it as training set for obtaining supervised WSD models. It is worth noting that since no other Persian WSD training set is available, we only compare the obtained results against knowledge-based alternatives. To this end, we make use of knowledge-based benchmarks presented by Rouhizadeh et al. (2020). The WSD approaches include:

- **Most Frequent Sense approach (MFS)**: We used Most Frequent Sense (MFS) approach as our baseline. The approach is context-independent and always choose the most frequent sense of each word in PerSemCor, as the most suitable one.
- **Part-of-Speech based approaches**: These models represent each target word by PoS tags of its surrounding words. For instance, consider the word w_i in a context C including 6 nouns, 2 verbs, 2 adjectives and 1 adverb. We represent w_i with the feature vector $[4, 2, 3, 1]$, where the features are representative of the number of nouns, verbs, adjectives, and adverbs in C, respectively.
- **Word embedding based approaches**: Word embedding models leverage contextual information of raw data to represent words and phrases in a semantic space. They have shown to be useful in many NLP tasks including WSD(Iacobacci et al., 2016). Following Saeed et al. (2019), we carried out several experiments to demonstrate the benefit of using such models in the training phase of WSD models. In addition, we were interested to check the impact of different word embedding models on the performance of WSD models. To this end, we trained two word embedding models, i.e. word2vec (Mikolov et al., 2013) and Glove (Pennington et al., 2014) on Persian-news corpus (see section 2) and carried out the same experiments with them. For each target word w_i in a context $C = \{w_1, ..., w_m\}$, we represent w_i with a n-dimensional vector (n is the size of embedding vectors) which is the average of word vectors of C.

		Noun			Verb			Adj			Adv			All		
		P	R	F1	P	R	F1	P	R	F1	P	R	F1	P	R	F1
FN 1st sense		48.4	48.4	48.4	43.5	43.5	43.5	81.1	81.1	81.1	90.0	90.0	90.0	55.0	55.0	55.0
MFS		58.0	51.8	54.8	70.0	56.8	62.7	84.8	74.6	79.3	93.6	79.3	85.9	66.1	68.2	61.7
MLP	POS	61.0	55.2	58.0	77.2	65.2	70.7	89.6	79.3	84.2	90.1	81.0	85.7	72.3	63.0	67.3
	W2V	64.0	58.0	60.8	77.9	65.8	71.3	90.1	79.8	84.7	90.1	81.0	85.7	74.3	64.8	69.2
	Glove	64.1	58.0	61.0	78.4	66.2	71.8	89.7	79.4	84.2	90.1	81.0	85.7	74.4	64.8	69.3
DT	POS	58.3	52.8	55.4	76.5	64.6	70.0	88.9	78.6	83.4	90.1	81.0	85.7	70.4	61.4	65.6
	W2V	61.5	55.8	58.5	75.5	63.7	69.2	90.5	80.2	85.0	90.1	81.0	85.7	72.5	63.2	67.5
	Glove	61.7	55.8	58.6	70.3	59.3	64.3	89.3	79.0	83.8	90.1	81.0	85.7	71.5	62.1	66.5
KNN	POS	58.8	53.2	55.8	70.1	64.7	67.3	90.3	80.0	84.9	90.1	81.0	85.7	69.8	61.9	65.6
	W2V	62.9	57.0	59.8	71.4	65.8	71.4	90.6	80.2	85.1	90.1	81.0	85.7	72.7	64.3	68.2
	Glove	62.1	56.2	59.0	71.8	66.2	71.7	**91.2**	**80.8**	**85.7**	90.1	81.0	85.7	72.4	64.0	68.0
SVM	POS	62.4	56.5	59.3	77.2	65.3	70.7	90.0	79.6	84.4	90.1	81.0	85.7	73.2	63.8	68.21
	W2V	**64.2**	**58.2**	**61.1**	78.6	66.3	72.0	90.4	80.0	84.9	90.1	81.0	85.7	**74.6**	**69.5**	**69.5**
	Glove	62.8	56.9	59.7	**78.8**	**66.6**	**72.3**	91.0	80.6	85.5	90.1	81.0	85.7	71.9	65.5	68.5

Table 3: Precision (P), Recall (R) and F-1 (F) performance of supervised WSD systems on SBU-WSD-Corpus

	Noun	Verb	Adjective	Adverb	All
MFS	54.8 — 59.2	62.7 — 65.0	79.3 — 84.2	85.9 — 90.1	61.7 — 65.8
MLP	61.0 — 64.9	71.8 — 73.1	84.2 — 89.5	85.7 — 90.1	69.3 — 72.4
DT	58.5 — 63.2	69.2 — 71.5	85.0 — 90.1	85.7 — 90.1	67.5 — 70.6
KNN	59.8 — 64.8	71.4 — 73.7	85.1 — **90.2**	85.7 — 90.1	68.2 — 71.4
SVM	61.1 — **65.0**	72.0 — **74.3**	84.9 — 90.0	85.7 — 90.1	69.5 — **72.7**

Table 4: Comparison between performance of the supervised WSD systems when the MFS back-off strategy is disabled (the number to the left of each cell) or enabled (the number to the right of each cell).

Machine learning algorithms: Following (Saeed et al., 2019), we employed four machine learning techniques, i.e. Support Vector Machine (SVM) (Cortes and Vapnik, 1995), K-Nearest Neighbor (KNN) (Altman, 1992) , Decision Tree (DT) (Black, 1988), and Multilayer Perceptron (MLP) (McCulloch and Pitts, 1943), which utilize the feature vectors, obtained by mentioned approaches, to train WSD models. We also compare the performance of the supervised models with MFS as the baseline of the supervised systems. In addition, we compare the results with FarsNet first sense approach[8] as the former baseline of Persian WSD (Rouhizadeh et al., 2020).

Results and analysis: In Table 3, we compare the performance of different machine learning algorithms when trained by different approaches. It is worth noting that PerSemCor is capable of covering most context words of SBU-WSD-Corpus (see Table 2). In order to clearly show the effect of PerSemCor in the final performance WSD systems, we report the precision (P), recall (R), and the harmonic mean (F1) of different systems, broken by PoS, when no back-off strategy was used.

As expected, the F1-performance of all systems on nouns is lower than other parts-of-speech. This can be explained by the ambiguity level of nouns in the SBU-WSD-Corpus as it is greater than all the other parts-of-speech. As can be seen, MFS can outperform the FarsNet 1st sense approach on disambiguating nouns and verbs by a large margin (10% on nouns and 18% on verbs). It clearly shows the potential of PerSemCor in providing information about sense distribution of Persian words.

Comparing different approaches, the results show that all machine learning algorithms achieve the highest performance when they use word embedding approaches as feature vectors for training. It clearly shows the great impact of using embedding vectors in a WSD pipeline. However, as can be seen, the use of different word embedding models does not greatly affect the final performance of the systems. Comparing machine learning algorithms, SVM outperforms all the other ones in almost all cases. In addition, the best results obtained when SVM trained with the word embedding based feature vectors.

Additional experiments:

1. **Applying Back-off strategy**: A back-off strategy is an alternative method that is used when our system is unable to decide the meaning of the

[8]The approach simply chooses the first sense of FarsNet as the best meaning of each word

		Noun	Verb	Adjective	Adverb	All
Supervised Systems	MFS	59.2	65.0	84.2	90.1	65.8
	MLP	64.9	73.1	89.5	90.1	72.4
	DT	63.2	71.5	90.1	90.1	70.6
	KNN	64.8	73.7	**90.2**	90.1	71.4
	SVM	**65.0**	**74.3**	90.0	90.1	**72.7**
Knowledge Based Systems	FarsNet 1st sense	48.4	43.5	81.1	90.0	55.0
	Basile14	62.7	66.3	83.6	82.9	67.8
	UKB (ppr)	58.4	70.5	82.4	83.6	65.7
	UKB (ppr-w2w)	58.3	71.5	84.4	84.5	66.2

Table 5: F-1 performance of different supervised and knowledge-based models on SBU-WSD-Corpus

input word. For instance, for the words occurring only with one meaning in the training data, we can use MFS as the back-off strategy[9]. This technique has shown to be helpful in several developed WSD systems (Raganato et al., 2017b). To test the effect of using a back-off strategy, we, therefore, decided to perform additional experiments on PerSemCor when the MFS back-off strategy is used[10]. As can be seen in Table 4, all the WSD models achieve higher performance when MFS back-off is used. It is indicative of the usefulness of applying this technique in multiple WSD pipelines.

2. **Comparison with knowledge-based systems**

In Table 5, we compared the F1 performance of supervised models against knowledge-based benchmarks (Rouhizadeh et al., 2020), including Basile14 (Basile et al., 2014), UKB (Agirre et al., 2018) and FarsNet 1st sense (baseline of knowledge-based models). The results show that supervised systems outperform knowledge-based models on all parts-of-speech. It clearly shows the high ability of PerSemCor on training WSD models as it leads simple supervised baselines to state-of-the-art performance when compared against the most recent knowledge-based models. More interestingly, the simplest supervised approach, i.e. MFS approach, is able to achieve competitive results with state-of-the-art knowledge-based systems. It will be more impressive considering that PerSemCor generated without any human intervention.

[9]Note that for the words which never occur in the training data, we consider the first sense of FarsNet as the most predominant one (Raganato et al., 2017b)(Rouhizadeh et al., 2019)

[10]For each machine learning technique, we only report the result of best performing setting

5 Related Work

Knowledge acquisition bottleneck i.e, producing a large amount of lexical-semantic data, can be mentioned as one of the most important problems in WSD. It is more crucial when it comes to supervised WSD as these types of systems need sense annotated data for training a machine learning model. Over recent decades, a variety of approaches have been proposed to mitigate this issue. They can be grouped into two main categories:

Manual annotation, where all the sense tags of the corpora are provided by human efforts. SemCor is one of the first manually annotated corpora for English, developed by the WordNet Project research team at Princeton University. It was initially tagged with senses for WordNet 2.1 and contains more than 200k sense annotated instances. Although SemCor has lead the supervised systems to achieve state-of-the-art performance in English WSD, obtaining such corpora is hard and time-consuming. To reduce or eliminate human intervention for obtaining semi-automatically or fully automatically sense-annotated corpora, a range of approaches have been proposed

Automatic annotation, where a semi-automatic or fully automatic approach is used to generate sense tags.

OMSTI (One Million Sense-Tagged Instances) (Taghipour and Ng, 2015) can be mentioned as one the largest and most predominant sense-tagged corpora for English, created in a semi-automatically manner. The authors of the paper leveraged a large English-Chinese parallel corpus and manual translations of senses to obtain one million training instances. Another group of systems make use of formerly annotated corpora in English, SemCor for instance, to create a new sense-tagged corpora for a second language. Bentivogli et al. (2004) and

Bond et al. (2012) used a parallel corpus (a subset of the SemCor) to create a sense-annotated corpus for the Italian and Japanese languages, respectively. Both approaches utilized word level alignments between the sentences of the parallel corpora to semantically annotate the target instances. Bovi et al. (2017) utilized Babelfy (Moro et al., 2014) as a language independent WSD system and NASARI (Camacho-Collados et al., 2016) as a vector representation of concepts to develop a parallel sense-annotated corpus for four European languages. Pasini and Navigli (2017) and Pasini and Navigli (2020) eliminated the requirement of parallel corpora by proposing Train-O-Matic, which makes use of structural-semantic information from a lexical network to automatically annotate the context words. Scarlini et al. (2019), also proposed a system which leverages Wikipedia categories and semantic vector of concepts to perform automatic sense annotation. The most similar method to our work is proposed by Barba et al. (2020). They make use of multi-lingual BERT and BabelNet to project senses from SemCor to the sentences in low-resource languages. However, the proposed system relies on high-performance pre-processing tools which are not available for Persian. In addition, the only available All-Words WSD test set for Persian is SBU-WSD corpus which is tagged based on FarsNet 3.0 senses, and as a result, the proposed approach can not be evaluated on Persian.
Considering the unavailability of key components of the formerly developed approaches for Persian (English-Persian word alignment tool: (Bond et al., 2012), (Bentivogli et al., 2004)), large English-Persian parallel corpora: (Bovi et al., 2017), high-performance tokenizer, and lemmatizer: (Pasini and Navigli, 2017) ,(Pasini and Navigli, 2020), (Scarlini et al., 2019), (Barba et al., 2020)), we propose a fully automatic approach to obtain a sense annotated corpus for the Persian language. In contrast to the most aforementioned approaches, which only provide sense-annotated nominal instances, our approach provides sense-annotated samples for all parts-of-speech (nouns, verbs, adjectives, and adverbs).

6 Conclusion

In this paper, we presented PerSemCor, a fully-automatic constructed sense-annotated corpus for the Persian language. Our approach for building PerSemCor includes no human intervention as it uses semantic inter-language relations to annotate the Persian words. Moreover, we eliminated the burden of high-performance pre-processing tools, i.e. tokenizer and lemmatizer, as they can be a source of error in constructing training data sets for the Persian Language. We evaluated the built corpus, PerSemCor, both intrinsically and extrinsically, and proved that it can count as a high-quality sense-annotated corpus for training supervised Persian WSD models. As the future work, we plan to create a Persian sentence-level sense-annotated corpus by employing a 'BoW2seq' approach, i.e. an approach which takes a set of shuffled words of a sentence as input and reorder them like a real sentence.

References

Eneko Agirre, Oier López de Lacalle, and Aitor Soroa. 2018. The risk of sub-optimal use of open source NLP software: UKB is inadvertently state-of-the-art in knowledge-based WSD. In *Proceedings of Workshop for NLP Open Source Software (NLP-OSS)*, Melbourne, Australia. Association for Computational Linguistics.

Naomi S Altman. 1992. An introduction to kernel and nearest-neighbor nonparametric regression. *The American Statistician*, 46(3):175–185.

Edoardo Barba, Luigi Procopio, Niccolo Campolungo, Tommaso Pasini, and Roberto Navigli. 2020. Mulan: Multilingual label propagation for word sense disambiguation. In *Proc. of IJCAI*, pages 3837–3844.

Pierpaolo Basile, Annalina Caputo, and Giovanni Semeraro. 2014. An enhanced lesk word sense disambiguation algorithm through a distributional semantic model. In *Proceedings of COLING 2014, the 25th International Conference on Computational Linguistics: Technical Papers*, pages 1591–1600.

Luisa Bentivogli, Pamela Forner, and Emanuele Pianta. 2004. Evaluating cross-language annotation transfer in the multisemcor corpus. In *COLING 2004: Proceedings of the 20th International Conference on Computational Linguistics*, pages 364–370.

Ezra Black. 1988. An experiment in computational discrimination of english word senses. *IBM Journal of research and development*, 32(2):185–194.

Francis Bond, Timothy Baldwin, Richard Fothergill, and Kiyotaka Uchimoto. 2012. Japanese semcor: A sense-tagged corpus of japanese. In *Proceedings of the 6th global WordNet conference (GWC 2012)*, pages 56–63. Citeseer.

Claudio Delli Bovi, Jose Camacho-Collados, Alessandro Raganato, and Roberto Navigli. 2017. Eurosense: Automatic harvesting of multilingual sense annotations from parallel text. In *Proceedings of the 55th Annual Meeting of the Association for Computational Linguistics (Volume 2: Short Papers)*, pages 594–600.

José Camacho-Collados, Mohammad Taher Pilehvar, and Roberto Navigli. 2016. Nasari: Integrating explicit knowledge and corpus statistics for a multilingual representation of concepts and entities. *Artificial Intelligence*, 240:36–64.

Devendra Singh Chaplot and Ruslan Salakhutdinov. 2018. Knowledge-based word sense disambiguation using topic models. In *AAAI*.

Corinna Cortes and Vladimir Vapnik. 1995. Support-vector networks. *Machine learning*, 20(3):273–297.

Luyao Huang, Chi Sun, Xipeng Qiu, and Xuanjing Huang. 2019. Glossbert: Bert for word sense disambiguation with gloss knowledge. *arXiv preprint arXiv:1908.07245*.

Ignacio Iacobacci, Mohammad Taher Pilehvar, and Roberto Navigli. 2016. Embeddings for word sense disambiguation: An evaluation study. In *Proceedings of the 54th Annual Meeting of the Association for Computational Linguistics (Volume 1: Long Papers)*, pages 897–907.

Fatemeh Khalghani and Mehrnoush Shamsfard. 2018. Extraction of verbal synsets and relations for farsnet. In *Proceedings of the 9th Global WordNet Conference (GWC 2018)*, page 424.

Fuli Luo, Tianyu Liu, Zexue He, Qiaolin Xia, Zhifang Sui, and Baobao Chang. 2018a. Leveraging gloss knowledge in neural word sense disambiguation by hierarchical co-attention. In *Proceedings of the 2018 Conference on Empirical Methods in Natural Language Processing*, pages 1402–1411.

Fuli Luo, Tianyu Liu, Qiaolin Xia, Baobao Chang, and Zhifang Sui. 2018b. Incorporating glosses into neural word sense disambiguation. *arXiv preprint arXiv:1805.08028*.

Niloofar Mansoory, Mehrnoush Shamsfard, and Masoud Rouhizadeh. 2012. Compound verbs in persian wordnet. *International Journal of Lexicography*, 25(1):50–67.

Warren S McCulloch and Walter Pitts. 1943. A logical calculus of the ideas immanent in nervous activity. *The bulletin of mathematical biophysics*, 5(4):115–133.

Tomas Mikolov, Ilya Sutskever, Kai Chen, Greg S Corrado, and Jeff Dean. 2013. Distributed representations of words and phrases and their compositionality. In *Advances in neural information processing systems*, pages 3111–3119.

George A Miller, Richard Beckwith, Christiane Fellbaum, Derek Gross, and Katherine J Miller. 1990. Introduction to wordnet: An on-line lexical database. *International journal of lexicography*, 3(4):235–244.

George A Miller, Claudia Leacock, Randee Tengi, and Ross T Bunker. 1993. A semantic concordance. In *HUMAN LANGUAGE TECHNOLOGY: Proceedings of a Workshop Held at Plainsboro, New Jersey, March 21-24, 1993*.

Andrea Moro, Alessandro Raganato, and Roberto Navigli. 2014. Entity linking meets word sense disambiguation: a unified approach. *Transactions of the Association for Computational Linguistics*, 2:231–244.

Steven Neale, Luís Gomes, Eneko Agirre, Oier Lopez de Lacalle, and António Branco. 2016. Word sense-aware machine translation: Including senses as contextual features for improved translation models. In *Proceedings of the Tenth International Conference on Language Resources and Evaluation (LREC'16)*, pages 2777–2783.

Tommaso Pasini, Francesco Maria Elia, and Roberto Navigli. 2018. Huge automatically extracted training sets for multilingual word sense disambiguation. *arXiv preprint arXiv:1805.04685*.

Tommaso Pasini and Roberto Navigli. 2017. Train-o-matic: Large-scale supervised word sense disambiguation in multiple languages without manual training data. In *Proceedings of the 2017 Conference on Empirical Methods in Natural Language Processing*, pages 78–88.

Tommaso Pasini and Roberto Navigli. 2020. Train-o-matic: Supervised word sense disambiguation with no (manual) effort. *Artificial Intelligence*, 279:103215.

Jeffrey Pennington, Richard Socher, and Christopher D. Manning. 2014. Glove: Global vectors for word representation. In *Empirical Methods in Natural Language Processing (EMNLP)*, pages 1532–1543.

Simone Paolo Ponzetto and Roberto Navigli. 2010. Knowledge-rich word sense disambiguation rivaling supervised systems. In *Proceedings of the 48th annual meeting of the association for computational linguistics*, pages 1522–1531.

Alessandro Raganato, Claudio Delli Bovi, and Roberto Navigli. 2017a. Neural sequence learning models for word sense disambiguation. In *Proceedings of the 2017 Conference on Empirical Methods in Natural Language Processing*, pages 1156–1167.

Alessandro Raganato, Jose Camacho-Collados, and Roberto Navigli. 2017b. Word sense disambiguation: A unified evaluation framework and empirical comparison. In *Proceedings of the 15th Conference of the European Chapter of the Association for Computational Linguistics: Volume 1, Long Papers*, pages 99–110.

Hossein Rouhizadeh, Mehrnoush Shamsfard, and Masoud Rouhizadeh. 2019. Knowledge-based word sense disambiguation with distributional semantic expansion. In *Proceedings of the 2019 Workshop on Widening NLP*.

Hossein Rouhizadeh, Mehrnoush Shamsfard, and Masoud Rouhizadeh. 2020. Knowledge-based word sense disambiguation with distributional semantic expansion for the persian language. In *2020 10th International Conference on Computer and Knowledge Engineering (ICCKE)*. IEEE.

Masoud Rouhizadeh, Mehrnoush Shamsfard, and Mahsa A Yarmohammadi. 2007. Building a wordnet for persian verbs. *GWC 2008*, page 406.

Masoud Rouhizadeh, A Yarmohammadi, and Mehrnoush Shamsfard. 2010. Developing the persian wordnet of verbs: Issues of compound verbs and building the editor. In *Proceedings of 5th Global WordNet Conference*.

Ali Saeed, Rao Muhammad Adeel Nawab, Mark Stevenson, and Paul Rayson. 2019. A word sense disambiguation corpus for urdu. *Language Resources and Evaluation*, 53(3):397–418.

Bianca Scarlini, Tommaso Pasini, and Roberto Navigli. 2019. Just "onesec" for producing multilingual sense-annotated data. In *Proceedings of the 57th Annual Meeting of the Association for Computational Linguistics*, pages 699–709.

Bianca Scarlini, Tommaso Pasini, and Roberto Navigli. 2020a. Sense-annotated corpora for word sense disambiguation in multiple languages and domains. In *Proceedings of The 12th Language Resources and Evaluation Conference*, pages 5905–5911.

Bianca Scarlini, Tommaso Pasini, and Roberto Navigli. 2020b. Sensembert: Context-enhanced sense embeddings for multilingual word sense disambiguation. In *AAAI*, pages 8758–8765.

Mehrnoush Shamsfard, Akbar Hesabi, Hakimeh Fadaei, Niloofar Mansoory, Ali Famian, Somayeh Bagherbeigi, Elham Fekri, Maliheh Monshizadeh, and S Mostafa Assi. 2010. Semi automatic development of farsnet; the persian wordnet. In *Proceedings of 5th global WordNet conference, Mumbai, India*, volume 29.

Kaveh Taghipour and Hwee Tou Ng. 2015. One million sense-tagged instances for word sense disambiguation and induction. In *Proceedings of the nineteenth conference on computational natural language learning*, pages 338–344.

Mahsa A Yarmohammadi, Mehrnoush Shamsfard, Mahshid A Yarmohammadi, and Masoud Rouhizadeh. 2008. Sbuqa question answering system. In *Computer Society of Iran Computer Conference*, pages 316–323. Springer.

Zhi Zhong and Hwee Tou Ng. 2010. It makes sense: A wide-coverage word sense disambiguation system for free text. In *Proceedings of the ACL 2010 system demonstrations*, pages 78–83. Association for Computational Linguistics.

HisNet: A Polarity Lexicon based on WordNet for Emotion Analysis

Merve Özçelik
Starlang Yazılım Danışmanlık
merve@starlangyazilim.com

Bilge Nas Arıcan
Starlang Yazılım Danışmanlık
bilge@starlangyazilim.com

Özge Bakay
Boğaziçi University
ozge.bakay@boun.edu.tr

Elif Sarmış
Starlang Yazılım Danışmanlık
elif@starlangyazilim.com

Nilgün Güler Bayazıt
Yıldız Technical University
guler@yildiz.edu.tr

Özlem Ergelen
Boğaziçi University

Olcay Taner Yıldız
Özyeğin University
olcay.yildiz@ozyegin.edu.tr

Abstract

Dictionary-based methods in sentiment analysis have received scholarly attention recently, the most comprehensive examples of which can be found in English. However, many other languages lack polarity dictionaries, or the existing ones are small in size as in the case of SentiTurkNet, the first and only polarity dictionary in Turkish. Thus, this study aims to extend the content of SentiTurkNet by comparing the two available WordNets in Turkish, namely KeNet and TR-wordnet of BalkaNet. To this end, a current Turkish polarity dictionary has been created relying on 76,825 synsets matching KeNet, where each synset has been annotated with three polarity labels, which are positive, negative and neutral. Meanwhile, the comparison of KeNet and TR-wordnet of BalkaNet has revealed their weaknesses such as the repetition of the same senses, lack of necessary merges of the items belonging to the same synset and the presence of redundant narrower versions of synsets, which are discussed in light of their potential to the improvement of the current lexical databases of Turkish.

1 Introduction

A wordnet can be described as a highly comprehensive dictionary which provides semantic relationships such as synonymy, hypernymy, hyponymy, meronymy, homonymy etc. These rich lexical sources are used for many tasks such as word sense disambiguation, text analysis, information retrieval, and sentiment analysis. There are two WordNets for Turkish, namely TR-wordnet of BalkaNet (Tufis et al., 2004a) (hereafter, TR-wordnet, which means Turkish wordnet) and KeNet (Ehsani et al., 2018; Bakay et al., 2019b; Bakay et al., 2019a; Ozcelik et al., 2019; Bakay et al., 2020). Whereas TR-wordnet has been created earlier with a smaller scope of synsets, KeNet has been created later with a much wider range of synsets than that of TR-wordnet (See Section 2 for a more detailed comparison). Although the newer WordNets such as KeNet are more exhaustive than the earlier ones due to their increased number of synsets, it must be noted that it is also possible to come across instances where the less inclusive wordnets, TR-wordnet can actually reveal the shortcomings of the larger ones. Therefore, comparisons of the available synsets for a given language are a good way to improve the available sources as they, by complementing one another, give us the chance to combine the powerful aspects of different wordnets and develop a more thorough dataset for performing various tasks such as sentiment analysis.

In recent years, sentiment analysis studies have gained significance in NLP applications. Currently, popular sentiment analysis applications frequently employ data regarding product interpretation, film interpretation, service evaluation and political events, mostly extracted from social media platforms. The aim of sentiment analysis is to reveal all emotions and commentary present in the data examined. There are several applicable methods for this purpose, one of which is the dictionary-based method where a polarity dictionary is employed.

Exploiting a dictionary-based method necessitates the construction of a specific polarity dictionary in the same language as the data-to-be-analyzed. The reason behind this necessity stems from the improbability of creating a universal polarity dictionary due to both grammatical and cultural asymmetries between languages. For instance, a certain historical event can have positive connotations in one culture and negative connotations in another culture. Thus, it is an essential step to create a language specific polarity dictionary.

In our study, we present a polarity dictionary to provide an extensive polarity dictionary for Turkish that dictionary-based sentiment analysis studies have been longing for[1]. Our primary objective is to provide a more refined and extensive polarity dictionary than the previous SentiTurkNet. In doing so, we have resorted to a different network from the referenced study. We have identified approximately 76,825 synsets from Kenet, which then were manually labeled as positive, negative or neutral by three native speakers of Turkish. Subsequently, a second labeling was further made on positive and negative words as strong or weak based on their degree of positivity or negativity.

In this paper, we will first discuss the literature on WordNets and polarity lexicons in Section 2, then proceed to present the comparison of KeNet and TR-wordnet in Section 3. In section 4, we explain how we have constructed our comprehensive polarity lexicon, HisNet. Subsequently in Section 5, we present the statistical comparison of HisNet to SentiTurkNet. Lastly, we make our concluding remarks in Section 6.

2 Literature Review

2.1 Wordnets

The first wordnet project was Princeton WordNet (PWN), which was initiated in 1995 by George Miller (1995). Currently, the latest release of PWN, version 3.1 has 117,000 synsets 206,941 word-sense pairs. Although WordNets for other languages were constructed shortly after the release of PWN, their coverage is not as extensive as that of PWN, (Vossen, 1997; Black et al., 2006). For Balkan languages, BalkaNet (Tufis et al., 2004a) is the most comprehensive work up to date. For the TR-wordnet of BalkaNet (Bilgin et al., 2004a), researchers automatically extracted synonyms, antonyms and hypernyms from a monolingual Turkish dictionary. Although TR-wordnet includes 14,626 number of synsets, KeNet is a more comprehensive Turkish WordNet, which has 80,000 synsets covering 110,000 word-sense pairs (Ehsani et al., 2018; Bakay et al., 2019b; Bakay et al., 2019a; Ozcelik et al., 2019; Bakay et al., 2020).

2.2 Polarity Lexicons

The first examples of polarity dictionary work could be found in English. SentiWordNet 1.0, the very first study on English polarity dictionaries, was presented by Esuli and Sebastiani (2006). Considerable research has been conducted to improve these resources with the aim of making them more precise. For example, the polarities of the objective words in SentiWordNet have been reassessed by Hung and Lini (2010). SenticNet (Cambria et al., 2014), another well-known dictionary in English, is created by rescoring words based on five different criteria, which are happiness, attention, sensitivity, ability and general polarity. Thus, it is evident that SenticNet is a polarity dictionary that provides a more extensive emotional evaluation than SentiWordNet.

There are polar dictionaries created in major languages other than English. However, these dictionaries were found to be insufficient in terms of the number of words. Brooke et al. (2009) aimed to translate English polarity sources to Spanish. At first, the methods established independent from the target language were found adequate, yet in the long term it was noticed that these methods were costly and inaccurate. Employing language-dependent resources to improve this system was deemed more feasible. Remus et al. (2010) have created a German sensitivity dictionary named SentiWortschatz for the German language. For the purpose of creating a feeling dictionary, over 3500 German words were assigned positive and negative values in the range of [-1, 1], using PosTags. Abdaoui et al. (2017) have created the FEEL: a French Expanded Emotion Lexicon polarity dictionary for French. Moreno-Sandoval et al. (2017) have created the Combined Spanish Lexicon polarity dictionary for Spanish.

Besides major languages such English, French and Spanish, polarity lexicon work has been extended to less-resourced languages such as Basque. Saralegi and Vicente (2013) created lexicons for Basque and evaluated them against the

[1]https://github.com/StarlangSoftware/TurkishSentiNet
https://github.com/StarlangSoftware/TurkishSentiNet-Py
https://github.com/StarlangSoftware/TurkishSentiNet-Cy
https://github.com/StarlangSoftware/TurkishSentiNet-C#
https://github.com/StarlangSoftware/TurkishSentiNet-CPP

standard datasets in varying domains. Das and Bandyopadhyay (2010) have proposed a method for designing a sentiment dictionary for the Indian languages, Bengali and Telugu. This proposal aims to translate all three languages using SentiWordNet and SubjectivityWordList (Wilson et al., 2005) as the source.

There was no known polarity dictionary study in Turkish up until 2015. The first study was conducted by Dehkharghani et al. (2016) drawing on the Turkish WordNet (Bilgin et al., 2004b), which is a part of the BalkaNet (Tufis et al., 2004b) project aiming to develop a multi-lingual dictionary database of separate WordNets for Balkan languages. To this end, this study aims to compare the two available WordNets for Turkish by revealing their weaknesses and presents HisNet, which is a more detailed polarity lexicon derived from KeNet.

3 Comparison of TR-wordnet and KeNet

3.1 Extracting Matchings

In order to compare KeNet and TR-wordnet, we have extracted the matchings between the two. Initially, the synsets containing only synset numbers are discarded from both KeNet and TR-wordnet. Since the number of synsets in KeNet by far outmatches the number of synsets in TR-wordnet, we concentrate on TR-wordnet. For each synset S_b in TR-wordnet, we display each synset S_k in KeNet, where S_k contains at least one synset number from S_b.

In general, the synsets containing the same synset number are taken as candidates for a possible match between TR-wordnet and KeNet. In total, there are 9,787 synsets from TR-wordnet which matches 27,314 synsets from KeNet. This extracted list has been, then, displayed on Google sheets and the comparisons have been analyzed by two trained annotators. Table 1 shows five example cases taken from the extracted list. In this table, whereas Case 1 shows a situation where one synset in Tr-wordnet matches with two synsets in KeNet, each of the Case 2, 3 and 4 exemplifies a one-to-one match between the WordNets. More specifically, in Case 2, the synset in TR-wordnet includes two lemmas as opposed to the single lemma in KeNet. Cases 3 and 4 demonstrate the lack of definitions for the given synsets in TR-wordnet. Case 4 and 5 exemplify the matching of a single synset in KeNet with two different synsets in TR-wordnet.

3.2 Weaknesses of KeNet

The first advantage of this comparison is that it shows several shortages of KeNet, which need to be improved. Firstly, a comparison of KeNet senses with the ones from TR-wordnet helps us see the organization of KeNet senses in a better way. After comparing the matching senses between TR-wordnet and KeNet, it has been found that more than 1,300 of senses in KeNet need to be re-written to cover the range of meanings given in the synsets. To exemplify, as it can be seen in case 1 in Table 2, whereas the TR-wordnet sense for the given synset is broader, the one provided in KeNet needs to be improved. Secondly, as synsets of KeNet have been extracted from different sources, there are some redundant synsets, which are the copies of some synsets, only with different IDs. For example, Case 2 in Table 2 shows two separate synsets for "İzlanda" in KeNet, one of which is redundant. With this comparison, we have been able to detect these repetitive synsets that need to be removed from KeNet, the number of which has been found to be 58.

Thirdly, this comparison has revealed the incorrect mergings in KeNet synsets. 310 mistakenly-merged synsets have been found and they were later split up based on their sense distinctions (Bakay et al., 2019b). Such a split procedure will first create new synsets and a comparison of these new synsets with TR-wordnet can later be used to further investigate how the scope of the sense disambiguation among the two Wordnets differs. As an example, in Case 3 in Table 2, we see the mergings in these synsets with the use of pipes (—) in between the senses. In this example, the comparison of the merged synset of "idaresiz gevşek" in KeNet with "gevşek" in TR-wordnet shows that the synset in KeNet is to be split up as it covers two different senses. Lastly, there are synsets that are actually referring to the same entities but wrongly separated and given as different ones due to a wrong split or a lack of merging. The display we have used in this work has enabled us to recognize these cases as these imitative synsets are matched with the same synsets in TR-wordnet. Case 4 in Table 2, for instance, shows that the two different synsets of KeNet that are matched with "steril aseptik" in TR-wordnet are, in fact, items belonging to the same synset. Thus, 816 numbers

Table 1: Candidate Matchings from TR-wordnet and KeNet

	TR-wordnet			KeNet		
Case	Id	Synset	Definition	Id	Synset	Definition
1	BILI-00000001	amca (uncle)	Babanın erkek kardeşi	TUR10-0066770 TUR10-0032550	baba yarısı emmi amca (uncle) amca (uncle)	Babanın erkek kardeşi Yaşlı erkeklere saygı için kullanılan bir seslenme sözü
2	BILI-00000022	sipahi tımarlı sipahi (cavalryman)	Tımar sahibi, atlı Osmanlı askeri	TUR10-0695630	sipahi (cavalryman)	Osmanlılarda tımar sahibi bir sınıf atlı asker
3	BILI-00000354	Bozcaada (district name)	-	TUR10-0975880	Bozcaada (district name)	Çanakkale iline bağlı ilçelerden biri
4	ENG20-04237061-n	tapınak (temple)	-	TUR10-745420	tapınak ibadethane mabet (temple)	İçinde ibadet edilen, tapınılan yapı
5	ENG20-04237290-n	tapınak (temple)	İçinde tanrıya kulluk edilen, tapınılan yapı	TUR10-745420	tapınak ibadethane mabet (temple)	İçinde ibadet edilen, tapınılan yapı

of such synsets have been merged into the other existing synsets which have the same senses.

3.3 Weaknesses of TR-wordnet

In addition to the advantage of showing the shortcomings of KeNet, this comparison has also shed light onto the weaknesses of TR-wordnet and thus, why it needs to be improved. First of all, as in KeNet, some senses in TR-wordnet are incomplete such that they are either in English or have only exemplary sentences instead of actual senses. Overall, in the dataset of TR-wordnet used in this comparison, 1,975 senses out of 9,787 (20.18%) are in English and 416 (4.25%) have exemplary sentences instead of senses. Furthermore, for 3,174 (32.43%) number of synsets, no sense definition is provided.

Similar to the case in KeNet as explained in the previous section, there are redundant synsets in TR-wordnet, as well. This one-to-one comparison between TR-wordnet and KeNet has showed us the cases where one single synset in KeNet is matched with more than one synset in TR-wordnet (see cases 1, 2 & 3 in Table 3). We must note that such matchings could mean that for more than one synset in TR-wordnet, there is only one available synset in KeNet as their equivalent. Such multiple matchings of the same synset could be interpreted as the lack of necessary sense distinction in KeNet. However, it is not the case in any of the multiple matchings. On the other hand, there are three reasons for such repeated use of the same senses with multiple matchings in TR-wordnet: they are (i) simply the copies of the same senses in TR-wordnet, only with different IDs (see Case 1), (ii) a result of the lack of the necessary merging of the synsets (see Case 2) or (iii) a result of the presence of a narrower and a wider synsets, the former of which should be removed as the latter already covers it (see Case 3). The numbers of such cases where one synset in KeNet matches with multiple senses in TR-wordnet for one of these three reasons is 416 in total.

Another significant difference between KeNet and TR-wordnet is the addition of new lemmas in KeNet synsets. Case 4 in Table 3 exemplifies the inclusion of the lemmas of "kokuşmak" and "taaffün etmek" in addtion to the existing lemma of "kokmak" in TR-wordnet. These additional lemmas can be taken as a clear reflection of the wider coverage of KeNet. Whereas the equivalents of these synsets in KeNet are also given in TR-wordnet, these extra lemmas in KeNet show that by using a more comprehensive dataset, KeNet has

Table 2: Examples for the Weaknesses of KeNet

	TR-wordnet			KeNet		
Case	Id	Synset	Definition	Id	Synset	Definition
1	ENG20-01406785-v	kaçış kaçma firar (escape)	Bulunulması gereken yerden izin almaksızın	TUR10-0395580	kaçış (escape)	kaçma işi veya biçimi
2	ENG20-08397969-n	İzlanda (Iceland)	İzlanda Adasında kurulu, cumhuriyetle yönetilen ülke	TUR10-1228520	İzlanda (Iceland)	İzlanda Adasında kurulu, cumhuriyetle yönetilen ülke
				TUR10-1228510	İzlanda (Iceland)	Atlas Okyanusu'nun kuzeyinde Grönland'ın güneydoğusu ile İskandinavya ve Britanya Adası'nın kuzeybatısında bulunan bir ada ve Avrupa ülkesi
3	ENG20-02029683-a	gevşek (laidback)	not fixed firmly or tightly	TUR10-0360900	idaresiz gevşek (laidback)	İdare etmesini bilmeyen, gevşek, beceriksiz kimse
4	ENG20-02050662-a	steril aseptik (sterile)	free of or using methods to keep free of pathological microorganisms	TUR10-0709320	sterilize steril (sterile)	Her çeşit mikroptan arınmış
				TUR10-0048950	aseptik (sterile)	Her türlü mikroptan arınmış

accomplished to widen its scope.

The last crucial discrepancy between TR-wordnet and KeNet is that some senses of TR-wordnet are matched with more than one sense in KeNet. To put differently, a single sense in TR-wordnet cannot be provided with only one sense in KeNet, which provides a sense distinction between the combined sense in TR-wordnet. The required distinction is given with either two or three separate senses in KeNet. Therefore, as it can be seen in Cases 5 and 6 in Table 4, although they are merged in a single synset in TR-wordnet, KeNet captures the necessary distinctions between the senses by having two separate synsets to correspond to a single synset in TR-wordnet. This lack of necessary distinctions in TR-wordnet can be taken as a significant issue of TR-wordnet to improve, which has been successfully given in the more comprehensive Turkish wordnet, KeNet.

4 Polarity Lexicon Generation: HisNet

This study aims to enlarge SentiTurkNet in terms of synset number by using a different Turkish WordNet. For this study, we used the most comprehensive word network available as the Turkish WordNet: KeNet (Ehsani et al., 2018; Bakay et al., 2019a; Bakay et al., 2019b; Ozcelik et al., 2019; Bakay et al., 2020). was created with the data obtained from the current items in Turkish lexicon, and emerged following the Turkish WordNet. Compared to Turkish WordNet, KeNet has a larger synset rate, which is the reason why we opted for KeNet over Turkish WordNet for the purposes of this study.

As the first step of our project, we have identified approximately 76,825 synsets from Kenet. Subsequently, all of these synsets were manually labeled as positive, negative or neutral by three native speakers of Turkish. This recursive labeling process is necessary to train the classifiers where the polarity values will then be determined.

Table 3: Examples for the Weaknesses of TR-wordnet (I)

	TR-wordnet			KeNet		
Case	Id	Synset	Definition	Id	Synset	Definition
1	ENG20-01406785-v ENG20-01412135-v	çekmek (to pull) çekmek (to pull)	Bir şeyi tutup kendine veya başka bir yöne doğru yürütmek Bir şeyi tutup kendine veya başka bir yöne doğru yürütmek	TUR10-0879570	çekmek (to pull)	Bir şeyi tutup kendine veya başka bir yöne doğru yürütmek
2	ENG20-01663909-n ENG20-01664028-n	Eunectes Eunectes cinsi (Eunectes) anakonda (anaconda)	- -	TUR10-1203400	Eunectes Eunectes cinsi anakonda (Eunectes)	Güney Amerika'nın tropik bölgelerinde yaşayan, boyu 8-10 metreye ulaşan bir boa yılanı cinsi
3	ENG20-02543258-v ENG20-02543409-v	teşkil etmek oluşturmak (to create) teşkil etmek oluşturmak meydana getirmek (to create)	- Burada gördüğümüz kuru otlar, bu evin çatısını teşkil ediyor	TUR10-1098960	meydana getirmek düzmek oluşturmak teşkil etmek (to create)	olmasını sağlamak, oluşturmak
4	ENG20-02062936-v	kokmak (to smell)	Kötü bir koku çıkarmak	TUR10-0467010	kokmak kokuşmak taaffün etmek (to smell)	Çürüyüp bozularak kötü bir koku çıkarmak—pis kokmak

The first labelling process resulted in 3,100 positive, 10,191 negative and 63,534 neutral data, during which decisions were based on the meaning and connotation of each word. As the polarity of such connotations are subjective by nature, and thus, we have attended to the majority's label when there is a discrepancy between the annotators. For instance, the word for flower, "çiçek," may have positive connotations for an individual, yet another individual may find flowers repulsive because of their allergies. After the first round of labeling, the words tagged as "neutral" consisted the majority.

Following the first labelling, a second labelling process was conducted for the words which were labeled as positive and negative in the first round. To be more specific, the words were re-labeled based on the degree of their positivity or negativity as strong or weak. There was no second labeling on objective words. After the second marking, we found that the weak positive and weak negative tags were more prominent. For instance, the word mükemmel (excellent) in Turkish has been marked three times. Thus, three different views were obtained for the value of this word. In this example, after it was decided that the value of the word

Table 4: Examples for the Weaknesses of TR-wordnet (II)

	TR-wordnet			KeNet		
Case	Id	Synset	Definition	Id	Synset	Definition
5	ENG20-13177331-n	konsensüs fikir birliği (consensus)	agreement in the judgment or opinion reached by a group as a whole	TUR10-0038950	antant uyuşma barışma uzlaşı itilaf mutabakat konsensüs uzlaşım (agreement)	Devletler arası siyasal, ekonomik, kültürel vb. alanlarda yapılan uzlaşma ve bu uzlaşmanın tespit edildiği belge
				TUR10-1238370	fikir birliği (consensus)	Bir fikrin herkesçe paylaşılması durumu
6	ENG20-12716857-n	geri besleme geri bildirim (feedback)	Çıktının girdiyi etkileyerek gelecek çıktıyı belirlemesi	TUR10-0222170	dönüt geri bildirim (feedback)	Gönderilen bilgi ve talimatın alıcıda yaptığı etkiye ilişkin edinilen bilgi
				TUR10-1031080	geri besleme (feedback)	Bir düzeneğin çıktısından alınan kuvvetin veya bilginin bir bölüğünün o düzeneğin girdisi ile bağlaşımı

Table 5: Number of synsets in each category.

Polarity Level	# of SynSets
Strongly positive (1.00)	1,038
Very positive (0.75)	451
Positive (0.50)	456
Weakly positive (0.25)	1,234
Objective (0.00)	65,767
Strongly negative (-1.00)	4,430
Very negative (-0.75)	1,465
Negative (-0.50)	1,238
Weakly negative (-0.25)	3,360

mükemmel (excellent) was positive, it was evaluated whether the positive value was weak or strong in the second stage. While selecting the appropriate label, the compatibility of the labels selected by the three labelers was also evaluated. To put it differently, if a positive word receives strong label from all three annotators, it is regarded as strong positive. If it receives two strong and one weak label, it is considered as very positive. If it is labelled as strong once and as weak twice, it means it is just positive. Finally, if it receives weak label from all three annotators, it is considered as weak positive. The same is also true for the words labelled as negative. Table 5 shows the number of synsets annotated in each categories and their degree of positivity and negativity. It is clear from this table that weakly positives/negatives and strongly positives/negatives outnumber very positives/negatives and plain positives/negatives. If this task had been conducted with the random assignment of these labels, the outcome would have been the opposite with very positives/negatives and plain positives/negatives constituting the majority. This could be interpreted as the high degree of consistency between the annotators since at least two of the annotators obviously agree with each other in most cases.

Finally, the automatic analysis processes will be easier and more accurate in Turkish with the assignment of such polarity values to words. We believe that tagging words from KeNet data and comparing them to WordNet in English will lead us to conduct better analyses. Moreover, providing the sentiment analysis solutions with marked data will enhance their performance.

5 Annotation Statistics

5.1 Agrement of Annotators: Fleiss's Kappa statistic

The consistency between annotators is very important for creation of a reliable polarity lexicon.

Table 6: Fleiss's Kappa values for polarity synsets.

Polarity	Kappa	Strength
Positive	0.618	Good
Negative	0.652	Good

Table 7: Fleiss's Kappa values for polarity synsets.

	Annotator	Kappa	Strength
Positive	1-2	0.694	Good
	1-3	0.461	Moderate
	2-3	0.695	Good
Negative	1-2	0.720	Good
	1-3	0.534	Moderate
	2-3	0.701	Good

Table 8: Numbers of polarity tagged synsets.

Polarity	HisNet	SentiTurkNet
Positive	3,100	1,039
Negative	10,191	2,619
Neutral	63,534	11,038
Total	76,825	14,696

There are several methods to calculate the consistency between annotators such as Cohen's Kappa, Fleiss Kappa, Gwet's AC1 and Krippendorff's Alpha.

In our study, we have employed Fleiss Kappa statistic to measure the level of agreement between annotators in this work. Fleiss kappa coeffient (Fleiss, 1971), which is a generalization of Scott's pi coeffient (Scott, 1955), can be applied to more than two, an arbitrary number of raters. As with Cohen's Kappa and Scott's pi coeffient, how much of the agreement between these raters cannot be attributed to chance is expressed as a number between 0 and 1. As shown in Table 6 and Table 7, the results have demonstrated that the agreement between the annotators is significant.

5.2 Comparison of HisNet and SentiTurkNet

In this section, we present the results of the statistical comparison of HisNet and SentiTurkNet. Since the TurkishWordNet Ids of the synonyms in SentiTurkNet have not been defined, the mappings have been performed using the English synonyms. Afterwards, the faulty mappings have been corrected manually.

When the synsets in the KeNet and the synsets in WordNet were mapped, only the 19,835 of synsets matched. Therefore, we used a subset of HisNet's in comparisons with other sentiment lexicons. Table 8 shows the number of polarity tagged synsets in both lexicons. As shown in Table 8, the volume of HisNet is approximately five times larger than that of SentiTurkNet. Furthermore, a large percentage of the synonym synsets in polarity lexicons is labelled as neutral. Table 9 shows mapping of HisNet synsets polarities to SentiTurkNet synsets polarities. The level of agreement between two polarity lexicons turned out to have Fleiss's Kappa value of 0.405 (moderate). In a nutshell, it is clear that HisNet presents a more comprehensive polarity lexicon than SentiTurkNet while preserving its consistency with the latter in moderate level.

Table 9: Mapping of HisNet synset polarities to SentiTurkNet synset polarities

		SentiTurkNet		
HisNet	Polarity	Positive	Negative	Neutral
	Positive	120	12	136
	Negative	7	332	200
	Neutral	408	350	7,639

6 Conclusion

Dictionary-based sentiment analysis studies in languages except English are very limited due to the scarcity of sources regarding polarity. We conclude that translating sources of polarity from English to Turkish is not a viable approach to create a Turkish polarity dictionary since not all terms in one language have equivalent terms in other languages. Furthermore, the same terms may have different degrees of polarity due to the cultural discrepancies. To this end, the most prominent contribution of this study is to present HisNet, a new polarity lexicon for Turkish by extending the volume of SentiTurkNet, the existing first and only polarity dictionary available in Turkish. We expect that HisNet can prove itself as a useful tool for sentiment analysis applications in Turkish thanks to its exhaustive coverage of the synsets in Turkish WordNet.

In this paper, we have also presented a comparison of two available WordNets for Turkish, which is crucial to do so when there are multiple sources for a given language for further improvements. Our comparison has shown that both TR-wordnet and KeNet have their shortcomings. To sum up, such comparisons may present a detailed picture of what steps need to be taken to improve the available WordNets as they provide the available sources for a language in a comparative way.

References

A. Abdaoui, J. Azé, S. Bringay, and P. Poncelet. 2017. *Feel: a French expanded emotion lexicon*, volume 833–855. Language Resources and Evolution.

O. Bakay, O. Ergelen, and O. T. Yildiz. 2019a. Integrating Turkish WordNet KeNet to Princeton WordNet: The case of one-to-many correspondences. In *Innovations in Intelligent Systems and Applications*.

O. Bakay, O. Ergelen, and O. T. Yildiz. 2019b. Problems caused by semantic drift in wordnet synset construction. In *International Conference on Computer Science and Engineering*.

O. Bakay, O. Ergelen, E. Sarmis, S. Yildirim, A. Kocabalcioglu, B. N. Arican, M. Ozcelik, E. Saniyar, O. Kuyrukcu, B. Avar, and O. T. Yıldız. 2020. Turkish WordNet KeNet. In *Proceedings of GWC 2020*.

O. Bilgin, O. Cetinoglu, and K. Oflazer. 2004a. Building a wordnet for Turkish. *Romanian Journal of Information Science*, 7:163–172.

O. Bilgin, O. Cetinoglu, and K. Oflazer. 2004b. Building a wordnet for Turkish. *Romanian Journal of Information Science and Technology*, 7(1–2):162–172.

W. Black, S. Elkateb, H. Rodriguez, M. Alkhalifa, P. Vossen, A. Pease, and C. Fellbaum. 2006. Introducing the Arabic wordnet project. In *International Wordnet Conference*, pages 295–300. Masaryck University, Brno, Czeck Republic.

J. Brooke, M. Tafiloski, and M. Taboada. 2009. Cross-linguisric sentiment analysis: From English to Spanish. pages 50–54. RANLP.

E. Cambria, D. Olsher, and D. Rajagopal. 2014. Senticnet 3: a common and common-sense knowledge base for cognition-driven sentiment analysis. In *Proceedings of the fourth conference on Applied natural language processing*, pages 1515–1521. AAAI conference on artificial intelligence.

A. Das and S. Bandyopadhyay. 2010. Sentiwordnet for Indian languages. pages 56–63. Eighth Workshop on Asian Language Resources.

R. Dehkharghani, Y. Saygin, B. Yanikoglu, and K. Oflazer. 2016. Sentiturknet: a Turkish polarity lexicon for sentiment analysis. *Language Resources and Evaluation*, 50(3):667–685.

R. Ehsani, E. Solak, and O.T. Yildiz. 2018. Constructing a wordnet for Turkish using manual and automatic annotation. *ACM Transactions on Asian and Low-Resource Language Information Processing (TALLIP)*, 17(3):24.

A. Esuli and F. Sebastiani. 2006. Sentiwordnet: A publicly available lexical resource for opinion mining. pages 417–422. 5th Conference on Language Resources and Evaluation (LREC).

J. L. Fleiss. 1971. Measuring nominal scale agreement among many raters. volume 76, page 378.

C. Hung and H.K. Lini. 2010. In *Using objective words in SentiWordNet to improve word-of-mouth sentiment classification.*, page 0047–54. IEEE Intelligent Systems.

G.A. Miller. 1995. Wordnet: a lexical database for English. *ACM Communications*, 38:39–41.

L. G. Moreno-Sandoval, P. Beltran-Herrera, J. A. Vargas-Cruz, C. Sanchez-Barriga, A.P. Quimbaya, J. A. Alvarado-Valencia, and J. C. Garcia-Diaz. 2017. Csl: A combined Spanish lexicon-resource for polarity classification and sentiment analysis. pages 288–295. 19th International Conference on Enterprise Information Systems.

R. Ozcelik, S. Parlar, O. Bakay, O. Ergelen, and O. T. Yildiz. 2019. User interface for Turkish word network KeNet. In *Signal Processing and Communication Applications Conference*.

R. Remus, U. Quasthoff, and G. Heyer. 2010. Sentiws-a publicly available German-language resource for sentiment analysis. pages 1161–1178. Seventh International Conference on Language Resources and Evaluation (LREC).

X. Saralegi and I. San Vicente. 2013. In *CSL: A Combined Spanish Lexicon - Resource for Polarity Classification and Sentiment Analysis*. Workshop on Sentiment Analysis at SEPLN (TASS2013).

W. A. Scott. 1955. Reliability of content analysis: The case of nominal scale coding. *Public Opinion Quarterly*, pages 321–325.

D. Tufis, D. Cristea, and S. Stamou. 2004a. BalkaNet: Aims, methods, results and perspectives. a general overview. *Romanian Journal of Information Science*, 7:9–43.

D. Tufis, D. Cristea, and S. Stamou. 2004b. Balkanet: Aims, methods, results and perspectives, a general overview. *Romanian Journal of Information Science and Technology*, 7(1–2):9–43.

P. Vossen. 1997. Eurowordnet: a multilingual database for information retrieval. In *DELOS workshop on Cross-language Information Retrieval*. Vrije Universiteit, Amsterdam, Czech Republic.

T. Wilson, J. Wiebe, and P. Hoffmann. 2005. Recognizing contextual polarity in phrase-level sentiment analysis. pages 347–354. Human Language TEchnology Conference and Conference on Empirical Methods in Natural Language Processing.

Turkish WordNet KeNet

Özge Bakay
Boğaziçi University
bakayozge@gmail.com

Özlem Ergelen
Boğaziçi University

Elif Sarmış
Starlang Yazılım Danışmanlık
elif@starlangyazilim.com

Selin Yıldırım
Özyeğin University
selin.yildirim@ozyegin.edu.tr

Atilla Kocabalcıoğlu
Boğaziçi University

Bilge Nas Arıcan
Starlang Yazılım Danışmanlık
bilge@starlangyazilim.com

Merve Özçelik
Starlang Yazılım Danışmanlık
merve@starlangyazilim.com

Ezgi Sanıyar
Starlang Yazılım Danışmanlık
ezgi@starlangyazilim.com

Oğuzhan Kuyrukçu
Starlang Yazılım Danışmanlık
oguzhan@starlangyazilim.com

Begüm Avar
Boğaziçi University

Olcay Taner Yıldız
Özyeğin University
olcay.yildiz@ozyegin.edu.tr

Abstract

Currently, there are two available wordnets for Turkish: TR-wordnet of BalkaNet and KeNet. As the more comprehensive wordnet for Turkish, KeNet includes 76,757 synsets. KeNet has both intralingual semantic relations and is linked to PWN through interlingual relations. In this paper, we present the procedure adopted in creating KeNet, give details about our approach in annotating semantic relations such as hypernymy and discuss the language-specific problems encountered in these processes.

1 Introduction

Information regarding words and meanings are traditionally stored in dictionaries. With the advancement of natural language processing studies, a need for machine-readable dictionaries has arisen (Miller, 1995). In an attempt to answer that need, wordnets which store lexicographic information in a format that is adaptable to modern computing have emerged. Wordnet, in its broader definition, is a highly comprehensive dictionary that is built on distinct word senses along with their definitions. Most of the words in a wordnet are open-class words such as nouns, verbs, adjectives and adverbs. Main building blocks of a wordnet are *synsets*, which are comprised of synonym synset members. Synsets are the distinct units in wordnets and all the mappings including intra- and inter-lingual ones are constructed based on the synsets. In lexical semantics, it is argued that words can be defined based on the relations between them. Adopting this principle, wordnets map semantic relations such as hypernymy, meronymy or antonymy through synsets.

Turkish wordnet of BalkaNet (TR-wordnet) (Bilgin et al., 2004) is the first wordnet created for Turkish. TR-wordnet of BalkaNet includes 14,626 synsets and 19,834 internal semantic relations. In this paper, we present our work on creating a more comprehensive wordnet for Turkish, namely KeNet[1,2] (Ehsani et al., 2018) and discuss the creation of semantic relations such as hypernymy. We present the literature review on wordnets for other languages in Section 2, describe the process of synset construction in KeNet in Section 3, present intralingual semantic relations including hypernymy in Section 4, explain the interlingual mapping of KeNet to Princeton WordNet in Section 5, summarize the challenges we have encountered in all these processes in Section 6 and conclude in Section 7.

2 Literature Review

Constructing a wordnet, whether from scratch or by expanding a previous one, is a labor intensive process that requires several steps and ex-

[1] "Ke" in KeNet comes from "kelime" (word) in Turkish.

[2] KeNet can be freely and publicly downloaded under an open source licence from:
https://github.com/StarlangSoftware/TurkishWordNet
https://github.com/StarlangSoftware/TurkishWordNet-Py
https://github.com/StarlangSoftware/TurkishWordNet-Cy
https://github.com/StarlangSoftware/TurkishWordNet-C#
https://github.com/StarlangSoftware/TurkishWordNet-CPP

tensive use of both human labor and automated systems. Since the creation of the first wordnet Princeton WordNet (PWN) in 1995 (Miller, 1995), many other wordnets have been created for several languages (e.g., Finnish WordNet FinnWordNet (Linden and Carlson, 2010), Polish WordNet (Derwojedowa et al., 2008), Norwegian WordNet (Fjeld and Nygaard, 2009), Danish WordNet (Pedersen et al., 2009), French WordNet WOLF (Sagot, 2008)). In addition, multilingual wordnets linking the wordnets of multiple languages have been created. To exemplify, EuroWordNet (EWN) is a multilingual WordNet project that consists several European languages (English, Dutch, Italian, Spanish, German, French, Czech and Estonian) (Vossen, 2007). In EWN, the wordnets were created for each language separately and then linked through an Inter-Lingual-Index based on PWN. BalkaNet, similar to EWN, is a multilingual wordnet project consisting of six Balkan languages (Bulgarian, Czech, Greek, Romanian, Serbian, and Turkish) (Tufis et al., 2004). This project was done to produce a multilingual semantic network, fully compatible with EWN and its extensions.[3]

Different approaches were adopted in creating wordnets and mapping them with those for other languages. Two of the most-commonly used approaches in the literature are *expand approach* and *merge approach*. In the expand approach, a set of synsets from PWN, including their semantic database, are first translated into the target language and then the relations that are transferred from English are checked in a manual fashion. For example, the Finnish WordNet FinnWordNet (Linden and Carlson, 2010) and the French WordNet WOLF (Sagot, 2008) were constructed with this approach. In the merge approach, on the other hand, the first step in creating a new wordnet is to build the intralingual relations from scratch, without any links to English. The monolingual wordnet is then mapped onto English. Exemplary wordnets that were created with this approach are Polish WordNet (Derwojedowa et al., 2008), Norwegian WordNet NorNet (Fjeld and Nygaard, 2009) and Danish WordNet DanNet (Pedersen et al., 2009). In a comparison of these two approaches, it is argued that the expand approach is more practical and less time-consuming since it enables us to have many correct monolingual relations that are extracted from PWN automatically. This automatic extraction of relations from PWN is especially beneficial for languages which show a similar pattern to English in their semantic associations, such as in the case of French (Sagot, 2008).

In the following sections, the details in creating KeNet is presented.

3 Synset Construction

The very first step in constructing KeNet, as in every other wordnet, was to create synsets. Synset can be defined as a group of words sharing the same sense and part of speech (POS). The structure of a sample synset in KeNet is as follows:

```
<SYNSET>
  <ID>TUR10-0038510</ID>
  <synset member>anne<SENSE>2</SENSE>
  </synset member>
 <POS>n</POS>
 <DEF>...</DEF>
 <EXAMPLE>...</EXAMPLE>
</SYNSET>
```

An exemplary set of synsets from KeNet is given in Table 1. In this table, examples of the four most frequent parts of speech in KeNet are listed, i.e., noun, adjective, verb and adverb, respectively. For each of these examples, the first column shows the ID of the synset. The characters that are separated with "-" from the ID gives the POS of the synset (*n* for noun, *v* for verb, *a* for adjective, *adv* for adverb). The second column lists the synset members; the synset members that are listed in the same synset are synonyms. The third column demonstrates the definitions and lastly, the fourth column presents an exemplary sentence (if there is any) including one of the synset members.

Regarding the construction of these synsets, the first version of the database was constructed through mining of the latest Contemporary Dictionary of Turkish (CDT) (2011's print) published by the Turkish Language Institute (TLI) (Ehsani et al., 2018). By convention, CDT marks synonyms by using commas such that synonyms of a word are given after its definition with a separation of comma. To decide on true synonyms that must occur in the same synsets, we sliced the definitions at commas and listed the comma-separated lemmas and the rest of the definitions as candidates of synonyms. Then, those lists were displayed for

[3]Further details about the wordnets that are discussed above and many others can be found on the website for the Global WordNet Association (GWA).

Table 1: Exemplary Synsets

Synset ID	Synset Members	Definition	Example Sentence
TUR10-0000030-n	su ab âb "water"	Hidrojenle oksijenden oluşan, oda sıcaklığında sıvı durumunda bulunan, renksiz, kokusuz, tatsız madde	
TUR10-0000220-a	abajurlu "with lampshade"	Abajuru olan	Üstünde lacivert abajurlu, parlak bir madenden lamba.
TUR10-0000350-v	abanmak "to lean over"	Eğilerek bir şeyin, bir kimsenin üzerine kapanmak	Efendi, sen de ne üstüme abanıyorsun?
TUR10-0000520-adv	abartısız mübalağasız "without exaggeration"	Abartmadan, abartısız olarak, mübalağasız bir biçimde	

linguistically-informed human annotators who decided on the synonymy relation between the lemmas and the definitions. 49,774 pairs were annotated at the end of this phase. Although some of them were included as separate entries in CDT, passivized and causativized forms of verbs were deleted from KeNet as they share the same root with their active forms.

Although the vast majority of the synsets were constructed during this process, there was a need for follow-up procedures to improve the organization of the current synsets. Since the main problem encountered in synset construction was the semantic relatedness of the synset members, two other procedures were followed in order to control the synonymy relations within the synsets: the *merge* process and the *split* process. These two processes are discussed next.

3.1 Merge Process

In the merge process, different synsets that should be grouped together were identified and grouped as a single synset. Three things were crucial while merging the synsets: (i) having a single and unique definition for each synset, (ii) having true synonyms as synset members in each synset and (iii) having a representative first synset member in each synset. Firstly, the synsets that were created by combining the synset members with identical senses had as many definitions as the number of synset members in them since the definitions were also merged while merging the synset members. The definitions of the merged synsets were initially combined with a pipe symbol in between them. A new definition for each merged synset was written so that each synset had a single and unique definition that covers the meaning of all its synset members. None of the synset members of a synset appeared in its definition. In this process, new definitions for 10,612 number of synsets were written by the human annotators.

Secondly, some synsets were found to include unrelated synset members. Therefore, another goal of the merge process was to include only the synset members that were synonyms. 1,144 number of synsets with unrelated synset members that had been identified in other parts of the work were transferred to the split process (see Section 3.2 for details). Additionally, there were cases where the synsets were missing some of the necessary synset members. Whereas some of these missing synset members were present in KeNet, some were not. Those that were already present in KeNet were merged with the current synsets. Those that were not present in KeNet were added as distinct synset members in the existing synsets. At the end of this process, 122 number of synsets were enriched with new synset members.

Lastly, the order of the synset members in the synsets was checked in this process. Due to time limitation, only the first synset member was checked. The most frequently-used synset members in the synsets were placed as the first to appear in order to have a representative display. The ordering of the rest of the synset members was noted as a future task.

3.2 Split Process

In the split process, the synsets that included synset members with different senses were split and separate synsets were created for each group of related synset members. In order to fix this

Table 2: Number of Synsets in KeNet

Part of Speech	# of Synsets
Nouns	44,074
Verbs	17,791
Adjectives	12,416
Adverbs	2,550
Interjections	3342
Pronouns	68
Conjunctions	60
Postpositions	29
Total	77,330

problem, we created a pool where we collected all the synsets that had unrelated synset members. We displayed these synsets on Google Sheets. Linguistically-informed human annotators then split these wrongly-merged synsets and wrote new definitions for the newly-created ones.

There were three main reasons for the wrong mergings: meaning-related drifts, POS-related drifts and morphology-related problems (Bakay et al., 2019c). For meaning-related drifts, the synset members that were semantically related but not true synonyms, e.g., nouns with close meanings such as *dere* "brook" and "*ırmak nehir* "river", had been mistakenly conjoined. For POS-related drifts, synset members which were semantically related but had different POS, e.g., a noun and an adjective with a similar meaning or coming from the same root such as *güç* "difficult" and *güç* "strength", had been mistakenly combined. Lastly, for morphology-related drifts, morphologically-related synset members, e.g., verbs that are morphologically related but have different meanings and different argument structures such as *sopalamak* "to beat somebody" and *sopalanmak* "to get beaten by somebody", had been mistakenly grouped under the same synsets. These synsets were split and different synsets were created for each group.

4 Semantic Relations

Currently, there are 77,330 synsets, 109,049 synset members and 80,956 distinct synset members in KeNet. The POS categories that are included are nouns, adverbs, adjectives, adverbs, interjections, pronouns, postpositions and conjunctions (see Table 2 for numbers). Regarding the number of words in synset members, although the majority of the synset members are one- (72,436 - 66.48%) or two-word (31,705 - 29.36%) synset members, there are synset members including up to seven words. Lastly, 19,776 number of synsets have exemplary sentences (25.57%). Including an exemplary sentence for each synset was noted as future work.

In KeNet, eight intralingual semantic relations were included: hypernymy, derivational relatedness, domain topic, part holonymy, antonymy, instance hypernymy, member holonymy, substance holonymy and attribute (see Table 3 for examples and the current number of matchings for these relations). For all these relations, the main word class that was annotated was nouns whereas antonymy and attribute were mainly annotated for adjectives.

There can be various approaches to constructing semantic relations in a wordnet such as translating an already constructed wordnet from another language into the target language or building one from scratch. Both approaches have their advantages and disadvantages, which will change drastically from one language to another. Translating a previously constructed wordnet into another language, while seems to be the easier approach, comes with a lot of disadvantages, especially in languages like Turkish which are morphologically and syntactically different from English.

In KeNet, in the creation of all these eight semantic relations, we consulted the semantic relations in the English WordNet PWN, but none of the relations were automatically translated from English. That is, in constructing the semantic relations, possible relations between Turkish synsets were listed based on their dictionary translations in English PWN and the relations between the English synsets in PWN. Then, human annotators checked these relations manually; the correct relations were added to KeNet whereas the incorrect ones were eliminated. For example, as Table 4 shows, two candidate antonymy relations for the Turkish synset *ağır* "heavy" were listed: *yeğni hafif* "light" and *hafif* "light". These candidate antonyms were extracted based on the English translations of the Turkish synsets *ağır* and *hafif* and the existing antonymy relations between their English equivalents "heavy" and "light". For this example, the antonymy relation between *ağır* and *yeğni hafif* were correct and it was added to KeNet, but the antonymy relation between *ağır* and *hafif* were not correct and it was not kept. This procedure was followed for all the semantic rela-

Table 3: Semantic Relations in KeNet

Semantic Relation	Example	# of Mappings
Hypernymy	gürgen - ağaç "alder tree - tree"	45,389
Derivational Relatedness	kitap - kitaplık "book - bookshelf"	39,682
Domain Topic	işlemci - bilgisayar bilimi "processor - computer science"	15,366
Part Holonymy	kulp - bardak "handle - glass"	2,718
Antonymy	sıcak - soğuk "hot - cold"	1,884
Instance Hypernymy	Antartika - kıta "Antarctica - continent"	1,345
Member Holonymy	ebeveyn - aile "parent - family"	862
Substance Holonymy	hidrojen - su "hydrogen - water"	367
Attribute	ılık - sıcaklık "warm - heat"	226

Table 4: Building Antonymy Relations in KeNet based on PWN

TR synset	Sense	TR synset	Sense	ENG synset	Sense	ENG synset	Sense
ağır	tartıda çok çeken	yeğni hafif	tartıda ağırlığı az gelen	heavy	of comparatively great physical weight or density	light	of comparatively little physical weight or density
ağır	tartıda çok çeken	hafif	kalınlığı veya yoğunluğu az olan	heavy	of comparatively great physical weight or density	light	of comparatively little physical weight or density

tions. However, building hypernymy relation was more complicated and it included some additional steps. The details of hypernymy relation in keNet is presented next.

4.1 Hypernymy

For now KeNet has a semantic hierarchy tree only for the noun category. In this section, we explain how we built the hypernymy relations only for the nouns in KeNet.

We started building hypernymy relations based on the Turkish Estate WordNet (Parlar et al., 2019) and Turkish Tourism WordNet (Arican et al., 2020) because these wordnets were built based on KeNet but they were much smaller than KeNet in terms of their scope due to being domain-dependent. Both Turkish Estate WordNet and Turkish Tourism WordNet had synsets that were and were not present in KeNet. Thus, we first created two lists on Google Sheets: a list with the synsets that occurred in both Turkish Estate WordNet and KeNet and another with those that occurred in both Turkish Tourism WordNet and KeNet. This enabled us to focus on a smaller size of synsets from KeNet in the first place that belonged to the same domain. Then, the corresponding English synsets from PWN were then found for the Turkish synsets in these lists by human annotators and placed next to the Turkish synsets. Based on the hypernymy relations between the corresponding English synsets, hypernymy relations between the Turkish synsets were created. This enabled us to have small hierarchical trees for the synsets in KeNet.

After building some preliminary hypernymy relations in domain-dependent wordnets, we decided to start forming the comprehensive hierarchical tree from the top. Therefore, our second step was to find the nodes that would occur on the top of the hierarchical tree. In order to find these nodes, we extracted a list of approximately 700 words that repeated the most in the hypernymy relations in Turkish Estate WordNet and Turkish Tourism WordNet. When we had the

Table 5: Constructing Hypernymy Relations in KeNet based on PWN

EN ID	EN synset member	EN Definition	TR synset member	TR Definition1	TR Definition2
ENG31-00001740-n	entity	that which is perceived or known or inferred to have its own distinct existence	varlık	Doğumla ölüm arasında yaşanan süre	Her türlü taşınır ve taşınmaz maddi varlık
ENG31-00001930-n	physical entity	an entity that has physical existence	fiziksel varlık		
ENG31-00002684-n	object physical object	a tangible and visible entity	nesne	Belli bir ağırlığı ve hacmi, rengi, maddesi olan her türlü cansız varlık, şey, obje	Geçişli fiili bütünleyen yalın veya belirtme durumunda bulunan tümleç
ENG31-00003553-n	whole unit	an assemblage of parts that is regarded as a single entity	bütün	Birlik, birleşmiş olma durumu	Bölünmezliği içeren yalın bütün
ENG31-00022119-n	artifact artefact	a man-made object taken as a whole	yapı	Türlü amaçlarla kullanılan, insan yapısı, taşınabilir cansız nesnelerin bütünü	Yapılmakta olan konut, yol, köprü vb. inşaat
ENG31-04348764-n	structure construction	a thing constructed	yapı	Yapılmakta olan konut, yol, köprü vb. inşaat	Canlı bir varlığın ruh veya beden özelliklerinin tümü, bünye, strüktür
ENG31-03302664-n	establishment	a public or private structure including buildings and equipment for business or residence	kurum	Bir kurum veya kuruluşun yönetildiği yer veya makam	Ocak bacalarında biriken veya çevrede savrulan kalın is
ENG31-03959296-n	place of business	an establishment where business is conducted, goods are made or stored	işletme	İstihdam edilen kişilerin çalıştığı, üretimin yapıldığı yer	İş yeri
ENG31-03753653-n	mercantile establishment retail store	a place of business for retailing goods	satış noktası	Perakende satış yapan esnafın, küçük zanaat sahiplerinin satış yaptıkları veya çalıştıkları yer	

list for the most repetitive synsets in these wordnets, human annotators formed hypernymy relations among these synsets. At the end of this process, the majority of the nodes that would appear on top of the hierarchical tree in KeNet, e.g., *varlık* "entity" (see Table 5) was formed. In this process, we also noticed that some of the uppermost nodes that were present in PWN did not have equivalents in Turkish. For example, there was no corresponding synset for "physical entity" in KeNet (see Table 5). When such synsets were crucial to have in the hierarchical tree, new synsets were created for those in KeNet by translating them from PWN to Turkish.

Thirdly, as in the construction of other semantic relations, possible hypernymy relations between the synsets in KeNet were extracted based on their dictionary translations in English PWN and the relations between the synsets in PWN. A list of these possible hypernymy relations was listed on Google Sheets and checked by human annotators one by one. The relations that were correct were added to KeNet. This step again allowed us to have small hierarchical trees that were to be combined in order to form a single hierarchical tree.

The forth step was thus to place these small trees that were created in the first and the third steps under the topmost nodes. To exemplify, in this step, the synsets *nesne* "object" and *bütün* "whole unit" that had a hypernymy relation between from earlier processes was placed under *fiziksel varlık* "physical entity", as shown in Table 5.

After the placement of small hierarchical trees into a single tree, we were left with free-standing synsets that were not currently attached to any node in the hierarchical tree. In the final step, these free-standing synsets were listed in a java program where they were attached to their hypernyms one by one by human annotators. The biggest problem at this stage was that there were no guides to follow and the annotators had to decide where to place free-standing synsets in the tree.

Several strategies have been employed by our team to successfully place the free-standing items. The first strategy was to rely on the definitions of the synsets. For instance, a free-standing synset such as *etimoloji* "etymology", which is defined as "a branch of linguistics", would be placed under *dilbilim* "linguistics". Another useful approach was to refer to PWN to see where the corresponding English synset was placed in PWN. Following from the previous example, if the synset "etymology" was placed under 'linguistics' in PWN, its counterpart in Turkish, i.e., *etimoloji* "etymology", can be placed under the equivalent of its hypernym in Turkish, i.e., *dilbilim* "linguistics". A third strategy was to perform a domain-specific top-down analysis. That is, when we encountered a synset in the tree that could possibly host several hyponyms, we searched for its possible hyponyms in the list of free-standing items and placed them under their hypernyms. For example, when we came across with the synset *dilbilim* "linguistics", we looked for its possible hyponyms such as syntax, semantics or phonology and placed them under it. This was especially useful for domain-related synsets. The last strategy was to consider the sister synsets of the synset in question. If we were not sure of the correct hypernym of a given synset, but placed its sister synset in the hierarchical tree in earlier stages, we would find the hypernym of its sister synset and place the synset in questions under its hypernym. Again, following from the same example, knowing that *sentaks* "syntax" and *etimoloji* "etymology" were sister synsets, a simple search for the hypernym of *sentaks* "syntax" would provide us with the correct hypernym for the synset in question: *dilbilim* "linguistics".

In addition to these strategies, one advantage we had was that as the same team members worked on the same hierarchy for extended periods of time, e.g., 15 hours per week for 5-6 months, they became familiar with the general structure of the tree and placing the free-standing synsets into the tree became easier with practice.

5 Interlingual Relations

With the creation of wordnets in several languages, the idea of matching these wordnets to English and/or to one another has gained importance since the linking of wordnets across languages would enable us to use these resources in machine translation.

As discussed in Section 1, there are two available wordnets for Turkish, which are TR-wordnet of BalkaNet and KeNet. Having been created as part of BalkaNet (Tufis et al., 2004), TR-wordnet of Balkanet was integrated to PWN through an interlingual index (ILI) (Bilgin et al., 2004). As opposed to TR-wordnet, in our work, we used the merge approach and matched the synsets in KeNet with those in PWN manually (Bakay et al., 2019b). Additionally, as in building intralingual semantic relations, we extracted candidate multilingual relations based on dictionary translations and listed these potential interlingual relations on Google Sheets. Two human annotators checked the accuracy of these candidate relations one by one.

In TR-wordnet of BalkaNet, only one-to-one mappings between Turkish synets and the English synsets in PWN were included due to the use of ILI (Bilgin et al., 2004). In KeNet, on the other hand, although one-to-one matchings made up the majority of the interlingual relations between Turkish and English, one-to-many mappings between the two languages were also included (Bakay et al., 2019b). One-to-many mappings between KeNet and PWN were mainly used when selecting a single synset in one of the languages was not possible. That is, the two most common cases where one-to-many matchings were needed were (i) when a sense distinction in English is not reflected in Turkish, e.g., the English synsets "inequitable unjust", "unfair unjust", "unrighteous", "undue unjustified unwarranted" and "unlawful wrongful" all correspond to *haksız nahak* in Turkish or (ii) vice versa; when a sense distinction that is present in Turkish is not reflected in English, e.g., the Turkish synsets *hafiflemek*, *hafiflemek azalmak* and *kırılmak yatışmak* all correspond to the English synset "abate let up slack off slack die away".

Overall, the inclusion of one-to-many matchings in KeNet allowed for a better matching between the two languages.At the end of the manual interlingual matching between KeNet and PWN, 19,398 synsets in Turkish were associated with 19,208 synsets in English. 3,500 were one-to-one and 1,250 of them were one-to-many matchings. Furthermore, out of 5,000 most frequent senses in English, 4,417 (88%) were matched with their Turkish equivalents in order to have the matchings of the synsets that are most commonly used.

6 Challenges

We have faced many resource-related and language-related challenges in creating KeNet. We faced an important resource-related problem in the creation of synsets due to not having a Turkish dictionary that marks the synonymy relation in a systematic fashion. We also encountered language-related problems in constructing synsets. For example, some synsets in KeNet included synset members with different POS categories. The reason for this was that in Turkish some words can be used in different POS categories with similar meanings. This resulted in wrong groupings of synonyms, which we had to deal with in the split process. In building the hypernymy relations, one of our biggest challenges was that some synsets in PWN did not have corresponding synsets in KeNet. When this was the case in the upper parts of the tree, we came up with new synsets that would connect the lower parts of the tree with the upper parts as the tree would otherwise be missing some transitionary nodes. Moreover, in building interlingual relations, we realized that having only one-to-one mappings would not be a correct matching for Turkish and English and hence, we decided to include one-to-many mappings, which was a time-consuming process to conduct. Lastly, we had to devote a huge amount of time and labor in all the stages in creating KeNet as in most of the stages, we could not refer to earlier work and conducting the stages automatically would be misleading, thus human annotators had to work manually. This was mainly due to the structural and lexical differences between Turkish and other highly-investigated languages such as English.

7 Conclusion

In this paper, we presented the process for creating the Turkish wordnet KeNet and discussed the challenges that we encountered. Our biggest challenge was to work on a low-resource language since most of the studies in the field focus on highly-investigated languages like English. The differing morphological and syntactic properties of Turkish also prevent us from adopting the exact approaches used in these studies. Although structural differences have created problems mostly for morphological analyses, we also encountered cases where semantic mappings and/or relations in English could not be directly copied to Turkish. This discrepancy was observed in both intra- and inter-lingual semantic relations. Overall, unavailability of sources which can be easily linked to Turkish forced us to include a huge amount of manual annotations.

KeNet has been used as a source in other NLP studies on Turkish such as Turkish PropBank TRopBank (Kara et al., 2020), Turkish SentiNet HisNet (Ozcelik et al., 2020), Turkish FrameNet (Marsan et al., 2020) and domain wordnets for Estate (Parlar et al., 2019) and Tourism (Arican et al., 2020). Having a common wordnet source for different NLP studies in a given language can be a great advantage for the linking of these sources. That is, when the sense categorization between two different sources of a given language do not match well, as in the case of English PropBank and English WordNet PWN (Bakay et al., 2019a), the linking of the available sources becomes more challenging.

References

B. N. Arican, M. Ozcelik, D. B. Aslan, E. Sarmis, S. Parlar, and O. T. Yıldız. 2020. Creating Domain Dependent Turkish WordNet and SentiNet. In *Proceedings of GWC 2020*.

O. Bakay, B. Avar, and O. T. Yıldız. 2019a. Comparing Sense Categorization between English PropBank and English WordNet. In *Proceedings of GWC 2019*, pages 307–314.

O. Bakay, O. Ergelen, and O. T. Yildiz. 2019b. Integrating Turkish WordNet KeNet to Princeton WordNet: The Case of One-to-Many Correspondances. In *ASYU*.

O. Bakay, O. Ergelen, and O. T. Yildiz. 2019c. Problems caused by semantic drift in wordnet synset construction. In *UBMK*.

O. Bilgin, O. Cetinoglu, and K. Oflazer. 2004. Building a wordnet for Turkish. *Romanian Journal of Information Science*, 7:163–172.

M. Derwojedowa, M. Piasecki, S. Szpakowicz, M. Zawisławska, and B. Broda. 2008. Words, Concepts and Relations in the Construction of Polish WordNet. In *Proceedings of GWC 2008*, pages 162–177.

R. Ehsani, E. Solak, and O.T. Yildiz. 2018. Constructing a WordNet for Turkish Using Manual and Automatic Annotation. *ACM Transactions on Asian and Low-Resource Language Information Processing (TALLIP)*, 17(3).

R. V. Fjeld and L. Nygaard. 2009. Nornet - a monolingual wordnet of modern Norwegian. In *NODALIDA 2009 workshop: WordNets and other Lexical Semantic Resources - between Lexical Semantics, Lexicography, Terminology and Formal Ontologies*, pages 13–16.

N. Kara, D. B. Aslan, B. Marsan, K. Ak, and O. T. Yıldız. 2020. TRopBank: Turkish PropBank V2.0. In *Proceedings of LREC 2020*, pages 2763–2772.

K. Linden and L. Carlson. 2010. Construction of a FinnWordNet. *Nordic Journal of Lexicography*, 17:119 - 140.

B. Marsan, N. Kara, M. Ozcelik, B. N. Arican, N. Cesur, A. Kuzgun, E. Saniyar, O. Kuyrukcu, and O. T. Yıldız. 2020. Building the Turkish FrameNet. In *Proceedings of GWC 2020*.

G.A. Miller. 1995. WordNet: a lexical database for English. *ACM Communications*, 38:39–41.

M. Ozcelik, B. N. Arican, O. Bakay, E. Sarmis, N. B. Bayazit, O. Ergelen, and O. T. Yıldız. 2020. HisNet: A Polarity Lexicon based on WordNet for Emotion Analysis. In *Proceedings of GWC 2020*.

S. Parlar, B. N. Arican, M. Erkek, K. Cayirli, and O. T. Yildiz. 2019. Emlak Alanına Özgü Kelime Ağı. In *Proceedings of the Signal Processing and Communication Applications Conference*.

B. S. Pedersen, S. Nimb, J. Asmussen, N. H. Sørensen, L. Trap-Jensen, and H. Lorentzen. 2009. DanNet: the challenge of compiling a wordnet for Danish by reusing a monolingual dictionary. *Language resources and evaluation*, 43:269–299.

B. Sagot. 2008. Building a free French wordnet from multilingual resources. page 24. ACM.

D. Tufis, D. Cristea, and S. Stamou. 2004. BalkaNet: Aims, methods, results and perspectives. a general overview. *Romanian Journal of Information Science*, 7:9–43.

P. Vossen. 2007. EuroWordNet: A multilingual database for information retrieval. In *DELOS workshop on Cross-Language Information Retrieval*.

Enriching plWordNet with morphology

Agnieszka Dziob and Wiktor Walentynowicz
G4.19 Research Group, Department of Computational Intelligence
Wrocław University of Technology, Wrocław, Poland
{agnieszka.dziob,wiktor.walentynowicz}@pwr.edu.pl

Abstract

In the paper, we present the process of adding morphological information to the Polish WordNet (plWordNet). We describe the reasons for this connection and the intuitions behind it. We also draw attention to the specificity of the Polish morphology. We show in which tasks the morphological information is important and how the methods can be developed by extending them to include combined morphological information based on WordNet.

1 Introduction

plWordNet is a very large wordnet of Polish. The 4.1 version presented in Dziob et al. (2019) contains 192,495 lemmas, 290,366 lexical units (henceforth, LUs), and 224,179 synsets belonging to four parts of speech: verbs, adjectives, adverbs and nouns. Since 2012, there have been carried out ongoing works on its connection to Princeton WordNet (Rudnicka et al., 2012).

For the description of synsets and LUs, lexical-semantic relations are used, the concept of which was taken from Princeton WordNet (Fellbaum, 1998) and EuroWordNet (Vossen, 2002). In the course of those works, the need emerged to create new relations specific to the Polish language (Piasecki et al., 2012). It is related to the necessity of describing derivational dependencies for a language with a rich derivational morphology. Inflectional morphology was not dealt with in plWordNet. Following Miller (1995), we assumed that describing inflectional morphology is the task of a separate resource that is morphological dictionaries for the Polish language, which support the use of plWordNet.

In plWordNet meaning is defined according to the assumptions of relational semantics (Lyons, 1977) that is as a bundle of lexico-semantic relations it enters. Thus, LUs having different relations in the language system cannot be treated as synonyms and belong to the same synset (Derwojedowa et al., 2008). Maziarz et al. (2013) formulated the concept of constitutive relations and constitutive features, i.e. those which differentiate the meaning. They include all synset relations, except fuzzynymy, and LU features, such as stylistic register, aspect for verbs, and semantic classes for adjectives and verbs (Maziarz et al., 2016). Therefore, there are no theoretical and methodological assumptions, which would allow to define inflectional features as distinguishing meanings of an LU in plWordNet. At the same time, it was also not explicitly stated that morphological features cannot influence meaning.

Lexicographic works are ongoing, and currently focus on completing the structure of plWordNet with new LUs, increasing the density of lexico-semantic relations, and correcting errors resulting from manual work. The most recent work has consisted of connecting morphological descriptions from the Grammatical Dictionary of Polish (pol. *Słownik Gramatyczny Języka Polskiego*, henceforth SGJP) (Saloni et al., 2007). This process has four practical objectives: 1) investigating the influence of morphological characteristics of LUs on their semantic description; 2) verifying the membership to parts of speech of morphologically ambiguous LUs and lemmas; 3) completing the semantic description of the existing lemmas with new senses, based on their morphological description in the SGJP; 4) building a practical resource, combining semantic and morphological description, for tasks related to the processing of the Polish language. The result of this work is plWordNet combined with the morphological description from SGJP, created automatically with a manual disambiguation of morphologically ambiguous lemmas, i.e. those which have more than one pattern of inflection.

The purpose of this paper is to present the results of combining resources and to indicate the applications of them.

2 The Problem of Morphology Description

2.1 The Morphological Description in Wordnets

The assumption of Princeton WordNet was a semantic description, i.e. including derivational, not inflectional morphology (Miller et al., 1990). Still, morphological data resources are developed as independent linguistic databases. One of them is CELEX – a lexical database for Dutch and English (Van der Wouden, 1990), extended in 2.0 version with German (Baayen et al., 1995). It contains orthographic, phonological, morphological (also inflectional), syntactic, and statistical information (frequency in text corpora), but it does not contain semantics.

The morphological description of the derivation and inflection in CELEX offers great opportunities to enrich it with semantic information. Hathout (2002) describes combining the morphological resources of CELEX for the English language with Princeton WordNetto create a language-independent mechanism for obtaining semantic relational data (synonyms and derivatives). Similar studies with the use of CELEX and semantic-relational thesauri were conducted for Dutch (Kraaij and Pohlmann, 1996). This research is particularly applicable to the extraction of information and knowledge from text.

The inflectional morphology is less of a problem for languages with residual inflection, such as English, but a serious challenge for highly inflected languages. In the paper Henrich et al. (2012), semantic data from Princeton WordNet and GermaNet (Hamp and Feldweg, 1997) and morphological data for these languages from Wiktionary were used to create a method for sense-annotation and automatically annotated text corpora.

Slavic languages have an even more complicated inflection than Germanic ones. The paper of Pala and Hlaváčková (2007) presents the results of the work consisting of adapting a mechanism of the Czech morphological analyzer Ajka (Sedláček and Smrž, 2001) to extend the Czech WordNet with derivational relations. For Slavic languages, the research on derivational morphology has also been carried out on a larger scale for Bulgarian (Koeva, 2008).

The works that are the closest to those presented in this paper were described in Obradović and Stanković (2007). The authors have developed a tool for the creation of complex lexicographic data obtained from wordnets, morphological dictionaries, and text corpora.

It is possible to highlight several important aspects of morphological description in wordnets: 1) on a wider scale it describes derivational, not inflectional morphology; 2) there is a regular relationship between inflection and derivation, but these two levels of description are not treated as equivalent; 3) the combination of semantic and morphological description (both, at the inflectional and derivational level) is useful, e.g. for the tasks related to Word Sense Disambiguation and, in connection with it, the extraction of information from texts and building knowledge bases.

2.2 The Specificity of the Polish Morphology

As already mentioned, plWordNet describes four parts of speech: verbs, adjectives, adverbs, and nouns. In Polish, nouns and adjectives are inflected by seven cases in two numbers: singular and plural. Furthermore, adjectives are inflected for gender, while nouns are always lexically specified for grammatical gender.

There are five genders: three masculine (personal, animate, and inanimate), feminine and neuter (Lewandowska-Tomaszczyk et al., 2012). For example, *pies* (zw) 'dog' and *pies* (os) 'cop' (depreciative and colloquial) differ in their genders and, consequently, in the pattern of the inflection. The gender of adjectives depends on the gender of nouns they have syntactic relations in the text, e.g. *szafa* 'wardrobe', feminine, *czerwon-a* 'red' an adjective, feminine. Moreover, adjectives and adverbs have three degrees: positive, comparative, and superlative.

Verbs in Polish are inflected for two numbers and three persons for each of them, four tenses (including two future ones that differ with each other only grammatically), and three modes of expressing modality (indicative, conditional, imperative). They have an assigned aspect having grammatical and semantic functions (Dziob and Piasecki, 2018). They form gerunds and four types of participles, which are treated as forms of the verb. A semantic-syntactic feature of the verb (to a lesser extent also of other parts of speech) is valence, understood as the ability of predicates to attach arguments in specific forms and syntactic positions (Przepiórkowski et al., 2014). For example, the verb *jeść* 'to eat' opens three syntactic positions, for a subject, an object, and a circumstance. In this case, the object is expressed as a noun in the accusative case. Walenty is connected at the semantic layer to the plWordNet by using synsets to determine a semantic preference, e.g. 'jeść' + *jedzenie 2* 'food'.

Traditional Polish grammars cf. (Grzegorczykowa et al., 1998) distinguish a quite large group of numbers and pronouns. In syntactically oriented grammars, e.g. (Saloni, 2012), they are combined with other parts of speech (nouns, adjectives, adverbs, and verbs) depending on the pattern of the inflection and morphosyntactic functions. This solution was also applied in plWordNet.

2.3 The Morphological Description in the NLP Practice

Morphological analysis is widely used in the syntactic processing of the Polish language. The task of morphological tagging is to process a sequence of tokens – sentence – and assign each of them a unified morphological interpretation. In the task of morphosyntactic tagging the morphological analysis is most often used in two ways: 1) as a set of input features to the tagger (Waszczuk, 2012, Wróbel, 2017), 2) as a tagger output filter (Georgiev et al., 2019, Walentynowicz et al., 2019).

Indirectly, morphology can be used as a method of regularization tagger learning process (Straka et al., 2019). Also in the task of inflection language chunking, full morphological information is used (Goldberg et al., 2006).

The task which depends on the morphological information and, at the same time, has a semantic aspect, is lemmatization. Words have different patterns of inflection by case, depending on their meaning. Choosing the right base form affects the result of tasks occurring after the lemmatization process such as Word Sense Disambiguation or Named Entity Recognition.

The combination of morphological information with semantic information will allow for better results in syntactic tasks due to better differentiation of contexts of the occurrence of given expression forms. The semantic dimension, which WordNet contains, allows searching for new patterns in data.

3 Resources

3.1 Morfeusz and SGJP

SGJP (Saloni, 2012) aims to give grammatical characteristics of Polish words. The main element of this characteristic is an open description of the inflection of units taken into account by giving all their forms of inflection and determining their grammatical functions. The dictionary does not contain lexeme sense. Morfeusz2 (Woliński, 2014) is a morphological analyzer that can use data from SGJP as a basis for a dictionary. It has the ability to analyze word forms, without recognizing out-of-vocabulary words. It is also able to perform morphological synthesis – the creation of a modified word form by indicating the lemma and the desired inflection characteristics.

The above-mentioned combination of Morfeusz2 with the SGJP dictionary was used to prepare the projection of forms found in plWordNet on the morphology available in SGJP. The list of lemmas available in plWordNet was processed by Morfeusz2, and then all word form varieties were prepared with the help of a morphological synthesis. This process had to be supervised by a linguist, because not all lemmas change in the same way – depending on the sense of a word, differences in the inflection can occur. This is when a linguist decided which inflection scheme to use.

3.2 Combining of Resources

As already mentioned, plWordNet describes four parts of speech. For all of them, the morphological information has been drawn from the SGJP. However, as a result, not all units have been given a pattern of inflection, see 4.1. In the task described in this article, new patterns of inflection were not added. Morphological disambiguation consisted of manual removal of the excess patterns for ambiguous lemmas. The task of linguists was to leave a set of forms confirmed for a given meaning in text corpora, even when they were rare or used in a specific context. In the cases where the morphological description did not match any of the available meanings, it was removed, and a new LU has been added to plWordNet without any inflection. Five linguists and a coordinator, who controlled the quality of works, worked on this task. Each of the linguists worked on one set of morphological features. The inter-annotator agreement was not measured. The morphological information for these units shall also be added in the further iteration. The lexicographic works were realized using the WordNet Loom editing system (Naskret et al., 2018), using a specially constructed field to edit morphological data.

4 The Alliance of Morphology and Semantics

4.1 Morphological Disambiguation

Two lists of lemmas were the result of a comparison of plWordNet and SGJP. The first one indicated those lemmas, which are described in plWordNet, but not in the SGJP. The second list included lemmas that are morphologically ambiguous in plWordNet. Those lemmas were manually disambiguated at the level of LUs. In total, 3,733 lemmas were ambiguous, including 772 adjectives, 200 adverbs, 2,309 nouns, and 452 verbs.

Among the ambiguous lemmas were those that belong to the following groups: 1) lemmas that have an adjective and a noun pattern of inflection, e.g. *white 1* (color, adjective) and *white 1* 'White' (person, noun); 2) nouns which may have two grammatical genders depending on their meaning, e.g. *pies 1* 'dog' and *dog 4* 'cop'; 3) proper names (surnames and names of places), which in SGJP have a given masculine gender, in plWordNet are not described at all (the work of linguists consisted in removing excess patterns); 4) elements of multi-word LUs that are not one-words lemmas in plWordNet[1]; 5) lemmas, which in one meaning belong to parts of speech described in plWordNet, but not in another, e.g. noun *jeden 1* 'short, nip' and the numeral *jeden* 'one'; 6) lemmas which, depending on their meaning, may belong to: a) nouns or verbs (gerunds), e.g. *uczulenie* as a noun ('allergy') and gerund from the verb *uczulić* 'to sentitize'; b) adjectives or participles, e.g. adjective *zabłąkany*' as an adjective ('confused') and participles from the verb *zabłąkać się* 'get lost'; 7) two-aspectual verbs, i.e. those which have the same form in the perfective and imperfective, cf. (Grzegorczykowa et al., 1998), e.g. *izolować 1* 'to isolate (perflimperf)'; 8) lemmas marked by pragmatics (e.g. high, formal, book) and unmarked meaning, e.g. miły 1 'dear' has the general form of a comparative *milszy* and superlative *najmilszy* and a marked (old, book) comp. *milejszy* and sup. *najmilejszy*; 9) lemmas non-inflectable according to any Polish pattern of inflection, belonging to a part of speech disambiguated contextually, e.g. *extra* 'additionally' (adverb) and *extra* 'additional' (adjective).

These are the most common problems defined in the course of manual work. They result from the ambiguity of the Polish language and its rich grammar, on the one hand, and, on the other hand, from the way of defining the LU in plWordNet. And they also have their consequences for this definition.

5 Towards the Definition of *Meaning*

The third list, resulting from the manual connection of the resources, contains senses missing in plWordNet. It includes about 800 lemmas which appear in plWordNetin a different sense and whose missing sense was made possible to be completed by a morphological disambiguation.

Among them there are the following groups of senses which have been qualified as plWordNet LUs: 1) lemmas, which plWordNet contains only in the adjective meaning, but not in their noun meaning, e.g. *hotelowy* 'hotel' (adjective) and 'the person who serves guests in the hotel, boy' (noun)[2]; 2) the sub-group, which contains missing adjective senses, but not distinct also in traditional dictionaries; those lemmas have in texts the function of a subject or an object (like a noun), not an attributive (like an adjective), e.g. *otyły* 'fat' (adjective, described in plWordNet) and *otyły* 'a fat person' (noun, none); 3) missing sense, which are pragmatically marked; they are included in plWordNet only if their appearance can be confirmed in corpora (Maziarz et al., 2014), e.g. *napaść* 'to fatten', which has a different inflection than *napaść 1* 'to attack'; 4) uninflected lemmas belonging to a part of speech disambiguated by the context, e.g. *bordo* 'maroon' as an adjective (described) or adverb (none); 5) ambiguous nouns whose grammatical gender is contextually disambiguated, e.g. *kapo*-female 'female guard in a concentration camp' (in plWordNet is only *kapo*-male); 6) inflected nouns, which can have different grammatical genders, depending on their meaning, e.g. *przewodnik* 'guide' (person,

[1]The description of multi-words is planned for the further work by linking it to the SEJF Dictionary (Czerepowicka and Savary, 2015).

[2]This group includes many representatives of less popular or former occupations and positions (functions).

personal gender), *przewodnik* 'guidebook' (thing, inanimate gender), *przewodnik* 'guide dog' (none; animate); 7) bearers of features, in the case of which meanings can be distinguished by particular lexico-semantic relations, e.g. *garbusek* 'little hunchback' (person who has a hump) and *garbusek* 'little beetle' (car).

In addition to the above, the method of manually enriching plWordNet allows to reveal other LUs, the meaning of which is connected with less regular morphological processes. These are such LUs as e.g. *podskarbiostwo* 'the married couple, a former Polish court's clerk and his wife' *flop* 'the computer power unit', *flop* 'men's hairstyle' etc.

It is interesting that for many nouns with lemmas identical to adjectives, whose morphological disambiguation is contextual, plWordNet describes only masculine nouns, e.g. there is *gruby* as a 'fat person' but not *gruba* as a 'fat women'. Let us recall that nouns do not inflect by gender, but have their gender assigned. On this basis, it can be concluded that the existence of these meanings as separate is non-intuitive and not obvious in Polish.

The list of deficiencies also includes meanings that will not be included in plWordNet due to its theoretical-methodological limitations of defining meanings: 1) senses which are understood in the SGJP as adjectives, whereas in plWordNet interpreted as participles, e.g. *kupujący* 'someone who buys' (derived from the verb *kupować* 'to buy'); 2) occasionalisms, e.g. *bufetowa* 'the person managing the canteen' (the journalists called in this way the former Mayor of Warsaw, Hanna Gronkiewicz-Walz); 3) nouns that may be personal or non-personal, e.g. *pięciolatek* 'a person who is a five years old' or 'animal who is a five years old'; in plWordNet this is the same sense; 4) archaisms whose occurrence is not confirmed by corpora, e.g. *majorat* as a person; 5) lemmas which occur only in multi-word units cf. (Maziarz et al., 2015), e.g. *warcabnik* as 'butterfly' occurs only in species names *warcabnik ślazowiec* ' Carcharodus alceae' and *warcabnik szantowiec* 'Carcharodus floccifera'; 6) proper names not constituting the basis for derivation of relational adjectives used in general language, cf. (Maziarz et al., 2012), e.g. *Koło* 'a part of Warsaw's Wola district'; 7) acronyms from proper names which are not described in plWordNet, e.g. *LP* - Legiony Polskie 'Polish Legions'.

The most important conclusion for the methodology and procedure of distinguishing senses is that the morphological pattern cannot be treated as a distinguishing feature. Instead, it can be a strong argument for manual work, which consists of verifying in corpora previously not described LUs. This is especially true in the case of regularities connected with distinguishing LUs belonging to different parts of speech, as well as grammatical genders (masculine and feminine). The existence of two masculine patterns of inflection next to each other needs to be verified every time, because plWordNet often treats meanings more generally than it is established in the Polish grammatically oriented linguistics.

6 New Possibilities

A wordnet combined with morphological information can be used by NLP tools such as taggers and shallow parsers. The use of wordnet-based context vectors (Patwardhan and Pedersen, 2006) or the combination of word embeddings with wordnet information (Mao et al., 2018) have already been applied in NLP tasks. Current taggers most often rely on a vector-based word representation, so a wordnet-based context vector could be attached to the input representation to better represent the dependencies between tokens in a sentence. More semantic information should improve the lemmatization process, which cannot be based solely on morphological information, since there are cases where a pair of word forms and tags has several possible lemmas. The task of extracting key phrases requires morphological information to obtain good results. The word relations that are in wordnet are an additional element that should improve the results (Kardan et al., 2013). So far, this task has not used the combined morphology information with the data from wordnet.

The combination of information contained in wordnet and morphological dictionaries opens up new paths for the development of a method in various NLP tasks, like the ones mentioned above. Moreover, from the implementation side, such integration will allow reducing the number of dependencies in the already functioning methods, which use both the morphology and wordnet. Examples of such systems can be a system of clustering terms from the field of economics, which uses morphological information and relationships from wordnet (Mykowiecka and Marciniak, 2012), or wordnet-based morphological analysis (Geum and Park, 2016).

Acknowledgments

The work co-financed as part of the investment in the CLARIN-PL research infrastructure funded by the Polish Ministry of Science and Higher Education.

References

R Harald Baayen, Richard Piepenbrock, and Hedderick Van Rijn. The celex database. *Nijmegen: Center for Lexical Information, Max Planck Institute for Psycholinguistics, CD-ROM*, 1995.

Monika Czerepowicka and Agata Savary. Sejf-a grammatical lexicon of polish multiword expressions. In *Language and Technology Conference*, pages 59–73. Springer, 2015.

Magdalena Derwojedowa, Maciej Piasecki, Stanisław Szpakowicz, Magdalena Zawisławska, and Bartosz Broda. Words, Concepts and Relations in the Construction of Polish WordNet. In A. Tanács, D. Csendes, V. Vincze, Ch. Fellbaum, and P. Vossen, editors, *Proc. Fourth Global WordNet Conf.*, pages 162–177, 2008.

Agnieszka Dziob and Maciej Piasecki. Implementation of the Verb Model in plWordNet 4.0. In *Proceedings of the 9th Global Wordnet Conference*, 2018.

Agnieszka Dziob, Maciej Piasecki, and Ewa Rudnicka. plwordnet 4.1–a Linguistically Motivated, Corpus-based Bilingual Resource. In *Global Wordnet Conference 2019*, pages 353–362, Wrocław, 2019.

Christiane Fellbaum, editor. *WordNet – An Electronic Lexical Database*. The MIT Press, 1998.

Georgi Georgiev, Valentin Zhikov, Petya Osenova, Kiril Simov, and Preslav Nakov. Feature-rich part-of-speech tagging for morphologically complex languages: Application to bulgarian. *arXiv preprint arXiv:1911.11503*, 2019.

Youngjung Geum and Yongtae Park. How to generate creative ideas for innovation: a hybrid approach of wordnet and morphological analysis. *Technological Forecasting and Social Change*, 111:176–187, 2016.

Yoav Goldberg, Meni Adler, and Michael Elhadad. Noun phrase chunking in hebrew: Influence of lexical and morphological features. In *Proceedings of the 21st International Conference on Computational Linguistics and 44th Annual Meeting of the Association for Computational Linguistics*, pages 689–696, 2006.

Renata Grzegorczykowa, Roman Laskowski, and Henryk Wróbel. *Morfologia: gramatyka współczesnego jzyka polskiego*. Wydawn. naukowe PWN, 1998.

Birgit Hamp and Helmut Feldweg. Germanet-a lexical-semantic net for german. In *Automatic information extraction and building of lexical semantic resources for NLP applications*, 1997.

Nabil Hathout. From wordnet to celex: acquiring morphological links from dictionaries of synonyms. In *LREC*, 2002.

Verena Henrich, Erhard Hinrichs, and Tatiana Vodolazova. An automatic method for creating a sense-annotated corpus harvested from the web. *International Journal of Computational Linguistics and Applications*, 3(2):47–62, 2012.

Ahmad A Kardan, Farzad Farahmandnia, and Amin Omidvar. A novel approach for keyword extraction in learning objects using text mining and wordnet. *Global Journal of Information Technology*, 3(1), 2013.

Svetla Koeva. Derivational and morphosemantic relations in bulgarian wordnet. *Intelligent Information Systems*, 16: 359–369, 2008.

Wessel Kraaij and Renée Pohlmann. *Using Linguistic Knowledge in Information Retrieval Technical Report*. Citeseer, 1996.

Barbara Lewandowska-Tomaszczyk, Mirosław Bańko, Rafał L Górski, Piotr Pęzik, and Adam Przepiórkowski. Narodowy korpus języka polskiego. Wydawnictwo Naukowe PWN, 2012.

John Lyons. *Semantics*. 1977.

Rui Mao, Chenghua Lin, and Frank Guerin. Word embedding and wordnet based metaphor identification and interpretation. In *Proceedings of the 56th Annual Meeting of the Association for Computational Linguistics (Volume 1: Long Papers)*, pages 1222–1231, 2018.

Marek Maziarz, Stanisław Szpakowicz, and Maciej Piasecki. Semantic relations among adjectives in polish wordnet 2.0: a new relation set, discussion and evaluation. *Cognitive Studies*, (12), 2012.

Marek Maziarz, Maciej Piasecki, and Stanisław Szpakowicz. The chicken-and-egg problem in wordnet design: synonymy, synsets and constitutive relations. *Language Resources and Evaluation*, 47(3):769–796, 2013.

Marek Maziarz, Maciej Piasecki, Ewa Rudnicka, and Stan Szpakowicz. Registers in the system of semantic relations in plwordnet. In *Proceedings of the Seventh Global Wordnet Conference*, pages 330–337, 2014.

Marek Maziarz, Stan Szpakowicz, and Maciej Piasecki. A procedural definition of multi-word lexical units. In *Proceedings of the International Conference Recent Advances in Natural Language Processing*, pages 427–435, 2015.

Marek Maziarz, Maciej Piasecki, Ewa Rudnicka, Stan Szpakowicz, and Paweł Kędzia. plwordnet 3.0 – a Comprehensive Lexical-Semantic Resource. In Nicoletta Calzolari, Yuji Matsumoto, and Rashmi Prasad, editors, *COLING 2016, 26th International Conference on Computational Linguistics, Proceedings of the Conference: Technical Papers, December 11-16, 2016, Osaka, Japan*, pages 2259–2268. ACL, 2016.

George A Miller. Wordnet: a lexical database for english. *Communications of the ACM*, 38(11):39–41, 1995.

George A Miller, Richard Beckwith, Christiane Fellbaum, Derek Gross, and Katherine J Miller. Introduction to wordnet: An on-line lexical database. *International journal of lexicography*, 3(4):235–244, 1990.

Agnieszka Mykowiecka and Malgorzata Marciniak. Combining wordnet and morphosyntactic information in terminology clustering. In *Proceedings of COLING 2012*, pages 1951–1962, 2012.

Tomasz Naskret, Agnieszka Dziob, Maciej Piasecki, Chakaveh Saedi, and António Branco. Wordnetloom–a multilingual wordnet editing system focused on graph-based presentation. In *Proceedings of the 9th Global WordNet Conference (GWC2018)*, 2018.

Ivan Obradović and Ranka Stanković. Wordnet development using a multifunctional tool. In *Proceedings of the International Workshop Computer Aided Language Processing (CALP)'2007*, pages 25–32, 2007.

Karel Pala and Dana Hlaváčková. Derivational relations in czech wordnet. In *Proceedings of the Workshop on Balto-Slavonic Natural Language Processing*, pages 75–81, 2007.

Siddharth Patwardhan and Ted Pedersen. Using wordnet-based context vectors to estimate the semantic relatedness of concepts. In *Proceedings of the Workshop on Making Sense of Sense: Bringing Psycholinguistics and Computational Linguistics Together*, 2006.

Maciej Piasecki, Radoslaw Ramocki, and Marek Maziarz. Recognition of Polish Derivational Relations Based on Supervised Learning Scheme. In *LREC*, pages 916–922, 2012.

Adam Przepiórkowski, Elżbieta Hajnicz, Agnieszka Patejuk, Marcin Woliński, Filip Skwarski, and Marek Świdziński. Walenty: Towards a comprehensive valence dictionary of Polish. In Nicoletta Calzolari, Khalid Choukri, Thierry Declerck, Hrafn Loftsson, Bente Maegaard, Joseph Mariani, Asuncion Moreno, Jan Odijk, and Stelios Piperidis, editors, *Proceedings of the Ninth International Conference on Language Resources and Evaluation, LREC 2014*, pages 2785–2792. ELRA, 2014.

Ewa Rudnicka, Marek Maziarz, Maciej Piasecki, and Stan Szpakowicz. A Strategy of Mapping Polish WordNet onto Princeton WordNet. In *Proc. COLING 2012, posters*, pages 1039–1048, 2012.

Zygmunt Saloni. Podstawy teoretyczne „słownika gramatycznego języka polskiego". *Warszawa, online: http://sgjp.pl/static/pdf/Wst% C4% 99p% 20do% 20II% 20wydania% 20SGJP. pdf*, 1458313456, 2012.

Zygmunt Saloni, Włodzimierz Gruszczyński, Marcin Woliński, and Robert Wołosz. Grammatical Dictionary of Polish. *Studies in Polish Linguistics*, 4:5–25, 2007.

Radek Sedláček and Pavel Smrž. A new czech morphological analyser ajka. In *International Conference on Text, Speech and Dialogue*, pages 100–107. Springer, 2001.

Milan Straka, Jana Straková, and Jan Hajič. Udpipe at sigmorphon 2019: Contextualized embeddings, regularization with morphological categories, corpora merging. *arXiv preprint arXiv:1908.06931*, 2019.

Ton Van der Wouden. Celex: Building a multifunctional polytheoretical lexical data base. *Proceedings of BudaLex*, 88:363–373, 1990.

Piek Vossen. EuroWordNet General Document Version 3. Technical report, Univ. of Amsterdam, 2002.

Wiktor Walentynowicz, Maciej Piasecki, and Marcin Oleksy. Tagger for polish computer mediated communication texts. In *Proceedings of the International Conference on Recent Advances in Natural Language Processing (RANLP 2019)*, pages 1295–1303, 2019.

Jakub Waszczuk. Harnessing the crf complexity with domain-specific constraints. the case of morphosyntactic tagging of a highly inflected language. In *Proceedings of COLING 2012*, pages 2789–2804, 2012.

Marcin Woliński. Morfeusz reloaded. In Nicoletta Calzolari, Khalid Choukri, Thierry Declerck, Hrafn Loftsson, Bente Maegaard, Joseph Mariani, Asuncion Moreno, Jan Odijk, and Stelios Piperidis, editors, *Proceedings of the Ninth International Conference on Language Resources and Evaluation, LREC 2014*, pages 1106–1111, Reykjavík, Iceland, 2014. European Language Resources Association (ELRA). ISBN 978-2-9517408-8-4. URL `http://www.lrec-conf.org/proceedings/lrec2014/index.html`.

Krzysztof Wróbel. Krnnt: Polish recurrent neural network tagger. In *Proceedings of the 8th Language & Technology Conference: Human Language Technologies as a Challenge for Computer Science and Linguistics*, pages 386–391. Fundacja Uniwersytetu im. Adama Mickiewicza w Poznaniu, 2017.

Towards Expanding WordNet with Conceptual Frames

Svetla Koeva
Institute for Bulgarian Language "Prof. Lyubomir Andreychin"
Bulgarian Academy of Sciences
svetla@dcl.bas.bg

Abstract

The paper presents the project *Semantic Network with a Wide Range of Semantic Relations* and its main achievements. The ultimate objective of the project is to expand Princeton WordNet with conceptual frames that define the syntagmatic relations of verb synsets and the semantic classes of nouns felicitous to combine with particular verbs. At this stage of the work: a) over 5,000 WordNet verb synsets have been supplied with manually evaluated FrameNet semantic frames, b) 253 semantic types have been manually mapped to the appropriate WordNet concepts providing detailed ontological representation of the semantic classes of nouns.

1. Introduction

The paper presents and discuss the results of the research project *Semantic Network with a Wide Range of Semantic Relations* (2016 – 2020)[1]. The project targets to expand WordNet with conceptual frames that define the syntagmatic relations of verb synsets and the semantic classes of nouns felicitous to combine with particular verbs.

In Princeton WordNet, each verb synset is associated with a list of sentence frames illustrating the types of simple sentences in which the verbs in the synset can be used (Fellbaum 1990/1993: 55). WordNet sentence frames represent information for the number of frame elements, some semantic information – whether a given element is a human or not, and brief syntactic information – whether the element is realized as a noun, a prepositional phrase (in some cases the preposition is indicated), an adjective, an *-ing* form of the verb, a clause, an infinitive clause or a *that* clause. For example, the verbs from the synset {*hate*; *detest*} with a definition 'dislike intensely; feel antipathy or aversion towards' are associated with the sentence frames: ***Somebody ----s somebody*** and ***Somebody ----s something***. There are 35 generic frames and a sentence frame might be applicable to all literals within a synset or only to some of them. The frame information given on verbs in WordNet is not sufficient to indicate syntagmatic relations between synsets (syntagmatic relations are semantic relations that express the semantic compatibilities of words). For example, humans and some animals can run, thus most of the nouns from WordNet synsets marked as noun.person and many nouns marked as noun.animal can be linked with the verb *run* as its **Agent**.

To remedy the deficiency of syntagmatic relations in WordNet we introduce the notion of **conceptual frame**, which refers to the set of verbs having equal syntagmatic relations with nouns.

The framework of conceptual frames is built upon the WordNet morphosemantic relations introduced by Miller and Fellbaum (2003). Predetermined by the meanings of derivational affixes, the morphosemantic links express semantic relations between a verb synset and a noun synset (for example, *an inventor* is an **Agent** of the verb *invent*; *a hanger* is a **Location** of the verb *hang*, a dinner is an **Event** of the verb *dine*, etc.) (Fellbaum et al. 2007). In fact, the morphosemantic relations outline subclasses among the WordNet noun classes: e.g., nouns that can act as human **Agents**, nouns that can act as inanimate **Agents**, etc., and further, the existence of a morphosemantic relation between a verb synset

[1] https://dcl.bas.bg/en/semantichni-mrezhi/

and a noun synset can serve as an indicator for defining the respective conceptual frame.

The enrichment of the WordNet structure with conceptual frames is related with the implementation of the following steps:

a) identification of verb synsets that evoke a particular FrameNet semantic frame;

b) detailed ontological representation of semantic classes of noun synsets;

c) specification of frame elements relevant for the expression of syntagmatic relations;

d) assigning the frame elements with noun semantic classes or a combination of classes ensuring the words' compatibility;

e) definition of WordNet conceptual frames;

f) insertion of syntagmatic relations within the WordNet structure.

The assumption is that a relatively small number of conceptual frames, which represent the predicate – argument relations between verb and noun synsets, will introduce a large number of syntagmatic relations.

In the presented approach, we take the advantage of automatic mapping of existing resources and rely on the precision of manual assessment of the results. We integrated particular types of semantic knowledge represented basically in three resources: Princeton WordNet 3.0[2] (offering an extensive lexical coverage organized in a semantic network by means of semantic relations), FrameNet[3] (presenting a deep conceptual description of semantic frames), and PDEV (Pattern Dictionary of English Verbs) with the CPA (Corpus Pattern Analysis) semantic types (offering a large ontology of noun semantic classes).

We are going to present here briefly steps a) and b). In particular, we specify the WordNet noun semantic classes into a more fine-grained ontology by mapping WordNet noun hierarchies with the CPA ontology (Section 4) and combine verb hierarchies in WordNet with FrameNet frame semantics and PDEV verb patterns (Section

2. Introduction to Conceptual Frames

Conceptual frames are abstract structures which define the semantic and syntactic compatibility between verb predicates and noun arguments. A particular conceptual frame is: associated with a semantic class that expresses its general semantic properties (ideally, each conceptual frame will be assigned with a unique semantic class); represented by a set of verbs organized in the WordNet synonym sets, and described by a set of frame elements. The frame verbs can be one or several: linked between each other with lexical relations (synonymy, antonymy) and / or hierarchical relations (hypernymy, troponymy, entailment). The conceptual frame elements roughly correspond to the FrameNet core elements, which means that there is no one-to-one correspondence between FrameNet semantic frames and WordNet conceptual frames.

The selection of conceptual frame elements is based on the intuition about the core participants within a situation but also on the frame elements (implicit or explicit) of superordinates and subordinates in the WordNet hierarchies and on the information from the already available frame representations such as WordNet sentence frames, the FrameNet semantic frames (Ruppenhofer et al. 2016), the VerbNet verb classes (Palmer et al. 2017), the PropBank frames (Bonial et al. 2014), the PDEV patterns (Hanks 2013), the VerbAtlas frames (Di Fabio et al. 2019).

Each conceptual frame element is associated with a set of nouns that are compatible with the verb predicate. Again, the set could contain a single noun or several nouns linked between each other with lexical relations (synonymy, antonymy) and / or hierarchical relations (hypernymy, hyponymy). The association between the frame (verb synsets) and its elements (noun synsets) can be explicitly introduced in WordNet by means of syntagmatic relations. If more than one noun synset can express the frame element (which is the usual case), the syntagmatic relation links the verb synset with the top-most noun synset of the hierarchy, grouping nouns with the same semantic properties (semantic class). The diversity in the compatibilities between representatives of verb classes and noun classes drives the necessity for a detailed ontology of semantic classes.

We can generalize that a **conceptual frame** defines a unique set of syntagmatic relations between: a) verb synsets representing the frame, and b) noun synsets expressing the frame elements (Koeva 2020). Thereby, the notion of conceptual frame combines semantic knowledge presented in WordNet and FrameNet and builds upon it.

The framework of conceptual frames is closely related to the FrameNet semantic frames. Semantic frames are schematic representations of situations involving various participants, props,

---

[2] http://wordnetweb.princeton.edu [30 November 2020]

[3] https://framenet.icsi.berkeley.edu [30 November 2020]

and other conceptual roles, each of which is a frame element (Johnson and Fillmore 2000: 56). The semantic frames contain frame elements which have a name, a definition, a semantic type, a specification for their core status, and frame internal relations among the frame elements. The main difference between conceptual frames and the FrameNet semantic frames is that conceptual frames are explicitly linked with the noun synsets representing the words with which the verb predicate can be combined (to the extent this is possible due to WordNet structure and content and metaphoric language use).

For example, a conceptual frame which roughly corresponds to the FrameNet semantic frame **Experiencer_focused_emotion** is represented by the verb synsets: {dislike} 'have or feel a dislike or distaste for'; {hate, detest} 'dislike intensely; feel antipathy or aversion towards'; {like} 'find enjoyable or agreeable'; {love} 'have a great affection or liking for'. The conceptual frame elements are **Experiencer** and **Content** (if we keep the names of the FrameNet core elements). The semantic classes of nouns that they could be expressed with are [Human], [Animal], [Physical entity], and [Abstraction] and the combinations are the following:

Experiencer: {person, individual} – **Content:** {physical entity} ∪ {abstraction}

or

Experiencer: {animal} – **Content:** {physical entity}.

The syntagmatic links which can be introduced are:

{dislike} and {hate, detest} and {like}and {love} have **Experiencer$_1$** {person, individual} and have **Content$_1$** {physical entity} and have **Content$_1$** {abstraction};

{**dislike**} and {hate, detest} and {like} and {love} have **Experiencer$_2$** {animal} and have **Content$_2$** {physical entity}.

One verb synset can be linked by means of one and the same syntagmatic relation with either one or many noun synsets. Many to many syntagmatic relations do not exist.

Ideally, the conceptual frame of the top-most verb in a hierarchy should be the same as the frames of its subordinates. However, it is noticed that troponymy actually comprises various types of manner relation. For example, verbs of motion may specify the kind of transportation (*train*, *bus*, *truck*, *bike*) or the speed dimension (*walk*, *run*) (Talmy 1985: 62–72; Fellbaum 1990/1993: 47). This implies that verb hierarchies may be elaborated further and verb semantic classes (trees) may be divided in a more precise way. This would result in smaller trees; however, the generalizations for conceptual frames related with these trees would be more precise. Other problems with the generalizations in conceptual frames might arise from the way of conceptualization (for English or other languages), the level of granularity, the lack of consistency in representing causative and inchoative verbs, the lack of consistency in representing verb aspects for languages expressing this category and some others.

As for conceptual frames (if they are correctly defined), we can expect that the daughter verb synsets will inherit the conceptual frame assigned on the top of the verb tree and deviations are expected in two directions: differences in the explicitness of core frame elements and a reduction of the members of the set of nouns eligible to express a particular frame element (a general tendency is that verbs expressing more specific manners enforce more specific restrictions).

For example, the hyponyms of the verb {dislike} can be linked with the following syntagmatic relations:

{abhor, loathe, abominate, execrate} 'find repugnant' has **Experiencer** {person, individual} and has **Content** {physical entity};

{contemn, despise, scorn, disdain} 'look down on with disdain' and {look down on} 'regard with contempt' have **Experiencer** {person, individual} and have **Content** {person, individual}.

To summarize, some of the main advantages of both resources (WordNet and FrameNet) with regard to the conceptual description of the predicate – argument structure can be complemented and upgraded to expand WordNet with conceptual frames that represent verb predicate – argument syntagmatic relations.

3. Combining Semantic Information from Existing Semantic Resources

There are many rich semantic resources (mainly for English but also for other languages) that include different types of semantic information: WordNet (Miller et al. 1990/1993), FrameNet (Baker et al. 1998), VerbNet (Kipper et al. 2008), PropBank (Palmer et al. 2005), Ontonotes (Weischedel et al. 2011), PDEV (Hanks 2004), Yago (Suchanek et al. 2007), BabelNet (Navigli, Ponzetto 2012), VerbAtlas (Di Fabio et al. 2019), SynSemClass (Urešová et al. 2020), among others.

The main advantages of WordNet for semantic analysis focused on introducing conceptual frames are: a) the large number of concepts organized in a semantic network; b) the grouping of concepts in semantic classes according to their general meaning. The main advantages of FrameNet for implementing conceptual frames are: a) the extensive description of semantic knowledge about an event type and its participants; b) the linking semantic frames with semantic relations. The main advantages of PDEV with CPA for the specification of conceptual frame elements are: a) a description of the semantic types of the elements of verb patterns; b) the organization of semantic types in a shallow ontology. Bellow we briefly discuss the advantages of the three resources.

3.1. Princeton WordNet

WordNet (Miller 1986; Miller et al. 1990/1993: 1–9; Miller, Fellbaum 1991; Fellbaum 1998) is a lexical semantic resource that provides diverse and wide-ranging semantic information. In WordNet, the hypernymy relation (and its inverse relation, hyponymy) links more general concepts to more specific ones and organizes the noun synsets in hierarchies with the most abstract concepts being at the root of trees and the most specific concepts at the leaves of trees (Miller et al. 1990/1993: 12). The hierarchies of verbs are shallow: verbs at the roots of trees express more abstract concepts, while verbs at lower levels of the trees (troponyms) express more specific concepts that denote the manner of doing something (Fellbaum 1990/1993: 47). The inheritance principle of *is-a* relations (such as hypernymy and hyponymy/troponymy) states that anything that is true about the generic entity type A, must also be true about the specific entity type B. Any attributes of A, therefore, are also attributable of B (but not necessarily vice versa). Similarly, in whichever relation A can participate, B can participate also (Storney 1993: 461). In WordNet, a hyponym inherits all the features of the more generic concept and adds at least one feature that distinguishes it from its superordinate and from any other hyponyms of that superordinate (Miller et al. 1990/1993: 8).

Nouns and verbs are grouped in WordNet into more specific semantic classes (Miller 1990/1993: 16; Fellbaum 1990/1993: 41), describing their general meaning: noun.person, noun.animal, noun.cognition; verb.cognition, verb.change, etc. Nouns are classified into twenty-five semantic classes and verbs – into fifteen semantic classes: fourteen classes for events or actions and one class for verbs denoting states (Fellbaum 1990/1993: 41). For example, the verb synonyms {cook; fix; ready; make; prepare} with a definition 'prepare for eating by applying heat' have a sentence frame ***Somebody ----s something*** and a semantic class verb.creation which is inherited by their hyponyms like *dress out, deglaze, scallop, escallop, flambe, devil, precook*, etc. However, not every noun classified as noun.person can collocate with these verbs as their subject and not every noun that is not classified as noun.person can be their object (*the ex-spouse*, ?the neoliberal, *the infant *cooks dinner*, ?elephant, *books). In other words, the WordNet noun semantic classes could be further specified in order to correlate precisely with the verb-noun selectional preferences. An interdependence between the semantic classes of verbs and the sentence frames applicable to the verbs of one and the same class can be tracked, but such task is very ambiguous because of the small number of semantic classes and the small number of different sentence frames in WordNet. This implies that verb hierarchies may be elaborated further and verb semantic classes may also be divided in a more detailed way.

The following semantic information encoded in WordNet is most important for our research: the relations of inheritance in noun and verb synset trees; the semantic classes to which the noun and verb hierarchies belong; and the sentence frames assigned to the verb synsets. Language independent data can be shared while language specific properties are maintained (Bond et al. 2016).

3.2. Berkeley FrameNet

FrameNet is another language resource that contains lexical and conceptual knowledge (Fillmore 1982; Fillmore and Baker 2010; Ruppenhofer et al. 2016). FrameNet can be viewed as a semantic network (or a set of small semantic nets), whose nodes indicate the semantic frames and whose arcs represent semantic relations between frames. For the purposes of the presented research, the following information is employed: the sets of verb lexical units related with semantic frames, the inheritance relation between semantic frames, and the description of core and peripheral frame elements and their semantic types.

In FrameNet, all lexical units evoking a semantic frame have identical (or closely comparable) semantic descriptions: they denote the same part of a scene; have the same number and types of frame elements and the same relations between frame elements (Ruppenhofer et al. 2016: 11). For example, the verb *hate*, together with the verbs *abhor, abominate, adore, delight, despair, despise, detest, dislike, dread, empathize, enjoy, envy, fear, grieve, like, loathe, love, luxuriate, mourn, pity, relish, resent, rue, savour* (and some nouns, adjectives, and adverbs), evokes the frame **Experiencer focused emotion**. One and the same semantic frame might be evoked by lexical units which are encoded either as synonyms, or as hypernyms and hyponyms in the WordNet semantic structure. For example, the verb *hate* is a synonym of the verb *detest* in a synset expressing the meaning defined as 'dislike intensely; feel antipathy or aversion towards'. The synset {*hate, detest*} has a hypernym {*dislike*} with a definition 'have or feel a dislike or distaste for', a sister synset {*resent*} with a definition 'feel bitter or indignant about' and two hyponyms: the synset {*abhor, loathe, abominate, execrate*} with a definition 'find repugnant', and the synset {*contemn, despise, scorn, disdain*} with a definition 'look down on with disdain'. The verbs *loathe, execrate, contemn, scorn, disdain* are presented in WordNet only.

FrameNet includes a network of relations between frames. Several types are defined, of which the most important are: **Inheritance** (an *is-a* relation, the child frame is a subtype of the parent frame), **Using** (the child frame presupposes the parent frame as background); **Subframe** (the child frame is a sub-event of a complex event represented by the parent); **Perspective on** (the child frame provides a particular perspective on an unperspectivized parent frame) (Puppenhofer 2016: 80–83). Inheritance is the strongest relation between frames corresponding to an *is-a* relation in many ontologies. The basic idea of this relation is that each semantic fact about the parent must correspond to an equally specific or more specific fact about the child (Puppenhofer 2016: 80).

FrameNet allows for the characterization of 'role fillers' by semantic types of frame elements, which ought to be broadly constant across uses (Ruppenhofer et al. 2016: 12). However, not all frame elements are supplied with a semantic type or the semantic types are too general, and in some cases, they do not show the actual restrictions for lexical combinations. For example, the following frame elements of the semantic frame **Experiencer focused emotion** are equipped with semantic types: **Content** with the semantic type [Content]; **Event** with the semantic type [State of affairs]; **Experiencer** with the semantic type [Sentient]; **Degree** with the semantic type [Degree]; **Explanation** with the semantic type [State of affairs]; **Manner** with the semantic type [Manner]; **Time** with the semantic type [Time]. In summary, the lexical units in FrameNet are not grouped into semantic classes and the semantic types of frame elements, if any, are too general to characterize the class of words that can express the frame element (the annotation part of FrameNet illustrates the specific lexical and grammatical realization of the frame elements).

FrameNet contains extensive semantic information for the semantic frames which are evoked by the sets of lexical units. The value of the semantic information is intensified by the organization of the semantic frames in a semantic network.

3.3. Pattern Dictionary of English Verbs

The third semantic resource is the Pattern Dictionary of English Verbs (PDEV), where the verb arguments are described by means of the semantic types from the Corpus Pattern Analysis. The verb patterns capture the typical uses of verbs in context and represent the basic 'argument structure' of each verb (with semantic values stated for each of the elements of the patterns) (Hanks 2004: 87). The patterns consist of a fixed ordered set of semantic categories (the CPA), whose order corresponds to grammatical categories. The CPA semantic types refer to properties shared by a number of nouns that are found in verb pattern (argument) positions. The reliability of the semantic types is due to the fact that they are corpus-driven – they are formulated on the basis of real examples encountered in corpora.

This semantic resource can also be viewed as a semantic network whose nodes indicate the CPA semantic types and directly point to the subjects, objects, complements, and other positions within the verb patterns. The most important part of this semantic resource is the ontology of semantic types describing the properties of lexical units which are appropriate for filling the slots of verb patterns.

4. Ontology of Semantic Classes of Nouns

The semantic classes of nouns and verbs in WordNet might be subdivided into a set of semantic subclasses. For example, within the semantic class [Food] we can introduce the subclass of [Beverage] for nouns associated with verbs like *stir*, *sip*, *drink*, *lap*, etc. Such representation aims to specify the organization of concepts into an ontological structure which allows inheritance between the semantic classes down the hierarchy and ensures more precise specification of verb – noun compatibility.

One potential to extend the repository of WordNet semantic classes is to map the WordNet synsets to an existing hierarchy of semantic types, such as the CPA types. The semantic types (e.g. [Human], [Animal], [Part], etc.) refer to properties which can be expressed by words regularly found to participate in particular verb pattern positions (Hanks 2012: 57–59). In other words, the semantic types state the semantic preferences of verbs that determine the sets of nouns and noun phrases that are normally found in a particular clause role depending on a verb predicate. The CPA semantic types are organized in a shallow ontology which is based on the analysis of corpus data and which could be supplemented with new semantic types if such appear in new verb patterns. Some verb patterns may contain very general preferences, i.e., the semantic type [Anything], while others impose preferences for a limited set of lexical units grouped into more particular semantic types. For example, some verbs are associated with nouns characterized as [Body part]; however, the verb *shampoo* is associated with a more particular semantic type [Hair], the same is referred to the verb *nod*, which is associated with the type [Head], etc. Some verb patterns require a very small set of lexical units for a particular slot and in this case a semantic type is not formulated; instead, the concrete lexical units are listed in the verb pattern.

The expansion of WordNet semantic classes with CPA semantic types is performed manually by matching the CPA semantic types with WordNet synsets and choosing the most appropriate ones (Koeva et al. 2018).

The following general principles were followed:

- The WordNet semantic classes are preserved. New semantic types borrowed from the CPA ontology are attached to the WordNet synsets.
- The highest appropriate WordNet synset is chosen (within the hypernymy tree).

As a result of the mapping, the hyponyms of a synset to which a semantic type is mapped inherit not only the respective WordNet semantic class, but also the CPA semantic type. For example, the hyponyms of the WordNet synset {medium of exchange; monetary system} 'anything that is generally accepted as a standard of value and a measure of wealth in a particular country or region' mapped with the semantic type [Money] (for example, *currency*, *cash*, *paper money*, etc.) inherit not only the WordNet semantic class noun.possession, but also the more specific type [Money].

The 253 CPA semantic types are manually mapped to the respective WordNet concepts (synsets) as follows: 199 semantic types are mapped directly to one concept, i.e., [Permission] is mapped to {permission} 'approval to do something', semantic class noun.communication; [Dispute] is mapped to {disagreement} 'the speech act of disagreeing or arguing or disputing', semantic class noun.communication; 39 semantic types are mapped to two WordNet concepts, i.e., [Route] is mapped to {road; route} 'an open way (generally public) for travel or transportation', semantic class noun.artefact, and {path; route; itinerary} 'an established line of travel or access', semantic class noun.location; 12 semantic types are mapped to three concepts; 2 semantic types are mapped to four concepts; and 1 semantic type is mapped to five concepts (Koeva et al. 2018).

Automatic mapping of hyponym synsets to the inherited semantic types was performed. In the cases where a semantic type and its ancestor were both mapped to the same synset, the ancestor was removed. 82,114 WordNet noun synsets were mapped to the 253 semantic types of the CPA ontology, resulting in 172,991 mappings[4]. As there are multiple hypernymy relations in WordNet some of the inheritances are not correct, and further, the inheritance by multiple hypernyms will be manually evaluated, and if necessary, adjusted.

5. Mapping Verb Frames to WordNet

There are previous efforts at linking WordNet with different semantic resources such as FrameNet, VerbNet, PropBank, Levin's classes (Korhonen 2002; Shi and Mihalcea 2005; Palmer 2009; Baker and Ruppenhofer 2002; Fellbaum and Baker 2008; Baker and Fellbaum 2009; Fellbaum 2010; Tonelli and Pighin 2009; Laparra, Rigau 2010; Palmer et al. 2014; among others). These efforts resulted in different (but limited) coverage of the mapping and are hardly compatible because they use different release versions of WordNet, FrameNet, VerbNet and PropBank.

In our approach we rely on automatic mapping, automatic prediction for the mapping extension and manual evaluation of the results, something which has not been offered so far. All considered resources are manually crafted and our understanding is that their upgrading and extension (facilitated by automatic methods) should be manually evaluated and proved.

5.1. Mapping FrameNet Frames to WordNet

The new WordNet to FrameNet mapping is based on three lexical mappings: 2,817 direct mappings provided within FrameNet (Baker and Fellbaum 2009), 3,134 from eXtendedWordFrameNet (Laparra and Rigau 2010), and 1,833 from MapNet (Tonelli and Pighin 2009), and on 1,335 structural mappings with VerbNet. All in all, the unification of mappings resulted in 4,306 unique mappings of a WordNet synset onto a FrameNet frame (Leseva and Stoyanova 2020).

[4] http://dcl.bas.bg/PWN_CPA/

The procedures applied to improve and extend mapping coverage are based mainly on the relations of inheritance within WordNet and FrameNet. The frames assigned to 250 out of the 566 root verb synsets were manually evaluated: 75 mappings were corrected and 27 root synsets were additionally assigned a semantic frame. As a general procedure, the hypernym's frame was transferred to its hyponyms in the cases where the hyponyms are not directly mapped to FrameNet frames. As a result, **13,226 synsets** were automatically assigned a FrameNet frame

Further procedures were applied aiming at improving the quality of the mapping: a) checks for unmapped WordNet synsets and FrameNet frames; b) automatic or semi-automatic consistency checks; c) manual evaluation of the assigned frames (Leseva and Stoyanova 2020).

For synsets with frames inherited from their hypernyms, the following tests were applied:

- Searching for an additional match between literals in the given synset and the FrameNet lexical units in the related and sister frames; in any other frame in FrameNet; and in the frames assigned to the synset hyponyms and sisters.
- Calculation of similarity between the gloss of a verb synset and FrameNet lexical unit definitions, as well as between the glosses of derivationally related synsets and their hypernyms and FrameNet lexical unit definitions.
- Searching for a match between literals and words contained in the FrameNet frame name.

As a result of these steps, 9,341 new suggestions of more specific or other possible frames have been made for 5,661 synsets with inherited frames from their hypernyms.

Among all mappings 5,025 frames assigned to verb synsets in WordNet have been manually validated by experts[5].

Further, some frame elements and their subtypes are analyzed with regard to the selectional preferences imposed on their lexical expression (Leseva et al. 2020). Most of the frame elements are complex structures which prepossess a variety of more specific elements. For example, the frame element [Theme] can be characterized as not having control over the situation and not undergoing changes in its structure, form, function or essential properties; some of the defined subtypes of the [Theme] are: [Effected entity] associated with the synset {entity}; [Suspect] associated with the synsets {person, individual} ∪ {social group}; [Clothing] associated with the synset {clothing, article of clothing}, and so on. [Effected entity], [Suspect] and [Clothing] (and other sub-types) can be viewed as candidates for enriching the system of WordNet semantic types.

5.2. Mapping PDEV Patterns to WordNet

Mapping the PDEV verb patterns and WordNet sentence frames is used for expanding WordNet provided that: a) the semantic types from the CPA ontology are featured as arguments of a given predicate in the PDEV patterns; b) the WordNet noun synset hierarchy is already mapped onto the semantic type hierarchy in the CPA ontology.

A set of translation rules was applied to convert PDEV patterns into WordNet sentence frames and to preserve information of optional pattern arguments and alternative semantic types (Koeva et al. 2019a). After translating the PDEV patterns to WordNet frames, the result was used to assign patterns to the verb synsets in WordNet. For the assignment, we assumed the following:

For a synset S and a literal $L \in S$, PDEV pattern $P \in$ patterns(L) can be assigned to S if and only if frames(S) $\cap$ translations(P) $\neq \emptyset$.

We automatically assigned 2,904 of 4,048 unique PDEV verb patterns to 2,593 of the 13,767 verb synsets in WordNet by matching the verbs in the PDEV patterns to the literals and the translations of the patterns to the sentence frames of the synsets. This resulted in 6,898 synset pattern assignments (a single pattern may be assigned to more than one synset). 358 unique PDEV verb patterns were assigned to 148 of the 561 top verb synsets (altogether 453 synset pattern assignments).

The automatic mapping was subjected to manual validation (Koeva et al. 2019b). The exact matches were few and covered mainly one place predicates and two place predicates without (or with a few) alternative semantic types. In most cases, WordNet sentence frames were less detailed and involved only the obligatory arguments, while the PDEV patterns involved other constituents (adverbials, optional constituents, etc.), hence, it was expected for WordNet sentence frames to match the PDEV patterns only partially.

In cases where both the WordNet sentence frame and the PDEV pattern were evaluated as correct, but the PDEV pattern contained more information, we took the syntactic and semantic information from the PDEV pattern and the addi-

[5] https://dcl.bas.bg/en/semantic-relations-data/

tional CPA semantic types were applied to the WordNet sentence frames.

In fact, it is rather rare for patterns to be automatically assigned to more than two literals in a synset, and if they coincide, it is usually with respect to the type of participants (for example, the verbs {*yelp, yip, yap*} were assigned the patterns [Dog] *yelps*, [Dog] *yaps*), and at most with transitive verbs such as [Human] *watches* [Event], [Human] *sees* [Event]. The effect of manual validation and correction is shown at Table 1.

Total number of WordNet verb synsets covered by PDEV	**3,220**
Confirmed assignments	
Synsets with fully confirmed pattern assignment	1,488
Confirmed pattern assignments for all synsets	4,084
Manually added assignments	
Synsets to which new patterns were manually assigned	930
Manually assigned patterns in total for all synsets	1,568
Automatic assignments, removed at validation	
Synsets from which patterns were removed	1,143
Removed patterns from all synsets	2,815

Table 1: Manual validation of mapping WordNet sentence frames with PDEV patterns

The manually validated PDEV patterns were added to the XML version of the Princeton WordNet verb synsets used for this study, which is publicly available under the CC by license[6].

6. Conclusion and Future Work

The definition of conceptual frames representing the syntagmatic relations between verb synsets from a particular semantic class and noun synsets from particular semantic classes is (largely) language independent and applicable to any wordnet and other semantic networks. In general, languages differ in the syntactic, morphologic and lexical realization.

At this stage of our work we: a) supplied over 5,000 WordNet verb synsets with manually evaluated FrameNet semantic frames, b) provided a detailed ontological representation of the semantic classes of nouns in WordNet.

Further, selected verb synsets (part of basic vocabulary) will be analyzed with respect to: the FrameNet semantic frames assigned to the verbs with special focus to the core elements; the corresponding sentence frames in WordNet; as well as the PDEV verb patterns assigned to the verb synsets with a particular attention to the CPA semantic types. Through the course of the research other available semantic resources might be analyzed for comparison and evaluation of findings. The study will result in the formulation of conceptual frames represented by a set of verbs and described by a set of frame elements.

As it was pointed out, the main difference between a conceptual frame and a semantic frame (as defined in FrameNet) is that the structure of the conceptual frame includes description of the admissible classes of nouns that may be realized as elements of the frame. Thus, the definition of conceptual frames presupposes the explicit insertion of syntagmatic relations in WordNet and contributes to the effort directed to the enrichment of WordNet structures with multiple relations.

The obtained semantic and syntactic information will be analyzed both through corpus studies of the contexts in which the target verbs occur, as well as through manual evaluation by experts. Where necessary, the conceptual frames will be aligned with the data obtained from the corpus analysis and the conclusions of experts.

The presented research may contribute both to theoretical and contrastive linguistic studies and to the implementation of methods for syntactic parsing and semantic role labelling, important NLP tasks with applications in semantic analysis, word sense disambiguation, language understanding and generation and machine translation.

Conceptual frames offer opportunities for more precise (although still probabilistic) description of syntactic dependencies and semantics of frame elements. The integration of syntagmatic relations in WordNet structure will reveal the existing preferences in word compatibilities.

6 http://dcl.bas.bg/PWN_PDEV/

Acknowledgments

The studies published in this volume have been carried out as part of the projects: *Towards a Semantic Network Enriched with a Variety of Semantic Relations* funded by the National Science Fund of the Ministry of Education and Science of the Republic of Bulgaria under the Fundamental Scientific Research Program (Grant Agreement 10/3 of 14.12.2016) and *Enriching the Semantic Network WordNet with Conceptual Frames* funded by the National Science Fund of the Ministry of Education and Science of the Republic of Bulgaria under the Fundamental Scientific Research Program (Grant Agreement 49/13 of 30.11.2020).

References

Colin Baker, Charles J. Fillmore and John B. Lowe. 1998. The Berkeley FrameNet Project. *Proceedings of the 36th Annual Meeting of the Association for Computational Linguistics and 17th International Conference on Computational Linguistics*, Montreal, Canada, 10–14 August 1998:86–90.

Colin Baker and Josef Ruppenhofer. 2002. FrameNet's Frames vs. Levin's Verb Classes. Patrick Chew (ed.) *Proceedings of 28th Annual Meeting of the Berkeley Linguistics Society*:27–38.

Collin Baker and Christiane Fellbaum. 2009. WordNet and FrameNet as Complementary Resources for Annotation. *Proceedings of the Third Linguistic Annotation Workshop (ACL-IJCNLP'09)*, ACL, Stroudsburg, PA, USA:125–129.

Francis Bond, Piek Vossen, John McCrae and Christiane Fellbaum. 2016. CILI: The collaborative interlingual index. *Proceedings of the Eighth Global WordNet Conference*. Bucharest:50–57.

Claire Bonial, Julia Bonn, Kathryn Conger, Jena Hwang and Martha Palmer. 2014. PropBank: Semantics of New Predicate Types. *The 9th edition of the Language Resources and Evaluation Conference.* Reykjavik, Iceland:3013–3019.

Christiane Fellbaum. 1990/1993. English Verbs as a Semantic Net. *International Journal of Lexicography*, Volume 3, Issue 4, Winter 1990:278–301; reprinted in 1993:40–51.

Christiane Fellbaum. 1998. (Ed.). WordNet: An Electronic Lexical Database. Cambridge (MA): MIT Press.

Christiane Fellbaum. 2010. Harmonizing WordNet and FrameNet. *IceTAL*:2–3.

Christiane Fellbaum, Anne Osherson, and Peter E. Clark. 2007. Putting Semantics into WordNet's "Morphosemantic" Links. *Responding to Information Society Challenges: New Advances in Human Language Technologies*. Springer Lecture Notes in Informatics, vol. 5603:350–358. 2008.

Christiane Fellbaum and Colin Baker. 2008. Can WordNet and FrameNet be Made "Interoperable"? Jonathan Webster, Nancy Ide, and Alex Chengyu Fang. (Eds.) *Proceedings of the 1st International Conference on Global Interoperability for Language Resources*, Hong Kong, City University: 67–74.

Charles J. Fillmore. 1982. Frame semantics. *Linguistics in the Morning Calm*. Seoul: Hanshin:111–137.

Charles J. Fillmore and Collin Baker 2010. A frames approach to semantic analysis. *Oxford Handbook of Linguistic Analysis.* Oxford: Oxford University Press:313–341.

Andrea Di Fabio, Simone Conia and Roberto Navigli. 2019. VerbAtlas: a Novel LargeScale Verbal Semantic Resource and its Application to Semantic Role Labelling. *Proceedings of the 2019 Conference on Empirical Methods in Natural Language Processing and the 9th International Joint Conference on Natural Language Processing*, Hong Kong, China, November 3–7:627–637.

Peter Hanks. 2004. Corpus pattern analysis. Proceedings of the 11th EURALEX International Congress, (EURALEX 2004), Lorient, France, 6–10 July 2004:87–97.

Peter Hanks. 2012. How people use words to make meanings: Semantic types meet valencies. Alex Boulton and James Thomas (Eds.). *Input, Process and Product: Developments in Teaching and Language Corpora*. Brno: Masaryk University Press: 54–70.

Peter Hanks. 2013. *Lexical Analysis.* Cambridge (MA): MIT Press.

Christopher Johnson and Charles J. Fillmore. 2000. The FrameNet tagset for frame semantic and syntactic coding of predicate-argument structure. *Proceedings of the Applied Natural Language Processing Conference* (ANLP 2000):56–62.

Karin Kipper, Anna Korhonen, Neville Ryant and Marta Palmer. 2008. A Largescale Classification of English Verbs. *Language Resources and Evaluation*, 42(1):21–40.

Svetla Koeva. 2020. Semantic Relations and Conceptual Frames. Koeva, S. (ed.) *Towards a Semantic Network Enriched with a Variety of Semantic Relations*,.Professor Marin Drinov Publishing House of BAS:7–20.

Svetla Koeva, Tsvetana Dimitrova, Valentina Stefanova and Dimitar Hristov. 2018. Mapping WordNet Concepts with CPA Ontology. *Proceedings of the 9th Global WordNet Conference (GWC'2018).* Global WordNet Association, Singapore:70–77.

Svetla Koeva, Dimitar Hristov, Tsvetana Dimitrova, and Valentina Stefanova. 2019a. Enriching WordNet with Frame Semantics. *Proceedings of the International Annual Conference of the Institute for Bulgarian Language Prof. Lyubomir Andreychin*

(Sofia, 14th – 15th May 2019). Vanya Micheva, Diana Blagoeva, Siya Kolkovska, Tatyana Aleksandrova, Hristina Deykova (Eds.). Sofia: Prof. Marin Drinov Press of the Bulgarian Academy of Sciences:300–308.

Svetla Koeva, Tsvetana Dimitrova, Valentina Stefanova and Dimitar Hristov. 2019b. Towards Conceptual Frames. *Foreign Language Teaching*, 46, 6:551–564.

Anna Korhonen. 2002. Assigning Verbs to Semantic Classes via WordNet. *Proceed*ings of the 2002 Workshop on Building and Using Semantic Networks, vol. 11:1–7.

Egoitz Laparra and German Rigau. 2010. eXtended WordFrameNet. *Proceedings of the Seventh International Conference on Language Resources and Evaluation*, 17–3 May 2010, Valletta, Malta: 1214–1219.

Svetlozara Leseva and Ivelina Stoyanova. 2020. Beyond Lexical and Semantic Resources: Linking WordNet with FrameNet and Enhancing Synsets with Conceptual Frames. Svetla Koeva (Ed.). *Towards a Semantic Network Enriched with a Variety of Semantic Relations*. Sofia: Professor Marin Drinov Publishing House of BAS:21–48.

Svetlozara Leseva, Ivelina Stoyanova, Maria Todorova, and Hristina Kukova. Putting Pieces Together: Predicate-Argument Relations and Selectional Preferences. Svetla Koeva. (Ed.). *Towards a Semantic Network Enriched with a Variety of Semantic Relations*. Sofia: Professor Marin Drinov Publishing House of BAS:49–86.

George Miller. 1986. Dictionaries in the Mind. *Language and Cognitive Processes*, 1:171–185.

George Miller, R. Beckwith, Christiane Fellbaum, D. Gross, and K. J. Miller. 1990/1993. *Introduction to WordNet: An On-Line Lexical Database. International Journal of Lexicography*, 1990, 3(4), pp. 235–244; reprinted in 1993:1–9.

George Miller and Christiane Fellbaum. 1991. Semantic networks of English. *Cognition.* 41 (1-3): 197–229.

George Miller and Christiane Fellbaum. 2003. Morphosemantic links in Wordnet. *Traitement automatique des langues*, 44.2:69–80.

Roberto Navigli, Simone Ponzetto. 2012. BabelNet: The Automatic Construction, Evaluation and Application of a WideCoverage Multilingual Semantic Network. *Artificial Intelligence*, 193, Elsevier: 217–250.

Marta Palmer. 2009. Semlink: Linking PropBank, VerbNet and FrameNet. *Proceedings of the* 5th International Conference on Generative Approaches to the Lexicon, Pisa, Italy, 2009:9–15.

Marta Palmer, Daniel Gildea, Paul Kingsbury. 2005. The Proposition Bank: A Corpus Annotated with Semantic Roles. *Computational Linguistics Journal*, 31:1:71–106.

Marta Palmer, Claire Bonial, and Diana McCarthy. 2014. SemLink+: FrameNet, VerbNet and Event Ontologies. *Proceedings of Frame Semantics in NLP: A Workshop in Honor of Chuck Fillmore (1929–2014)*, Baltimore, USA, ACL:13–17.

Martha Palmer, Claire Bonial, Claire, and Jena D. Hwang. 2017. VerbNet: Capturing English verb behavior, meaning and usage. (Ed.) Susan Chipman. *The Oxford Handbook of Cognitive Science.* Oxford University Press.

Josef Ruppenhofer, Michael Ellsworth, Miriam R. L Petruck, Christopher R. Johnson, Collin F. Baker, and Jan Scheffczyk. 2016. *FrameNet II: Extended Theory and Practice.* <https://framenet.icsi.berkeley.e- du/fndrupal/the_book> [30.11.2020]

Lei Shi and Rada Mihalcea. 2005. Putting Pieces Together: Combining FrameNet, VerbNet and WordNet for Robust Semantic Parsing. Alexander Gelbukh, (Ed.). *Computational Linguistics and Intelligent Text Processing*. Lecture Notes in Computer Science, Springer, Berlin, Heidelberg, vol. 3406:100–111.

Veda Storey. 1993. Understanding Semantic Relationships. *The International Journal on Very Large Data Bases,* 2:455–488.

Fabian Suchanek, Gjergji Kasneci, and Gerhard Weikum. 2007. Yago – A Core of Semantic Knowledge. *Proceedings of the 16th International Conference on World Wide Web*, 16th International Conference on World Wide Web, Banff, Alberta, Canada, 8–12 May 2007:697–706.

Leonard Talmy. 1985. Lexicalization Patterns: Semantic Structure in Lexical Forms. Timothy Shopen (Ed.). *Language Typology and Syntactic Description*, vol. 3. Cambridge: Cambridge University Press:57–149.

Sara Tonelli and Daniele Pighin 2009. New Features for FrameNet – WordNet Mapping. *Proceedings of the Thirteenth Conference on Computational Natural Language Learning*, Boulder, USA:455–488.

Zdenka Urešová, Eva Fucíková, Eva Hajicová, and Jan Hajic. 2020. SynSemClass Linked Lexicon: Mapping Synonymy between Languages. *Proceedings of the Globalex Workshop on Linked Lexicography, Language Resources and Evaluation Conference* (LREC 2020), Marseille, 11–16 May 2020:10–19.

Ralph Weischedel, Eduard Hovy, Mitchell Marcus, Marta Palmer, Robert Belvin, Sameer Pradhan, Lance Ramshaw, and Nianwen Xue. 2011. Ontonotes: A large training corpus for enhanced processing. Olive, J., C. Caitlin, J. McCary (Eds.). *Handbook of Natural Language Processing and Machine Translation.* Springer:54–63.

OdeNet: Compiling a German Wordnet from other Resources

Melanie Siegel
Darmstadt University
of Applied Sciences
melanie.siegel@h-da.de

Francis Bond
School of Humanities
Nanyang Technological University
bond@ieee.org

Abstract

The Princeton WordNet for the English language has been used worldwide in NLP projects for many years. With the OMW initiative, wordnets for different languages of the world are being linked via identifiers. The parallel development and linking allows new multilingual application perspectives. The development of a wordnet for the German language is also in this context. To save development time, existing resources were combined and recompiled. The result was then evaluated and improved. In a relatively short time a resource was created that can be used in projects and continuously improved and extended.

1 Introduction

The goal of this initiative is to have a German resource in a multilingual wordnet initiative, where the concepts (synsets) of the languages are linked, and where the resources are under an open-source license, being included in the NLTK language processing package ((Bird et al., 2009)) via the Wn package ((Goodman and Bond, 2021)).

Wordnet resources are largely used in NLP projects all over the world. Our idea is to create a German resource that starts from a crowd-developed thesaurus; is open; and included in the NLTK package. Then it can be further developed by researchers while using the resource for their NLP projects.

For the first version, we combined existing resources: The OpenThesaurus German synonym lexicon,[1] the Open Multilingual Wordnet[2] (OMW: Bond and Foster, 2013) the English resource, the Princeton WordNet of English (PWN: Fellbaum, 1998)). The OMW data (Bond and Foster, 2013) was made by matching multiple linked wordnets to Wiktionary (Wikimedia, 2013) and the Unicode Common Locale Data Repository (Unicode, 2012). The OpenThesaurus is a large resource, generated and updated by the crowd. The PWN resource is a well-developed resource for English concepts. It includes many relations between the concepts and is linked to resources for multiple languages. The synsets from the OMW data have an estimated accuracy of 90%. We call our new resource "OdeNet", from "Offenes deutsches Wordnet - open German wordnet". The first version of OdeNet was automatically compiled. We also describe the efforts to extend and correct the entries.

[1] https://www.openthesaurus.de/

[2] http://compling.hss.ntu.edu.sg/omw/

2 Related Work

In the Open Multilingual Wordnet initiative (Bond and Paik, 2012; Bond et al., 2015), wordnets for several languages were developed and linked.

A manually well-designed wordnet resource for German is GermaNet (Hamp and Feldweg, 1997). GermaNet was developed over 20 years now and is very stable and precise. The problem is that it is not under an open-source license and is therefore not broadly used in language technology applications. Further, the restricted license makes it impossible to include GermaNet in the Open Multilingual Wordnet initiative. This is the reason why we decided to build up a new resource. In order not to violate the license terms, we do not use anything from GermaNet in OdeNet.

Vossen (1998, p11) describes two basic approaches to develop new wordnet resources: In the first case (**expand**), existing PWN synsets are taken and lexical entries added for the specific language. In the second case (**merge**), language-specific resources are built and then linked to the PWN.

An example of expand is the Japanese wordnet

(Isahara et al., 2008). It is based on translations of PWN to Japanese. The Japanese wordnet is not fully automatically built: most translations are manually checked. The authors found that there are differences between concept structures in English and Japanese, such that several synsets could not be translated.

The Russian wordnet (Alexeyevsky and Temchenko, 2016) is an example of the merge approach. It is based on a monolingual dictionary and the word definitions in these. The idea is that definitions contain hypernyms of the defined words, often in the form of WORD:HYPERNYM …, and that this information can be used to set up hierarchical structures in the wordnet.

The approach of the OdeNet initiative is merge. We use an existing synonym dictionary and try to link the synsets to PWN.

Braslavski et al. (2016) describe the creation of a large thesaurus for Russian by means of crowd sourcing. The data is directly collected in a wordnet style, but synsets are not linked to the OMW. The basic data for OdeNet is also generated in a crowd sourcing style, in the OpenThesaurus project. The OpenThesaurus project (Naber, 2004) is a crowd initiative to set up a German synonym lexicon. The version we downloaded in April 2017 has about 120,000 lexical entries in about 36,000 synsets.

2.1 German

The establishment of an ontology for the lexical information of a language requires an in-depth study of ambiguities and multi-word lexemes. In German, compounds are also an issue. There are many examples of lexical ambiguities in German, such as *Mutter* "mother, nut" or *umfahren* "bypass, to knock over". These are in many cases (especially in the case of homonyms) not parallel to English ambiguities, which makes the translation more difficult (for the purpose of linking in OMW). In most cases, ambiguities remain within a syntactic category (POS). The capitalization of German nouns prevents ambiguities between nouns and other syntactic categories, as is often the case in English (e.g. *change* "money" or "transform"). Morpho-syntactic ambiguities, which occur frequently in German, are not relevant for OdeNet because only lemmata are included. There are some words that can be used both as verbs and adjectives, such as *verlegen* "to place, to relocate, to publish - embarrassed". Other POS ambiguities are not relevant for this work because they refer to finer POS distributions than we can provide at the moment (particles - prepositions, demonstrative pronouns - articles).

In the area of multi-word lexemes we are concerned with support verb constructions, such as *Abschied nehmen* "to say goodbye" or *in Rechnung stellen* "to invoice". In addition, there are idioms such as *das geht auf keine Kuhhaut* "it beggars description". Especially for idioms it is difficult to automatically determine the syntactic category.

However, complex nouns are not realized - as in English - by means of multi-word expressions, but with compounds. Nominal compounds are very productive in German. They can be very long, like the well-known example *Donaudampfschifffahrtskapitänsmütze* "Danube steamship captain's cap". They can constantly be newly created. Automatic extraction and analysis from text data is complex because there are ambiguities here too.

In the case of regular German compounds, there is a hyponymy relationship between the head and the compound. For example, *Wassereis* is an ice that consists of water, while *Eiswasser* is water that is ice-cold. Different relations can exist to the modifier. The regularity of the hyponymy relationship to the head of German compounds is used to add relations to OdeNet.

3 Process of Creating OdeNet

The first version of OdeNet was completely automatically created by compilation from OpenThesaurus. In the following, manual corrections were made in the domains of project management and business reports. German definitions were introduced, relations were corrected and supplemented and CILI links (links to the multilingual concepts in OMW) were added. Then we worked on the syntactic categories. The main focus was on correcting the POS tags of multi-word lexemes.The next step was the annotation of basic German words[3]. We annotated all lexical entries (except for function words) of this list with

```
dc:type="basic_German"
```

We then added missing entries and corrected synsets manually. Then, we implemented an anal-

[3]as listed in http://pcai056.informatik.uni-leipzig.de/downloads/etc/legacy/Papers/top1000de.txt

ysis of German nominal compounds and used this information for the addition of hypernym relations.

3.1 Linking OpenThesaurus Synsets with the Multilingual Wordnet

The OpenThesaurus data can be downloaded as txt. The text file contains one synset per line, such that the lexical items in each synset are divided by semicolons, e.g.:

```
Mobilität;Unabhängigkeit;Beweglichkeit
```

The target of the transfer process of this synset is to have three lexical entries and a synset entry. The format is described in Bond et al. (2016). We start with the synset:

```
<Synset id="de-9784-n"
  ili="i62097"
  partOfSpeech="n"
  dc:description="the quality of moving
                          freely">
  <SynsetRelation
                targets='odenet-23172-n'
                relType='hypernym'/>
</Synset>
```

The synset has a unique synset ID, a link to the international wordnet IDs in "ili", a POS, a definition, and relations to other synsets.

The first task is to find POS information. POS information is not included in the OpenThesaurus download data. We use the Python library TextBlob for POS annotation.[4] OdeNet just uses "n", "v" and "a" as POS tags, such that we map the Penn Treebank POS tags that TextBlob gives to these. In the case of multi-word expressions, such as *moralische Werte* "ethical values", we take the POS value of the last word in the expression, which is the head word in most cases.

The second task is to find an English synset that can be linked. We translate the words in the synset to English using google-translate.[5] Using a statistical machine translation system instead of a dictionary has the advantage that the translation is based on the context. In case of ambiguous words, the decision is context-based, with the context being the other words in the synset. Using the NLTK wordnet API, we then search for synsets with these English words in the PWN and access their synset ID.

[4]https://textblob.readthedocs.io/en/dev/

[5]https://translate.google.de/

```
(id="de-39-n",pwn="in-05890249-n"),
```

We could link 19,845 German synsets to synsets in the PWN, about 55 % of the German synsets. Synsets that could not be linked were often multi-word expressions and metaphorical, such as: *es kann Gott weiß was passieren; für nichts garantieren können; mit allem rechnen müssen* "God knows what can happen; can't guarantee anything; have to count on everything". The link gives direct access to the definition in PWN, such that we could copy these into OdeNet in `dc:description`. Thus, we have an English definition as long as German definitions are still missing. The synset relations in PWN link to English synsets. We searched for German synsets with the `ili` that links to the target of a relation in the PWN and added these as targets.

3.2 Lexical Entries and Senses

These are the lexical entries for the words in the synset above:

```
<LexicalEntry id="w39185">
    <Lemma writtenForm="Mobilität"
         partOfSpeech="n"/>
        <Sense id="w39185_9784-n"
            synset="odenet-9784-n">
        </Sense>
</LexicalEntry>

<LexicalEntry id="w33556">
    <Lemma writtenForm="Beweglichkeit"
                partOfSpeech="n"/>
        <Sense id="w33556_8203-n"
              synset="odenet-8203-n"/>
        <Sense id="w33556_9784-n"
               synset="odenet-9784-n"/>
        <Sense id="w33556_11420-n"
             synset="odenet-11420-n"/>
         <Sense id="w33556_19087-n"
              synset="odenet-19087-n"/>
</LexicalEntry>

<LexicalEntry id="w35624">
    <Lemma writtenForm="Unabhängigkeit"
                  partOfSpeech="n"/>
        <Sense id="w35624_8795-n"
               synset="odenet-8795-n"/>
        <Sense id="w35624_9784-n"
               synset="odenet-9784-n"/>
        <Sense id="w35624_28976-n"
              synset="odenet-28976-n"/>
</LexicalEntry>
```

The lexical entries in a synset belong to one sense with the same sense ID. Further senses for lexical entries come from other synsets in the OpenThesaurus. Each lexical entry has a unique word ID, a lemma, and a part of speech (POS).

When a synset gets its ID and link to PWN, all words in the synset are added to a tuple with this ID, as for example:

```
("Beweglichkeit",
"odenet-8203-n", "in-05003850-n"),
("Beweglichkeit",
"odenet-9784-n", "in-04773351-n"),
("Beweglichkeit",
"odenet-11420-n", "in-04875728-n"),
("Backlogged",
"odenet-19087-n", "in-05003850-n"),
```

The sense relations (antonym and pertainym) again are taken from the PWN and linked back to German.

4 Corrections and Extensions

4.1 POS Corrections

In a first evaluation, we found that POS information in OdeNet was only correct in 77% of the cases. With many multi word expressions in OdeNet, standard procedures to POS assignment do not seem to be sufficient. The basic idea for corrections was that a synset should in principle contain only lexical items of the same syntactic category. Therefore, we extracted all synsets containing lexical items with different POS information and manually corrected them. The evaluation showed an increase of correct POS to 90%. The next idea was to look at endings of lexemes. In German, words ending in *-ung*, *-heit*, and *-keit* are always nouns, while words ending in *-lich* are adjectives. Further, nouns are capitalized. We used this information to automatically correct further POS assignments. The evaluation showed an increase of correct POS to 93.3%.

4.2 Using German Compounds for Hypernym Relations

Regular German nominal compounds have a hypernym relation to their head, as explained above. A large part of the German compounds are regular and many synsets contain compounds. We decided to make use of these facts in order to add relations to OdeNet.

The idea is to use the regularity of German compounds to automatically generate hypernym relations for OdeNet. For this purpose, we have implemented a compound analysis tool that recognizes the head of the compound. Using this tool, we then analyzed all lexical items that are not multi-word expressions in OdeNet and extracted compounds and their heads.

Basis for the compound analysis is a list of nouns extracted from the TIGER tree bank (Brants et al., 2004). If the word to analyze consists of less than three letters, it is not a compound. If there are hyphens in the word (such as *Lehr-Lern-Forschung*, teaching-learning-research), the compound is split at these.

Using the pyphen module,[6] we split the compound into syllables. If the word to analyze consists only of one syllable (as in the case of *Stuhl* "chair"), it is not a compound. If the word consists of two noun components with one syllable each, as in the case of *Haustür* "front door", then both components are searched for in the TIGER lexicon. If they exist as entries, then the result of the analysis is a list with both components, such as *([Haus],[Tür])*. If the two syllables do not exist as words, then an attempt is made to delete a linking element from the first syllable and then look it up again. This is e.g. the case with *Wirtshaus* "pub", consisting of *Wirt* + *s* + *Haus*. If there are more than two syllables, different combinations of syllables are tested, as in the case of *Herstellungskosten* "production costs", until it can be split into parts that can be found in the noun list:

```
("Herstellungskosten")
SYLLABLES:
 ['Her', 'stel', 'lungs', 'kos', 'ten']
SYLLABLE COMBINATIONS:
  ['Herstel', 'Stellungs', 'Lungskos',
  'Kosten', 'Herstellungs',
  'Stellungskos', 'Lungskosten',
  'Herstellungskos', 'Stellungskosten']
COMPONENTS:
 ['Herstellungs', 'Kosten']
```

If the analysis with syllables does not lead to a result, we look up all combinations of n-grams in the word, considering fugen elements.

We ran our compound analyzer on all lexical entries that are not multiword entries and could identify 3,630 compounds. In case that the head has a singular sense in OdeNet, we added a hypernym relation to that synset and a hyponym relation backwards. Using synsets instead of lexical entries results in relations not only between single words, but also between groups of words. For example, because of the analysis of the word *Butterbrot* "sandwich" as consisting of *Butter* "butter" and *Brot* "bread", we added a hyponym relation between the synsets 11770-n ['Brotlaib', 'Wecken', 'Brot'] and 10073-

[6] https://pyphen.org/

n ['Knifte', 'belegtes Brot', 'Scheibe', 'Butterbrot', 'Schnitte', 'Bemme', 'Stulle'].

There are some exceptions to the hypernym relation of compound and compound head. In some cases, the compound is synonym to its head, as in the case of *Fachterminus* "technical term" and *Terminus* "term". In these cases, both appear in the same synset and could therefore be automatically excluded.

More complicated are negations in compounds. A *Nichtraucher* "non-smoker" is not hyponym to *Raucher* "smoker", but antonym. On the other hand, *Nichteisenmetall* "non-ferrous metal" is a kind of *Metall* "metal". Thus, we manually checked all compounds with negations. Another problem are expressions with *Pseudo* "pseudo" or *Schein* "phantom". Is a pseudo-documentation a documentation? Is a *Scheinschwangerschaft* "phantom pregnancy" a pregnancy? We decided to not treat these as hyponyms. The compound analysis found 19,115 nominal compounds in OdeNet. In 12,132 cases, the found head was ambiguous between multiple senses and did not get a relation entry. In 1,810 cases, there was no entry for the head in OdeNet, such that these were also ignored.

For all hypernym relations that we added, we added the backward hyponym relation as well. 10,346 relations were added to the OdeNet synsets by this method. OdeNet contains around 35,000 synsets, such that we could add information for 29% of all synsets.

For the evaluation we randomly extracted 100 compounds from OdeNet. The compound analysis found 83 of these. Only one of the 83 analyzed compounds got a wrong analysis: *Blockdiagramm* (block diagram) was analyzed as ['Block', 'Dia', 'Gramm'] (block - slide - grams). This analysis is syntactically fine, but semantically nonsense. Thus, the precision of the compound analysis is very high (0.99), while the recall is moderate (0.83). For our purpose, extending OdeNet, precision is highly important, while a moderate recall is fine.

The 100 entries had 41 hypernym relation entries that originated from compound analyses. One of the relation entries was wrong: in the case of *Fleischsaft* "meat juice", the compound analysis was correct (['Fleisch', 'Saft']), but the hypernym relation led to the synset ['Strom', 'Saft', 'Elektrizität'] (electricity). The German word *Saft* is ambiguous between *juice* and *electricity*, but

Synset relation	Number
hypernym relations	9,907
hyponym relations	10,101
member holonyms	84
part holonyms	647
member meronyms	74
part meronyms	282

Table 1: Number of synset relations

had only the electricity entry in OdeNet, which is wrong. If there was more than one sense for a word, there was no hypernym relation added to avoid such errors.

Therefore, for 100 synsets that had compounds, we could add 40 good hypernym relations by this method, and one wrong relation, which is a precision of 98%.

5 Current State of OdeNet

The resulting wordnet resource (v1.3) contains about 120,000 lexical entries in about 36,000 synsets. About 20,000 of these synsets are linked to synsets in the English PWN and then to the multilingual CILI numbers. There are 2,664 antonym relations and 1,053 pertainym relations linking lexical entities. The number of synset relations can be seen in table 1.

For evaluation of preciseness, we randomly chose 90 lexical entries, 30 with POS "n", "v" and "a" respectively, and evaluated them manually, see Table 2.

The **POS information** was correct in 93.3% of the cases. In 5 cases of 6 wrong POS assignments, the lemma was a multi-word lexeme, such as *nicht unumstößlich* "not unalterable". POS tagging of multi-word lexemes needs more sophisticated procedures than the ones we used here, as standard POS taggers do not tag multi-word expressions. A good part of this problem could be solved with POS corrections in synsets that had lexical items with different POS. The linked English synsets could also give a hint that there might be a problem, as they have POS assigned, which often would be the same for German. A further attempt to improve OdeNet could therefore be to search for cases where the synsets are linked and the POS tags of the English and German synsets do not match.

The German synsets that are linked to English ones, contain the **definitions** from the correspond-

Tested	Correct	Comment
POS	93%	many multi-word lexemes
DEFINITIONS	82%	in cases of errors, POS of the English words are often different
RELATIONS	61%	in cases of errors, definitions are also wrong

Table 2: Precision of 90 randomly chosen lexical entries

ing English synsets. We checked if the definitions are correct (and therefore the synsets are correctly linked). 55 of the 90 cases had a link to an English synset, and therefore a definition. In 45 of the 55 cases (82%), these definitions were correct.

There were 41 cases, where **relations** on the lexical or the synset level were assigned (34%). 12 of these cases had wrongly assigned relations (39%). In 5 of these cases, the link to PWN was also wrong, and the relation was taken over from the English synset. In one case, the relation from the English synset was wrong, while the relation that was automatically added by the compound analysis was correct. The next correction step will have to address the linking.

We have annotated the entries with a default confidence of **0.6**, with entries that have been manually validated given a confidence of **1.0** and those from the extended OMW a confidence of **0.85**.

Release

The wordnet is released through GitHub, as a compressed tar file containing the wordnet itself, its license (CC-BY-SA 4.0)[7] and canonical citation.[8] This can be loaded directly into the Wn Python library (Goodman and Bond, 2021), which allows easy use: either on its own or linked to other wordnets through CILI.

6 Discussion and Future Plans

It has been possible to set up a wordnet for the German language in a couple of years. We have benefited both from OpenThesaurus and the knowledge in the OMW. In this way, we were able to build a very large resource, with the synsets being created manually in the OpenThesaurus project, and therefore very precise. We have used NLP techniques to add more information, namely POS and the relations to OMW and CILI. We have used the knowledge in the OMW to supplement relations between the German synsets - parallel to the relations in the other wordnets.

The Open Multilingual Wordnet initiative is a great chance to get highly linked and standardized language resources for multiple languages. The standardization makes it possible to include these resources in NLP packages, such as NLTK or spaCy.

We have shown that it is possible using NLP techniques to combine language resources such as the OpenThesaurus and the English PWN to gain a new resource in this standardized multilingual context, with a reasonable precision.

The next step will be to further work on the quality of OdeNet. We have already started to implement methods that allow the semi-manual correction and extension:

- A tool for adding more hyponym relations in case of compounds that shows the user different synsets for a compound head and asks which one to set the relation to. It then adds the relation to OdeNet automatically.
- A tool that shows the user all information for a word and gives her multiple possibilities to correct and extend it.
- A tool that allows to search for a word in PWN and give the corresponding CILI(s) and allows the user to add the CILI to OdeNet.

Further, it will again be compared to the English PWN, such that cases where linked synsets differ in their POS assignment will be further investigated. Another source of problems is multiword lexemes, where we will have to search for better POS tagging methods.

A problem is that the automatic translation method added links of CILIs from multiple German synsets, which is undesirable. We need to focus on better linking quality. One approach could be to look at the cases where the POS of German and English differs.

We started to work on the basic German words, adding and correcting information. This will be

[7] https://creativecommons.org/licenses/by-sa/4.0/

[8] https://github.com/hdaSprachtechnologie/odenet/releases/tag/v1.3

a valuable information source for simplified language projects.

Through the Wn library (Goodman and Bond, 2021) the resource will be available to NLTK, such that it can be used in NLP projects. The open-source idea will help to let researchers working on German language further improve and expand OdeNet. We ourselves plan to use it in information extraction in the business domain and sentiment analysis projects. By this approach, we will add synsets from the business domain and sentiment polarity for many words.

We will add a user interface to make crowd development possible, in order to extend and correct OdeNet.

We would also like to tag some German texts.

The resource is available on GitHub under an open-source license: `https://github.com/hdaSprachtechnologie/odenet`.

Acknowledgments

We would like to thank Michael Wayne Goodman for his help in preparing the GitHub release.

References

Daniil Alexeyevsky and Anastasiya V. Temchenko. 2016. WSD in monolingual dictionaries for Russian WordNet. In *Proceedings of the Eighth Global WordNet Conference*. Bucharest, Romania.

Steven Bird, Ewan Klein, and Edward Loper. 2009. *Natural language processing with Python: Analyzing text with the natural language toolkit*. O'Reilly Media, Inc., Beijing.

Francis Bond, Luis Morgado Da Costa, and Tuan Anh Le. 2015. Imi—a multilingual semantic annotation environment. *Proceedings of ACL-IJCNLP 2015 System Demonstrations*, pages 7–12.

Francis Bond and Ryan Foster. 2013. Linking and extending an open multilingual wordnet. In *Proceedings of the 51st Annual Meeting of the Association for Computational Linguistics*, pages 1352–1362. Sofia. URL `http://aclweb.org/anthology/P13-1133`.

Francis Bond and Kyonghee Paik. 2012. A survey of wordnets and their licenses. *Small*, 8(4):5.

Francis Bond, Piek Vossen, John P McCrae, and Christiane Fellbaum. 2016. CILI: The Collaborative Interlingual Index. In *Proceedings of the Global WordNet Conference*, volume 2016.

S. Brants, S. Dipper, P. Eisenberg, S. Hansen-Schirra, E. König, W. Lezius, C. Rohrer, G. Smith, and H. Uszkoreit. 2004. TIGER: Linguistic interpretation of a German corpus. *Research on language and computation*, 2(4):597–620.

P. Braslavski, D. Ustalov, M.l Mukhin, and Y. Kiselev. 2016. Yarn: Spinning-in-progress. In *Proceedings of the 8th Global WordNet Conference, GWC 2016*, pages 58–65.

Christiane Fellbaum, editor. 1998. *WordNet: An Electronic Lexical Database*. MIT Press, Cambridge, MA.

Michael Wayne Goodman and Francis Bond. 2021. Intrinsically interlingual: The Wn Python library for wordnets. In *11th International Global Wordnet Conference (GWC2021)*. (to appear).

B. Hamp and H. Feldweg. 1997. GermaNet - a lexical-semantic net for German. In *Proceedings of ACL workshop Automatic Information Extraction and Building of Lexical Semantic Resources for NLP Applications*. Madrid.

Hitoshi Isahara, Francis Bond, Kiyotaka Uchimoto, Masao Utiyama, and Kyoko Kanzaki. 2008. Development of the Japanese wordnet. In *Sixth International conference on Language Resources and Evaluation (LREC 2008)*. Marrakech.

Daniel Naber. 2004. Openthesaurus: Building a thesaurus with a web community. *Retrieved January*, 3:2005. URL `https://www.openthesaurus.de/download/openthesaurus.pdf`.

Inc. Unicode. 2012. Unicode, inc. license agreement - data files and software. URL `http://www.unicode.org/copyright.html`.

Piek Vossen, editor. 1998. *Euro WordNet*. Kluwer.

Wikimedia. 2013. List of wiktionaries. (accessed on 2013-09-12).

Comparing Similarity of Words Based on Psychosemantic Experiment and RuWordNet

Valery Solovyev
Kazan Federal University,
Kazan, Russia,
maki.solovyev@mail.ru

Natalia Loukachevitch
Lomonosov Moscow State University,
Moscow, Russia,
louk_nat@mail.ru

Abstract

In the paper we compare the structure of the Russian language thesaurus RuWordNet with the data of a psychosemantic experiment to identify semantically close words. The aim of the study is to find out to what extent the structure of RuWordNet corresponds to the intuitive ideas of native speakers about the semantic proximity of words. The respondents were asked to list synonyms to a given word. As a result of the experiment, we found that the respondents mainly mentioned not only synonyms but words that are in paradigmatic relations with the stimuli. The words of the mental sphere were chosen for the experiment. In 95% of cases, the words characterized in the experiment as semantically close were also close according to the thesaurus. In other cases, additions to the thesaurus were proposed.

1 Introduction

Semantic proximity of words is an important parameter required in various tasks of natural language processing. It can be estimated in different ways: by corpus, using distributional methods (Mikolov 2013, Bojanowski et al., 2017), expert assessments; from psychosemantic experiments; using thesauri such as WordNet (Fellbaum, 1998).

The general concept of *semantic similarity* can be subdivided to paradigmatic (taxonomical) similarity and semantic associations (Agirre et al., 2009; Hill et al., 2015; Kliegr and Zamazal, 2018; Majewska et al., 2020). Paradigmatic similarity can be defined in terms of shared superordinate category or shared semantic features. Semantic associations correspond to co-occurrence (syntagmatic relations) in texts.

To study automatic methods of word similarity calculation, specialized datasets are created. Some researchers try to create datasets distinguishing different subtypes of semantic similarity of words, which requires additional efforts and guidelines. Agirre et al. (2009) subdivided the existing semantic word dataset WordSim353 (Finkelstein et al., 2002) into two subsets: WordSim353-similarity and WordSim353-relatedness datasets. SimLex-999 guidelines (Hill et al., 2015) aim to distinguish word pairs in taxonomical semantic similarity relation (synonyms, hypernyms, hy ponyms) from remaining types of relations (antonymy, co-hyponyms). The authors of WIN353 dataset (Kliegr and Zamazal, 2018) ask respondents about word similarity based on word interchangeability in sentences.

We can also try to use human scores of word semantic similarity to assess the quality of descriptions in electronic lexical-semantic resources (thesauri). Such resources are built on the basis of synsets – sets of synonyms – linked by semantic relations such as hyponymy, hypernymy, antonymy, and some others. The automatic use of thesauri requires high quality descriptions of semantic senses and semantic relations between them.

In this paper, we compare the results of a survey of respondents and the similarity of words according to the RuWordNet thesaurus (Loukachevitch et al., 2018) for the Russian language. Currently, the published RuWordNet version comprises about 110 thousand Russian words and expressions. A new version of RuWordNet is being prepared and RuWordNet data are tested from different points of view.

In the psychosemantic experiment the respondents were asked to list synonyms for stimuli words without any guidelines. We found that their answers mainly contain paradigmatically similar words, practically without words related via any other similarity relationships, which makes it possible to check the taxonomic structure of the thesaurus.

The paper is structured as follows. Section 2 provides information on related work. Section 3 describes a psychosemantic experiment to determine the semantic proximity of words. Section 4 analyzes the data obtained. Section 5 discusses the results of the experiment.

2 Related work

The paper concerns two directions of studies: revision and updating existing lexical-semantic resources for natural language processing (thesauri) and studies on relation types exploited by native speakers in word association experiments.

2.1 Revision of Existing Lexical Semantic Resources

Procedures for revising and verifying resources are important for the developers of WordNet-like resources. Some ontological tools have been proposed to check the consistency of relationships in WordNet (Guarino and Welty, 2004; Alvez et al., 2018). Rambousek et al. (2018) considered a crowdsourcing tool allowing a user of the Czech wordnet to report errors. Users may propose an update of any data value. These suggestions can be approved or rejected by editors. Visualization tools can also help to find problems in wordnets (Piasecki et al. 2013; Johannsen et al. 2011). Cristea et al. (2004) and Rudnicka et al. (2012) reported on the revision of mistakes and inconsistencies in their wordnets in the process of linking the wordnet and the English WordNet.

McCrae et al. (2019) discussed a new project: Open-Source WordNet for English, which is based on the Princeton WordNet. This project has already fixed errors found in the current version of WordNet, including spelling mistakes in definitions and examples. Some problematic issues were reported (for example, synset duplicates, missed or incorrect relationships) for further revision.

Recently, verification and enrichment methods have been systematically developed for the RuWordNet thesaurus. In (Loukachevitch, 2019), the following method for enriching the RuWordNet thesaurus was proposed. For a large text corpus, words are searched for which 20 words closest in the corpus (based on the standard method for evaluating the semantic similarity of words) are located far from each other in the thesaurus. The distance between words in the thesaurus is the length of the shortest path between them in the graph of semantic relations. For found words with such properties, the reasons for such discrepancy are analyzed. The analysis of the data presented in (Loukachevitch, 2019) was continued in (Bayrasheva, 2019).

In work (Soloviev et al., 2020), RuWordNet synsets were compared with synonymous sets according to published 10 dictionaries of Russian synonyms. The work (Erofeeva et al., 2020) presents the results of an experiment in which the respondents were asked to list synonyms for a given word. The results are compared with the RuWordNet synsets. Usmanova et al. (2020) analyzed pairs of quasi-synonyms and the distance between them in RuWordNet. It was expected that quasi-synonyms, as semantically close words, should be located at a short distance in the thesaurus.

The general result of above-mentioned studies of RuWordNet is as follows. RuWordNet data, including the composition of synsets and the structure of semantic relations, correlate well with all the other considered sources of information about semantically close words. At the same time, a number of gaps in RuWordNet were identified, taking into account of which allows improving descriptions in the thesaurus. This article continues research in this direction.

2.2 Lexical relations in associations experiments

One of the most known associative experiments for Russian was organized by Karaulov in 1986-1997 (Karaulov et al., 2002). In experiments such demographic information such as age, gender, specialization, and location was also considered and recorded. Currently, these data are considered as outdated.

Many researchers classify word associations into syntagmatic and paradigmatic relations (Fitzpatrick, 2006). The researchers study the structure of associations for language learners (Fitzpatrick, 2006), patients (Arias-Trejo et al., 2018), children (Wojcik and Kandhadai, 2019), and other social groups.

Vylomova et al. (2018) study types of relations in associative responses of Russian native speakers in dependence on socio-demographic characteristics. They organized associative experiments in various Russian regions, including Siberia and the Urals. The age of participants ranged from 16 to 26, most of them were university students of approximately 50 specialties. In their analysis, Vylomova et al. (2018) classified the lexical relations in associations to syntagmatic (they calculated word co-occurrences in a text corpus) and paradigmatic (according to RuWordNet thesaurus). The authors found that men more frequently list paradigmatic associations whereas women are more likely to produce syntagmatic associations. It was also revealed that most students of technical specializations and natural sciences demonstrate high scores for paradigmatic association types.

Sinopalnikova (2004) studies approaches to extract useful lexical relations from existing word association thesauri to assist in developing new wordnets.

3 Experiment Setting

In the current study we present the results of a psychosemantic experiment, carried out in accordance with the methodology described in (Petrenko, 2010). The experiment reveals semantically close words (synonyms) as seen by native speakers. In (Erofeeva et al., 2020) only synonyms from the RuWordNet synsets were considered, in this work all semantic relations are involved.

The experiment is as follows. The respondents (Russian native speakers) receive a number of words, and they have to list synonyms for these words in a limited time. The respondents are students (18-23 years old, 200 people) of Kazan Federal University (Kazan, Russia). About half of the students are philologists, the second half are non-philological students. The definition of a synonym is not explained to the respondents; we rely on intuitive understanding of synonyms by native speakers. For the experiment, words related to the mental sphere are selected. This semantic area is the most difficult for clear differentiation of synonym sets and their semantic relations.

The results of philologists and non-philologists differ insignificantly. However, it is worth noting that synonyms for word *мечта* (mechta – dream as imaginative thoughts) listed by philologists and non-philologists have interesting distinctions. So, for philologists, the word *фантазия* (fantasia – fantasy) is in 3rd place, and for non-philologists, the word *стремление* (stremleniye – aspiration) is in the 3rd position. Conversely, for philologists, *stremlenie* (aspiration) is listed in the 5th place, and for non-philologists, *fantasia* (fantasy) is in the 4th position. It seems that the figurative thinking of philologists, the reading and study of fiction, which form their linguistic personalities, are reflected in the results of the experiment: for them, the word *mechta* (dream) is associated with fantasy and dreams, that is, with something unreal, ephemeral. Not-philologists are more pragmatic: the third position in their lists is occupied by the word *stremlenie* (aspiration), in the semantics of which the presentation of concrete results is conveyed (Erofeeva et al., 2020).

Further we will write Cyrillic Russian words in Latin transcription.

Since the respondents, naturally, did not use the criteria of synonymy, such as interchangeability in different contexts and did not have much time to complete the task, they suggested words that have something semantically in common with the given word, but not necessarily synonyms in the strict sense of the term. For example, for the word *mechta* (dream as imaginative thoughts), the following words were listed as synonyms in RuWordNet: *gresa, mechtaniye, fantasia* (fantasy). The respondents most often indicated the following words: *zhelaniye* (desire), *tsel'* (goal), *fantasia* (fantasy), *gresa, stremleniye* (aspiration), *nadezhda* (hope). Only two of them are synonymous. The rest of the words – *zhelaniye* (desire), *tsel'* (goal), *stremleniye* (aspiration), *nadezhda* (hope) – at first glance may seem like associations with the given word dream. However, this assumption is not true.

In the Karaulov's dictionary of Russian associations (Karaulov et al., 2002), the word *mechta* (dream) has the following most frequent associations: *goluboy* (blue), *zhizn'* (life), *moya* (mine), *sbylas'* (come true), *idiota* (idiot), *nesbytochnaya* (unrealizable), *rozovaya* (pink). The words *zhelaniye* (desire), *stremleniye* (aspiration), *nadezda* (hope) are not mentioned as associations at all, and the word *tsel'* (goal) is mentioned only once in 101 responses. We can see that in fact words having syntagmatic relations with the original one are also mentioned as associations by respondents. In the current experiment, the respondents indicated words that were not in syntagmatic but in paradigmatic relations with the stimulus. Rather, they can be characterized as belonging to the semantic field of the original word or as its analogues.

It is worth noting that in the dictionary (Apresian, 2004) the words *namereniye* (intention) and *mysl'* (thought) are considered as analogues (near-synonyms) of the word *mechta* (dream) (its synonyms are not given in the dictionary). For the verb *mechtat'* (to dream), the synonyms, according to (Apresyan, 2004), are *khotet'* (to want), *zhelat'* (to desire), and the analogue is the word *nadeyat'sya* (to hope). Thus, the words indicated by the respondents are close in meaning to the word *mechta* (dream). Our experiment can be characterized as aimed at identifying paradigmatic associations, while the Karaulov's dictionary (Karaulov et al., 2002) in fact mixes paradygmatic and syntagmatic associations.

4 Analysis of Results

In this work, the associations for the words *obida* (offense, as a feeling caused being offended), *radost'* (joy), *talant* (talent), *strast'* (passion), *lyubov'* (love), *mysl'* (thought), *vostorg* (delight) are considered. For each stimulus word, six most frequently mentioned responses are studied.

***Обида* (offense feeling)**. The informants most often indicated the words: *ogorcheniye* (grief), *dosada* (annoyance), *bol'* (pain), *grust'* (sadness), *razocharovaniye* (disappointment), zlost' (anger). The first of them is interpreted in RuWordNet as a hypernym for *obida.* The word *grust'* (sadness) in RuWordNet also has a direct connection with *obida* – it is a hypernym-hypernym for *obida. Dosada* (annoyance) is a co-hyponym for *obida,* having the common hypernym *nedovol'stvo* (discontent).

There is also a short path between the words *obida* and *razocharovaniye* (disappointment): *obida* (offense) – *nedovol'stvo* (discontent) – *dushevnoye perezhivaniye* (emotional experience) – *razocharovaniye* (disappointment). There is a similar path between the words *obida* (offense) and *razocharovaniye* (disappointment): offense – discontent – emotional experience – disappoitment. Finally, the path between the words *bol'* (pain) and *obida* is only slightly longer: pain – suffering – emotional experience – discontent – offense. Semantic distances of 4 steps or less are treated in (Loukachevitch, 2019) as short. All semantic relations are hypo-hypernymic.

***Radost'* (joy)**. For this word, respondents indicate the following word associations: *schast'ye* (happiness), *vostorg* (delight), *vesel'ye* (fun), *ulybka* (smile), *likovaniye* (exultation), *udovol'stviye* (pleasure).

The words *veseliye* (fun), *likovaniye* (exultation), *udovol'stviye* (pleasure) are hyponyms in relation to *radost'* (joy). The words *vostorg* (delight) and *schast'ye* (happiness) are co-hyponyms with *radost'* (joy) with a common hypernym – *dushevnoye perezhivaniye* (emotional experience). But between the words *radost'* (joy) and *ulybka* (smile) there is only a very long way: *radost'* (joy) – *dushevnoye perezhivaniye* (emotional experience) – *mental'nyy ob"yekt* (mental object) – *abstraktnaya sushchnost'* (abstract entity) – *kachestvo* (quality) – *vneshnost'* (appearance) – *vyrazheniye litsa* (facial expression) – *ulybka* (smile). Such a long path reflects the fact that in RuWordNet the word *ulybka* (smile) is interpreted only as a facial expression and, accordingly, *radost'* (joy) and *ulybka* (smile) in RuWordNet refer to different spheres — the mental world and the physical.

Princeton WordNet presents the point of view that a person smiles to communicate something to others about his condition (to change one's facial expression by spreading the lips, often to signal pleasure[1]) and thus it is classified as communication. Still, it should be noted that a person can smile at own thoughts, pleasant memories while alone with yourself, i.e. a smile is also possible outside the communication situation. As we can see, the situation here is very difficult. According to the Russian explanatory dictionary (Ozhegov and Shvedova, 1997), *ulybka* (smile) has the following definition: "mimic movement of the face, lips, eyes, showing disposition to laughter, expressing pleasure or ridicule and other feelings (translation from Russian)". This definition takes into account both facial expressions and communicative intentions.

It is possible to take into account the intuition of native speakers and the dual nature of a smile by making certain changes to the thesaurus. It can be described with the entailment relationship between concepts *ulybat'sya* (to smile) and *radovat'sya* (to joy). If a person smiles, then usually this person is really happy, or at least seeks to show happiness to others. Conversely, if a person is really happy about something, then this manifests itself in a smile.

Talant (talent). For this word, the respondents indicate the following synonymous words: *sposobnost'* (ability), *dar* (gift), *umeniye* (skill), *darovanie, odarenost'* (giftedness), *talent, geniy* (genius). In RuWordNet *darovaniye* (giftedness),

[1] http://wordnetweb.princeton.edu/perl/webwn

дар (gift), are listed as synonyms to the word *talant* (talent). *Sposobnost'* (ability) is a hypernym for *prirodnaya sposobnost'* (natural ability), which is a hypernym for *talant* (talent). *Umeniye* (skill) is a co-hyponym with *talant* (talent) through the general hypernym *prirodnaya sposobnost'* (natural ability). *Odarennost'* (giftedness) is a hyponym in relation to *sposobnost'* (ability), i.e. is at distance 3 from the word *talant* (talent). The word *geniy* (genius) is a hyponym to *odarennost'* (giftedness), at a distance 4 from the word *talant* (talent).

***Strast'* (passion)**. For the word *strast'* (passion), the respondents indicate the synonymous words: *zhelaniye* (desire), *vlecheniye* (attraction), *любовь* (love), *uvlecheniye* (infatuation), *pokhot'* (lust), *интерес* (interest). In RuWordNet, *uvlecheniye* (infatuation) is a hypernym for *strast'* (passion). The word *interes* (interest) is a hypernym of the hypernym for the word *strast'*(passion). The words *vlecheniye* (attraction), *zhelanie* (desire), *lyubov'* (love) are co-hyponyms with the word *uvlecheniye* (infatuation) with a common hypernym, *dushevnoye perezhivaniye* (emotional experience), i.e. are at a distance of 3 from *strast'* (passion). The word *pokhot'* (lust) is a hyponym in relation to *vlecheniye* (attraction), i.e. is at a distance of 4 from the initial word *strast'* (passion).

The scheme of semantic relations in this group of words can be represented in Fig. 1. This is a typical scheme for the student answers in the experiment. The arrows show links from hypernyms to hyponyms.

***Lyubov'* (love)**. For this word, the respondents indicated such words as *privyazannost' (attachment), vlyublennost'*(falling in love), *sympatia* (sympathy), *nezhnost'*(tenderness), *vlecheniye* (attraction).

We saw above that *lyubov'* (love) is at a distance of 3 from *strast'* (passion) and 2 from *vlecheniye* (attraction). *Privyazannost' (attachment))* is a hypernym for *lyubov'* (love). The words *lyubov'* (love) and *vlyublennost'* (falling in love) are co-hyponyms with a common hypernym *dushevnoye perezhivaniye* (emotional experience). The word *sympatia* (sympathy) is a co-hyponym with word *vlyublennost'* (falling in love) through a hypernym *lichnostnyye otnosheniya* (personal relationships). Thus, between the words *sympatia* (sympathy) and *lyubov'* (love) there is a distance of length 4. But *nezhnost'* (tenderness) is interpreted in RuWordNet only as a character trait (two other senses: *nezhnost'* 1 (soft, gentle to the touch), *nezhnost'* 3 (fragile, too weak) are not here discussed as irrelevant), and not as mental experience and there is no close way between them.

In fact, in RuWordNet one of the senses of the word *nezhnost'* (tenderness) is missing. In the dictionary (Ozhegov and Shvedova, 1997), *nezhnost'* (tenderness) refers to the word *nezhnyi* (tender), which is interpreted (in this sense) as "affectionate, full of love: tender feelings". According to the dictionary (Apresian, 2004) "*nezhnyi* (tender) – showing a feeling of love or affection in communication with a person."

Thus, in the interpretation of this word, the word *lyubov'* (love) invariably appears, indicating the correctness of the students' assessment. Therefore, it is recommended to add a new sense of the word *nezhnost'* (tenderness) in RuWordNet, in accordance with the above-mentioned dictionary definitions.

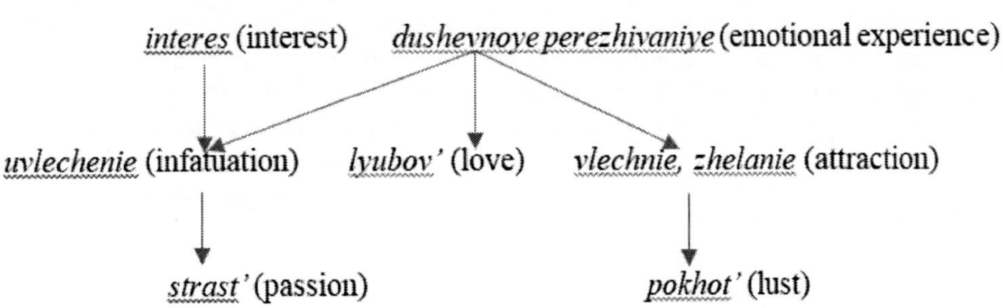

Fig1. Scheme of semantic relations of words-reactions to the stimulus *strast'* (passion)

Vostorg (delight). Respondents indicate the following words: *radost'* (joy), *voskhishcheniye* (admiration), *udivleniye* (surprise), *schast'ye* (happiness), *likovaniye* (jubilation), *voodushevleniye* (inspiration).

In RuWorNet, *vostorg* (delight) and *voskhishcheniye* (admiration) are synonyms, *schast'ye* (happiness), *udivleniye* (surprise) and *radost'* (joy) are co-hyponyms with *vostorg* (delight) with the common hypernym *dushevnoye perezhivaniye* (emotional experience). Word *likovaniye* (jubilation), as noted above, is a hyponym in relation to *radost'* (joy), i.e. is at a distance of 3 from *vostorg* (delight). *Voodushevleniye* (inspiration) is a co-hypernym with the word *radost'* (joy) with the common hyponym *euphoria*, i.e. is at a distance of 4 from *vostorg* (delight).

***Mysl'* (thought)**. Respondents indicate the following words: *ideya* (idea), *duma* (thought), *mneniye* (opinion), *dogadka* (guess), *soobrazheniye* (consideration), *suzhdeniye* (judgment).

Words *soobrazheniye* (consideration) and *duma* (thought) are synonymous with *mysl'* (thought). *Ideya* (idea) is a hyponym for *mysl'* (thought), *suzhdeniye* (judgment) is a hypernym for *mysl'* (thought). *Mneniye* (opinion) is a co-hyponym with *mysl'* (thought) via common hypernym *suzhdeniye* (judgment).

Between the words *mysl'* (thought) and *dogadka* (guess) there is a path of length 4: *mysl'* (thought) – *suzhdeniye* (judgment) – *mneniye* (opinion) – *dopushcheniye* (assumption) – *dogadka* (guess).

5 Discussion

We analyzed 40 word pairs (out of a total of 7x6 = 42 pairs, two pairs were repeated). In 38 cases (95%), word pairs listed by the respondents as synonyms are also close according to the thesaurus descriptions: 13 pairs are at a distance of 1; 12 pairs are at a distance of 2; 7 pairs are at a distance of 3; 6 pairs are at a distance of 4. The number of mentioned words located at a certain path distance in the thesaurus decreases monotonically with increasing distance. In all these cases, it turned out to be sufficient to consider only hypo-hypernymic relations. In two cases, it is necessary to make certain changes in the thesaurus to obtain smaller distance for semantically close words. These pairs of words are as follows: *lyubov'* (love) – *nezhnost'* (tenderness) and *radost'* (joy) – *ulybka* (smile). In the first case, it is proposed to add a new sense of the word *neznost'* (tenderness) to the thesaurus and to establish the necessary additional relation of hyponymy, in the second case we suggest to add the relation of entailment.

Thus, most words frequently mentioned by respondents are located close to the stimulus word in RuWordNet, which indicates good consistency of the thesaurus with the intuition of native speakers. At the same time, taking into account the data of a psychosemantic experiment makes it possible to identify some problem areas in the thesaurus. Let us consider whether there is a correlation between the frequency with which the response word is chosen by the respondents and the distance in the thesaurus from the stimulus word to the response word. We sort words-reactions according to the frequency of their mention.

Table 1 summarizes the data, sorted by the frequency of the words in the respondents' answers. The asterisk indicates the distances that will take place after the implementation of the above-mentioned suggestions for improving the thesaurus structure. We can see that the words mentioned more often are at a shorter distance from the stimulus word in the thesaurus, which is also a good confirmation of the correct structure of the thesaurus and the adequacy of the experiment.

6 Conclusion

Thesauri are created by professionals who rely on both the theory of language and their ideas about the semantics of linguistic units. However, semantics are not described in the literature in as much detail as required by the thesaurus developers. Taking this into account, it is of natural interest to compare thesaurus data with the linguistic intuition of native speakers, manifested in psychosemantic experiments.

Stimulus word	Obida (offense)	Radost' (joy)	Talant (talent)	Strast' (passion)	Lyubov' (love)	Mysl' (thought)	Vostorg (delight)	Average
Words in the 1st places of the respondents' associations								
Frequency (%)	24	49	55.5	43.5	26	61.5	48.5	40.3
Relation dist.	1	2	2	3	1	1	2	1.7
Words in the 2nd places of the respondents' associations								
Frequency (%)	19	34.5	44.5	28.5	24.5	28.5	39.5	31.3
Relation dist.	3	2	1	3	4	1	1	2.1
Words in the 3d places of the respondents' associations								
Frequency (%)	16	32	30	17.5	22	12.5	29.5	22.7
Relation dist.	2	1	2	3	2	2	2	2.0
Words in the 4th places of the respondents' associations								
Frequency (%)	14	12	14	12.5	20.5	11	13.5	13.9
Relation dist.	4	1	3	1	3	1	2	2.1
Words in the 5th places of the respondents' associations								
Frequency (%)	13.5	10.5	13	11.5	18	10.5	12.5	12.7
Relation dist.	3	3*	4	2	2	1	3	2.6
Words in the 6th places of the respondents' associations								
Frequency (%)	13	7	11.5	9.5	14.5	9	8.5	10.4
Relation dist.	2	1	1	4	2*	4	4	2.6

Table 1. Positions, frequencies (percentage of answers) and RuWordNet distances of word associations. The sign *) means distances after the suggested corrections.

Most words frequently mentioned by respondents or synonyms with the stimulus word or are located close to it in RuWordNet, which indicates good consistency of the thesaurus with the intuition of native speakers. This confirms the high quality of the RuWordNet thesaurus. The experimental results also support the choice of distance 4 as a measure of the semantic proximity of words in the thesaurus. At the same time, taking into account the experimental data made it possible to identify some problem areas in the thesaurus.

Acknowledgments
This research was financially supported by RFBR, grants № 18-00-01238 and № 18-00-01226 as parts of complex project № 18-00-01240 (K).

References

Agirre, E., Alfonseca, E., Hall, K., Kravalova, J., Pasca, M.,and Soroa, A. 2009. A study on similarity and relatedness using distributional and WordNet-based approaches. In *Proceedings of NAACL-HLT*: 19–27.

Alvez, J., Gonzalez-Dios, I., and Rigau, G. 2018. Cross-checking WordNet and SUMO using meronymy. 2018. *Proceedings of the Eleventh International Conference on Language Resources and Evaluation (LREC-2018).*

Apresian, I.D. *New explanatory dictionary of Russian synonyms.* Moscow, Vena: Iazyki slavianskoi kul'tury, 2004. (in Russian)

Arias-Trejo, N., Minto-García, A., Luna-Umanzor, D. I., Ríos-Ponce, A. E., Mariana, B. P., and Bel-Enguix, G. 2018. Word-word relations in Dementia and typical aging. In *Proceedings of the first international workshop on language cognition and computational models*:85-93.

Bayrasheva, V. 2019. Corpus-based vs thesaurus-based word similarities: expert verification. *The XXth International Scientific Conference "Cognitive Modeling in Linguistics"*. Proceedings:56-63.

Bojanowski, P., Grave, E., Joulin, A., and Mikolov, T. 2017. Enriching word vectors with subword informa-tion.Transactions of the ACL, 5:135–146.

Cristea, D., Mihaila, C., Forascu, Trandabat, D., Husarciuc, M., Haja, G., and Postolache, O. 2004. Mapping Princeton WordNet synsets onto Romanian WordNet synsets. *Romanian Journal of Information Science and Technology*, 7(1-2):125-145.

Erofeeva, I., Solovyev, V., and Bayrasheva, V. 2020. Psychosemantic experiment as a tool for objectifying data on the ways of representing synonymy in modern Russian language. *Bulletin of the Volgograd State University*. Series 2: Linguistics. 2020. - T. 19, No. 1:178–194 (in Russian).

Fellbaum, Ch. 1998. *WordNet: An electronic lexical database*. MIT Press. 1998.

Finkelstein, L., Gabrilovich, E., Matias, Y., Rivlin, E., Solan,Z., Wolfman, G., and Ruppin, E. 2002. Placing searchin context: The concept revisited. *ACM Transactions on Information Systems*, 20(1):116–131.

Fitzpatrick, Tess. 2006. "Habits and rabbits: Word associations and the L2 lexicon." *EuroSLA Yearbook* 6.1 (2006):121-145.

Guarino, N., and Welty, Ch. 2004. An overview of OntoClean. *Handbook on ontologies*. Springer, Berlin, Heidelberg:151-171.

Hill, F., Reichart, R., and Korhonen, A. 2015. SimLex-999: Evaluating semantic models with (genuine) similarity estimation. *Computational Linguistics*, 41(4):665–695.

Johannsen, A. and Pedersen, B. 2011. Andre ord"–a wordnet browser for the Danish wordnet, DanNet." *Proceedings of the 18th Nordic Conference of Computational Linguistics (NODALIDA 2011)*.

Karaulov, Yu.N., G.A. Cherkasova, N.V. Ufimtseva, Yu.A. Sorokin, E.F., and Tarasov. 2002 *Russian associative dictionary*. In 2 volumes. M.: AST-Astrel, 2002. 784 p. (in Russian)

Kliegr T., and Zamazal O. 2018. Antonyms are similar: Towards paradigmatic association approach to rating similarity in SimLex-999 and WordSim-353. *Data & Knowledge Engineering*. V. 115:174-193.

Loukachevitch N., Lashevich G., and Dobrov B. 2018. Comparing Two Thesaurus Representations for Russian. *Proceedings of Global WordNet Conference GWC-2018*:35-44.

Loukachevitch, N. 2019. Corpus-based Check-up for Thesaurus. *Proc. of the 57th Annual Meeting of the Association for Computational Linguistics ACL-2019*: 5773-5779.

Majewska, O., McCarthy, D., van den Bosch, J., Kriegeskorte, N., Vulić, I., and Korhonen, A. 2020. Spatial Multi-Arrangement for Clustering and Multi-way Similarity Dataset Construction. In *Proceedings of The 12th Language Resources and Evaluation Conference*: 5749-5758.

McCrae, J., Rademaker, A., Bond, F., Rudnicka, E., and Fellbaum, Ch. 2019. English WordNet. An Open Source WordNet for English. In *Proceedings of Global WordNet Conference GWC-2019*.

Mikolov, T., Chen, K., Corrado, G. S., and Dean, J. (2013). Efficient estimation of word representations in vectorspace.CoRR, abs/1301.3781.

Ozhegov, S.I. and Shvedova, N.Yu. 1997. *Explanatory Dictionary of the Russian Language*. Russian Academy of Sciences. Institute of the Russian Language named after V.V. Vinogradov. - 4th ed., Add. - M .: Azbukovnik,. (in Russian).

Petrenko, V.F. 2010. *Fundamentals of psychosemantics*. M .: Eksmo. (in Russian)

Piasecki, M., Marcińczuk, M., and Maziarz, M. 2013. WordNetLoom: a WordNet development system integrating form-based and graph-based perspectives. *International Journal of Data Mining, Modelling and Management*, 5(3) :210-232.

Rudnicka, E., Maziarz, M., Piasecki, M., and Szpakowicz, S. 2012. A strategy of Mapping Polish WordNet onto Princeton WordNet. In *Proceedings of COLING 2012* :1039-1048.

Sinopalnikova, A. 2004. Word association thesaurus as a resource for building wordnet. *Proceedings of the 2nd International WordNet Conference*: 199-205.

Soloviev, V., Gimaletdinova, G., Khalitova, L., and Usmanova, L. 2020. Expert Assessment of Synonymic Rows in RuWordNet. *Proc. of Analysis of Images, Social Networks and Texts AIST-2020 cnference*. CCIS, vol. 1086:174-183.

Usmanova, L, Erofeeva, I., Solovyev, V., and V. Bochkarev. 2020. Analysis of the Semantic Distance of Words in the RuWordNet Thesaurus. 2020. *Proceedings of the DAMDID/RCDL'2020 Conference*.

Vylomova, E., Shcherbakov, A., Philippovich, Y., and Cherkasova, G. 2018. Men Are from Mars, Women Are from Venus: Evaluation and Modelling of Verbal Associations. In: *Analysis of Images, Social Networks and Texts. AIST 2017*. Lecture Notes in Computer Science, vol 10716. Springer, Cham:106-115.

Wojcik, E. H., and P. Kandhadai. 2019. Paradigmatic associations and individual variability in early lexical–semantic networks: Evidence from a free association task. *Developmental Psychology*. 56(1):53-69.

Text Document Clustering: Wordnet vs. TF-IDF vs. Word Embeddings

Michał Marcińczuk♣, Mateusz Gniewkowski♣, Tomasz Walkowiak♣, Marcin Będkowski♢

♣ Wrocław University of Science and Technology, Poland
{michal.marcinczuk,mateusz.gniewkowski,tomasz.walkowiak}@pwr.edu.pl

♢ University of Warsaw, Poland
mbedkowski@uw.edu.pl

Abstract

In the paper, we deal with the problem of unsupervised text document clustering for the Polish language. Our goal is to compare the modern approaches based on language modeling (doc2vec and BERT) with the classical ones, i.e., TF-IDF and wordnet-based. The experiments are conducted on three datasets containing qualification descriptions. The experiments' results showed that wordnet-based similarity measures could compete and even outperform modern embedding-based approaches.

1 Introduction

The aim of the paper is to evaluate different semantic distance calculation methods using clusterization by the Agglomerative Clustering method regarding qualifications collected in the Integrated Qualifications Register (IQR). It is a Polish public register supporting the Integrated Qualifications System (IQS) and regulated by the Act of 22 December 2015 on the Integrated Qualifications System. The IQR enables broad access to qualifications functioning in the national education system and enhances its transparency, as well as encourages the development of lifelong learning (IBE, 2020, p. 50).

As a repository of information about qualifications, the IQR does not meet the definition of Big Data — at least not yet — but still, it can benefit from the use of natural language processing methods allowing the calculation of similarity of documents and their clustering. The project entitled "Operating and Developing the Integrated Qualifications Register" financed by the European Social Fund aims at developing several applications supporting citizens in their career decisions and policy-makers in their strategic choices.

The main problem was how to compare and find similar qualifications from different sources, e.g., higher education (HE) diplomas and vocational education and training (VET) certificates, and group them in meaningful and interpretable clusters.

At the beginning of our work, we aimed at exploring content-based semantic similarity of qualifications, so we relied mostly on unsupervised clustering methods. Eventually, we covered both unsupervised and supervised techniques. We evaluated traditional methods and modern ones, as we wanted to test several approaches regarding their efficiency, interpretability, and feasibility. Here, we will present part of our work dealing with unsupervised methods.

2 Datasets

The dataset covers several thousand documents containing descriptions of qualifications (out of a total number of about 10000 qualifications included in the IQS and IQR). These descriptions mainly consist of so-called learning outcomes statements (LOs), which characterize the knowledge, skills, and attitudes required to obtain a given qualification. LOs can be broken down into three main components: an action verb, a skill object, and a context of the performance demonstration, e.g., "(Person) creates documents using word processing software".

Learning-outcomes-based qualifications framework is intended to "provide a common language allowing different stakeholders in education and training, as well as the labor market and society at large, to clarify skills needs and to respond to these in a relevant way" (Cedefop, 2017, p. 26). It is assumed that LOs allow for comparison of qualifications across the sector, institutional, and national borders, which was why we started with a content-based semantic similarity of qualifications and clustering techniques.

Qualification name	Category	Label
Web application and database development and administration	market qualification	IT
Computer graphics design	market qualification	IT
IT technician	VET qualification	IT
Programming, development and administration of websites and databases	VET qualification	IT
Computer science	HE diploma	IT
Game and virtual space design	HE diploma	IT
Dental technician	VET qualification	Medicine
Veterinary technician	VET qualification	Medicine
Psychooncologist	market qualification	Medicine
Supplying stores with mass-produced medical products	market qualification	Medicine
Medical rescue	HE diploma	Medicine
Medicine	HE diploma	Medicine

Table 1: Sample clusters of qualifications

Dataset name	Documents	Tokens/doc	Labels
PPKZ	633	539–17810	13
Market	362	48–888	18
Higher education	2029	29–11355	21
ALL	3024	29–17810	36

Table 2: Datasets used in the experiments

The IQR is a source of information about qualifications functioning in the IQS. However, it does not contain descriptions and learning outcomes for some qualifications, especially HE diplomas. This information is available on university and government websites, usually in PDF files. To obtain the data, we used web-scraping and OCR techniques. As a result, the IQR data has been complemented by about 2000 descriptions.

In the experiment, we used four manually labeled datasets (see Table 2). The labels denote the sectors to which the qualifications belong (see Table 1).

3 Text Similarity

3.1 Wordnet

The literature describes several metrics used to calculate the semantic similarity between two words based on their position in the wordnet structure. Here are the more known metrics:

- shortest path — the similarity is computed based on the shortest path between synsets. The similarity is in the range of 0 to 1, where 1 represents words identity;
- Leacock-Chodorow (Leacock and Chodorow, 1998) — the similarity is computed based on the shortest path between synsets and synsets' depth in the wordnet structure;
- Lin (Lin, 1998) — the similarity is computed based on *Least Common Subsumer (LCS) and* Information Content (IC). LCS is the most specific ancestor node, and IC is a measure of synset specificity (higher values are associated with more specific concepts, and lower values are more general). The similarity is in the range of 0 to 1, where 1 represents words identity;
- Wu-Palmer (Wu and Palmer, 1994) — it is a specific case of Lin measure, where the information content is the same for each synset;
- Jiang-Conrath (Jiang and Conrath, 1997), Resnik (Resnik, 1995) — other metrics which also utilize *Least Common Subsumer and* Information Content.

Budanitsky and Hirst (2006) showed that Lin metric obtained the highest correlation with human intuition. Because Polish wordnet does not contain information content, thus we could not use this metric directly. We decided to utilize the Wu-Palmer metric as it is a specific case of Lin, which does not require information content. We-Palmer metric is calculated according to Formula 1. In the formula, $depth$ is the length of the shortest path from the synset to the wordnet root.

The similarity between documents is computed according to Formula 2 (Mihalcea et al., 2006). In the formula, T_1, T_2 represent sets of synsets for the documents, and $maxSim(w, T_2)$ is the highest similarity value for a synset $w \in T_1$ and any synset from T_2. Since the clustering algorithm requires a distance matrix, we converted the similarity measure using Formula 3 (the similarity from Formula 2 is within the range 0 to 1)

In the experiments, we used Słowosieć 3.2 (Maziarz et al., 2016) (a wordnet for Polish) and

$$wu - palmer(s_1, s_2) = 2 * \frac{depth(LCS(s_1, s_2))}{depth(s_1) + depth(s_2)} \quad (1)$$

$$sim(T_1, T_2) = \frac{1}{2} * \left(\frac{\sum_{w \in T_1} (maxSim(w, T_2) * idf(w))}{\sum_{w \in T_1} idf(w)} + \frac{\sum_{w \in T_2} (maxSim(w, T_1) * idf(w))}{\sum_{w \in T_2} idf(w)} \right) \quad (2)$$

$$distance = 1 - sim \quad (3)$$

WoSeDon (Janz et al., 2018) — a tool for word sense disambiguation. To calculate the document similarity we used the *wnsim* tool[1].

3.2 TF-IDF

The most classical method for building a vector representation of texts is a bag of words. This approach's key assumption is that the text can be expressed using an unordered set of frequencies of words (terms) in text. The number of selected features (words) can be often reduced by transforming the words into their generic form (stemming, lemmatization). The text frequency (TF) representation is very often modified by the Inverted Document Frequency (Salton and Buckley, 1988) (IDF), giving a TF-IDF representation of texts. In performed experiments, we have used a tagger for Polish to lemmatize the text and TF-IDF representation of lemma 1-, 2-, and 3-grams.

3.3 Language Models

Language modeling is a modern approach to text analysis based on the assumption that individual words or even whole sentences can be represented by high-dimensional feature vectors. It is based on the hypothesis that relationships (distances) between vector representations of words or sentences can be related to semantic similarities of words/sentences. The models are built on large text corpora by observing the co-occurrence of words in similar contexts.

3.3.1 doc2vec

One of the most popular techniques of language modeling, *word2vec*, is based on neural networks (Le and Mikolov, 2014). In the so-called skip-gram approach, the aim is to predict context words from a given word. In the classical word2vec (Le and Mikolov, 2014) technique, each word (form from the text) is represented by a distinct vector, which might be a problem for a language with large vocabularies and rich inflection like Polish is. In (Bojanowski et al., 2017) authors extend the skip-gram model by building a vector representation of character n-grams and constructing the word representation as a sum of the character n-grams embeddings (for n-grams appearing in the word). It allows generating word embeddings for words not seen in the training corpus. In performed experiments, we used pre-trained vectors for Polish language (Kocoń and Gawor, 2019)[2]. Since texts differ in document length, the feature vectors representing a document were gained by averaging vector representations of individual words. This approach is known as doc2vec (Le and Mikolov, 2014).

3.3.2 BERT

The newest approaches to language modeling are inspired by deep-learning algorithms and context-aware methods. The state of the art is BERT (Devlin et al., 2018). Due to its bidirectional representation, jointly built on both the left and the right context, BERT looks at the whole sentence before assigning an embedding to each word in it. Therefore, the embeddings are context-aware. In performed experiments, we used a BERT model for Polish: Polbert[3]. The model is capable of analyzing up to 512 subwords. Therefore longer texts were cut. As a feature vector, we have used the first (with index zero) token from the last Transformer layer.

3.4 Document similarity

The TF-IDF, doc2vec, and BERT methods represent documents as vectors in multi-dimensional space. Most of the clustering methods are distance- or similarity-based. Therefore we need

[1] `https://github.com/CLARIN-PL/wnsim`

[2] `http://hdl.handle.net/11321/606`

[3] `https://huggingface.co/dkleczek/bert-base-polish-cased-v1`

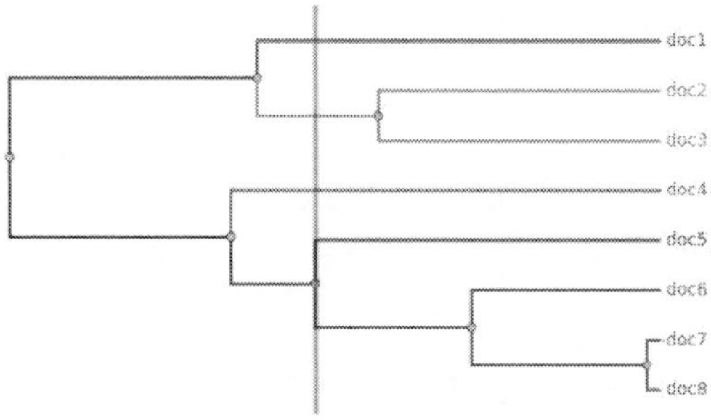

Figure 1: Example dendrogram (5 clusters)

Symbol	Description
X, Y	set of classes/clusters
H	entropy
MI	mutual information
NMI	normalized mutual information
AMI	adjusted mutual information
x_i, y_i	*i*-th element of *X*/*Y* (class or cluster)
$P(x_i), P(y_i)$	probability of the document being in *i*-th class or cluster
$P(x_i \hat{y}_j)$	intersection of $P(x_i)$ and $P(y_j)$
$E(MI)$	expected value of MI

Table 3: Symbols description

to calculate the distance between vector-based representations of documents. We used popularly in natural language processing problems a cosine distance. It works well with sparse high-dimensional space (like TF-IDF is), and it is less noisy than Euclidean distance (Kriegel H-P., 2012). Moreover, it does not distinguish proportional vectors, which is often a desirable feature for word embedding.

4 Clustering Method

In our work, we decided to use the Agglomerative Clustering algorithm (Day and Edelsbrunner, 1984). The method iteratively joins samples into subgroups basing on a linkage criterion (in this case, an average distance).

The obtained dendrograms allowed us to determine the set of flat clusters for each different threshold defined by the joining points. A sample dendrogram with a fixed threshold is shown in Figure 1.

5 Quality Metrics

To evaluate the results, we decided to use *Adjusted Mutual Information* (Hubert and Arabie, 1985) score that allows comparison between two different clusterings. We may have used another measure (such as the Adjusted Rand Index), but according to Romano et al. (2016), AMI is the better choice because it performs well for unbalanced datasets. The score was calculated between the ground truth labels and all sets of labels obtained from the clustering algorithm.

Adjusted mutual information score is one of the information-theoretically based measures. It is based on mutual information (MI), which comes naturally from entropy.

$$H(X) = \sum_i P(x_i) \log \frac{1}{P(x_i)}$$

$$MI(X, Y) = \sum_i \sum_j P(x_i \cap y_j) \log \frac{P(x_i \cap y_j)}{P(x_i)P(y_i)}$$

The problem with mutual information is that the maximum is reached not only when labels from one set (clusters) match perfectly those from the other (classes), but also when they are further subdivided. The simple solution for that is to normalize MI by mean of entropy of X and Y:

$$NMI(X, Y) = \frac{MI(X, Y)}{(H(X) + H(Y))/2}$$

Normalized mutual information can be further improved ("corrected for a chance") by subtracting the expected value of MI from nominator and denominator:

$$AMI(X, Y) = \frac{MI(X, Y) - E(MI)}{(H(X) + H(Y)/2 - E(MI)}$$

6 Evaluation

6.1 Configuration

For word2vec, TF-IDF, and Wu-Palmer methods, we used four variants with a different subset of words:

- *allposes* — all words, i.e., nouns, verbs and adjectives,
- *noun*, *verb* and *adj* — only nouns, verbs and adjective were used, respectively.

6.2 Results

For all four datasets, the BERT method obtained significantly lower results than the other methods (see Figure 2). The problem might be related to

Method	ALL			PPKZ			Market			Higher education		
	n	AMI	rank	n	AMI	rank	n	AMI	rank	n	AMI	rank
bert	179	0.360		50	0.095		104	0.344		370	0.287	
doc2vec-allposes	375	0.508	3	36	0.390	3	82	0.498	3	154	0.449	
doc2vec-verb	512	0.333		106	0.262		85	0.293		570	0.275	
doc2vec-adj	358	0.494		51	0.386	4	68	0.392		94	0.464	3
doc2vec-noun	414	0.474		75	0.343		80	0.476		128	0.438	
tfidf-allposes	81	0.497		65	0.333		24	**0.550**	1	39	0.418	
tfidf-verb	139	0.430		90	0.302		47	0.379		193	0.353	
tfidf-adj	73	0.529	2	90	0.289		37	0.460		22	**0.507**	1
tfidf-noun	106	0.501	4	65	0.317		25	0.505	2	46	0.435	
wupalmer-allposes	258	0.488		37	**0.452**	1	69	0.496	4	203	0.458	4
wupalmer-verb	208	0.321		183	0.213		156	0.217		584	0.259	
wupalmer-adj	207	**0.536**	1	36	0.441	2	63	0.398		57	0.499	2
wupalmer-noun	503	0.454		43	0.386		75	0.470		275	0.398	

Table 4: Summary of AMI scores for all dataset and method variants. The table contains the highest value of MRI score and the number of groups for which the score was obtained.

how the vector representing a document is generated — only the first 512 subwords are taken. At the same time, the documents are much longer, and some information is lost. However, experiments on supervised classification (which are not discussed herein) using the same BERT model (Polbert plus classification layer, working on the first 512 subwords) show that BERT tuned on a downstream task gives better results than doc2vec, and TF-IDF approaches. This, as well as results reported by Walkowiak and Gniewkowski (2019), could suggest that document features generated directly from the BERT language model (without retraining on a downstream task) are not suitable for the document to document similarity analysis.

In Table 4, we presented the highest AMI scores obtained for each method and dataset. For the ALL dataset, the highest scores were obtained by Wu-Palmer and TF-IDF, both using adjectives only. The AMI values were 0.536 and 0.529, respectively. A slightly lower result was obtained by doc2vec using all words — AMI value of 0.508.

For two out of three datasets, the best score was obtained by the TF-IDF. For the Market dataset, the advantage over any other method was significant and came to 0.05 points. In turn, for the Higher education dataset, the advantage over Wu-Palmer was lower than 0.01 points. For PPKZ, the Wu-Palmer method obtained the highest score, and the advantage over other methods was significant — 0.6 points (see Figure 3).

We also observed that for all methods based solely on verbs, the scores were significantly lower by 0.1–0.2 than for adjectives and nouns. For the ALL, PPKZ, and Higher education datasets the top scores were obtained on adjectives solely. The advantages over nouns and verbs were significant. Figure 4 presents the difference between Wu-Palmer variants on the ALL dataset.

6.3 Performance

We measured the computation time for two stages separately:

- document preprocessing (pre) — morphological tagging and word-sense disambiguation (for Wu-Palmer only). For preprocessing, we used CLARIN-PL web services[4] (Walkowiak, 2018) — a MorphoDita tagger (Walentynowicz, 2017) and WoSeDon (Janz et al., 2018) — a WSD tool.
- similarity computing (sim) — time required to generate the distance matrix on a single CPU thread.

Method	Pre	Sim	Total
doc2vec	2.0	3.6	5.6
TF-IDF	2.0	24.5	26.5
Wu-Palmer	7.0	563.0	570.0
BERT	2.0	1234.0	1236.0

Table 5: Processing times (in minutes) for different methods for the ALL dataset.

In Table 5, we present times required to process the ALL dataset. The fastest was doc2vec, which required only less than 6 minutes to process 3024 documents. TF-IDF was five times slower and required ca. 26 minutes. Wu-Palmer was 100 times slower than doc2vec, and BERT was 200 times slower.

[4] https://ws.clarin-pl.eu/wsd.shtml

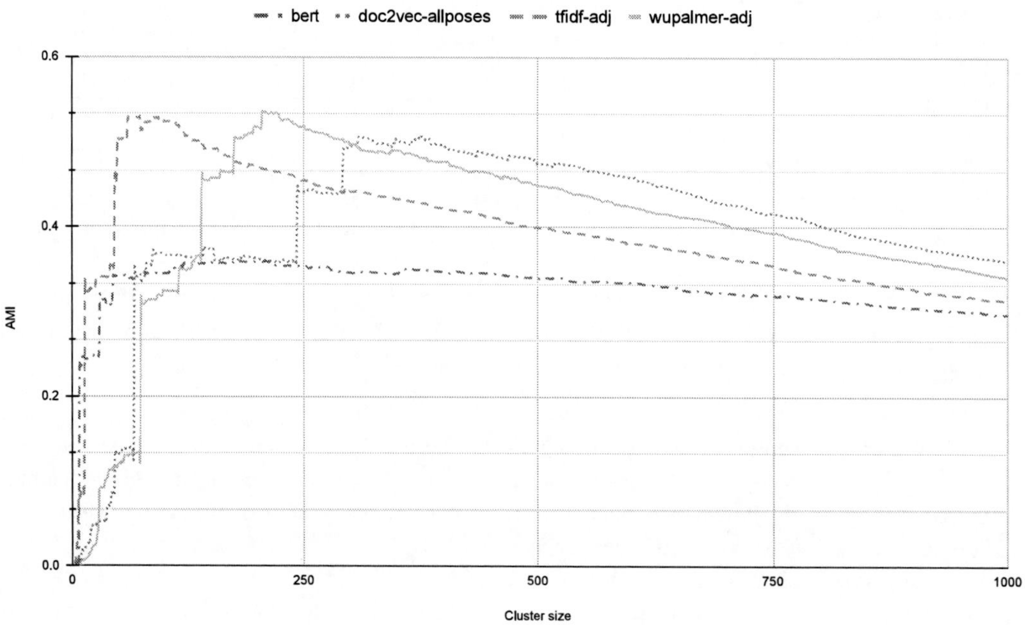

Figure 2: AMI values for the best-performing variants for each method on the ALL dataset.

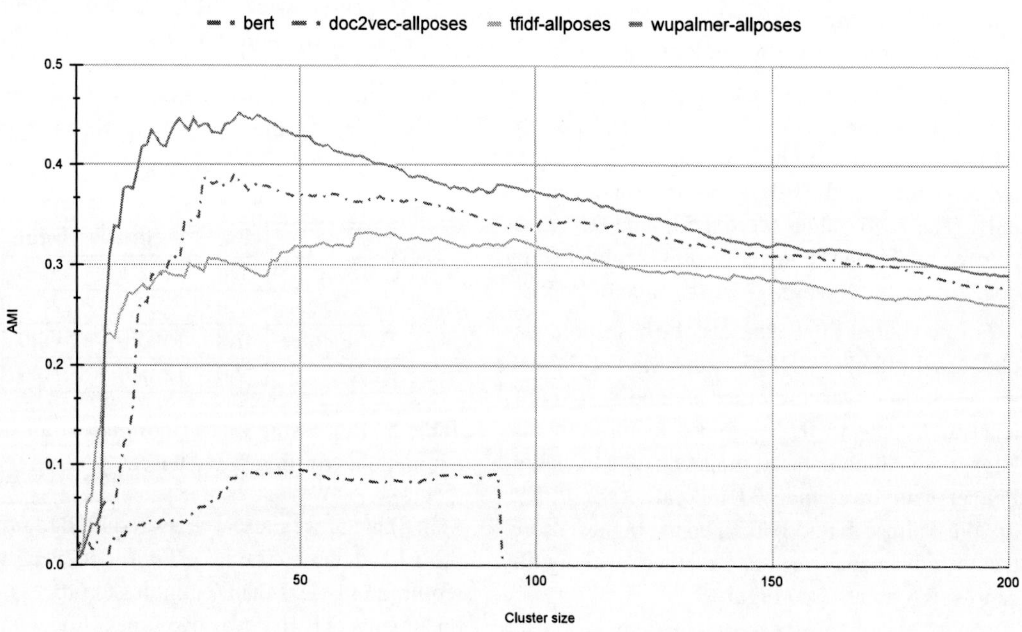

Figure 3: AMI values for the best-performing variants for each method on the PPKZ dataset.

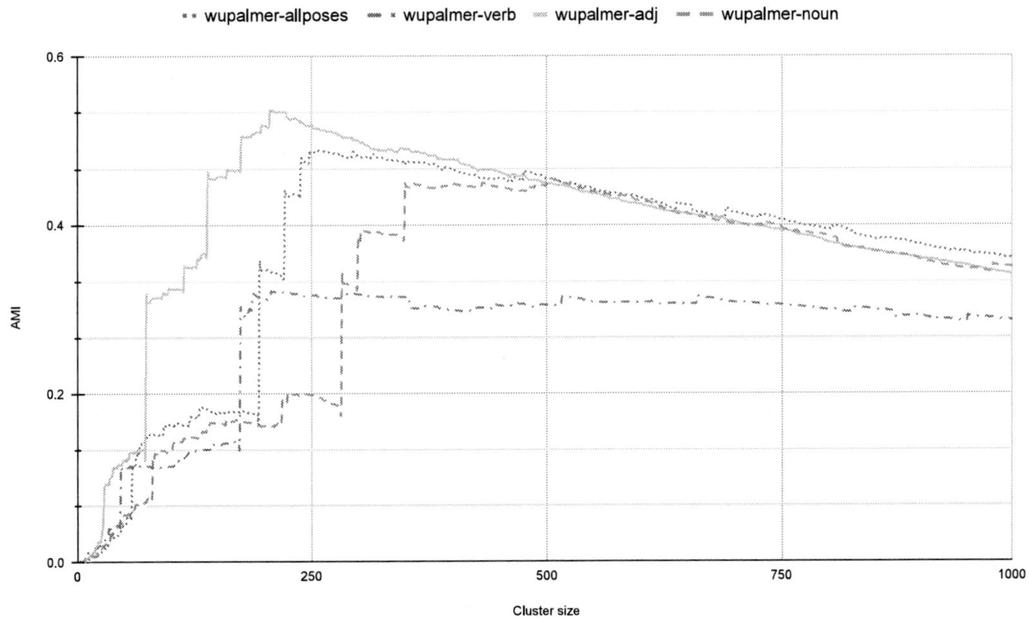

Figure 4: AMI values for each Wu-Palmer variant on the ALL dataset.

The Wu-Palmer method could be easily accelerated by paralleling — for 64 threads, the computation time can be reduced from 563 to 18 minutes. Another way to improve the processing speed would be reducing the number of synsets used to represent the document — as the number of synsets increases, processing time increases exponentially. We could apply the same technique as for TF-IDF — limit the number of synsets by defining the minimal document frequency for synsets.

7 Conclusion

The obtained results confirm the importance of developing dictionaries, knowledge bases, and domain ontologies. Wordnet-based measures of similarity may compete with embedding-based approaches in the task of text document clustering. Our research shows that the Wu-Palmer similarity metric can obtain comparable or even better (for the PPKZ dataset) results than the classical TF-IDF method and the modern doc2vec approach.

As far as the similarity of qualifications based on learning outcomes is concerned, one of the challenges discovered during our work was that the domain similarity and groups of qualifications were distorted by their source. Qualifications from the same source, e.g., from the same university or curriculum, tend to contain common, formulaic phrases. This problem will be addressed in further work.

Acknowledgements

The paper was prepared as part of the project "Operating and Developing of the Integrated Register of Qualifications" implemented by the Educational Research Institute as commissioned by the Ministry of National Education, co-financed by the European Union under the Operational Programme Knowledge Education Development.

References

Piotr Bojanowski, Edouard Grave, Armand Joulin, and Tomas Mikolov. 2017. Enriching word vectors with subword information. *Transactions of the Association for Computational Linguistics*, 5:135–146.

Alexander Budanitsky and Graeme Hirst. 2006. Evaluating wordnet-based measures of lexical semantic relatedness. *Computational Linguistics*, 32(1):13–47.

Cedefop. 2017. Defining, writing and applying learning outcomes: A european handbook.

William H. E. Day and Herbert Edelsbrunner. 1984. Efficient algorithms for agglomerative hierarchical clustering methods. *Journal of Classification*, 1(1):7–24, Dec.

Jacob Devlin, Ming-Wei Chang, Kenton Lee, and Kristina Toutanova. 2018. Bert: Pre-training of deep bidirectional transformers for language understanding. *arXiv preprint arXiv:1810.04805*.

Lawrence Hubert and Phipps Arabie. 1985. Comparing partitions. *Journal of Classification*, 2(1):193–218, Dec.

IBE. 2020. Qualifications registers in selected european union countries.

Arkadiusz Janz, Paweł Kędzia, and Dominik Kaszewski. 2018. Word sense disambiguation tool WoSeDon. CLARIN-PL digital repository.

Jay J. Jiang and David W. Conrath. 1997. Semantic similarity based on corpus statistics and lexical taxonomy. *CoRR*, cmp-lg/9709008.

Jan Kocoń and Michal Gawor. 2019. Evaluating KGR10 polish word embeddings in the recognition of temporal expressions using bilstm-crf. *CoRR*, abs/1904.04055.

Zimek A. Kriegel H-P., Schubert E. 2012. A survey on unsupervised outlier detection. *Statistical Analysis and Data Mining*, pages 363–387.

Quoc Le and Tomas Mikolov. 2014. Distributed representations of sentences and documents. In *International Conference on Machine Learning*, pages 1188–1196.

C. Leacock and M. Chodorow. 1998. Combining local context and wordnet similarity for word sense identification. In Christiane Fellfaum, editor, *MIT Press*, pages 265–283, Cambridge, Massachusetts.

Dekang Lin. 1998. Automatic retrieval and clustering of similar words. In *Proceedings of the 17th international conference on Computational linguistics*, pages 768–774, Morristown, NJ, USA. Association for Computational Linguistics.

Marek Maziarz, Maciej Piasecki, Ewa Rudnicka, Stan Szpakowicz, and Paweł Kędzia. 2016. PlWordNet 3.0 – a Comprehensive Lexical-Semantic Resource. In Nicoletta Calzolari, Yuji Matsumoto, and Rashmi Prasad, editors, *COLING 2016, 26th International Conference on Computational Linguistics, Proceedings of the Conference: Technical Papers, December 11-16, 2016, Osaka, Japan*, pages 2259–2268. ACL, ACL.

Rada Mihalcea, Courtney Corley, and Carlo Strapparava. 2006. Corpus-based and knowledge-based measures of text semantic similarity. volume 1, 01.

Philip Resnik. 1995. Using information content to evaluate semantic similarity in a taxonomy. In *IJCAI'95: Proceedings of the 14th international joint conference on Artificial intelligence*, pages 448–453, San Francisco, CA, USA. Morgan Kaufmann Publishers Inc.

Simone Romano, Nguyen Xuan Vinh, James Bailey, and Karin Verspoor. 2016. Adjusting for chance clustering comparison measures. *The Journal of Machine Learning Research*, 17(1):4635–4666.

Gerard Salton and Chris Buckley. 1988. Term-weighting approaches in automatic text retrieval. *Inf. Process. Manag.*, 24(5):513–523.

Wiktor Walentynowicz. 2017. MorphoDiTa-based tagger for polish language. CLARIN-PL digital repository.

Tomasz Walkowiak and Mateusz Gniewkowski. 2019. Evaluation of vector embedding models in clustering of text documents. In *Proceedings of the International Conference on Recent Advances in Natural Language Processing (RANLP 2019)*, pages 1304–1311, Varna, Bulgaria, September. INCOMA Ltd.

Tomasz Walkowiak. 2018. Language Processing Modelling Notation – Orchestration of NLP Microservices. In Wojciech Zamojski, Jacek Mazurkiewicz, Jarosław Sugier, Tomasz Walkowiak, and Janusz Kacprzyk, editors, *Advances in Dependability Engineering of Complex Systems*, pages 464–473, Cham. Springer International Publishing.

Zhibiao Wu and Martha Palmer. 1994. Verbs semantics and lexical selection. pages 133–138, 01.

Extracting Synonyms from Bilingual Dictionaries

Mustafa Jarrar
Birzeit University
Palestine
mjarrar@birzeit.edu

Eman Karajah
Birzeit University
Palestine
1105486@student.birzeit.edu

Muhammad Khalifa
Cairo University
Egypt
m.khalifa@grad.fci-cu.edu.eg

Khaled Shaalan
The British University in Dubai
United Arab Emirates
khaled.shaalan@buid.ac.ae

Abstract

We present our progress in developing a novel algorithm to extract synonyms from bilingual dictionaries. Identification and usage of synonyms play a significant role in improving the performance of information access applications. The idea is to construct a translation graph from translation pairs, then to extract and consolidate cyclic paths to form bilingual sets of synonyms. The initial evaluation of this algorithm illustrates promising results in extracting Arabic-English bilingual synonyms. In the evaluation, we first converted the synsets in the Arabic WordNet into translation pairs (i.e., losing word-sense memberships). Next, we applied our algorithm to rebuild these synsets. We compared the original and extracted synsets obtaining an F-Measure of 82.3% and 82.1% for Arabic and English synsets extraction, respectively.

1 Introduction

The importance of synonyms is growing in a number of application areas such as computational linguistics, information retrieval, question answering, and machine translation among others. Synonyms are also considered essential parts in several types of lexical resources, such as thesauri, wordnets (Miller et al., 1990), and linguistic ontologies (Jarrar, 2021; Jarrar, 2006).

There are different notions of synonymy in the literature varying from strict to lenient. In ontology engineering (see e.g., Jarrar, 2021), synonymy is a formal equivalence relation (i.e., reflexive, symmetric, and transitive). Two terms are synonyms *iff* they have the exact same concept (i.e., refer, intentionally, to the same set of instances). Thus, $T_1 =_{Ci} T_2$. In other words, given two terms T_1 and T_2 lexicalizing concepts C_1 and C_2, respectively, then T_1 and T_2 are considered to be synonyms *iff* $C_1 = C_2$. A less strict definition of synonymy is used for constructing Wordnets, which is based on the substitutionablity of words in a sentence. According to Miller et al. (1990), "two expressions are synonymous in a linguistic context *c* if the substitution of one for the other in *c* does not alter the truth value". Others might refer to synonymy to be a "closely-related" relationship between words, as used in distributional semantics, or the so-called *word embeddings* (see e.g., Emerson, 2020). Word embeddings are vectors of words automatically extracted from large corpora by exploiting the property that words with a similar meaning tend to occur in similar contexts. But it is unclear what type of similarity word vectors capture. For example, words like red, black and color might appear in the same vector which might be misleading synonyms.

Extracting synonyms automatically is known to be a difficult task, and the accuracy of the extracted synonyms is also difficult to evaluate (Wu et al., 2003). In fact, this difficulty is also faced when modeling synonyms manually. For example, words like *room* (غرفة) and *hall* (قاعة) are synonyms only in some domains like schools and events organization (Daher et al., 2010). Indeed, synonymy can be general or domain-specific; and since domains and contexts are difficult to define (Jarrar, 2005), and since they themselves may overlap, constructing a thesaurus needs special attention.

Another difficulty in the automatic extraction of synonyms is the polysemy of words. A word may have multiple meanings, and its synonymy relations with other words depend on which meaning(s) the words share. Assume e_1, e_2, and e_3 are English words, and a_1, a_2 and a_3 are Arabic words, we may have e_1 participating in different synonymy and translation sets, such as, $\{e_1, e_2\}=\{a_2\}$ and $\{e_1, e_3\}=\{a_3\}$. For example {table, tabular array}={جدول} and {river, stream}={جدول}.

In this paper, we present a novel algorithm to automatically extract synonyms from a given bilingual dictionary. The algorithm consists of two phases. First, we build a translation graph and extract all paths that form cycles; such that, all nodes in a cycle are candidate synonyms. Second, cyclic paths are consolidated, for refining and improving the accuracy of the results. To evaluate this algorithm, we conducted an experiment using the Arabic WordNet (AWN) (Elkateb et al., 2016). More specifically, we built a flat bilingual dictionary, as pairs of Arabic-English translations from AWN. Then, we used this bilingual dictionary as input to our algorithm to see how much of AWN's synsets we can rebuild.

Although the algorithm is language-independent and can be reused to extract synonyms from any bilingual dictionary, we plan to use it for enriching the Arabic Ontology - an Arabic wordnet with ontologically clean content (Jarrar, 2021; Jarrar, 2011). The idea is to extract synonyms, and thus synsets, from our large lexicographic database which contains about 150 Arabic-multilingual lexicons (Jarrar at el, 2019). This database is available through a public lexicographic search engine (Alhafi et al., 2019), and represented using the W3C lemon model (Jarrar at al., 2019b).

This paper is structured as follows: Section 2 overviews related work, Section 3 presents the algorithm, and Section 4 presents its evaluation. Finally, Section 5 outlines our future directions.

2 Related work

Synonyms extraction was investigated in the literature mainly for constructing new Wordnets or within the task of discovering new translation pairs. In addition, as overviewed in this section, some researchers also explored synonymy graphs for enhancing existing lexicons and thesauri.

A wordnet, in general, is a graph where nodes are called *synsets* and edges are *semantic relations* between these synsets (Miller et al., 1990). Each synset is a set of one, or more synonyms, which refers to a shared meaning (i.e., signifies a concept). Semantic relations like hyponymy and meronymy are defined between synsets. After developing the Princeton WordNet (PWN), hundreds of Wordnets have been developed for many languages and with different coverage (see *globalwordnet.org*).

Many researchers proposed to construct Wordnets automatically using the available linguistic resources such as dictionaries, wiktionaries, machine translation, corpora, or using other Wordnets. For example, Oliveira and Gomes (2014) proposed to build a Portuguese Wordnet automatically by building a synonymy graph from existing monolingual synonyms dictionaries.

Candidate synsets are identified first; then, a fuzzy clustering algorithm is used to estimate the probability of each word pair being in the same synset. Other approaches proposed to also construct wordnets and lexical ontologies via cross-language matching, see (Abu Helou et al., 2014; Abu Helou et al., 2016).

A recent approach to expand wordnets, by Ercan and Haziyev (2019), suggests to construct a multilingual translation graph from multiple Wiktionaries, and then link this graph with existing Wordnets in order to induce new synsets, i.e., expanding existing Wordnets with other languages.

Other researchers suggest to use dictionaries and corpora together, such as Wu and Zhou (2003) who proposed to extract synonyms from both monolingual dictionaries and bilingual corpora. First, a graph of words is constructed if a word appears in the definition of the other, and then assigned a similarity rank. Second, a bilingual English-Chinese corpus (pairs of translated sentences) is used to find links between words if they appear in the same pair, with a probability rank. Third, a monolingual Chinese corpus is used to find words co-occurring in the same context. These three results are then combined together using the ensemble method. A more recent approach, by Khodak et al. (2017), proposed to use an unsupervised method for automated construction of Wordnets using PWN, machine translations, and word embeddings. A target word is first translated into English using machine translation, and these translations are used to build a set of candidate synsets from PWN. Each candidate synset is then ranked with a similarity score that is calculated using the word embedding-based method.

A similar attempt to build Arabic and Vietnamese Wordnets was proposed by Lam et al. (2014). They proposed a method to automatically construct a new Wordnet using machine translation and existing Wordnets. Given a synset in one or more Wordnets, all words in this synset (in multiple languages) are translated using machine translation into the target language. The retrieved translations, which contain wrong translations because of polysemy, are ranked based on their relative frequencies, and the highest ranked translations are retrieved. This approach was extended by Al-Tarouti et al. (2016) by introducing word embeddings to better validate and remove irrelevant words in synsets.

Other related work to synonymy extraction is the task of finding new translations, such that, given translation pairs between multiple languages, one may discover new translation pairs that are not explicitly stated. For example, Villegas et al. (2016) presented an experiment to produce new translations from a translation graph constructed from the Apertium dictionaries. Given a set of multilingual translation pairs, a translation graph is constructed, from which cycles are extracted. New translation pairs are then identified if they participate in the extracted cycles. The experiment illustrated that some wrong translations might be detected because of polysomy, thus a path density score was assigned to each path, such that low densities are excluded. More recently, Torregrosa et al. (2019) presented three algorithms for automatic discovery of translations from existing dictionaries, namely, cycle-based, path-based, and multi-way neural machine translation. In the cycle-based approach, a translation graph is constructed from a multilingual dictionary, and cycles of length 4 are identified. However, in the path-based approach, a frequency weight is assigned to each path based on the number of translation pairs participating in this path, such that paths of lower length and higher frequency get lower weights. In the third algorithm, multilingual parallel corpora were used to train a multi-way neural machine translation, and continued the training based on the output of the other two algorithms. An experiment by the authors shows a very low recall and a reasonable precision (25-75%) for the three approaches.

The main differences between these approaches and our approach, is that we aim at extracting synonyms rather than translation pairs, and that we assume the translation graph to be formed of nodes from two languages only. Having two languages in the translation graph produces a different number of paths; thus, different disambiguation complexity.

A lexicon-based algorithm called CQC was proposed by Flati and Navigli (2012). The algorithm takes a bilingual dictionary as input, then builds a translation graph, from which only cyclic and quasi-cyclic paths are extracted. These paths are then ranked, such that shorter paths are given higher ranks than longer ones. Words, and words senses, encountered in the cycles or quasi-cycles are likely to be synonymy candidates. This approach is mainly used for validating and enriching the Ragazzini-Biagi English-Italian dictionary, but it can be also used for extracting synonyms. The accuracy of this approach depends on the structure of input dictionaries, which is assumed to contain senses, e.g., an English word and its set of equivalent Italian translations. This implies that these Italian words are themselves synonyms.

In our approach, we assume that a word in a given language is translated to only one word in the other language, i.e., only translation pairs, without synonymy relations. In other words, we assume the bilingual input to be the most ambiguous.

As will be discussed in Section 4, our algorithm does not assume any pre-existing conditions or assumptions about the input data, and does not use part-of-speech or any other morphological features. Designing an algorithm without any pre-existing assumption, makes the algorithm more reusable (Jarrar et al., 2002) for other languages and other types of lexicons. Nevertheless, and as described in the future work Section, using linguistic features would improve the algorithm's accuracy.

3 Our Algorithm

The problem we aim to tackle in this paper is described as the following: given a set ***B*** of bilingual translation pairs of the form (a_i, e_j), where a_i is a word in language l_1 and e_j is its translation in language l_2. Our goal is to extract a set ***R*** of bilingual synonyms, such that $\{a_1,..,a_k\} = \{e_1,..,e_l\} \in \boldsymbol{R}$.

To extract the set ***R*** of bilingual synonyms from ***B***, our algorithm performs two steps:

Step 1: Extract cyclic paths

Given ***B***, an undirected graph is built, where each node represents a word of either language and two edges (in both directions) connect any two nodes that represent a word-translation pair. Then, we use Johnson's algorithm (Johnson, 1977) to find all cycles in the directed graph. A cycle is a path of nodes that starts and ends in the same node, such as $a_1 \rightarrow e_1 \rightarrow a_2 \rightarrow e_2 \rightarrow a_1$. Nodes participating in the same path are considered candidate synonyms, and converted into bilingual synsets, e.g., $\{a_1, a_2\} = \{e_1, e_2\}$. To avoid very long cycles, we modify Johnson's algorithm to stop expanding a path beyond the pre-specified maximum cycle length *k*. Figure 1 illustrates an Arabic-English translation graph extracted from the Arabic WordNet. The graph starts from the word ġābaẗ (غَابَة), expands its English translations, then expand the Arabic translations of each English word, and so on, up to 7 levels (*k*=7).
The expansion stops in these cases:

1) The root node is found, i.e., cycle,
2) No more translations are found, which are underlined (e.g., woodland), or
3) The max *k* level is reached.

The output of this step is a set of candidate bilingual synsets extracted from the nodes participating in cyclic paths, such as:

1. {forest, woods} = {غَابَة, غَاب}
2. {forest, woods} = {غَابَة, أدْغَال}
3. {forest, wood} = {غَابَة, أدْغَال}
4. {forest, wood}={غَابَة, غَاب}
5. {wood, woods } = {غَابَة, غَاب}
6. {wood, woods} = {غَابَة, أدْغَال}
7. {forest, wood, woods} = {أدْغَال, غَابَة, غَاب}

Step 2: Consolidation

This step aims to merge synsets that have the same sets of translations. In other words, Arabic synsets are consolidated (i.e., unioned) if they have the same English synsets, such as synsets 1 and 2, 3 and 4, and 5 and 6, in the previous example. Similarly, English synsets are consolidated if they have the same Arabic synsets. This step is repeated until no more consolidations are found. The output of this phase is the final sets of bilingual synonyms, such as:

{forest, wood, woods} $=_{ci}$ {أدْغال, غابَة, غاب}

As will be shown in the evaluation section, the consolidation phase is important, in order to minimize the impact of paths that might not be sufficiently expanded, if k is small. The consolidation phase is designed based on the following heuristics:

(i) It is less likely for a set of bilingual synsets, especially long synsets, to refer to multiple concepts. In other words, the longer a synset (i.e., more bilingual words in the synset), the less likely the synset to be polysemous and to refer to multiple meanings.

(ii) It is less likely that a synset, especially long synsets, to be a subset of another synset. That is, it is possible in practice to have different synsets, like $\{a, b, c, d\}$ and $\{a, b, c\}$, where the former is a subset of the later, which may negatively affect the accuracy of our algorithm. However, such cases are less likely to happen, especially in case of long synsets.

(iii) It is less likely for the same English synset, especially long synsets, to be translated into multiple Arabic synsets. An English synset may have multiple concepts and thus multiple Arabic synsets, such as $\{e_1, e_2, e_3, e_4\}=_{c1}\{a_1, a_2, a_3, a_4\}$ and $\{e_1, e_2, e_3, e_4\}=_{c2}\{a_5, a_6, a_7, a_8\}$. Such cases may negatively affect our accuracy, but they are rare in practice.

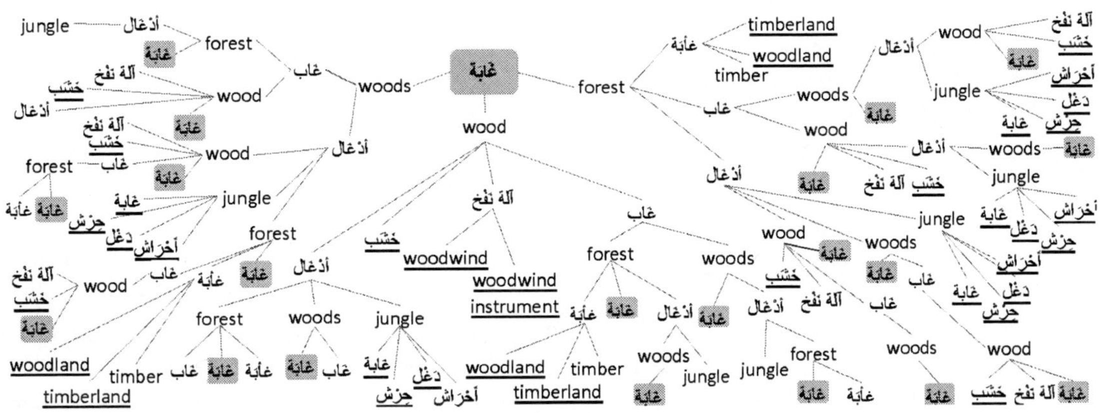

Figure 1: Example of a translation graph

4 Evaluation and Discussion

To evaluate the extent to which our synonyms extraction algorithm is able to produce correct results, we used the Arabic Wordnet (AWN). The AWN, which is a set of bilingual synsets, is converted into a flat bilingual dictionary (i.e., translation pairs), such that all synonymy links between words are lost. Then, we use our algorithm to restore these links (extract bilingual synsets), and compare the extracted with original synsets.

Our choice of evaluating the algorithm using the AWN data is because this resource contains highly polysemous words, and thus evaluates the algorithm in challenging cases. In addition, and in order to evaluate the algorithm in unguided conditions or any pre-existing assumption, and make it reusable for other languages, we did not apply any fine-tuning or language-specific preprocessing or treatment. Thus, we assume that the input translation pairs do not have any tag indicating their part of speech (POS) or other morphological features, or whether words are MSA or dialect (Jarrar et al., 2017). We also assume that Arabic words with different diacritic signs, even if they are compatible (Jarrar et al., 2018), are different words. For example (غابَة) and (غَابَة) are considered different words because of slightly different diacritics. Tuning the algorithm to take into account such morphological features, inflections, and diacritics, would very likely improve the accuracy of the results; but this is not a goal in this paper and is left as a future work.

As evaluation metrics, we use the precision, recall and F-measure to compare the extracted synsets with the original AWN as the gold standard. We use the Cosine similarity to compute the match between two given synsets.

For precision, we count the number of correctly extracted synsets divided by all the extracted synsets. In cases of partial match between two synsets *x* and *y*, we use the max similarity with all the gold sets as the "correctness" of the extracted synset:

$$Precision = \frac{\sum_{x \in extracted} \; max_{y \in AWN} \, Cosine(x, y)}{|Extracted\ synsets|}$$

where $Cosine(x, y) \in [0,1]$. Recall and F-measure are computed as:

$$Recall = \frac{\sum_{y \in AWN} \; max_{x \in Extracted} \, Cosine(x, y)}{|AWN|}$$

$$F\text{-}Measure = 2 * \frac{Precision . Recall}{Precision + Recall}$$

Tables 1 and 2 show the evaluation metrics when extracting Arabic and English synsets, respectively. Clearly, the proposed consolidation step has a positive effect on the algorithm by boosting the F-measure from 74.4% to 82.3% and from 70.1% to 82.1% for Arabic and English, respectively for a path length *k*=6.

	Precision	Recall	F-Measure
k=6, no consolidation	62.5	**91.9**	74.4
k=6, with consolidation	**80.5**	84.2	**82.3**
k=8, with consolidation	64.4	84.3	73.0

Table 1: Results on the AWN for Arabic synsets extractions using the proposed algorithm.

	Precision	Recall	F-Measure
k=6, No consolidation	57.6	**89.8**	70.1
k=6, with consolidation	**80.4**	83.8	**82.1**
k=8, with consolidation	64.7	**84.0**	73.1

Table 2: Results on the AWN for English synsets extractions using the proposed algorithm

The results also show that having longer paths (e.g., *k*=8) does not improve the accuracy, which is most likely in case of highly polysemous words, where some irrelevant nodes are generated in longer paths.

Last but not least, the Arabic Wordnet contains about 10K synsets, and most of the words in these synsets are, by definition, highly polysemous Arabic and English words. This is because these 10K synsets are called Common Base concepts, and assumed to be frequently used and exist in many languages. As discussed earlier such high polysemy is likely to affect the accuracy; thus, evaluating our algorithm on less polysemous words is likely to produce better accuracy.

5 Conclusions and Future Work

We presented our progress in developing a novel algorithm to extract synonyms from bilingual dictionaries. Although the algorithm was evaluated on extracting English-Arabic bilingual synsets, it is reusable for other languages, especially since it does not assume any language-specific treatment or preprocessing. Our choice of using AWN in the evaluation, which contains highly polysemous words, illustrates that our algorithm produces realistic results in such challenging cases.

We plan to extend our algorithm in different directions. We plan to take into account part of speech tags and other morphological features when generating candidate synonyms. Similarly, words with different, but compatible, diacritics, inflections, and forms need a special treatment. Such extensions and fine-tunings are very likely to produce higher accuracy.

Acknowledgments

This research is partially supported by the Research Committee at Birzeit University.

References

Alhafi, D., Deik, D., & Jarrar, M. (2019): Usability Evaluation of Lexicographic e-Services. In Proceedings – 2019 IEEE/ACS 16th International Conference on Computer Systems and Applications, Abu Dhabi (pp.1-7). IEEE. doi:10.1109/AICCSA47632.2019.9035226

Daher, J., & Jarrar, M. (2010). Towards a Methodology for Building Ontologies – Classify by Properties. In Proceedings – 3rd Palestinian International Conference on Computer and Information Technology (PICCIT), Palestine.

Elkateb, S., Black, W., Vossen, P., Farwell, D., Pease A., & Fellbaum, C. (2006). Arabic WordNet and the Challenges of Arabic. In Proceedings – Arabic NLP/MT Conference (pp. 665-670).

Emerson, G. (2020). What are the Goals of Distributional Semantics. In Proceedings of the 58th Annual Meeting of the Association for Computational Linguistics. ACL. (pp. 7436-7453).

Ercan, G., & Haziyev, F. (2019). Synset expansion on translation graph for automatic wordnet construction. Information Processing & Management, 56(1), 130-150.

Helou, M. A., Palmonari, M., & Jarrar, M. (2016). Effectiveness of Automatic Translations for Cross-Lingual Ontology Mapping. Journal of Artificial Intelligence Research, 55, 165-208. doi:10.1613/jair.4789

Helou, M. A., Palmonari, M., & Jarrar, M., Fellbaum, F. (2014). Towards Building Lexical Ontology via Cross-Language Matching. In Proceedings – 7th Conference on Global WordNet. Global WordNet Association. (pp. 346–354). EID: 2-s2.0-84859707947

Jarrar, M., & Meersman, R. (2002). Scalability and Knowledge Reusability in Ontology Modeling. In Proceedings – International Conference on Advances in Infrastructure for Electronic Business, Science, and Education on the Internet (SSGRR 2002s). Scuola Superiore G Reiss Romoli. Rome, Italy.

Jarrar, M. (2005). Towards Methodological Principles for Ontology Engineering. Doctoral dissertation, Vrije Universiteit Brussel, Belgium.

Jarrar, M., (2006). Towards the Notion of Gloss, and the Adoption of Linguistic Resources in Formal Ontology Engineering. In Proceedings – 15th international conference on World Wide Web, (pp.497-503). ACM. doi: 10.1145/1135777.1135850

Jarrar, M. (2011): Building A Formal Arabic Ontology (Invited Paper). In Proceedings – Experts Meeting on Arabic Ontologies and Semantic Networks, Tunis. ALECSO, Arab League.

Jarrar, M., Habash, N., Alrimawi, F., Akra, D., & Zalmout, N. (2016). Curras: An Annotated Corpus for the Palestinian Arabic Dialect. Language Resources and Evaluation, 50(219), 1-31. doi:10.1007/S10579-016-9370-7

Jarrar, M., Zaraket, F., Asia, R., & Amayreh, H. (2018). Diacritic-based Matching of Arabic Words. ACM Transactions on Asian and Low-Resource Language Information Processing (TALLIP), 18(2), 1-21. doi: 10.1145/3242177

Jarrar, M., & Amayreh, H. (2019). An Arabic-Multilingual Database with a Lexicographic Search Engine. In Proceedings – 24th International Conference on Applications of Natural Language to Information Systems (NLDB 2019). Lecture Notes in Computer Science (vol. 11608, pp. 234-246). Springer. Doi:10.1007/978-3-030-23281-8_19

Jarrar, M., Amayreh, H., & McCrae, J. (2019): Representing Arabic Lexicons in Lemon – a Preliminary Study. In Proceedings – 2nd Conference on Language, Data and Knowledge, Leipzig, Germany. CEUR-WS (vol. 2402, pp. 29-33).

Jarrar, M. (2021). The Arabic Ontology - An Arabic Wordnet with Ontologically Clean Content. Applied Ontology Journal, IOS Press.

Johnson, D. B. (1975). Finding all the elementary circuits of a directed graph. SIAM Journal on Computing, 4(1), 77-84.

Khodak, M., Risteski, A., Fellbaum, C., & Arora, S. (2017). Automated WordNet construction using word embeddings. In Proceedings of the 1st Workshop on Sense, Concept and Entity Representations and their Applications (pp. 12-23).

Lam, K., Tarouti, F., & Kalita J. (2014). Automatically constructing Wordnet synsets. In Proceedings of the 52nd Annual Meeting of the Association for Computational Linguistics (Volume 2: Short Papers) (pp. 106-111).

Miller, J., Beckwith, R., Fellbaum, C., Gross D., & Miller, K. (1990). Introduction to Wordnet: An on-line Lexical Database. International Journal of Lexicography, 3(4), 235-244.

Oliveira, H., & Gomes, P. (2014). ECO and Onto. PT: a flexible approach for creating a Portuguese wordnet automatically. Language resources and evaluation, 48(2), 373-393.

Tarouti, F., & Kalita, J. (2016). Enhancing automatic wordnet construction using word embeddings. In Proceedings – Workshop on Multilingual and Cross-lingual Methods in NLP (pp. 30-34).

Tiziano, F., & Navigli. R. (2012). The CQC algorithm: Cycling in graphs to semantically enrich and enhance a bilingual dictionary. Journal of Artificial Intelligence Research, 43, 135-171.

Torregrosa, D., Mihael, A., Ahmadi, S., & McCrae, J. (2019). TIAD 2019 Shared Task: Leveraging knowledge graphs with neural machine translation for automatic multilingual dictionary generation. Translation Inference Across Dictionaries.

Villegas, M., Melero, M., Gracia J., & Bel, N. (2016). Leveraging RDF graphs for crossing multiple bilingual dictionaries. In Proceedings of the Tenth International Conference on Language Resources and Evaluation (LREC'16) (pp. 868-876).

Wu, H., & Zhow M. (2003). Optimizing synonym extraction using monolingual and bilingual resources. In Proceedings of the second international workshop on Paraphrasing (pp. 72-79).

Neural Language Models vs Wordnet-based Semantically Enriched Representation in CST Relation Recognition

Arkadiusz Janz, Maciej Piasecki, Piotr Wątorski
Wrocław University of Science and Technology, Poland
{arkadiusz.janz|maciej.piasecki|piotr.watorski}@pwr.edu.pl

Abstract

Neural language models, including transformer-based models, that are pre-trained on very large corpora became a common way to represent text in various tasks, including recognition of textual semantic relations, e.g. Cross-document Structure Theory. Pre-trained models are usually fine tuned to downstream tasks and the obtained vectors are used as an input for deep neural classifiers. No linguistic knowledge obtained from resources and tools is utilised. In this paper we compare such universal approaches with a combination of rich graph-based linguistically motivated sentence representation and a typical neural network classifier applied to a task of recognition of CST relation in Polish. The representation describes selected levels of the sentence structure including description of lexical meanings on the basis of the wordnet (plWordNet) synsets and connected SUMO concepts. The obtained results show that in the case of difficult relations and medium size training corpus semantically enriched text representation leads to significantly better results.

1 Introduction

Recognition of semantic relations linking text fragments may provide insight into the semantic-pragmatic structure of text or be a basis for human-like reasoning. The Cross-document Structure Theory (CST) (Radev, 2000) defines a system of semantic relations connecting topically related texts. However, due to the large number of relations and often subtle differences between them, CST relation recognition is known to be much harder than Textual Entailment (TE) recognition. TE depends on a binary decision whether one piece of text semantically entails another one due to their content, while CST is a model of more general use, but more difficult to achieve good results, especially when a classifier is trained on a domain different than the domain of its application.

CST relations are based on relations between semantic content of the text fragments, like *Subsumption* or *Background*. Such semantic oppositions are not trivial in the case of several relation types. For instance, differences in the definitions of *Description*, *Follow-up* or *Elaboration* indicate some potential difficulties that may arise when we want to recognize certain types of relations. In case of Description, the new additional information is about the current, non-historical nature of an event, e.g. the first sentence describes an object or entity appearing in the second sentence. Elaboration provides some additional details regarding the event, but generally the sentences convey the same core information. Follow-up provides some unrevealed facts about the event but appearing after occurrence of this event, thus it may be some kind of description for related events.

Janz et al. (2018) showed that enriched graph based representation of sentences that combines elements from the levels of words, syntactic structures and also semantic structures results in significant improvement of the recognition performance in comparison to less informed approaches of simpler representation models. The semantic parts of graphs included wordnet synsets, SUMO (Pease, 2011) concepts, proper names and selected semantic relations from noun phrases, where the wordnet and SUMO based graph elements dominates. The recent rapid development of approaches based on word embeddings, neural language models and deep neural classifiers shows that novel end-to-end methods can be very successful when applied to downstream tasks. In our work we want to verify this common claim by comparing approaches utilising more complex text representation with those based on versatile neural language models or word embeddings. The goal of this paper is to compare two approaches: a typical 'neural' approach and the elaborated method of Janz et al. (2018), as well as their combination, as the first step into this domain. The approach was presented on the basis of a well built, but medium size corpus. This may be an exemplar of a practical problem: in practice many tasks are sparingly illustrated by annotated data, and, thus, poses challenges to 'neural' methods as they require large resources to fine tune representations based on pre-trained neural models (contextual embeddings) to the problem. For the comparison we used the same annotated corpus and exactly the same representation as in (Janz et al., 2018) and neural language models pre-trained on very large corpora, and fine tuned on the same annotated corpus. Our aim is to verify a claim that knowledge-based representation, especially wordnet-based, may be still useful in such cases.

2 Related Work

In Zhang et al. (2003) CST relations were recognised by a supervised approach with boosting on the basis of lexical, syntactic and semantic features extracted from sentence pairs. The evaluation was performed in two steps: binary classification for relationship detection, and multi-class classification for relationship recognition. (Zhang and Radev, 2005), in addition to labelled data, exploited also unlabelled instances that improved the performance. Boosting technique was used in combination with the same set of features to classify the data in CSTBank (Radev et al., 2004). Relation detection was significantly improved to F1-score = 0.8839. However, recognition of the relation type was still unsatisfactory.

(Aleixo and Pardo, 2008) is one of few works that address the problem of CST relations recognition for languages other than English. They utilised CST in search for topically related Portuguese documents. They applied a supervised approach based on similarity measures calculated for sentence pairs from different documents: cosine similarity and a variant of the Jaccard index. Cut-off thresholds for the similarity were studied in combination with the performance of classifiers. Aleixo and Pardo (2008) constructed a CST corpus for Portuguese and used it to conduct their study.

Zahri and Fukumoto (2011) applied the supervised learning to recognise a a subset of CST relations: *Identity*, *Paraphrase*, *Subsumption*, *Elaboration* and *Partial Overlap*. SVM algorithm was used and examples from CSTBank. The features of Aleixo and Pardo (2008) were expanded with: cosine similarity of word vectors, Jaccard Index to measure intersection of common words, longer sentence indicator, and uni-directional word coverage ratio.

Kumar et al. (2012a) followed Zahri and Fukumoto (2011), but restricted the set of relations to four and used only four features: tf-idf based cosine sentence similarity, words coverage ratio, sentence length difference, and longer sentence flag. The performance of SVM in relation recognition was between (F1): 0.54 and 0.91 For the same relations Kumar et al. (2012b) presented results obtained with SVM, a Feed-Forward neural network and CBR (Case-based Reasoning). The features of Zahri and Fukumoto (2011) were extended with the Jaccard based similarity of noun phrases and verb phrases from the compared sentences. The best result was achieved with CBR based on the cosine similarity measure: from 0.722 to 0.966.

Due to the ambiguity in the interpretation of certain CST relationships, Maziero et al. (2014) proposed several refinements to CST in order to reduce the ambiguity. They improved definitions by introducing several additional constraints on the co-occurrence of different relations in texts. The CST taxonomy was amended by adding a division based on the form and information content of relations. The improved model was used in evaluation of supervised CST relation recognition The applied features included: sentence length difference, ratio of shared words, sentence position in text, differences in word numbers across PoSs, and the number of shared synonyms between sentences. The J48-based classifier achieved the best average score of 0.403.

In similar task of implicit discourse relation recognition (Cianflone and Kosseim, 2018) used encoder- decoder (RNN) trained directly on character-level data from a large training corpus of annotated relations (reported F1 between 0.3 and 0.8, depending on the relation type). (Bai and Zhao, 2018) used ELMo (Gardner et al., 2017) and subword-level encoding as an input to a stack of a convolutional encoder, and a recurrent encoder and a multiple layer perceptron with softmax layer as the classifier – F1 between 0.36 and 0.51 was obtained. (Guo et al., 2018) represented input data by pre-trained word embeddings and next trained a neural tensor network on a large corpus of annotated sentences obtaining F1: 0.38 – 0.72.

However, (Ponti and Korhonen, 2017) used topic model word vectors as representation, but also enriched it with features extracted by dependency parser to recognise causal relations between events – a similar task to ours, but narrower.

3 Dataset

For comparison, we utilised exactly the same dataset as in (Kędzia et al., 2017; Janz et al., 2018), i.e. of sentence pairs annotated with CST relations from the KPWr Corpus (Broda et al., 2012), henceforth *WUT CST*. The underlying corpus used to build the dataset contained 11 949 complete documents that were clustered and split into groups of 3 news, each including the most similar and potentially related documents. A set of bundles for manual annotation process was prepared – every one with 10 triples $\{D_1, D_2, D_3\}$ of most similar documents, that were randomly assigned to the annotators. Finally, 96 bundles covering more than 2800 documents were analysed in order to discover new instances of CST relations. The imposed similarity structure facilitated searching for sentence pairs linked by a CST relation. Manually annotated pairs of sentences (by at least by 3 annotators each) representing new instances of CST relations formed the gold reference subcorpus introduced for the first time by Kędzia et al. (2017). Each annotator was exploring the corpus independently. The annotators followed the guidelines used for the construction of CSTBank (Radev et al., 2004) adapted to Polish.

However, for the final corpus *WUT CST*[1] we have rejected uncertain CST instances with inconsistent annotations. This means that our *WUT CST* corpus contains only CST instances with almost homogenous annotations assigned by at least $n-1, n>2$ annotators. The final distribution of collected CST instances in our *WUT CST* corpus is presented in Figure 2.

A corpus, with similar distribution of discourse relations linking multiple documents (texts from journals in Brazilian Portuguese), was also introduced in (Cardoso et al., 2011).

We updated the original dataset to eliminate data redundancy and improve its quality by removing noisy sentence pairs. To deal with highly imbalanced class distribution we decided to completely remove specific minor classes as their sample size was too small to prepare a robust and effective supervised model in a supervised setting. The updated dataset is available at `https://clarin-pl.eu/dspace/handle/11321/781`.

4 Neural Representation

Successful applications of transformer-based language models in many NLP tasks seem to be grounded in transfer learning methods and intensive model pre-training on large textual corpora. As pre-trained neural language models became very successful pushing the limits in many different natural language tasks we decided to start off with the most popular transformer-based language models and prepare baseline solutions for CST task. To prepare our baseline solutions we decided to choose ELMo and BERT (Devlin et al., 2019) pre-trained language models as it has been shown that they express good performance in Natural Language Inference (NLI) tasks e.g. Textual Entailment (TE). This choice was motivated by the fact that NLI tasks and CST theory are strongly interconnected.

4.1 Pre-trained Language Models

In recent years the general interest in neural language modeling has led to emergence of new pre-trained language models for many different natural languages and Polish language is no exception here. In this paper we used the largest freely available language models pre-trained on selected Polish corpora.

4.2 Multilingual BERT

BERT is a popular and very successful transformer-based architecture for language modeling. It uses masked language modeling with next sentence prediction as an auxiliary objective for training. In this work we use the Multilingual Cased model. The authors used Wikipedia dump extracted for over 100 languages to prepare the model. Still, the language modeling abilities of this model can vary across different languages due to the differences of Wikipedia dump size and thematic representativeness for different languages.

[1] `https://clarin-pl.eu/dspace/handle/11321/305`

Historical Background
Phoenix wylądował 25 maja 2008 na północnym biegunie Marsa z 3 miesięczną misją badania planety.
Phoenix landed on the Mars' North Pole on 25th May 2008 in a three month mission to explore the planet.

Z tego powodu NASA podejmuje okresowe nasłuchy lądownika.
Due to this reason NASA undertakes periodical listening for the landing module.

Fulfilment
21 lutego 2008 po północy (wg czasu polskiego) miało miejsce całkowite zaćmienie Księżyca.
21st February 2008 past midnight (Polish time) a total Lunar eclipse took place.

21 lutego 2008 po północy (w Polsce) będzie można zaobserwować całkowite zaćmienie Księżyca.
21st February 2008 past midnight (in Poland) it will be possible to observe a total Lunar eclipse.

Follow up
Były premier Leszek Miller będzie kandydował do wyborów parlamentarnych z listy Samoobrony.
The former prime minister Leszek Miller will candidate in parliamentary election from the Samoobrona list.

2007-09-15: Leszek Miller odszedł z SLD
2007-09-15: Leszek Miller left SLD.

Figure 1: Examples of sentence pairs linked by CST relations in WUT CST dataset.

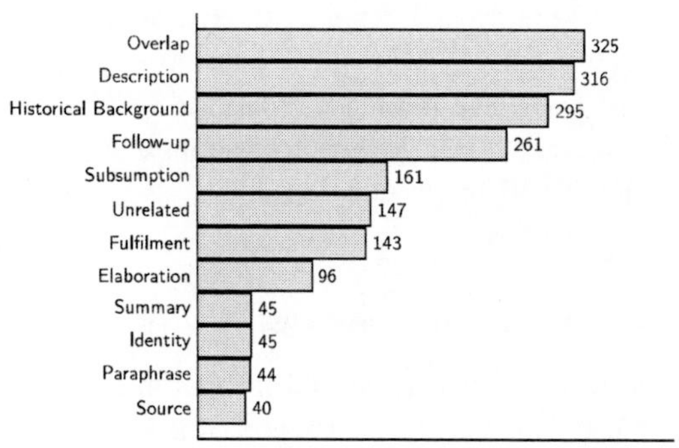

Figure 2: Relations distribution in *WUT CST*.

4.3 Polish BERT-based Models

As it was stated in previous section, the quality of pre-trained language models is mainly dependent on the quality of training corpora. A large part of Polish NLP community in the last few years was focused on adopting well-known language models and training them on publicly available Polish corpora due to the insufficient performance of models trained on Polish Wikipedia only.

HerBERT[2] is a new Polish language model (Rybak et al., 2020) pre-trained on multiple open Polish corpora. The model itself is mainly based on BERT architecture but it also uses dynamic masking as it was originally proposed in RoBERTa (Liu et al., 2019) language model.

4.4 Polish ELMo

ELMo is a language model based on stacked bidirectional LSTM architecture with character-level convolutions. We decided to choose a publicly available model [3] trained on KGR10 corpora as it was the only one model of this kind fully pretrained on large Polish data from scratch. The KGR10 (Kocoń and Gawor, 2019) is one of the largest Polish corpora of over 4 billion words.

The model was tested extrinsically in selected Polish benchmarks prepared for different NLP tasks e.g. Named Entity Recognition (NER), Sentiment Analysis (SA), or Recognition of Temporal Expressions.

5 Complex Representation

We started from the representations proposed by Janz et al. (2018). In the original work the best result were reported for the combination of manually engineered features and complex graph-based similarities. We preserve the original setting and we shortly recollect features inspired by the literature in Sec. 5.1 and the graph-based features in Sec. 5.2. Finally, both groups of features are concatenated into one single vector as a sentence representation in the experiments discussed in Sec. 8.

[2] https://huggingface.co/allegro/herbert-klej-cased-v1

[3] https://clarin-pl.eu/dspace/handle/11321/690

As graph-based features are those making the differences, cf (Janz et al., 2018), the combined representation will be referred as graph-based representation (or features).

5.1 Bag-of-Elements Representation

The simplest representation of a sentence is a bag of words (a collection of words), i.e. a set of pairs: words plus their frequencies. This basic idea was expanded to bags of diverse elements resulting from rich pre-processing of analysed data.

As it was proposed by Janz et al. (2018) we applied the following pre-processing steps: text lemmatisation and morphosyntactic tagging (Radziszewski, 2013), dependency parsing (Wróblewska and Woliński, 2012; Wróblewska, 2014) in parallel with chunking (Radziszewski and Pawlaczek, 2013), named entity recognition (Marcińczuk et al., 2013), multi-word expression recognition (Radziszewski et al., 2011), and word sense disambiguation (Kędzia et al., 2015; Piasecki et al., 2016). Selected semantic relations inside nominal phrases were recognised by hand-crafted rules (Kedzia and Maziarz, 2013).

The output from word sense disambiguation tool was used to map words to the appropriate synsets of plWordNet 3.0. As plWordNet 3.0 synsets were semi-automatically mapped onto concepts from SUMO ontology (Pease, 2011), thus, the words could be also mapped to their corresponding concepts. We used the metadata obtained by applying aforementioned pre-processing steps to reproduce graph-based representations of the sentences from WUT CST dataset.

5.2 Graph-based Representation

The graph-based representation proposed by Janz et al. (2018) represents a single sentence as a collection of graphs where the nodes correspond to the elements of the detected linguistic structure (e.g. words, lemmas, senses, or ontology concepts) and links reflect relations held between these elements. Concerning the latter a relation can be a simple linear precedence in text, but also a syntactic or semantic link recognised by an appropriate tool. All graphs used are directed.

Some of them include elements external to the sentence structure originating from the linked knowledge resources, e.g. an ontology. A pair of sentences may be described not only by a pair of graphs themselves, but also by values of different similarity measures defined on their graphs.

Many graph types were generated and used in (Janz et al., 2018) by combining different types of nodes with a variety of edge types. Four node types are used:

1. *Lemma* – a graph node represents a lemma of the word w_i converted to lowercase; all words from the sentence with the same lemma (irrespectively of PoS) are represented by the same node;

2. *Lemma PoS* – a node represents a lowercased lemmas, but concatenated with the PoS label, e.g. the Polish word *piec* can be morphologically disambiguated as a verb or noun *Kasia piecze:v ciasto w piecu:n* 'Kasia is baking a cake in the oven'. Using *Lemma lower* type, the words *piecze* '[he/she] bakes' and *piecu* 'an oven:inst' will be represented by a single node labelled as *piec*, while in *Lemma PoS lower* type there will be two different nodes: *piec:n* and *piec.v*.

3. *Synset* – a node represents a plWordNet synset of a given word; the synsets are obtained by applying word sense disambiguation tool to input sentences,

4. *Concept* – a node is a SUMO concept identified on the basis of the disambiguated synset of a word and its mapping to a SUMO concept (Kędzia and Piasecki, 2014).

The edge types originate from the automatically recognised lexical and semantic relations in a sentence. The edge direction reflects the original link direction:

word order – edges represent the word order,

head order – an edge represents the relative order of the heads of *agreement phrases* in a sentence – phrases and their heads are recognised by IOBBER chunker, edges signal the linear order of the heads,

NE order – similar to the head and word orders, but it represents the linear order of the named entities *NE* in a sentence,

syntactic dependency – represents the dependency relations, recognised by the Polish Malt parser (Wróblewska and Woliński, 2012), *nominal structure* relations – similar to the *syntactic dependency*, but relations come from *Defender* parser based on IOBBER and introduce deeper syntactic-semantic relation structures into the representation of NPs, cf (Kedzia and Maziarz, 2013).

semantic role – represents semantic roles from *NPSemrel*[4], a Polish shallow semantic parser (Kedzia and Maziarz, 2013), e.g. *agent*, *theme*.

An example sentence with one of its graph representations is presented in Fig. 3. The lemmas were replaced with the equivalent *Synset* nodes from plWordNet after disambiguating them with word sense disambiguation tool.

Constructed graphs can be enriched and generalised to some extent by expanding them with additional nodes from the linked semantic resources. Janz et al. (2018) used for this purpose plWordNet 3.0 and SUMO ontology. For all node pairs from the original graph the shortest paths going across given semantic resource are identified and then included into the expanded graph, cf (Janz et al., 2018). This means that the additional nodes are included together with the resource-specific relations comprising the paths.

All types of edges and nodes and their combinations characterised above were used for the description of pairs of sentences in the experiments by (Janz et al., 2018) and also in ours[5]. As a result, 12 possible graph types in total can be generated, i.e. 4 types of nodes and 3 types of resource expansion, namely: *Lemma lower* graph expanded with SUMO, *Lemma PoS lower* expanded on the basis of plWordNet, *Concept* expanded with SUMO (additional structures, generalisation by higher level concepts) and *Synset* graph expanded with both plWordNet and SUMO (as one connected semantic network). To generate the features we used all of possible graphs we could obtain with this procedure.

Graphs created for a pair of sentences – a training/testing case – were mainly used to calculate their similarity. The computed values of similarity measures were included in vector space representation describing given classification case. To compute similarities six different measures were applied Janz et al. (2018):

1. *Graph Edit Distance* (Fernández and Valiente, 2001) (GED) – the minimal sum of the costs of atomic operations transforming one graph into the other;

2. *Maximum Common Subgraph* (MCS) (Bunke and Shearer, 1998) – the size of maximum common subgraph normalised by the size of the bigger graph;

3. Measure *WGU* (Wallis et al., 2001) – the size of the maximum common subgraph normalised by the sum of the sizes of both graphs minus it.

4. *UGU* (Bunke, 1997) is simply $|G_1| + |G_2| - 2 \cdot |mcs(G_1, G_2)|$, where G_1 and G_2 are sentence graphs, and $mcs(...)$ returns the maximum common subgraph.

5. *MMCS* Fernández and Valiente (2001) expresses the dissimilarity of graphs G_1 and G_2: $|MCS(G_1, G_2)| - |mcs(G_1, G_2)|$.

6. *Contextual BOW* – based on the application of the *Jaccard* measure to sets of nodes of both graphs expanded with their direct neighbour nodes (Janz et al., 2018).

The calculated similarity values are next used as features – elements of input vectors – during training a classifier. By changing the way of constructing the graphs and computing their similarity we are able to control the representation of sentences in classification process and put more attention to characteristic properties of textual semantic relations (CST relations). This could be a possible way to tune the models by pre-selecting graph representations for the downstream task. However, in this work we do not attempt to perform any tuning procedure using prior graph selection.

[4]The construction of *NPSemrel* is based on hand-written lexicalised syntactic-semantic constraints. They mostly express high precision, i.e. around 60% in the worst cases, but the majority of them is close to 100%. However, the recall is much lower, so F1 measure is typically around 0.5, see (Kedzia and Maziarz, 2013).

[5]More specifically, for every single sentence pair we combine all of possible graph configurations (including possible expansions i.e. plWordNet and SUMO) with all available similarity metrics that can be used to generate similarity-based features. The possible graph configurations were generated in a following way: {[*Lemma*], [*Lemma PoS*], [*Synsets*], [*Concepts*], [*Lemma – plWordNet exp.*], [*Lemma – SUMO exp.*], [*Lemma – plWordNet & SUMO exp.*], [*Lemma PoS – plWordNet exp.*], [*Lemma PoS – SUMO exp.*], [*Lemma PoS – plWordNet & SUMO exp.*], [*Synsets – plWordNet exp.*], ..., [*Concepts – plWordNet & SUMO exp.*]} and so on.

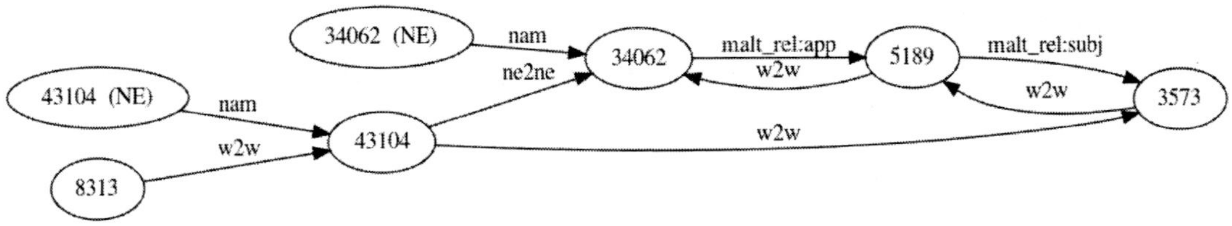

Figure 3: Graph built for the example sentence with *Synset* node type and full set of edges types (*w2w* – word order, *ne2ne* – NE order) (Janz et al., 2018).

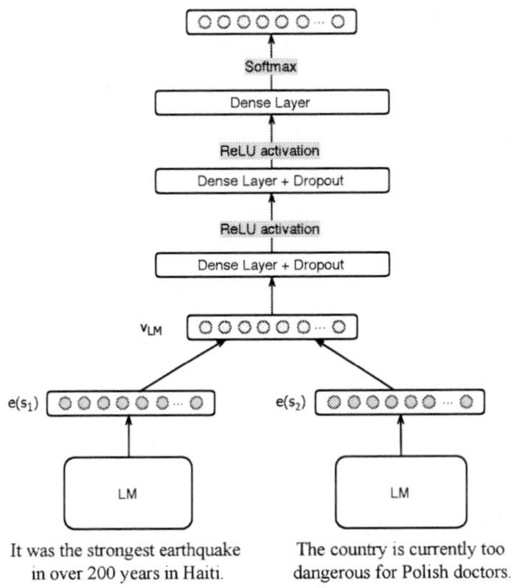

Figure 4: Baseline architecture with transformer-based language modeling and feed forward neural network with multiple dense layers. The language model is used to generate sentence embeddings.

6 CST Relation Recognition

In this section we describe the architecture of the baseline solutions as well as the architecture of their extensions. The architectures are generally based on contextual word embeddings computed by applying pre-trained language models to given sentence pairs. Our main aim was to evaluate existing modern language models and compare them with various wordnet-based features in the task of the recognition of discourse relations. As the task itself is closely related to other NLI tasks, we had assumed that the applied neural language models should bring very good results.

The first architecture uses contextual word embeddings to generate sentence embeddings of sentence pairs from the WUT CST corpus. Given a sentence pair (s_1, s_2) we generate an input vector space representation of this pair $v_{LM} \in \mathcal{R}^{2d_{LM}}$ by concatenating the representations of its sentences $e(s_1) \in \mathcal{R}^{d_{LM}}$, $e(s_2) \in \mathcal{R}^{d_{LM}}$ computed by a given language model LM. The concatenated vector $v_{LM} = [e(s_1), e(s_2)]$ is then passed through a multi-layer dense classification network with Dropout and ReLU activations on its hidden layers, and Softmax in the output layer. The baseline architecture is presented in figure 4.

Since the architecture itself is very simple we are easily able to extend it and incorporate supplementary features by concatenating precomputed vector space representations of input sentences v_{LM} with a vector v_{GF} of additional features coming from the graph-based representation (including similarity values calculated for various graphs) $v_{input} = [v_{LM}, v_{GF}]$. As a result the baseline architecture is expanded with pre-computed graph-based features mentioned in section 5.2.

7 Experimental Setting

To conduct the experiments we used the updated version of *WUT CST* dataset as it was mentioned in Sec. 3. We divided the dataset into three distinct parts to train, tune and evaluate selected neural models and their extensions. To prepare and test the models we applied popular transformer library called Hugging Face[6] Most of the language models used in this work were fine-tuned to the task to obtain the best possible results. We found that fine-tuning the models slightly increases their performance. The ELMo appeared to be difficult to tune, thus, we decided to test only the pre-trained version of this model (ELMo$_{nFT}$). For each pair of sentences we compute their vectors using given language model and classify them with the same baseline architecture presented in figure 4. The extended models used additional graph-based features as an input to classification network (see Sec. 6). As a baseline approach we used Logistic Model Tree (LMT) (Landwehr et al., 2005) trained on graph-based features only as it was proposed

[6] `https://huggingface.co`

Model	Overlap	Description	Background	Follow-up	Subsumption	Unrelated	Fulfilment	Elaboration	Summary	Identity	Paraphrase	Source	Accuracy
BERT	0.35	**0.89**	0.78	0.56	0.40	0.61	0.62	0.25	0.13	0.84	0.15	0.31	0.58
RoBERTa	0.41	0.85	0.83	0.61	0.55	0.68	0.57	0.32	0.21	1.00	0.47	0.36	0.63
HerBERT	0.37	0.84	0.78	0.55	0.30	0.62	0.52	0.14	**0.22**	0.63	0.00	0.29	0.57
ELMo$_{nFT}$	0.36	0.76	0.72	0.51	0.28	0.69	0.67	0.26	0.00	0.50	0.00	0.00	0.55
GF–LMT	0.69	0.68	0.83	0.74	0.75	0.95	0.60	0.40	0.00	0.95	0.53	**0.75**	0.71
GF–BERT	**0.82**	0.77	**0.86**	**0.88**	0.76	**0.97**	0.54	0.00	0.00	**1.00**	0.53	0.67	**0.78**
GF–RoBERTa	0.82	0.76	0.76	0.87	**0.78**	0.95	0.68	0.17	0.00	0.89	**0.55**	0.67	0.74
GF–HerBERT	0.79	0.85	0.81	0.86	0.71	0.88	0.79	0.15	0.00	0.84	0.36	0.67	0.77
GF–ELMo$_{nFT}$	0.80	0.80	0.84	0.87	0.65	0.87	**0.76**	**0.42**	0.20	0.86	0.36	0.67	0.77

Table 1: F1-scores of evaluated solutions computed with respect to CST relation type. The last column presents the final accuracy of the models.

in (Janz et al., 2018). We selected the default parameters offered by WEKA framework (Hall et al., 2009).

8 Results

The overall results are presented in Table 1 which includes the final F1-scores of four baseline language models, as well as their versions expanded with graph-based representation – marked by GF prefix. They are compared to graph-based only baseline solution GF–LMT – using Logistic Model Trees as a classifier and graph-based representation only. The baseline GF–LMT model, identical to the one of (Janz et al., 2018) achieved significantly better results, especially for many under-represented classes. The language models were fine-tuned multiple times to our task to ensure that we obtain the best possible results. The language models enhanced with the same graph-based features as our baseline model – GF–BERT, GF–HerBERT, GF–RoBERTa, and GF–ELMo appeared to beat their initial results as it was expected.

9 Conclusions

Neural language models (word and sentence embeddings) are capable to express enormous amounts of knowledge about possible language contexts, if pre-trained on a corpus that is large enough and representative. We applied models which have been built on very large corpora and showed very good performance when used as a basis in many applications. However, the complexity of such pre-trained models causes that machine learning algorithm must cope with it, unless they are fine tuned to a given problem on a dataset large enough. In order to do this, one requires appropriate data, both in terms of the good representation of the problem, and, very important, substantial size. Extraction of elements of linguistic structures introduces generalisation, highlighting most important markers and a kind of mapping to an abstract space. We showed that such enriched representation may help in problems where we do not have enough training data. A future challenge is to find a way of balancing and combining the two approaches.

Acknowledgments

The work financed as part of the investment in the CLARIN-PL[7] research infrastructure funded by the Polish Ministry of Science and Higher Education.

References

Priscila Aleixo and Thiago Alexandre Salgueiro Pardo. 2008. Finding Related Sentences in Multiple Documents for Multidocument Discourse Parsing of Brazilian Portuguese Texts. In *Companion Proceedings of the XIV Brazilian Symposium on Multimedia and the Web*, WebMedia '08, pages 298–303. ACM, New York, NY, USA.

Hongxiao Bai and Hai Zhao. 2018. Deep enhanced representation for implicit discourse relation recognition. In *Proceedings of the 27th International Conference on Computational Linguistics*, pages 571–583. Association for Computational Linguistics, Santa Fe, New Mex-

[7] `http://clarin-pl.eu`

ico, USA. URL https://www.aclweb.org/anthology/C18-1048.

Bartosz Broda, Michał Marcińczuk, Marek Maziarz, Adam Radziszewski, and Adam Wardyński. 2012. KPWr: Towards a Free Corpus of Polish. In Nicoletta Calzolari (Conference Chair), Khalid Choukri, Thierry Declerck, Mehmet Uğur Doğan, Bente Maegaard, Joseph Mariani, Asuncion Moreno, Jan Odijk, and Stelios Piperidis, editors, *Proceedings of the Eight International Conference on Language Resources and Evaluation (LREC'12)*. European Language Resources Association (ELRA), Istanbul, Turkey.

H. Bunke. 1997. On a Relation Between Graph Edit Distance and Maximum Common Subgraph. *Pattern Recogn. Lett.*, 18(9):689–694.

Horst Bunke and Kim Shearer. 1998. A Graph Distance Metric Based on the Maximal Common Subgraph. *Pattern Recogn. Lett.*, 19(3-4):255–259.

Paula C.F. Cardoso, Erick G. Maziero, María Lucía Castro Jorge, Eloize R.M. Seno, Ariani Di Felippo, Lucia Helena Machado Rino, Maria das Gracas Volpe Nunes, and Thiago Alexandre Salgueiro Pardo. 2011. CSTNews - A discourse-annotated corpus for single and multi-document summarization of news texts in Brazilian Portuguese. In *Proceedings of the 3rd RST Brazilian Meeting*, pages 88–105. Cuiabá, Brazil.

Andre Cianflone and Leila Kosseim. 2018. Attention for implicit discourse relation recognition. In *Proceedings of the Eleventh International Conference on Language Resources and Evaluation (LREC 2018)*. European Language Resources Association (ELRA), Miyazaki, Japan. URL https://www.aclweb.org/anthology/L18-1306.

J. Devlin, Ming-Wei Chang, Kenton Lee, and Kristina Toutanova. 2019. Bert: Pre-training of deep bidirectional transformers for language understanding. In *NAACL-HLT*.

Mirtha-Lina Fernández and Gabriel Valiente. 2001. A Graph Distance Metric Combining Maximum Common Subgraph and Minimum Common Supergraph. *Pattern Recogn. Lett.*, 22(6-7):753–758.

Matt Gardner, Joel Grus, Mark Neumann, Oyvind Tafjord, Pradeep Dasigi, Nelson F. Liu, Matthew Peters, Michael Schmitz, and Luke S. Zettlemoyer. 2017. Allennlp: A deep semantic natural language processing platform.

Fengyu Guo, Ruifang He, Di Jin, Jianwu Dang, Longbiao Wang, and Xiangang Li. 2018. Implicit discourse relation recognition using neural tensor network with interactive attention and sparse learning. In *Proceedings of the 27th International Conference on Computational Linguistics*, pages 547–558. Association for Computational Linguistics, Santa Fe, New Mexico, USA. URL https://www.aclweb.org/anthology/C18-1046.

Mark Hall, Eibe Frank, Geoffrey Holmes, Bernhard Pfahringer, Peter Reutemann, and Ian H Witten. 2009. The weka data mining software: an update. *ACM SIGKDD explorations newsletter*, 11(1):10–18.

Arkadiusz Janz, Paweł Kędzia, and Maciej Piasecki. 2018. Graph-based complex representation in inter-sentence relation recognition in polish texts. *Cybernetics and Information Technologies Journal*, 18(1):152–170.

Pawel Kedzia and Marek Maziarz. 2013. Recognizing semantic relations within Polish noun phrase: A rule-based approach. In *RANLP*.

Paweł Kędzia, Maciej Piasecki, and Arkadiusz Janz. 2017. Graph-based approach to recognizing CST relations in Polish texts. In *Proceedings of the International Conference Recent Advances in Natural Language Processing, RANLP 2017*, pages 363–371. INCOMA Ltd., Varna, Bulgaria. URL https://doi.org/10.26615/978-954-452-049-6_048.

Jan Kocoń and Michał Gawor. 2019. Evaluating KGR10 polish word embeddings in the recognition of temporal expressions using BiLSTM-CRF. *arXiv preprint arXiv:1904.04055*.

Yogan Jaya Kumar, Naomie Salim, Ahmed Hamza, and Albarraa Abuobieda. 2012a. *Automatic identification of cross-document structural relationships*, pages 26–29.

Yogan Jaya Kumar, Naomie Salim, and Basit Raza. 2012b. Cross-document Structural Relationship Identification Using Supervised Machine Learning. *Appl. Soft Comput.*, 12(10):3124–3131.

Paweł Kędzia and Maciej Piasecki. 2014. Ruled-based, Interlingual Motivated Mapping of plWordNet onto SUMO Ontology. In Nicoletta

Calzolari, Khalid Choukri, Thierry Declerck, Hrafn Loftsson, Bente Maegaard, Joseph Mariani, Asunción Moreno, Jan Odijk, and Stelios Piperidis, editors, *Proceedings of the Ninth International Conference on Language Resources and Evaluation (LREC-2014), Reykjavik, Iceland, May 26-31, 2014.*, pages 4351–4358.

Paweł Kędzia, Maciej Piasecki, and Marlena Orlińska. 2015. Word sense disambiguation based on large scale Polish CLARIN heterogeneous lexical resources. *Cognitive Studies / Études cognitives*, 15:269–292. URL https://ispan.waw.pl/journals/index.php/cs-ec/article/download/cs.2015.019/1765.

Niels Landwehr, Mark Hall, and Eibe Frank. 2005. Logistic model trees. *Machine learning*, 59(1-2):161–205.

Yinhan Liu, Myle Ott, Naman Goyal, Jingfei Du, Mandar Joshi, Danqi Chen, Omer Levy, Mike Lewis, Luke Zettlemoyer, and Veselin Stoyanov. 2019. Roberta: A robustly optimized bert pretraining approach. *arXiv preprint arXiv:1907.11692*.

Michał Marcińczuk, Jan Kocoń, and Maciej Janicki. 2013. Liner2 – a customizable framework for proper names recognition for Polish. In Robert Bembenik, Łukasz Skonieczny, Henryk Rybiński, Marzena Kryszkiewicz, and Marek Niezgódka, editors, *Intelligent Tools for Building a Scientific Information Platform*, pages 231–253.

Erick Galani Maziero, Maria Lucía Del Rosário Castro Jorge, and Thiago Alexandre Salgueiro Pardo. 2014. Revisiting Cross-document Structure Theory for Multi-document Discourse Parsing. *Inf. Process. Manage.*, 50(2):297–314.

Adam Pease. 2011. *Ontology: A Practical Guide*. Articulate Software Press, Angwin, CA.

Maciej Piasecki, Pawel Kędzia, and Marlena Orlińska. 2016. plWordNet in Word Sense Disambiguation task. In *GWC 2016, Proceedings of the 8th Global Wordnet Conference, Bucharest, 27-30 January 2016 Osaka, Japan*, pages 280–290.

E. Ponti and A. Korhonen. 2017. Event-related features in feedforward neural networks contribute to identifying implicit causal relations in discourse. In *Proceedings of the 2nd Workshop on Linking Models of Lexical, Sentential and Discourse-level Semantics*, pages 25–30.

Dragomir R. Radev. 2000. A Common Theory of Information Fusion from Multiple Text Sources Step One: Cross-document Structure. In *Proceedings of the 1st SIGdial Workshop on Discourse and Dialogue - Volume 10*, SIGDIAL '00, pages 74–83. Association for Computational Linguistics, Stroudsburg, PA, USA.

Dragomir R. Radev, Jahna Otterbacher, and Zhu Zhang. 2004. Cst bank: A corpus for the study of cross-document structural relationships. In *LREC*. European Language Resources Association.

Adam Radziszewski. 2013. *A Tiered CRF Tagger for Polish*, pages 215–230. Springer Berlin Heidelberg, Berlin, Heidelberg. URL https://doi.org/10.1007/978-3-642-35647-6_16.

Adam Radziszewski and Adam Pawlaczek. 2013. *Language Processing and Intelligent Information Systems: 20th International Conference, IIS 2013, Warsaw, Poland, June 17-18, 2013. Proceedings*, chapter Incorporating Head Recognition into a CRF Chunker, pages 22–27. Springer Berlin Heidelberg, Berlin, Heidelberg.

Adam Radziszewski, Adam Wardyński, and Tomasz Śniatowski. 2011. WCCL: A morpho-syntactic feature toolkit. In *Proceedings of the Balto-Slavonic Natural Language Processing Workshop (BSNLP 2011)*. Springer.

Piotr Rybak, Robert Mroczkowski, Janusz Tracz, and Ireneusz Gawlik. 2020. Klej: Comprehensive benchmark for polish language understanding. *arXiv preprint arXiv:2005.00630*.

W. D. Wallis, P. Shoubridge, M. Kraetz, and D. Ray. 2001. Graph Distances Using Graph Union. *Pattern Recogn. Lett.*, 22(6-7):701–704.

Alina Wróblewska and Marcin Woliński. 2012. *Preliminary Experiments in Polish Dependency Parsing*, pages 279–292. Springer Berlin Heidelberg, Berlin, Heidelberg.

Alina Wróblewska. 2014. *Polish Dependency Parser Trained on an Automatically Induced Dependency Bank*. Ph.D. dissertation, Institute of Computer Science, Polish Academy of Sciences, Warsaw.

Nik Adilah Hanin Binti Zahri and Fumiyo Fukumoto. 2011. *Multi-document Summariza-*

tion Using Link Analysis Based on Rhetorical Relations between Sentences, pages 328–338. Springer Berlin Heidelberg, Berlin, Heidelberg.

Zhu Zhang, Jahna Otterbacher, and Dragomir Radev. 2003. Learning Cross-document Structural Relationships Using Boosting. In *Proceedings of the Twelfth International Conference on Information and Knowledge Management*, CIKM '03, pages 124–130. ACM, New York, NY, USA.

Zhu Zhang and Dragomir Radev. 2005. Combining Labeled and Unlabeled Data for Learning Cross-document Structural Relationships. In *Proceedings of the First International Joint Conference on Natural Language Processing*, pages 32–41. Springer-Verlag, Berlin, Heidelberg.

What is on Social Media that is not in WordNet? A Preliminary Analysis on the TwitterAAE Corpus

Cecilia Domingo*, Tatiana Gonzalez-Ferrero*, and Itziar Gonzalez-Dios**

*University of the Basque Country (UPV/EHU)
**Ixa group, HiTZ center, University of the Basque Country (UPV/EHU)
[cdomingo003, tgonzalez023]@ikasle.ehu.eus, itziar.gonzalezd@ehu.eus

Abstract

Natural Language Processing tools and resources have been so far mainly created and trained for standard varieties of language. Nowadays, with the use of large amounts of data gathered from social media, other varieties and registers need to be processed, which may present other challenges and difficulties. In this work, we focus on English and we present a preliminary analysis by comparing the Twitter-AAE corpus, which is annotated for ethnicity, and WordNet by quantifying and explaining the online language that WordNet misses.

1 Introduction

Natural Language Processing (NLP) tools and resources have usually been developed for major and standard varieties of language. Maintaining and updating these resources is expensive (Aldezabal et al., 2018), but recently open-source methodologies are being used to update the English WordNet (McCrae et al., 2020). However, well-known state-of-the-art tools in data processing that are used in industry and offer semantic analysis, such as NLTK (Loper and Bird, 2002) or knowledge-based word sense disambiguation tools like UKB, still rely on Princeton WordNet (Miller, 1995), which has not been updated for a long time.

On the other hand, NLP tools are being used nowadays in many industrial, marketing and social analysis projects and mainly social media text is being used. It is well known that social media may present several challenges when it comes to data processing, since, among others, non-standard varieties of languages or slang are used. Other problems related to this kind of texts are the length of the produced texts (sentences are rather short) and the difficulty of identifying useful information in order to separate it from what is not useful, such as hashtags, mentions or user-names (Farzindar and Inkpen, 2016).

In this paper, we explore the coverage of sociolects in WordNet to see what information state-of-the-art knowledge-based NLP tools may miss when analysing social media. In this preliminary analysis we use the TwitterAAE corpus (Blodgett et al., 2016), which contains geographic and census information. Exactly, we follow this methodology: a) we select a corpus with geographical/sociological information; b) we extract a sample of each group and we preprocess it; c) we compare it against an NLP resource, in our case, WordNet, and carry out a quantitative and qualitative analysis of the differences.

As a contribution of this preliminary study, we want to raise awareness of, on the one hand, how much linguistic diversity can be found in common data sources and, on the other hand, how risky it may be to use generic NLP tools and resources to process these diverse linguistic registers (colloquial, informal, internet language...) and sociolects for which the tools were not designed.

This paper is structured as follows: in Section 2 we present the corpus we have used and its preprocessing, in Section 3 we compare quantitatively and qualitatively the most frequent lemmas in the corpus to WordNet, in Section 4 we discuss our findings and expand upon some issues that concern the whole project. Finally, in Section 5 we conclude and outline the future work.

2 Corpus selection and preprocessing

The dataset used in this project was the publicly available TwitterAAE corpus (Blodgett et al., 2016), which consisted of 59.2 million publicly posted geolocated tweets (F. Morstatter and Carley, 2013). These data were collected in the United States in 2013. Each message was annotated considering the U.S. Census block-group geographic area from which it was posted, meaning that ethnicity and race information associated with that district was taken into account. Four different covariants were established for the annotation: (non-Hispanic) Black, Hispanic (of any race), (non-Hispanic) Asian, and (non-Hispanic) White. This grouping reflects the main categories observed in the US census data, removing some smaller categories like "Native Hawaiian and Other Pacific Islander", and thus naturally as limited in nuance as the census categories may be (e.g. the census report groups all Black identities together, whether the respondents are African-American, African, Caribbean...). The terminology used in this paper will therefore reflect this simplified classification. For every user, the demographic values of all their tweets within the dataset were then averaged resulting in a length-four vector. The demographic data associated to each user and their corresponding tweets were then used by Blodgett and O'Connor (2017) to develop a mixed-membership probabilistic model that linked linguistic features with ethnicity. This model, the TwitterAAE model, assigned ethnicity values to the messages according to census data, giving each ethnicity a different proportion based on the "weight" of that ethnicity in the area where the tweet was written. If a tweet was assigned a proportion of more than 0.8, that meant that the tweet had a strong association with one of the previously mentioned demographic groups. A small sample of example messages belonging to each of the four covariants can be found in Table 1.

2.1 Sample selection

NLP tools are mainly trained to handle the standard variety of languages. Given that 2017 US census data reports 72.3 % of the population as exclusively white,[1] we assumed that tweets more strongly associated with the White demographic would be the most representative of standard English, although, as will be discussed after presenting our results, tweets even by the majority demographic present much non-standard language. To extract this sample of assumed standard English, we collected a subcorpus of tweets with the highest possible value of association with the White demographic, which was a proportion of 0.99 or higher. The new subcorpus consisted of around a million tweets.

In order to make a comparison, we needed to create other subcorpora of approximately the same size containing the messages of the other three demographic groups accounted for in the dataset. To create these subcorpora it was necessary to reduce the association value slightly, to a proportion of 0.9 or more, since otherwise the 'very' Black, Hispanic and Asian subcorpora size would have been significantly smaller than that of the 'very' White one.

2.2 Preprocessing

Prior to performing the analysis it was necessary to not only preprocess the subcorpora, but also the lemmas included in WordNet.

The Natural Language Toolkit (NLTK) provided us with the list of all lemmas included in WordNet. We used this version because it is the one that is used in NLP pipelines and applications. Since our goal was to identify the textual information that cannot be processed by WordNet, we needed to extract all the information that is in fact included in WordNet. We first filtered all the Multi-Word Expressions (MWE). It was necessary to work firstly with MWE and then with single-word lemmas separately in order to avoid overlap between the two (e.g. a MWE like "around the bend" has to be extracted first to avoid extracting the single-word lemmas "around" and "bend" separately and incorrectly). At the end of this process, we obtained two lists of lemma types to compare our corpora against.

Regarding the subcorpora, we selected 25 000 tweets for this preliminary analysis. We removed hashtags, mentions, emoticons, numbers, punctuation marks, white spaces, and other elements that did not provide useful information (Blodgett et al., 2018). Afterward, we removed all MWEs from the subcorpora by making use of the previously created file that listed all MWEs in WordNet. The next step was to extract Named-Entities with spaCy.[2] The remaining words were then lowercased, tokenized, and lemmatized, again with the aid of spaCy. Finally, we extracted all the single-word lemmas that were in the WordNet list, leaving only the tokens that could not be recognized.

Moreover, the Asian and Hispanic subcorpora contained a large number of tweets in languages other than English. The tweets in Spanish and Por-

[1] `data.census.gov/cedsci/table`

[2] `https://spacy.io/`

Tweet	Black	Hispanic	Asian	White
One min itss dhis, dhen another min itss dhat	**0.902**	0.0	0.0	0.098
Wont look out fa dis punk no mo	**0.91**	0.057	0.002	0.03
Well truth be told, I do not speak great Mexican	0.01	**0.936**	0.008	0.045
Okay, since I got no one to text, a dormir putos!	0.001	**0.93**	0.031	0.037
Y.O.L.O =[Y]ou [O]bviously [L]ove [O]reos	0.008	0.01	**0.956**	0.026
First person to bring me a midol at work wins best friend card for life. GO!	0.0	0.0	**1.0**	0.0
Spongebob will get his license before Taylor Swift finds love	0.0	0.005	0.001	**0.992**
I need to not be an old lady and learn to stay up past 8:30 #idontknowwhy #ihaveaproblem	0.0	0.0	0.0	**1.0**

Table 1: Examples from the Black, Hispanic, Asian and White subcorpora.

tuguese, due to their large number and the availability of language models, were also processed with spaCy to obtain data for the qualitative analysis. However, as Wordnet is an English resource, only the tweets in English were compared against the lists of Wordnet lemmas and used in the quantitative analysis. To detect the language of each tweet, the langid library[3] was used, as it showed the best combination of detail in output and accuracy of classification among the tools tested. The threshold to classify a tweet as English was set as 40; we arrived at this figure after several tests, to achieve optimal precision without much loss in recall.

3 Comparison to WordNet

In this section, we present a quantitative analysis of the lemmas found in each of the subcorpora and in WordNet. On the one hand, we have analyzed the number and percentage of lemmas and unique lemmas not found in WordNet. On the other hand, we have calculated the intersection of the subcorpora with the White subcorpus. Moreover, in the qualitative analysis we present the commonalities and the specifics of each subcorpus.

3.1 Quantitative Analysis

In Table 2, we show the number and percentage of lemmas[4] (repeated and unique) not found in WordNet for each subcorpus.

When we compare the two corpora that were almost fully in English, we observe that the White corpus contained 3501 more words that were not found in WordNet (not counting the words removed in preprocessing). However, removing the repetitions and counting each unique lemma only once reveals the opposite: there are 1994 more unique lemmas in the list of not-found lemmas from the Black corpus. This can be partly explained by the fact that the White corpus contained 8224 more pronouns. When we separate the lemmas found in both the Black and White corpora and look at the lemmas that are different, the list of unique not-found lemmas remains longer for the Black corpus than for the White one.

Looking at the data for the Hispanic and Asian corpora, it again seems that the White corpus posed the biggest challenge for WordNet, but this conclusion can again be discarded: if we include the tweets that were only classified as English with low confidence or that were classified as another language, the number of not-found lemmas rises to 79678 for the Asian corpus, and 31983 for the Hispanic. With regard to the unique lemmas, the number also rises significantly. The majority of these lemmas are in languages other than English. In the Hispanic corpus, however, there is a more balanced mix of Spanish and English lemmas.

When looking at the total amount of not-found lemmas in WordNet, there are 9542 fewer lemmas in the Hispanic subcorpus compared to the White one. Moreover, although the completely opposite happened with the Black corpus, the count of unique lemmas not found in WordNet for the White subcorpus was again considerably higher than those for the Hispanic one, more specifically 1160 lemmas of difference between them.

[3] https://github.com/saffsd/langid.py

[4] The (cleaned) lemma lists are available at ixa2.si.ehu.eus/notinwordnetwordlists.

Subcorpus	Total words (without tags, etc.)	Lemmas not found in WN	% of total tokens	Unique lemmas not found in WN	% of total tokens
Asian (only English tweets)	7290	916	12.706	218	3.023
Hispanic (only English tweets)	138222	20790	15.041	2061	1.491
Black	163549	26831	16.405	5215	3.188
White	228794	30332	13.257	3221	1.407

Table 2: Lemmas not found in WordNet, in absolute terms and relative to the size of each subcorpus

If we take a look at the rates of repeated lemmas, the Black and Hispanic corpora had the highest rate of not-found lemmas; for unique lemmas, it was the Asian and again the Hispanic corpora which had the highest rate. These data suggest that, even when people tagged as Asian and Hispanic users tweet in English, their language deviates more than that of the users tagged as Black and White from the standard English vocabulary recorded in WordNet. Users tagged as Black also seem to employ words not present in WordNet very frequently, but with less variety than the people tagged as members of the Asian group, who use more non-standard words, though with lower frequency. Overall, the users tagged in the Hispanic group proved the most problematic for an analysis reliant upon WordNet.

With regard to the Asian subcorpus, it must again be noted that its linguistic heterogeneity impedes any reliable quantitative comparisons. We will only mention that, even when we express the comparisons in relative terms to compensate for the small size of the English-language tweets of the Asian corpus, the Asian corpus has the lowest rate of unique lemmas in common with the White corpus. This suggests that the English written by the Asian and Black population according to the corpus may be the most different from the variant of the people tagged as White.

In Table 3, we present the intersection between the subcorpora and some illustrative examples. As we are comparing corpora of very different sizes, though we provide some quantitative data, we will focus on the qualitative analysis, which we believe will be of more value and which can be found below in Section 3.2.

3.2 Qualitative Analysis

As can be seen in Table 2, there is a large number of unique lemmas not found in WordNet that appear on one corpus but not on the one it is compared with. The only exception would be the Asian corpus, but this is easily explained by the small number of tweets in this corpus that were classified as English. The overall numbers seem indicative of a significant difference in the lexicon used by speakers of the sociolects reflected in each corpus. This difference can be corroborated by looking at some of the most common lemmas exclusive to each corpus. Due to the large number of lemmas to analyze, we only comment on the most frequent ones since lemmas ranked outside the top 30 already show very low frequencies.

3.2.1 Commonalities of all corpora

As was mentioned in the quantitative analysis, the corpora are not perfectly comparable, as the Asian and Hispanic corpora contain a large proportion of tweets in a language other than English. Still, a general look at all the corpora allows us to see some general characteristics of internet speech that are challenging for NLP tools, regardless of the user's dialect, or even language. It is important to bear in mind, though, that functional parts of speech are not included in WordNet, so understandably the list of common lemmas includes standard pronouns, prepositions or conjunctions. However, there are also many non-standard English (and Spanish and Portuguese) words in the list, and those are the kinds of words that seem to be characteristic of online writing:

- Onomatopoeia and forms of laughter: awww, hahahaha, lmao, kkkk (in Portuguese), jajaja (in Spanish)...
- Words with additional letters at the end: yess,yesss,yessss,yesssss...
- Acronyms: lbs, omg, smh, wtf...

Subcorpora	Exclusive lemmas	Examples
{BLACK (not WHITE)}	4787	*anotha, fckmuhlife, smoken*
{HISPANIC (not WHITE)}	1680	*definitly, samething, burritos*
{ASIAN (not WHITE)}	205	*twittrr, veryone, oleelo*
{WHITE (not BLACK)}	2793	*accidently, cheez, forsureeee*
{WHITE (not HISPANIC)}	2840	*memoryin, sweeet, hdache*
{WHITE (not ASIAN)}	3208	*bdtime, finaallly, hunny*
{BOTH BLACK and WHITE}	428	*badass, freakin, gurl*
{BOTH HISPANIC and WHITE}	381	*yike, pendeja, hungover*
{BOTH ASIAN and WHITE}	13	*anything, boooo, skype*

Table 3: Count of unique lemmas not found in WordNet that exist in only one of the two corpora compared or that exist in both

- Joint words: bestfriend, forreal, goodnight, lemme, wassup...
- Shortened words: bday, dnt, prolly, txt...
- Words related to technology: retweet, Facebook, whatsapp...

Aside from these types of words and standard words in languages other than English, all the lists of lemmas not found in WordNet contained errors related to preprocessing:

- Named entities that were not recognized as such, possibly due to miscapitalization, and sometimes perhaps because they did not have the typical form of a named entity (e.g. the TV show "Buckwild", mentioned in several tweets, could be mistaken for an adjective or adverb).
- Lemmatization issues in English text, for example, "to poop" was incorreclty lemmatized despite being a well-established word, used in the currently most common sense since at least 1903, according to Merriam Webster's dictionary.[5] We also encountered something similar with the verb "to text", lemmatized as "texte". This error is more understandable, as "to text" has only existed for two decades; still, though perhaps this verb was not so much in vogue when WordNet was created, a modern lemmatizer should be able to deal with such a common verb.
- Lemmatization issues with other languages. Even though the focus of this project was on English-language processing, as spaCy also included models for Spanish and Portuguese, we tried its lemmatizer for the tweets in those languages and encountered more lemmatization problems. These were of a different nature: when a word could be an inflected form of more than one lemma, the lemmatizer tended to select the less frequent one (e.g. the Spanish and Portuguese preposition "para" was interpreted as a form of the verb "parir, meaning "to give birth").

3.2.2 The Black corpus

The meager length of the list of not-found lemmas common to the Black and White corpora strongly suggests a big difference between the sociolects reflected in each corpus. In the analysis of the most frequent lemmas of the Black corpus that were not found in WordNet, firstly, whereas among the lemmas from the White corpus we barely saw any mild profanity (e.g. "douchebag"), here we find several acronyms with "f" and two alternative spellings of the word "shit". All this is not to say that there is no actual strong profanity in either corpus: both corpora feature numerous instances of derivations and inflections of "fuck", but this is a standard word that is included in WordNet. Still, it is interesting to see that a search for forms of "fuck" returns almost twice as many hits for the Black corpus than for the White corpus. Though in online speech we see many acronyms and alternative spellings overall, in the case of profanity these transformations of words might actually serve a purpose: escaping

[5]`https://www.merriam-webster.com/` (Accessed on 2020-06-16)

filters so that posts are not removed by moderators. Alternative spellings are overall very common in the Black subcorpus, as reflected by our list of frequent lemmas (e.g. "bruh", "nomore", etc.), sometimes reflecting non-standard pronunciations (e.g. "thang"), that are known to be characteristic of African-American English (AAE) (Kohler et al., 2007; Patton-Terry and Connor, 2010). Even though the list of lemmas from the White corpus was sparser, the alternative spellings in the top 28 most frequent lemmas from the Black corpus not found in WordNet had relatively high frequencies, which would justify more efforts to adapt NLP tools to accommodate them, at least if those tools are to process colloquial English.

3.2.3 The Asian corpus

For this corpus, given the small number of tweets written in English, the comparison between the Asian and the White corpus is of little relevance (less than 2 % of tweets in the Asian corpus were classified confidently as English). The English part of this subcorpus contained a large number of tweets from a traffic channel, which distorted the results and took most positions in the top-frequency words. Other frequent lemmas were laughter onomatopoeia in English and Portuguese. Nonetheless, tweets in English were a minority in this corpus (no more than 15 %, if we add the ones classified less confidently as English), so the majority of lemmas not found in WordNet were classified as Spanish and Portuguese. As WordNet is a resource for English, these lemmas were nothing exceptional, but rather ordinary Spanish and Portuguese words (e.g. in both languages the most frequent lemma that was not a preposition or adverb was the equivalent of "make" or "do"). Something less ordinary were the 135 variations of the "jaja" laughter onomatopoeia in the Spanish file - illustrative of the wide variety of laughing expressions used online.

3.2.4 The Hispanic corpus

Although it also applies to the previously described subcorpora, it is surprising that, along with the acronyms and the most varied representations of laughter ("lmao", "xd", "hahah") and agreement ("yeahh", "yess"), joint words have a strong presence in the Hispanic subcorpus. This may well be due to the appearance of hashtags that have not been recognized as such in the pre-processing, and therefore have not been removed (e.g. "onedayilllooklike", "whataburger", "wordsyouneverwanttohear"), or because the user has intentionally got rid of the spaces between words since there is a character limit in the Twitter platform when writing messages. Whatever the reason, the employed NLP tools have not been able to recognize this phenomenon, and even though the lemmas that make up the joint words might be easily found in WordNet, they have remained unrecognized. However, and as one could have expected, the most characteristic feature of this subcorpus is the presence of Spanish words, even if the analysed tweets have been mostly written in English. Evidently, these terms are not found in WordNet. Lastly, it is worth mentioning that the Hispanic subcorpus contains several misspellings. One could say that the type of the observed typos are made quite recurrently by Spanish native speakers ("seriuosly", "pasword", "ecspecially").

3.2.5 The White corpus

As in the Hispanic subcorpus, a noticeable characteristic of the list of lemmas of the White corpus is the variety of expressions denoting laughter (e.g. "hahah", "hahahah", "lolol"). Despite the variability, the most frequent onomatopoeias seem to be the shortest (two or three syllables) with a regular pattern of "(ha)*h". Though very few onomatopoeia exist in WordNet (e.g. onomatopoeia that also function as verbs, like "moo"), the frequency of appearance of these laughter onomatopoeia would justify their inclusion in any NLP tool that could be considered suitable for handling tweets. As has been described, with a few exceptions, there seems to be a regular pattern in the formation of the different forms of laughter, so lemmatizers could be adapted to tackle the most frequent forms. Other frequent lemmas refer to technology (e.g. "snapchat", "ipad"), understandably too modern to be processed by resources that are not updated regularly.

It is also interesting how some named entities escaped the NER filter applied during preprocessing. This highlights how named entities may adopt different forms in online discussions. For instance, the name of the Canadian singer Justin Bieber, though often spelled full and thus correctly spotted through NER, may also appear as simply "Bieber", and something similar might happen with other celebrities. Also, we see an example of the popular internet trend of referring to TV shows or other popular sagas/bands/etc. by an acronym;

the American TV show Pretty Little Liars thus becomes "PLL". When the acronym is capitalized, it is recognized by our NER tool (only as an organization, though), but users online often do not care much for capitalization, and "pll" cannot be recognized as a named entity. Lastly, we must mention that several of the lemmas in the list of "white" lemmas were introduced by a single user, a weather channel ("wx", "lotemp", "hitemp").

4 Discussion

This preliminary experiment has allowed us to see that general NLP tools' performance on online, colloquial speech is suboptimal, especially with texts written by users outside the White demographic according the annotations of the corpus. We used the spaCy lemmatizer and NER tool, which are very popular nowadays, but even these modern tools had issues with some phenomena of internet speech: new terms, alternative spellings, new named entities and disregard for capitalization.

We have seen that WordNet was developed with standard English in mind and has not been updated for many years, so it fails to account for "modern" terms (we are considering tweets from 2013 relatively modern), online slang and diverse dialects. Interestingly, we saw that WordNet includes many multiword expressions (over sixty thousand), but the trend online seems to go in the opposite direction: expressions are shortened into acronyms (e.g. "lol", "omg"), and even single words are shortened (e.g. "bday, "txt").

As vast amounts of text are produced online daily, and this is of interest to businesses and researchers, there are initiatives that try to better deal with the type of language used online. For instance, Colloquial WordNet (McCrae et al., 2017) aims to be a more modern version of WordNet, one that includes popular, colloquial terms used online and SlangNet (Dhuliawala et al., 2016) gathers slang words and neologisms from the internet structured like in WordNet. It would certainly be worthy of study whether these resources recognize Twitter lexicon better; in our study, however, we did not perform any analysis using Colloquial WordNet, due to the difficulty in extracting its list of lemmas, at least in comparison with the easy method available in WordNet (a line of Python code suffices and returns text with no inconvenient tags) and SlangNet is not available.

WordNet does not include certain parts of speech, such as prepositions; it only includes "open class words". Nonetheless, as we have seen, internet users create new versions of "closed class words" (e.g. "eht" as a synonym of "at") or create words that merge words from both classes (e.g. "lemme", meaning "let me"). A deeper analysis of the words from our corpus belonging to or containing PoS not present in WordNet would be valuable, to consider whether such words should be added to semantic databases, or whether lemmatizers should be adapted to extract the standard form when processing new variants.

Though the focus of this project was on English-language text, it is important to emphasize the large number of tweets written in languages other than English, especially in the case of the Asian subcorpus. Therefore, any toolkit employed to process tweets from the US will need to include language detection and analysis tools for languages other than English - processing only English leaves many users behind and reduces the validity of any conclusions that might be extracted from analyzing tweets.

Future studies in this area, when possible, should also analyze a larger section of the TwitterAAE corpus. It is important to have a large corpus size to prevent a single user's repetitive lexicon from distorting the results. Alternatively, this type of users could be detected as part of preprocessing and their tweets excluded.

Even though the corpus has been very useful and is relatively modern, considering how fast language can change online, it would be necessary to replicate the methodology of Blodgett and O'Connor (2017) to annotate more recent tweets. The methodology could also be applied to other languages for which NLP tools and demographic data are available (e.g. to analyze dialects of Spanish or German). The resulting datasets would be very valuable for sociolinguistic studies, but also to assess NLP tools' inclusivity – are NLP tools leaving some groups of people behind? Nonetheless, it must be noted that, as any model, the one employed to annotate the dataset used here showed some inaccuracies. Though the sociolinguistic validation performed by Blodgett and O'Connor (2017) proved it quite accurate for AAE, classification in other categories seemed more problematic (e.g. the large number of Spanish tweets in the Asian category). This may be due partly to the even larger diversity of Asian and Hispanic groups, which makes classifiying people into four categories overly simplistic at times (e.g. where do Brazilians go, being racially very diverse and culturally close to the Hispanic demographic but outside it?). Problems may also have arisen due to the source of the data used to build the model: the US Census is known to undercount minorities.[6] Even though race and ethnicity are self-reported, the way the data are aggregated is problematic for some groups, such as Middle-Eastern populations, Afro-Latinos or Portuguese speakers.[7] Moreover, the way the Census data were linked to the tweets may have also introduced some inaccuracies: geolocation may not have been perfectly exact,[8] and it may sometimes have been false, given the large number of internet users who connect through VPN.[9]

Finally, we would like to emphasize the same message that Blodgett and O'Connor (2017) leave at the end of their paper: African Americans are underrepresented in the Computer Science community, which makes it much harder for their voices to be taken into account. This conclusion is also valid for the Hispanic demographic, though for the Asian demographic there seems to be adequate representation.[10]

5 Conclusion and future work

In this paper, we have carried out an analysis of a corpus with geolocated tweets and we have compared the lemmas used to WordNet. As the corpus contained text from social media, we have dealt with non-standard language and we have seen that it still presents a challenge for mainstream NLP resources, which may put them at risk of leaving behind some speakers and varieties. As a result of this study, we encourage linguistic work on different registers and non-standard varieties.

In the future, we plan to expand the analysis to a bigger sample of the corpus and apply this methodology to study other languages e.g. Spanish with *Corpus de Referencia del Español Actual* (CREA) corpus. Moreover, we are preparing a list of candidate synsets to propose to the English WordNet (McCrae et al., 2020) following the open source and collaborative initiative. Moreover, we would like to study the possibility of adding register/ geographical information to synsets as e.g. Huber and Hinrichs (2019) are proposing for the Swiss variety of German. Analysing other Twitter tokens such as hashtags or mentions that were left out in the preprocessing could lead also to other studies.

[6] https://journalistsresource.org/studies/government/2020-census-research-undercount/

[7] https://www.census.gov/topics/population/race/about/faq.html

[8] https://www.singlemindconsulting.com/blog/what-is-geolocation/

[9] https://blog.globalwebindex.com/chart-of-the-day/vpn-usage-2018/

[10] https://www.wired.com/story/computer-science-graduates-diversity/

Acknowledgments

This work has been partially funded by the project DeepReading (RTI2018-096846-B-C21) supported by the Ministry of Science, Innovation and Universities of the Spanish Government, Ixa Group-consolidated group type A by the Basque Government (IT1343-19) and BigKnowledge – Ayudas Fundación BBVA a Equipos de Equipos de Investigación Científica 2018.

References

Izaskun Aldezabal, Xabier Artola, Arantza Díaz de Ilarraza, Itziar Gonzalez-Dios, Gorka Labaka, German Rigau, and Ruben Urizar. 2018. Basque e-lexicographic resources: linguistic basis, development, and future perspectives. In *Workshop on eLexicography: Between Digital Humanities and Artificial Intelligence*.

S. L. Blodgett and B. O'Connor. 2017. Racial disparity in natural language processing: A case study of social media african-american english.

Su Lin Blodgett, Lisa Green, and Brendan O'Connor. 2016. Demographic dialectal variation in social media: A case study of african-american english. In *Proceedings of the 2016 Conference on Empirical Methods in Natural Language Processing*, pages 1119–1130.

Su Lin Blodgett, Johnny Wei, and Brendan O'Connor. 2018. Twitter universal dependency parsing for african-american and mainstream american english. In *Proceedings of the 56th Annual Meeting of the Association for Computational Linguistics (Volume 1: Long Papers)*, pages 1415–1425.

Shehzaad Dhuliawala, Diptesh Kanojia, and Pushpak Bhattacharyya. 2016. SlangNet: A WordNet like Resource for English Slang. In *Proceedings of the Tenth International Conference on Language Resources and Evaluation (LREC'16)*, pages 4329–4332.

H. Liu F. Morstatter, J. Pfeffer and K. M. Carley. 2013. Is the sample good enough? comparing data from twitter's streaming api with twitter's firehose. In *Proceedings of the Seventh International AAAI Conference on Weblogs and Social Media*, pages 400–408.

A. Farzindar and D. Inkpen. 2016. Natural language processing for social media. *Computational Linguistics*, 42(4):833–836.

Eva Huber and Erhard Hinrichs. 2019. Including Swiss Standard German in GermaNet. In *Proceedings of the Tenth Global Wordnet Conference*, pages 24–32.

Candida T Kohler, Ruth Huntley Bahr, Elaine R Silliman, Judith Becker Bryant, Kenn Apel, and Louise C Wilkinson. 2007. African american english dialect and performance on nonword spelling and phonemic awareness tasks. *American Journal of Speech-Language Pathology*.

Edward Loper and Steven Bird. 2002. NLTK: The Natural Language Toolkit. In *Proceedings of the ACL-02 Workshop on Effective Tools and Methodologies for Teaching Natural Language Processing and Computational Linguistics*, pages 63–70.

John P McCrae, Ian Wood, and Amanda Hicks. 2017. The colloquial wordnet: Extending princeton wordnet with neologisms. In *International Conference on Language, Data and Knowledge*, pages 194–202. Springer.

John Philip McCrae, Alexandre Rademaker, Ewa Rudnicka, and Francis Bond. 2020. English WordNet 2020: Improving and Extending a WordNet for English using an Open-Source Methodology. In *Proceedings of the LREC 2020 Workshop on Multimodal Wordnets (MMW2020)*, pages 14–19.

George A Miller. 1995. WordNet: a lexical database for English. *Communications of the ACM*, 38(11):39–41.

Nicole Patton-Terry and Carol Connor. 2010. African american english and spelling: How do second graders spell dialect-sensitive features of words? *Learning Disability Quarterly*, 33(3):199–210.

Creating Domain Dependent Turkish WordNet and SentiNet

Bilge Nas Arıcan
Starlang Yazılım Danışmanlık
bilge@starlangyazilim.com

Merve Özçelik
Starlang Yazılım Danışmanlık
merve@starlangyazilim.com

Deniz Baran Aslan
Starlang Yazılım Danışmanlık
deniz@starlangyazilim.com

Elif Sarmış
Starlang Yazılım Danışmanlık
elif@starlangyazilim.com

Selen Parlar
Starlang Yazılım Danışmanlık
selen.parlar@boun.edu.tr

Olcay Taner Yıldız
Özyeğin University
olcay.yildiz@ozyegin.edu.tr

Abstract

A WordNet is a thesaurus that has a structured list of words organized depending on their meanings. WordNet represents word senses, all meanings a single lemma may have, the relations between these senses, and their definitions. Another study within the domain of Natural Language Processing is sentiment analysis. With sentiment analysis, data sets can be scored according to the emotion they contain. In the sentiment analysis we did with the data we received on the Tourism WordNet, we performed a domain-specific sentiment analysis study by annotating the data. In this paper, we propose a method to facilitate Natural Language Processing tasks such as sentiment analysis performed in specific domains via creating a specific-domain subset of an original Turkish dictionary. As the preliminary study, we have created a WordNet for the tourism domain with 14,000 words and validated it on simple tasks.

1 Introduction

WordNet is a semantic network that represents semantic relations between different concepts by providing a graph consisting of nodes and links. A semantic network is a sine qua non of NLP applications which aim to integrate domain knowledge and lexical knowledge. To this end, since the primary purpose of using WordNet is obtaining the similarities and relations between words, WordNets have been employed in various fields of NLP such as word sense and root word disambiguation, information retrieval, machine translation, and sentiment analysis.

Sentiment analysis interprets and classifies the emotions in a data through natural language processing learning. It can be performed on a word, a sentence, or even a paragraph. With sentiment analysis, many data such as surveys, texts, customer comments and social media content can be analyzed. Especially in the business world, it has a very important place in understanding customers, so that products and services can be arranged to meet the needs.

Among many fields of NLP emplying WordNet, sentiment analysis, or opinion mining, refers to the study of people's opinions, sentiments, appraisals, attitudes, and emotions towards entities, which might include products, services, organizations, issues, individuals or events (Liu, 2015). Sentiment analysis primarily deals with opinions that express or imply positive, negative or neutral sentiments. In order to conduct such analyses, WordNets are of great importance since they provide data in an organized way, especially when the study relies on domain-specific data as in this study. Usually created for general usage, a WordNet can also be created and used for specific domains such as tourism, textile or technology, each of which may inherently contain different senses and relations of the same words. That is to say, depending on the WordNet one draws on, the output of sentiment analysis may change. To illustrate, being 'thick' has positive connotations for a carpet whereas it is often undesirable for smart phones. Therefore, conducting a sentiment analysis in a specific domain necessitates the creation of a domain-specific WordNet.

Prior to the creation of a WordNet, a lexicon with broad coverage should be created in the first place. However, there is no limit for the number of words in a lexicon for agglutinative languages like

Turkish. In addition to agglutination, polysemy, i.e., the coexistence of many possible meanings for a word creates hundreds of basic semantic inconsistencies, which indicates that covering all the words and their senses in a language is a highly demanding task. For instance, a Turkish lexicon carries more than 50,000 words; nevertheless, employing such a vast lexicon for a specific domain brings out ambiguous results since it leaves out the words that are not prevalent in daily usage but common in that specific domain.

To this end, this study aims to address the issue of utilizing an immense WordNet for a specific domain, namely tourism. The data for the study consists of online user reviews and preferences of a tourism company located in Turkey. Drawing on this data, we have initially corrected the misspelled words, put them into groups depending on their part of speech (noun, proper noun, adjective, verb and adverb), and finally tagged them based on the linguistic features of Turkish. These steps have provided us with a 14,000-word lexicon covering not only commonly used words but also domain-specific words. Compared to currently used Turkish dictionaries, this newly created dictionary has approximately four times fewer words, which is the reason why we draw on this dictionary while creating the domain-specific WordNet. As expected, the meanings of the words in this domain specific dictionary vary based on their area of usage. That is to say, the meanings of some words in general use acquire new meanings in the domain-specific dictionary, according to which we have arranged the hierarchy of the words.

The necessary data for SentiNet, which is a domain-dependent resource for sentiment analysis, have been drawn from the Tourism WordNet we created. It should be said that the data used for sentiment analysis were matched with their counterpart in Turkish WordNet again after annotating. The Tourism WordNet and SentiNet data are linked to each other via senses. The synset IDs of SentiNet and Tourism Wordnet data are the same on both sides. In the annotating phase, care has been taken to annotate all data with more than one annotator and to ensure these annotators do not have information about each other's preferences. Although the line of objectivity is not possible for sentiment analysis markings, it is aimed to present a study that yields more successful results with these items that we pay attention to in the marking stages.

This paper is organized as follows: We first discuss the relevant literature on WordNets in Section 2. We explain how we generated the domain dependent WordNet and SentiNet in Sections 3 and 4. We provide details on the word-sense disambiguation task using our domain dependent wordnet in Section 5. The statistics and experimental results regarding our WordNet and SentiNet are given in Section 6. Lastly, we conclude in Section 7.

2 Literature Review

The first WordNet project is a lexical database for English, namely Princeton WordNet (PWN), which was initiated in 1995 by George Miller, (1995). Currently, the latest release of PWN, version 3.1, has 117,000 synsets, and 206,941 word-sense pairs. A more detailed history and description of PWN is given in (Fellbaum, 1998). Shortly after the release of PWN, WordNets for other languages have been constructed although their coverage is not as extensive as that of PWN, (Vossen, 1997), (Black et al., 2006). For Balkan languages, BalkaNet (Tufis et al., 2004) is the most comprehensive work up to date. For the Turkish WordNet part of BalkaNet (Bilgin et al., 2004), the researchers automatically extracted the synonyms, antonyms and hyponyms from a monolingual Turkish dictionary. The most comprehensive Turkish WordNet is KeNet, which has 80,000 synsets covering 110,000 word-sense pairs (Ehsani et al., 2018; Bakay et al., 2019b; Bakay et al., 2019a; Ozcelik et al., 2019; Bakay et al., 2020).

All this body of work mentioned above has been created and used for general purposes. However, the creation of a domain-specific WordNet is a more recent phenomenon, of which there are relatively few examples. ArchiWordNet is a WordNet created specifically for the architecture and construction domain drawing on Italian/English bilingual resources. Similarly, Jur-WordNet is another example of a domain-specific WordNet which was created as an extension for the legal domain of ItalWordNet by providing multilingual access to legal information sources. Specifically created to be used for software engineering tasks, SEthesaurus is a dictionary constructed based on informal discussions about programming on social platforms. By generating a WordNet specific to the tourism domain, we hope to contribute to this body of work, and provide inspiring ideas for future studies (Sagri et al., 2004; Bentivogli et al., 2003; Chen et al., 2019).

Regarding sentiment analysis, to the best of our knowledge, there have been no studies conducting a domain-specific sentiment analysis relying on a domain-specific WordNet. Therefore, it would be plausible to assert that we are presenting a pioneering study in this field.

3 Domain Dependent WordNet

3.1 Preprocessing

As stated in Section 1, the data used for this study consist of online customer reviews or customer preferences from the tourism domain. Since users usually prefer daily, informal language not paying attention to grammatical correctness but focusing mainly on the semantics, it is not feasible to perform further natural language processing based on the original input. Therefore, we employ the final version of the data following a preprocessing pipeline. The first step of this preprocessing is sentence splitting, where we divide paragraphs into sentences and each sentence into words, then perform case-folding to convert all the words to a particular case. Subsequently, we conduct the stemming process for which we only consider basic Turkish suffixes. For instance, we remove the plural suffix '*-lar, -ler*' ('-s, -es'), locative case suffix '*-de, -da*' (in, on, by), ablative case suffix '*-den, -dan*' (from, of), and dative case suffix '*-a, -e*' (to, towards). This stemming process provides us with tokens by unveiling distinct words.

Following the sentence splitting and stemming processes, the remaining single tokens need to be deasciified since not all tokens are spelled correctly by users. That is, we convert erroneously written Turkish characters into their correct forms. For instance, the word '*Türkçe*' (Turkish) which contains language-specific characters ('ü, ç') is mostly written by using English characters as '*Turkce*', which has no meaning in the lexicon. Moreover, if a word cannot be morphologically analyzed, after all, we interchange each letter with its closest neighbor. Provided that the resulting string still cannot be analyzed, we suggest the most similar word in the lexicon based on the Levenshtein distance between words. At the end of this preprocessing, we tokenize and retrieve the distinct words which are ready to be analyzed morphologically.

Table 1: Example words from the Tourism WordNet

Word	Instance Hypernym
Sicily	Island
Metrogarden	Mall
Nestle	Food brand
Izmir	City
Mimarova	Neighborhood
Merlin	Hotel
Italy	Country

3.2 Dictionary

Relying on the words and comments from the online system of a tourism company, a dictionary is prepared for the creation of the WordNet by three Turkish native speakers, who specialize in Turkish linguistics. This makes sure that the dictionary reflects the most commonly used words in the domain such as meals, hotel names, holiday items, etc. Based on their part of speech, these words are tagged as a proper noun, noun, verb, adjective or adverb, which determines the area of usage for each word. In addition to these main categories, some words receive extra labels such as vowel harmony tags while verbs are re-grouped based on their grammatical features.

In addition, we have created a set of "misspelling data" consisting of the misspelled words, which contain 120,000 entries. In this way, we have identified the words that are most frequently misspelled by users so that these words can be automatically corrected for future studies.

3.3 WordNet

In a WordNet, which plays a crucial role in NLP, words are first grouped based on their part of speech under the categories of proper nouns, nouns, verbs, adjectives, and adverbs, after which the words in each category are clustered depending on their semantic relations. In our Tourism Dictionary, there are three major part of speech categories (See Table 1, which are proper noun, noun, and adjective.

Following the categorization of the words, each category is exclusively studied on its own. The words in the noun category are organized depending on several semantic relations, namely synonym, antonym, member holonym, substance holonym, part holonym, domain topic, and attribute. Regarding the proper noun category, we have paid attention to the areas that the words belong to; therefore, all proper nouns that do not have a particular importance are grouped under the same category, the majority of which consists of hotel names. However, given names and surnames have been removed from the data. Finally, the adverb category has been dismissed from the scope of this study due to the small number of words in that category.

4 Doman Dependent SentiNet

Since sentiment analysis focuses on whether entities are positive, negative or neutral, the words in our tourism corpus have been labeled as positive, negative or neutral by three annotators, who are native speakers of Turkish. Following the first labeling process, the words labeled as positive and negative have been subjected to a second labeling process, marked as strong or weak since the degree of positivity or negativity may vary as in the difference between the words "güzel" (beautiful) and "harika" (excellent). This allows a more precise analysis of the positive or negative value that the word adds to the sentence. Furthermore, we have paid attention to both the dictionary meaning of the word and the way it is used in daily life in this specific domain. In cases where a word was labeled differently by the annotators, we have relied on the opinion of the majority.

Following the labeling process, we have found that the majority of the words are neutral while the ratio of negative words is higher than positive words. Moreover, we have found that the weak positive and weak negative tags are more prevalent than the strong positive and strong negative. In addition, the automated analysis of the sentences are accelerated since the positive, negative and neutral values of the words can be better processed by the algorithm. Therefore, we believe that the automatic analysis of the words will be much easier and faster.

5 Usage of WordNet in Semantic Annotation: All-Words Sense Annotation

The study has been conducted on a 20,000-sentence corpus created using data from the tourism domain. The words and their definitions have been drawn from the Tourism WordNet. Two interfaces have been created to employ in the semantic annotation process, which consisted of two steps. The sentences were processed by the annotators after each word was subjected to morphological analysis and matched with its equivalent in the Turkish WordNet. Four annotators worked simultaneously in the first step using the interface that displays each sentence individually. As can be seen in Figure 1, each word can be annotated individually, and the buttons at the top are used to navigate the corpus. When a word is clicked on, a list of every possible definition is displayed. The annotators chose the appropriate definition manually. Punctuation marks were annotated automatically. The annotators also made use of the "annotate each occurrence of the word with the same definition" feature, making the process semiautomatic and increasing efficiency. This feature annotates all occurrences of the selected word in the corpus with the same definition from the list. Through this feature, words that happen to only have a single definition, in general or in this specific domain, have been annotated more easily. Sentences that produced errors in the morphological analysis phase were corrected manually using the same analyzer. Each word was annotated primarily using the definitions in the Tourism WordNet. The definitions in the Turkish WordNet were made use of where the Tourism WordNet was not sufficient.

At the end of the first step, there were still words without annotations. The second step was an effort to fill in these gaps and check the results manually. A different interface displaying all sentences simultaneously was used in this step. The words were arranged alphabetically, and grouped based on their sentences. In this way, the words were compared to one another in different contexts, and their definitions were decided on by reviewing the entire corpus. The missing annotations were completed based on the existing ones. Two annotators worked on this step in cooperation in order to ensure consistency between their annotations.

In the annotation process, an optional automatic annotation function was also employed. This function automatically matches the words with only one definition in the dictionary with that one definition without asking the annotator. Afterwards, these were verified by the annotators and corrected when necessary. The semantic annotation interface can also detect multi-word expressions, which allows the annotation of words that come together to form a single unit of meaning.

Table 2: An example of positive marking

Annotation	ID	Word	Definition
p	TUR10-0318100	güzel (beautiful)	Göze ve kulağa hoş gelen, hayranlık uyandıran (Pleasing to the eye, admirable)

Table 3: An example of neutral marking

Annotation	ID	Word	Definition
o	TUR10-0016080	ahşap (wood)	Ağaçtan, tahtadan yapılmış (Made of wood)

Table 4: An example of negative marking

Annotation	ID	Word	Definition
n	TUR10-0335560	Çığlık (scream)	Acı, ince ve keskin ses, feryat (Painful, subtle and sharp sound, howl.)

Table 5: Markings in the second stage of a positive sample

Ann.1	Ann.2	Ann.3	ID	Word	Definition
s	s	s	TUR10-0318100	Güzel (beautiful)	Göze ve kulağa hoş gelen, hayranlık uyandıran (Pleasing to the eye, admirable)
w	s	w	TUR10-0246270	Empati (empathy)	Aynı duyguları paylaşma (Sharing the same emotions)
w	w	w	TUR10-0421970	Hesaplı (economic)	Az masraflı, kazançlı, hesaplı, iktisadi (Low-cost, profitable, affordable, economic)

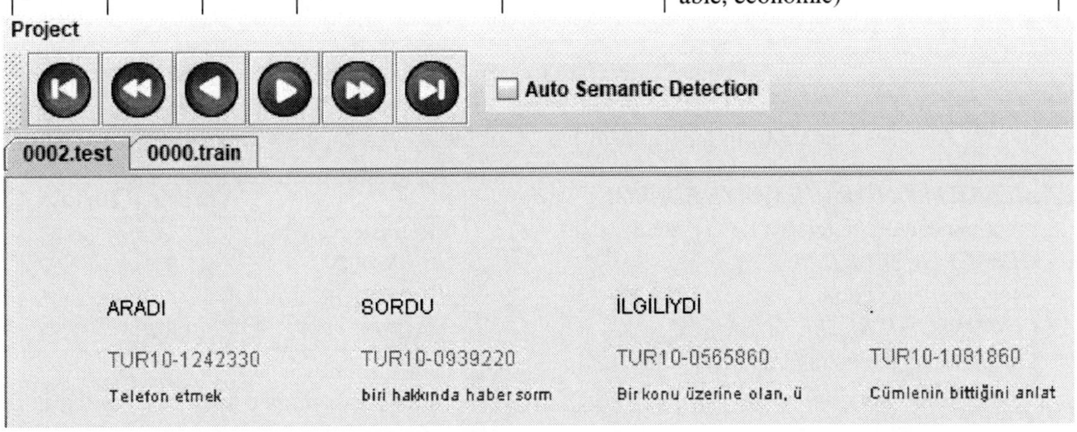

Figure 1: Interface used in the first phase

Turkish has a great volume of two-word verbal expressions (e.g. "kabul etmek", to accept; "memnun kalmak", to be satisfied"), which is reflected in the tourism corpus. The senses that do not show up when these words occur by themselves are included in the list of possible definitions if they appear consecutively in the right order, which the annotators chose manually.

6 Results

6.1 Statistics About WordNet and SentiNet

Designing WordNets and dictionaries entails working with a huge body of data, which is the reason why this study relies on a large amount of data from online user reviews and user preferences from the tourism domain. Before the study, for the tourism domain, we created a lexicon of 14,000 entries by using the words extracted from the most common 20,000 reviews by users, e.g., the customers of a holiday resort, or a tour, an example of which can be seen in Table 7.

Generally, users do not pay attention to the conventions of standard grammar or spelling while typing their comments in online surveys. Therefore, we have enacted several pre-processing steps described in Section 3 in order to retrieve the cor-

Table 6: Markings in the second stage of a negative sample

Ann.1	Ann.2	Ann.3	ID	Word	Definition
s	s	s	TUR10-0827940	Yalan (lie)	Aldatmak amacıyla bilerek ve gerçeğe aykırı olarak söylenen söz (A word that is not true)
s	w	s	TUR10-0600400	Öksüz (orphan)	Anası veya hem anası hem babası ölmüş olan çocuk (Child whose mother or father has died)
w	w	w	TUR10-0201160	Dezavantaj (disadvantage)	Avantajlı olmama durumu (A disadvantaged situation.)

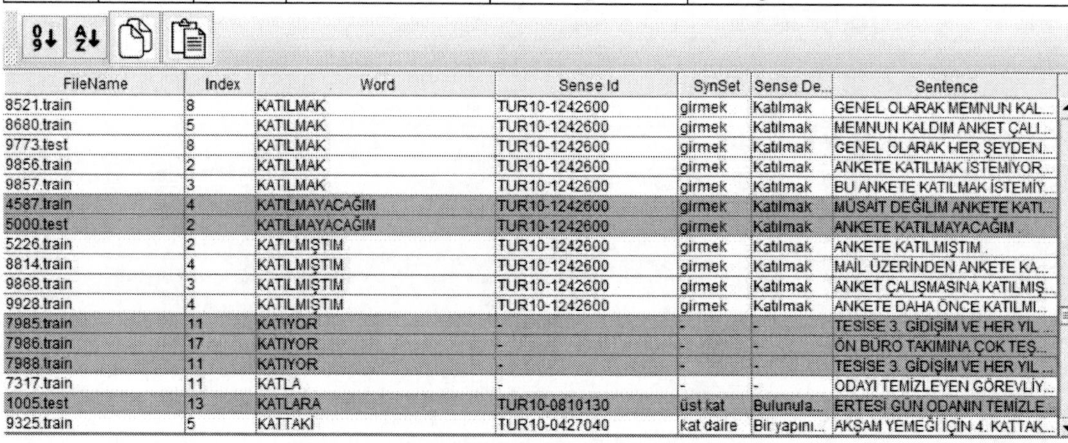

Figure 2: Interface used in the second phase

Table 7: A review sample from the Tourism Domain

AİLE OTELİ OLARAK TAVSİYE EDERİM .
I recommend the hotel as a family hotel.
HERŞEY GÜZELDI .
Everything was good.
ÇOCUKLU AILELERE ÖNERIRIM .
I recommend the hotel to families with children.
DENIZI ÇOK GÜZELDI .
The sea was nice.

rected sentences for the annotations. For instance, the sentence *"HERŞEY GÜZELDI ."* is not orthographically correct since the lemma *ŞEY* (thing) should be written separately from the previous word *HER* (every) according to the standard orthographic conventions of Turkish. Moreover, since there is a *capital i* (İ) in the Turkish alphabet, the *I* should be corrected as *İ*. In this case, the correct form of this sentence would be *"HER ŞEY GÜZELDİ ."*.

Following the pre-processing of the data, we manually assign POS tags to each word in order to perform morphological analysis. For instance, the word *"Samsun"*, which is a city in Northern Turkey, is a proper name and its tag is represented as "IS_OA" in the dictionary. Similarly, the word *"ev"* (house) is a common noun and it is represented as "CL_ISIM" in the dictionary. Table 8 shows the percentages of the four most frequently used POS tags in the Tourism and Turkish dictionaries, which are IS_OA (proper name), CL_ISIM (common name), CL_FIIL (verb), and IS_ADJ (adjective) respectively.

Table 8: Percentage of frequently used POS tags of 2 dictionaries.

	Tourism	Turkish
PROPER NOUN	32.44	36.87
NOUN	45.92	53.07
VERB	8.42	8.35
ADJECTIVE	13.53	7.38

Since users or customers generally use the daily language in texts, the Tourism Dictionary has a lot of words in common with the Turkish Dictionary, which accounts for the result that 70.5% of the Tourism Dictionary is identical to the Turkish Dictionary. Table 9 shows the percentage of the POS tags of the intersecting words in the Tourism and Turkish dictionaries.

Table 9: Percentage of frequently used POS tags of common words in Tourism-Turkish dictionaries.

	Tourism-Turkish
PROPER NOUN	28.41
NOUN	51.27
VERB	9.19
ADJECTIVE	12.64

Table 10: The percentages of the top 5 hypernym relations in the Tourism WordNet

Otel (Hotel)	42.74
İlçe (District)	4.17
Ülke (Country)	2.23
Şehir (Town)	1.90
İl (City)	1.61

Table 11: Percentages of analyzed sentences and words with different sizes of tourism dictionaries and a Turkish Dictionary.

Dictionary	Size	Sentence	Word
Tourism	5,000	98.52	99.66
Tourism	10,000	98.93	99.75
Tourism	14,000	98.92	99.75
Turkish	51,552	95.97	99.07

Furthermore, we have extracted the hypernym relation, i.e., the hierarchy of word-senses from WordNet to obtain a more precise picture of the data. Table 10 shows the top 5 hypernyms in the tourism domain. As expected, the tourism dictionary predominantly consists of hotel names under the word hotel.

6.2 Morphological Analysis Tests

We have created a domain-dependent dictionary and WordNet using the dataset described in Section 6.1, and performed some analyses with the newly created domain-specific dictionary WordNet, and the general Turkish Dictionary. In order to validate our lexicon, we have tested it on tourism datasets and compared the results with that of the general Turkish Dictionary on the same datasets.

Table 11 shows the results of two analyses, a sentence-based and a word-based analysis, for three different sizes of tourism dictionaries and a Turkish dictionary. For the sentence-based analysis, we check the Tourism Dictionary's ability to correctly perform a morphological analysis of 20,000 sentences. For the word-based analysis, we check the accuracy of the performance of a morphological analysis on each of the 93,483 words

Table 12: Morphological analyses of size 1 using different dictionaries

	% of Morphological Analyses
Tourism	61.05
Turkish	54.11

Table 13: The 20 topmost annotated synsets and their counts

Id	SynSet	Count
TUR10-1081860	.	19,995
TOU01-1010440	çok	3,016
TUR10-0388960	iyi	2,529
TUR10-0105580	bir	1,981
TOU01-1063690	memnun kalmak	1,929
TUR10-0000000	(özel isim)	1,759
TUR10-0624490	personel	1,557
TUR10-0318110	güzel	1,396
TUR10-0513570	yemek	1,330
TUR10-0495010	tesis	1,247
TUR10-0816400	ve	1,221
TUR10-0346660	hizmet	1,042
TUR10-0593590	otel	1,014
TUR10-1121820	puan vermek	1,010
TUR10-0318100	güzel	957
TUR10-0097260	bey	924
TUR10-0582130	oda	915
TUR10-0187890	değil	769
TUR10-0473520	konum	740
TUR10-0565860	ilgili	708

separately. It can been observed that there is a 2.55% improvement in the sentence-based analysis, and the results of the word-based analysis are also similar. Nevertheless, after the dictionary size reaches 10,000 entries, no sufficient improvement is observed.

Having multiple morphological analyses for a word introduces an ambiguity problem. With our approach, we aim to address this ambiguity issue by diminishing the dictionary size. To do so, we include only the domain-related senses of words, and discard the rest. To test its performance, we count the number of the words that have only one possible morphological analysis. This leads to a 7% improvement in the tourism domain as shown in Table 12. Thus, it is plausible to assert that reducing the dictionary size is an effective method to solve the disambiguation problem.

6.3 Semantic Annotation Statistics

Following the processing of 20,000 sentences, 93,653 words were annotated semantically, during which a total of 1,849 senses were used. While only 111 of these were from the Tourism WordNet, the remaining 1,737 were from the Turkish WordNet. As for the words, while 8,455 were annotated with senses from the Tourism WordNet, the remaining 85,186 were annotated from the Turkish WordNet. The results showed that 4,788 entries among the 13,555 in the Tourism WordNet were specific to the tourism domain whereas the remaining 8,767 were from the Turkish WordNet.

As can be seen in Table 13, function words such as "değil (not), bir (a), ve (and)" are highly frequent, which is an expected case regardless of domain. However, the domain effects are observable through content words such as "personel" (staff), "tesis" (facility), "hizmet" (service) and "otel" (hotel)", which make up a significant portion of the corpus. As the data is comprised of customer reviews, adjectives such as "iyi (good), güzel (good / pretty)" are also highly frequent. Furthermore, due to the inclusion of punctuation, the full stop at the end of each sentence appears as the most frequent "word". Other frequent words that are not listed in Table 13 include evaluative adjectives such as "yeterli (sufficient), kötü (bad)" and of course the comma. Finally, another anticipated result is the frequent occurrence of proper names such as the names of hotels and hotel staff.

As mentioned previously, multi-word expressions were also included in the annotation process. Table 14 shows that the majority of these were expressions such as "memnun kalmak" (to be satisfied) or "puan vermek" (to give points), frequently used in customer reviews. The inclusion of multi-word expressions were not limited to two-word expressions; thus, the occurrence of three and even four-word expressions was also frequent.

As shown in Table 15, the majority of the sentences in the corpus have a length of three to six words, while there are also sentences longer than 10 words, which make up a minority. At the end of the two-step process, approximately 100.000 words have been annotated, and a significant portion of these annotations have been observed to be a small set of frequently repeated expressions. Most of these frequent expressions have been annotated semi-automatically. Therefore, the words that took the longest time to annotate were the least frequent ones, occurring once or twice in the entire corpus.

Table 14: The 20 topmost annotated multi-word synsets and their counts

Id	SynSet	Count
TOU01-1063690	memnun kalmak	926
TUR10-1121820	puan vermek	404
TUR10-1154960	tavsiye etmek	321
TUR10-1181550	tercih etmek	187
TUR10-0728240	güler yüzlü	154
TUR10-0893550	yardımcı olmak	113
TUR10-1160460	teşekkür etmek	102
TUR10-0181700	damak tadı	51
TUR10-0847620	yeme içme	47
TOU01-1063820	aile oteli	45
TUR10-0839560	sağ olsun	43
TUR10-0227360	haberdar olmak	42
TUR10-1199410	bilgi vermek	34
TOU01-1041440	aqua park	30
TUR10-0089100	hoşuna gitmek	26
TOU01-1063770	çocuk dostu	24
TUR10-0004240	açık büfe	20
TUR10-0019600	dört dörtlük	19
TUR10-0565860	ilgi alaka	17
TUR10-0084000	her zaman	16

Table 15: Number of words in a sentence and their occurrences

# of Words	# of Occurences
2	824
3	4,475
4	6,761
5	4,584
6	1,632
7	601
8	341
9	157
10	134

7 Conclusion

Overall, we have created a domain-specific lexicon with user reviews and preferences from the tourism domain. Based on this newly created lexicon, we have designed a novel WordNet, and employed it for domain-specific sentiment analysis. By doing so, we have managed to mitigate the disambiguation problem for this specific domain. Finally, we have improved the performance of sentence-based morphological analysis by approximately 7% in the tourism domain.

References

Ozge Bakay, Ozlem Ergelen, and Olcay Taner Yildiz. 2019a. Integrating Turkish WordNet KeNet to Princeton WordNet: The case of one-to-many correspondences. In *Innovations in Intelligent Systems and Applications*.

Ozge Bakay, Ozlem Ergelen, and Olcay Taner Yildiz. 2019b. Problems caused by semantic drift in wordnet synset construction. In *International Conference on Computer Science and Engineering*.

O. Bakay, O. Ergelen, E. Sarmis, S. Yildirim, A. Kocabalcioglu, B. N. Arican, M. Ozcelik, E. Saniyar, O. Kuyrukcu, B. Avar, and O. T. Yıldız. 2020. Turkish WordNet KeNet. In *Proceedings of GWC 2020*.

L. Bentivogli, A. Bocco, and E. Pianta. 2003. Archiwordnet: Integrating wordnet with domain-specific knowledge.

O. Bilgin, O. Cetinoglu, and K. Oflazer. 2004. Building a wordnet for Turkish. *Romanian Journal of Information Science*, 7:163–172.

W. Black, S. Elkateb, H. Rodriguez, M. Alkhalifa, P. Vossen, A. Pease, and C. Fellbaum. 2006. Introducing the Arabic wordnet project. In *International Wordnet Conference*, pages 295–300. Masaryck University, Brno, Czeck Republic.

X. Chen, C. Chen, D. Zhang, and Z. Xing. 2019. Sethesaurus: Wordnet in software engineering. *IEEE Transactions on Software Engineering*, pages 1–1.

R. Ehsani, E. Solak, and O.T. Yildiz. 2018. Constructing a wordnet for Turkish using manual and automatic annotation. *ACM Transactions on Asian and Low-Resource Language Information Processing (TALLIP)*, 17(3):24.

C. Fellbaum. 1998. *Wordnet: an electronic lexical database. Cambridge*. MIT Press, MA, USA.

G.A. Miller. 1995. Wordnet: a lexical database for English. *ACM Communications*, 38:39–41.

Riza Ozcelik, Selen Parlar, Ozge Bakay, Ozlem Ergelen, and Olcay Taner Yildiz. 2019. User interface for Turkish word network KeNet. In *Signal Processing and Communication Applications Conference*.

Maria Teresa Sagri, Daniela Tiscornia, and Francesca Bertagna. 2004. Jur-wordnet.

D. Tufis, D. Cristea, and S. Stamou. 2004. Balkanet: Aims, methods, results and per- spectives. a general overview. *Romanian Journal of Information Science*, 7:9–43.

V. Vossen. 1997. Eurowordnet: a multilingual database for information retrieval. In *DELOS workshop on Cross-language Information Retrieval*. Vrije Universiteit, Amsterdam, Czech Republic.

Towards a Linking between WordNet and Wikidata

John P. McCrae
Data Science Institute
NUI Galway
Ireland
john@mccr.ae

David Cillessen
Data Science Institute
NUI Galway
Ireland
D.CILLESSEN1@nuigalway.ie

Abstract

WordNet is the most widely used lexical resource for English, while Wikidata is one of the largest knowledge graphs of entity and concepts available. While, there is a clear difference in the focus of these two resources, there is also a significant overlap and as such a complete linking of these resources would have many uses. We propose the development of such a linking, first by means of the hapax legomenon links and secondly by the use of natural language processing techniques. We show that these can be done with high accuracy but that human validation is still necessary. This has resulted in over 9,000 links being added between these two resources.

1 Introduction

English WordNet (McCrae et al., 2019, 2020), derived from Princeton WordNet (Miller, 1995; Fellbaum, 2012, PWN)[1], is the most complete wordnet for English, while Wikidata[2] provides one of the largest collection of encyclopedic facts in machine readable form. Moreover, as Wikidata is an open resource to which anyone can contribute and data is published without any license, it is quickly becoming a central database to which knowledge graphs can link. As such, a linking between WordNet and Wikipedia would provide value to users of both resources, and potentially make it easier to extend WordNet in the future with new synsets. However, there are significant differences between the scope of the two projects, with WordNet specialising on providing information about the use of words in English, including verbs, adjectives and adverbs, whereas Wikidata describes entities, mostly by means of proper nouns, although lexical information is currently being added to Wikidata (Nielsen, 2020). Still, there is a significant overlap in terms of the proper and common nouns in WordNet and providing links to Wikidata would help to improve and extend the usage of WordNet.

A linking between the proper nouns in WordNet and Wikipedia was constructed by McCrae et al. (2018) and as a side part of this work we updated and contributed this list to Wikidata including manually remapping 156 links that had become stale. However, we also see that for most common nouns it is still possible to match most of the senses to a concept in Wikidata, for example of the eight senses of 'work' in WordNet, six of them can easily be mapped to a concept in Wikidata and only two abstract definitions 'activity directed toward making or doing something' and 'applying the mind to learning and understanding a subject (especially by reading)' are not obviously available in Wikidata. In fact, out of 122,147 noun lemmas in English WordNet 67,569 (55.3%) are represented by an entry in Wikidata and as such we believe that the majority of noun senses in WordNet should have a counterpart in Wikidata.

Given the size of the task of this linking, it is obvious that we should have some automatic help to improve the linking process; however, neither resource would accept fully automatic linking as has been applied in other resources such as BabelNet (Navigli and Ponzetto, 2010) and UBY (Gurevych et al., 2012). As such, in this paper we start the process of using automatic tools to construct the links between the datasets and manually validating. For the purpose of this paper, our first focus is on what we refer to as *hapax* links, that is links for which there is only a single sense for the lemma in WordNet and for which only one page in Wikidata has this lemma as the English title. We then consider how we could extend this further to the links where there is ambiguity in the lemma. Finally, we consider how this linking could

[1] We use 'WordNet' to refer to either resource

[2] `https://www.wikidata.org/wiki/Wikidata:Main_Page`

be used to contribute back to English WordNet and extend the existing categories there.

2 Related Work

Most of the focus to date has been on the development of automatic linking between WordNet and encyclopedic knowledge graphs based on Wikipedia such as DBpedia (Auer et al., 2007) or Wikidata. One of the most prominent examples of this is BabelNet (Navigli and Ponzetto, 2010), which mapped WordNet to Wikipedia using a word sense disambiguation algorithm, in which the surrounding elements in the synset graph and article text were used as context for disambiguation. In their work (Navigli and Ponzetto, 2012), the authors report an F-Measure of 82.7% in their linking, and while this is strong it cannot be considered to be a gold standard. Another approach has been through the use of Personalised PageRank (PPR) (Agirre and Soroa, 2009), which was first attempted by Toral et al. (Toral et al., 2009) and later improved by Meyer and Gurevych (Meyer and Gurevych, 2011) to create the UBY resource (Gurevych et al., 2012). A similar resource, YAGO (Suchanek et al., 2008), has also been constructed by means of automatic linking and while they report very high accuracy (97.7%) this referred to only a limited number of concepts that are linked. There have also been attempts to link WordNet to other resources including the SemLink (Bonial et al., 2013; Palmer et al., 2014) that have provided links to other lexical resources and ontologies. In contrast to these works, this work is developing a manual linking that aims to be usable as a gold standard.

3 Hapax Linking

3.1 Methodology

One of the most obvious ways to get a good linking is to focus on the elements in the two resources that are *hapax legomenon* in the resource, that is that they only occur a single time in the resource. By this, we mean that for English WordNet, a synset only occurs in a single noun synset and for Wikidata the label is unique for this concept. As such, we first base our approach on identifying and linking these elements between the two resources based on an exactly matching hapax lemma in both resources. An initial analysis of this showed that there were quite a large number of links; however, we noticed that due to the large number of entities that are available in Wikidata there were often spurious links. In order to mitigate this, we took a couple of quick heuristics before evaluation

- Each Wikidata entity is identified with a 'Q' code that is assigned sequentially. A quick analysis suggested that 'Q' numbers over 10,000,000 generally referred to entities of such little significance that it was extremely unlikely they would be mentioned in English WordNet.
- We filtered out all entities whose definition contained "Wikipedia disambiguation page" or "Wikimedia disambiguation page" as these were not real-world entities in Wikidata.
- We also filtered out all entities whose definitions were of the form of 1-3 words followed by the word "by" and then 1-4 words. A very large number of entities matching this pattern were irrelevant entities such as "song/album/film" by "band/author/director".

In total, using this method we discovered 16,452 candidates for this hapax linking, which represents 19.5% of all noun synsets in WordNet.

3.2 Evaluation

In order to evaluate the quality of the hapax linking, and automatically check for any errors in the linking, we set up an evaluation program using a simple spreadsheet to evaluate the hapax links. We provided the evaluators with enough information to evaluate the quality of the linking, in particular: the lemma and Wikidata identifier, the definitions of the concept given in both resources and the (instance) hypernyms of the concepts in each resource. The results of this can be seen in Table 1, where we give four examples of the linkings extracted, where the first three were the first three rows randomly presented to our evaluators. The fourth row, 'Occam' gives an interesting example of a spurious match, where the philosopher is linked to a programming language named after the philosopher. As part of the annotation guidelines, annotators were instructed to consider matches as long as they were broadly correct, so for example 'prunus triloba' refers to a species of plants in Wikidata but as a tree in English WordNet, but as they clearly refer to the same plant they are considered matching even though ontologically a species is not a tree.

Wikidata ID	Lemma	Wikidata Definition	WordNet Definition	Wikidata Hypernyms	WordNet Hypernyms
Q2663273	boasting	to speak with excessive pride and self-satisfaction about one's achievements, possessions, or abilities [...]	speaking of yourself in superlatives	*none*	speech act
Q514686	aphonia	medical condition leading to loss of voice	a disorder of the vocal organs that results in the loss of voice	voice disorder	defect of speech, speech disorder, speech defect
Q105719	Jean Harlow	American film actress	United States film actress who made several films with Clark Gable (1911-1937)	human	actress
Q838062	Occam	Concurrent programming language	English scholastic philosopher and assumed author of Occam's Razor (1285-1349)	programming language; procedural programming language	philosopher
Q2727171	prunus triloba	species of plant	deciduous Chinese shrub or small tree with often trilobed leaves grown for its pink-white flowers	Prunus	almond tree

Table 1: Examples of the Hapax linking and the information give to annotators to evaluate the results.

So far the annotation has been completed up to 1,997 entities and of those 1,920 have been accepted (96.1%) indicating that the hapax linking is overall very reliable. The annotators quickly noted that some Wikidata classes contained many entities not found in English WordNet, in particular 'album', 'band', 'single', 'video game', 'film', 'television series', 'family name', 'written work', 'song' and 'television program'. These elements account for 35 of the false links and if they were excluded the overall accuracy of the hapax linking would be 98.4%. In addition, we also evaluated the inter-annotator agreement of the linking using two annotators over 497 evaluations and a Cohen's kappa score of 81.4% was obtained indicating strong agreement between the annotators. In fact, 8 of the 11 disagreements between the annotators were errors by the annotators and only 3 were due to the nature of the task. This suggests that the annotators are able to make clear judgements in the vast majority of cases.

3.3 Publishing

The links have been made available through Wikidata by means of the property `P5063`, which links the elements to the GWA InterLingual Index (ILI) (Bond et al., 2016). These were contributed to the Wikidata project by means of QuickStatements. In addition, the data is made available as a comma-separated value list on the English WordNet project.

4 Towards a complete linking

The hapax linking above, while it has a very high accuracy is also not sufficient in order to create a complete linking between two resources, as such we have attempted to evaluate how easily this can be extended to a complete linking of the two re-

Q7366	song
Q7889	video game
Q11424	film
Q101352	family name
Q134556	single
Q207628	musical composition
Q215380	musical group
Q222910	compilation album
Q386724	work
Q482994	album
Q3305213	painting
Q5398426	television series
Q5741069	rock band

Table 2: List of classes in Wikidata that do not frequently occur in English WordNet

sources using the Naisc system (McCrae and Buitelaar, 2018), so that we can also link entities where there is some ambiguity in the potential matching labels.

4.1 Extending the linking with Naisc

The first step in creating the linking is to extract the relevant facts about the entities from WordNet and Wikidata. From English WordNet, we extracted the definitions and labels as well as the synset links, and similarly for Wikidata we extracted the English labels and definitions, as well as the links between synsets. As the size of Wikidata was very large, we limited this extraction to entities whose terms occurred in English WordNet and hypernyms of these terms. As previously, we filtered these entities using heuristics, namely the "X by Y" pattern, disambiguation pages and discarding Q IDs over 10,000,000 as before. In addition, we also developed a reject list and removed all elements that were hyponyms of this list, which is shown in Table 2. We then applied the Naisc methodology consisting of the following analysis

- The system identified the hapax links as in the previous step and accepted them automatically due to the high precision of these links established in the previous step. This created a merged graph containing the links between the Wikidata concepts, the links between the English WordNet synsets and the hapax links.

- The definitions were compared using the Jaccard similarity of the two definitions both at word-level and character-level, as in previous word similarity approaches (McCrae and Buitelaar, 2018).

- In addition, we analysed the similarity of each element according the Personalised PageRank (PPR) algorithm (Page et al., 1999), using the Fast-PPR implementation (Lofgren et al., 2014), as in Meyer and Gurevych (Meyer and Gurevych, 2011).

- This generated three scores, which were normalized in the range [0,1], by means of percentile ranking, so that the score which corresponds to the lowest of the top 10% of scores was mapped to 0.1.

- A simple average of the three scores (character-level Jaccard, word-level Jaccard and PPR) was used to rank each potential match.

- We used a bijective assumption, that each entity in WordNet matches only a single element in Wikidata, and as such the problem can be cast as an *assignment problem* (Munkres, 1957), which can be solved with the Hungarian algorithm (Kuhn, 1955). However, due to the very large size of the datasets, we instead used a simple greedy approach.

4.2 Evaluation of the Extended linking

The evaluation of the linking was completed by two annotators who evaluated 100 links predicted by the system. They agreed on an accuracy between 65-66% with a Cohen's Kappa of 0.934 of the automatic linking. The primary disagreements were on two examples "snack bar" defined as "inexpensive food counter" or a "usually inexpensive bar" and "brother" defined as "Hong Kong internet slang" or "used as a term of address for those male persons engaged in the same movement". Divided by the prediction scores, those links predicted with a confidence of less than 60% by the system were all incorrect (0.0% accuracy), those with a 60-80% accuracy were correct 23/39 times (59.0% accuracy) and those with a greater than 80% confidence were correct 42/49 times (85.7% accuracy). These statistics indicate that the system's confidence was a good predictor of the accuracy of links.[3]

[3]These scores were not shown to the annotators in the manual evaluation

5 Discussion

One of the key objectives of this project is to enable the extension of WordNet with more entities achieving a similar goal to that of Bond and Bond (2019) of developing wordnets of geographic place names, but for more categories than just place names. Given that we have 9,149 links now confirmed between WordNet and Wikidata, we can make inference about likely extra entities that could be added to WordNet. For example, if we know that 'Paris' (`i83645`) is an instance of 'national capital' (`i82619`) and we have now linked this to Wikidata (`Q90`) which asserts that this is an instance of 'capital' (`Q5119`), then we could establish the link between the categories for 'national capitals' and 'capitals' and add capitals that are missing from WordNet, such as 'Juba' (`Q1947`). We are currently investigating the potential to create an extended WordNet from this linking, however there are challenges due to the difference in structure between WordNet and Wikidata. For example, 'George Washington' (`i97352/Q23`) is asserted as an instance of 'general' (`i90718`) and 'President of the United States' (`i92216`) in WordNet but only as a 'human' (`Q5`) in Wikidata. Instead, Wikidata uses different properties, namely 'occupation' (`P106`) and 'position held' (`P39`) to assert the facts expressed in WordNet. It is unclear how best these inconsistencies should be resolved in the context of WordNet.

6 Conclusion

In this work we have analysed the task of linking the noun hierarchy of WordNet with Wikidata. We found that the approach relying on hapax linking can be achieved with very high accuracy, although this does still produce occasional errors. However, for ambiguous senses the task of linking is still much harder and the automatic methods need to be further refined to produce high quality results. As a result of this we have increased the amount of links between Wikidata and WordNet to nearly 10,000 and have made them available in Wikidata and English WordNet[4]. We hope that this can be a seed to further the integration of the two projects and close the gap between the lexical and encyclopedic information in the two resources.

[4] `https://github.com/globalwordnet/english-wordnet`

Acknowledgements

This work is supported by the EU H2020 programme under grant agreements 731015 (ELEXIS - European Lexicographic Infrastructure) and by a research grant from Science Foundation Ireland, co-funded by the European Regional Development Fund, for the Insight Centre under Grant Number SFI/12/RC/2289.

References

Eneko Agirre and Aitor Soroa. 2009. Personalizing pagerank for word sense disambiguation. In *Proceedings of the 12th Conference of the European Chapter of the ACL (EACL 2009)*, pages 33–41.

Sören Auer, Christian Bizer, Georgi Kobilarov, Jens Lehmann, Richard Cyganiak, and Zachary Ives. 2007. DBpedia: A nucleus for a web of open data. In *The Semantic Web*, pages 722–735. Springer.

Francis Bond and Arthur Bond. 2019. GeoNames Wordnet (gnwn): extracting wordnets from GeoNames. In *Proceedings of the 10th Gloabl WordNet Conference*, pages 387–393.

Francis Bond, Piek Vossen, John P. McCrae, and Christiane Fellbaum. 2016. CILI: the Collaborative Interlingual Index. In *Proceedings of the Global WordNet Conference 2016*.

Claire Bonial, Kevin Stowe, and Martha Palmer. 2013. Renewing and revising SemLink. In *Proceedings of the 2nd Workshop on Linked Data in Linguistics (LDL-2013): Representing and linking lexicons, terminologies and other language data*, pages 9–17.

Christiane Fellbaum. 2012. Wordnet. *The encyclopedia of applied linguistics*.

Iryna Gurevych, Judith Eckle-Kohler, Silvana Hartmann, Michael Matuschek, Christian M Meyer, and Christian Wirth. 2012. UBY-a large-scale unified lexical-semantic resource based on LMF. In *Proceedings of the 13th Conference of the European Chapter of the Association for Computational Linguistics*, pages 580–590.

Harold W Kuhn. 1955. The Hungarian method for the assignment problem. *Naval research logistics quarterly*, 2(1-2):83–97.

Peter A Lofgren, Siddhartha Banerjee, Ashish Goel, and C Seshadhri. 2014. FAST-PPR: scaling personalized pagerank estimation for large graphs. In *Proceedings of the 20th ACM SIGKDD international conference on Knowledge discovery and data mining*, pages 1436–1445.

John P. McCrae. 2018. Mapping WordNet Instances to Wikipedia. In *Proceedings of the 9th Global WordNet Conference*.

John P. McCrae and Paul Buitelaar. 2018. Linking Datasets Using Semantic Textual Similarity. *Cybernetics and Information Technologies*, 18(1):109–123.

John P. McCrae, Alexandre Rademaker, Francis Bond, Ewa Rudnicka, and Christiane Fellbaum. 2019. English WordNet 2019 – An Open-Source WordNet for English. In *Proceedings of the 10th Global WordNet Conference – GWC 2019*.

John Philip McCrae, Alexandre Rademaker, Ewa Rudnicka, and Francis Bond. 2020. English WordNet 2020: Improving and Extending a WordNet for English using an Open-Source Methodology. In *Proceedings of the Multimodal Wordnets Workshop at LREC 2020*, pages 14–19.

Christian M Meyer and Iryna Gurevych. 2011. What psycholinguists know about chemistry: Aligning Wiktionary and WordNet for increased domain coverage. In *Proceedings of 5th International Joint Conference on Natural Language Processing*, pages 883–892.

George A Miller. 1995. WordNet: a lexical database for English. *Communications of the ACM*, 38(11):39–41.

James Munkres. 1957. Algorithms for the assignment and transportation problems. *Journal of the society for industrial and applied mathematics*, 5(1):32–38.

Roberto Navigli and Simone Paolo Ponzetto. 2010. BabelNet: Building a very large multilingual semantic network. In *Proceedings of the 48th annual meeting of the association for computational linguistics*, pages 216–225.

Roberto Navigli and Simone Paolo Ponzetto. 2012. BabelNet: The automatic construction, evaluation and application of a wide-coverage multilingual semantic network. *Artificial Intelligence*, 193:217–250.

Finn Nielsen. 2020. Lexemes in Wikidata: 2020 status. In *Proceedings of the 7th Workshop on Linked Data in Linguistics (LDL-2020)*, pages 82–86, Marseille, France. European Language Resources Association.

Lawrence Page, Sergey Brin, Rajeev Motwani, and Terry Winograd. 1999. The PageRank citation ranking: Bringing order to the web. Technical report, Stanford InfoLab.

Martha Palmer, Claire Bonial, and Diana McCarthy. 2014. Semlink+: Framenet, verbnet and event ontologies. In *Proceedings of Frame Semantics in NLP: A Workshop in Honor of Chuck Fillmore (1929-2014)*, pages 13–17.

Fabian M Suchanek, Gjergji Kasneci, and Gerhard Weikum. 2008. YAGO: A large ontology from Wikipedia and WordNet. *Journal of Web Semantics*, 6(3):203–217.

Antonio Toral, Oscar Ferrandez, Eneko Agirre, and Rafael Munoz. 2009. A study on Linking Wikipedia categories to Wordnet synsets using text similarity. In *Proceedings of the international conference RANLP-2009*, pages 449–454.

Toward the creation of WordNets for ancient Indo-European languages

Erica Biagetti
University of Pavia / Bergamo
Pavia / Bergamo, Italy
erica.biagetti01@universitadipavia.it

Chiara Zanchi
University of Pavia
Pavia, Italy
chiara.zanchi01@unipv.it

William M. Short
University of Exeter
Exeter, United Kingdom
W.Short@exeter.ac.uk

Abstract

This paper presents the work in progress toward the creation of a family of WordNets for Sanskrit, Ancient Greek, and Latin. Building on previous attempts in the field, we elaborate these efforts bridging together WordNet relational semantics with theories of meaning from Cognitive Linguistics. We discuss some of the innovations we have introduced to the WordNet architecture, to better capture the polysemy of words, as well as Indo-European language family-specific features. We conclude the paper framing our work within the larger picture of resources available for ancient languages and showing that WordNet-backed search tools have the potential to re-define the kinds of questions that can be asked of ancient language corpora.

1 Introduction

This paper presents the work in progress toward the creation of a family of WordNets for ancient Indo-European (IE) languages, namely Sanskrit (Skt.), Ancient Greek (AG), and Latin (Lat.). This ongoing project is being jointly developed by an international team of scholars at the University of Exeter, the University of Pavia, the Center for Hellenic Studies at Harvard University, and the Alpheios Project, spearheaded by William M. Short. The design, as well as the specific content, of these WordNets builds on several previous (but, as far as we know, now defunct) attempts in the field (for AG, Bizzoni et al., 2014, Boschetti, 2019; for Lat., Minozzi, 2009),[1] extending and elaborating this work in certain critical respects (in particular, by bringing the framework under theories of meaning from Cognitive Linguistics). Crucially, these WordNets share the same data organization and exploit of the same pool of sense designations (synsets), enabling comparison of linguistic – above all semantic – structures cross-linguistically through the use of a common set of definitional elements.

In this paper, we discuss some of the innovations we have introduced to the WordNet architecture, to better capture the polysemy of words (including their figurative metaphorical and metonymic uses) as well as IE language family-specific features. We finally frame our family of WordNets in the wider picture of linguistic resources available for ancient languages.

2 Representing meaning in ancient language WordNets

Like previous WordNets (Fellbaum, 1998), our ancient language WordNets are lexical databases in which meaning is stored in a relational way. WordNets comprise nodes for lemmas to which meanings are associated in the form of synsets,

[1] The previous Ancient Greek and Latin WordNets can be partly consulted here: http://www.languagelibrary.eu/new_ewnui/. Boschetti (2019) references to an ongoing project on the Homeric lexicon, named Homeric Greek WordNet, which at the time, when the paper was published, was being developed at ILC, CNR, Pisa. Currently, the website https://cophilab.ilc.cnr.it/hgwnWeb/ requires a username and password to be accessed, and detailed information on the status of the project does not seem to be available online.

i.e., sets of synonymous words and phrases accompanied by brief definitions. Lemmas are connected to each other through lexical relations, whereas semantic relations establish connections among synsets.

Different lemmas can share one or more synset(s), which means that they are (partly) synonymous. Other semantic relations are typically tagged in WordNets, which mostly interconnect synsets associated with lemmas of the same part of speech: for example, the HYPONYMY-HYPERNYMY relation connects nouns to nouns (e.g. AG *ikhthûs* 'fish' and *zôion* 'animal'), the ENTAILS relation connects verbs to verbs (e.g. AG *pléō* (ACT) 'sail' and *kinéomai* (M/P) 'be in motion'), etc. (for similarities and differences between the traditional and our set of relations, see Section 3.4). Like in previous WordNets, our set of semantic relations fails to capture semantic solidarity due to belonging in the same Frame (Fillmore *et al.*, 2003) or semantic field (Fellbaum, 1998: 10 *tennis problem*). Thus, for example, no semantic relation links the AG words in (1):

(1) *ikhthûs* 'fish', *thálassa* 'sea', *naûs* 'ship', *naútēs* 'sailor', *pléō* 'sail'

However, *naútēs* is morphologically derived from *naûs*, which is annotated among lexical relations.

Like in other WordNets, lemmas can be assigned multiple synsets, which indicates polysemy. We have decided to frame our lexicographic work within a cognitive linguistic approach (e.g. Lakoff and Johnson, 1980; Tyler and Evans, 2003; on Cognitive Linguistics applied to the study of ancient languages, see Mocciaro and Short, 2019) and thus have embraced a principled view of polysemy. This entails (a) avoiding exaggerating the number of distinct senses associated to a lemma; (b) assuming that all senses of a lemma can be organized in a structured semantic network. Roughly, literal senses are detected based on their early attestation, concreteness, and predominance in the network (Tyler and Evans, 2003: 45-50), whereas non-literal senses are derived from literal ones through the cognitive processes of metaphor and metonymy. For example, in the Princeton WordNet, three senses are associated with the adjective *salty*, reported in (2):

(2) a. containing or filled with salt;
b. one of the four basic taste sensations; like the taste of sea water;
c. engagingly stimulating or provocative.

The sense in (2)a is the basic one, as *salty* morphologically derives from the noun *salt*. The sense in (2)b can be derived from (2)a via a metonymic process: a word denoting a state is employed to denote the physical sensation that such state triggers. The metaphoric meaning in (2)c can be connected with (2)a via the metonymic sense in (2)b: *being salty* is as positively or negatively engaging for the palate as *being stimulating/provocative* is for the spirit. The difference between cognitive metonymy and metaphor is that, with the former, the senses associated with the polysemous word belong to the same conceptual domain, whereas with the latter two senses belonging to different conceptual domains are mapped to one another.

Crucially, in our WordNets, we are implementing this principled view of polysemy by asking annotators to avoid multiplying the number of synsets associated to lemmas and to tag only senses that clearly do not emerge from context. Moreover, our annotators are required to maximize the usage of the synsets deriving from the Princeton WordNet for English, in order to enhance the compatibility of our WordNets with existing ones and to establish a common base of sense definitions. Finally, while tagging senses of lemma entries, our annotators are asked to distinguish among synsets that correspond to literal, metonymic, and metaphoric meanings.

For example, 16 synsets are currently associated to the AG word for 'salt', *háls*, and classified into three groups, viz. literal (4 synsets), metonymic (4 synsets) and metaphoric (8 synsets) senses, exemplified in (3)a, (3)b, and (3)c, respectively.

(3) a. literal sense 'salt'
n#05846273 | white crystalline form of especially sodium chloride used to season and preserve food
b. metonymic sense 'body of salty water'
n#10771040 | water containing salts
c. metaphoric sense 'wit'
n#05075890 | a message whose ingenuity or verbal skill or incongruity has the power to evoke laughter

As discussed above, the difference between metonymy and metaphor relies in being vs. not-being part of the same conceptual domain. Clearly, the senses of 'salt' and 'body of salty water' both pertain to the domain of SEA; by contrast, the senses of 'salt' and 'wit' belong to two different domains (cf. the meanings of *salty*, remembered above in this section).

As we are dealing with corpus languages that enjoy centuries of attestation and a long tradition of studies, each of the identified literal, metonymic, and metaphoric synsets will be tagged for its periodization(s), literary genre(s), and optionally *loci*, i.e., exemplifying attestations referred to by author(s) and work(s). Thus, for example, the senses in (3)a-c are enriched with the following diachronic and stylistic metadata:

Sense	Period	Genre	Loci
(3)a	Archaic (8th-6th BCE)	poetry epic historiography narrative	Il.9.214, Od.11.123 Ar.Ach.835 Hdt.4.53
(3)b	Hellenistic (323-31 BCE)	-	Call.Fr.50
(3)c	Roman (31 BCE-290 CE)	philosophy treatise	Plut.2.685 Plut.2.854

Table 1: Diachronic and stylistic metadata associated with the sense of *háls* in (3)a-c

We expect this information to be extremely useful for philologists, lexical typologists, and historical linguists interested in semantic change. On the one hand, as our WordNets will also include etymological information (Section 3.1), users will be able to investigate whether Skt., AG, and Lat. cognate words lexicalize comparable arrays of concepts (see Section 4). On the other hand, users will be able to track whether and how word meanings change over time and vary across literary genres and authors.

3 Family-specific attributes and relations

3.1 Annotation of lemmas

As anticipated in Section 2, etymological information completes the diachronic picture. Etymological information for each database entry is hierarchically structured and consists of:

a. ETYMOLOGY proper: e.g. PIE **pleu-* 'float' for AG *pléō* 'sail' and Skt. *plu-* 'float, swim';
b. ETYMON: a discrete form in the history of a word's etymological development (e.g. Lat. *pulmo* < AG *pleumon* < AG *pneumon* 'lung' < PIE **pleu-* 'float');
c. MORPHEME: a discrete element within the etymon (e.g. *-*ti-* in Skt. *plu-ti-* 'flood', AG *plú-si-s* 'washing').

Each of the three levels of etymological information is stored as a separate entry in the database, which allows lemmas to be linked via their etymological constituents at many different levels (root, stem, morphemes, etc.).

For AG, a dedicated field gives information on dialectal variants (e.g. Attic *ploûs* 'sailing, voyage', Ionic *plóos* 'id.').

Unlike in other WordNets, each lemma is provided with morphological information in our databases. Beside specification of the part of speech, morphological information is stored in three fields:

a. MORPHO: we employ a modified version of the tagging schema developed for the *Perseus Digital Library*[2] for encoding morphological properties of tokens. The schema consists of a ten-place character string, where each place corresponds to a grammatical category (e.g. AG *limḗn* 'harbor' n-s---mn3n).
b. MORPHOLOGY: this field consists of a subfield PRINCIPAL PARTS, where relevant parts of the paradigm are listed, and a subfield PROSODY providing vowel length when relevant. For instance, AG *háls* 'salt' has a principal part *halós*, which corresponds to its genitive form. Prosody, instead, is provided in cases such as Lat. *occīdo* 'to strike down' as distinct from *occĭdo* 'to fall; die'.
c. FORM TOKENS: it consists of a token with its morphological tag, specifying whether this is 'irregular' and/or 'alternative'. Since irregular forms may be case- or number-specific, this field constitutes an exception to the exclusion of inflected word forms from our WordNet. One instance is again represented by AG *háls* 'salt' with its two dative plural forms *halsí* and *hálasi*: the latter, being built on a different stem, is annotated as an alternative form (Form n-p---md3-, Token *hálasi*, Alternative).

Table 2 displays the annotation associated to the AG lemma *háls* 'salt':

Field	Subfield	Value
Etymology	_	PIE **séh$_2$l-* 'salt'
Lemma	_	*háls*

[2] http://www.perseus.tufts.edu.

POS	_	Noun
Morpho	_	n-s---mn3-
Morphology	Prin. Parts	*halós*
	Prosody	_
Form Tokens	Form	n-p---md3-
	Token	*hálasi*
	Alternative	✓

Table 2: Lemma annotation for AG *háls*.

3.2 Lexical databases

Previous WordNets comprise lemmas belonging to open class parts of speech only, that is, nouns (N), adjectives (A), verbs (V), and adverbs (Adv). In our WordNets, a new part of speech was added, that of prepositions (P), for a number of reasons. First, because of the importance these elements hold in the grammar systems of IE languages. Following the literature on AG (e.g. Chantraine, 1953), we take *preposition* as a catch-all term for a class of uninflected morphemes that feature high semantic and syntactic flexibility in IE, functioning either as local adverbs, adpositions or preverbs (Reinöhl and Casaretto, 2018; Zanchi, 2019: Ch. 3). Second, prepositions are originally associated with concrete meanings, which constitute the starting point for developing more abstract meanings thanks to the cognitive mechanisms of metonymy and metaphor (Section 2). Therefore, they are of particular importance in Cognitive Linguistics, as they constitute a privileged viewpoint for studying how discrete senses associated to a lemma organize in a structured network. Finally, including prepositions in WordNet allows us to study the semantic interaction between simplex and compound verbs. A compound verb such as AG *ap-eîpon* 'deny' illustrates the points above: in combination with the communication verb *eîpon* 'say', the preverb *apó-* 'away' gains an abstract meaning and expresses refusal, making the meaning of the compound verb non-compositional (Zanchi 2019: 67).

Sometimes, prepositions occur in *multi-word units* (Fellbaum, 2015), such as Lat. *sub divo* 'in the open air'. In our WordNets, the lemma list will include such multi-word units that show a word-like distribution and feature some degree of semantic idiomaticity and of structural fixedness (on multi-word expressions, see also Masini, 2019 with references). Other examples are Lat. *res publica* 'state, republic' and AG *thalássia érga* 'navigation'.

3.3 Lexical relations

In WordNet, lexical relations include both morphological relations, such as derivation and composition, and the semantic relation of antonymy. The reason for including antonymy among lexical relations is that, in a word association test, two antonyms are always given as the most common response one of the other (Deese, 1964; 1965); therefore, *heavy/light* are antonyms, but *weighty/light* are not, and antonymy is defined as a semantic relation between words rather than synsets (Miller, 1998: 48). However, since we cannot rely on speakers' judgments, we have decided to split the antonymy relation into a lexical (i.e. morphological) and a semantic relation. Morphological antonyms are lemma pairs, where one of the antonyms is derived from the other through the privative prefix *a-*: Skt. [*a-mítra-* 'non-friend, enemy'] IS PRIVATIVE OF [*mítra-* 'friend']. Note that lexical antonymy is asymmetric: if we take the base as a starting point, we get [*mítra-* 'friend'] HAS PRIVATIVE [*a-mítra-* 'non-friend, enemy'].

In order to represent the rich derivational morphology of IE languages, we have decided to extend the set of lexical relations as follows:

a. Derivation: asymmetric relation holding between a base and a word derived from it either by conversion (Skt. *nāga-* A 'serpentine' > *nāga-* N 'a kind of serpent') or by affixation: AG [*makró-tēs* 'length'] IS DERIVED FROM [*makrós* 'long']. The inverse relation is IS RELATED TO: [*makrós*] IS RELATED TO [*makró-tēs*].
b. Parasynthesis: asymmetric relation holding between a base and a word derived from it by simultaneous conversion and affixation: AG [*ánoos* A 'without understanding'] IS PARASYNTHETIC OF [*nóos* N 'mind']. The inverse relation is HAS PARASYNTHETON: [*nóos*] HAS PARASYNTHETON [*ánoos*].
c. Composition: asymmetric, many-to-many relation holding between a compound word and its constituents: Skt. [*rāja-putra-* 'a king's son, prince'] IS COMPOSED OF [*rāja-* 'king'], [*rāja-putra-*] IS COMPOSED OF [*putra-* 'son']. The inverse relation is COMPOSES: [*rāja-*] COMPOSES [*rāja-putra-*].
d. Inclusion: asymmetric many-to-many relation holding between a multi-word unit and its parts: AG [*thalássia érga* 'navigation'] INCLUDES [*thalássios* 'related to the sea'], [*thalássia érga*] INCLUDES [*érgon* 'work'].

The inverse relation is IS INCLUDED IN: [*thalássios*] IS INCLUDED IN [*thalássia érga*], [*érgon*] IS INCLUDED IN [*thalássia érga*];

e. Participle: asymmetric relation holding between a participle and its base verb: Skt. [*sát-* 'true'] IS PARTICIPLE OF [*as-* 'be'].

Table 3 summarizes newly added lexical relations:

Rel.	Label	Inverse
Anton.	IS PRIVATIVE OF	HAS PRIVATIVE
Der.	IS DERIVED FROM	IS RELATED TO
Paras.	IS PARASYNTHETIC OF	HAS PARASYNTHETON
Comp.	IS COMPOSED OF	COMPOSES
Incl.	INCLUDES	IS INCLUDED IN
Part.	IS PARTICIPLE OF	HAS PARTICIPLE

Table 3: Family-specific Lexical Relations.

3.4 Semantic relations

Semantic relations constitute the core of WordNet architecture. In order to ensure compatibility of our WordNets with the existing ones, we tried to stick to the established set as closely as possible. However, some differences must be mentioned:

a. Semantic antonymy: contrary to morphological antonymy (Section 3.3), and to antonymy in other WordNets, semantic antonymy holds between synsets. Thus, semantic antonymy does not link e.g. AG *kalós* 'good' and *kakós* 'bad' themselves, but rather the synsets to which they belong; contrary to morphological antonymy, semantic antonymy is a symmetric relation: {n#01963712 "of moral excellence"} HAS ANTONYM {n#01078381 "having undesirable or negative qualities"}.

b. Similar to / Also see: in other WordNets, the relation IS SIMILAR TO links satellite synsets to one of the antonyms in a cluster of adjectives; ALSO SEE, instead, links the half cluster to another half cluster related to it. Since semantic antonymy links synsets in our WordNets, we avoid using both relations and employ IS NEAREST TO as a catch-all relation for similar synsets: {n#01893072 "a young pig"} IS NEAREST TO {n#01892895 "domestic swine"} for AG *khoîros* and *sûs*.

c. Verbal sense group: symmetric relation linking verbs related by aspectual, voice- or valency-related properties: {v#00399347 "become conscious of"} VERBAL SENSE GROUP {v#00401762 "possess knowledge or information about"} for AG *gignṓskō* (PRS) 'perceive, know' and *oîda* (PF) 'know'.[3]

d. Qualifies event as: asymmetric relation holding between an adverb and an adjective: {r#00162139 "for an extended time or at a distant time:"} QUALIFIES EVENT AS {a#01380813 "being or indicating a relatively great or greater than average duration or passage of time or a duration as specified"} for AG *makrán* 'at length' and *makrós* 'long'; the inverse relation is QUALIFIES ENTITY AS.

Table 4 summarizes family-specific semantic relations:

Rel.	Label	Inverse
Anton.	HAS ANTONYM	HAS ANTONYM
Near.	IS NEAREST TO	IS NEAREST TO
Verb. Sense Group	VERBAL SENSE GROUP	VERBAL SENSE GROUP
Qual. event as	QUALIFIES EVENT AS	QUALIFIES ENTITY AS

Table 4: Family-specific Semantic Relations.

4 Integrating ancient language WordNets with existing resources

The Skt., AG, and Lat. WordNets have been designed to be fully interoperable, as well as integrated into the larger ecosystem of digital lexical and textual resources for ancient languages. What is more, they make available a standard API (application programming interface) permitting any user, or computer application, to programmatically access their lexical and semantic content in a consistent manner, regardless of language (or simultaneously for all languages). For example, it would be trivial to discover the words in Skt., AG, and Lat. that correspond to the meaning 'a short stabbing weapon' (i.e., a dagger) – represented by synset n#02542418 – simply by querying the endpoint */api/synsets/n/02542418/lemmas/* at the address of the relevant WordNet. More sophisticated queries could take advantage of the rich semantic, morphological, etymological, and figurative data

[3] In IE studies, *oîda* (PF) 'know' is said to be a defective form, which thus enters paradigms of other verbal roots.

that, while characterizing specific structures of a given language, are encoded through a set of language-independent (as it were, 'etic') elements. In fact, because they share certain linguistic structures (including etymological primitives) at a fundamental level, the Sanskrit, Greek and Latin WordNets represents the first systematic attempt in classical language lexicography to deliver a basis for comparative semantic research (Section 2).

Beyond interoperability, the architecture of the Skt., AG and Lat. WordNets aims to facilitate their integration with other lexical and textual resources. The Lat. WordNet, for instance, is now being aligned with the ERC-funded *Linking Latin* project (https://lila-erc.eu), which aims to standardize different resources around a single set of lemma-based URIs. This will enable users to easily tie together information available from disparate lexical and textual resources by guaranteeing the correct identification of lemmas (e.g., in the case of ambiguous word forms). Similarly, the Sanskrit WordNet is tightly integrated with the *Digital Corpus of Sanskrit* (http://www.sanskritlinguistics.org/dcs/index.php), which will allow users of this corpus to query semantic data utilizing pre-existing identification tags. The morphological encoding schema is compatible with the quasi-standard system used in most annotated corpora of Greek and Latin, adding two further fields to provide greater specificity in lexical categorization (see Section 3.1). This is meant to enable scholars to inject semantic information, along with syntactic information, into natural language processing pipelines for the first time. At the same time, this means that other NLP tools already available for the ancient languages can automatically and immediately take advantage of the WordNet data to improve their functionality, accuracy, and scope.

The Sanskrit, Greek and Latin WordNets are, finally, designed to work hand-in-hand with electronic corpora of semantically annotated texts – what we call "sembanks" on the model of syntactic "treebanks". The creation of the WordNets, on one hand, and of sembanks, on the other, in fact constitute two prongs of a single effort to bring research on ancient language semantics under computational approaches. For this reason, efforts are currently underway to produce a robust but flexible XML schema, following standards established by the Text Encoding Initiative (http://tei-c.org) for use in annotating texts with WordNet constructs (above all, synsets) in order to capture the senses of words or larger textual units, as they occur in specific contexts. This schema incorporates the concept of a *semtagm* as a semantically meaningful unit consisting of one or more tokens and that of a *reading*, representing one discrete possible interpretation of the given semtagm. So, for example, the mark-up of the first sentence of the preface of Cato's *De Agri Cultura* would consist of a sequence of semtagm elements, whose values correspond straightforwardly to definite synsets: *est* = v#01775163, 'have an existence, be extant'; *interdum* = r#00020741, 'on certain occasions'; *praestare* = v#01246259, 'value more highly'; *mercaturis* = n#00707408, 'the commercial exchange of goods and services' and so on.

Because the ancient language WordNets also include information about the figurative senses of words and the conceptual structures that underpin these senses (Section 2), it is further possible to annotate the figurative senses of words. For example, in the following annotation of Ovid's *Metamorphoses* 13.11, the synset glossed "a hostile meeting of opposing military forces in the course of a war" (n#00610417) has been encoded as the contextual sense of *Mars*, which is indicated as a metonymical usage of the god's name and includes a designation of the conceptual metonymy that motivates this interpretation:

```
<semtagm n="73"
urn="latinLit:phi0959.phi006.perseus-lat1"
cite="13.11:11:7">
    <token n="1" form="Marte" lemma="Mars"
        uri="50193" morpho="n-s---mb3-">
        <reading n="1" synset="n#00610417"
                figure="#" mapping="247" />
    </token>
</semtagm>
```

This annotation schema is designed, moreover, to help capture the polysemy that tends to characterize word usage in literary contexts – due to textual problems arising from the process of transmission, intentional or unintentional lexical ambiguities, or genuine disagreements of interpretation in critical analysis – by permitting annotators to tag lexical or phrasal tokens with multiple sense designations. Thus, for example, the famous ambiguity of Catullus's *pudicitiam matris indicet ore*, where *os* can be interpreted either as 'face' or (more specifically) as 'mouth' and again by metonymy, "speech", is represented by two *reading* elements within a single semtagm, to simultaneously encode synsets n#03683012, 'outward or visible aspect of a person or thing' and n#05319899, 'communication by word of mouth' as this word's possible interpretations.

When combined with a next-generation corpus search tool like Cylleneus,[4] WordNet-based semantically annotated texts will enable users to query ancient texts on the basis not only of their morphological and syntactic properties, but also of their semantic properties – that is, on the basis of the meanings of words as well as of the kinds of grammatical constructions in which they appear. For example, someone interested in ancient "courage" would easily be able to find occurrences of this concept in Sanskrit, Greek, or Latin literature, simply by searching for a specific synset or some higher-order semantic category (semfield) – without needing to conduct separate searches for each lemma. This would make identifying semantic intertextualities, for instance – the ways in which one text creates new meanings by reworking the themes and ideas (not merely the verbal elements) of other texts – almost trivial. More generally, whereas current corpus search methodologies require painstaking and time-consuming "brute force" searching in order to identify patterns of usage, by abstracting away from the lexicon and thus permitting efficient queries of whole semantic fields (in conjunction with morphosyntactic queries), WordNet-backed search tools have the potential to redefine the kinds of questions that can be asked of ancient language corpora.

Acknowledgements

The innovations we introduced in the architecture of our WordNets partly implement suggestions made by students at the University of Pavia, who volunteered to annotate the data. We are extremely grateful to them for their time and insightful comments and to Silvia Luraghi for leading the Pavia research unit in this project.

The present paper results from intense collaboration of the three authors. For academic purposes, Erica Biagetti is responsible of Section 3, William M. Short of Section 4, and Chiara Zanchi of Sections 1 and 2.

References

Federico, Boschetti. 2019. Semantic Analysis and Thematic Annotation. In: Monica Berti (ed.), *Digital Classical Philology.* De Gruyter, Berlin, DEU.

Pierre Chantraine. 1953. *Grammaire homérique*, Tome 2: Syntaxe. Klincksieck, Paris, FR.

Yuri Bizzoni, Federico Boschetti, Harry Diakoff, Riccardo Del Gratta, Monica Monachini and Gregory R. Crane. 2014. The Making of Ancient Greek WordNet. In: Nicoletta Calzolari et al. (eds.), *Proceedings of the Ninth International Conference on Language Resources and Evaluation* (LREC, vol. 2014), Reykjavik, Iceland, may 2014, 1140-1147. Accessed online at https://www.aclweb.org/anthology/L14-1054/.

James Deese. 1964. The associative structure of some common English adjectives. *Journal of Verbal Learning and Verbal Behavior* 3(5):347-357.

James Deese. 1965. *The Structure of Associations in Language and Thought.* John Hopkins Press, Baltimore, MD.

Christiane Fellbaum (ed.). 1998. *WordNet: An electronic lexical database.* MIT Press, Cambridge, MA.

Christiane Fellbaum. 2015. The treatment of multi-word units in lexicography. In: Philip Durkin (ed.), *The Oxford handbook of lexicography.* OUP, Oxford, UK, 411-424.

Charles. J. Fillmore, Christopher Johnson, and Miriam R. L. Petruck. 2003. Background to Framenet. *International Journal of Lexicography*, 16(3):235-250.

Francesca Masini. 2019. *Multi-Word Expressions and Morphology.* Accessed online at https://oxfordre.com/linguistics/view/10.1093/acrefore/9780199384655.001.0001/acrefore-9780199384655-e-611.

Katherine J. Miller. 1998. Modifiers in WordNet. In: Christiane Fellbaum (ed.), *WordNet: An electronic lexical database*. MIT Press, Cambridge, MA, 47-67.

Stefano Minozzi. 2009. The Latin WordNet Project. In: Peter Anreiter and Manfred Kienpointner (eds.), *Latin Linguistics Today. Akten des 15. Internationalem Kolloquiums zur Lateinischen Linguistik*, Innsbrucker Beiträge zur Sprachwissenschaft 137, Innsbruck, AUT, 707-716.

Egle Mocciaro and William M. Short. 2019. *Toward a Cognitive Classical Linguistics. The Embodied Basis of Constructions in Greek and Latin.* De Gruyter, Berlin, DEU.

Uta Reinöhl and Antje Casaretto. 2018. When grammaticalization does not occur—Prosody-syntax mismatches in Indo-Aryan. *Diachronica* 35(2):238-276.

[4] http://github.com/cylleneus/cylleneus.

Andrea Tyler and Vyvyan Evans. 2003. *The Semantics of English Prepositions: Spatial Scenes, Embodied Meanings and Cognition.* CUP, Cambridge, UK.

Chiara Zanchi. 2019. *Multiple preverbs in ancient Indo-European languages.* Narr, Tübingen.

DanNet2: Extending the coverage of adjectives in DanNet based on thesaurus data

Sanni Nimb
Society for Danish Language and Literature
sn@dsl.dk

Bolette S. Pedersen
University of Copenhagen, CST
bspedersen@hum.ku.dk

Sussi Olsen
University of Copenhagen CST
saolsen@hum.ku.dk

Abstract

The paper describes work in progress in the DanNet2 project financed by the Carlsberg Foundation. The project aim is to extend the original Danish wordnet, DanNet, in several ways. Main focus is on extension of the coverage and description of the adjectives, a part of speech that was rather sparsely described in the original wordnet. We describe the methodology and initial work of semi-automatically transferring adjectives from the Danish Thesaurus to the wordnet with the aim of easily enlarging the coverage from 3,000 to approx. 13,000 adjectival synsets. Transfer is performed by manually encoding all missing adjectival subsection headwords from the thesaurus and thereafter employing a semi-automatic procedure where adjectives from the same subsection are transferred to the wordnet as either 1) near synonyms to the section's headword, 2) hyponyms to the section's headword, or 3) as members of the same synset as the headword. We also discuss how to deal with the problem of multiple representations of the same sense in the thesaurus, and present other types of information from the thesaurus that we plan to integrate, such as thematic and sentiment information.

1. Introduction to the project

In this paper, we provide a project description of the recently initiated 'DanNet2' project financed by the Carlsberg Foundation. The project runs from 2019-2022 and aims at investigating to which degree a recently compiled Danish Thesaurus, DDB (Nimb et al. 2014a; Nimb et al. 2014b) can be used to facilitate the extension of the lexical coverage of the Danish wordnet DanNet (cf. Pedersen 2009). Where the first version of DanNet was semi-automatically compiled on the basis of the isolated information on genus proximum in the manuscript of The Danish Dictionary (Hjorth & Kristensen 2003-2005, henceforth DDO) and covers 50% of its senses, we now want to exploit that 90% of the DDO vocabulary is thematically and semantically grouped in a newly compiled thesaurus. The three lexical resources share id numbers at sense level, making it possible to develop methods where data from one are transferred to the other. This was already exploited in the compilation of many thesaurus sections. DanNet data constituted for example the basis of the sections on diseases, garment and furniture based on information on ontological type in the wordnet. Like the current version of DanNet, also the extended version compiled in the DanNet2 project will be open source and downloadable via CLARIN-DK and github.

The main focus in DanNet2 is on the upgrade of the coverage and description of adjectives in DanNet, which in the thesaurus are richly represented, but rather sparsely described in the wordnet with a quite limited coverage of approx 3,000 adjective synsets. Our goal is by the end of the project to reach a more or less complete coverage of approx. 13,000 adjectival synsets.

We start out in Section 2 with related work on the treatment of adjectives in wordnets and similar resources, and move on to the way they are currently described in DanNet.

In Section 3 we describe how adjectives in the thesaurus are presented along topical chapters, sections and subsections, a structure that we want to use as source for the semi-automatic extension of adjectives in DanNet.

Section 4 presents the semi-automatic transfer method, where we employ a multistep procedure, first manually encoding the headwords of each section into DanNet, and thereafter automatically enlarging the DanNet vocabulary by encoding the semantic similarity of the other adjectives in the subsection with a default relation to the headword.

Section 5 addresses additional information to be transferred from DDB to DanNet such as thematic and sentiment information. Finally in Section 6 we conclude.

2. Adjectives in wordnets and similar resources

Adjectives are generally recognized as being indeed very challenging to categorize from a lexical-semantic perspective, mainly because of their plasticity in the sense that they have an extreme ability to take colour from their surroundings. In other words, a core semantic description which is somewhat stable across a certain number of contexts seems even more difficult to provide for adjectives than for other content words (cf. Cruse 1986; Pustejovsky 1995; Bick 2019; Peters & Peters, 2000; and others).

While the structuring feature of wordnets is basically the hyponymy relation between synsets, it has been argued that adjectives are maybe better characterized by their polarity and antonymy relations, their scalarity, their connotation (positive, negative), or simply by the semantics of the external argument (typically a noun) that they prototypically affiliate to.

Consequently, in many wordnets adjectives are to some extent only rudimentarily described and with a not too specific taxonomic labeling. This can be seen as a pragmatic approach in order to be able to cope with their extensive semantic variability.

Exceptions to this are wordnets that have developed their own very elaborate feature scheme for adjectives after thorough analysis, such as GermaNet (Hamp & Feldweg, 1997) with a specific class hierarchy for adjectives of around 100 types relating basically to the semantics of the prototypical external argument of the adjective. Maziarz et al. (2015) describes a set of adjective relations in the Polish WordNet 2.0 based on the principles of especially PWN and EuroWordNet combined with specific lexico-semantic features of the Polish language. Bick (2019) also suggests an annotation scheme of approx 100 taxonomically structured tags partly based on the semantics of the external argument (such as Human, Action, and Semiotic product etc.).

In comparison, Peters & Peters (2000) provides a slightly different description model for adjectives with a primary distinction between Intentional (as in *former president*) and Extensional (as in *American president*), respectively, and a further subdivision according to meaning components such as social, physical, temporal, intensifying etc. The model was developed for the computational lexicon project SIMPLE (Lenci et al. 2001), but was to our knowledge never implemented at a larger scale - maybe due to its complexity.

Previous pilot studies on the Danish adjectival data (Nimb & Pedersen 2012) support the idea that the semantics of the external argument of the adjective can actually function as an appropriate classification scheme, indicating for instance that *bekymret* ('worried') is a prototypical property of human beings whereas for instance *groftskåren* ('coarsely cut') prototypically relates to food items. For Danish, these features can for some of the adjectives be derived from the DDB and might be considered in future transfer of lexical information from the thesaurus to the wordnet.

In DanNet as it stands, the adjectives, like nouns and verbs, are mainly structured according to the EuroWordNet Topontology (Vossen et al. 1998). They are encoded primarily in terms of the ontological type Property combined with a limited set of meaning components, such as Mental and Physical as seen in table 1.

Property
Property + Existence
Property + LanguageRepresentation
Property + Location
Property + Mental
Property + Physical
Property + Physical + Colour
Property + Physical + Condition
Property + Physical + Form
Property + Social
Property + Stimulating + Physical
Property + Time

Table 1: Ontological types assigned to adjectives in DanNet

In fact, these meaning components can also be interpreted as referring indirectly (and coarsely) to the type of the external argument of the adjective in context. In other words, an adjective of the type Property + Mental will relate to humans, as in *en bekymret* *politimand* ('a worried policeman'), whereas an adjective of the type Property + Time will have a temporal entity as its external argument, as in *en lang uge* ('a long week').

In addition, some adjectives are encoded wrt. their positive or negative connotation.

3. Adjectives in the DDB

In contrast, the thesaurus DDB presents adjectives from a thematically point of view in 22 named chapters (e.g. *Følelser* ('Feelings, emotions')), 888 named sections (e.g. *Vrede* ('Anger') and *Tristhed* ('Sadness')), which are furthermore divided into subsections, initiated with a headword. All the other words in the same subsection are closely semantically related to the headword. The grade of similarity ranges from full synonymy over near synonymy to weaker similarity like hyponymy or just relatedness.

The adjectives in DDB are linked to the sense inventory of the DDO dictionary. The sense links between the two resources and the keyword information in DDB have already shown very useful for the automatic presentation of near synonyms to senses in the online DDO (ordnet.dk/ddo), see Nimb et al. (2018). Exactly which adjectives to extract and present is based on the automatic calculation of the scope of the headword as well as on the further division of the headwords' subsection into even smaller groups of very related words, expressed in terms of dots in the boxes in figure 1. The figure illustrates the near synonyms of the adjective *cool* ('cool; smart') in the online DDO. The focus of the DanNet2 project is to investigate to which degree these principles can be reapplied in the semi-automatic extension of the number of adjectives in DanNet.

The thesaurus contains most of the approx. 13,000 DDO adjective lemmas and represents 90% of the 17.000 adjective senses of the dictionary. Most of them, also the headwords, are not yet included in DanNet where only 17% of the senses are represented. To illustrate this, consider the subsection headword *smittefarlig* ('contagious') in figure 2 where neither the headword, nor any of the semantically related adjectives in its subsection are presently in DanNet, these being *smittebærende* ('contagious'), *virulent* ('virolent'), *patogen* ('pathogen'), *smitsom* ('contagious'), *kontaminøs* ('contaminated'), and *epidemisk* ('epidemic'). However, the noun *smittefare* ('risk of infection') is.

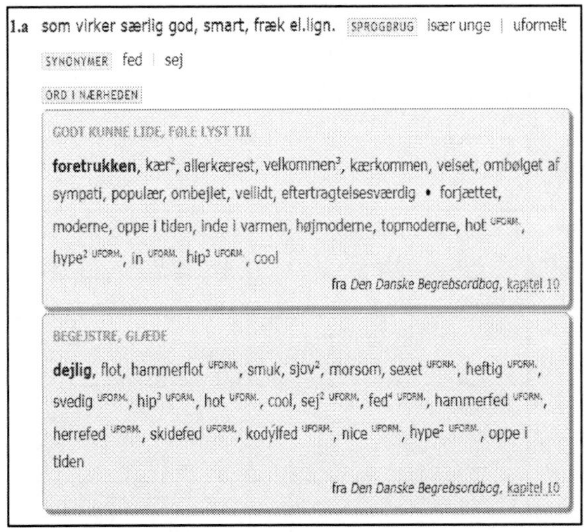

1.a som virker særlig god, smart, fræk el.lign. SPROGBRUG især unge | uformelt

SYNONYMER fed | sej

ORD I NÆRHEDEN

GODT KUNNE LIDE, FØLE LYST TIL

foretrukken, kær^{2}, allerkærest, velkommen^{2}, kærkommen, velset, ombølget af sympati, populær, ombejlet, vellidt, eftertragtelsesværdig • forjættet, moderne, oppe i tiden, inde i varmen, højmoderne, topmoderne, hot UFORM., hype^{2} UFORM., in UFORM., hip^{3} UFORM., cool

fra *Den Danske Begrebsordbog*, kapitel 10

BEGEJSTRE, GLÆDE

dejlig, flot, hammerflot UFORM., smuk, sjov^{2}, morsom, sexet UFORM., heftig UFORM., svedig UFORM., hip^{3} UFORM., hot UFORM., cool, sej^{2} UFORM., fed^{4} UFORM., hammerfed UFORM., herrefed UFORM., skidefed UFORM., kodylfed UFORM., nice UFORM., hype^{2} UFORM., oppe i tiden

fra *Den Danske Begrebsordbog*, kapitel 10

Figure 1. The adjective *cool* ('cool, smart') in the online DDO, with thesaurus data presented in boxes. The first box is extracted from the section *Godt kunne lide; føle lyst til* ('to like, to be fond of, fancy') initiated by the headword *foretrukken* ('preferred'). The second box is extracted from the section *Begejstre; glæde* ('please, make happy') initiated by the headword *dejlig* ('nice').

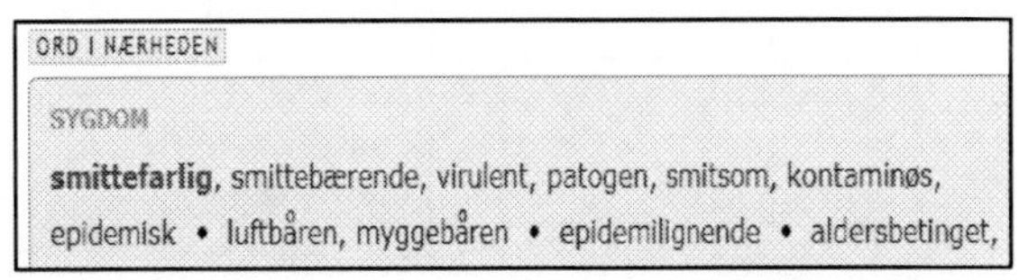

ORD I NÆRHEDEN

SYGDOM

smittefarlig, smittebærende, virulent, patogen, smitsom, kontaminøs, epidemisk • luftbåren, myggebåren • epidemilignende • aldersbetinget,

Figure 2. The headword *smittefarlig* ('contagious') in DDB. None of the 7 adjectives in the subsection limited by the first dot are presently part of DanNet.

Four out of five sections in the thesaurus contain adjectives (710 of the 888 sections). In particular, the chapters regarding human thinking, behavior and appearances do. There are many adjectives describing feelings and emotions (chapter 10), as well as volition and action (chapter 9), and also many describing social life (chapter 15). This also goes for 'physical' life (chapter 2) where we find the many adjectives for looks and physical conditions, e.g. diseases. Also thesaurus sections describing understanding, knowledge and opinions (chapter 11) contain quite a lot of adjectives. We find lesser adjectives in chapters on e.g. artifacts and food. See table 2.

DDB chapter number and name (in English)	%	Examples of adjectives (in English)
10.Feelings, emotions	11	'angry', 'happy'
15.Social life	9	'famous', 'hostile', 'married', 'foreign'
9.Will, volition, act, action	9	'lazy', 'active', 'stubborn'
2.Life	8	'young', 'blond', 'ill'
11.Cognition, thinking, reflection, reasoning	7	'wise',' clever', 'thought out'
7.Sense, impression, sensation, state of matter	6	'cold', 'warm', 'fluid', 'gaseous'
5.Condition,characteristics	6	'possible', 'optional', 'sudden'
4.Size, amount, number, degree	5	'big', 'small', 'huge', 'numerous'
12.Sign, communication, language	5	'French', 'open-mouthed', 'clear'
6.Time	4.6	'late',' early', 'simultaneous'
20.Economy, finance	4	'economical',' rich', 'poor'
18.Society	3.5	'political', 'conservative', 'ministerial'
13. Science	3	'scientific', 'mathematical'
3.Space, shape	3	'round', 'triangular'
19.Equipment, machinery, devices, artifacts	2.7	'wowen', 'patterned', 'computer-based'
21.Court, legal system, ethics	2.4	'legal', 'illegal', 'immoral'
1.Nature, environment	2	'polar', 'rainy', 'ecological'
16.Food and drink	2	'hungry', 'spicy', 'hard boiled
8.Place, motion	1.8	'fast', 'slow', 'trafficked'
14.The arts and culture	1.7	'artistic', 'cultural', 'poetic'
22.Religion, supernatural	1.3	'religious',' islamic', 'Christian'
17.Sport and leisure	1	'well-trained', 'football-wise'

Table 2. The 22 chapters and their share of the total number of adjectives in DDB, ranged from the highest share (11%) to the lowest (1%) (average 4.5%).

4. Transfer method and data

The transfer is carried out in three steps:

Initially the 766 adjectives which are headwords in the thesaurus (some of which in more than one section), are manually inserted into the wordnet hierarchy representing properties. This includes manual assignment of the appropriate ontological type and is a time-consuming task. The hypothesis is that the headword senses are probably also good candidates for central concepts in the wordnet. The lexicographer carefully studies the headword and its surrounding words in the thesaurus, as well as the existing wordnet hierarchies and the ontological values of the already encoded adjective synsets before the new adjective synset is created and linked to a hypernym, preferably at the very top level of the taxonomy. Already existing 'top' adjective synsets in DanNet sometimes also have to be adjusted according to the new adjectival taxonomy.

Secondly, all other adjectives from the headword group in the thesaurus are extracted into synsets in DanNet. They are selected automatically by applying the same method as illustrated in figure 1 (see Nimb et al. 2018), and assigned a) the ontological type of the headword and b) the default relation 'near synonym' to the headword.

As a third and final step, the automatically transferred synsets are manually validated. When appropriate, they are changed into co-synset members or hyponyms of the headword instead of the default value 'near synonym'. This step will be combined with extracted information on synonyms in DDO in order to insert some of the adjectives as an extra synset member instead of the default value 'near-synonym'.

Most of the adjective senses in DDB (64 % 11,000) only have one representation, making the method straightforward to follow in these cases. However, 22 % of them are part of two sections, 10 % of three, and 4% of even four or more sections. These cases of multiple representations of the same adjectival sense in the thesaurus are a challenge. We have chosen to let headword representations overrule non-headword representations. In the case where the adjective sense is never a headword but represented more than once, we relate it to the headword having the largest number of words in its scope. According to this rule, *cool* in figure 2 would be inserted as a near-synonym to *dejlig* ('nice') in

DanNet, and not to *foretrukken* ('preferred') in the second box.

The method also allows us to improve the thesaurus. We plan to look closer into the approx. 200 adjectives which are represented in five or more sections. Especially the 20 adjective senses which are represented in 6 up to 9 sections will be checked in order to see whether they are in fact overrepresented and should rather be removed from some sections.

5. Additional information on adjectives that can be transferred

In the initial phase of DanNet2, we also compile a sentiment list with a high lexical coverage based on the polarity values of DDB thesaurus sections. We plan to transfer also this *polarity information* to the wordnet (which already contains this information for a small part of the vocabulary as previously mentioned) relying again on the shared id numbers across our resources. By doing so, we enable DanNet to be used for sentiment analysis. The DanNet2 sentiment list is compiled in a rather efficient way due to the fact that many thesaurus sections contain almost only positive or negative words, respectively. The manual annotation of the 888 DDB sections was the starting point. ¼ of the 888 sections were estimated to contain polarity words based on the section name – 122 annotated to be negative (e.g. 'Unimportant' and 'Sadness'), 80 to be positive (e.g. 'Important', 'Admire' and 'Friendship, amity'), and 12 to be more unclear cases, however estimated to be relevant to include in a sentiment lexicon (e.g. 'Reputation' and 'Protest, uprising'). The annotated values were transferred to all the words in the section and manually checked, and words that did not convey polarity of any kind were assigned a zero value.

The more challenging part of this task is to find an objective way of including scalable values to the default polarity annotation. We study the polarity degree of the words in existing sentiment lexica for Danish (Nielsen 2011) with a much smaller lexical coverage. The high negative or positive degree is expanded manually to the near-synonyms in the thesaurus sections when appropriate. Following this line further, also the section and chapter numbers and names from DDB (all translated into English) might be valuable information to include in DanNet. It allows for the identification of *thematically related vocabulary* in the wordnet addressing what is sometimes labelled 'the tennis problem' of wordnets (meaning that wordnets generally do not resemble thematic relatedness well). This could be useful especially when it comes to adjectives that are difficult to categorize from a taxonomical point of view.

6. Conclusions

In this paper we have accounted for the aims and initial steps of the DanNet2 project. The first phase of the project has focused on examining the DDB adjective data, and establishing a qualified procedure for semi-automatic transfer of the adjective vocabulary from DDB into DanNet based on the same principles that have already proved useful in the automatic presentation of selected thesaurus data in the online dictionary DDO. In the case of the transfer of thesaurus data to a wordnet, a major challenge is the possible multiple representation of the same word sense in the thesaurus, reflecting again the previously discussed feature of variability which is so characteristic for adjectives This is the case for 1/3 of the adjective senses we plan to transfer. We have discussed different ways of dealing with this problem and described a method which combines the manual encoding of a rather small part of the adjectives, namely those that are headwords in the thesaurus, with the semi-automatic transfer of the rest and much larger part of the adjective vocabulary.

We intend to do a validation of the manually inserted headwords along with the validation of the automatically transferred synsets in order to ensure consistency. Since the method is based on carefully edited and already validated data in the published DDB, we expect to end up with high quality data. Another issue not quite clear yet is how much time and resources the transfer task will require.

Last but not least, we have looked into how sentiment information from a sentiment word list which we simultaneously compile in the DanNet2 project, and which is also based on the thesaurus, could be fruitfully integrated into DanNet. Furthermore we have discussed some future ideas on how to transfer thematic information from the thesaurus into the wordnet.

References

Bick, Eckhard (2019). A Semantic Ontology of Danish Adjectives. In *Proceedings of the 13th nternational Conference on Computational Semantics - Long Papers.* Gothenburg, Sweden, 2019.

Cruse, D.A. (1986). *Lexical Semantics.* Cambridge University Press.

Hamp, Birgit and Helmut Feldweg (1997). GermaNet - a Lexical-Semantic Net for German. In *Automatic Information Extraction and Building of Lexical Semantic Resources for {NLP} Applications.* https://www.aclweb.org/anthology/W97-0802.

Hjorth, Ebba & Kristensen, Kjeld (eds.) (2003-2005). *Den Danske Ordbog, volume 1-6*, Det danske Sprog- og Litteraturselskab/Gyldendal, Copenhagen, Denmark. Online: ordnet.dk/ddo

Lenci, A.; Bel, N.; Busa, F.; Calzolari, N.; Gola, E.; Monachini, M.; Ogonowski, A.; Peters, I.; Peters, W.; Ruimy, N.; Villegas, M. & Zampolli, A. (2000). 'SIMPLE – A General Framework for the Development of Multilingual Lexicons'. In: *International Journal of Lexicography 13.* 249–263.

Maziarz, Marek, Stanislaw Szpakovicz, Maciej Piasecki (2015). Semantic Relations among Adjectives in Polish WordNet 2.0. A New Relation Set, Discussion and Evaluation. In Cognitive *Studies | Études cognitives.* 149-179. https://doi.org/10.11649/cs.2012.011.

Nielsen, Finn Årup (2011). A new ANEW: evaluation of a word list for sentiment analysis in microblogs. In *Proceedings of the ESWC2011 Workshop on 'Making Sense of Microposts': Big things come in small packages.* Volume 718 in CEUR Workshop Proceedings: 93-98.

Nimb, Sanni, Nicolai Hartvig Sørensen & Thomas Troelsgård (2018). From standalone thesaurus to integrated related words in the Danish Dictionary. In: *Proceedings from Euralex 2018*, Ljubliana, Slovenia.

Nimb, Sanni, Henrik Lorentzen, Liisa Theilgaard, Thomas Troelsgård (2014). *Den Danske Begrebsordbog*, Det Danske Sprog- og Litteraturselskab & Syddansk Universitetsforlag.

Nimb Sanni, Lars Trap-Jensen, Henrik Lorentzen (2014). The Danish Thesaurus: Problems and Perspectives. In: Andrea Abel, Chiara Vettori & Natascia Ralli (eds.), *Proceedings of the XVI EURALEX International Congress: The User in Focus.* 15-19 July 2014. Bolzano/Bozen: EURAC Research, pp. 191-199.

Nimb, Sanni, and Bolette S. Pedersen (2012). Towards a richer wordnet representation of properties – exploiting semantic and thematic information from thesauri." In *LREC 2012 Proceedings.* Istanbul, Turkey, 2012.

Pedersen, Bolette Sandford, Sanni Nimb, Jørg Asmussen, Nicolai Hartvig, Sørensen, Lars Trap-Jensen & Henrik Lorentzen. 2009. DanNet: the challenge of compiling a wordnet for Danish by reusing a monolingual dictionary. *Language Resources and Evaluation* 43(3). 269–299. https://doi.org/10.1007/s10579-009-9092-1.

Peters, Ivonne & Wim Peters (2000). The treatment of adjectives in SIMPLE: Theoretical observations. In *LREC 2000 Proceedings.* Athen, Greece, 2000.

Pustejovsky, J. (1995). *The Generative Lexicon.* The MIT Press, Cambridge, Massachusetts.

Vossen, Piek & Bloksma, Laura & Calzolari, Nicoletta & Roventini, Adriana & Bertagna, Francesca & Alonge, Antonietta. (1998). *The EuroWordNet Base Concepts and Top Ontology.*

Teaching Through Tagging — Interactive Lexical Semantics

Francis Bond, Andrew Kirkrose Devadason,
Teo Rui Lin, Melissa and **Luís Morgado da Costa**
School of Humanities, Nanyang Technological University
bond@ieee.org, andrewtemerarious@gmail.com
trlm31@outlook.com, lmorgado.dacosta@gmail.com

Abstract

In this paper we discuss an ongoing effort to enrich students' learning by involving them in sense tagging. The main goal is to lead students to discover how we can represent meaning and where the limits of our current theories lie. A subsidiary goal is to create sense tagged corpora and an accompanying linked lexicon (in our case wordnets). We present the results of tagging several texts and suggest some ways in which the tagging process could be improved. Two authors of this paper present their own experience as students. Overall, students reported that they found the tagging an enriching experience. The annotated corpora and changes to the wordnet are made available through the NTU multilingual corpus and associated wordnets (NTU-MC).

1 Introduction

This paper introduces a method of incorporating lexical semantic research into the teaching of semantics, as a form of experiential learning (Kolb, 1984). The main goal is to lead students to discover how we can represent meaning and where the limits of our current theories lie. A subsidiary goal is to create sense tagged corpora and an accompanying linked lexicon (in our case wordnets).

The first author (Francis) teaches HG2002: Semantics and Pragmatics, a core course in linguistics with 70-100 students. The course is survey-oriented (Pullum, 1984, p152), summarising various theories without dwelling on any overarching theme. It is easy for students to become bewildered by the variety of concepts, particularly in the absence of concrete applications. To alleviate this, from 2011, each semester a text was introduced, which students would try to analyse using the various approaches. The decision was also influenced by our university's encouraging stance towards involving students in research. The NTU computational linguistics lab is heavily involved in lexical semantics and wordnets, including building and extending wordnets and sense tagged corpora for multiple languages. We thus integrated some tagging into the course as a way to give students hands-on experience with a semantics-oriented research project.

This course later formed the base for a general elective (GE), which is offered to any student in the university.[1] This was an interdisciplinary course, developed and co-taught with colleagues from the English and Chinese departments. To make it more appealing, we focused on Sherlock Holmes — HG8011: Detecting Meaning with Sherlock Holmes. Roughly half the course deals with interpreting the texts using semantics, a quarter with placing the stories in their literary context, including a discussion of fan-fiction, and the rest with Sherlock in film and in translation. The course has proved popular, with over 200 students every time it is offered, and long wait lists.

The pedagogical goals for both courses were fourfold:

- P-1 Apply semantic theories to real-world texts
- P-2 Show students the difficulties of defining and identifying senses. For example they need to look at more than prototypical cases; identify gaps in the lexicons and add new entries; and consider the problems of tokenization and MWEs.
- P-3 Expose them to annotation and resource building (common sources of employment for humanities students)
- P-4 Teach the students about inter-annotator agreement

There were four main research goals:

- R-1 Produce sense tagged corpora, with all concepts disambiguated, in multiple languages
- R-2 Experiment with how to sense tag: What is the best interface? What information do annotators need?

[1] Due to the content overlap with *Semantics and Pragmatics* a student cannot take both.

R-3 Identify interesting phenomena that can lead to student assignments or theses

R-4 Identify potential student research assistants

For teaching a subject like this, it is impossible to do a quantitative evaluation where half the class does the annotation and half does not. Instead, in this paper two students who took these classes share their experiences as students in Section 3. They both did well in the subjects and are keen on working further with wordnets. As such, their expressed views may not be representative of the student population at large. Therefore, we also looked at comments by the students in their assignments, and in the anonymous student course evaluation.

One project that is very similar to our annotation in spirit is the Georgetown University Multilayer Corpus (GUM: Zeldes, 2017). GUM is collected and expanded by students as part of the curriculum in LING-367 Computational Corpus Linguistics at Georgetown University. The course has around 20 students, mainly postgraduate. The students are more computational than in our courses, so there is more emphasis on using external tools to annotate. The corpus selection is opportunistic, aiming to represent different communicative purposes, while coming from sources that are readily and openly available (mostly Creative Commons licenses). The results of this project show that high quality, richly annotated resources can be created effectively as part of a linguistics curriculum. The main difference is that the course at Georgetown is specifically about corpora, while for my courses, the corpora are not the main focus.

Wordnets have also been used widely in teaching computational linguistics (Lemnitzer and Kunze, 2004; Bird et al., 2009, 2010), but as far as we know this is the first time they have been a core part of a general linguistics course.

The paper is structured as follows: in Section 2 we describe the actual practice of annotation. In Section 3 we present the student experience. In Section 4 we look at what work is necessary to make the corpus ready for release. We finish with some conclusions and ideas for future work in Section 5.

2 Annotating Texts

There is some overlap between the linguistics and GE course, but enough differences that we will describe them separately. Our university teaches in English, and the majority of the students are native speakers of English, although we have some international students (more in the GE class). Many students are also fluent in another mother tongue (mainly Mandarin Chinese, Standard Malay and sometimes Tamil) and many of the linguistics students have studied a second language to a level in which they can annotate meaning (with Japanese and Korean being the most popular).

2.1 Linguistic Students

Each year, students read one (or part) of a given texts After reading the text, and hearing lectures on word and sentence level semantics, each student tags a short passage (roughly 300 concepts: 20-30 sentences). Most years we choose a text that can be completely tagged by the class, so typically 600-700 sentences. The students found the specialist computer science content in the Cathedral and the Bazaar hard to understand, and much preferred either locally salient text (like the Singapore Tourist Data) or short stories. In 2015 we had a very multilingual group so we picked a shorter story and the students annotated the original Japanese as well as Chinese, English, and Malay translations. From 2018 we tagged a longer novel.

The texts annotated are listed below:

2011 Singapore Tourist Data (website)

2012 The Cathedral and the Bazaar (essay) (Raymond, 1999)

2013 The Adventure of the Speckled Band (Doyle, 1892)

2014 The Adventure of the Dancing Men (Doyle, 1905)

2015 **蜘蛛の糸** *Kumo no Ito* "The Spider's Web" (芥川, 1918)

2018–2020 The Hound of the Baskervilles (Doyle, 1902)

Each sentence is assigned at least three annotators. At first, three or four students tagged each passage. Since 2018 we have added an automatic tagger as the third annotator. This gives the students experience with automatic sense disambiguation, and allows us to tag more text. In order to make the automatic tagging predictable, we used a simple most-frequent sense based annotator, trained on frequencies in Princeton Wordnet combined with the already tagged short stories.

During the tagging, students look at every content word and find its corresponding meaning in a dictionary (wordnet). If there is an appropriate sense, then they select it. When such a meaning is absent from the wordnet, a new synset should be proposed. For the last three years, students have also annotated positive or negative sentiment (-100 to $+100$) at the sense level, using the set up described in Bond et al. (2016a). If there is an error in the corpus (such as incorrect tokenization or lemmatization or just a typo) the student tag it as '**e**', if there is a problem with the wordnet (no appropriate sense or indistinguishable senses) the students tag it as '**w**'. If a word should not be tagged (for example if it is a closed class word such as preposition or auxiliary) then it is tagged as '**x**'.

When students complete tagging individually, we calculate and show the agreement. A new text is made tagged with the majority tag for each concept, and students must then retag anything with no majority tag (and can, of course, retag anything at all). If any two taggers agree, their tag is selected: the automatic tagger thus only has an effect when two students disagree. Students tagging the same sentences meet up to discuss disagreements and then retag. Overall, the tagging takes roughly 5-6 hours for each round.

Finally, they write up a joint report on their findings (worth 30% of their final grade). In the final write-up, the students are asked to: (i) describe the strengths and weaknesses of using a lexical resource such as wordnet to define word meaning, (ii) give concrete examples from the text you analyzed. (iii) discuss cases where you disagreed with other annotators, on reflection, do you think: you were right; they were right; the definition is bad; or is there some other reason? (iv) For words with senses missing in wordnet, they should write a comment with enough information to create a new entry for them consisting of, at minimum, a definition, a relational link to an existing synset and an example.

2.2 General Elective Students

The GE students have no tutorials, and generally are expected to cover the material at a slightly easier level. For this class, students only tag Sherlock Holmes stories, and only in English.

NTU offers elective classes as part of General Education with discipline branches in Liberal Arts, Science and Technology, and Business. *HG8011: Detecting Meaning with Sherlock Holmes* falls under Liberal Arts. The course teaches semantics, some literature, film theory and translation studies. The assignments follow the same structure as *HG2002: Semantics and Pragmatics*, except that a written report is not required. The stories tagged are:

2016 The Redheaded League (Doyle, 1892)

2018 A Scandal in Bohemia (Doyle, 1892)

2019 The Hound of the Baskervilles (Doyle, 1902)

The stories are chosen from the most popular of the short stories (Doyle, 1927), plus the most popular novel.

The project is broken into three parts for these students: tag individually (20%), tag as a group (20%), tag sentiment (20%). Each passage is given to three or four students as the drop out rate for general electives is around 10% — this means that some groups end up with fewer than three for the comparison. We also add the automatic tagger. The GE students are not asked to write a report, instead they are judged on the comments they enter when they tag.

2.3 Interface

We used an enhanced version of the annotation tool IMI described in Bond et al. (2015). As well as selecting the sense, it allows annotators to tag senses in context with sentiment (from -100 to +100).

Figure 1 shows a passage that has been tagged. The text is shown on the left. Words with positive and negative sentiment are shown with red and green underlines respectively. The annotator thinks that there is no suitable sense for the word being tagged (***hell-hound***) so has suggested a new entry in the comments. Existing senses for ***hell-hound*** are shown on the right.

The students only tag a small sample, so they tag as a **sequential** task: annotating chunks of text word-by-word. **Targeted** tagging (annotating by word type) is known to be more accurate (Langone et al., 2004). Our tool, IMI, supports both and the RAs typically use targeted tagging when they add new senses or correct common errors.

2.4 Wordnets

The senses are tagged with enhanced versions of the Princeton WordNet of English (PWN: Fellbaum, 1998), the Chinese Open Wordnet (COW: Wang

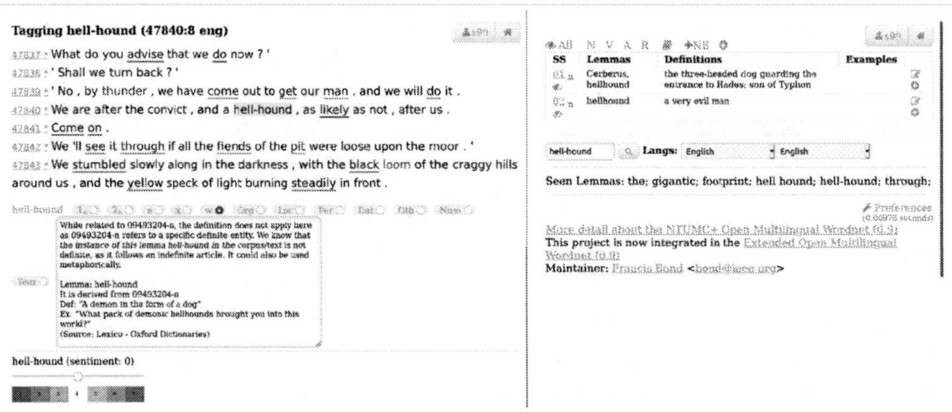

Figure 1: The Sequential Tagging Interface

and Bond, 2013), the Wordnet Bahasa (Bond et al., 2014) and the Japanese wordnet (Isahara et al., 2008). They included systematic extensions for pronouns, chengyu,[2] exclamatives and classifiers (Seah and Bond, 2014; Ho et al., 2014; Morgado da Costa and Bond, 2016) extended with many new senses and semantic relations. For English, 71% of taggable words are tagged with PWN senses, 23% are pronouns, 3.2% are named entities and 2.5% are other new senses we have added.

3 The Student Experience

In this section we provide a summary of students' feedback. Additionally, two students, one each from the linguistics and general elective classes talk about their experience, both as students and later as research assistants.[3]

3.1 Linguistics Students

The students who attained higher grades overall clearly enjoyed the task more. This was evident in their reading the entirety of the text (rather than only the portions assigned to them), and the time they took to deliberate their chosen tags. Several students reported that reading the whole passage through was very useful in helping them situate words, especially polysemous ones, within the broader textual context. Some found tagging only one meaning to be restrictive when multiple interpretations are possible; this reflects students' sensitiveness to multi-faceted words. The inter-annotator comparison segment was useful in resolving doubts and gaining insights towards fine-grained sense distinctions. Some students drew on their knowledge of other languages in referring to the multi-lingual gloss to distinguish between relatively similar words. Overall, student feedback suggests learning from wordnet tagging was a novel and enjoyable experience. Students' active involvement in research thus seems to benefit the processes of teaching, learning, and research.

Linguistics Student's Personal Experience

In the iteration of HG2002 I (Andrew) participated in, the cohort worked on the English-language version of *The Hound of the Baskervilles* by Sir Arthur Conan Doyle. Each section of the corpus was assigned to a pair of students, who would first tag the section without consulting each other. An automated naive annotator (a computer assigning the most frequent sense tag to each lemma) would also tag that section of the corpus (hereafter MFS). We were then presented with an automatically generated list of lemmas for which at least one of the three of us (two humans and one computer) had selected a tag that didn't match the others' choices, and given the go-ahead to discuss our choices with each other. We then worked to come to a consensus (amongst the two human participants) as to the most appropriate tag in each case.

As linguistics students with strongly held opinions and feelings about how language behaves and what words mean, it was useful to have the naive annotator as a third party. For my human annotation partner and myself, the MFS became a kind of common enemy that could not defend itself, and which could generally be relied on to be a worse tagger than we were. When discussing the points of conflict my an-

[2] 成語 *chengyu* "Chinese four character idioms".

[3] Note that students have the option to opt their data out any time up to one week after they get their results. So far no student has asked to do this.

notation partner and I had over our tagging choices (a process that she at one point described as "arguing"), we could generally at least fall back on agreeing that, whatever it was, the computer's choice was probably wrong.

However, the computer annotator was useful as more than a scapegoat. Its choices often did agree with ours (though we spent much less time discussing those cases, as there was no disagreement), affirming both its competence and our own. It was also most interesting to me when its mistakes exposed its own workings. For example, it failed to recognise *finger-tips* as linked to the lemma ***fingertip***, leading me to realise that while punctuation does not usually alter a word's surface form past recognition for a human reader, it might do so for a computer. It was also interesting to me that, while I assumed that a computer program would abide strictly by procedures, its behaviour flaunted some of the instructions we were given as annotators. For example, we were instructed to only tag the highest level of meaning in a multiword expression, as in ***whip up*** as a single lemma, with ***with*** and ***up*** individually marked as '**x**'. However, the computer annotator would routinely assign meaningful tags to both (or multiple) levels.

As someone who grew up reading and enjoying the Sherlock Holmes stories, I was delighted to hear that we would be using them as the source material for this exercise. I also assumed that I would have no trouble with tagging any of the words in the story, as I did not think the language was particularly challenging or archaic. However, once I began using the wordnet, I realised that my initial assumption was far from correct.Beyond simply being familiar with the connotations and denotations of words, and the ways in which they are used, the exercise demanded that I be able to pick out the precise shades of meaning being invoked in any particular instance. Coming from a background of enjoying both literary analysis and creative writing, in which ambiguous or multiple coexisting meanings are rarely subjected to forcible disambiguation, this was an unexpected paradigm shift for me.

A particularly interesting case in which my ideas about fine-grained meaning were challenged was in tagging the lemma ***unimaginative*** in the context of the phrase *practical and unimaginative*. My annotation partner and I both took the collocation of *practical* (which we agreed indicated an interest in concrete concerns) with *unimaginative* into consideration in choosing a sense for ***unimaginative***. I thought that the collocation meant that the two words should have similar senses (thus interpreting ***unimaginative*** as indicating a concern with concrete facts), as two similar ideas placed together for rhetorical emphasis. However, my annotation partner thought that the collocation meant that the two words should have different senses (thus interpreting ***unimaginative*** as "uncreative"), so as to avoid redundancy. Our disagreement in this instance led me to reflect on the ways I use and interpret language in ways I had not previously considered.

Selecting particular senses was an important part of the annotation process. In pursuing this task, we were also forced to attend to the parts of the corpus which we were **not** meant to annotate, including dummy pronouns, auxiliary and modal verbs, conjunctions, and prepositions. While the documentation we were provided with clearly explained that these items should not receive semantically meaningful tags (and should instead be tagged as '**x**'), we were not always clear about what fell into these categories. While some of this confusion was simply reflective of our inexperience at the time, in many cases we felt that leaving these items without meaningful tags would be omitting important semantic information. This was particularly true of modal verbs and prepositions, as we felt that they contributed significantly to the text's meaning. In the case of prepositions, we also faced some confusion, as some more complex prepositions did appear to be available as tags in the wordnet.

This attention to what should not receive meaningful tags alongside what should also revealed to me how closely interdependent the tags (and by extension, the interpretations) we chose were. For example, in dealing with the phrase *were set forth*, the first word (*were*, for the lemma ***be***) should be tagged as '**x**' as auxiliary verb if ***set forth*** were interpreted as a verbal phrase. However, if ***set forth*** were understood as an adjective, ***were*** would become the main verb and would require an appropriate tag.

Working with the wordnet was ultimately a rewarding experience, both as a way of gaining experience with language in actual use and in terms of feeling like I was able to contribute something to a larger project. I also found the interface enjoyable to use and fun to explore; in many ways, the hyperlinked format reminded me of playing a sort of computer game. Being able to compare my annotation with both a human and non-human partner was also invaluable in terms of prompting me to think more deeply about my strategies in sharing and interpreting meaning.

3.2 General Elective Students

Basing the class on Sherlock Holmes was an attractive factor for the majority of students. Most have previously been acquainted with Holmes through media adaptations, but reading the original stories (a class requirement) was a new experience. They were pleased with Arthur Conan Doyle's usage of innovative phrases such as *swamp adder* and *pea jacket*. It removed the impression of the original Holmes texts as too historically stuffy to be understood in modern times. Additionally, using Holmes as a medium to teach linguistics made the subject's technicalities less daunting for students. A student commented, *"I thought it was a really creative idea and since Sherlock Holmes is really popular, it could easily get students interested in linguistics."* Most students were new to wordnets but were brought up to speed with the clear instructional guide to every assignment.

GE Student's Personal Experience

I (Melissa) recall *Detecting Meaning with Sherlock Holmes* as the most carefree yet meaningful class in my undergraduate studies thus far. As a social science major, class content tends towards pessimism. Sociology's assessment mostly takes the form of essays, hence it was refreshing to be graded in this class through another medium (i.e. Wordnet). The class workload was relatively manageable and I could enjoy learning.

Class content was presented in digestible bites of Powerpoint slides, with the right ratio of semantics to more technical linguistic concepts. It was an enjoyable experience of "detecting meaning" with myself, giving names to semantic phenomena I was previously aware of on an intuitive level, but did not know the proper terminology and definitions, especially for the more formal semantics (quantifiers and logical connectives).

On to "detecting meaning" with Sherlock Holmes! The tagging interface is fairly easy to navigate and get accustomed to for a first-time user. I found it rather delightful to dissect words, to pause and ponder its individual meaning, simultaneously separate from and while within the sentence. The assignments took on a personal activity component, as I read through the list of meanings of each word, I referenced them against my personal vocabulary. When I encountered meanings I was previously unaware of, it enhanced the learning factor and expanded my vocabulary. Conversely, I encountered moments of disorientation when the meaning (and sometimes POS) I had in mind was absent from wordnet. On closer inspection, the meaning was often present but tagged with a different morphological form.

The disjunction in meaning took on another dimension during the group project component. Students were grouped with three other classmates who were assigned the same set of sentences in the individual assignment. The task was to confer and settle on one tagged meaning per word. Retagging as a group was an arduous journey for we had varying understandings of the text. Those who spent marginally less time on the first assignment (did not read HOUND in its entirety), tended to tag words literally and out of context. Doubly adding on to the challenge was: One, our visualisation of the story's events were based on different media adaptations of Sherlock Holmes and preexisting knowledge of the Victorian era, or possibly just based on a figment of imagination. Two, our assigned section was a conversation between Dr. Watson and Stapleton as they witnessed a pony get sucked into the Grimpen Mire. It is an abstract conversation when read separately from the main story. Doyle's anthropomorphism of the mire added on to the confusion of whose body part (pony or the mire) some words were referring to.

I was anticipating putting into practice (tagging) everything I learned in class, to encounter and decipher all the possible word puzzle theories. We were assigned 15 sentences each, the length and the literary challenge of which depended on luck. I was a tad disappointed despite knowing it is not feasible for a text to encompass instances of every semantic device. I was hoping for more tagging practice and the chance to make real changes to the corpus beyond proposing suggestions for new entries (part of the assessment criteria). Semantically close reading a text was a new experience, becoming attuned to the finer grains of a text allowed me to forge a deeper appreciation of the effort authors go through in selecting their words.

3.3 Students and Research Output

Most course iterations reveal students who are both outstanding and interested in continuing to contribute to our research goals – something that has happened with the authors of the shared accounts, above. Admittedly, this happens most often with Linguistics students but has also, on occasion, happened with students enrolled in the General Elective course. These longer-term contributions take one of many forms: i) some join the NTU Computational Linguistics Lab as a student research assistant (RA); ii) some decide to write their Final Year Project (FYP) about a related topic; and iii) a selected few join our lab through a program called URECA (Undergraduate Research Experience on CAmpus), designed to cultivate a research culture among the outstanding undergraduate students.

Over the years, our lab has had dozens of student members that were selected from their contributions to the tagging task described in this paper. Most of these students end up making substantial contributions to research problems that emerge and are defined through multiple layers of quality control of the tagging done by our students (discussed in the next section). Some published research that relied on student contributions include: work on Japanese derivational relations (Bond and Wei, 2019); on pronoun representation for Japanese, Mandarin and English (Seah and Bond, 2014); as well as work on exclamatives and classifiers (Mok et al., 2012; Morgado da Costa and Bond, 2016). Other important contributions that came either in the form of theses or research reports include extensive work cleaning up and expanding the Wordnet Bahasa. The resources have been used by students for sentiment analysis (Le et al., 2016; Bond et al., 2019), cross-lingual sense annotation (Bonansinga and Bond, 2016), multilingual crosswords (Tan, 2012) and more.

4 Quality Control and Expert Tagging

Given that the annotation that happens in our classrooms is done by untrained students from diverse backgrounds and often lacking linguistic intuition, it is not surprising that our corpus needs to go through multiple layers of quality control before being suitable for release.

The large majority of this quality control is done by student RAs. This usually happens in phases, and each phase (or RA) focuses on a particular task. These different tasks include: i) review comments left by students during their tagging exercise (e.g. references to possible metaphors, named entities, etc.); ii) review and fix the corpus where problems concerning lemmatization or corpus structure were flagged (i.e. **e** tags); iii) review and address reported gaps in the wordnet coverage (i.e. **w** tags); iv) ensure students made adequate use of the tag **x** (i.e. using it only for words that should not be tagged); and v) review and retag any mistakes in the student annotations. Much of this work ends up rejecting the suggestions made by students, as they often identify real issues without finding the best solution, due to unfamiliarity with wordnets.

To accomplish these tasks, student RAs make use of a set of tools not usually available to other students, including the **targeted** tagging tools (introduced above); the Corpus Fixer which allows the annotator to change the tokenization, POS and lemmatization, as well as to add new multi word expressions; and OMWEdit which allows the annotator to add to or change the wordnets. (Morgado da Costa and Bond, 2015). Some of the non-intuitive aspects of these tools require some training before they can be used but, most importantly, require a deeper understanding of many layers of lexical analysis (e.g. POS tags, lemmatization, multi-word expressions, etc.).

Student RAs without a computational background are often both baffled and amused with problems caused by POS and lemmatization issues (e.g. when words like *graves* are lemmatized as *graf* through a misapplication of the same rule that produces *shelf* from *shelves*), but are quick to grasp these more mechanical aspects of the quality control process.

Most of the other tasks involve more difficult problems, such as judging whether an expression is compositional or not, or whether a distinction in meaning is significant enough to warrant the creation of a new synset. Wordnets are fairly complex, and our student RAs learn about it *on the job*. The task of changing a wordnet feels quite daunting at first, and it only becomes easier once our RAs get familiarized with the wordnet's structure.

Once the decision to create a new synset is made, other layers of complexity arise. Our RAs have to balance the coverage of new senses (i.e. how broad or narrow should the new synset be – taking into consideration other existing synsets). Finding the appropriate semantic links between new and preexisting synsets is also not always straightforward. If the decision is to try to use an existing synset to accommodate a missing sense, then there are other issues to take into account. The main concern is the extent to which an existing synset can be edited to accommodate this alternative meaning. This often requires detailed lexicographic work, observing examples inside and outside our corpus to determine if the proposed changes are warranted by real data.

Many of the more difficult decisions are discussed within larger lab meetings, where multiple student RAs and senior lab members join in. As it was discussed above, some of the problems encountered by our RAs end up deserving a more in depth treatment or discussion, and are taken up by smaller focused teams within our lab, or as the topic of a project/dissertation.

Every time we teach one of the courses described above, a new set of data requiring quality control is created. From our experience, this amounts to roughly 3-4 weeks full-time work for a trained annotator for 600-700 sentences of text. This is often done taking into consideration the written reports submited by students (when available), which also gives our RAs an insight into the common problems that faced student annotators. Whenever possible, these insights are also used to improve the documentation made available to students during their annotation task – with the goal of making this documentation intuitive for students who may feel overwhelmed by the amount of information they need to absorb.

This is not the most efficient way to annotate text, but a good result is obtained in the end, and we can involve many students. One problem we found was that as we refined the tokenization and wordnet guidelines, the corpora got out of sync. For example, when we added pronouns, we had to go back and tag them in the older corpora. More interestingly, we occasionally change our tokenization guides: *long-legged* we used to tokenize as *long* and *-legged* but now tokenize as *long*, *-*, *-legged*. We also need a new tag for the noun: NND (noun inflected like a pas-participle), which we lemmatize to ***leg***. We are currently working on further using the tagged corpora to find examples in this class; as a source text in corpus linguistics, and for the digital edition of the tagged stories.

4.1 Multilingual Tagging

Many of our student RAs are confident enough to tag and review tagging in other languages present in our corpus (i.e. Mandarin, Japanese, Indonesian or Malay). When this happens, in addition to the quality control process described above, these students are also paid as expert taggers and tag data using their language of choice.

The corpora are made available at `https://github.com/bond-lab/NTUMC/`..

4.2 Dynamic Resources

Our research on lexical semantics is part of a broader attempt to understand language, where we also look at syntax and lexical semantics. Oepen et al. (2004) show that treebanking is an essential part of grammar development — identifying the correct parses from the grammar for a large corpus is the best way to verify its correctness. They suggest a cyclical model of grammar development, where the grammar is revised based on the results of treebanking and then the treebank is updated with the new grammar. To achieve complete coverage, many iterations are necessary. In the same way, we consider sense tagging the best way to verify the coverage and correctness of a wordnet.

Our tagging process looks something like that shown in Figure 2. (i) First the text is pre processed: tokenized, POS tagged and lemmatized. (ii) Then multiple annotators annotate a passage independently, making notes about issues with the corpus or wordnet. (iii) They then compare their annotations and discuss their differences and possibly write up a report. This is the end of the teaching. (iv) The instructor and some RAs go through all entries with comments or as errors. Where necessary, they fix the corpus and/or the wordnet. (v) Finally (although in practice often simultaneously with the previous step) they retag the corpus with the fixed tokenization and lemmatization using the enhanced wordnet. This is then repeated for the next class. The new students start off with a better wordnet, and potentially better preprocessing, tagging tools and guidelines, as enhancements are made based on last year's issues. Thus their task should be easier and the final annotated text better. This is similar to the **spiral** model of software development described by software developers such as Boehm (1988); Gilb (1989); Larman and Basili (2003). At each loop the development cycle (here we consider we are developing the wordnet, corpus and tools) the process becomes gradually better.

We feel that the wordnets needs to go through several more iterations of tagging and fixing before all the commonly appearing issues are fixed, and of course annotation in new domains will bring new families of problems. One non-trivial problem is coordinating our improvements with others: we are

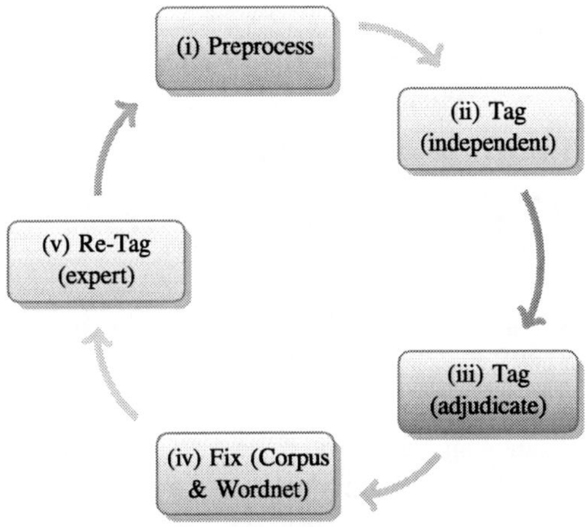

Figure 2: Sense Annotation Spiral

doing our best to coordinate with the English Wordnet (McCrae et al., 2019) and linking through the Collaborative Interlingual Index (CILI Bond et al., 2016b). However, this integration is not seamless.

There are still many questions left unsolved. We still have many lexical semantic phenomena not covered: auxiliary verbs, conjunctions and prepositions; light verb+noun combinations; decomposable semantics (e.g. *unADJ* is productively the antonym of *ADJ*); multiple interpretations, ...These are often taken up by students as final year projects or research projects in other classes.

5 Conclusion and Future Work

We need more annotated text: linking text to analysis is an important task. We expect linking to lead to changes in the linked resource: it is important to support this. Access to more data makes more interesting projects possible. Students learn a lot by attempting real tasks, and enjoy working on interesting stories. We can take advantage of this to improve the quantity and quality of our wordnets and corpora.

One of the goals of this paper is to encourage other similar courses around the world to integrate similar strategies to annotate more text. We have had success supporting colleagues at the University of Pisa in order to tag an Italian translation of *the Speckled Band* as art of a semantics course. We would like to like to coordinate with more lecturers in other countries to extend the task to other languages. This is also why we commit to open-source practices, and make both our data and our tools[4] available on GitHub.

Acknowledgements

This paper started off as an invited talk at the Linked Data in Linguistics workshop (LDL 2018). We would like to thank all the students involved in the tagging: HG2002 (2011–2015, 2018–2020) HG8011 (2016,2018,2019), the URECA projects, FYPs and student assistants. And of course we thank all the wordnet developers, especially Christiane Fellbaum. We would like to thank Alessandro Lenci, Giulia Boanasinga and Tommaso Petrolito for their help with preparing and tagging the Italian data.

For ideas and information about Sherlock Holmes, we would like to thank the Sound of the Baskervilles for their encouragement and advice and Alexis Barquin of the Arthur Conan Doyle Encyclopedia, who kindly allowed us to access his database of texts.

Some of this work was funded by the following grants: MOE Tier 2 grant *That's what you meant: a Rich Representation for Manipulation of Meaning* (MOE ARC41/13, Singapore), *Inter-lingual equivalence in lexical databases* (NSC, Poland) and *Joint Research on Multilingual Semantic Analysis* (Fuji-Xerox Corporation, Japan).

References

Stephen Bird, Ewan Klein, and Edward Loper. 2009. *Natural Language Processing with Python*. O'Reilly. (`www.nltk.org/book`).

Stephen Bird, Ewan Klein, and Edward Loper. 2010. *Nyumon Shizen Gengo Shori [Introduction to Natural Language Processing]*. O'Reilly. (translated by Hagiwara, Nakamura and Mizuno).

Barry Boehm. 1988. A spiral model of software development and enhancement. *IEEE Computer*, 21(5):61–71.

Giulia Bonansinga and Francis Bond. 2016. Exploring cross-lingual sense mapping in a multilingual parallel corpus. In *Proceedings of the 8th Global Wordnet Conference (GWC 2016)*, pages 45–49.

Francis Bond, Arkadiusz Janz, and Maciej Piasecki. 2019. A comparison of sense-level sentiment scores. In *Proceedings of the 11th Global Wordnet Conference (GWC 2019)*.

[4] `https://github.com/bond-lab/NTUMC/` (data) `https://github.com/bond-lab/IMI/` (tools)

Francis Bond, Lian Tze Lim, Enya Kong Tan, and Hammam Riza. 2014. The combined wordnet Bahasa. *Nusa: Linguistic studies of languages in and around Indonesia*, 57:83–100.

Francis Bond, Luís Morgado da Costa, and Tuấn Anh Lê. 2015. IMI — a multilingual semantic annotation environment. In *ACL-2015 System Demonstrations*.

Francis Bond, Tomoko Ohkuma, Luís Morgado da Costa, Yasuhide Miura, Rachel Chen, Takayuki Kuribayashi, and Wenjie Wang. 2016a. A multilingual sentiment corpus for Chinese, English and Japanese. In *6th Emotion and Sentiment Analysis Workshop (at LREC 2016)*. Portorož.

Francis Bond, Piek Vossen, John McCrae, and Christiane Fellbaum. 2016b. CILI: The collaborative interlingual index. In *Proceedings of the 8th Global Wordnet Conference (GWC 2016)*, pages 50–57.

Francis Bond and Ryan Lim Dao Wei. 2019. Generating derivational relations for the japanese wordnet: The case of agentive nouns. In *2019 Pacific Neighborhood Consortium Annual Conference and Joint Meetings (PNC)*, pages 1–7. IEEE.

Arthur Conan Doyle. 1892. *The Adventures of Sherlock Homes*. George Newnes, London.

Arthur Conan Doyle. 1902. *The Hound of the Baskervilles*. George Newnes, London.

Arthur Conan Doyle. 1905. *The Return of Sherlock Homes*. George Newnes, London. Project Gutenberg `www.gutenberg.org/files/108/108-h/108-h.htm`.

Arthur Conan Doyle. 1927. How I made my list. *Strand Magazine*.

Christine Fellbaum, editor. 1998. *WordNet: An Electronic Lexical Database*. MIT Press.

Tom Gilb. 1989. *Principles of Software Engineering Management*. Addison Weslet Longman.

Wan Yu Ho, Christine Kng, Shan Wang, and Francis Bond. 2014. Identifying idioms in Chinese translations. In *Ninth International Conference on Language Resources and Evaluation (LREC 2014)*. Reykjavik.

Hitoshi Isahara, Francis Bond, Kiyotaka Uchimoto, Masao Utiyama, and Kyoko Kanzaki. 2008. Development of the Japanese WordNet. In *Sixth International conference on Language Resources and Evaluation (LREC 2008)*. Marrakech.

David A. Kolb. 1984. *Experiential Learning: Experience as the Source of Learning and Development*. Prentice-Hall.

Helen Langone, Benjamin R. Haskell, and George A. Miller. 2004. Annotating wordnet. In *Workshop On Frontiers In Corpus Annotation*, pages 63–69. ACL, Boston.

Craig Larman and Victor R Basili. 2003. Iterative and incremental development: A brief history. *Computer*, 36(6):47–56.

Tuan Anh Le, David Moeljadi, Yasuhide Miura, and Tomoko Ohkuma. 2016. Sentiment analysis for low resource languages: A study on informal Indonesian tweets. In *Proceedings of The 12th Workshop on Asian Language Resources*, page 123–131. Osaka.

Lothar Lemnitzer and Claudia Kunze. 2004. Using wordnets in teaching virtual courses of computational linguistics. In *Proceedings of the 2nd Global Wordnet Conference (GWC 2004)*, pages 150–156.

John P. McCrae, Alexandre Rademaker, Francis Bond, Ewa Rudnicka, and Christiane Fellbaum. 2019. English WordNet 2019 —an open-source wordnet for English. In *Proceedings of the 11th Global Wordnet Conference (GWC 2019)*.

Hazel Shuwen Mok, Eshley Huini Gao, and Francis Bond. 2012. Generating numeral classifiers in Chinese and Japanese. In *Proceedings of the 6th Global WordNet Conference (GWC 2012)*. Matsue. 211-218.

Luís Morgado da Costa and Francis Bond. 2015. Omwedit - the integrated open multilingual wordnet editing system. In *Proceedings of the 53rd Annual Meeting of the Association for Computational Linguistics and the 7th International Joint Conference on Natural Language Processing of the Asian Federation of Natural Language Processing, System Demonstrations (ACL 2015)*, pages 73–78. Beijing, China. URL `static/pubs/acl2015-omwedit-demo.pdf`.

Luís Morgado da Costa and Francis Bond. 2016. Wow! what a useful extension to wordnet! In *10th International Conference on Language Resources and Evaluation (LREC 2016)*. Portorož.

Stephan Oepen, Dan Flickinger, and Francis Bond. 2004. Towards holistic grammar engineering and testing — grafting treebank maintenance into the grammar revision cycle. In *Beyond Shallow*

Analyses — Formalisms and Statistical Modelling for Deep Analysis (Workshop at IJCNLP-2004). Hainan Island. URL `http://www-tsujii.is.s.u-tokyo.ac.jp/bsa/`.

Geoffrey K. Pullum. 1984. If it's tuesday, this must be glossematics. *Natural Language & Linguistic Theory*, 2(1):151–156. URL `http://www.jstor.org/stable/4047563`.

Eric S. Raymond. 1999. *The Cathedral & the Bazaar*. O'Reilly.

Yu Jie Seah and Francis Bond. 2014. Annotation of pronouns in a multilingual corpus of Mandarin Chinese, English and Japanese. In *10th Joint ACL - ISO Workshop on Interoperable Semantic Annotation*. Reykjavik.

Jeanette Yi Wen Tan. 2012. *Automatic Generation of Multilingual Crossword Puzzles with WordNet*. Final year project, Linguistics and Multilingual Studies, Nanyang Technological University.

Shan Wang and Francis Bond. 2013. Building the Chinese Open Wordnet (COW): Starting from core synsets. In *Proceedings of the 11th Workshop on Asian Language Resources, a Workshop at IJCNLP-2013*, pages 10–18. Nagoya.

Amir Zeldes. 2017. The GUM corpus: Creating multilayer resources in the classroom. *Language Resources and Evaluation*, 51(3):581–612.

竜之介芥川. 1918. 蜘蛛の糸. 赤い鳥.

Towards the Addition of Pronunciation Information to Lexical Semantic Resources

Thierry Declerck
German Research Center for AI
Multilinguality and Language Technology
Stuhsatzenhausweg 3
D-66123 Saarbrücken Germany
declerck@dfki.de

Lenka Bajčetić
Austrian Centre for Digital Humanities and
Cultural Heritage
Sonnenfelsgasse 19
Wien 1010, Austria
lenka.bajcetic@oeaw.ac.at

Abstract

This paper describes ongoing work aiming at adding pronunciation information to lexical semantic resources, with a focus on open wordnets. Our goal is not only to add a new modality to those semantic networks, but also to mark heteronyms listed in them with the pronunciation information associated with their different meanings. This work could contribute in the longer term to the disambiguation of multi-modal resources, which are combining text and speech.

1 Introduction

The work described in this paper aims at enriching lexical semantic databases by adding the modality of pronunciation, primarily targeting in our current work the Open English WordNet (McCrae et al., 2019a, 2020).[1] Pronunciation information is typically not associated with WordNet, but can be particularly relevant within the vision of contributing directly or indirectly to integrated lexical resources and architectures, like the ELEXIS Dictionary Matrix (McCrae et al., 2019b) or BabelNet (Navigli and Ponzetto, 2010), as well as text-to-speech systems which use WordNet or WordNet-based lexical resources or tools.

In a number of cases, homographs with different meanings are also characterised by different pronunciations. This can be the case across syntactic categories, but also within one category, like for example for the noun "lead",[2] which is having a different pronunciation per sense, as this is exemplified in the combination of the IPA[3] code [/lɛd/] and the definition:

> ("A heavy, pliable, inelastic metal element, having a bright, bluish color, but easily tarnished; both malleable and ductile,though with little tenacity. It is easily fusible, forms alloys with other metals, and is an ingredient of solder and type metal. Atomic number 82, symbol Pb (from Latin plumbum).")

and of the IPA code [/liːd/] and the definition:

> ("The act of leading or conducting; guidance; direction, course").

This phenomenon is called "heteronymy". Although they share the same spelling, heteronyms have two different possible pronunciations that are associated with two (or more) different meanings (Martin et al., 1981). By definition, these words are homographs which are not homophones. They can be considered as the opposite of polyphones, which are words with different pronunciations that are not associated with different meanings. Typical heteronym examples in English include "tear" , "bow", and "row".

The frequency of heteronymy varies across different languages. For example, as for today, Wiktionary counts 723 cases for English,[4] while only 21 cases are listed for French.[5] But the number of concerned entries increases considerably if we take into account all the derived terms (including

[1] See also https://github.com/globalwordnet/english-wordnet.

[2] The two pronunciation and definition pairs for the noun "lead" displayed here are taken from the XML dump of the English edition of Wiktionary. The human readable page can be consulted at https://en.wiktionary.org/wiki/lead#Noun.

[3] IPA stands for "International Phonetic Alphabet". See also https://www.internationalphoneticassociation.org/.

[4] https://en.wiktionary.org/wiki/Category:English_heteronyms, [consulted: 2021.01.28]

[5] https://en.wiktionary.org/wiki/Category:French_heteronyms, [consulted: 2021.01.28]

compounds and phrasal expressions) in which a heteronym entry is occurring. So, for the "metal" sense of the "lead" entry, Wiktionary is listing 77 derived terms, 32 of them being currently included as an entry in the dictionary. Some of them are carrying pronunciation information ("leadsman"), and some are not ("lead pencil"). Similarly, for the "curved" sense of "bow" Wiktionary lists 19 derived terms, like for example "longbow", all included as an entry in the dictionary. Some of them are also not carrying pronunciation information, like for example "bow harp". Hence, a much larger number of Wiktionary entries can be considered as instances of heteronymy, if one lexical item in a compound or in a phrasal entry is itself included in Wiktionary as a heteronym.

2 Targeted Lexical Databases

Although our current work is primarily intended at enriching WordNet, ultimately we aim at adding disambiguated pronunciation information to a series of lexical databases. Once the phonetic transcriptions are correctly stored in WordNet, this information can be propagated to BabelNet (Navigli and Ponzetto, 2012)[6] and all other lexical resources which are making use of WordNet.

2.1 Wordnets

As each WordNet is a sense inventory, it is particularly relevant to associate pronunciation information with the heteronyms it lists. Recently we witnessed the development of a new WordNet for English (McCrae et al., 2020), which is based on the Princeton WordNet (PWN, see (Fellbaum, 1998)), but aiming at an open source development policy. This makes this version of WordNet a good candidate for testing in a near future the addition of pronunciation information in a collaborative manner, using the corresponding GitHub platform.[7] The Open English WordNet (OEW) data can be downloaded in various formats, including XML, LMF[8] and RDF.

2.2 BabelNet

While BabelNet already combines wordnets and wiktionaries, as well as many other resources, it does not yet provide the phonetic transcription that it has extracted from various language versions of Wiktionary. Although BabelNet provides sound files in its word entries, those pronunciations are given by an external library that do not read from IPA codes. This library seems to be connected to the text-to-speech modules of the browser accessing the server, and utilises it to add pronunciation to some textual information on the BabelNet pages, like the entry and its associated definition(s) and example sentence(s).

Experimenting with BabelNet, we discovered that in fact a unique pronunciation for homographs is provided, leading thus to a number of wrong pronunciation examples. In this case we can see the importance of considering the IPA phonetic transcriptions for all senses of a heteronym. This way, the disambiguated IPA code of each sense could be used as input to the sound file generator of BabelNet. We hope that our work will prove beneficial in this endeavour.

2.3 ELEXIS – Dictionary Matrix

The Dictionary Matrix, under development within the ELEXIS project,[9] is a collection of linked dictionaries. The goal of this matrix is to enhance interoperability across resources and languages. For this, ELEXIS provides services for linking resources semi-automatically across languages at various matching levels such as headword, sense and lexeme. We plan to add pronunciation information to WordNet resources that are included in this linking exercise, as this can help in the particularly challenging sense linking task.

3 Our Approach

The first step of our work consisted in accessing the XML dump of the English Wiktionary resource,[10] and extracting from there, with the help of customised Python scripts, the pronunciation information associated with nouns, verbs, adjectives, and adverbs. As we can see in Figure 1, we also extracted the corresponding senses and associated examples sentences, as we need to keep the relation of

[6]See also https://babelnet.org/.

[7]Open English WordNet is accessible at https://github.com/globalwordnet/english-wordnet It is also accessible via a GUI: https://en-word.net/.

[8]LMF stands for "Lexical Markup Language", an ISO standard (Francopoulo et al., 2006), which has also be employed for encoding WordNet, as this is described for example in (Henrich and Hinrichs, 2010).

[9]https://elex.is/.

[10]The XML dumps of recent versions of the English edition of Wiktionary are available at https://dumps.wikimedia.org/enwiktionary/.

the pronunciation information with the corresponding meaning and the associated example sentences, if any is provided.

While we can report good progress in this task, there are still a few issues to solve, mainly due to the sometimes idiosyncratic way of encoding information in Wiktionary. While the overall XML structures of the lexical entries in Wiktionary is quite consistent, the linguistic information itself is encoded by making use of the Wiki mark-up language and with a number of options left to the (volunteering) encoders of the entries, so that extra lines of codes are necessary for dealing with those recurrent idiosyncratic cases. Still, we have extracted a large amount of lexical information that we have checked for validity. The numbers are given and discussed in the next section.

3.1 Some Figures

In this section we give some quantitative details on our current extraction work from Wiktionary.[11] A Wiktionary page is selected for processing if it contains within its English section one or more of the following Parts-of-Speech (PoS): noun, verb, adjective or adverb. This was the case for 829.342 Wiktionary pages, out of which the following lexical information was detected and extracted:

- nouns: 584.021
- verbs: 141.938
- adjectives: 139.887
- adverbs: 21.413
- pronunciation information for 72.067 entries (out of a total of 887.259 entries)

A note on the terminology is appropriate here. We call "Wiktionary pages" the Web resources that are accessed by a Wiktionary URL. So for the "lead" example, we access the Wiktionary page by typing "https://en.wiktionary.org/wiki/lead" in a browser. The element name "page" is in fact also used in the XML dump for marking an entry. A Wiktionary page typically covers more than one language (4 languages in our example). We are concentrating here on the English language, and in this case we see that 3 "etymologies" are listed, while two of them include the noun part-of-speech and all three include the verb part-of-speech. Those elements are the ones we call "entries" in the list of figures displayed just above.

On average, there is only 1,07 entries per English section in the selected pages. Many Wiktionary pages are about morphological variants of a lemma form, and those typically do not include PoS ambiguities. Therefore, we do not observe a significant amount of such PoS ambiguities in the English section of the total amount of selected Wiktionary pages, but there are many more ambiguities to be seen, if one concentrates on the Wiktionary pages that are leading to the lemma forms.

We observe that 815.192 English entries are without pronunciation information. Inspecting those, we see that in many cases the entries are in fact dealing with morphological variations (e.g. plural) of the ground form. In such cases we see the relatively straightforward possibility to automatically accommodate the pronunciation information of the lemma to the derived form. Also compound words are most often lacking the pronunciation information. An example of this is the adjective "leadlike". Although this would be more complicated, it could still be possible to derive the pronunciation of the compound word, as explained in the Future Work section.

We show the (shortened) output of our program for the extraction of nouns from the Wiktionary page "lead" in Figure 1.[12]

4 Formal Lexical Representation

In order to make the information we extracted from Wiktionary available in an interoperable and reusable format, we make use of the OntoLex-Lemon model, resulting from the W3C Community Group "Ontology Lexica" (Cimiano et al., 2016).[13] Figure 2 displays the general organisation of the core module of the OntoLex-Lemon model.

4.1 The RDF Encoding of the Open English WordNet

Our decision to use OntoLex-Lemon for representing the extracted lexical information from Wiktionary is also motivated by the fact that the Open English WordNet (OEW) has an export of its data in the so-called Global-Wordnet-RDF format,[14]

[11] We were using the XML dump of May 2020.

[12] At this stage of development, wiki mark-up signs are still included. In future versions, the data will be cleaned-up.

[13] See for more details `https://www.w3.org/2016/05/ontolex/`.

[14] For details and examples of the encoding, see `http://globalwordnet.github.io/schemas/#rdf`.

```
title: lead
   ety
       pos : noun
       plural : 'leads'
       senses : [" {{lb|en|uncountable}} A heavy, pliable, inelastic metal element,
       having a bright, bluish color, but easily tarnished; both malleable and
       ductile, though with little tenacity. It is easily fusible, forms alloys
       with other metals, and is an ingredient of solder and type metal.
       atomic|Atomic number 82, symbol Pb (from Latin ''plumbum'').", ... ]
       {{lb|en|uncountable|typography}} Vertical space in advance of a row or
       between rows of text. Also known as ''leading''.", ... ]
       examples : [(" {{lb|en|uncountable|typography}} Vertical space in advance of
       a row or between rows of text. Also known as ''leading''.", "{{ux|en|This
       copy has too much '''lead'''; I prefer less space between the lines.}}\n"),
       (" {{lb|en|plural '''leads'''}} A roof covered with lead sheets or terne
       plates.\n", "I would have the tower two stories, and goodly '''lead'''s upon
       the top", ....)]
       pronunciation : [' {{enPR|lĕd}}, {{IPA|en|/lɛd/}}\n']
   ety
       pos : noun
       plural : 'leads'
       senses : [' {{lb|en|countable}} The act of leading or conducting; guidance;
       direction, course', ... ]
       examples : [(' {{lb|en|countable}} The act of leading or conducting;
       guidance; direction, course', "{{ux|en|to take the '''lead'''}}\n"), ...]
       pronunciation : [' {{a|RP}} {{enPR|lēd}}, {{IPA|en|/li:d/}}\n', ' {{a|GA}}
       {{IPA|en|/lid/}}\n']
```

Figure 1: The extracted information from the Wiktionary page "lead", focused on nouns, listing the PoS, the associated senses and examples, as well as the pronunciation belonging to each sense. (shortened)

which is using also the OntoLex-Lemon model. We display in the next 3 listings the way OEW is encoding information about "lead" in the Global-Wordnet-RDF format.[15] This representation is the one that will be used for automatically linking the disambiguated heteronym pronunciations to OEW.

In Listing 1 we see the way OEW encodes the original Princeton WordNet synset for the *metal* meaning of "lead".

```
pwnid:ewn-14667645-n
  owl:sameAs ili:i113959 ;
  wn:partOfSpeech wn:noun ;
  dc:subject "noun.substance" ;
  wn:definition [ rdf:value
    "a soft heavy toxic malleable
    metallic element; bluish white
    when freshly cut but tarnishes
    readily to dull grey"@en ] ;
  wn:hypernym pwnid:ewn-14649636-n ;
  wn:holo_substance pwnid:ewn-14700071-n ;
  wn:holo_substance pwnid:ewn-14694339-n ;
  wn:hyponym pwnid:ewn-14929227-n ;
  wn:hyponym pwnid:ewn-14929348-n ;
  wn:hyponym pwnid:ewn-15008253-n ;
  wn:hypernym pwnid:ewn-92464177-n ;
  a ontolex:LexicalConcept .
```

Listing 1: The Global-Wordnet-RDF representation of the Open English WordNet synset for the concept associated with *lead* in the *metal* sense (listing also semantic relations the synset is involved in)

[15]The encodings are taken from https://en-word.net/lemma/lead.

Listing 2 below is displaying a meaning of "lead" that is a lexicalized sense of the synset introduced in Listing 1.

```
<#lead-ewn-14667645-n>
   ontolex:isLexicalizedSenseOf
      pwnid:ewn-14667645-n ;
   a ontolex:LexicalSense .
```

Listing 2: The Global-Wordnet-RDF representation of an OEW sense associated with the LexicalConcept pwnid:ewn-14667645-n

Listing 3 is then showing the OEW representation of the nominal lexical entry "lead", with all its senses.

```
<#lead-n>
  ontolex:canonicalForm [
    ontolex:writtenRep "lead"@en
  ] ;
  ontolex:sense <#lead-ewn-05164526-n> ;
  ontolex:sense <#lead-ewn-14667645-n> ;
  ontolex:sense <#lead-ewn-05835238-n> ;
  ontolex:sense <#lead-ewn-01259362-n> ;
  ontolex:sense <#lead-ewn-13915822-n> ;
  ontolex:sense <#lead-ewn-06281532-n> ;
  ontolex:sense <#lead-ewn-13617665-n> ;
  ontolex:sense <#lead-ewn-10668135-n> ;
  ontolex:sense <#lead-ewn-08609721-n> ;
  ontolex:sense <#lead-ewn-06664322-n> ;
  ontolex:sense <#lead-ewn-06281845-n> ;
  ontolex:sense <#lead-ewn-05058239-n> ;
  ontolex:sense <#lead-ewn-03658258-n> ;
  ontolex:sense <#lead-ewn-03656591-n> ;
  ontolex:sense <#lead-ewn-03656410-n> ;
  ontolex:sense <#lead-ewn-03610056-n> ;
```

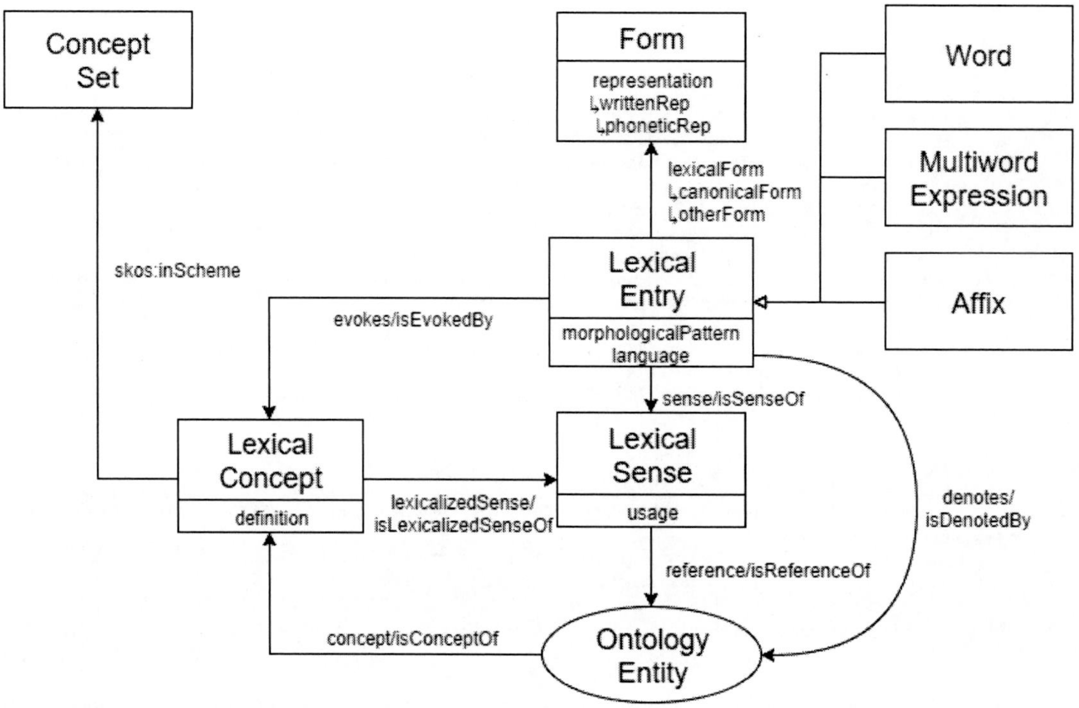

Figure 2: The core module of OntoLex-Lemon. Graphic taken from `https://www.w3.org/2016/05/ontolex/`.

```
ontolex:sense <#lead-ewn-01258857-n> ;
wn:partOfSpeech wn:noun ;
a ontolex:LexicalEntry .
```

Listing 3: The Global-Wordnet-RDF representation of the OEW entry "lead"

In this representation, the canonical form is included as the value of a blank node that just gives information about its written representation. We aim at adding the phonetic representation. But as not all the senses listed in this entry are related to the same concept, we can not assume one canonical form with the same pronunciation for all senses, and we have to depart from the modelling displayed in Listing 3.

4.2 Adapting the Representation

In this section we present the current OntoLex-Lemon representation we suggest for elements of the lexical information extracted from Wiktionary, for the example of "lead", in its *metal* meaning.

Listing 4 is just displaying the Lexical Concept representation for "lead", similar in part to the representation shown in Listing 1, but without semantic relations. A major difference is that the definition is now "outsourced", as we introduce definitions as instances of a class ":Definition", as can be seen in Listing 5. We are also adding a link to a Wikidata page.

```
:LexicalConcept_1
  rdf:type ontolex:LexicalConcept ;
  rdfs:label "\"lead\""@en ;
  skos:definition
    :Definition_Concept_1_English_Lead_1 ;
  skos:topConceptOf :ConceptSet_1 ;
  ontolex:isConceptOf
    <https://www.wikidata.org/wiki/Q708> ;
  ontolex:isEvokedBy :lex_lead_1 ;
  ontolex:lexicalizedSense :sense_lead_1 ;
.
```

Listing 4: Our suggested OntoLex-Lemon representation for the OEW entry "lead"

```
:Definition_Concept_1_English_Lead_1
  rdf:type :Definition ;
  rdfs:label "\"A heavy, pliable,
  inelastic metal element, having
  a bright, bluish color, but easily
  tarnished; both malleable and
  ductile, though with little tenacity.
  It is easily fusible, forms alloys
  with other metals, and is an ingredient
  of solder and type metal. Atomic number
  82, symbol Pb (from Latin plumbum). ;
.
```

Listing 5: A Wiktionary definition for "lead" as an instance of the class ":Definiton"

Listing 6 introduces one sense for the *metal* meaning of "lead" in Wiktionary.

```
:sense_lead_1
  rdf:type ontolex:LexicalSense ;
  rdfs:label "\"lead\""@en ;
  ontolex:isLexicalizedSenseOf
    :LexicalConcept_1 ;
  ontolex:isSenseOf :lex_lead_1 ;
  ontolex:reference
    <https://www.wikidata.org/wiki/Q708> ;
  ## ontolex:usage lexinfo:singular ;
.
```

Listing 6: Introducing a sense for on the meanings of "lead" in Wiktionary

The reader can see that we link this sense to a specific lexical entry for "lead", as we have now two entries for this word. The commented line "##ontolex:usage lexinfo:singular" shows the possibility to express that this sense requires the word to be used in singular. But we disregard this encoding here, as we are introducing also different forms for the noun "lead", one per pronunciation. One case is shown in Listing 7.

```
:lex_lead_1
  rdf:type ontolex:Word ;
  lexinfo:partOfSpeech
     lexinfo:noun ;
  rdfs:label "\"lead\""@en ;
  ontolex:canonicalForm
     :form_lead_singular_1 ;
  ontolex:evokes :LexicalConcept_1 ;
  ontolex:otherForm
     :form_lead_plural_1 ;
  ontolex:sense :sense_lead_1 ;
.
:form_lead_singular_1
  rdf:type ontolex:Form ;
  lexinfo:number lexinfo:singular ;
  rdfs:label "\"lead\""@en ;
  ontolex:phoneticRep
    "\textipa{[/lEd/]}/en-GB-fonipa" ;
  ontolex:writtenRep "\"lead\""@en ;
.
```

Listing 7: The specific lexical entry and its related form – with the pronunciation information

Related conclusive experiments were also done for encoding lexical information extracted from the German Wiktionary (Declerck et al., 2020). It is suggested in (Declerck et al., 2020) that one could link specific senses of an entry to a lexical form carrying a specific pronunciation (by the use of the ontolex:phoneticRep) by applying restrictions that are defined in the lexicog module ((Bosque-Gil et al., 2019)[16] of OntoLex-Lemon. However, in our current experiment, we think that it might be more effective to just duplicate the lexical forms along the line of their pronunciation (even if they have the same gender and number features), and to point to those from the lexical sense via the corresponding lexical entry.

5 Sense Linking

In the following phase of our work, we plan to connect the extracted information with the correct WordNet synsets. After extracting the pronunciation information from Wiktionary, the subsequent step of our work lies in sense disambiguation and linking. More specifically, this task requires correctly inferring which of the heteronym synsets is the right match for the pronunciation information we have extracted from the Wiktionary entry. In order to disambiguate the word sense, we can utilize the WordNet synsets of the heteronymous senses as well as their description and examples from Wiktionary.

Our initial approach relies on comparing the document similarity between WordNet synsets and the matching Wiktionary entries. Firstly, we create 'documents' by concatenating the definitions and examples for all the senses of the ambiguous word. In the case of "lead", we have decided to combine all the possible sub-senses using their PoS tag. In this way, according to WordNet, we end up with two broader senses for "lead": a broad noun sense and a broad verb sense. These two documents need to be compared with the two documents extracted from Wiktionary, using the same approach. After tokenization, punctuation cleaning and stopwords removal, document similarity is calculated using TFIDF and the bag-of-words approach. For this purpose we have utilized the Docsim library from Gensim[17].

The preliminary work shows promising results. In Table 1 we can see these similarity comparisons for the example word "lead". Columns represent the sense documents extracted from Wiktionary, represented by their pronunciations, while rows represent the senses extracted from WordNet. The highest similarity scores are for the correct combinations of senses, which is the outcome we would expect. We believe that this approach, with modifications, can be used for automatic heteronym sense linking on a greater scale. However, joining all the sub-senses is certainly not the best solution.

[16] See `https://www.w3.org/2019/09/lexicog/` for more details of the specifications of the module.

[17] The Docsim library is explained here: https://radimrehurek.com/gensim/similarities/docsim.html

IPA code	[lɛd]	[li:d]
lead.noun	0.4272	0.0672
lead.verb	0.2176	0.4581

Table 1: Similarity scores for sense matching

The noun sense of the word lead can also refer to an advantage held by a competitor in a race, in which case the correct pronunciation is the second one. So we can see that sense granularity is also an important aspect when it comes to heteronym disambiguation.

6 Related Work

Our work with the English Wiktionary is an extension and a refinement of a first experiment dealing with the German version of Wiktionary, with the aim of enriching a new open WordNet for German with pronunciation information (Declerck et al., 2020). In both cases, we make use of the OntoLex-Lemon community standard for encoding the heteronyms (and other entries). Our current development is aiming at including the results into various integrated or interlinked lexical databases. We are also aiming at automatically adding pronunciation information to derived terms, on the base of sense-linking algorithms.

The work presented in (Declerck, 2020) describes an approach for linking the Open Dutch WordNet to external lexical resources, including the Dutch version of Wiktionary, with the goal of enriching the lemmas in the WordNet entries with morphological variants. But the work was not dealing with pronunciation information.

(Schlippe et al., 2010) assess the quality of pronunciation information in Wiktionary for four languages (English, French, German, and Spanish) and come to satisfying results, especially in the case of French, when it comes to the evaluation of the coverage and also to the impact on automatic speech recognition (ASR) systems, especially in the case of Spanish. This already older study comforted us in the opinion that extracting pronunciation information from Wiktionary can deliver a relevant source of data for our experiment consisting in equipping wordnets with pronunciation information.

In recent years, relevant research regarding heteronyms is done in the field of speech synthesis. For example, the work of (Samsudin and Rahim, 2019) focuses on handling heteronym ambiguity for a text-to-speech (TTS) system for Malay language. Although there are only 12 unique heteronyms in Malay, this research emphasises the importance of conducting a specific study on heteronym words and their pronunciation by TTS systems. Other important work in this field includes the patents of (Henton and Naik, 2014) and (Wang et al., 2011). Both models focus on heteronym pronunciation for dialogue systems, using the user's input to correctly predict the pronunciation of the output heteronym.

7 Future Work

A crucial phase of the future work involves evaluation. For this we could use some existing dictionaries which contain pronunciation information. Since pronunciation is an inevitable part of translation dictionaries, extracting the information from such sources could substantially enlarge the underlying resource and also serve as a basis for evaluation.

One interesting possibility for an expansion of the scope of this work can be found in compound words and derived terms. After correctly disambiguating the heteronymous lemma, we can use this information to produce the IPA of the compound words which contain it. This would be done following the rules of metrical phonology (Kreidler, 2004). If that would prove too complex we could produce the IPA without stress information. We could also use etymology information from Wiktionary to produce pronunciation descriptions for compounds.

Acknowledgements

Contributions by the German Research Center for Artificial Intelligence (DFKI GmbH) were supported in part by the H2020 project Prêt-à-LLOD with Grant Agreement number 825182. Contributions by the Austrian Centre for Digital Humanities and Cultural Heritage at the Austrian Academy of Sciences were supported in part by the H2020 project "ELEXIS" with Grant Agreement number 731015. The work described in this paper was also pursued in part in the larger context of the COST Action CA18209 - NexusLinguarum "European network for Web-centred linguistic data science". We also thank the anonymous reviewers for their insightful comments.

References

Julia Bosque-Gil, Dorielle Lonke, Jorge Gracia, and Ilan Kernerman. 2019. Validating the OntoLex-lemon lexicography module with K Dictionaries' multilingual data. In *Electronic lexicography in the 21st century. Proceedings of the eLex 2019 conference.*, pages 726–746, Brno, Czech Republic. Lexical Computing CZ s.r.o.,.

Philipp Cimiano, John P. McCrae, and Paul Buitelaar. 2016. Lexicon Model for Ontologies: Community Report.

Thierry Declerck. 2020. Towards an extension of the linking of the open dutch wordnet with dutch lexicographic resources. In *Proceedings of the 2020 Globalex Workshop on Linked Lexicography*, pages 33–35. ELRA.

Thierry Declerck, Lenka Bajcetic, and Melanie Siegel. 2020. Adding pronunciation information to wordnets. In *Proceedings of the LREC 2020 Workshop on Multimodal Wordnets (MMW2020)*. ELRA.

Christiane Fellbaum, editor. 1998. *WordNet An Electronic Lexical Database*. The MIT Press, Cambridge, MA ; London.

Gil Francopoulo, Monte George, Nicoletta Calzolari, Monica Monachini, Nuria Bel, Mandy Pet, and Claudia Soria. 2006. Lexical markup framework (LMF). In *Proceedings of the Fifth International Conference on Language Resources and Evaluation (LREC'06)*, Genoa, Italy. European Language Resources Association (ELRA).

Verena Henrich and Erhard W. Hinrichs. 2010. Standardizing wordnets in the ISO standard LMF: wordnet-lmf for germanet. In *COLING 2010, 23rd International Conference on Computational Linguistics, Proceedings of the Conference, 23-27 August 2010, Beijing, China*, pages 456–464. Tsinghua University Press.

Caroline Henton and Devang Naik. 2014. Disambiguating heteronyms in speech synthesis.

Charles Kreidler. 2004. *Prefixes, Compound Words, and Phrases*, chapter 12. John Wiley Sons, Ltd.

M. Martin, G.V. Jones, and D.L. Nelson. 1981. Heteronyms and polyphones: Categories of words with multiple phonemic representations. *Behavior Research Methods & Instrumentation*, 13:299–307.

John P. McCrae, Alexandre Rademaker, Francis Bond, Ewa Rudnicka, and Christiane Fellbaum. 2019a. English wordnet 2019 – an open-source wordnet for english. In *Proceedigns of the 10th Global Wordnet Conference*. Global Wordnet Association. To appear.

John P. McCrae, Carole Tiberius, Anas Fahad Khan, Ilan Kernerman, Thierry Declerck, Simon Krek, Monica Monachini, and Sina Ahmadi. 2019b. The elexis interface for interoperable lexical resources. In *Proceedings of the eLex 2019 conference*, pages 642–659. CELGA-ILTEC, University of Coimbra, Lexical Computing CZ, s.r.o.

John Philip McCrae, Alexandre Rademaker, Ewa Rudnicka, and Francis Bond. 2020. English wordnet 2020: Improving and extending a wordnet for english using an open-source methodology. In *Proceedings of the LREC 2020 Workshop on Multimodal Wordnets, MMW@LREC 2020, Marseille, France, May 2020*, pages 14–19. The European Language Resources Association (ELRA).

Roberto Navigli and Simone Paolo Ponzetto. 2010. BabelNet: Building a very large multilingual semantic network. In *Proceedings of the 48th Annual Meeting of the Association for Computational Linguistics*, pages 216–225, Uppsala, Sweden. Association for Computational Linguistics.

Roberto Navigli and Simone Paolo Ponzetto. 2012. BabelNet: The automatic construction, evaluation and application of a wide-coverage multilingual semantic network. *Artificial Intelligence*, 193:217–250.

N. Samsudin and L. N. Rahim. 2019. Rapid heteronym disambiguation for text-to-speech system. In *2019 4th International Conference and Workshops on Recent Advances and Innovations in Engineering (ICRAIE)*, pages 1–6.

Tim Schlippe, Sebastian Ochs, and Tanja Schultz. 2010. Wiktionary as a source for automatic pronunciation extraction. In *11th Annual Conference of the International Speech Communication Association, Makuhari, Japan*. Interspeech 2010.

Xi Wang, Xiaoyan Lou, and Jian Li. 2011. Speech synthesis with fuzzy heteronym prediction using decision trees.

Testing agreement between lexicographers: A case of homonymy and polysemy

Marek Maziarz,[◇] **Francis Bond**[♠] **and Ewa Rudnicka**[◇]
[♠] Nanyang Technological University, Singapore
[◇] Wrocław University of Science and Technology, Poland
bond@ieee.org, {marek.maziarz|ewa.rudnicka}@pwr.edu.pl

Abstract

In this paper we compare Oxford Lexico and Merriam Webster dictionaries with Princeton WordNet with respect to the description of semantic (dis)similarity between polysemous and homonymous senses that could be inferred from them. WordNet lacks any explicit description of polysemy or homonymy, but as a network of linked senses it may be used to compute semantic distances between word senses. To compare WordNet with the dictionaries, we transformed sample entry microstructures of the latter into graphs and cross-linked them with the equivalent senses of the former. We found that dictionaries are in high agreement with each other, if one considers polysemy and homonymy altogether, and in moderate concordance, if one focuses merely on polysemy descriptions. Measuring the shortest path lengths on WordNet gave results comparable to those on the dictionaries in predicting semantic dissimilarity between polysemous senses, but was less felicitous while recognising homonymy.

1 Introduction

We talk about *polysemy* when different word senses are semantically related. Homonymy is the opposite phenomenon in which etymologically unrelated senses are signified by the same word-form (Lyons, 1995, pp. 54-60).[1] The main source of homonyms is the diachronic process of word shortening due to their frequent use (Fenk-Oczlon and Fenk, 2008, p. 59). Though homonyms are frequent in text and speech, they remain a tough nut to crack for Natural Language Processing (Hauer and Kondrak, 2020; Klimenkov and Pokid, 2019; McCarthy, 2006; Mihalcea, 2003). One of the reasons is that wordnets lack any explicit links between the related meanings of the same word and do not discern between the two types of lexical ambiguity (Freihat et al., 2013).

The goals of this paper are two-fold: (i) we check the degree of agreement between polysemy descriptions in two general English dictionaries, namely Oxford Lexico and American English Merriam-Webster Dictionary, and in WordNet, (ii) we test the applicability of WordNet in measuring semantic similarity between senses (that is assessing polysemy vs. homonymy distinctions). For these purposes, we have created a data set of 57 nouns, noted by the three lexicons (Sec. 3.1). We represented dictionary microstructures as graphs with the equivalent WordNet synsets attached to them (Sec. 3.2). The approach resulted in 889 sense pairs in total. The set of the mapped synsets served as a common denominator for the subsequent comparisons between the three lexical resources. Measuring distances between particular sense pairs allowed us to compare the polysemy/homonymy description in the two dictionaries with the structural description in WordNet (via lexico-semantic relations, Sec. 3.3 and 4).[2] It turned out that the dictionaries are in high concordance with each other, if we consider the homonymy-polysemy distinction, and in moderate agreement, if we look at polysemy descriptions (in terms of Spearman's correlation coefficient). WordNet did not differ much from Lex-

[1]For the needs of this paper, we define *homonyms* (*homographs*) as a pair of senses which are characterised by the same part of speech, share the same lemma, but are not related semantically and etymologically (Svensén, 2009, pp. 96-7). A pair of polysemous senses (*polysemes*) – on the contrary – is constituted by the two senses of the same POS category, sharing the same lemma, semantically related and of the same etymology.

[2]The resource was published under the CC-BY 4.0 licence and is available from: `https://github.com/MarekMaziarz/HomoPoly`.

ico and Merriam-Webster in its capability to describe similarity between polysemous senses. It was homonymy that made the difference (Sec. 5).

2 Related Work

In Natural Language Processing accessing word or sense dissimilarity via measuring distances in lexical networks is a well-known procedure (Meng et al., 2013; Pedersen et al., 2004; Richardson et al., 1994). Among many measures, some are of special interest for semantic relatedness assessment, that is path-based indices (the shortest-path, Wu-Palmer's, Leakcock-Chodorow's or Li's measures) and information content-based measures (Resnik's, Lin's or Jiang's methods, see Meng et al. (2013)). In the context of recognising polysemous sense proximity, Wu-Palmer's measure was used to calculate concept similarity within the taxonomy of *The Historical Thesaurus of English* (Ramiro et al., 2018). Each sense was compared with all other word senses, then the obtained matrices of similarity were used to arrange polysemous word meanings into a chain of extended senses. In (Youn et al., 2016) polysemy networks for many world languages were compared with the use of path distances between Swadesh' concepts mapped to them. The authors found the distance distribution of polysemy structures universal across languages, despite clearly different geographical and cultural conditions. Out of various measures of semantic relatedness, we made use of one of the simplest – the shortest path length. Since our graphs were weighted, we utilised Dijkstra's distance algorithm (Dijkstra et al., 1959) which finds the geodesics for weighted networks. We applied it to measuring semantic distances in both English dictionaries and in WordNet.

Many traditional dictionaries depict word senses in the form of nested clusters of definitions. Starting from the basic sense (Atkins, 2008, p. 41), (Svensén, 2009, pp. 363-4), they unfold a network of inter-dependencies in the form of a sense hierarchy. In such structured polysemy nets main senses are linked into meaning chains with groups of subsenses attached to them (Svensén, 2009, p. 211-2, 350-1, 363). Hierarchical sense differentiation is more intuitive for dictionary users than a flat arrangement. In such a set-up senses are ordered according to their semantic "closeness" (Atkins, 2008, p. 41). Lexico and Merriam-Webster both represent this type of polysemy structuring.

The problem of consistency of lexicographic entries is widely acknowledged (Stock, 2008). The same word may be differently treated in different dictionaries (Svensén, 2009, pp. 205-6). Splitting or merging senses is not an easy task even for a specialist. The issue seems highly intuitive and decisions are supposed to be highly arbitrary. This is not entirely true. In distinguishing senses lexicographers rely on specific rules, like observing usage restrictions (e.g., for specialised vocabulary), differences in syntactic frames (cf. transitive - intransitive frame) or other grammatical properties, like grammatical number (cf. *pluralia* and *singularia tantum*) (Svensén, 2009; Jackson, 2002). Yet another way to tame lexicographers' intuitions is to rely on taxonomic and other sense relationships, in such a way *genus proximum* (a hypernym) and *differentia specifica* (a meronym/holonym, antonym etc.) might be captured (Stock, 2008, p. 153).

The lexicographic process of splitting and clustering senses was widely studied in the context of Word Sense Disambiguation (e.g. Passonneau et al. (2010)). We relate to several research studies which are most relevant to our approach. Resnik and Yarowsky (1999) proposed a method of measuring sense distances on *Hector* – a hierarchical dictionary (Atkins, 1992, cf. Tab. 3). They postulated that the penalty applied to a homonymous pair should be much higher than the cost of a polysemy step. In some aspects our methodology resembles this approach to the construction of an adjacency matrix.[3] Chugur et al. (2002) counter-argued against the possibility of an honest measure based on hierarchical dictionaries. The argument is as follows: since in metaphorical shifts extended senses completely change their semantic domain, dictionary provided sense relations do not mirror mental lexicon sense proximities. To this plea we answer that polysemy topologies are often multi-centred (Brugman and Lakoff, 2006) and are governed by their own rules (naming $\neq$ knowing, see (Malt et al., 1999)).

Véronis (1998) executed experiments in the assessment of the number of word senses obtained from a tagged corpus which was collated with dictionary data (*Petit Larousse*). The Spearman's

[3] We give homonymy links the distance of infinity, transformed later into the value of maximum distance of the whole polysemy network plus one. The crucial difference lies in the fact that we attach subsenses directly to the main sense, while Resnick and Yarowsky chained them. However, the idea to derive semantic dissimilarity measure out of the existing dictionaries and their hierachies remains the same.

rank correlation equal to 0.5 was reported for nouns. In various SENSEVAL editions research teams also reported rather mediocre agreement values between annotators (Artstein and Poesio, 2008, p. 587), e.g., Mihalcea et al. (2004) in SENSEVAL-3 observed ca. 70% ITA (percentage agreement) and $\kappa = 0.58$; similar results were obtained by Palmer et al. (2007). According to Artstein and Poesio (2008), "[w]ord sense tagging is one of the hardest annotation tasks."

3 Method

3.1 Lexico and Merriam-Webster Graphs

Two dictionaries were used to obtain distances between PWN senses: Oxford Lexico[4] and American English dictionary – Merriam-Webster[5].[6] 25 lemmas representing polysemy/homonymy distinction in English, according to these dictionaries, were chosen (the set S_{HP}), as well as 31 solely polysemous noun lemmas (the set S_P).[7] For each lemma two distinct graph structures were constructed out of the dictionaries, taking into account sense orderings. Both dictionaries apply similar lexicographic rules. Senses of different etymology are split into distinct entries. Then, main senses are ordered into a chain, according to their semantic closeness (cf. (Atkins, 2008, p. 41)), starting from the primal sense. Subsenses, if they exist, are attached to their superordinate meanings. The whole sense arrangement reflects semantic relationships, sense proximity and dissimilarity, being the result of the evolutionary sense extending process (as seen by each dictionary lexicographer team).

For instance, for the noun *sink* we found in Lexico the following microstructure[8]:

sink^2 noun

- 1. 'A fixed basin with a water supply and outflow pipe';
- 2. 'A pool or marsh in which a river's water disappears by evaporation or percolation;
- 2.1. technical 'A body or process which acts to absorb or remove energy or a particular component from a system';
- 3. short for *sinkhole*;
- 4. 'A place of vice or corruption';
- 4.1. British usually as modifier 'A school or estate situated in a socially deprived area'.

We transformed it into the set of bidirectional relations in such a manner that main meanings were linked into chains of consecutive senses ($1 \leftrightarrow 2 \leftrightarrow 3 \leftrightarrow 4$), and subsenses were joint to their superordinates ($2.1 \leftrightarrow 2$ and $4.1 \leftrightarrow 4$). Subsenses were dealt differently. In a polysemy graph they were given equal distances from their superordinate sense.[9]

3.2 Mapping PWN onto Dictionaries

PWN nominal senses representing the same lemma were mapped on the Lexico graph by two professional linguists in three steps (the set S_{HP}). (1) In the first phase, the mapping of the homonymous lemmas was done independently by the two annotators, then (2) disagreement cases were again independently annotated for the second time. (3) Finally, in the 3rd phase the remaining discrepancies were resolved in discussion. Cohen's κ was not worse than 0.8 in the task. Figure 1 presents the growth of kappa from the stage (1) to (2). Having assumed high agreement between lexicographers, polysemous senses from the set S_P were mapped by one of the annotators.

Thus, PWN sense *sink*-n-2 ('*technology* a process that acts to absorb or remove energy or a substance from a system') was linked to the sense sink^2-n-2-1, while PWN *sink*-n-1 ('plumbing fixture consisting of a water basin fixed to a wall...') was mapped onto the Lexico sense sink^2-n-1 resulting in the following graph structure (0s and 1s in superscripts represent relation weights) and Dijkstra's distance of two steps between the WordNet senses.

[4]`https://www.lexico.com/`

[5]`https://www.merriam-webster.com/`

[6]The dictionary entries were manually copy-pasted from the sites and then transformed into relation triples using regular expressions.

[7]The full list of the chosen words is as follows: *angle, band, bank, bark, bat, board, can, chapter, chop, clip, concealment, crest, cylinder, date, degree, duck, fall, fame, file, fly, gloss, intellect, lump, master, match, palm, pasturage, plant, ring, rock, rose, saw, scale, score, sentence, shilling, sink, skimmer, spring, stage, stalk, table, term, tie, tongue, trepan, trip, tune, veneer, vermin, victim, voucher, well, whirl, wrapping* and *wreck*.

[8]`https://www.lexico.com/definition/sink`

[9]In large hierarchies chaining subsenses would lead to inadequate similarity measures. Consider a hypothetical microstructure $G = (V, E)$: $V = \{1, 2, 2.1, 2.2, 2.3, 3\}$, $E = \{1 \leftrightarrow 2, 2 \leftrightarrow 3, 2.1 \leftrightarrow 2, 2.2 \leftrightarrow 2.1, 2.3 \leftrightarrow 2.2\}$. Let us measure the distance between the sense 2 and its subsense 2.3, which is $dist(2.3, 2) = 3$ steps. On the other hand, main senses 3 and 2 are only $dist(3, 2) = 1$ step ahead of each other, which seems counter-intuitive.

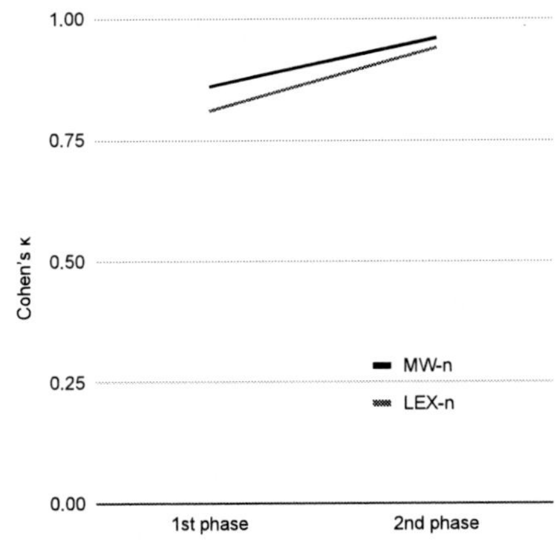

Figure 1: Cohen's κ measure of the agreement between two independent annotators for the WordNet-Lexico (LEX) and WordNet-Merriam-Webster (MW) nouns mappings, set S_{HP}.

- sink^{2}-n-1 $\overset{1}{\leftrightarrow}$ sink^{2}-n-2
- sink^{2}-n-2-1 $\overset{1}{\leftrightarrow}$ sink^{2}-n-2
- sink^{2}-n-2 $\overset{1}{\leftrightarrow}$ sink^{2}-n-3
- sink^{2}-n-3 $\overset{1}{\leftrightarrow}$ sink^{2}-n-4
- sink^{2}-n-4 $\overset{1}{\leftrightarrow}$ sink^{2}-n-4-1
- sink^{2}-n-1 $\overset{0}{\leftrightarrow}$ PWN-sink-n-1
- sink^{2}-n-2-1 $\overset{0}{\leftrightarrow}$ PWN-sink-n-2

The corresponding Merriam-Webster microstructure is the following[10]:

sink^{2} noun

- 1a. 'a pool or pit for the deposit of waste or sewage: cesspool';
- 1b. 'a ditch or tunnel for carrying off sewage: sewer';
- 1c. 'a stationary basin connected with a drain and usually a water supply for washing and drainage';
- 2. 'a place where vice, corruption, or evil collects';
- 3. 'sump: the lowest part of a mine shaft into which water drains';
- 4a. 'a depression in the land surface especially : one having a saline lake with no outlet';
- 4b. 'sinkhole';
- 5. 'a body or process that acts as a storage device or disposal mechanism: such as';
- 5a. 'heat sink broadly : a device that collects or dissipates energy (such as radiation)';
- 5b 'a reactant with or absorber of a substance forests are a sink for carbon dioxide'.

From which we obtain the relational graph of polysemy instances:

- sink^{2}-n-2 $\overset{1}{\leftrightarrow}$ sink^{2}-n-1
- sink^{2}-n-3 $\overset{1}{\leftrightarrow}$ sink^{2}-n-2
- sink^{2}-n-4 $\overset{1}{\leftrightarrow}$ sink^{2}-n-3
- sink^{2}-n-5 $\overset{1}{\leftrightarrow}$ sink^{2}-n-4
- sink^{2}-n-1-a $\overset{1}{\leftrightarrow}$ sink^{2}-n-1
- sink^{2}-n-1-b $\overset{1}{\leftrightarrow}$ sink^{2}-n-1
- sink^{2}-n-1-c $\overset{1}{\leftrightarrow}$ sink^{2}-n-1
- sink^{2}-n-4-a $\overset{1}{\leftrightarrow}$ sink^{2}-n-4
- sink^{2}-n-4-b $\overset{1}{\leftrightarrow}$ sink^{2}-n-4
- sink^{2}-n-5-a $\overset{1}{\leftrightarrow}$ sink^{2}-n-5
- sink^{2}-n-5-b $\overset{1}{\leftrightarrow}$ sink^{2}-n-5
- sink^{2}-n-1-c $\overset{0}{\leftrightarrow}$ PWN-sink-n-1
- sink^{2}-n-5 $\overset{0}{\leftrightarrow}$ PWN-sink-n-2
- sink^{2}-n-5-a $\overset{0}{\leftrightarrow}$ PWN-sink-n-2
- sink^{2}-n-5-b $\overset{0}{\leftrightarrow}$ PWN-sink-n-2

This example shows that while in Lexico the relation between the senses 'plumbing fixture' and 'the absorption or removal of energy' is seen as more direct (through the Lexico sense sink^{2}-n-2 'a pool or marsh'), the corresponding path in Merriam-Webster is much longer due to more fine-grained sense distinctions and different conceptualisation of the sense extending path (via the senses: 5 'body/process' $\leftrightarrow$ 4 'depression/sinkhole' $\leftrightarrow$ 3 'sump' $\leftrightarrow$ 2 'place of evil' $\leftrightarrow$

[10] `https://www.merriam-webster.com/dictionary/sink`

1 'cesspool/ditch/basin' $\leftrightarrow$ 1-c 'drainage basin', 5 steps in total).

We assumed that senses $s_1 \in PWN$ and $s_2 \in Dict$ were to be considered equivalent iff their extensions had a non-empty and non-trivial intersection. Let $S_1 = \{x : s_1(x)\}$ and $S_2 = \{x : s_2(x)\}$ be the sets of denotata of concepts s_1 and s_2, respectively. They were mapped iff

$$S_1 \cap S_2 \notin \emptyset \Leftrightarrow \exists x[(s_1(x) \implies s_2(x)) \wedge (s_2(x) \implies s_1(x))] \quad (1)$$

and the set of shared denotata $S_1 \cap S_2$ was intuitively not to small. The specificity of the task of linking dictionaries limited the space of choices only to different senses of the same word in WordNet (PWN) and in Lexico or Merriam-Webster ($Dict$), hence the requirement of non-triviality was easy to employ. Such an approach resulted in many-to-many mappings. An example of the process is shown in Fig. 2 (the noun *stalk*).

3.3 Semantic Distance

Having constructed semantic nets for both dictionaries and having mapped them onto PWN synsets we turned to measuring semantic distance between nodes in the graphs. For each PWN sense pair we calculated Dijkstra's distance. For 57 nominal lemmas we obtained, through combinatorics, 889 sense pairs and corresponding 889 distance values between the meanings. Homonymy groups constituted separate graphs, thus some possible paths were disjoint. Homonymy paths were given infinite lengths, while polysemy couplings obtained finite distance values. There were also cases of missed PWN meanings (a dictionary lacked any description of a given PWN sense). In such a situation we treated isolated (missed) sense exactly like homonymous ones. Table 1 jointly presents cardinalities of sets of finite ("<Inf") and infinite paths ("Inf"). As a result, we got 85% identical choices (the percentage agreement) and Cohen's κ = 0.67. Half of the remaining disagreement instances were missed senses (61 cases) and the other half were cases of real discrepancies in the homonymy/polysemy distinction (68 instances). Such a high agreement suggests that the dictionaries were pretty consistent in describing pairs of senses either as homonymous or polysemous.

Figure 3 represents a 2D histogram of actual Dijkstra's distances for the whole set of pairs.

		LEX	
		<Inf	Inf
MW	Inf	42	224
	<Inf	536	87

Table 1: Disjoint ("Inf") and finite ("<Inf") paths between PWN senses in Lexico ("LEX") and Merriam-Webster ("MW").

Homonymy couplings are posited in the top-right corner of the square. For the needs of correlation measurements, we transposed infinitives into finite values, i.e. $Inf \rightarrow max(dist) + 1$, which for Lexico was 8, and for Merriam-Webster was 9. Merriam-Webster has slightly longer sense chains than Lexico (because of deeper sense hierarchies). The concordance between Lexico and Webster was measured with Spearman's and Pearson's correlations ($\rho = .60$, $r = .60$).

Since investigating the coverage of a dictionary in terms of the noticed senses was not the aim of this research, we linked missed senses manually to the closest PWN senses (with weights equal to 1). This supplementary set of missed sense linkages was used in consecutive experiments as the shared extension of both dictionary graphs and Princeton WordNet. Having attached the set, we obtained the correlation of $\rho = .71$ and $r = .80$, see Table 2. The calculations show that our dictionaries give a similar semantic depiction of polysemy (lower distance values) and unrelated homonymous meanings (maximal distances).

Figure 4 illustrates the relationship between Lexico and Merriam-Webster after the removal of senses with infinite paths (homonymy cases). Now, correlations decrease to moderate values ($\rho = 0.43$ and $r = 0.41$). This proves that particular paths in each dictionary for the very same sense pair must differ (as we saw in the case of the PWN noun *sink*, senses 1 and 2).

4 Comparison with WordNet

Dictionaries are in high agreement when we consider both homonymy and polysemy, and in moderate concordance when we look solely at polysemy. The moderate correlations in polysemy depiction are not surprising. If one took into account the fact that our dictionaries might have differently clustered meanings, subsenses and meaning shades; might have distinguished more or less

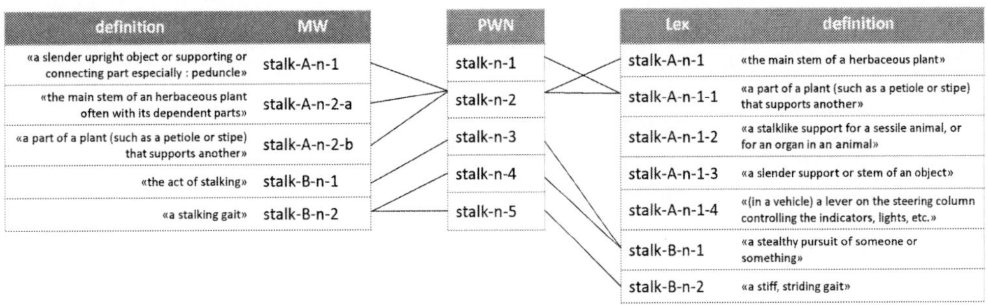

Figure 2: Mapping the equivalents of the noun *stalk* in Princeton WordNet (PWN), Lexico (Lex) and Merriam-Webster (MW). The number of possible choices was 25 for Merriam-Webster (5×5) and 35 (5×7) for Lexico, ca. $\frac{1}{5}$ of the combinatorial possibilities was real semantic equivalence, as defined by the proposition 1.

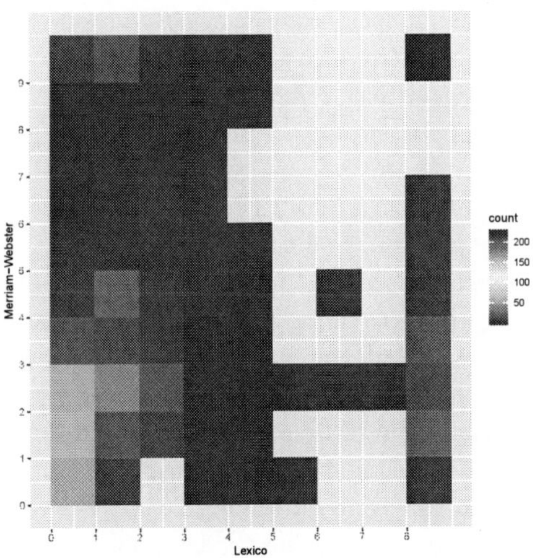

Figure 3: 2D histogram of Dijkstra's distances between PWN senses (in steps). This time the overlooked senses landed in the top-most and right-most sides of the square.

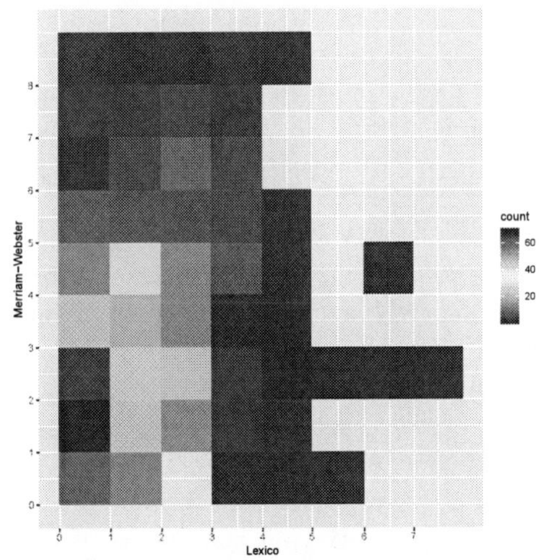

Figure 4: 2D histogram of Dijkstra's distances between PWN senses (in steps) for polysemous sense pairs noted in both dictionaries.

ρ	MW	
	HP	P
LEX	.71	.43
CI	$(0.65, 0.76)$	$(0.38, 0.53)$

Table 2: Spearman's rank correlation ρ between Lexico (LEX) and Merriam-Webster (MW) graph distances in two testing scenarios: HP – homonymy and polysemy cases, P – only polysemy cases. 'CI' signifies 99% jackknife pseudovalue intervals, $n = 57$ lemmas, cf. (Efron and Stein, 1981).

sense distinctions; might have merged and split the same semantic space in various ways – it would become obvious that they should differ. Eventually, differences do not necessarily indicate errors and may be signs of equally justified semantic descriptions.

We calculated Dijkstra's shortest path lengths between PWN senses mapped on the two dictionaries within WordNet 3.0. The undirected graph of WordNet was used. It contained 365,000 bidirectional relation instances. All relation instances were treated democratically, receiving weights of 1.

Table 3 presents the comparison between Lexico, Merriam-Webster and WordNet in terms of Spearman's correlation ρ for polysemy and homonymy cases. In general, WordNet distances behaved obviously worse than dictionaries, when homonymy was considered altogether with polysemy ('HP' scenario). However, when hints from the oracle were applied (the 'OHP' case), the results became fully comparable with the Lexico-Merriam-Webster agreement. When we cut off homonymy pairs, we found the WordNet-based measure performed almost as well as both dictionary-based distances (it achieved the lower confidence limit). It seems that what dictionaries and WordNet differ in is the proper treatment of homonymy pairs. In dictionaries the information is provided by etymologists; WordNet lacks it.

	WN		
ρ	HP	OHP	P
LEX	.46	**.70**	.36
MW	.46	**.67**	.38
minML	.47	**.68**	.38
LEX-MW CI	$(0.65, 0.76)$		$(0.38, 0.53)$

Table 3: Spearman's rank correlation ρ between WordNet (WN) and dictionary graph distances in three testing scenarios. Symbols: HP – homonymy & polysemy cases; OHP – homonymy cases given by the oracle; P – homonymy cases excluded ($n = 680$ sense pairs, 57 lemmas); LEX – Lexico, MW – Merriam-Webster, minML $= min(dist'_{LEX}, dist'_{MW})$, the lowest of two distance values, where $dist'$ signifies the standardisation of distance measures. In bold we indicated results that fitted corresponding 99% confidence intervals for the LEX-MW comparison.

When one merges the information from both dictionaries (see Table 3, *minML* measure), the Spearman's correlation increases. We calculated the minimum value from standardised distances on both dictionaries, i.e.

$$minML = min(dist'_{LEX}, dist'_{MW}). \quad (2)$$

The obtained scores indicate that dictionaries might have presented rather complementary pieces of sense description than inconsistent information.

5 Conclusions

The performed experiments aimed at comparing how similarly two dictionaries described semantic distances in polysemy and homonymy. We found out that traditional English dictionaries showed traces of positive correlation between Dijkstra's path lengths on corresponding polysemy nets (0.7 for polysemy and homonymy, and $\rho = 0.4$ for sole polysemy). With regard to the homonymy/polysemy binary distinction, we obtained Cohen's $\kappa = 0.67$ and 85% percentage agreement.

The agreement with WordNet was moderate in the case of homonymy and polysemy ($\rho \sim 0.46$). When the oracle was considered (hints on the status of homonymous pairs), the correlation rose to the level of $\rho = 0.7$ which value was comparable to the confidence interval calculated for dictionaries. The values calculated for the sole polysemy (i.e. excluding homonymy) were slightly smaller than those obtained from the Lexico and Merriam-Webster comparison. The achieved results resembled agreement measurements reported in the literature (see Sec. 2 above).

The performed experiments gave an insight into the debate on the quality of dictionary descriptions. It turned out that lexicographers from different publishing companies provided very similar semantic description of homonymy – senses were similarly grouped according to their shared etymology. Dictionaries comparably described also semantic distance between related senses, when measured shortest paths on entry microstructures (micro-hierarchies). WordNet proved its usefulness in capturing the strength of polysemy links, but failed in homonymy recognition.

Acknowledgments

This research was financed by the National Science Centre, Poland, grant number 2018/29/B/HS2/02919, and supported by the CLARIN-PL[11] research infrastructure, and the NTU Digital Humanities Research Cluster.

References

Ron Artstein and Massimo Poesio. 2008. Inter-coder agreement for computational linguistics. *Computational Linguistics*, 34(4):555–596.

Beryl TS Atkins. 1992. Tools for computer-aided corpus lexicography: the hector project. *Acta Linguistica Hungarica*, 41(1/4):5–71.

Sue Atkins. 2008. *Practical Lexicography: A Reader*, chapter Theoretical Lexicography and

[11] http://clarin-pl.eu

Dictionary-making, pages 31–50. Oxford University Press.

Claudia Brugman and George Lakoff. 2006. *Cognitive Linguistics: Basic Readings*, chapter Radial network: Cognitive topology and lexical networks, pages 185–239. Mouton de Gruyter: Berlin.

Irina Chugur, Julio Gonzalo, and Felisa Verdejo. 2002. A study of polysemy and sense proximity in the senseval-2 test suite. In *Proceedings of the ACL-02 workshop on Word sense disambiguation: recent successes and future directions*, pages 32–39.

Edsger W Dijkstra et al. 1959. A note on two problems in connexion with graphs. *Numerische mathematik*, 1(1):269–271.

Bradley Efron and Charles Stein. 1981. The jackknife estimate of variance. *The Annals of Statistics*, pages 586–596.

Gertrud Fenk-Oczlon and August Fenk. 2008. *Language Complexity: Typology, contact, change*, chapter Complexity trade-off between subsystems of language, pages 1–15. John Benjamins Publishing.

Abed Alhakim Freihat, Fausto Giunchiglia, and Biswanath Dutta. 2013. Regular polysemy in wordnet and pattern based approach. *International Journal On Advances in Intelligent Systems*, 6.

Bradley Hauer and Grzegorz Kondrak. 2020. One homonym per translation. In *Proceedings of the AAAI Conference on Artificial Intelligence*, volume 34, pages 7895–7902.

Howard Jackson. 2002. *Lexicography: An Introduction*. Routledge.

Sergey Klimenkov and Alexander Pokid. 2019. Designing a model of contexts for word-sense disambiguation in a semantic network.

John Lyons. 1995. *Linguistic semantics: An introduction*. Cambridge University Press.

Barbara C Malt, Steven A Sloman, Silvia Gennari, Meiyi Shi, and Yuan Wang. 1999. Knowing versus naming: Similarity and the linguistic categorization of artifacts. *Journal of Memory and Language*, 40(2):230–262.

Diana McCarthy. 2006. Relating wordnet senses for word sense disambiguation. In *Proceedings of the Workshop on Making Sense of Sense: Bringing Psycholinguistics and Computational Linguistics Together*.

Lingling Meng, Runqing Huang, and Junzhong Gu. 2013. A review of semantic similarity measures in wordnet. *International Journal of Hybrid Information Technology*, 6(1):1–12.

Rada Mihalcea. 2003. Turning wordnet into an information retrieval resource: Systematic polysemy and conversion to hierarchical codes. *International journal of pattern recognition and artificial intelligence*, 17(05):689–704.

Rada Mihalcea, Timothy Chklovski, and Adam Kilgarriff. 2004. The senseval-3 English lexical sample task. In *Proceedings of SENSEVAL-3, the Third International Workshop on the Evaluation of Systems for the Semantic Analysis of Text*, pages 25–28. Association for Computational Linguistics, Barcelona, Spain. URL `https://www.aclweb.org/anthology/W04-0807`.

Martha Palmer, Hoa Trang Dang, and Christiane Fellbaum. 2007. Making fine-grained and coarse-grained sense distinctions, both manually and automatically. *Nat. Lang. Eng.*, 13(2):137–163.

Rebecca J Passonneau, Ansaf Salleb-Aouissi, Vikas Bhardwaj, and Nancy Ide. 2010. Word sense annotation of polysemous words by multiple annotators. In *LREC*.

Ted Pedersen, Siddharth Patwardhan, Jason Michelizzi, et al. 2004. Wordnet:: Similarity-measuring the relatedness of concepts. In *AAAI*, volume 4, pages 25–29.

Christian Ramiro, Mahesh Srinivasan, Barbara C. Malt, and Yang Xu. 2018. Algorithms in the historical emergence of word senses. *Proceedings of the National Academy of Sciences*, 115(10):2323–2328.

Philip Resnik and David Yarowsky. 1999. Distinguishing systems and distinguishing senses: New evaluation methods for word sense disambiguation. *Natural language engineering*, 5(2):113–133.

Ray Richardson, A Smeaton, and John Murphy. 1994. Using wordnet as a knowledge base for measuring semantic similarity between words.

Penelope F. Stock. 2008. *Practical Lexicography: A Reader*, chapter Polysemy, pages 1–15. Oxford University Press.

Bo Svensén. 2009. A handbook of lexicography. *The theory and practice of dictionary-making. Cambridge: CUP.*

Jean Véronis. 1998. A study of polysemy judgements and inter-annotator agreement. In *Programme and advanced papers of the Senseval workshop*, pages 2–4. Citeseer.

Hyejin Youn, Logan Sutton, Eric Smith, Cristopher Moore, Jon F. Wilkins, Ian Maddieson, William Croft, and Tanmoy Bhattacharya. 2016. On the universal structure of human lexical semantics. *Proceedings of the National Academy of Sciences*, 113(7):1766–1771.

Association for Computational Linguistics
209 N. Eighth Street
Stroudsburg, Pennsylvania 18360

ISBN 978-1-7138-2910-2

CURRAN ASSOCIATES INC.
proceedings
.com